WHITE BONES RED ROT BLACK SNAKES

Also by Bhikkhu Sujato through Santipada

Sects & Sectarianism
How tranquillity worsted insight in the Pali canon

Beginnings
There comes a time when the world ends...

Bhikkhuni Vinaya Studies
Research & reflections on monastic discipline for Buddhist nuns

A Swift Pair of Messengers
Calm and insight in the Buddha's words

Dreams of Bhaddā
Sex. Murder. Betrayal. Enlightenment. The story of a Buddhist nun.

A History of Mindfulness
How insight worsted tranquillity in the Satipaṭṭhāna Sutta

SANTIPADA is a non-profit Buddhist publisher. These and many other works are available in a variety of paper and digital formats.

http://santipada.org

WHITE BONES RED ROT BLACK SNAKES

A Buddhist mythology of the feminine

BHIKKHU SUJATO

SANTIPADA

SANTIPADA
Buddhism as if life matters

Published in 2012 by Santipada.
Printed and distributed by Lulu.com.

ISBN: 978-1-921842-03-0

Typeset in Gentium using LuaLaTeX.

As a mother covers her son
with the hem of her cloak
so cover him thou, O earth.

CONTENTS

1 *The Lady & the Tree* 1

2 *A Myth of Origins* 14

3 *The Death of the Goddess* 25

4 *The Little Stick Collector* 39

5 *A Magic Birth* 57

6 *How Māyā Became a Goddess* 67

7 *She Who Ate the Children* 73

8 *The King Sacrificed* 87

9 *The Real Māyā* 104

10 *Let's Play* 116

11 *Perception, Symbol, Myth* 125

12 *On Using Jung* 136

13 *The Dhamma of Gender* 149

14 *Mythic Fact, Historic Fiction* 157

15 *The Other First Bhikkhuni* 166

16 *A Buddhist Femme Fatale* 174

17 *The Weaving of the Web* 187

18 *Fears of the Future* 193

19 *The Flood* 204

20	*The Serpent*	218
21	*The Deepest Taboo*	225
22	*How to Kill a Dead Nun*	237
23	*A Very Grievous Text*	245
24	*The Hero Departs*	257
25	*The Hero Wakes*	278
26	*The Hero Returns*	290
27	*Building the Legend*	303
28	*The Wicked Stepmother*	313
29	*The Princess & the Dragon*	332
30	*The Sacred Stepmother*	352
31	*Rescuing the Hero*	365
32	*The Hard Twin*	380
33	*The Sage & the Golden Maiden*	394
34	*The Soft Twin*	409
35	*What a Woman Wants*	422
36	*The Heroine*	431
37	*That Indefinable Yearning*	439
38	*The Flowering of the World*	445
39	*Her Dreaming*	460
40	*Things Hidden Since the Beginning*	468
	Thanks	478
	Bibliography	479
	Figures	496
	Notes	499

Figure 1: *Māyā, the Bodhisatta, and the tree*

CHAPTER 1

THE LADY & THE TREE

WHO DOES NOT KNOW THE IMAGE of the Buddha's mother, 'Queen Māyā'? Half-way between her maternal home, Devadaha, and the father's city of Kapilavatthu, she stands in the grove at Lumbini. In a relaxed, sensual pose, she clasps a flowering *sāl* branch, which bent down so that she might pluck one of the blossoms. With her slim body and small breasts, she presents, by the voluptuous standards of Indian art, a delicate, spiritualized image. Her arms, gracefully entwined with the branch, touch it at just one point, forming a circle which frames the beatific serenity of her face. Her legs, too, are crossed and form a second circle, with just a hint of a playful kick. The baby Buddha-to-be has emerged from her side and stands above the ground, firm upon a lotus, encompassed by the aura of his own glory; and in the air deities wait in attendance.

2 This delightful image appears throughout Buddhist literature, and is lusciously depicted in paintings and sculptures. In my favorite portrayal, the stone is black and heavy, polished smooth by the loving hands of the anonymous artist, so that the physicality of the rock recedes behind the luster of the surface, the light concealing the darkness.

Figure 1.1: *Sālabhañjikā, Bhahrut*

3 The lady who holds the bent branch does not confine her graces to the Buddhist faith, for the image is a classic Indian motif, the *sālabhañjikā* celebrated in art and literature. She favors the regions frequented by the Buddha, and is especially common in Jain art. The motif retained its popularity until colonial times, where syncretic styles featuring Persian and European influences are found.[1] She makes an appearance at the earliest Buddhist sites, such as Sanchi and Bāhrut, in her 'native' form, not yet adopted as the Buddha's mother. At these sites, in astonishing contrast with the Buddhist ascetic ideal, voluptuous naked fertility goddesses are everywhere, in numbers second only to the Buddha and his symbols.[2]

4 Such is our second example, cruder both in carving and in meaning: for she remains entwined with the tree, caught in the very act of emerging. While Māyā has just one delicate arm wrapped around a branch, our *sālabhañjikā* clasps with both arms and a leg. Her arms are apart, so she is less complete, less herself as a person. And the intimate wrapping of the leg with the tree reveals the erotic origin of Māyā's more elegant stance. Seeing her immodesty, it's no surprise to find the word *sālabhañjikā* among the rich Indian vocabulary for a prostitute.[3] Again, while the *sālabhañjikā*'s legs are separated, Māyā's connect: she is integrated, whole, while the *sālabhañjikā* is not yet distinct from the tree.

5 The next *sālabhañjikā* fills the gap between the previous two. She has emerged in front of and is clearly distinct from the tree. Her arms are not united, she is not as whole. And she displays a more obviously sexual femininity, with raunchy hips and adornments drooping over her breasts, which shine from long handling: rubbing them is a fertility charm.

6 It is believed that the touch of the tree could bring fertility to the woman; or alternatively, that the touch of the woman, perhaps a little kick with those dancer's feet, would excite the tree to blossom. In these quaint relics of very old magical beliefs, the woman as source of human fertility is identified with the earth, source of the world-fruits. Their relation is not exactly causal as we would understand it. It is an association, a pretense, a being-in-one that somehow flows from their seeming-as-one. But as time goes on, the distinction between the woman and her attributes becomes clear. She becomes differentiated from, yet in harmony with, the eternal symbols.

Figure 1.2: *Sālabhañjikā, Karnataka*

7 In the subtle distinctions between these images we see a feminine figure in evolution, gracefully emerging from the half-light of divinity, becoming a true woman.

❖

8 The topic was dignified with a learned treatise by Gustav Roth, a German philologist.[4] His analysis of the etymology and appearance of the *sālabhañjikā* throughout Indian art and literature was adorned with a reminiscence of his time living in India. He went to a party in Patna, where he joined in the children's games. They were playing a kind of 'catch'. And when the young girl was chased, she escaped by running to a flowering tree and clasping the branch, the very living picture of the *sālabhañjikā*. There she was safe, and the other children could not get her. But as soon as she let go she was caught!

9 What's so bad about being 'it'? Why do children believe that, whatever happens, they must avoid that dreadful fate? While no-one wishes it for themselves, for the game to work, someone must be 'it'. Eventually, all must take their turn. The girl is safe as long as the tree/goddess protects her; that is, as long as the physical touch ensures the symbolic (or magical) identification of woman with tree. She is embraced and enhanced within that glory, lifted out of herself. When she loses touch, her own symbols betray her and she is vulnerable, mortal, lost. Somehow, children remain closer to such basic truths. Perhaps the cares of life have not yet dimmed their memories of the deep past.

10 Roth pointed out that the connections between the girl holding the flowering branch and play can be traced throughout the Indian literature. Even Siddhattha's birth is drawn within this matrix of associations. Our sources tell us that the Buddha's mother-to-be was traveling from the father's home at Kapilavatthu to Devadaha to give birth in the maternal family home in accordance with custom. She saw the delightful blossoming grove of *sāl* trees and thought that she wished to go into the park 'to play'.[5]

❖

11 The 53rd story of the Avadānaśātaka, an ancient Sanskrit collection of Buddhist tales, tells us of a girl not coincidentally called Sālabhañjikā, who

collected the flowers of the *sāl* tree for play.[6] She wished to offer flowers to the Buddha, but the blossoms in the tree nearby were beyond her reach. She should have heeded the warning: if she was meant to pluck them, the gods would have bent down the branches as they did for Māyā when she became a mother. But the brave child climbed the tree to get the flowers, only to fall and dash out her young life upon the cruel ground. Due to her pure intention, however, she was reborn in the Tāvatiṁsa heaven in a mansion adorned with *sāl* flowers.

12 While for Māyā the magic tree reaches down to embrace her, forming a circuit of tree, woman, and ground, the unlucky *sālabhañjikā* girl left her ground and strayed too high, too soon. This story, with its senseless death redeemed by glorious rebirth, set in a context of religion and fertility, dimly echoes of darker things: child sacrifice.[7]

❖

13 The plucking of the flower reminds me of a story told in far distant lands, Aeneas and the Golden Bough.[8] Aeneas was the leader of the refugees who fled the calamity of the Trojan war. With the fragmented remains of his people, he wandered the oceans in search of a promised new home. At a time of crisis, when he despaired of accomplishing his goal, Aeneas consulted the Cumean Sybil, Deiphobe. Possessed by Apollo, she told him to seek the Golden Bough, which would serve as talisman for his last, critical adventure before arriving at his new homeland: the entry into and, more importantly, the return from the grim realm of Death. Aeneas could only find the hidden object by means of a sign from heaven, a pair of doves sent by his mother Aphrodite. They led him to Avernus, the 'birdless' entrance to the dread Underworld. There he saw the Golden Bough gleaming among the dark trees, like the mistletoe that is golden in the midwinter while all around is dead.[9]

14 The 'plucking' of the branch represents death, the separation of the soul from the body. In the word *sālabhañjikā*, this is probably the original meaning of the element *-bhañjikā*, 'breaker'.[10] But Māyā's mortality is made softer, as the branch is not broken, merely bent. The story from the Avadānaśātaka, where the girl breaks the branch and dies, stands nearer its primitive roots.

15 Like Deiphobe leading Aeneas into the Valley of Death, the goddess takes us by the hand and leads us into the deeps of time. How long the Indians have been her devotees we cannot know. Indian paleolithic art is not well documented, so there are few images to compare with the mother-goddess figurines found distributed from western Europe as far as Lake Baikal in south-eastern Russia. These 'Venuses' are dated to the upper paleolithic, typically 22 000–28 000 BCE, with some as early as 35 000 BCE or as late as 11 000 BCE.[11] The use of 'Venus' as generic name for such figures is perhaps unfortunate. There is no question of them being literally identical with the classical goddess of the same name; whether or not there is any historical link with the much later classical goddesses is disputed. The only comparable Indian image is from the Belan valley south of Mirzapur, a little way up the Ganges from Benares.[12] Carved of bone, with pendant breasts and broad hips, carbon-14 dating puts the Belan Venus around 15 000–20 000 BCE.

16 While we cannot say for certain, there is no reason to doubt that Her presence was as widespread in India as she was elsewhere. For when the curtain lifts again on Indian culture the goddess is there. The earliest feminine figures appear around 2500 BCE in Pakistan, near the modern towns of Quetta, Kulli, and Zhob, and in Afghanistan at Mundigak and Deh Morasi.[13] The Zhob figurines have the large eyes so typical of early deities,[14] and while they are not as exaggerated as the earlier 'Venus' figures, they are markedly feminine; several have the hands embracing the breasts and they feature elaborate hairstyles. Figures of men are absent from these sites, the masculine being represented by the bull.

17 The Zhob-type figurines are a part of the cultural matrix from which the first great Indic culture arose, the Indus Valley Civilization. At its height around 2600–1900 BCE this was the greatest civilization in the world, stretching from modern day Gujarat in the south to north of Kabul, and west into southern Iran. Artistic remains include hundreds of female images on seals as well as in the round. They are so prevalent that every household may have had one. The Indus images typically lack the exuberant emphasis on sexual or fertility motifs that is so striking in the goddess

images from the west. They tend, rather, to be somewhat slim, with the emphasis on the elaborately ornamented head.[15]

18 One of the enigmatic little seals from Mohenjo Daro (now Pakistan) shows a female figure within a Bodhi tree.[16] She is divine, adorned with a crescent-moon (or trident) head-dress, elevated, and fully included within the tree. She wears bangles on both arms—after the manner of Indian women until today—and wears her hair in one long plait.

19 Before her is a human head on a small altar, evidently a sacrificial offering. A bearded, long-nosed man, also wearing a trident, kneels in worship. He is a man of stature who bears a special relationship with the deity, like a king or a priest. Behind him stands a 'sphinx'—a giant bull or ram wearing a man's face like a mask. The 'sphinx', 'king', and decapitated head form one imagistic unit, and should be identified: the animal is totem for the king, while the head is his sacrificial destiny. Or perhaps this is a substitute sacrifice, in which case the symbolism works the other way: the death of the totem animal is 'as good as' the more direct method of regicide.

20 Seven apparently female figures stand in attendance at the base, each with long plaited hair, a single plumed headdress, bangles on both arms, and long skirts. The seven attendants are perhaps the goddess's celestial companions, perhaps her priestesses; they have been identified with the 'Seven Rivers' (*saptasindhu*),[17] or else the pleaides.[18] Along the top of the seal are several signs, and there is another at the base of the tree.[19] The meaning of the signs is unknown. The fish, which appears above the 'sphinx', is interpreted by Asko Parpola as a symbol of divinity and is said to represent a star.[20] The edges of the seal are worn from repeated handling.[21]

21 The details and implications of this intriguing image remain tantalizingly beyond our grasp. Who is the goddess? What was the manner of her worship? What relation, if any, did she have to the 'proto-Śiva' yogi who appears in other seals? Whatever we think, we must account for the central fact: a human head offered to a tree-goddess.

22 We have no direct evidence of human sacrifice in Her name in the Indus Valley Civilization.[22] But this is only because of the paucity of remains. The weight of evidence from images such as this, backed up by ethnology, history, and archaeology, renders the conclusion inevitable.[23]

***Figure 1.3:** Female deity in Bodhi tree. Mohenjo Daro, circa 2000 BCE.*

23 Our images of woman and tree show a progressive emergence. In the oldest image, from the Indus Valley Civilization, the goddess is embedded fully within the tree, and is clearly identified with it. As she grew up, however, she emerged from this primordial womb, and in the *sālabhañjikā* images the woman predominates, while the tree forms the setting, gradually receding into the background. While the artist wants to draw our attention to the woman, making her the center of our conscious focus, the tree—the Mother of the Mother—is receding to the unconscious. The stories associated with this stage show that the woman was independent and acted of her own volition, returning only occasionally to touch the place of her own birth as she participated in the next round of that most ancient of mysteries.

24 Next is the popular image of bhikkhuni Saṅghamittā, King Aśoka's daughter, who brought the sapling of the Bodhi tree to Sri Lanka.[24] She stands proudly on the ship as they approach the shore, the parasol of royalty raised over her head. Another parasol is raised above the sapling, the mirroring suggesting a twinning. The sapling is to her side, so that she and it share the center stage. The sapling is smaller than she, but raised on a high platform. It roughly centres where her halo would be; and it is surrounded by a soft glow of light. If we were unsure about whether the tree and she should be identified, the artist drives home his point by wrapping the base of the tree in the same kind of robe that she wears, the reddish robe of the ascetic. In the lower right corner King Devanampiyatissa has waded up to his chest in the water, nearly submersing his royal person, raising his hands in worship to receive her. As representative of the ordinary follower, he is largely immersed in the waters of the unconscious, but is emerging from them and aspiring towards the light; while she is a perfected being who bathes in the clear radiance of Awakening.

Figure 1.4: *Saṅghamittā arriving with the Bodhi tree*

25 The parallels with the Indus Valley seal are startling. It is the very same tree, the *ficus religiosa* or Bodhi tree. And the message is the same: the submission of the worldly powers to the sacred. But in the later Saṅghamittā image this submission appears merely as a temporary immersion of the body of the king. He keeps his head above the water, unlike his unfortunate predecessor in the Indus Valley, whose offering was more total. In this image, the woman and the tree are distinct but equal; the tree is the archetype, the woman is the person. While the tree emanates glory, the back-story, already familiar to all who might view the image, is that she took the sapling, showing her power over it, and brought it to Sri Lanka by a perilous sea voyage, along the way vanquishing the spirits of the waters.

26 In this story Saṅghamittā is the inverse of the vicious Tissarakkhitā, Aśoka's evil second wife, who, as the wicked stepmother, showed her jealousy and ambition for her own children by poisoning the Bodhi tree. She is the witch attempting to destroy the 'other woman', which for her was the tree.

❖

27 The connection between the Bodhi tree worshiped by all Buddhists and the far more ancient, more humble, rites of fertility associated with the *sālabhañjikā* did not go unnoticed in times past. The canonical authority for Bodhi tree worship is found in the Kāliṅga Jātaka.[25] The lay folk of Sāvatthī asked the Buddha's closest disciple Ānanda if a shrine could be provided for the sake of worship. The Buddha said that a Bodhi tree would be ideal, and so a fruit was brought from Bodhgaya for the purpose and planted in the Jetavana with all due ceremony. The tree became known as the 'Ānandabodhi' and its spiritual descendent is still worshiped in the Jetavana today. To mark the occasion the Buddha taught a story of the past.

28 A prince in exile was living in the forest. He bathed in a stream, and when he emerged a garland of flowers was caught in his hair. He knew that it must have been made by a fair young maiden. The maiden, as fate would have it, was herself a princess in exile, who had climbed a flowering mango tree to play and dropped the wreath. The prince found her, and asked what she was (evidently wondering whether she might be a divine being of some sort). She said that she was human; however, she didn't

wish to come down to consort with the strange man below, on account of her high birth. But he revealed his own birth to her, and they exchanged the secrets of their caste (*khattiyamāyā*). They were married, and their son became the ruler of all India.

29 One day the king decided to visit his parents, and went on his royal elephant with a great retinue. But he came to a place where he could not pass: it was the Bodhimaṇḍala, the region around the Bodhi tree where all Buddhas become enlightened. Not until he dismounted and paid worship to the tree with all his followers could he continue.

30 Here the fertility motif of the flowering tree could not be clearer. The encounter at the tree reads like an allegorical version of a marriage ritual. From this perfect match comes the greatest of kings, but even he must humble himself before the power of the Bodhi tree.

❖

31 Saṅghamittā did not destroy the tree; she gave it life. It is still alive today, the oldest historical tree in the world, surviving war, colonial rapacity, and terrorist attacks. And Saṅghamittā became the founder of the Sri Lankan lineage of bhikkhunis, or fully ordained nuns. It is from her arrival on the island that the four-fold assembly of Buddhism was complete: monks, nuns, laymen, and laywomen. Bhikkhunis later spread to China and today are found all over the globe. The bhikkhuni Sangha is the oldest order of sacred women in the world, with the possible exception of the Jain *sadhvis*. One might imagine this would be a cause for celebration in the Buddhist world. But despite the age and authenticity of this tradition, bhikkhunis are rejected by many followers of Theravāda and Tibetan Buddhism. Why? Well, that's a story that wants telling.

CHAPTER 2

A MYTH OF ORIGINS

THE MYSTERY LIES BEFORE US. Its existence is attested by the finest authorities. Bhikkhunis are seen as a threat, and the virulence of their threat is inscribed in the root-myth of the foundation of the nuns' order. While the story of Saṅghamittā is full of power and celebration, the tale of the supposed first bhikkhuni, the Buddha's step-mother Mahāpajāpatī Gotamī, is at best uneasy, at worst a curse: the Buddha repeatedly refuses her request for ordination, and when he finally acquiesces he declares that bhikkhunis are like a disease, a flood that will destroy Buddhism. Not an auspicious beginning.

2 To understand our predicament, we must enter into the minds and imaginations of those who have come before. Not by assuming that all the scriptures are the perfect emanation of Awakening, but by seeking within them humanity, with all its wisdom and its folly. We shall only progress if we hold closely the ambiguities and contradictions in the stories; for in the monks' treatment of bhikkhunis we can read all the confusion, attraction, and repulsion that men feel for women.

3 The traditional story of the first bhikkhuni, Mahāpajāpatī, is found in every popular account of the Buddha's life, and is seared unforgettably in the consciousness of traditional Buddhists. An abundance of text-critical studies has shown, again and again, the flaws and fracture lines in the text, yet still it breathes life into the emotional case for perpetuating the monastic institutions of modern Buddhism, which in Theravādin and Central Asian traditions means a male-only Sangha.[1]

4 This story is of decisive importance for understanding the emotional response of the Buddhist community towards nuns in particular and women's spirituality in general. It is the fundamental myth of origins, and like all myths it says the unsayable. It hides, under the veneer of reason, a deeply unconsidered inheritance of attitudes towards women. Overtly ambiguous, it both allows women the supreme spiritual attainments, and drags them back into the chthonic underworld.

❖

5 Talk of origins is always fraught, for we are peering into the twilight before the dawn. This is the fascination of it. We transgress the boundaries of knowledge and set free things that were perhaps better kept hidden. They are *ours*, they belong to *our* imagination. So it is *our* responsibility to take care of the monsters and fairies that lurk in the gloaming. How are we to relate to our demons? Do we use ancient myths to deny women their place in the Buddhist renunciate community? Or do we look for another way of seeing?

6 The myth of origin is not a historical record of the founding of the bhikkhuni order. This is entirely normal for myth. Just as 'prophecy' is a projection of present day issues into the future, myths of origin aim to authenticate present day customs by appeal to archaic authority.

7 While we can be sure that the text is a later compilation, it is much more difficult to say anything meaningful about what actually might have happened '*in the beginning*'. Rarely are such things conjured out of thin air. To dismiss the text as a fabrication is to avoid listening to it. But if we listen closely and carefully, little by little it starts to make a strange kind of sense...

❖

8 The story of Mahāpajāpatī exists in at least ten versions, none of which have any *a priori* claims to authenticity. The different versions tell more or less the same story, with the inevitable differences in detail. There is no question of any of these being a literal record of exact events. They have all been filtered through the perspectives of the authors and editors. A detailed text critical study can reveal much from these differences, but

would distract from our focus on the mythology. So for the time being we shall just focus on one telling.

9 Below I offer a translation of the Mahīśāsaka Vinaya version. The Mahīśāsaka was one of the 'eighteen' schools of early Buddhism. It was based on the mainland, possibly around Avanti, but was doctrinally similar to the school established at the Sri Lankan Mahāvihāra, which we know today as Theravāda. This particular text was brought from Sri Lanka to China by the pilgrim-monk Fa-xian, and translated (from a Sanskritic dialect) into Chinese by Buddhajīva and assistants in 434 CE.

10 I give the Mahīśāsaka rather than the Pali, since that version has been often translated into English before.[2] This version also has a number of unusual features. Reading a different account helps to deconstruct expectations, and invites consideration as to how the differences arose.

11 Some aspects of the Mahīśāsaka account are clearly later elements, such as the opening passage featuring Suddhodana. Suddhodana is not called 'king' in the earliest texts.

12 This version is also unusual in that it depicts the Buddha's father seeking ordination. It seems that this request, and its refusal, is a later development in imitation of Mahāpajāpatī's story. In other traditions, Suddhodana does not seek ordination, but lives and dies as a dedicated lay follower. Perhaps the question was asked as to why Suddhodana, if he was so dedicated, did not seek ordination, and the answer lay in a variation on Mahāpajāpatī's story. In any case, it raises the significant possibility that the rejection of Mahāpajāpatī may not be simply genderbased.

13 A peculiar aspect of this account is the statement that past and future Buddhas also forbid women's ordination. I believe this is unique to the Mahīśāsaka and does not represent the mainstream position, which always treats the fourfold assembly as the fundamental pattern of the dispensation of all Buddhas. Indeed, the Lokuttaravāda Vinaya has Ānanda, as a key means of persuasion at this point, asking the Buddha how many assemblies the Buddhas of the past had. He replies that they had four: bhikkhus, bhikkhunis, lay men, and lay women. Ānanda also uses this argument in his defense at the First Council according to the Mahāsaṅghika and Sarvāstivāda Vinayas.[3]

14 It is important to be conscious of what is happening here: different traditions, according to their preference, use unverifiable claims based on legendary time-frames to source conflicting details and argue for opposite conclusions; these mythological conclusions have a very real bearing on people's lives. Enough chat, here's the text.

❖

15 At that time the Blessed One, returning to She-Yi, had not yet arrived at Kapilavatthu and stayed at the root of the Nigrodha tree. [His father] King Suddhodana came out to welcome him, seeing the Blessed One coming in the distance, his face splendid like a mass of gold. He bowed down at the Buddha's feet and said the following verse:

16 'At your birth, the sooth-sayer prophesied
When I heard, I first bowed [to you]
When the tree bent, I bowed the head [again][4]
Now [you've] completed the path, I bow the third time.'

17 Having said these verses he sat down to one side. The Buddha taught him the excellent Dhamma in many ways, up until he gained the vision of the Dhamma, and the fruit. He rose from his seat, arranged his robe over the left shoulder, and kneeling with his hands in *añjalī*, said this to the Buddha, 'Blessed One, I wish to take the going forth and the full ordination.'

18 The Buddha then saw that the king would not obtain the going forth. So he said to the king, 'Don't be heedless—you should step by step gain the excellent Dhamma.' Thereupon [Suddhodana] requested to undertake the three refuges and five precepts. After he had undertaken the five precepts, the Buddha in many ways taught him the excellent Dhamma. In joy and benefit from the teaching, he returned to his dwelling. When the king had returned to his palace, in the middle of the courtyard he proclaimed three times, 'If you wish to obtain the going forth in the Tathāgata's Vinaya, pay attention!'

19 When Mahāpajāpatī Gotamī heard the king's proclamation, then surrounded by 500 Śākyan women, she took two new robes out to where the Buddha was staying. She bowed down at his feet and said to the Buddha, 'Blessed One, I wove these robes myself. Now I offer them up to you—please deign to accept them!'

20 The Buddha said, 'You should give to the Sangha, this is of great fruit.' [She] spoke again as above to the Buddha.

21 The Buddha said, 'You should give to the Sangha; I am counted among the Sangha.' Again she spoke as above. The Buddha said, 'I'll take one, and give one to the Sangha.' Then after accepting this advice, she gave to the Buddha and the Sangha.

22 Gotamī again said to the Buddha, 'May the Buddha allow the going forth and the full ordination for women in the true Dhamma!'

23 The Buddha said, 'Stop, stop, do not say that! For what reason? All Buddhas in the past did not allow women the going forth. All womankind can themselves take the Buddha as refuge, stay in the home, shave the head, wear the ochre robes, make an effort to practice, make an effort to progress, and gain the path and fruit.[5] In the time of future Buddhas, it will also be like this. For this reason, I now allow you to practice in this way.' Gotamī asked, as above, three times. The Buddha also, as above, did not allow it three times. Then Gotamī, weeping, bowed at the Buddha's feet and left.

24 The Buddha then left Kapilavatthu together with a great assembly of 1250 bhikkhus, and traveled through the countryside.[6] Gotamī and the 500 Śākyan women together shaved off their hair, put on the robes, and followed behind, weeping. They stayed where the Blessed One stayed. The Buddha, traveling by stages, arrived at Sāvatthī. He stayed at the Jetavana.[7]

25 Gotamī and the 500 Śākyan women, weeping, remained at the gate. Ānanda, when leaving in the morning, saw them, and asked the reason. They answered, 'Venerable, the Blessed One will not allow women the going forth and the full ordination. This is why we are so upset. We want you to speak, so we may fulfill our aspiration.'

26 Ānanda then went to the Buddha, paid respects and further pleaded with the Buddha. The Buddha stopped Ānanda also as above.

27 Ānanda again said to the Buddha, 'Soon after the Buddha was born, his mother passed away. Gotamī raised the Buddha with her own milk so that he might grow up. Should one not repay this great debt of gratitude?'

28 The Buddha said, 'Gotamī also owes me a great debt of gratitude. Relying on me, she has come to know the Buddha, Dhamma, and Sangha, and has aroused respect and faith. One who, through reliance on a good friend, knows the Buddha, Dhamma, and Sangha, and arouses faith and respect, could not repay this even if they were to give that person clothes, food, and medicine for the rest of their life.'

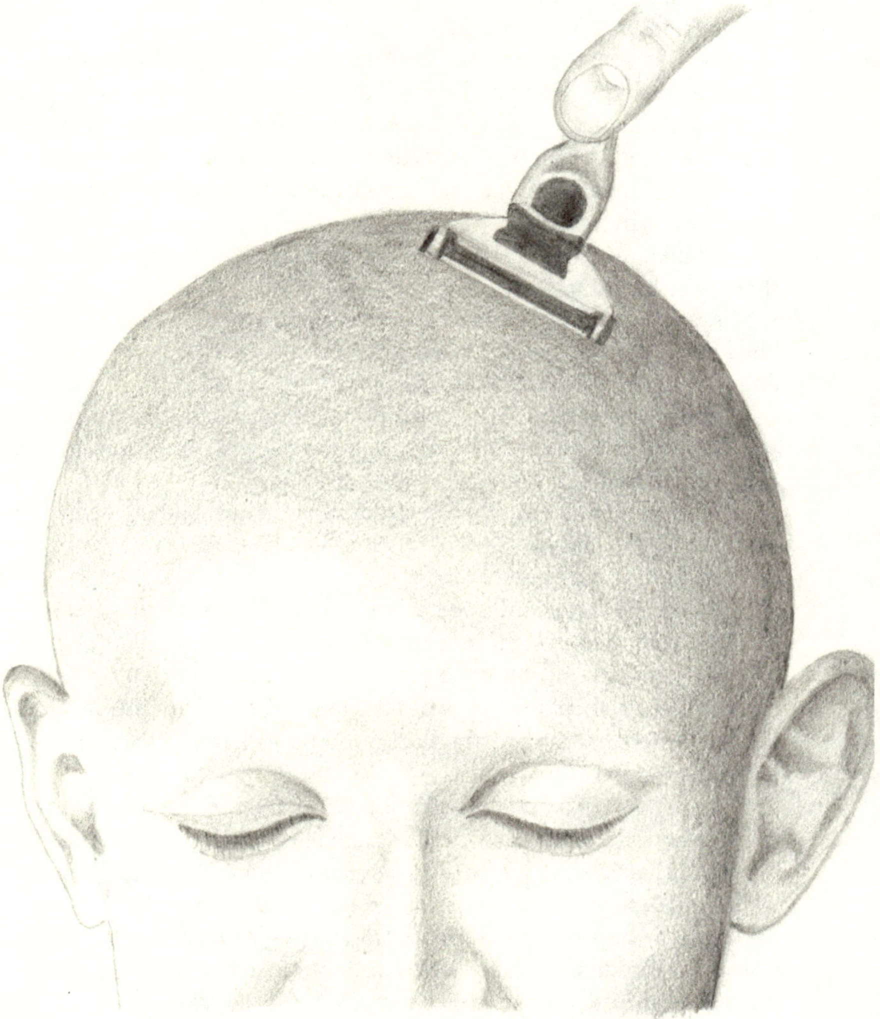

Figure 2.1: *Shaving a nun's head*

29 Ānanda then said to the Buddha, 'If women gain the going forth and full ordination, are they able to gain the four paths and fruits of the ascetic's life or not?'

30 The Buddha said, 'They can.'

31 Ānanda said, 'If they can gain the four paths, why does the Buddha not allow the going forth and the full ordination?'

32 The Buddha said, 'Now I allow Gotamī to undertake the eight *garudhammas*. That will be her going forth and full ordination. What eight?

33 1) The bhikkhunis should ask for an instructor from the bhikkhus every fortnight [*uposatha*].

34 2) A bhikkhuni should not spend the annual rains residence where there is no bhikkhu.

35 3) At *pavāraṇā* time [at the end of the annual rains residence] the bhikkhunis should invite the bhikkhus regarding three things: wrongdoings that are seen, heard, and suspected.

36 4) A *sikkhamānā* [trainee], having trained for two years in the precepts, should receive the full ordination [*upasampadā*] in the midst of the twofold Sangha.

37 5) A bhikkhuni is not allowed to abuse bhikkhus. She is not permitted to say to laypeople that bhikkhus are of bad ethics, of wrong conduct and wrong views.

38 6) A bhikkhuni is not allowed to bring up a bhikkhu's faults, but a bhikkhu is allowed to criticize a bhikkhuni.

39 7) If a bhikkhuni commits a grave fault, she should carry out a *mānattā* penance before the twofold Sangha for a fortnight. After practicing *mānattā* for a fortnight she should seek rehabilitation before each Sangha of twenty.

40 8) Though a bhikkhuni be ordained 100 years, she should bow in homage and rise to greet a newly ordained bhikkhu.'

41 Ānanda learnt that teaching. He went and said to Gotamī, 'Listen well, I will repeat what I have learnt in the Buddha's presence.'

42 Gotamī arranged her robe neatly and paying respect in the direction of the Buddha, she knelt with her hands in añjali, and with one mind she listened. Ānanda explained in detail as above.

43 Gotamī said, 'Just like a young man or woman, their bodies pure and clean after bathing, would be happy putting on fresh clothes, and a kind person were to give a garland of *vassika*, *uppala*, *atimuttaka*, or *tagara* flowers, and that person in joy and happiness were to take them in both hands and lift them over their head; the Blessed One's

Dhamma instruction is just like this, so I now undertake these [*garu-dhammas*] as the highest.'

44 Then she further said to Ānanda, 'I wish you to say something more, if this can be told to the Blessed One. I have already undertaken these eight rules as the highest. Of these eight rules, I wish to beg for one indulgence: may bhikkhunis bow to bhikkhus in accordance with seniority—how can a bhikkhuni ordained for 100 years bow to a newly ordained bhikkhu?' Ānanda returned and told the Buddha.

45 The Buddha said to Ānanda, 'It is not possible for me to allow the bhikkhunis to bow to bhikkhus in accordance with seniority. Women have five obstacles: they cannot become Sakka, ruler of Gods; Māra the king of gods; Brahmā king of gods; a wheel-turning monarch; or righteous king of the three realms. If women had not been allowed the going forth and the full ordination, the Buddha's true Dhamma would remain in the world 1000 years. Now that the going forth has been administered, this will decrease to 500 years. Just like a household with many women and few men, that family would decay and end, and would not last long.'

46 Again, he said to Ānanda, 'If women did not gain the going forth and full ordination in my Dhamma, after my passing away all the lay men and lay women followers would bring the four requisites for the bhikkhus, saying: "Venerable Sir, please accept my offerings out of compassion." If going out, seeing [a bhikkhu] they would take his arm and say: "Venerable Sir, I have such gratitude, when passing on alms-round come and sit, this will be beneficial for me." Whenever meeting [a bhikkhu] on the road, they would release their hair and lay it out so that the bhikkhu could step on it. But now I have allowed the going forth, this thing is finished.'

47 When he heard, Ānanda, deeply grieved, burst into tears. He said to the Buddha, 'Blessed One, previously I did not hear, did not know this teaching when I sought to allow the going forth and full ordination for women. If I knew this in the first place, how could I have asked three times?'

48 The Buddha said to Ānanda, 'Don't cry any more! Māra covered your mind, this is why you [acted thus]. Now it is allowed for women to take the going forth and full ordination, they should be obedient and practice what I have laid down without transgressing. What I have not established should not be wrongly established.'

49 Ānanda left and told this instruction to Gotamī. Gotamī, pleased and delighted, went to practice it. Now that the going forth and full

ordination was obtained, she returned and said to Ānanda, 'How can these 500 Śākyan women also gain full ordination? Please speak for us once more.'

50 Ānanda went and told the Buddha. The Buddha said, 'Now allow Pajāpatī, acting as preceptor in an assembly of ten bhikkhus, to give full ordination by an act with four announcements. I allow ordination of three people on one occasion, not four.'[8]

❖

51 I have lived with this story for so long, it is an effort to imagine life without it. For Buddhist nuns this story resonates in all kinds of ways. It is an emotional crucible, a spoken or unspoken background to all those who wish to pursue the Buddhist spiritual path in a body that happens to be female. Buddhist practice is all about deconstructing our notions of self and identity. There is no place for any conception of inherent gender. And yet, when faced with the living challenge of accepting women, far too many Buddhists revert to an unthinking sexism that is breathtaking in its denial and rigidity. And always this text hides in the background, whispering.

52 There is nothing within Buddhism that can help understand why this may be so. The text does not explain itself, and lies open to imagined motivations and rationalizations. I have not found any of these to be persuasive, and prefer to look at the story as a myth, the myth of origins for the bhikkhuni Sangha.

❖

53 There is one crucial aspect of the mythology that is omitted in the Mahīśāsaka version. This is concerning the all-important dangers that our text claims bhikkhuni ordination will bring to Buddhism. The Mahīśāsaka version says that, since bhikkhunis are ordained, the life of Buddhism is reduced from 1000 to 500 years; and that having women in the Sangha will weaken it, like a village with many women and few men. These statements are widely found among different versions.[9] However, the following dangers, concerning the reduction in gains and honor paid to the Sangha, are less widely attested and are another sign of lateness in this text.[10] Moreover, the Mahīśāsaka omits perhaps the most memorable and shocking

of images, which compare the entrance of bhikkhunis to a disease and a flood, or the destructive power of rain and hail. Similar imagery is found in most versions.[11] Here is a translation from the Pali.

> 54 'Just as, Ānanda, when the disease called "white bones" descends upon a field of wheat, that field of wheat does not last long; in the same way, Ānanda, in whatever Dhamma and Vinaya women gain the going forth from the home into homelessness, that holy life does not last long.
>
> 55 'Just as, Ānanda, when the disease called "red rot" descends upon a field of sugar cane, that field of sugar cane does not last long; so too, Ānanda, in whatever Dhamma and Vinaya women gain the going forth from the home into homelessness, that holy life does not last long.
>
> 56 'Just as, Ānanda, a man would build a dyke as a precaution to contain a large dam, so that the water would not overflow; in the same way, Ānanda, I have, as a precaution for the bhikkhunis, laid down these eight *garudhammas*, not to be transgressed as long as life lasts.'[12]

❖

57 The most critical power that the Mahāpajāpatī myth negotiates is the manner of ordination. This is absolutely fundamental for any monastic order. For a celibate community, controlling ordination is controlling reproduction. In an earlier work I have shown that the earliest, most authentic literature dealing with ordination of nuns, the bhikkhunis' own *pāṭimokkha* and Therīgāthā, speak only of the nuns themselves performing ordinations.[13] The Mahāpajāpatī story, on the other hand, claims that ordination for nuns must be performed by both nuns and monks. From now on, any new nuns must receive the seal of approval from the monks, and the nuns can never again maintain their own independent communities. The men have taken control of the nuns' reproductive rights, just as the patriarchal gods took the role of creator from the mother.

58 This tale repeats a pattern that was around long before the Buddha. A Sumerian myth of creation tells of a drunken game between the god Enki and the earth-goddess, his wife Ninhursag, in our most ancient story of gender alienation. They compete with each other to create the worst deformities in human beings. The wacky fun that gods get up to when they're drunk! Ninhursag creates all manner of monsters, all of whom the

clever Enki finds a place for in the world. When it comes to Enki's turn, however, the goddess cannot cope with his bizarre creations, until she is driven to a mad rage—and a vow of revenge.

59 'My city is destroyed, my house wrecked,
My children have been taken captive.
I have been exiled from the mountain city of the gods:
Even I escape not thy hand!
Henceforth you shall dwell neither in heaven nor on earth.'[14]

60 The woman's natural role as creator has been usurped: the man has the same power, and uses it to drive her to madness. It's not surprising that the children of such a dysfunctional relationship should be malformed; what is more astonishing is how the lesson has been so little observed. When men create patriarchy, the outcome is conflict.

CHAPTER 3

THE DEATH OF THE GODDESS

WHY IS THE MYTHOLOGY SO PROBLEMATIC for the bhikkhunis? And why does this mythology continue to exert power today?

2 These problems are usually dealt with by either fundamentalist literalism (the texts record the exact and unerring words of the Buddha), or modernist rationalism (the Buddha taught a rational ethic, and the myths are a later accretion by naïve followers). These approaches lead to impoverished and untenable readings of a complex, many-faceted array of stories and images.

3 The problem is a myth, and the answer lies in re-entering the realm of myth, a realm that we learned to scoff at in our teens, this time with imagination, sympathy, and intelligence. As long as we insist in seeing Mahāpajāpatī and the other characters in Buddhist stories as *people*, with inner feelings and thoughts much like ours, we will never understand them. They are not people, they are characters in myth. They exist only as images in the minds of those who listen to the myths.

❖

4 Try as we might, it is impossible for us to appreciate the power that myth held in ancient religious communities. The voices of the past are fragmented and dubious, and the evidence is vanishing before our eyes, through the accelerated crumbling of the physical remains, and more

so because as rational moderns we increasingly experience religion as a dream or a fiction.

5 The philosopher René Girard warns that, as traditional religions continue to disappear, we are also witnessing the disappearance of evidence. Societies are evolving on a trajectory of scepticism that follows that of ethnology and science in general. It will not be long before we find it hard to believe that anyone ever took the miracles and extravagences of religion seriously. We will convince ourselves that the ethnologists were deluded, subject to their own feverish dreams, or tricked by informers who got a kick out of playing mind-games with the ethnologists and their colonial prejudices.[1]

6 We cannot imagine the terror of the sacred, the awe of the rumbling All-Father as he roars and flashes his might across the desert, plain to see, incontrovertible in his majesty. Alienation and doubt have come to define our relationship with the divine.

7 Do not think, however, that the Death of God is a new thing, a radical innovation of skeptical 19th century philosophers. Our oldest records tell of the disappearance and vanishing of God, and the struggle to keep a relationship with the divine in the face of betrayal, jealousy, and death. In Babylonian cuneiform inscriptions of the 2nd millennium BCE we read:

> 8 My god has forsaken me and disappeared, my goddess has failed me and keeps at a distance, the good angel who walks beside me has disappeared.[2]

9 The Babylonian king Tabi-utul-Enlil around 1750 BCE recorded a long lament on alienation from his God:

> 10 Mine eyeballs he obscured, bolting them as with a lock; Mine ears he bolted, like those of one deaf... I cried to my god, but he did not show his face, I prayed to my goddess, she did not raise her head...[3]

11 We are used to reading the Bible as the story of God's relationship with his people. But look afresh: the Bible begins with the alienation of God and man. Once Adam and Eve leave the Garden, their descendants meet their God less and less frequently, and the relationship becomes ever more traumatic. Jahweh's followers, in their fearfulness, imagined a God who punishes them relentlessly for their naughtiness.

> 12 'On that day I will become angry with them and forsake them; I will hide my face from them, and they will be destroyed.'[4]

> 13 'I will show them my back and not my face in the day of their disaster.'[5]

> 14 'I will hide my face from this city because of all its wickedness.'[6]

15 By the time of Christ, God had become so alienated from his chosen people that he could only establish a connection through his son. Divinity could no longer be announced with authority and power from the skies, but had to be sought in the suffering and degradation of the Cross. While the surface message of Christianity is the relationship with God, is it not strange that at the center of Christian worship is the image of the dead son of an absent god, one whose last words were: 'My god, my god, why have you forsaken me?'[7]

16 Everywhere we find the same doubts, echoing through the ages and across the lands. The Ṛg Veda, around 1000 BCE, asks the great question, and gives an answer that has never been surpassed.

> 17 Who really knows? Who will here proclaim it? Whence was it produced? Whence is this creation? The Gods came afterward, with the creation of this universe. Who then knows whence it has arisen? Whence this creation has arisen—perhaps it formed itself, perhaps it did not—the one who looks down on it, in the highest heaven, only he knows—or perhaps he does not know.[8]

18 'Perhaps he does not know…'. After 3000 years of theology, can we improve on this in any way? Whether West or East, thoughtful people have, since the beginning of our records, questioned their relationship with the divine. In around 20 BCE Virgil wrote of the African king Iarbas, the son of Jupiter by a local nymph, who raised prayers full of doubt to his divine father.

> 19 'Do you observe these things? Or are we foolish to shudder when you shoot fire, O Father, foolish to be dismayed by lightning that is quite aimless and thunder that growls without meaning?… If indeed you are there, and we do not worship a vain myth.'[9]

20 The Jātaka stories, on their reduced scale, tell us over and again of the disappearance of the divine. One tale tells of two nymphs (*kinnara*) who

lived on the Mountain of the Moon in the rainy season, and only came down to the haunts of man in the dry. But a king, while a-hunting, shot the male fairy, so that his wife lamented: 'Are there, after all, no divine Guardians of the World? Or do they dwell apart? Or are they dead? For they do not protect my dear husband!' Sakka (the Indian Zeus) revived the fallen fairy, and warned them: 'From this day, do not go down from the Mountains of the Moon among the paths of men, but stay here.'[10]

21 The world of the Jātakas, like Narnia, is filled with talking beasts. They are a normal feature of the landscape, treated as characters just like the humans. In the Phandana Jātaka, however, when a black lion speaks to a wheelwright he cried out, 'A miracle! Never before this have I heard of a lion that could talk like a man.'[11] The wheelwright has come to find wood for cartwheels, and he assumes that the lion will be an expert on the subject. However, the lion has conceived a grudge against the deity of the tree under he had been sleeping, and so he recommended the wood of that tree. The deity in his turn recommended the skin of a black lion as the best for binding the rim of the wheel. And so the magical denizens of the wild become disunited and betray each other, even the lion and the tree, the mightiest of all animal and plant symbols. Meanwhile, the wheel of technology rolls on: the cart-wright kills them both.

❖

22 Just as our science has killed God, our history has killed myth. We have felled the forests, slaughtered the monsters, and tamed the wilderness. Are we surprised the gods have fled from us? Loss of faith doesn't just mean changing one's beliefs, like putting on a new suit of clothes. It is an agonizing revaluation of all values. Try as we may, we can't live inside myth any more, but only operate upon it, analyze, compare, and criticize.

23 Myth, like the gods themselves, strives for and vainly claims to achieve eternity. But it is forever haunted by the ghost of its future. In its very bombast it reveals its fear. Zeus is the greatest of the gods, and rules in glory having vanquished the earlier gods. But there is a deadful prophecy: he will be killed by his own son. Zeus has so many sons, and he is forever anxious—which will it be? Who possesses a weapon that can overcome the mightiest of gods? Zeus owns the lightning, the fiercest weapon of all. Not by sword can he be overcome, nor yet by axe nor by bow.

24 In the end, his deadly son is Cadmus; the murder weapon—letters. Zeus is killed by writing, which banishes the experience of divinity, and objectifies the words of the gods so they may be treated like any other profane object. Once the Commandments are writ in stone, we no longer need a prophet to wrestle in agony with the spirit of the Lord, but a grammarian to explicate the etymology.

25 Myth is the water in which ancient cultures swim, the air that they breathe. Myths are inexhaustible in their variety, profuse in their imagination. But they share one common factor: existence. They remain, they have a fixity and a stability that places them outside the fluidity of folk storytelling and grants them a privileged, apparently eternal, ontological status. They become reified as external objects, whether the obsessively perfect memory of the Vedas, or the monuments of the Egyptians, or the ten Commandments carved in stone, or the perfection of priestly ritual.

26 Once the myth has achieved this privileged ontology it exists outside the consciousness of any one of its participants. This is quite different to a tribal storytelling tradition, where the teller weaves a different pattern with each telling. Myth stays the same while circumstances change—which starts to become a problem. Now, in the spring festival, we give thanks to the gods for their fecundity. This is what we do every year. But this year there is drought, the crops fail and we starve. Why? Why have the gods forsaken us? And most importantly: who is to blame?

27 It is thus that all myth tells the story of the ending of myth. Every tale of the gods followed to its conclusion tells of the death of the gods. This is no coincidence, it is a logical necessity. The only myths that we can encounter are those that survive: this is a fact of evolution. But the world is not eternal, and no cycle is perfect. Old stories live on in a world of change, and from time to time there are disjuncts between myth and reality. These disjuncts invite questioning and reflection; and as soon as one does that one is no longer participating in myth, one is standing outside and acting upon it.

28 Despite its pretenses, myth is, of course, not actually eternal and does change according to circumstances. If the thing itself has become reified and unchangeable, like a received canon of scripture, the anomaly is accommodated through interpretation, through non-literal readings of the text. It is in this way that the very idea of interpretation arises.

❖

29 Our oldest myth of all, Gilgamesh, already pivots on just this problem. The spiritual crisis of the story is caused by the jealous, spiteful lust of a sacred woman. The background is this. Gilgamesh has met his match, Enkidu, created as an equal and a balance for Gilgamesh's unrestraint. They fight, these brutal twins, but then become the closest of friends. They accomplish a great adventure, felling the monster Humbaba, guardian of the cedars of Lebanon, thereby obtaining the materials to fulfill Gilgamesh's dream of building a great city. The triumphant hero Gilgamesh is approached by the goddess Ishtar, who says to him, 'Be my sweet man'. Gilgamesh refuses her, justifying himself with the earliest effort at comparative mythology.

30 'Which of your husbands did you love forever?
Which could satisfy your endless desires?
Let me remind you of how they suffered,
how each one came to a bitter end.[12]

31 'Remember what happened to that beautiful boy
Tammuz: you loved him when you were both young,
then you changed, you sent him to the underworld
and doomed him to be wailed for, year after year.

32 'You loved the bright-speckled roller bird,
then you changed, you attacked him and broke his wings,
and he sits in the woods crying *Ow-ee! Ow-ee!*

33 'You loved the lion, matchless in strength,
then you changed, you dug seven pits for him,
and when he fell, you left him to die.

34 'You loved the hot-blooded, war-bold stallion,
then you changed, you doomed him to whip and spurs,
to endlessly gallop, with a bit in his mouth,
to muddy his own water when he drinks from a pool.

35 'And for his mother, the goddess Silili,
you ordained a weeping that will never end...'[13]

36 Even at the beginning, she was already old, offering pleasure and dealing out death, deformity, pain. Enraged by Gilgamesh's refusal, Ishtar murdered Enkidu, prompting Gilgamesh's magnificent grief and his quest for immortality.

37 Thus the old feminine divinity is challenged by a newly assertive masculinity, a masculinity that is defined by its capacity to remember the old stories, to critically reflect upon them, to restrain the lusts of the flesh, and to not merely acknowledge, but to initiate change. The meeting with this feminine principle is the crisis point in the male hero's story. Up until then, Gilgamesh's interests had been worldly—fame, wealth, power, sex. His trip to the forest with Enkidu had been for no higher purpose than guaranteeing building supplies. But with Enkidu's death at the bloody hands of the goddess, he departs on a strange and ambiguous quest for the deathless. For all the tragedy, if it were not for the goddess's intervention Gilgamesh would have died a lesser man—and his name would not have endured through the ages, far longer than his city.

❖

38 As gods and goddesses disappear, whether by vanishing into the abstract heavens of the philosophers, being killed off by the next generation, or simply becoming irrelevant and pensioned off, their stories become tortured, twisted, trivialized. At best they remain as a quaint cultural relic, like the Easter bunny, and at worst an excuse for the most horrific depravities. We live in a world so inconceivably bizarre that its very existence is threatened by a manic, feverish insistence on the literal truth of a few ancient myths. Don't mistake it: textual fundamentalism is one of the most dangerous forces on our planet. It may destroy us all.

39 So how are we of the twilight to understand the stories from the dawn times? How are we to unearth the 'things hidden since the beginning'? We have lost so very much, yet we have one great advantage: knowledge. We can survey the religions of the world in a way that has never before been possible and see, as well as the distortions and corruptions, a spark of genuine light. In the continuity of religions' symbolic language, we can glimpse, perhaps for the last time, the dying embers of the numinous, before they disappear forever into the footnotes.

40 Nietzsche crystallized this ancient spiritual crisis when he spoke of the 'Death of God'. We are conscious of the hole He leaves in our psyche. The death of the Goddess, on the other hand, happened long ago, at the hands of that same, recently deceased, male deity. We have almost forgotten her, and must make conscious efforts to remember.

Figure 3.1: *Minoan snake goddess*

❖

41 We have already spoken of the ancient 'Venus' images that are such a striking part of paleolithic European culture. There is a long continuity between such images and modern worship of Mary. Half-way between these stand the goddesses of the mythic age, found throughout Greece, Crete, Syria, Egypt and so on. These were already old, for our most ancient sources speak of how their goddess descends from an earlier time. Virgil's *Aeneid* tells the origin myth of the then-modern empire of Rome, authorizing it by divine decree from the fall of Troy, already a millennium-old myth. But ancient Troy, it is said, received the Great Mother from still more ancient Crete.[14]

42 Figures of power, grace, sex, and violence, goddesses dominate the religious imagery of the time. And just as in the Indic sphere we can trace an evolution from the primordial goddess to the modern woman, the West also tells how mere woman emerged from her divine trappings.

43 Eve is known in the West as the first woman. To historians of religion she is no historical person, but an incarnation of the ancient Canaanite Mother, who went by many names—Asherah, Ishtar, and so on—and who was so thoroughly anathemized by the patriarchal redactors of the Bible.[15] Etymologically she descends from the Hurrian goddess Hebat. And we have been so conditioned to think of the Middle-east as the home of patriarchy that it comes as a surprise to learn that the king of Jerusalem during the Amarna period (1330s BCE) was named Abdi-Heba: 'servant of Eve'.

44 She was of old the wife of Jehovah, but they underwent a highly traumatic divorce. Having gained the ascendancy, Jehovah, unlike his counterparts Zeus or Indra, was not satisfied merely to rule over her, but tried to legislate her out of existence.[16] The ferocity of his attack merely reveals the hold that she had (and has) over his mind. The Old Testament constantly reviles the unfaithfulness of the Hebrew people. Not that they lacked faith, but they had faith in the wrong divinities. Her symbols were among the classic repertoire of the goddess: the serpent and the tree. This is evidenced through the Old Testament and archaeological findings of tree or wooden poles and serpents as cultic objects in ancient Israel, and is maintained in Christian tradition, where the serpent is depicted as a woman.

Figure 3.2: *Adam, Eve, and the Serpent*

45 What happened in the Garden was not, as might appear, a personal drama between conflicting parties. Eve, the goddess, was not seduced by a separate power in the serpent: she was betrayed by her own powers. Genesis tells how Eve became alienated from her symbols, shorn from their protection, and expelled from the Garden, where she truly becomes the first woman, that is, the first non-divine human female. Only then, not as punishment but as natural result of cause and effect, must she experience suffering and death. Her suffering is the suffering of humanity, especially women, as they become alienated from their sacredness. But sentimentality is out of place here: it is precisely this suffering that enables her to grow, and eventually to become a postmodern feminist.[17]

❖

46 So then: men are bad, women are good. Patriarchy destroyed the timeless wisdom of the Divine Feminine and ushered in an age of violence and technological conquest. So runs a prominent strain of modern feminist mythology. Such ideas are common enough in New Age circles, but they tell less than half a truth. It's true, men have done disgraceful things to the Goddess, but it would be disrespectful to think that She was a model of gentleness and nurturing, sipping peppermint tea as She tended her garden of flowers and organic healing herbs. This is just another modern fantasy.

47 In the real world, sacrifice is her right. Everywhere, she must be sated with blood. This is attested in the entire continuity of Indic tradition. We have seen that the roots of the Indic traditions in the Indus Valley depict human sacrifice for the goddess, just as do the red-daubed 'Venus' images of Old Europe. But these are not forgotten memories of the old times. At the spring festival of Kālī in 1871, 20 buffaloes, 250 goats, and 250 pigs were slaughtered each day. The pit of sand underneath the altar was soaked with blood and replaced thrice daily, to be buried in the fields as a fertility charm.[18] In late 2009, the world was aghast at the spectacle of over 200 000 beasts being slaughtered for the Nepalese Hindu festival of Gadhimai.[19] The justification for this slaughter has changed not at all through the ages. A Hindu priest of the temple, Chandan Dev Chaudhary, pleased with the festival's high turnout, said tradition must be kept. 'The goddess needs blood,' he said. 'Then that person can make his wishes come true.'[20]

48 Even more grisly offerings persist in the darker corners of India. In 2002 a 15 year old girl called Manju Kumari was murdered as an offering to the dark goddess Kālī. The ritual prescribed that the victim must be willing, must fully understand what was going on, must watch the knife and make no attempt to stop it. But the perpetrator, Khudu Karmakar, confessed to police that he, his wife, daughter, and three accomplices first drugged Manju Kumari, then gagged her and pinned her to the floor in front of the shrine. As she struggled, terrified, they wafted incense and sprinkled holy water from the Ganges, stripped off her blue skirt and pink t-shirt, shaved her, and anointed her with fat. Then they sawed off her hands, breast, and left foot and in imitation of Kālī's iconography, which depicts the goddess surrounded by dismembered body parts, they offered these at a shrine consisting of a photograph of Kālī soaked in blood. Blood spurted in arcs over the walls.[21]

49 This story is by no means isolated. Although ritual murder is a capital offence in India, condemned by the vast majority of Hindus, it is still reported on a fairly regular basis. Practitioners are motivated by the usual worldly concerns: wealth, revenge, fertility. The growing material wealth of India plays its part. Some are left behind and, unable to progress by more orthodox means, they return to Her for such blessings. The triangulation of desire renders the ancient TV-less state of nature intolerable, and they must enter the select community of the blessed by whatever means are available.

50 Manju Kumari was just one of millions of poor little Indian girls, and we would never have heard of her were it not for her awful fate. We have come to know of her, not as a human being of inherent dignity and worth, but as an incarnation of an archetype, the sacrificial victim. Creepily, her name 'Sweet Maiden' is fitting; she is the Maiden Sacrificed, not just a terrified little girl. In the days of old, the stories tell us that the sacrificial victims were honored and in many cases were volunteers. They had surrendered to their universal aspect, which can never die. But in our personalistic times such surrender is no longer possible. Though she does not know it, Manju Kumari has indeed become a symbol; her life has assumed a meaning that has outlasted her short, sad life. The external facts of her

life now inform our own consciousness, alerting us to the evil inherent in perverse religiosity.

51 Kālī is a multivalent and complex deity. In her earliest recorded forms such as the 5th century Devī Māhātmyam she has a cosmic significance as the cleansing force of destruction that annihilates evil.[22] This sophisticated mythology, however, must have been developed on the basis of a long history of more primitive but unrecorded beliefs in folk religion. In later Hinduism she is usually worshiped in benign forms. Yet the ancient devouring goddess is still close to the surface of her mythos. Her dark power has made her a favorite for appropriation for feminist or New Age purposes. There is a good reason for this. The incorporation of deadly, destructive, and horrific elements in the divine feminine is realistic and therefore healthy, and their denial in modern Western religion is an unmistakable warning sign. Yet as Manju Kumari will not let us forget, when you have a cult of a goddess of red tongue, adorned with skulls, trampling on corpses, and surrounded by dismemberment, some people will put this into practice in a perfectly straightforward way. To think otherwise is sheer naïvety.

❖

52 The divine has disappeared, and who can blame us if we despair? What's left is but a travesty, a perversion. Since Nietzsche declared the death of god, the Western world has equated the loss of the divine with the overturning of all values. For Buddhists, on the other hand, the simple fact that god dies, like all else, is a basic tenet of our philosophy, and is the very foundation of a mature ethical responsibility. The death of god is no existential or moral crisis, but the simple acknowledgment of how things are.

53 Death, for Buddhists, is no absolute or unprecedented disaster, but just another marker of change. The loss of the numinous experience in modernity sets up a tension that will resolve itself one way or the other; either by a retreat to superstition, or by an evolution in our experience of the sacred.

54 Remember the image of Saṅghamittā with the Bodhi tree. She has become separated from her divinity, but remains in harmony with it. She is a real woman, a historical figure, associated with a sacred meaning, and so the artist correctly depicts her in partnership with the sacred symbols,

neither submerged nor alienated. As a historical figure, she is subject to factual inquiry: When did she live? What did she do? Who were her relatives and companions? But the picture reminds us that this is not all there is to it. As well as the historical dimension, she plays a symbolic role in the sacred life of Buddhists. And that symbolic aspect cannot be dissected as fact, but may be entered into with imagination and reverence. If we are to understand Māyā, Mahāpajāpatī, and the other exemplars of the spiritual feminine in Buddhism, we must spend time with them, get to know them. They are family.

CHAPTER 4

THE LITTLE STICK COLLECTOR

WHEN MĀYĀ MAKES HER WAY TO THE WOODS TO PLAY, she does not do so as a stranger. In ages far past, she was a humble stick-collecting girl, who conceived and gave birth to the Bodhisatta in a forest. This story is recounted in the Kaṭṭhahāri Jātaka.[1] Within its narrow compass this little tale finds room for an extraordinary range of the deepest mythic themes. It shows not only how Buddhist literature remembers spiritual truths far older than itself, but also how the Theravādin storyteller, uninterested in myth, turned an existential drama into a somewhat dubious moral homily against matrilinear succession. Our story is some 2000 years old, and already deep myth is well on its way to becoming a child's tale.

2 The context is provided in another story, the Bhaddasāla Jātaka,[2] and we should briefly retell that story before going on to our main tale.

3 King Pasenadi of Kosala sought a bride from the Śākyans, but their notorious pride would not allow them to send a full-blood princess.[3] This put the Śākyans in a tight spot, as they acknowledged the sovereignty of Kosala. So they sent Vāsabhakhattiyā, daughter of the Śākyan prince Mahānāma and a slave girl, to Pasenadi, pretending she was of noble birth—which was not entirely untrue. The marriage was a success, and the royal couple deeply in love. The son of Pasenadi and Vāsabhakhattiyā was called Viḍūḍabha.

4 After coming of age, Viḍūḍabha returned to Kapilavatthu to visit his Śākyan family. He was surprised that no-one would return his greetings, even though he bowed 'until his back ached'. After they had left, one of his party had to return to collect a forgotten spear, and he saw a servant washing Viḍūḍabha's seat with milk-water, and muttering about Viḍūḍabha, that 'son of a slave-girl'. When Viḍūḍabha learnt of the deception, he vowed to wash the Śākyan palace with the blood of their throats.[4] His vengeance had to wait until he came to the throne; but then he destroyed the Śākyans utterly.[5]

5 When King Pasenadi heard of the Śākyan slave ripoff, he was appalled by the deceit and immediately consigned his wife Vāsabhakhattiyā and his son Viḍūḍabha to the slave quarters. But the Buddha consoled him, saying that although Viḍūḍabha's mother was a slave, the great kings of old valued the patrilinear succession. He told the following story of the days of yore. After hearing the story the king restored Viḍūḍabha and Vāsabhakhattiyā to their former glory.[6]

❖

6 King Brahmadatta of Benares, with a magnificent retinue, was wandering through a park, desirous of fruits and flowers, when he saw a certain maiden singing while gathering branches. Filled with desire, they consummated the act of love. She immediately felt her belly become heavy, as if filled with the thunderbolt of Indra.

7 She told the king that she was bearing his child. The king gave her his ring as a token of parentage, and instructed her to spend the ring on the upbringing if the child was a girl; but if it turned out to be a son, to bring the infant to the king together with the ring. Then he left.

8 Now, the child was indeed a boy, who was brought up by his mother. When he was playing, the other children would tease him, saying, 'No-Father has hit me!' So he went to his mother and asked who his father was. She told him the whole story, upon which he begged to be taken to the king.

9 Seeing her child's determination, she took him to the gate of the palace, and had their coming announced to the king. They were summoned within. She entered, bowed to the king, and declared, 'Your Highness, this is your son!'

10 But the king was ashamed before his court, and so he denied his own son. When she produced the signet-ring as proof, he said, 'This is not my ring.'

11 The mother boldly addressed him, 'O king, I have no witness except for the Truth. If this child be your son, may he remain in mid air. If not, may he fall to the ground and die!'

12 She took the child by the foot and tossed him in the air. The Wonderful Child—who was of course the Bodhisatta—sat cross-legged in mid air, and sang in sweet tones:

13 'Great king, I am your son!
You should rear me, O Protector of the People.
The king rears others, still more
He should look after his own child!'

14 When the king heard the Dhamma thus taught, he cried out, 'Come, my child!' And he stretched out his hands, saying, 'I myself shall rear you! I myself shall rear you!' Though a thousand hands were stretched out to save the boy, he descended into the king's hands and sat in his lap. The king made the child the crown prince, and the mother became the chief queen.

❖

15 At the end of the story, the Buddha revealed the connections in the present day: the king was reborn as the Buddha's father Suddhodana, the queen as the Buddha's mother Māyā, and he himself was the prince.

16 Traditional interpretations do not take us very far in unraveling this fable. The Buddha is made to draw a straightforward anti-matriarchal lesson, saying that the pundits of old have declared: 'What is the mother's clan? The father's clan alone is the measure!'[7] This stands in contrast with the message rather more plausibly attributed to the Buddha in the Saṁyutta Nikāya. Pasenadi comes to him, and is disappointed when he learns that his wife has just given birth to a girl. The Buddha bucks him up, saying, 'Sometimes a daughter is even better than a son.'[8]

17 There is a counter-moral to this patriarchal message: the father has the responsibility to take care of his children, or at least the sons. The affair consummated in the park would have been, in Indian eyes, a valid marriage. Ancient Indians were not hung up on the European idea of only one valid form of marriage, any more than they were hung up on the idea of

worshiping only one true god. There was an elaborate system of different kinds of marriage, each named after the various levels of celestial beings. The least honorable, though still acceptable, form was the spontaneous union of two willing partners, known as the Gandharva wedding, or the *muhutta*, 'instant wedding'. Thus the king was merely fulfilling his accepted duty in acknowledging his responsibility for the child. This is, to be sure, a perfectly respectable moral for the story, but it hardly scratches the surface.

18 The trick of relying on his emotional attachment to establish parenthood is a variation on a ploy that is more commonly used to judge a case where two women claim to be the mother. The child is placed between the two women. They must pull the child towards them; and however pulls hardest wins the baby. But of course the real mother lets go, for she would never harm her child. This fable is found in the Jātakas, and was used as the central metaphor of Brecht's *Caucasian Chalk Circle.*[9] It's a neat example of a piece of folk wisdom that has survived for 2000 years and a journey from India to Germany. Perhaps it has lasted so long because it speaks a truth about a mother's love: if she really loves her child, she knows when to let go.

❖

19 So much for the traditional explanations of the Kaṭṭhahāri Jātaka. The commentators are not interested in mythic structures, archaic cultural relics, or metaphysical metaphors. They were immersed in the world of myth, and were trying to elevate their culture to what they felt to be a more rational ethic (whatever we think about their values in this case). The mythic themes are not of interest in themselves, but are employed solely because they lend an aura, a resonance, a glory to the story. As detailed by Carl Jung, and as known to every Hollywood scriptwriter since *Star Wars*, the subliminal use of archetypal images unleashes an energy, or *libido*, from the unconscious. This lends the force of eternity to the merely human figures whose story comprises the surface narrative.

20 The shallowness of the traditional commentary is of immense value. The commentators were not conscious of the deeper dimensions, and yet they still assigned meaning to the story, in particular through the connections

between the characters in the past and the present. This reveals their unexpressed motivations in a way that self-justifying reasoning never can.

❖

21 To begin delving beneath the surface, let us think of names. To name someone is to give them a 'mark' (*saññā*), a label that sums up who they are. One of the purposes of the Kaṭṭhahāri Jātaka seems to be to explain the curious name of King Kaṭṭhavāhana, the 'Stick Carrier'. The girl is referred to as a *kaṭṭhahārī*, 'stick-bearer', and, while there is no denying the simple sweetness of the tale of the Royal Personage who spies a singing maiden and swoons in her arms,[10] we might yet wonder at the nature of this 'Stick-bearer' who is able to entrance a king.

22 Kaṭṭhahārī is identified with Māyā, and Māyā at the moment of giving birth to Siddhattha is identified with the greatest Stick-bearer of them all: the tree. It is the tree who takes the raw material of Mother Earth and raises it on high, transmuting it into a graceful form, provider of food, fuel, and shade. This is the Tree of Life, sibling to the Tree of Knowledge under which the Buddha sat, and from whose presence Eve was expelled. If we are allowed this much, then the branches appear in a more poignant light: the dead, cast off from the Tree of Life like the Golden Bough or the *sāl* flowers, gathered back into the insatiable belly of the same Mother Earth who gave them birth.

❖

23 The tender maiden is at the same time the maw of death. This is a classic mytheme, embodying the cycles of the seasons, bringing life with death, death with life. Perhaps the best-known exemplar is that other maiden of the wild country, in lands far to the West: Persephone.

24
> She was playing with the deep-bosomed daughters of Okeanos and gathering flowers over a soft meadow, roses and crocuses and beautiful violets, irises also and hyacinths; and the narcissus, which Gaia made to grow at the will of Zeus and to please Polydektor (the Host of Many), to be a snare for the bloom-like girl—a marvelous, radiant flower. It was a thing of awe whether for deathless gods or mortal men to see: from its root grew a hundred blooms and it smelled most sweetly, so that all wide heaven above and the whole earth and the

> sea's salt swell laughed for joy. And the girl was amazed and reached out with both hands to take the lovely toy: but the wide-pathed earth yawned there in the plain of Nysa, and the lord, Polydegmon (Host of Many), with his immortal horses sprang out upon her—the Son of Kronos, Polynomos (He of Many Names).
>
> 25 He caught her up reluctant on his golden car and bare her away lamenting. Then she cried out shrilly with her voice, calling upon her father, [Zeus] the Son of Kronos, who is most high and excellent. But no one, either of the deathless gods or mortal men, heard her voice, nor yet the olive-trees bearing rich fruit.[11]

26 The driver of the chariot is Hades, Lord of Death, taking Persephone the Girl to be his queen. She reigned in the Underworld beside him. Demeter, her mother and the goddess of the grains, was distraught to lose her child; seeking everywhere, her lament dried up the earth. So Persephone was allowed to return, as long as she would spend a season below the ground with her Lord, while the winter covered the land and nothing grew. Persephone, who is only indistinctly differentiated from Demeter, presided over a cult of death and rebirth in the mysteries of Eleusius. She is, at one and the same time, the tender maiden, the fertile wife, and Death's keeper.

27 Could a family relationship be admitted, however distant, between our Stick-bearer at home in the woods and Persephone the Queen of Death? She is an innocent country lass; a queen raised to sit in glory beside her king; and the collector of corpses. Thus she reveals herself as the ancient goddess in her threefold aspect: maiden, wife, and crone.

❖

28 And she sings! According to Julian Jaynes, all the earliest religious texts we have are in verse, especially those parts that speak the essence, the inspired utterances that resonate with the ancient wisdom of the gods.[12] Such are the Vedas, the ancient Indo-European 'hymns of knowledge', passed down orally since—who knows?—maybe 1700–1000 BCE. These verses would always be sung to a simple tune, as they are still in India today. The singers of the Vedas were divinely inspired Seers (*ṛṣi*), who did not compose their verses but 'channeled' them directly from the gods. Some of these 'gods', such as Soma—variously identified with the fly agaric

mushroom, ephedra, hemp, harmal, or the lotus—are still potent today, and their devotees still produce divinely inspired song and verse.[13]

29 The divine inspiration is typically female. For the Greeks, the Muses were always women, from the very beginning, the Iliad's tremendous opening line: 'Sing, O Goddesses, of the wrath of Achilles!' The idea of poetic inspiration as goddess worship became the central obsession of Robert Graves, leading him to declare, 'The function of poetry is religious invocation of the Muse; its use is the experience of mixed exaltation and horror that her presence excites.'[14] Scholars dismiss Graves' historical fancies; yet this does not help us understand why his very personal re-visioning of history has taken such a hold of the western psyche, a continual inspiration for modern New Age/Wicca writers.[15] In looking to the goddess for poetic inspiration, Graves was convinced that he had access to a profound source of ancient wisdom, for she had always been there and had witnessed everything. Thus the greatest of Latin poets, Virgil, invoked the goddess to furnish his mythic imagination with the details of events of the forgotten past, saying 'you remember it all and can recount it'.[16] Such beliefs are by no means alien to the Buddhist tradition: depictions of the Buddha defeating Māra show him calling the Earth Goddess to witness his past deeds. She had always been present and knew the depths of his spiritual achievements.

30 On the other hand, a male deity may take the Muse's place. Vālmīki spontaneously invented the *śloka* metre, overcome with sorrow (*śoka*) when he saw a beautiful bird cruelly slain while making love. But Brahmā appeared to him and told him that he, Brahmā, was the true creator of the metre, so that Vālmīki could tell of the exploits of Rāma, without hesitation or flaw.[17] Modern poets would recognize the melancholic origin of poetic inspiration here.

31 In an earlier and simpler time, Agni inspired of the 'bright word' that filled the hearts of the Vedic seers and overflowed into 'flashing hymns'.[18]

32 While the deity may be incarnated as male or female, in all cases they spring from the well of creative power that is essentially feminine, the domain of the goddess as Mother of All. Such was the conclusion of Erich Neumann in his Jungian analysis of the archetype of the Great Mother. He spoke of the woman as seeress, whose murmuring springs and fountains

bring the wisdom of the unconscious to the surface as an ecstatic vision or inspiration, flowing forth as magic, song, or poetry.[19] Plato said it long ago: '... all good poets, epic as well as lyric, composed their beautiful poems not by art, but because they are inspired and possessed.'[20]

33 Hence at the emotive and spiritual climax of our Jātaka, when the hero is suspended in mid-air, the story suddenly shifts from linear prose to inspired verse. The songs of Kaṭṭhahārī or Persephone would have been ballads, of love maybe, or love's loss, simple country tunes, earthy and sensual. The Bodhisatta is didactic, he sings of justice and is not shy to tell the king of his duties. But each of these songs marks a crisis point, a climactic shift in the fates of the protagonists.

❖

34 Our little Stick-bearer has been taken by the spirit of the goddess as she does her ambiguous work in the woods; thus she is ripe for a lightning strike. While we moderns inevitably take the king to be a mortal, more or less like us, this is a distinctly minority position. Kingship always has a divine dimension. In ancient India it was believed that if the king was righteous, the rain would fall, flowers would bloom, and the fruit would be sweet throughout his realm. Seers could assess the justice of the king's rule merely by tasting the fruit.[21] The divine aspect of our story is insisted on, for the maiden knows immediately that she has become pregnant. Intercourse between gods and human women invariably results in pregnancy, because the point of the story is not to depict a human relationship, but to authorize the kingly lineage.

35 The actual intercourse may take any form, from an idealized romance to outright rape. On one level this is a perfectly realistic social comment on the sexual behavior of kings. Nevertheless, such encounters cannot be reduced to human terms. Often enough, indeed, the conception comes about by magical means: a thumb placed on the belly, a prayer to a deity, or even eating a mango.[22] Divine seduction is not subject to human laws.

36 Yet as the sacred is inexorably worn away, taboos are leached of power, and it becomes possible to subject the gods to the same ethical standards that we expect of humans. On the day the gods are criticized for rape, their humiliation is near complete. Euripides has Apollo's son Ion, born of the rape of Creüsa, reproach his father:

37 > What is wrong with him? He rapes virgins and then abandons them. Begets children and then abandons them too—to die? No, Apollo. Do not abuse your great power. Seek only virtue. If you have it that the mortal who sins gets punished by the gods, well then, how can you commit sins and not be punished yourselves? And if you don't want to do this—for argument's sake—then make it legal for the mortals also to have illegal unions. Then you will see Poseidon and you, too, Zeus how your temples will empty as punishment for your crimes. You go off pursuing your own pleasure without a care for the consequences. Why should people say that men are wicked for imitating acts the gods consider acceptable? No, it is the men's teachers one must blame![23]

38 Like all fundamental mythemes, divine sex is essentially an existential motif. The ethical dimension is secondary, and becomes a storytelling trope to evoke an emotional reaction, or as an excuse to discuss ethical issues of the day. The fact that one and the same story can be told as both a forcible, violent rape and as a loving union proves that the ethical issues are not fundamental. The late sophisticate Ovid, for example, depicts Europa as forcibly abducted by Zeus, while earlier depictions show her gracefully acquiescing.

39 As imagined by Roberto Calasso, divine rape expresses a shocking, arbitrary state of possession, a sudden, unpredictable, and dangerous overwhelming of one's limited being as it is exposed to forces that are orders of magnitude greater than a mere mortal can endure.[24] A full exposure to the godhead would leave the victim dead, so the divinity must assume a variety of masks to veil its majesty.[25] In one of his most penetrating moods, Jung remarks:

40 > The incomparably useful function of the dogmatic symbol is that it protects a person from a direct experience of God as long as he does not mischievously expose himself. But if he leaves home and family, lives too long alone and gazes too deeply into the dark mirror, then the awful event of the meeting may befall him. Yet even then the traditional symbol, come to full flower through the centuries, may operate like a healing draught and divert the final incursion of the living godhead into the hallowed spaces of the church.[26]

41 Jung has captured the thing in gentleness, but his words are all too true: the purpose of religious forms is to protect us from divinity. Divinity is

the world around us, the unfathomable, the mysterious, the unexpressed potency, the unseeable manifest. This itself is the truth from which we hide. The churches have become, not houses of God, but prisons for God, trapping Him in liturgy and dogma. And in just the same way, the temples have become, quite literally, tombs of the Buddha. Very often, the greatest expense and devotion in a Buddhist temple goes into building the stupa, which is nothing more than a tomb for the Buddha's supposed physical remains, his relics. The very size and weight of the construction reveals the force that is required to keep the Buddha down.

42 Always and without exception, the true encounter happens to the brave soul who dares venture outside. The Bodhisatta only approached the truth when he rejected, not only the physical comforts of home life, but the more insidious comfort of the religious dogma that he learnt from his first teachers.

❖

43 Our sweet maiden is alone in the woods, without the artifice of religion to protect her from the divine. The king, outside the strictures of court, removes the mask that hides his divinity and so she experiences him as a thunderbolt, the thinnest of disguises. This violent imposition of the Other, so characteristic of the Sky-Father religions, contrasts with the timeless immanence of the nature cults, which experience divinity rather in the slow, predictable growth of the crops and trees.

44 The divine Father who appears as the 'thunderbolt in the belly' is irresistibly reminiscent of Zeus, with his countless amorous escapades. Zeus-like, too, is the lightness of the encounter, the playful-yet-serious tone, exactly halfway between the primordial devouring Leviathan and today's divas, rock gods, and American Idols. Thus the king is associated with the Indo-European patriarchal gods, just as the Stick-collector is identified with Mother Earth.

45 The Indo-European fathers were not bound to the slow, profound, morbid rhythms of Nature's cycles, patiently waiting for this season's death to yield up next season's life. They sped in their horse-drawn chariots over the plains, accompanied by the winds and the storms, striking like lightning and taking what they willed. The king intrudes at his own whim

into the maiden's dim, timeless demesne, in search of 'fruits and flowers' for his own pleasure.[27]

46 Such myths have long been taken to record a cultural memory of an ancient conflict between the indigenous goddess cults of the Neolithic (or earlier), and the patriarchal gods of the nomadic invaders. In India, this conflict has been localized in the incursion of the Indo-European culture, perhaps around 2000 BCE. While there is scant textual or archeological evidence for any large scale invasion or immigration from outside India, recent genetic research suggests that the Indian upper castes are more similar to Europeans, while the lower castes are more similar to Asians.[28] This suggests that immigrants from the northwest into India were mainly absorbed in the upper castes, especially the ruling and priestly castes, where their cultural influence would be great, despite their limited numbers.

47 The socio-historical memory of tribal conflict appears in a curiously blatant way in the background story to the Jātaka, where the Stick-collector is introduced in comparison with Vāsabhakhattiyā, the slave-girl deceitfully married to Viḍūḍabha.[29] The name Vāsabhakhattiyā suggests a successful adoption into the Khattiya class; but her mother is called Nāgamuṇḍā.[30] Both Nāga and Muṇḍa—and probably the very word *dāsa*, which we translate as 'slave'—are non-Indo-European names of indigenous Indian tribes.[31] Viḍūḍabha, too, is a curious name, which the commentary explains as being given by mistake, after a deaf servant misheard the real name.[32] However, the repeated retroflex consonants, so unlike the Indo-European languages of the ruling classes, betray its indigenous origins; which is why it was given by a servant.

48 These names hint at the tribal roots of the goddess fertility cult. Like dozens of stories in the international mythic corpus, the Indo-European sky-god of the thunderbolt impregnates the chthonic goddess, telling of a historical shift from feminine to masculine religious orientations. Read historically, the evasiveness and denial of parentage reflects the reluctance of the patriarchal cults to acknowledge their neolithic roots. But it also reflects a very personal concern, the need to know the truth of paternity.

❖

49 The uncertainty of paternity is reflected in many other stories, both Brahmanical and Buddhist. We think of the key Mahābhārata myth of

Duṣyanta and Śakuntalā, which mirrors almost exactly the form of the present Jātaka. Closer still is the Uddālaka Jātaka; there the Bodhisatta, a chaplain under King Brahmadatta, takes the part of the random father in the park; a 'gorgeous prostitute' is the mother; and the child, since he cannot take his father's name, is named Uddālaka, after the tree beside which he was conceived. But in this story the ring is recognized.[33]

50 Or consider the Upaniṣadic story of Satyakāma, 'Truth-lover'.[34] Like the Bodhisatta in our story, he was brought up by his mother alone. On coming of age, he conceived the wish to study the scriptures. Knowing that the Brahmanical teacher would inquire about his parentage, he approached his mother to ask who his father was. His mother openly admits that when she was young she 'got around a lot as a maid' and did not know who the father was. Satyakāma, undaunted, went to the teacher Gautama Haridrumata and told him exactly the truth. Gautama said: 'One who was not a brahman could not have spoken thus!'

51 As well as the obvious parallels in structure, in each story the Truth plays the crucial role. This emphasis arises from the basic problem with patrilinear societies: you never really know who the father is. This is just as problematic today. As many as 19% of women in the USA who receive child support have named the wrong man as father.[35]

52 If we chase this mythic pattern into the deep past, it would seem that this concern with paternity is more than an example of the benefits of truth-telling. It was a critical social force that elevated Truth to a decisive moral concern. We know who the mother was, and so there is little need to tell stories establishing maternity.[36] Mother-stories are concerned not with truth, but with meaning. Only the ascendance of the Father demands a more literal conception of the Truth. Here we see a critical juncture, where the distinction between myth and history, religion and science, value and fact lies in embryo, just starting to unfurl. It was the men who started compiling lists of 'patriarchs', whether tribal or religious, where time was a succession of individuals, rather than a cycle of emergence and decay. The Brahmanical tradition is full of such lists, stretching into an improbably distant past. The early generations of Buddhists adopted this Brahmanical custom, forming the basis of the lineage lists that are so crucial to the monastic Sangha's sense of self-identity today.[37]

53 It is no coincidence, then, that the story of the First Lie tells the origins of the patriarchal lineages of the kings.[38] In ages far past the first king was named Mahāsammata.[39] The line of kings descended from him culminated in Upacāra, who could walk through the air, was defended by four deities, and exuded the fragrance of sandalwood and lotus. Upacāra's priest was Kapila, who had a younger brother called Korakalamba. But when Kapila left the king's service to become an ascetic, the coveted post of royal priest was granted to his son, not his brother Korakalamba. The king promised to make Korakalamba the priest by means of a lie. The people went about asking: 'What sort of thing is a lie? Is it blue or yellow or some other color?' King Upacāra, though he was warned by Kapila, asserted in public that Korakalamba was the senior and deserving of the priesthood. His guardian angels fled and he was dragged to hell; but his sons sought the advice of Kapila and established five kingdoms.

54 Mother-stories are not trying to prove anything. They speak of life, of love, of the pain of loss. How different is the king in the Kaṭṭhahārī story! There is no question of the king responding to his child from simple love. Only when the lineage is proven does he feel a connection. His love arises from the son's injunction to an abstract notion of duty, arguing from the king's duty to all people to his duty for his son. This inference goes against all natural psychology; a man should love his son first and from there expand his sphere of concern.[40] Our king has become so immersed in his patriarchy that natural love is dependent on abstract justice, not the other way around.

❖

55 For Satyakāma, as for the Bodhisatta in our Jātaka, the mother remains passive during the childhood period. She is content to let matters lie, and is only stirred to action on the volition of the son. The male is the doer.[41] Satyakāma is removed from the circle of the women, where he has spent his younger years, and is initiated into the circle of men, an essential step in his own growth towards manhood.

56 In the Kaṭṭhahāri Jātaka, this moment of transition is vividly drawn: the Bodhisatta is suspended between the sky and the earth, between the mother and the father. If anything goes wrong, the mother's threat will

come true. He will fall to the earth and die, failing to make the transition to manhood, and being absorbed back into the chthonic realm.

57 Tossing her child into the sky, the goddess as murderer emerges with disturbing clarity. The king rescues the child; this gives a further moral subtext to the story, as the patriarchal religions typically saw one of their chief civilizing effects being the abolition of human sacrifice. This reform is remembered in such tales as Abraham, who substituted a goat for his son; or Tantalus, who so outraged the gods by feeding them human flesh that they decreed everlasting torment. The gods were aware of Tantalus' intent, so they avoided the horrific feast. Only Demeter, distraught and distracted by the loss of Persephone, ate part of a shoulder. Demeter is an incarnation of the Great Mother of old, and it is entirely fitting that she should be the last of the gods to fully give up the old ways.

58 In Buddhism this ethical revolution is brought about, of course, by the Bodhisatta. In the Takkāriya Jātaka the Bodhisatta persuades the king to sacrfice a dead goat on the site of the city gate instead of a brahman.[42] In the Khaṇḍahāla Jātaka the Bodhisatta persuades his father the king to stop his evil plan of sacrificing all his family to gain heaven.[43] In both of these cases the instigator of the sacrifice was a corrupt brahman, who is using his spiritual authority to get rid of his enemies by pretending they need to be sacrificed. Even here, in these stories over two millennia old, there is no question of an authentic cosmic meaning to such sacrifice. It is taken for granted that those conducting the rituals were sheer hypocrites. Those who conduct the rituals believe them least.

❖

59 Our story reaches its fulfillment through a reciprocal transgression. The king entered Her domain, the wild and unpredictable realm of the goddess, where he did indeed encounter the wild and unpredictable. This trope is found in countless Jātakas: the king of culture only reaches maturity when he masters the 'other', nature, the wilds, the unconscious.[44] He passes through the woods, but he cannot remain. Leaving the woods, he escapes immediate death, but he cannot escape the cycle of necessity. The ring is the circle that binds the family. While the shape of the ring is wholeness, its golden substance is purity and eternity. The ring is the incorruptible One, and to recognize it is to find your soul.[45]

60 The circle of the ring brings the mother back into the sphere of the father. This time it is she who transgresses the male domain, an unlettered country lass in the court of kings. She challenges the king to a higher awareness, a fuller acceptance of humanity, but the problem is not surmounted until the Wonderful Child, in between the male and female, intervenes. He is the promise of things higher, of a life more complete. With the appearance of the Child as the Mysterious Third, the male and female can find fulfillment in each other at last.

61 Throughout our story, the male is the agent of culture, the female is the embodiment of nature. And when, prompted by the son, the mother at last makes her magnificent stand on Truth, she is raised into a higher level of culture. Her previous existence as a nature-child was an immature expression of her femininity. Now she is the Queen, as the full flowering of her glory unfolds.

❖

62 The crown, the scepter, the magnificence of royalty are the numinous halo of archetypal realization, behind which her mere person recedes as behind a mask, or behind the bridal veil. We respond emotionally to these symbols, even if our political sympathies are thoroughly democratic.

63 The wedding might be seen, on a crude level, as a license to have sex. But this would be a mistake. Sexual promiscuity is the norm of nature. It takes a powerful cultural construct, hallowed by traditions, blessed by the Elders, and wrapped in ritual, to restrict the couple's sexual activity to each other.[46] Even with this full weight of cultural expectation, the promiscuity of nature reasserts itself often enough. But adultery is still felt to be a transgression, a falling away from cultural and personal aspirations. This bounding of sexuality comes with the acceptance of each other's humanity. One marries a person, not a sexual organ.

64 The mother grasps the child by the foot; again, this motif occurs in countless stories. Achilles' mother, the goddess Thetis, grasped him by the heel when she dipped him in the river Styx, rendering all of his body immortal and invulnerable, except for the heel. Achilles' proverbial heel is the most well-known. But for Oedipus, Jason, Kṛṣṇa,[47] and countless others the foot, which stands on Mother Earth, is closest to her power, and is the last part of the body to be freed from her perilous beneficence.

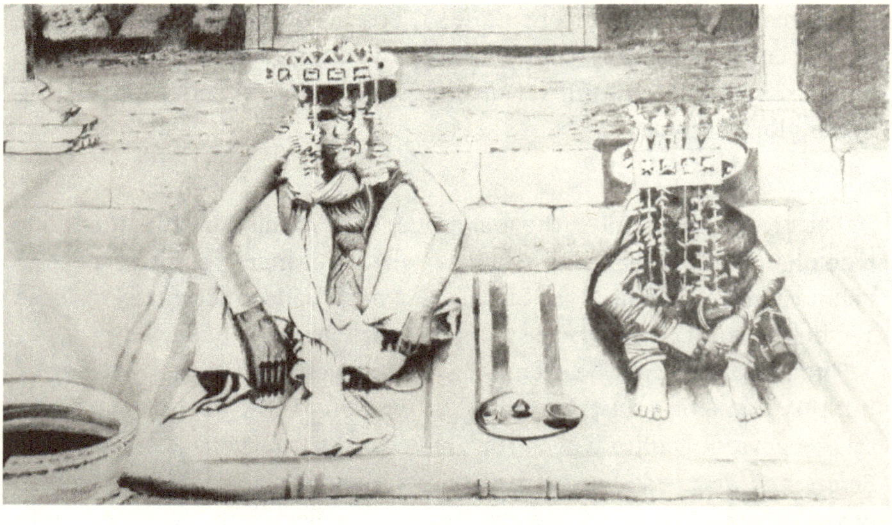

Figure 4.1: *Bridal couple, Mali, India*

65 Having been tossed by the mother the Wonderful Child remains still in the air. This is the ambiguous posture of the hero, outside the normal gamut of possibilities. Suspension in ambiguity is a critical feature of coming of age rituals for both boys and girls, as shown at length by Frazer in his chapter 'Between Heaven and Earth'.[48] Suspended in the twilight zone between mother and father, neither touching the earth, nor flying the sky, anything can happen; he is potentiality, not actuality. But he cannot sustain this poise, and returns to the father, who then replaces the mother in nurturing the child, crying out: 'I alone will raise him'. Thus the Sky Father usurps the Creator role from the Earth Mother.

66 The father's boast is not entirely truthful. He marries the girl, and the child is brought up by man and wife together. The pre-conscious separation from the father while an infant; the conscious separation from the mother to rediscover the father: these are the agonizing pre-requisites of wholeness. But this is not the end of the matter. It is merely the attainment of fullness, not the transcendence of emptiness. For that, our Bodhisattva must learn to remain seated in the sky.

67 He will not achieve this until his final birth, when he is not born onto the ground. Held aloft by the gods, he stands poised between all dualities, and from this place of pure potential his Awakening becomes possible. In iconography, this poise is captured in the baby Bodhisatta's hand gestures: one hand points to the sky, the other to the earth.

68 This stance is prefigured in the Bodhisatta's last birth story, the Vessantara Jātaka, where it is suggested by his name. In the Pali the name is given a suspiciously jejune explanation:

> 69 'My name came not from the mother's side nor the father's.
> As I was born in Vessa Street, Vessantara's my name.'[49]

70 That *vessantara* indicates something more interesting than an address is suggested by the Upāli Sutta, where it is an epithet of the Buddha.[50] Like Viḍūḍabha, the unusual name prompted a dubious explanation. But while Viḍūḍabha is probably not Indo-European, Vessantara is made of *vessa* (= Sanskrit *viśva*), 'all', and *antara*, 'in-between'.[51] The Sanskrit is Viśvaṇtara, the one who 'Crosses Over All'.[52] Vessantara is the one who is 'In-between All', or 'Crosses Over All', neither mother nor father.

71 Another reading is possible. *Viśva* is the 'all' in the sense of the entire cosmos; and *antara* can mean the innermost part, the secret heart of something. So Vessantara is not only the one who Crosses Over All, he is the Secret Heart of the Cosmos. In the Kaṭṭhahāri Jātaka, the Bodhisatta's pose, suspended in mid-air between mother and father, was resolved by choosing the father, and then integrating the two through marriage. But now, his spiritual progress nearly complete, he identifies with none; and yet at the same time he is the hidden seed of Awakening in each person.

CHAPTER 5

A MAGIC BIRTH

In speaking of little Siddhattha's birth, our sources say again and again that the events are *dhammatā*, the way of nature, a universal truth. How are we to understand this? When Buddhist modernists speak of *dhammatā*, they point to philosophical Suttas which describe the laws of causality, or impermanence, for example, as universal principles.[1] They were not invented by the Buddha; they were discovered by him, and taught for those who seek liberation. In this sense *dhammatā* is a natural law, a description of reality. How can the events around a miraculous birth be a 'law of nature'? Here are the items listed, all said to be *dhammatā*.

❖

2 Mindful and clearly comprehending, the Bodhisatta passed away from Tusita heaven and was reborn in his mother's womb.

3 When the Bodhisatta was conceived, an immeasurable splendor filled the dark reaches of the cosmos, so that even the creatures existing in the abysmal reaches of space could recognize each other for the first time.

4 The divine Four Great Kings guard the Bodhisatta and his mother from all harm.

5 When pregnant, the Bodhisatta's mother naturally keeps the five precepts.

6 She has no thought of lust for a man.

7 She is endowed with all sensual delights.

8 She does not become ill, is happy and unfatigued.

9 She sees the Bodhisatta within her womb, as clearly as one can see a thread running through a fine gem.

10 Seven days after the Bodhisatta's birth, his mother dies and is reborn in Tusita heaven.

11 She carries the Bodhisatta for exactly 10 months.

12 She gives birth standing.

13 Deities first receive the infant, then humans.

14 While the Bodhisatta has still not reached the earth, the Four Great Kings announce to the mother: 'Rejoice, O Queen! A son of great majesty has been born to you.'

15 When emerging from the womb, both the Bodhisatta and his mother are entirely clean, with no mucus or blood or any impurities, just like a pure gem resting on a clean cloth.

16 Two streams of water appear in the air for washing the mother, one cool, one warm.

17 Mindful and clearly comprehending, the Bodhisatta stands on his own feet, faces the North, takes seven mighty strides with a white umbrella raised over him, surveys the quarters, and roars with the voice of a bull: 'I am Foremost in the world! I am Eldest in the world! I am Greatest in the world! This is my last birth, now there is no further existence!'

18 When the Bodhisatta emerged from the womb, an immeasurable splendor filled the dark reaches of the cosmos, so that even the creatures existing in the abysmal reaches of space could recognize each other for the first time.[2]

❖

19 In some of these miracles we can discern *dhammatā* in a meaningful sense. For example, the superhuman prodigies displayed by the baby Bodhisatta prefigure his future career as a Buddha. Standing on his own feet he demonstrates his own self-Awakening; facing the North (*uttara*) he signifies his orientation to the 'beyond' (*uttara*); seven 'mighty strides' indicate his crossing over the cycles of creation (and, in doing so, usurp the three great strides of Viṣṇu[3]); the umbrella is the purity of liberation; surveying the quarters shows his unobstructed knowledge of the spiritual capacities of beings; and his bull's roar of supremacy presages the future rolling forth of the Wheel of Dhamma. This symbolic biography in miniature describes the essential qualities of all Buddhas. It is impossible to imagine a Buddha

who does not have these qualities, and so this 'miracle' is readily comprehensible as a mythic expression of a natural principle, albeit a supernatural natural principle.

20 In other cases such an explanation is not possible. The Four Great Kings guarding the mother, and jets of water bathing her, lights in the sky, and the rest; these do not have any meaningful connection with the Buddha, and are just the kind of miracles that might be associated with the birth of any great religious teacher.

21 The text itself playfully undermines its own mythic pretensions, for after Ānanda has finished enunciating all of these 'wonderful and marvelous' qualities, the Buddha responds by telling Ānanda a further quality: the Buddha is mindfully aware of feelings, perceptions, and thoughts as they arise, persist, and cease.[4] With typically quiet irony this marginalizes the miraculous in preference for the psychological. The meditative practice mentioned here is elsewhere said to be the way to develop 'mindfulness and clear comprehension'.[5] This ties up with the beginning of the discourse: if the Bodhisatta is already mindful when he is born, it must have been because of his meditative practice in past lives.

22 In this early discourse the rational trumps the mythic, but even here the mythic/magical aspect is irreducible. And for later generations the meditative aspect of this scripture became entirely neglected. We cannot argue away the fact that, regardless of the historicity of the passage, the redactors felt the need to express a mythic dimension to the Buddha's birth, whether or not they literally believed in these miracles. And it is therefore in a mythic sense that dhammatā must be understood here.

❖

23 *Dhammatā* suggests inevitability. It implys that the characters in our story, while appearing to make choices and decide their own lives, are actually conforming to necessity. Their lives reiterate cosmic patterns, in the same way that, for example, the lives of fertility and vegetation deities such as Tammuz, Osiris, or Demeter would constantly replay the cycle of the seasons. Such fatalism is characteristic of the old goddess; as the three Fates, she weaves the destiny of the world.

24 My suggestion that the *dhammatā* of the birth must be understood in a mythic sense is no arbitrary one, for our textual sources for the birth are

overtly mythic. The prime source for the archetypal pattern of Buddhism, ever-recurring through 91 æons of cosmic expansion and contraction, is the Mahāpadāna Sutta.[6] The birth is depicted as we have seen above; it is entirely archetypal and has no personal connection with Siddhattha. The Sutta goes on to list the names, parents' names, castes, chief disciples, Awakening Trees, etc. of the seven Buddhas before telling in detail of Vipassī's going forth. Here we find the canonical source for the legend of the 'Four Divine Messengers', which the later tradition retold with Siddhattha as the principal character.

25 While the 'Four Divine Messengers' episode was, it seems, adopted from Vipassī's story and included in Siddhattha's, for the most part the Mahāpadāna Sutta retells Siddhattha's story, glorifying the mundane details: while Siddhattha lived for 80 years, Vipassī lived for 80 000; while Siddhattha had 1250 arahant disciples, Vipassī had 6 980 000. The teachings remain the same, but the drama is played out on a cosmic scale. The facts become impossible and hence inevitable: *dhammatā*.

26 Comparing the stories of Siddhattha and Vipassī I am more than a little reminded of the *Iliad*, where the worldly conflicts and alliances of the warriors are mirrored in the intrigues and rivalries of the 'deathless gods'. Closer to home, this pattern echoes the form of hundreds of Jātakas, where the mythic events of the past become the archetype for events in the Buddha's lifetime.

27 The birth is also described in the Acchariya-abbhuta Sutta.[7] In this Sutta, Ānanda reports the miracles associated with the birth as things he has 'heard from the Blessed One's lips'. This suggests that he was quoting, perhaps from the Mahāpadāna Sutta itself.[8] Thus the whole cycle of miracles originally occurred within a mythic time-frame, which the devotional tradition (represented by Ānanda) drew into 'historical' time.

❖

28 Of all the miracles, perhaps the most suggestive is that Māyā can see the child in her womb, 'like a thread running through a gem'. This motif is represented exactly in Christian iconography, where Mary is depicted with a fully visible, radiant boy Jesus in her womb, through whom runs a thread, the thread she is weaving.[9] The bright clarity contrasts with the dark obscurity of normal birth, a magical process that no-one ever sees or

understands; yet we have all lived through it and the continuance of our species depends on it. Now this is raised to full consciousness, announcing a radically different kind of birth, which heralds a radically different kind of death. The thread, in the literal Buddhist interpretation, is the *bhavanetti*, the 'thread of life', the craving that knits our lives together by creating identity, an 'I' who is the subject of the stories we tell ourselves: the Hero of our imagination. It is the thread of destiny, woven by karma, which in popular Buddhism takes over from the Fates.

29 Why thread? Such a persistent, widespread metaphor does not take hold of language and imagination for no reason. The 'yarn', the 'spinning of the tale', happened in the real world. Weaving is women's work; and in the telling and the retelling, whiling away the hours as the repetitive, never-ending work goes on, the yarn is spun over and over again, until the fabric of the tale is as familiar and comforting as a robe of fine cloth. It's the thing that holds a people together. And the destiny of the soul is woven in the pattern.

❖

30 Māyā's magical pregnancy and birthing were bright, clean, happy, crystalline, as far from the noisy, sweaty, blood-soaked pain of a real birth as is possible to imagine. Such a fantasy could only have been invented by men. Māyā is made, even while still human, separate from the seamy side of her womanhood.

31 The story is that hackneyed old cliché, the 'virgin birth', by which the heroes of old were all born. The affinity between the Buddha's birth and those of other heroes was noted around 400 CE by the Christian patriarch Jerome, as he defended Jesus' virgin birth from the rationalists of his day.

32 > To come to the Gymnosophists of India, the opinion is authoritatively handed down that Budda, the founder of their religion, had his birth through the side of a virgin. And we need not wonder at this in the case of Barbarians when cultured Greece supposed that Minerva at her birth sprang from the head of Jove, and Father Bacchus from his thigh. Speusippus also, Plato's nephew, and Clearchus in his eulogy of Plato, and Anaxelides in the second book of his philosophy, relates that Perictione, the mother of Plato, was violated by an apparition of Apollo, and they agree in thinking that the prince of wisdom was

> born of a virgin. Timus writes that the virgin daughter of Pythagoras was at the head of a band of virgins, and instructed them in chastity. Diodorus, the disciple of Socrates, is said to have had five daughters skilled in dialectics and distinguished for chastity, of whom a full account is given by Philo the master of Carneades. And mighty Rome cannot taunt us as though we had invented the story of the birth of our Lord and Savior from a virgin; for the Romans believe that the founders of their city and race were the offspring of the virgin Ilia and of Mars.[10]

33 This does not mean that Māyā the maiden had never had sex. Physical intactness is not essential to the mythic ideal of the virgin mother. It is just another symbol. Mary, after giving birth to Jesus, remains 'ever virgin' in the eyes of the Catholic Church (although they're still tying themselves in exegetical knots to explain away his brothers and sisters.[11]) This remains true even today: young women who wish to 'renew' their virginity may do so either through surgery or simply by affirming vows of abstinence.[12] Virginity is a state of mind. Nor is the puritanical ideal of motherly celibacy essential, although it has found its way into Māyā's story of the marvelous birth.

34 The essence of mythic virginity, rather, is the transcendence of normal cycles of generation. In western myth, virgin heroines such as Atlanta, Artemis, and the rest, were powerful and independent actors, not subject to the control of the males.[13] This reflects the social reality in a world before contraception. Such independence makes the woman barren and hence useless in the eyes of conventional norms, but for the virgin mothers it announces the entry of something new into the cycle, something that will break open the old ways of being.

35 Siddhattha's paternity is twofold: his human father, with whom he would have such troubled relations, and who would resist so manfully his son's spiritual destiny; and the divine father—Siddhattha the father of Siddhattha, who deliberately descends from Tusita heaven to enter his mother's womb. We are used to simply thinking of Suddhodana as the father, but he, like Mahāpajāpatī, is merely the one who raised Siddhattha. The traditions did not think of him as the literal father, for Suddhodana was absent the night of the conception.[14] Thus Siddhattha became known as the Svayambhūnātha, 'The Self-originated Lord'.

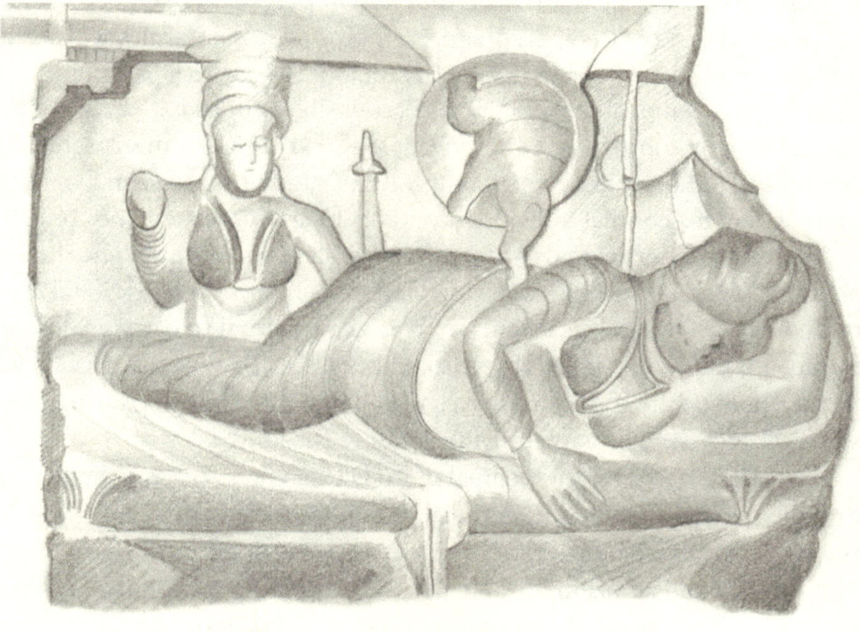

***Figure 5.1:** Māyā's dream: the conception of the Bodhisatta*

36 Later tellings fancied Māyā lying languid in a mystic dream as a white, six-tusked elephant entered her womb.[15] The appearance as an elephant, however, is not 'just a dream', for the Bodhisatta consciously takes on this form, which is experienced by his mother as a dream. The elephant is the divine impregnation, comparable to the multitude of forms taken by Zeus in his amorous adventures, one of which we have already met: the thunderbolt. The elephant, with six tusks and trunk held erect, makes the phallic symbolism entirely explicit, even blatant.

37 Siddhattha conflicts with his father and impregnates his mother, and so we are within the Oedipal sphere. For many people of faith it will seem little short of scandalous to reduce the Buddha's story to a psychological theory that is unpalatable and incomprehensible. But the 'Oedipal' motif in one form or another pervades mythology.[16] A Freudian interpretation is possible: Siddhattha's attachment for and sudden separation from his mother, and his conflict and later atonement with his father. The conflict is resolved in later legends when the Buddha helps Suddhodana attain arahantship on his deathbed. Having played the limiting, oppositional role of diverting Siddhattha's attention from the spiritual to the worldly, he finally embraces the value of spiritual liberation. This legend, as well as its psychological dimension, serves the political agenda of exalting the spiritual above the profane, the monk above the king.

38 Ultimately, however, the Oedipal motif is existential, not psychological or political, and certainly not ethical. It depicts a coming-to-be, and sets the stage for an extraordinary life by describing an extraordinary birth. The wonder and amazement of Awakening, bursting all bonds of reality, requires an appropriately incredible backstory. The most extraordinary birth of all is the creation of the cosmos, which must always be a kind of 'self-generation'. This is taken for granted by the mythographers. Their job is to render this in terms suitable for the scale and nature of the particular myth at hand. The crude and violent imagery of, say, the Egyptian Atum creating his children through masturbation,[17] or the Greek Kronos' castration of his father Uranus with a sickle at the urging of his mother,[18] is in the Buddhist myth suitably replaced by the symbol of the Royal Elephant, embodiment of power and nobility.[19]

39 Such motifs in myth spring from the very deepest reaches of time, and have nothing to do with real or imagined incest in our modern sense. 'Incest' can only be conceived once the boundaries delimiting kinship have been drawn; that is to say, when culture, language, and society have evolved. The very idea of incest is predicated on a duality of 'kin' and 'not-kin', a duality that underpins all logic. But these motifs speak from within a primal, undifferentiated consciousness, from which point of view the achievement of sheer humanity is the 'pearl of great price', to be attained through unstinting effort and sacrifice. The Bodhisatta's 'self-generation' is entirely appropriate for he who was to become 'selfawakened'.

❖

40 Dramas such as *Oedipus Rex* derive their power from the questioning of these primitive mythemes by an emerging sense of critical, personal ethics. This is the appalling glory of myth from this period, the 'axial age' centered around 500 BCE, when both Indian and Greek culture burst into flower. The oldest mythic layers, neolithic or earlier, emerged through spontaneous inspiration, without conscious reflection. Later generations inherited the archaic themes, revered them as an authentic out-pouring of the human heart, and grappled to reconcile them with rational, ethical concerns.[20] The mythographers invoked the emotional power of the ancient stories in the very act of announcing their destruction. Axial legends, including the life of the Buddha, stand halfway between myth and history; but they also stand halfway between myth and the novel.[21]

41 In Sophocles' *Oedipus Rex*, the drama pivots on the terrible clash of unconscious destiny and 'conscious' ethical values. It is Oedipus' success that leads him to his downfall. First he overthrows the Sphinx through answering her riddle: 'What speaks with but one voice, and walks on four feet, two feet, and three feet?'[22] The answer: the human beast. For as an infant we crawl on all fours, when grown we stand upright, and in old age we lean on a stick. Oedipus' victory, by which he wins the queen and the throne, relies not on force of arms, but on self-realization. But he does not realize that, although the riddle was about 'feet', his own feet were wounded, damaged, when as a baby he was abandoned to the wilderness by his parents, who were driven to this inhumanity by the fear of an oracle. When he was found, his feet were bound and pierced. Hence his name, so heavy with

etymology and punning that it overbears its bearer: 'child of the swelling sea'; 'alas, two-footed'; 'swollen-foot'; but also: 'I am the knower'.[23]

42 Accordingly, as king he is a decisive, forceful ruler, who personally drives the investigation, seeking every word that will reveal his own unconscious crimes. But all the while, although he believes he has vanquished the monstrous She in the form of the Sphinx, he brings to fruition the inexorable dictates of the Fates as revealed through the priestesses of the Oracle. The unconscious has not been uprooted, but merely banished from awareness. In his search for knowledge he denies his innate knowing; he is cut off, dissociated, from his parents, yet his life draws itself back into their circle, driven by love, the terrible love that cannot admit its pain.[24] The crime of his parents leads down the road to his own crimes, all encoded in his name. And the ultimate victim of this spiral of family crime is love, which forever loses its innocence.

43 In the axial age, mythic inevitability collides with personal choice. Myth embodies life and death, and must speak of universals, while in a personal story an individual constructs their own life through their choices. Siddhattha's spiritual development was, in truth, a matter of his own choice. He was not abandoned by his parents, he chose to leave them. Unlike heroes such as Oedipus, who struggle to assert their will against fate, the Buddha created his own destiny. His choices were so authentic and had such a profound universal resonance that myth was the only container big enough to hold them. And the easiest event to mythologize is the birth, since an infant's experience is the closest that real life comes to experiencing myth as reality.

CHAPTER 6

HOW MĀYĀ BECAME A GODDESS

BAD FAITH: TO DENY THE OVERWHELMING FACT OF OUR FREEDOM, to pretend that we are in the grip of destiny, passive and choiceless. This is the seductive illusion of the birth as *dhammatā*, as if by taking matters out of his hands Siddhattha's acts become even more heroic. Authentic passages on Siddhattha's spiritual career contain no trace of bad faith. They emphasize the immediacy of Siddhattha's choices. The birth story is perhaps the first trace of bad faith in the telling of the Buddha's life. From now on, the story assumes its now-familiar artificial sheen. The Buddha over-acts his part, gestures become theatrical, larger than life. Smiles are required by contract, and the actor's own feelings become irrelevant.

2 There is, however, one detail in Siddhattha's birth that escapes this flaw. The Buddha's birth is a miraculous event of cosmic dimensions, embodying the inevitability of nature; but it does not merely dress itself up in virginal purity and dancing deities. It acknowledges the Dark Side, the Kālī aspect: after seven days, Māyā must die. Death is the only inevitability in life, and in conforming to the *dhammatā* of death our text authentically represents not only the profane facts of life, but also the fundamental truth embodied by myth.

3 It cannot be chance that this 'wonderful and marvelous' event is the only detail of the birth that is mentioned outside the miraculous context.

Ānanda and the Buddha discuss the 'marvelous' death of the Bodhisatta's mother.

> 4 … Venerable Ānanda said to the Blessed One: 'It is incredible, Bhante! It is amazing, Bhante! How short-lived was the Blessed One's mother! Seven days after the Blessed One was born, the Blessed One's mother passed away, and was reborn in Tusita heaven.'
>
> 5 'So it is, Ānanda: short-lived are the Bodhisattas' mothers. Seven days after the Bodhisattas are born the Bodhisattas' mothers pass away and are reborn in Tusita heaven.'
>
> 6 Then the Blessed One, knowing the meaning of this, on that occasion uttered the following utterance:
>
> 7 'Whatever beings there will be
> All will fare on having abandoned their body.
> The clever one, knowing all this,
> Ardently lives the holy life.'[1]

8 The emphasis here is not on the magical purity and miraculous splendor of the birth, but on the everyday tragedy that birth always comes with death. Perhaps this little fragment preserves the historical seed around which the miraculous birth narrative crystallized. As a historical fact, it suggests that Māyā, like countless other women, succumbed to the awful fate of death in childbirth, or due to complications arising from birth. This was—and is—an all-too-common tragedy, and must figure as a deep imprint of fear in the minds of women, especially in times and places where maternal mortality is prevalent.[2] Siddhattha, whose mature teaching would center on the fact that birth is the cause of death, received his first lesson from his own mother.

9 The Buddha's reply makes two subtle changes to Ānanda's question. The first is that Ānanda refers to the 'Blessed One', a term used only of the Buddha as enlightened Master, whereas the Buddha reminds him that when born he was merely the Bodhisatta, not yet Awakened. Ānanda's wording suggests the tendency towards deifying Siddhattha from the start of his life, making his Buddhahood inevitable.[3]

10 The second shift is that the Buddha shifts from singular to plural; in other words, from a personal biographical statement to a universal truth. So distant is the Buddha's tone that he speaks not of Māyā or of 'my mother' but of the *bodhisattamātā*, the 'Bodhisattva's mother', an impersonal term

he also used when telling of the Bodhisatta Vipassī. His coolness is a blank field inviting the projection of our own emotions into his story. We are not told of his sorrow, yet we cannot help feeling it. This non-personal aspect appears from without as a part of the cosmology. But from within, from the Buddha's own perspective, it reflects his own experience of his mother.

11 The infant Siddhattha could not have formed an idea of Māyā as a mere person. For him, she would have been forming a totality of the world as love, a world in which he and she were not yet distinct.

12 The perceptual world of the young infant bears a remarkable similarity to the world of magic, of *māyā*. This similarity did not escape the notice of Jean Piaget, the foundational theorist on infant mental development. He says an object that has vanished from the infant's immediate presence is not, for the infant, a permanent object that has been moved away, but rather a 'mere image' which disappears into the void, and re-emerges from it for no apparent reason.[4] Space and time have not yet been organized into groups and series, nor is causality spatially located in objects. There is no clear separation of subject and object, and hence no recognition of the limitations such separation brings.[5] An infant is yet to learn that they can exert control over their body but not the bodies of others. Piaget compares such perception with the workings of magic; like an occult spirit, a vanished object obeys no natural laws, but may sometimes be caught by a magician.[6] What seem to us to be objectively existing things, therefore, appear to the infant as magic, as 'mere image', as *māyā*.

13 This undifferentiated ('uroboric') state is an enduring symbol of the bliss of peace and contentment, but it also presents a grave danger. For if the mother and I are one, then if the mother disappears—not if, when—then part of my Self disappears with her.

> 14 The infant's experience has a profound influence on mythic imagery. The mother is the creator, the source of life, nuture, bounty, comfort. In her love the infant forms a wholeness that shapes the development of a healthy person. But no mother can be there always, or supply every wish that an infant might have—nor should they. A

> mother should prepare their child for the whole of life, which will always include loss and disappointment. The moment when the mother is absent when needed is experienced by the infant as a trauma, and so from the beginning the image of the mother in the infant's mind is associated not just with beatitude and fullness, but also with separation and loss. This ambiguity lies at the root of the imagery of the Goddess, the loving, devouring, blessed murderer. Myth is far too honest to indulge in sentimentalities of motherhood.[7]

15 This separation, which echoes dimly in story and nightmare, is a far more fundamental, existential threat than our adult experience of grief and loss. Our grief is precisely knowing that we must go on while they have disappeared, while the infant has not yet established a sense of enduring selfhood, or the realization that objects that have left their field of perception have not ceased to exist.

16 This formless, shifting ambiguity is reflected everywhere in images of the Mother of mythology. Kālī's tongue delights in licking up the blood of her children, yet she is also the goddess Annapūrṇā, 'Abundance of Food'. Isis is the goddess of death, wielder of power over the deadly serpent, yet she is at the same time the 'moon shining over the sea', protector of the poor, mother of heaven and earth. Hecate is a goddess of the liminal and ambiguous, haunter of doorways and crossroads, depicted in tripartite form; she is worshipped with blood at midnight, bringing bounty just as easily as she takes it away. In mythology as in the mind of the infant, the mother is source of all, both good and bad.[8]

17 Siddhattha, like all of us, had been born already countless times. This cycle of birth and death leaves a deep-rooted pattern embedded in all our minds. While in our normal mature, waking, conscious minds we are unaware of these patterns, they remain and may be accessed through deep meditation. But children stand closer to this reality than we.[9] Children who remember experiences from past lives typically lose the memories as they mature. The concrete, individual experiences that Siddhattha had as a baby would evoke, not a conscious personal response, but a numinous association or resonance with the 'Mothers' of the past, countless millions of them. This is expressed in mythic form when the Jātakas say that Māyā had been the Bodhisatta's mother repeatedly in his past lives.

❖

18 Māyā scarcely exists as a person in the early texts. She is mentioned in only one place, and there we merely hear her name.[10] This is in the Mahāpadāna Sutta, the bulk of which, as we have seen, is an account of the life of Buddha Vipassī 91 æons ago. The literalists will insist that Māyā is merely a personal name, and only by chance is it related with the spiritual/mythic concept of *māyā*. After all, many women are called 'Eve' or 'Mary' (or Diana or Bridget or Julie or Sarah or Helen or Sophia or…) and we don't imagine that they are goddesses.

19 But this argument simply follows the prejudice of the rationalizing mind. In the early texts, apart from the bare mention of her name in one mythic text, Māyā is *solely* an archetypal representation. Aside from the time of pregnancy, birth, and death, she does not exist. Only much later would we learn of her genealogy, her relations, and her love of playing among the *sāl* blossoms. She is a generic young woman, whose beauty and virtue are entirely conventional.[11] It is little short of perverse to insist on making Māyā exclusively personal when the earliest texts are concerned solely with her archetypal nature. Her 'glory', the miraculous glow that surrounds her, is not her personal possession. It would have meant as little to her as the 'honor' of being sacrificed meant to Manju Kumari. Rather, her glory is the nimbus of little Siddhattha's 'coming-to-know', the joy of dawning consciousness as it first perceives the love, the wonder, and the creative magic of the world. Or, more to the point, it is how Buddhist traditions imagined that this experience must be like. And so, like 'Sweet Maiden', Māyā's mortal destiny evokes the universal aspect of her name.

20 This archetypal, and hence divine, nature is consummated in her death after seven days. The number seven is featured repeatedly in the contexts of the Buddha's birth (taking seven steps to the north), Awakening (staying in *samādhi* for seven days, the dragon Muñcalinda encircling him with seven coils for seven days, etc.), and death (seven days between the Parinibbāna and the arrival of Mahākassapa). Such repeated use of 'seven' is a mythic identifier, informing the reader that we are no longer in our mundane world, but in that mystic realm where space is infinity and time is eternity.[12] The number seven, inheriting mystical associations from its astronomical roots, evokes 'the entire cycle of creation and death'.[13] The

unity of birth and death is the key to the magical logic of the sacrifice. Since all life has death for its food, we can only ensure an increase of life through a deliberate slaying: murder.

21 Whether considered as a medical fact of history, or as the evocation of an archetype, the Bodhisatta's birth—gently, lovingly, inexorably—guarantees his mother's death.

CHAPTER 7

SHE WHO ATE THE CHILDREN

LIKE SĀLABHAÑJIKĀ THE LITTLE FLOWER GIRL, Māyā makes her way straight to heaven after her death.[1] Having fulfilled the role that destiny has laid out for her, human life has no purpose. From then on she is unabashedly a goddess, and has left behind even the faint traces of human personality that we imagine we glimpse in her life.

2 According to later legend, she was visited on one occasion by the Buddha. The Theravādin Elders of the Mahāvihāra like to imagine that the Buddha taught her the Abhidhamma at that time. They also like to imagine that she was reborn as a male deva; no doubt in recognition of her good kamma.[2] The commentators, despite the Buddha's statements to the contrary, apparently cannot bring themselves to think that a woman's lot could actually be happy, that she might be quite content to remain as a woman. This reflects the monastic situation in which they lived, a man's world where a woman's highest aspiration is to be reborn as a man.

3 In a roundabout way the Abhidhamma is perfectly appropriate for this setting, since, like the goddess Māyā, it has been divested of its earthly context and presents only the universal, bloodless Dhamma. Māyā, having so delicately touched the world of the profane at the moment of giving birth, completes her patriarchal destiny by learning the Dhamma in its most abstract, rationalized form.[3]

Figure 7.1: *Hārītī with her husband*

4 Other sources retain a Māyā much closer to her motherly wellsprings. They say that when Māyā heard that her son had become the Buddha, milk gushed forth from her breasts as from white lotuses and shot across the heavens into the Buddha's mouth, an impromptu offering which must have come as a bit of a surprise. The Buddha rose to the heavens to visit his mother, and she spoke some verses, most of which were in praise of the 'Mother of Demons': Hārītī.

5 For some reason the traditions were concerned to bring these two ladies, otherwise so different, within the same sphere. Māyā is the highest authority for the feminine divine in Buddhism, so her words must have come as an encouraging endorsement for her sister. Here, from the lips of Māyā, is the story of Hārītī.[4]

❖

6 The Buddha in his mercy
Hid the son of the Mother of Demons,
Who ceaselessly devoured the children of men,
Making him invisible.

7 In the depths of despair, she searched everywhere
But knew not at all the place where he was.
Then she came and questioned the Buddha,
Asking him to point out where her son was.

8 The Tathāgatha used a method of salvation.
Reversing roles, he questioned her:
'This is because you yourself love your son
That you hurry about eagerly asking to see him.

9 'Why therefore with so much cruelty
Do you ceaselessly devour the children of others?
Reflect, so that your feelings are a lesson for you.
Kill no longer, torment no longer,
If you are capable of reforming your heart.
You will instantly see your son again.'

10 As soon as she heard these words
She was seized with joy and worshiped the Buddha,
Her face to the ground.
And furthermore, in order to see again her son,
Joining her hands together, she said to the Buddha:

11 'Henceforth for this entire existence
I reject all evil intentions!'
Then going forward, she received the five precepts
And likewise obtained the fruit of the law.

12 And so, this mother of demons,
Because she loved her own son,
Extended her love to other people
And, finally, forever ceased the killing.

13 I ask you, oh Venerable Great Merciful Benevolence
That it be so now.
By your compassion for the mother who gave you birth
Extend this compassion to every living being!

14 I ask you to open in haste the Way of the Law
And ensure that all hear and receive it.[5]

❖

15 The Buddha was the teacher of Hārītī, able to tame and convert even such a ferocious monster to the ways of peace. But notice how the teaching here is inverted: Māyā is telling the story of Hārītī as an example for the Buddha, and encouraging him to reflect and act from the same place, the redemptive love of a mother for her child. It is the same reasoning that Ānanda used to persuade the Buddha to grant ordination for women. In each case, the mother's milk becomes a metaphor for a more universal love, one that includes the feminine.

16 This Hārītī is a fascinating figure; a child-devouring *yakkhinī* (ogress), goddess of smallpox, who on conversion to Buddhism became protector of the children, worshiped as a fertility deity within the monasteries.[6] It seems that, while Māyā is invoked as a fertility goddess in some places, notably Nepal, she was too removed, too spiritual to be really effective in that role. The more earthy *yakkhinīs* like Hārītī do a much better job.

17 Her name is a little obscure. It might be derived from *hari* 'green', making Hārītī the 'Green Lady', wife of the well known 'Green Men' who symbolize the rebirthing power of nature in myth west and east. The 'Green Men' are depicted wreathed in leaves or flowers, not unlike Māyā in the *sāl* tree. If this fertile, nurturing role is too positive for a smallpox deity, we can trace the second part of her name to *īti*: 'plague, calamity'. Hārītī then

becomes the 'Green Plague'. Alternatively, her name might stem from √*har* or 'Carrier'. If the latter, we are moving into the same semantic realm as our Stick-gatherer 'Kaṭṭhahāri'. And there can be little doubt what she is carrying: the bodies of the dead children which, as goddess of smallpox, belong to her.[7]

18 Hārītī, who enters our story by devouring the children of Rājagaha, is later found with her husband Pañcika in Kaśmīr, where they were cowed by the power of the monk Majjhantika in the time of Aśoka.[8] She had a fabulous career. She was worshiped throughout India, she is closely associated with the syncretic Greco-Indic art of Gandhārā, she makes an appearance in the Mendut shrine near Borobudur in Java, and she retains her popularity today in far-off Japan.[9] Not bad for a cannabalistic ogress.

19 Despite her successful conversion to Buddhism, which meant she had to give up eating children, her ferocious origins have never been entirely forgotten. She is one of the earliest examples of the Buddhist worship of wrathful deities, whose appeasement is made all the more urgent since in the back of the mind lurks the little fear that if she is not properly worshiped, she might revert to her old ways. Just don't make her angry!

❖

20 Hārītī was by no means lonely in her role as a ogress converted to Buddhism.[10] On the contrary, she enjoyed abundant fellowship, a lively club of demons who lived within the very walls of the monasteries. From the earliest times, Buddhist scriptures have told similar stories, as attested in the Yakkha Saṁyutta. This features several ogres who either express strikingly un-ogreish sentiments ('It is better each day for the mindful one/And he is freed from enmity.'[11]) or whose violent attitude is softened by the Buddha, such as Āḷavaka, who threatens to rip out the Buddha's heart and hurl him across the Ganges, but is quickly converted.[12] Oddly enough, several ogres express their profound faith in the bhikkhunis Sukkā and Cirā, while none express similar sentiments for the bhikkhus.[13] Close parallels to Hārītī are found in the stories of *yakkhinīs* such as Piyaṅkara, who takes her children to listen to Dhamma being recited by Anuruddha at dawn, gently hushing her children and encouraging them to listen carefully.[14] The *yakkhinī* Punabbasu's Mother similarly exhorts her children to

hush and listen to the Buddha, only for her son to retort: 'My sister and I are quiet already, it is you who must pay attention!'[15]

21 The most intriguing precedent for Hārītī in the early texts is the dramatic story of Sānu and his mother.[16] Sānu was a devout young novice, who on reaching maturity returned to his mother's home, planning to disrobe. A *yakkha* (or *yakkhinī* according to the commentary) possessed him and, to his distraught mother, taught the Dhamma of restraint and doing good. When the spirit released Sānu, he didn't know what had happened, and asked his mother:

22 'They weep, mother, for the dead
Or for one living who isn't seen.
When you see, mother, that I'm alive,
Why, O mother, do you weep for me?'

23 'They weep, O son, for the dead [replied Sānu's mother]
Or for one living who isn't seen;
But when one returns to the home life
After renouncing sensual pleasures,
They weep for this one too, my son,
For though alive he's really dead.

24 'Drawn out, my dear, from hot embers,
You wish to plunge into hot embers.
Drawn out, my dear, from an inferno,
You wish to plunge into an inferno.'[17]

25 This clever tale neatly turns conventional morality on its head. The ferocious *yakkha* is actually a beneficent teacher (according to the commentary, Sānu's mother in a previous life) and a life-saver. While the ordination ritual is modelled after funeral rites—going forth is a dying to the world—here the return to the home life is said to be death. The mother is the supporter for the son's spiritual endeavors, based on her higher compassion for his welfare, which surmounts the elementary attachment to her son. This message, as any monastic would know, is still relevant today, as many mothers are still desperately reluctant to let their sons or daughters go forth. But the mythic imagery is equally interesting, for after his possession by the spirit, the son compares himself to the dead, thus invoking the notion of child sacrifice. This is kept very quiet, hidden far

in the background, in accordance with the gentle, humorous style of the Sagāthāvagga in which the text is found.[18]

❖

26 Hārītī's life is closely paralleled in the story of a certain divine lady known as Kuntī. There are, it seems, two Kuntīs to deal with, one from the southern and one from the northern sources.

27 One deity called Kuntī appears in the Sri Lankan chronicle the Mahāvaṁsa, as part of the cycle of stories in the time of Aśoka. She has no obvious connection with Hārītī. We are not told anything about her, except that she was a wood-nymph (*kinnarī*) who had two children with a man from Pāṭaliputta. The sons were named Kontiputta ('Son of Kuntī'); they ordained as monks and died young. We are not told why she would give up her children to be ordained. Here, as the seducer of mortals and mother of mortal heroes, she plays the part of a whimsical seductress. This is all we know of Kuntī the wood-nymph.

28 There is another Kuntī of a more malevolent sort: a fierce, child-devouring *yakkhinī*. This Kuntī is unknown in the Sri Lankan (Mahāvihāravāsin) sources, but her story is told in detail in such texts as the Mūlasarvāstivāda Vinaya, which stems from Mathura in the north.[19] The *yakkhinī* Kuntī met the Buddha on a legendary journey to the north-west of India, so she is a long way from Pāṭaliputta, the home of our woodnymph; but Hārītī spanned even greater distances with ease.

29 Kuntī the *yakkhinī*, after her conversion, asks for a monastery to be built on her behalf, where she, like Hārītī, would have received the offerings of the villagers to ensure the safety of their children. Here we see the methods that the Buddhists used to adopt local cults into Buddhism, making the deities dependent on the offerings of the Buddhist faithful.

30 There might seem to be little in common between the Kuntī who is a malicious child-eating ogress and the Kuntī who is a sweet nymph of the woods; except that the only thing we know of the nymph Kuntī is that she had two sons, who became monks and died. It seems to me that she too belongs in the Kuntī/Hārītī cycle. Her 'sons' are probably monks ordained in a temple devoted to her; this reminds us of the common Indic motif of the abandoned child brought up by a sage in the temple.[20] The Nigrodha Jātaka tells of a baby abandoned under a banyan tree, who was looked after

by the deity of the tree until he was discovered and raised with the name 'Banyan'.[21]

❖

31 Spreading our wings further afield, the Kuntani Jātaka is about a bird—curlew, heron, or stork—who was a messenger for the king of Benares.[22]

> 32 Once, when she was away, the boys of the palace killed her two young ones. In revenge she persuaded a tiger to eat the boys, and told the king what she had done. She then flew away to the Himālaya because, she said, there could be no friendship between the wrong-doer and the wronged one.[23]

33 Children killed, again.

34 Love and abandonment are constant themes in these tales of divine bird/women, as they are in the story of Māyā. The pattern is not just in Buddhist texts. The Mahābhārata, for example, tells of Śakuntalā, mother of Bharata. The love-child of a celestial nymph and a powerful rishi, she was abandoned at birth and raised in the wild by vultures, hence her name 'Bird'. The bird mediates the human and the divine: one moment tenderly caring for the young, the next disappearing into the sky.

35 The words *kunti* and *śakunti* hark back to a pre-Āryan Muṇḍa root, and were adopted into the Vedic language, where they already carry the meanings of a nymph, a tribe, and a bird.[24] Śakunī is the name of a ferocious ogress who, like Hārītī, brings disease to children.[25] This cluster of connotations has a tenacious persistence. They seem to stem from a very ancient strata of story, much as the disappearing Māyā stems from an ancient strata of the child's development.

36 The Mahābhārata further develops these themes in the story of Mandapāla. Although he was a great sage, try as he might he could not find peace of heart. Eventually he learnt the truth: sons were the path to heaven. So he must have sons. He considered what were the most fruitful of beings, and decided it was the bird. He took the form of a bird and found a mate called Jarita. They had four children, all learned in the Vedas. Though he dearly loved his children, he was away on an amorous adventure when Agni the Fire God approached in full glory, consuming the forest. The children begged their mother to save herself and leave them, and they all

thought they had been abandoned by their father. Little did they know that Mandapāla had meanwhile made a deal with Agni to spare his children: the flames bypassed the family. In the Buddhist version of this story, the baby quail, abandoned by his parents in the face of the flames, is fully aware of his exalted spiritual status, and averts the fire himself through the power of a Declaration of Truth.[26]

37 Once more: devotion and abandonment, together with the metamorphosis between human and divine forms. The bird, most fruitful of beings, is also the sage. The shaman, from the earliest cave paintings to modern times, is depicted as a bird; and, as the Dhammapada tells us, the path of the adept is trackless, like that of birds in the sky.[27]

38 The Mahābhārata completes this cycle of ambiguity in the story of yet another Kuntī. This time she is the mother of the five Pandava princes. While they were on the run, fugitives in their own land, they were sheltered by a brahman family. The town was Ekacakra, 'One Wheel', which, in the context of a bird-story, may symbolize the sun. Kuntī overheard the family lamenting. Their town, it seems, was haunted by ogres and trolls, and there was one *rakṣasa* in particular, name of Baka ('Heron'), who feasted on human flesh. The time had come for the brahman family to offer one of their own and, such was their nobility, each family member insisted on being the victim. None could stand to live with the family broken, and in the end they decided to all give themselves up. Kuntī knew that her sons, the greatest heroes of the age, could easily deal with a few trolls. She consoled the brahman family, and asked her strongest son, Bhīma, to destroy the *rakṣasa.* The elder son, Yudhiśthira, worried that she was sending her son into danger. But Kuntī prevailed, and Bhīma took on the troll. Its grin gaped from ear to ear; with red eyes, red hair, and red beard, the ground groaned at his step. Awesome in strength, the great fighters grappled, spreading devastation across the land; until Bhīma snapped the hill-huge monster in half and smote his ruin upon the earth.

39 The mythic cycles keep turning in upon themselves. The 'Heron' (*kuntī* and *baka*) is the protective mother, the sacrificer, and the child-eater. Kuntī saves the brahman children from sacrifice to the cannibal monster, but sends her own son to substitute. The brahmans' baby boy, taking a grass-

leaf in his hand as a sword, and lisping that he'll kill the bad guy, is also Bhīma, Kuntī's son who is the killer in fact.

40 The connotations of these birds were similar in the West.[28] The crane is associated with Hermes the messenger, who bridged the gods and humans; a suitable occupation for such a high-flying bird, and a conduit between the ancient winged deities of Mesopotamia and the modern angel. The idea of a winged deity, of course, assumes that the gods live in the sky, not the earth. And while Hermes would carry the messages of Zeus to humanity, in modern times Mother Goose carries the 'old wives' tales' from generation to generation for the children. The Sirens' song for Odysseus, while commonly imagined to be sensual temptation, was far more Greek: they promised knowledge of all things. And the bird carries a more substantial burden than mere knowledge; for while the stork of 19th century Germanic folklore was the bringer of children, the winged beings on the Greek sarcophagi of the 3rd century BCE carried the bodies of the dead to the underworld.[29]

41 The stork, the crane, and the pelican are all big birds, who swoop down to snatch their prey. They are like Death itself, striking without warning. And people might well fear that a pelican or similar could catch up a little baby in its beak, carrying it off to the unknown.

42 The stork is an abductor of children, yet it is also the bringer of children, a messenger who is quite capable of bridging the gap between the earth and the heavens, carrying with it a tiny person. Just so, the same ogress who is the murderer of children, if tamed in the Buddhist way and propitiated with offerings, would become the protector of children, like the heron in the Kuntani Jātaka, both the killer and protector of children. The bird's beak is a stabbing spear (*kunta*), both violent and sexual (*kunta* is also a word for passion, or the god of love); but also the bringer of food, a source of bounty from the beyond. And the bird's significance lies deeper than this: for the egg is nothing less than the totality of the cosmos, the self-generating seed of life itself. The mother, in bearing, protecting, and nurturing the egg, is the creator of all.

❖

43 O indefatigable reader, we fly over distant lands, chasing the tracks of birds in the sky! Like the falcon which, growing tired of its adventures,

folds its wings and returns to its nest,[30] we must return to Pāṭaliputta to roost, to our little story of Kuntī the wood-nymph.

44 The story is unknown to the more sober commentarial accounts, being an elaboration found in the Mahāvaṁsa. The text itself hints at its mythic status with the word *kira* ('it seems'). The 'history' behind the myth has to do with the adoption of local folk cults into a Buddhist monastery. The monastery may be named after the deity, and it is not unlikely that monks from the monastery would be called its 'sons', especially if they had been dedicated to the monastery as young children.

45 It is a curious fact that in our earliest concrete record for the personal names of Buddhist monks—that is, the reliquary caskets from Vedisa, dated before 100 BCE—several of the monks are named after cannabalistic monsters: Ālābagira (whose name recalls Āḷavaka the *yakkha*), Hāritīputa, Kotīputa, and perhaps Gotiputa.[31] Bizarre though it may seem, this theme is an important subtext reappearing constantly through the sources in this period. We have already noted the two 'Kontiputtas', sons of Kuntī who were monks in Pāṭaliputta. These may be identical with the Kotiputa of the inscriptions, or perhaps they hail from the same monastery.

46 Hāritīputa, the 'son of Hāritī', has left us relics in stupas at Sānchī and Andher.[32] Since Hārītī and Kuntī are both child-eating *yakkhinīs* with identical mythic backgrounds, the presence of these two names together on the inscriptions can be no coincidence.

47 The idea that 'children' of Hārītī were offered to the monastery is no mere speculation, for it forms the theme of a long passage from the Mūlasarvāstivāda Vinaya. This passage follows on from the details of Hārītī's birth, life, murderous activities and conversion, with the inevitable past life stories.[33]

> 48 In the same location as above, until Hārītī had received the three refuges and the five precepts of the Tathāgatha, she was tormented by the other *yakṣas*. Then she brought all her children and gave them to the Buddhist community. One day, seeing the monks going in search of their food, they changed into small children and followed behind. When the women of Rājagaha saw them, many of them were overcome by emotion and came to take them in their arms. They then disappeared.
>
> 49 The women asked the monks: 'Whose children are these?'

50 They replied: 'They are the children of Hārītī.'

51 The women said: 'Are these then the children of that *yakṣinī* so hateful and wicked?'

52 The monks answered: 'She has completely rejected all wickedness, and because of this, all the *yakṣas* torment her. This is why from this time forward she has given us these children.'

53 The women thought 'The *yakṣinī* has rejected her evil intentions and has given her children. Why would we then not give them ours also?' And they gave their children to the community. The community refused to take them.

54 The women said then: 'The saints have taken the children of that wicked *yakṣinī*. Why then will they not take ours?'

55 The monks took this opportunity in order to speak to the Buddha. The Buddha said: 'Receive them.'

56 The monks obeyed these instructions. But although they received the children, they were not supervised and they went everywhere to amuse themselves at their whim. The monks told this to the Buddha.

57 The Buddha said: 'Once a boy has been given to the community, a monk will receive him and will tie to his head a piece of old *kāsāya* [robe cloth] and will watch over him. If many boys have been given, the monks of all ranks, superior, average, and lower, will receive them and will share them according to their wish and will watch over them just as said before so that they will not be the target of suspicion.'

58 Then the parents came back bearing gifts in order to compensate (the expenses incurred by the children) and to withdraw them. The monks did not accept. The Buddha said: 'Accept.'

59 Subsequently, these children conceived affectionate feelings, and they returned bearing clothing which they offered to the monks in recognition of their good deeds. The monks, knowing their feelings, would not accept. The Buddha said: 'Receive them.'

60 As the Buddha was saying that they must receive the presents offered in exchange for the children, six monks went to ask the parents for the entire compensation. The Buddha said: 'Don't ask the price; learn to content yourselves to receive that which they give according to their wishes.

61 In the same location as above, the *yakṣinī* Hārītī gave all her sons to the community. During the night while they were sleeping, they were tormented with hunger and let out groans of complaint. Once morning came, the monks took this opportunity to tell the Buddha of this matter. The Buddha said: 'Once morning has come, take them

> something to eat while saying their name and rendering homage to them.'...
>
> 62 It happened also that during times of abstinence they wished to eat. The Buddha said: 'You must give food to them.'...
>
> 63 It happened also that they wished to eat at forbidden times. The Buddha said: 'You must give to them.'...
>
> 64 It happened also that they wished to eat that which was left at the bottom of the monks' bowls. The Buddha said: 'You must give it to them.'...
>
> 65 It happened also that they wished to eat of impure things. The Buddha said: 'You must give these to them.'

66 Unless the Mūlasarvāstivādins have gone to a great deal of trouble to invent a legal framework for a fairy tale, it seems that in ancient India children were offered to the monastery for the monks to look after as an expression of goddess worship. Such activity is connected with the worship of converted child-eating *yakkhinīs* within an institutional Buddhist context. The children of the local families may be substituted for those of the *yakkhinī*.

67 This mirrors the story of Hārītī's conversion: she had been killing the people's children, so the Buddha 'kidnapped' one of her children. She came seeking her child in distress, and the Buddha pointed out that the families of all the children she had murdered had suffered even greater distress. In that story, Hārītī's children substitute for the human children killed; in the cult, the women's children substitute for Hārītī's child who mysteriously disappeared.[34]

68 The children apparently lived for a period of time in the monastery, during which the monks saw fit to relax many of the more stringent requirements of monastic living. The practice must have been fairly widespread for it to have developed a complex background story and a whole series of rule-modifications based on precedent. This was not a one-off. After their period in the monastery, substantial compensation was offered, so there was plenty of incentive for the monks to play along.

❖

69 Now, it might seem a little strange to find that monks were ordaining, not, it seems, out of a sense of dispassion for the world and a longing to

dedicate themselves to the path, but to participate in goddess cults. Having been placed by their mother in the monastery at a young age, one would expect that a certain percentage of the boys would wish to stay on; such, it would seem, are the monks mentioned at Vedisa.

70 This is very similar to the custom of temporary ordination in contemporary Thailand and Myanmar. It is normal, even required, for boys (not girls, of course!) to spend a period of time in the monastery, ranging from a week to a few months. This custom is unknown in the Pali texts and is not found in Sri Lanka. It is usually rationalized as an opportunity for the boys to learn and practice Dhamma for a period before embarking on married life. There is some truth in this, and in good monasteries temporary ordinands do indeed learn a lot. But there are some not-so-good monasteries too, and the drinking and whoring both the day before ordination and immediately after disrobal does make one wonder. If you ask one of the ordinands why they are ordaining, typically the response has nothing to do with practice of Dhamma, rather, 'To make merit for my mother'. Does this not sound more than a little reminiscent of the mothers who 'sacrificed' their children for a period of time in the Mūlasarvāstivādin monasteries of northern India?[35]

71 By 'dying' to the world (remember Sānu), the sons set up an artificial, though temporary, barrier between themselves and all women, including their mother. This is always painful, but it is a crucial stage of growing up. They enter into the men's circle, where they discover their own masculine independence. On emerging from the cloistered time, they are 'ripe', and fit for marriage; that is, fit to enter upon a relationship with a woman their own age.

72 The crucial thing is that the mother must disappear—like Māyā, like the birds who feed their young and fly into the heavens, like the mothers who place their sons in a monastery—for the children to grow. She is the all-pervading goddess of infancy, and her domain retreats from the child's growing self-awareness, just as the wild things retreat before civilization. What happens if she does not retreat is one of the darker tales of our mythos. It is the story of the King Sacrificed.

CHAPTER 8

THE KING SACRIFICED

QUILACARE, SOUTHERN INDIA, 16TH CENTURY. At the completion of the twelfth year of his reign, the king performed a solemn festival with his people, ceremonially bathed, and worshiped the divinity for the last time. Accompanied by music and pomp, he mounted a wooden scaffold decorated all over with silk. Taking some sharp knives, he sliced off his nose, ears, lips, and all his members piece by piece, throwing the blood and gore about, until he came near to fainting, at which he sliced his own throat.[1]

2 Many ancient societies sacrificed their kings. In some cases this was a periodic rite determined by the calender. In other cases it was resorted to when danger threatened the realm (which is, after all, not so different from modern politics), or if the king showed signs of frailty. Such practices have been traced back to the roots of human culture, and their distant antecedents can be discerned even in primate behavior. We have already seen a strong suggestion of regicide in the Indus Valley at the very dawn of Indian civilization.

3 Modern awareness of regicide largely stems from Frazer, who made it a major theme of *The Golden Bough*. Frazer's underlying motive was to demonstrate that much of Christianity was derived from pagan sources. Substitute sacrifice is central to Roman Catholic ritual, for the host eaten at each Mass is solemnly declared to be literally the Son of God, changed from bread to flesh by the miracle of transubstantiation.[2] Frazer was quite right to point out that the beliefs and practices of 'higher' religions such

as Catholicism or Buddhism owe much to the more 'primitive' religious forms among which they evolved. Yet he erred on the side of reductionism. It is not what a religion inherits that defines its spiritual worth; it is what it makes of its inheritance.

4 Such practices were found all over the world. Many of Frazer's primary examples of this theme are drawn from the Indian cultural sphere. Here are a few of Frazer's cases.

5 > 'It is a singular custom in Bengal,' says an old native historian of India, 'that there is little of hereditary descent in succession to the sovereignty.... Whoever kills the king, and succeeds in placing himself on that throne, is immediately acknowledged as king; all the amirs, wazirs, soldiers, and peasants instantly obey and submit to him, and consider him as being as much their sovereign as they did their former prince, and obey his orders implicitly. The people of Bengal say, "We are faithful to the throne; whoever fills the throne we are obedient and true to it."' A custom of the same sort formerly prevailed in the little kingdom of Passier, on the northern coast of Sumatra."' The old Portuguese historian De Barros, who informs us of it, remarks with surprise that no wise man would wish to be king of Passier, since the monarch was not allowed by his subjects to live long. From time to time a sort of fury seized the people, and they marched through the streets of the city chanting with loud voices the fatal words, 'The king must die!' When the king heard that song of death he knew that his hour had come. The man who struck the fatal blow was of the royal lineage, and as soon as he had done the deed of blood and seated himself on the throne he was regarded as the legitimate king, provided that he contrived to maintain his seat peaceably for a single day. This, however, the regicide did not always succeed in doing. When Fernão Peres d'Andrade, on a voyage to China, put in at Passier for a cargo of spices, two kings were massacred, and that in the most peaceable and orderly manner, without the smallest sign of tumult or sedition in the city, where everything went on in its usual course, as if the murder or execution of a king were a matter of everyday occurrence. Indeed, on one occasion three kings were raised to the dangerous elevation and followed each other in the dusty road of death in a single day. The people defended the custom, which they esteemed very laudable and even of divine institution, by saying that God would never allow so high and mighty a being as a king, who

> reigned as his vicegerent on earth, to perish by violence unless for his sins he thoroughly deserved it.[3]

6 No doubt a dedicated king would be honored to serve the Divine in such a manner. Our sources make it quite plain that, no matter how strange it may seem to us, the sacrificial victims frequently acquiesced meekly to their fate. This is not as extraordinary as it might seem. After all, we all must die. For most of us the problem is how we are to give our life, and hence our death, some semblance of meaning. The sacrificial victim has no such problem. Their death is perfect; they are celebrated as the source of abundance, of new life.

7 Nevertheless, it might happen that the king, when called upon to instantiate his timeless sacred role as sacrificial victim to ensure the stability and fertility of the realm, would feel a little squeamish. Luckily it was found that he could be replaced by a family member, who would work just as well. Even a stranger could be temporarily anointed king and then rather more permanently disposed of, with no loss of effectiveness. Further tests revealed that a maiming, or an animal, or even a purely symbolic sacrifice such as damaging a statue would still do the trick. Among the early figures of gods and goddesses of ancient India, in certain sites it is rare to find any undamaged, suggesting they were ritually mutilated.[4]

8 Psychologically, the substitute represents the emergence of the individual from the archetype. For a king to gladly accept his own death, he must identify so totally with the eternal divine in himself that the passing of this mere physical shell is of little consequence. To the extent that the king feels himself to be a person distinct from the kings who came earlier and will come after, he will resist his sacred destiny.

9 Here are some examples of substitute sacrifice taken from Buddhist countries.

10

> In the month of Méac (February) the king of Cambodia annually abdicated for three days. During this time he performed no act of authority, he did not touch the seals, he did not even receive the revenues which fell due. In his stead there reigned a temporary king called Sdach Méac, that is, King February. The office of temporary king was hereditary in a family distantly connected with the royal house, the sons succeeding the fathers and the younger brothers the elder brothers just as in the succession to the real sovereignty.

Figure 8.1: *Sacrificing the king*

11 On a favorable day fixed by the astrologers the temporary king was conducted by the mandarins in triumphal procession. He rode one of the royal elephants, seated in the royal palanquin, and escorted by soldiers who, dressed in appropriate costumes, represented the neighboring peoples of Siam, Annam, Laos, and so on. In place of the golden crown he wore a peaked white cap, and his regalia, instead of being of gold encrusted with diamonds, were of rough wood. After paying homage to the real king, from whom he received the sovereignty for three days, together with all the revenues accruing during that time (though this last custom has been omitted for some time), he moved in procession round the palace and through the streets of the capital. On the third day, after the usual procession, the temporary king gave orders that the elephants should trample under foot the 'mountain of rice', which was a scaffold of bamboo surrounded by sheaves of rice. The people gathered up the rice, each man taking home a little with him to secure a good harvest. Some of it was also taken to the king, who had it cooked and presented to the monks.

12 In Siam on the sixth day of the moon in the sixth month (the end of April) a temporary king is appointed, who for three days enjoys the royal prerogatives, the real king remaining shut up in his palace. This temporary king sends his numerous satellites in all directions to seize and confiscate whatever they can find in the bazaar and open shops; even the ships and junks which arrive in harbor during the three days are forfeited to him and must be redeemed. He goes to a field in the middle of the city, whither they bring a gilded plough drawn by gaily-decked oxen. After the plough has been anointed and the oxen rubbed with incense, the mock king traces nine furrows with the plough, followed by aged dames of the palace scattering the first seed of the season. As soon as the nine furrows are drawn, the crowd of spectators rushes in and scrambles for the seed which has just been sown, believing that, mixed with the seed-rice, it will ensure a plentiful crop. Then the oxen are unyoked, and rice, maize, sesame, sago, bananas, sugar-cane, melons, and so on, are set before them; whatever they eat first will, it is thought, be dear in the year following, though some people interpret the omen in the opposite sense. During this time the temporary king stands leaning against a tree with his right foot resting on his left knee. From standing thus on one foot he is popularly known as King Hop; but his official title is Phaya Phollathep 'Lord of the Heavenly Hosts'. He is a sort of Minister of Agriculture; all disputes about fields, rice, and so forth, are referred

> to him. There is moreover another ceremony in which he personates the king. It takes place in the second month (which falls in the cold season) and lasts three days. He is conducted in procession to an open place opposite the Temple of the Brahmans, where there are a number of poles dressed like May-poles, upon which the Brahmans swing. All the while that they swing and dance, the Lord of the Heavenly Hosts has to stand on one foot upon a seat which is made of bricks plastered over, covered with a white cloth, and hung with tapestry. He is supported by a wooden frame with a gilt canopy, and two Brahmans stand one on each side of him. The dancing Brahmans carry buffalo horns with which they draw water from a large copper caldron and sprinkle it on the spectators; this is supposed to bring good luck, causing the people to dwell in peace and quiet, health and prosperity. The time during which the Lord of the Heavenly Hosts has to stand on one foot is about three hours. This is thought to prove the dispositions of the Devattas and spirits. If he lets his foot down he is liable to forfeit his property and have his family enslaved by the king, as it is believed to be a bad omen, portending destruction to the state, and instability to the throne. But if he stand firm he is believed to have gained a victory over evil spirits, and he has moreover the privilege, ostensibly at least, of seizing any ship which may enter the harbour during these three days, and taking its contents, and also of entering any open shop in the town and carrying away what he chooses.

13 The mechanism of sacred regicide, with its astrologically determined terms of office, elaborate ritual play and pretense, magical potency, and substitute sacrifice, is well attested in those countries that have long practiced Buddhism, where it takes forms no less surreal than are found elsewhere in the world. Buddhist rituals are, however, typically gentle, and it is rare, although not impossible, to find actual human sacrifice.[5]

14 The examples above emphasize fertility magic. The correct ritual performance of the sacrifice is essential to the fertility of the soil, on which the life of the people depend. Fertility magic always harks back to its roots in the Goddess, even when the brahmans, the kings, and the monks have taken control of the process. If we look closely it is not hard to find traces of her influence still lingering even in these late patriarchal adaptations of the old ways. Thus it is the 'old dames of the palace' who scatter the first seed of the season.

15 In the examples we have seen so far, although they are taken from the Indo-Buddhist cultural sphere, the actual Buddhist involvement is peripheral. But this was not always the case. Here is an amazing ritual from the 'real' Tibet.

> 16 In Tibet the ceremony of the scapegoat presents some remarkable features. The Tibetan new year begins with the new moon which appears about the fifteenth of February. For twenty-three days afterward the government of Lhasa, the capital, is taken out of the hands of the ordinary rulers and entrusted to the monk of the Debang monastery who offers to pay the highest sum for the privilege. The successful bidder is called the Jalno, and he announces his accession to power in person, going through the streets of Lhasa with a silver stick in his hand. Monks from all the neighboring monasteries and temples assemble to pay him homage. The Jalno exercises his authority in the most arbitrary manner for his own benefit, as all the fines which he exacts are his by purchase. The profit he makes is about ten times the amount of the purchase money. His men go about the streets in order to discover any conduct on the part of the inhabitants that can be found fault with. Every house in Lhasa is taxed at this time, and the slightest offence is punished with unsparing rigor by fines. This severity of the Jalno drives all working classes out of the city till the twenty-three days are over. But if the laity go out, the clergy come in. All the Buddhist monasteries of the country for miles round about open their gates and disgorge their inmates. All the roads that lead down into Lhasa from the neighboring mountains are full of monks hurrying to the capital, some on foot, some on horseback, some riding asses or lowing oxen, all carrying their prayer-books and culinary utensils. In such multitudes do they come that the streets and squares of the city are encumbered with their swarms, and incarnadined with their red cloaks. The disorder and confusion are indescribable. Bands of the holy men traverse the streets chanting prayers, or uttering wild cries. They meet, they jostle, they quarrel, they fight; bloody noses, black eyes, and broken heads are freely given and received. All day long, too, from before the peep of dawn till after darkness has fallen, these red-cloaked monks hold services in the dim incense-laden air of the great Machindranath temple, the cathedral of Lhasa; and thither they crowd thrice a day to receive their doles of tea and soup and money. The cathedral is a vast building, standing in the center of the

city, and surrounded by bazaars and shops. The idols in it are richly inlaid with gold and precious stones.

17 Twenty-four days after the Jalno has ceased to have authority, he assumes it again, and for ten days acts in the same arbitrary manner as before. On the first of the ten days the priests again assemble at the cathedral, pray to the gods to prevent sickness and other evils among the people, 'and, as a peace-offering, sacrifice one man. The man is not killed purposely, but the ceremony he undergoes often proves fatal. Grain is thrown against his head, and his face is painted half white, half black.' Thus grotesquely disguised, and carrying a coat of skin on his arm, he is called the King of the Years, and sits daily in the market-place, where he helps himself to whatever he likes and goes about shaking a black yak's tail over the people, who thus transfer their bad luck to him. On the tenth day, all the troops in Lhasa march to the great temple and form in line before it. The King of the Years is brought forth from the temple and receives small donations from the assembled multitude. He then ridicules the Jalno, saying to him, 'What we perceive through the five senses is no illusion. All you teach is untrue,' and the like. The Jalno, who represents the Grand Lama for the time being, contests these heretical opinions; the dispute waxes warm, and at last both agree to decide the questions at issue by a cast of the dice, the Jalno offering to change places with the scapegoat should the throw be against him. If the King of the Years wins, much evil is prognosticated; but if the Jalno wins, there is great rejoicing, for it proves that his adversary has been accepted by the gods as a victim to bear all the sins of the people of Lhasa. Fortune, however, always favors the Jalno, who throws sixes with unvarying success, while his opponent turns up only ones. Nor is this so extraordinary as at first sight it might appear; for the Jalno's dice are marked with nothing but sixes and his adversary's with nothing but ones. When he sees the finger of Providence thus plainly pointed against him, the King of the Years is terrified and flees away upon a white horse, with a white dog, a white bird, salt, and so forth, which have all been provided for him by the government. His face is still painted half white and half black, and he still wears his leathern coat. The whole populace pursues him, hooting, yelling, and firing blank shots in volleys after him. Thus driven out of the city, he is detained for seven days in the great chamber of horrors at the Samyas monastery, surrounded by monstrous and terrific images of devils and skins of huge serpents and wild beasts. Thence he goes away into the mountains of Chetang,

where he has to remain an outcast for several months or a year in a narrow den. If he dies before the time is out, the people say it is an auspicious omen; but if he survives, he may return to Lhasa and play the part of scapegoat over again the following year.

18 This quaint ceremonial, still annually observed in the secluded capital of Buddhism—the Rome of Asia—is interesting because it exhibits, in a clearly marked religious stratification, a series of divine redeemers themselves redeemed, of vicarious sacrifices vicariously atoned for, of gods undergoing a process of fossilization, who, while they retain the privileges, have disburdened themselves of the pains and penalties of divinity. In the Jalno we may without undue straining discern a successor of those temporary kings, those mortal gods, who purchase a short lease of power and glory at the price of their lives. That he is the temporary substitute of the Grand Lama is certain; that he is, or was once, liable to act as scapegoat for the people is made nearly certain by his offer to change places with the real scapegoat—the King of the Years—if the arbitrament of the dice should go against him. It is true that the conditions under which the question is now put to the hazard have reduced the offer to an idle form. But such forms are no mere mushroom growths, springing up of themselves in a night. If they are now lifeless formalities, empty husks devoid of significance, we may be sure that they once had a life and a meaning; if at the present day they are blind alleys leading nowhere, we may be certain that in former days they were paths that led somewhere, if only to death. That death was the goal to which of old the Tibetan scapegoat passed after his brief period of license in the market-place, is a conjecture that has much to commend it. Analogy suggests it; the blank shots fired after him, the statement that the ceremony often proves fatal, the belief that his death is a happy omen, all confirm it. We need not wonder then that the Jalno, after paying so dear to act as deputy-deity for a few weeks, should have preferred to die by deputy rather than in his own person when his time was up. The painful but necessary duty was accordingly laid on some poor devil, some social outcast, some wretch with whom the world had gone hard, who readily agreed to throw away his life at the end of a few days if only he might have his fling in the meantime. For observe that while the time allowed to the original deputy—the Jalno—was measured by weeks, the time allowed to the deputy's deputy was cut down to days, ten days according to one authority, seven days according to another. So short a rope was doubtless thought a long enough tether for so black

> or sickly a sheep; so few sands in the hour-glass, slipping so fast away, sufficed for one who had wasted so many precious years. Hence in the jack-pudding who now masquerades with motley countenance in the market-place of Lhasa, sweeping up misfortune with a black yak's tail, we may fairly see the substitute of a substitute, the vicar of a vicar, the proxy on whose back the heavy burden was laid when it had been lifted from nobler shoulders. But the clue, if we have followed it aright, does not stop at the Jalno; it leads straight back to the pope of Lhasa himself, the Grand Lama, of whom the Jalno is merely the temporary vicar. The analogy of many customs in many lands points to the conclusion that, if this human divinity stoops to resign his ghostly power for a time into the hands of a substitute, it is, or rather was once, for no other reason than that the substitute might die in his stead. Thus through the mist of ages unillumined by the lamp of history, the tragic figure of the pope of Buddhism—God's vicar on earth for Asia—looms dim and sad as the man-god who bore his people's sorrows, the Good Shepherd who laid down his life for the sheep.

19 Thus Frazer, in his inimitable Victorian prose, interprets this strange tale. Frazer seems to think that the office of the Dalai Lama itself was originally subject to periodic regicide. This is not the case. The ceremony of the Jalno must have been inherited from much older Tibetan customs. The ceremony he describes is, no doubt, lost forever in the ashes of old Tibet. But it serves, if nothing else, as a reminder of the intimate intertwining of Buddhist culture with far older cultural strands. Such strands involve us in an elaborate game of make-believe, by comparison with which the games of children are, well, childish.

❖

20 We should not imagine that such games only appeared in late, 'decadent' Buddhist cultures. On the contrary, the process of engagement between the Dhamma and the magical, mythical dimensions of religious culture has been ongoing since the beginning, and finds its distinctive forms in each Buddhist culture.

21 Sacred regicide is strongly suggested in a number of Jātaka stories, with the usual motif of the substitute. The Maṇicora Jātaka tells of a time when the Bodhisatta had been born as a householder in Benares.[6] He was wed

to a lovely young woman called Sujātā, who was as ravishing as a divine nymph. They lived together in love and harmony, 'rejoicing, with one heart'. One day King Brahmadatta spotted Sujātā and became besotted. To get rid of the Bodhisatta he had a jeweled crown dropped in his cart, and then claimed it had been stolen. The Bodhisatta was condemned to death. Sujātā, however, raised a lament, crying out that the gods must have disappeared to so allow cruelty to reign over men. Sakka heard her lament just as the executioner's axe was falling. He snatched away the Bodhisatta and placed the evil king's head on the block—and it was promptly severed. Sakka dressed the Bodhisatta in the royal pomp, and declared to the people that he was to be the new king. The old king, he averred, was unrighteous, and this was why no rain had been sent in due season.

22 The Sutana Jātaka offers another variation.[7] The king was at sport, hunting deer, when he came into the clutches of a man-eating *yakkha* who lived in a certain tree. The king made a deal: if the *yakkha* would be content to eat the deer for now, the king would ensure that every day in future he would send a man with a plate of rice. The *yakkha* agreed, being greedy for both rice and man-flesh. The king returned to Benares. From then on they sent a man each day to be sacrificed, starting with those in jail. But these were all consumed, so a prize was offered for anyone who would dare the *yakkha*. The Bodhisatta in those days was a poor man who had to support a family, so he volunteered. But he set a number of conditions for the king. He must have golden slippers ('not to touch the earth') and a golden umbrella ('not to see the sky'), for the *yakkha* would eat those who stood on the ground beneath the tree, or under the tree's shadow. Furthermore, he had a sword and a golden bowl of rice. When he arrived at the tree, he stayed out of the *yakkha's* reach, and cleverly appealed to his healthy self-interest. If the *yakkha* would be content with the delicious rice, and abjure the flesh of man, he will be fed every day. If he continues to insist on eating human flesh, men will avoid him or try to destroy him. Better to be content with a staple diet of civilized food. The *yakkha* is impressed with this reasoning. The Bodhisatta admonished him further, making him give up violence completely, and then offered to make him a new home by the city gates where he could receive the best offerings

every day. A win-win solution, and a neat demonstration of how old ways can be transformed by applying rationalized ethics.

23 I will draw one final example from a Chinese Dhammapada style text.[8] This tale stems from a similar period as the Jātakas—the developed form of early (pre-Mahāyāna) Buddhism—but it tells of events in the Buddha's lifetime. It is particularly interesting, as it sets forth the entire cycle of culture culminating in the compassionate ethics of the Buddha.

> 24 An official was expelled from Rājagaha for corruption.[9] He was sent to barbarous lands in the south, where no people lived and no food grew.[10] After he arrived, however, the spring waters flowed and the five kinds of grain grew in abundance.[11] People were attracted to those fertile lands, and the official gave each of them land, up to several thousand families.[12]
>
> 25 The elders consulted, and decided to invite the former official to be their king, saying, 'A land with no king is like a body with no head'.[13]
>
> 26 'If you wish to take me as your king,' he said, 'then we must conform with the laws of kingship. Officials must be appointed of the various grades and types, and an army must be established for the court. Women must be given to me. Taxes and trade should be regulated by law.'[14]
>
> 27 The people agreed, and began to build a grand city and palace for the king.[15] There was so much extra work, however, that the people began to complain and plot against the king.[16]
>
> 28 Wicked ministers took the king out hunting to a marshy wilderness; but they were intent on murder.[17]
>
> 29 When he realized their intentions, the king asked, 'Why would you kill me?'
>
> 30 'Formerly the people were happy,' they replied, 'they were fond of you and served you gladly. But now they are in distress and families are in ruin, so they have turned against the state.'
>
> 31 'Sirs,' replied the king, 'this is not my doing, but yours. If you unjustly kill me, the spirits will know. Let me have one wish.'[18] This they granted.
>
> 32 'When I first came to this land,' he said, 'it was a barren wasteland. I produced food, shared it with the people, so that all were happy. The people chose me as their king, and I have committed no crime against them. Let me, then, be reborn as an ogre, enter my old body, and have my vengeance!'[19]

> 33 They strangled him and left his corpse in the wasteland.[20] Three days later the king was reborn as a flesh-eating monster called Āḷavaka who re-entered the old body.[21] He went to the city, killed the new king, the harem, and the ministers.[22]
>
> 34 The three elders of the land tied themselves with rope of straw[23] and went to beg for mercy from the monster, claiming that neither they nor the people had nothing to do with the plot to kill the old king. They even offered him the chance to resume the kingship once more.[24]
>
> 35 'I am a demon!' roared the former king. 'How could I serve the people? I am violent by nature, and must have human flesh to eat!'[25]
>
> 36 To pacify the monster, the elders created a lottery to choose victims for him to eat. Each family had to give a child when their turn came.[26]
>
> 37 By chance the first family chosen by the lottery were the only Buddhists in the land. Yet they must sacrifice their little baby to the frightful monster. In despair, they traveled to see the Buddha and seek forgiveness. But the Buddha saw that he could save them all.
>
> 38 The Buddha flew to the demon's palace, radiant with light. Āḷavaka, outraged at his temerity, tried to crush him with a mountain, but it turned to dust. When Āḷavaka had exhausted his rage, the Buddha taught him the Dhamma. The vicious monster repented, accepted the Dhamma, and undertook the five precepts.
>
> 39 He sent for the child who was to be offered as sacrifice. All the people wailed and lamented. But Āḷavaka took the baby gently in his arms and offered him to the Buddha. The Buddha placed the baby in his begging bowl,[27] and took him back to the parents.
>
> 40 'Rejoice!' he said, 'for your child is safe. Take him now, and raise him in health and happiness.'

41 Once more, the Buddha converts the demon from violence, and puts an end to the depraved sacrifice of infants. Compassion has replaced fear as the dominant emotion, and now only harmless offerings will be made.

42 These examples show that the more recent examples of sacred regicide observed in Buddhist countries were no innovation, but are deeply rooted in ancient Buddhist culture. The Buddhist stories do not question the basic magical principles underlying regicide. They often reaffirm that the king is responsible for the fertility of the crops, for example.[28] They do, however, ethicize the magic. The Jātakas insist that the king's righteousness is the crucial factor. More primitive, pre-ethical motifs still persist, however,

even in the later times; the Thai festival of King Hop correlates the height of the crops to the height of the king's skirt—which says something about the importance of fashion in Thailand. Moreover, the Buddhist sources endorse the notion of substitute sacrifice. They were not, it seems concerned with the superstitious overtones of the local practices of making offerings to deities. It was only the violence that was problematic. Rather than condemn and exclude the worship of local deities, they transformed and civilized it.

❖

43 In the real world, the succession of kings is a highly problematic social institution. While a periodic sacrifice of one's leader might seem to be a brutal way to solve the problem, in practice it may have been gentler than the alternatives. Knowing that one is to die in a few years would deter less devoted aspirants to the throne. And it would ameliorate one of the most tragic aspects of kingship: patricide.

44 In the time of the Buddha, Bimbisāra was killed by his only son Ajātasattu, while Pasenadi was indirectly killed by his son Viḍūḍabha. The Saṁkicca Jātaka informs us that in his past lives, too, Ajātasattu was born as a prince called Brahmadatta in Benares, where he killed his father, King Brahmadatta.[29] Brahmadatta kills Brahmadatta, the personal element receding behind the eternal cycle.

45 The very name Brahmadatta is born by so many kings of Benares (we will meet others below) that it cannot be a personal name. It means 'Godgiven', and perhaps might be understood as 'given from God'; equally it could mean 'given to God', i.e. a sacrificial victim.[30] It should come as no surprise that Ajātasattu was murdered by his son; and he in turn by his son.... Or again, after Aśoka's brother committed the capital crime of donning the imperial regalia, Aśoka offered to turn his crown over to his brother for seven days, following which he must be killed.

46 The surface narrative of all these stories depicts the killing, not as a ritual or religious act, but as a result of the natural wish of the prince to gain power. Even in colonial times it was common in India for the local Rāja to build a palace for his sons at a considerable distance from his own home, to secure himself from his son's potentially murderous ambitions. The motivation is therefore essentially personal: power. This differs from

Frazer's emphasis on the sacred aspect of regicide, which has been criticized as being an external interpretation ('etic') which did not do justice to the complexities of the real social situation. No doubt there is some truth to this, and Frazer's theories tell only part of the story.

47 A more nuanced perspective emerges in a contemporary study by Märta Salokoski on sacred kingship and regicide in two Owambo kingdoms of Naminia. She perceives both secular and sacred forces at work in handling the succession; but these are presented very differently depending on the perspective of the sources.

48 German colonial sources depict the kings as tyrants who arbitrarily dole out life and death for their subjects. The clan members constantly assassinate their kin in the struggle for the throne. The throne is won through ruthlessness, violence, and kin-slaying, as well as cunningly-crafted alliances with neighbouring states.

49 Local sources, on the other hand, say that kingship is passed down by a careful selection from the eligible Elders of the clan of the dying king, with the consent of the queen. In preparation for kingship, the new candidate is ridiculed and humiliated by his subjects—which, as we have seen in the case of the Tibetan Jalno, is part of the stock ritual vocabulary—and must perform rituals as prescribed by the diviners or sorcerors. Moreover, since he ascended the throne by killing the previous king, he knows that he too will die when his powers wane, at the hands of his successor.

50 Salokoski's discussion shows that there was a ritualized, sacred aspect to the death of the king and succession to the throne. However, royal succession was not a smooth, clear-cut process, and would change with the individual conduct of the king and the surrounding political climate. Nevertheless, it is clear that the ritual aspects of succession were overlooked by the European interpreters, conditioned as they were to think of kingship in secular terms. Salokoski concludes that Frazerian sacred kingship and periodic ritual regicide was indeed operative in this culture, although operating in a nuanced way that was negotiated according to the particular circumstances of the royal transmission.

51 Our Indian sources, which portray an endemic pattern of regicide, especially by the crown prince, similarly involve both secular and sacred processes. The mythic structures are informing the way that narratives

of kingship and succession are constructed in the legendary 'Stories of the Past' and even for the supposedly historical events at the time of the Buddha and later. This is the unconscious form of kingship, even as the conscious story is entirely secular.

❖

52 The Jungian interpretation of this motif hinges on the idea that the king stands for the realized Self, the whole, integrated conscious individual at a mature stage of life, able to make choices and bear the responsibility for them. The sacrifice of the king, while a genuine historical practice, also represents a psychological stage, that is, the failure to emerge from the shadow of the engulfing mother of infancy. The king, in such undeveloped stages, can only dart out a little at a time from the mother, before running back to her, like a little joey that bounces headlong into the mother's pouch. In ritual, this is performed by killing the king to ensure the fertility of Mother Earth. In the case of substitute sacrifice the king will still give up something, such as his income and sovereignty for a limited period, but remains alive and whole.

53 The story of the Buddha and Devadatta now takes on a new light. Devadatta is the evil 'brother', a relative of the Buddha who embodies all the evil qualities that the Buddha has overcome. He nursed enmity to the Buddha through countless past lives. But there are certain details in his story that suggest that his conflict with the Buddha is not merely personal animosity.

54 Devadatta converted Ajātasattu, then the crown prince, to his cause by appearing to him in the form of a boy with a girdle of snakes.[31] For Ajātasattu, such mastery over the body's form was sufficient demonstration of Devadatta's might. But the image is specific.

55 Elsewhere, the Buddha warns of four things one should not despise because they are young: a fire (which though small may grow out of control), a snake (which though young may still harbour poison), a crown prince (who when he comes to power may extract vengeance for wrongs done to him as a child), and a bhikkhu (who while still young may have great spiritual might).[32] Here three out of four of these are present. The snake and the prince announce the overthrow of the old guard and the rise of the young.

56 Devadatta's identification with the serpent shows that his challenge to the Buddha, while on the surface merely a quest for fame and power, possesses a symbolic force as well. The girdle of snakes does not belong to Devadatta, for it is normally worn by Kālī or other dark goddesses.[33] The snake as a circle specifically represents the cycle of death-&-rebirth.

57 Devadatta presents his plot to the prince: Ajātasattu will kill his father Bimbisāra and become king, while Devadatta will kill the Buddha Gotama and become the new Buddha.[34] Ajātasattu succeeded in murdering his father, but Devadatta's attempts to murder the Buddha and take over the Sangha resulted only in his humiliation. In the end, the earth itself could not bear his crimes and he is dragged screaming into the maw of hell. This failure is not merely a slip-up, for it is impossible that a Buddha should die of violence. Devadatta's failure is, accordingly, an archetypal rather than a historical truth. Ajātasattu's 'success' is also archetypal. Not only, as we have seen, does the cycle of regicide extend into the past, it will continue on in the future. Ajātasattu's son, who he loves so dearly, will in time kill him; and so the pattern continues through the generations.

58 The Buddha is something new. He stands outside the cycle of death & rebirth enacted in the periodic regicide. He is the triumphant Master whose emergence from the unconscious is unshakeable. He no longer has to fear the submission to the forces of the wild or the primitive. When the drunken elephant Nāḷāgiri is unleashed by Devadatta in a murderous rampage, his disciples, except for ever-loyal Ānanda, flee in fear; but the Buddha remains unperturbed.[35] Nāḷāgiri bows on his knees before the Buddha, overwhelmed by the sheer force of the Buddha's loving kindness. Thus even the most awesome primal energies are encompassed, subsumed, and transformed by love. In this triumph of tenderness, the love of a mother is redeemed: no longer the stifling bonds of infantile attachment, but a freely given offering of the heart.

59 This is the essence of the lesson Siddhattha learned from Māyā, the ideal mother. Her love was truly divine, without fracture or flaw. Her departure was perfect suffering. Love, in its fullness and its sudden, inevitable absence. An ideal portrait; almost *too* ideal, one might think. After all, someone had to change the diapers.

CHAPTER 9

THE REAL MĀYĀ

MĀYĀ HAS LED US THROUGH THE MAZE of Buddhist history, illuminating aspects of Buddhist culture that remain in the shadows of modernist Buddhism. She is hard to know, and we have had to seek in associations and connotations: past life stories, images created centuries later, parallels with fairies, even ogresses. But notice that this whimsical journey, this magical mystery tour, has almost entirely avoided the issue: what was it *like* to be Māyā?[1]

2 We see her as an image, looking out from inside our own mind, and seeing her as 'outside' us. But this is, of course, just our projection, a figment of our own fantasy that has nothing to do with the 'real' Māyā.

3 In what sense could there be a 'real' Māyā? Did she even have an 'inside'? If so, how could we ever know it? Māyā is a mirage, endowed with a personal life only because we think that she *must have had* one. In myth, the contents of our psyche are depicted as if external to us. Partially realized structures ('complexes') appear as partially realized characters or images. The very blankness of her historicity leaves her wide open to receive our projections.

4 The traditions tell many stories of Māyā, which I have omitted here. They may be found in any popular recounting of the Buddha's life, told as if fact. And that is true, the stories do represent facts: the fact that they are beliefs. Reading her story, it is difficult to remember that almost all of it is, in all likelihood, sheer invention, the fancy of the poets, nothing more (or less). Merely hearing the story triggers our minds to begin constructing

an imagined historical context, which automatically creates meaning if we are indolent enough to allow it.

❖

5 Not only Māyā, but the Buddha's whole family background is shrouded in mystery. The Buddha's wife, for example, is known in the early texts merely as Rāhulamātā, the 'Mother of Rāhula'.[2] She is there purely to perform the function of being the mother to the Buddha's son. We know—or believe we know—that Rāhula was the Buddha's son, so we infer that Rāhulamātā was the Buddha's wife. But who is she, really? Her name is as various as that of the Goddess herself. She is Yasodharā or Yasovatī; or Bhaddakaccānā or Bhaddakaccā or Subhaddakā or Bhaddā; perhaps Bimbadevī or Bimbasundarī or just plain Bimbā; or else Gopā or Gopikā; unless it was Mṛgajā or Mṛgarājanyā. Her father was Daṇḍapāṇī or Mahānāma or Amitodana or Sukkodana or Suppabuddha or Kiṅkiniśvara. Her mother was Pamitā or Amitā, or perhaps Godhī. Her brothers may have been Ānanda or Devadatta.

6 Can we tease out a kernel of 'solid fact' about the name of Siddhattha's wife from such a confused mass of beliefs? Malalasekera, who (literally) wrote the book on Pali proper names, concluded that Bimbā is the more historically plausible candidate.[3] But *bimbā* means 'image, puppet', a delusory beguiling surface. It is used in exactly the same way as the English 'bimbo', though sadly there is no etymological connection.[4] So the rigors of philology lead us back to the maze of *māyā*. Calasso, as always, says it better:

> 7 His chosen wife was called Gopā. One thing we know about her is that she refused to wear a veil of any kind. Nobody could understand why.[5] It was an allusion to the preceding age: when Kṛṣṇa's *gopīs* heard his flute approaching, their plaits would come undone of their own accord and the veils supporting their breasts fell away. Yet something kept the memory of Kṛṣṇa at bay. For everything that happened to the Bodhisattva happened, as it were, at a remove, was the merest copy. He belonged to the many who are called on not to invent gestures but to repeat those of others. But he was also the only one who would be called upon to extinguish gesture itself. By the time the Bodhisattva appeared, all events of whatever kind seemed to have lost their epic

> profile. Their only value was as a pretext for thought. And it was there, perhaps, that something new was about to happen. There, ever since time began, something had been awaiting the arrival of the Buddha.
>
> 8 The Bodhisattva's life was coated by a uniform film, like the thin walls his father, Śuddhodana, had had built around the palace park. Whatever happened, there was always something slightly artificial and suspect about it. Why did the Bodhisattva only meet creatures of his own age? Why, whenever he approached the boundaries of the park, did the path veer off into thick vegetation that hid any trace of the walls and turn back? Was this the world—or a piece of temporary scenery whose real purpose was to hide the world?[6]

9 When we hear the story of the Bodhisatta trapped in his home, like a princess in her tower, his rule-making father determined to set the course of his life for him, we willingly suspend disbelief. Isn't the tale a bit fake? Siddhattha never saw an old person, or a sick or dead person for his entire life—really? It's too much—surely the authors of this tale could not have expected us to take it literally. So, boldly, we suggest that the story might have been *just a metaphor*. Of course Siddhattha saw sick people and the rest, but he never really *saw* them. He was so attuned to his world of youth and delight that he filtered out the less pleasant side of life. Only now did he consciously realize that the sickness, death, and suffering he saw around him applied to himself as well. He too would experience these things, as would all those he loved. The journey in the park, like so many journeys in story, was in reality an inward path, a voyage to self-discovery.

10 We delight in our insight, our mature approach to what more naïve followers take literally—or so we imagine. But we forget: there is no such thing as *just a metaphor*. All language, all story, is metaphor. It stands before us, plain and obvious, the letters and words that we know so well; but always pointing beyond itself, to something less knowable and more mysterious. Our insight into the metaphor of Siddhattha's story itself convinces us we have found the truth; complacent, we stop there. We have pierced one veil and believe we have found the truth. But the truth is that a million veils remain; and the hardest veil of all to lift is the one that whispers, 'I know the truth.'

❖

11 The unknowability of Māyā is, like everything else about her, nothing personal. Everywhere the goddess appears in beguiling, shifting forms, changing names as often as she changes clothes. And if you are unlucky enough to glimpse her while she is naked, when the veils fall from Gopā's face and reveal the reality beneath the *māyā*, the true form of the *bimbā*, you must endure the fate of Actaeon, who saw Artemis at her bath: he was ripped to shreds by his own hounds. As soon as we try to pin her down, to understand her, she slips from our grasp, to reappear in a new form, a different place. One can never know her truly and can only submit in awe of her everlasting, ever-changing majesty. No-one has captured this better than Apuleius, who crowned his bawdy novel *Metamorphoses* with a giddy rapture of the forms of the Goddess.

> 12 'I am Nature, the universal Mother, mistress of all the elements, primordial child of time, sovereign of all things spiritual, queen of the dead, queen also of the immortals, the single manifestation of all gods and goddesses that are.
>
> 13 'My nod governs the shining heights of Heaven, the wholesome sea-breezes, the lamentable silences of the world below. Though I am worshiped in many aspects, known by countless names, and propitiated with all manner of different rites, yet the whole round earth venerates me.
>
> 14 'The primeval Phrygians call me Pessinuntica, Mother of the gods; the Athenians, sprung from their own soil, call me Cecropian Artemis; for the islanders of Cyprus I am Paphian Aphrodite; for the archers of Crete I am Dictynna; for the trilingual Sicilians, Stygian Proserpine; and for the Eleusinians their ancient Mother of the Corn.
>
> 15 'Some know me as Juno, some as Bellona of the Battles; others as Hecate, others again as Rhamnubia; but both races of Ethiopians, whose lands the morning sun first shines upon, and the Egyptians who excel in ancient learning and worship me with ceremonies proper to my godhead, do call me by my true name—Queen Isis!'[7]

16 And in those lands to the East, where 'the morning sun first shines upon', the goddess is no less revered and no less elusive. She is still worshiped as Lalitā Sahaśranāmā, the Playful One of a Thousand Names.[8] Her elusiveness is disguised in her very ubiquity, her nakedness. In India she is obvious to all, displayed in countless variations of sensuous form; yet no-one would dare say that they truly know her.

17 Māyā is described in the later legends as the epitome of feminine beauty. The monks who lingered in composition of such rapturously sensual accounts as are found in the Lalitavistara, for example, are clearly devotees, in thrall to her loveliness. The traditional instructions for sculptors creating the *sālabhañjikā* insist that they become sensuously involved with their artwork during the creative process. But, obsessed with surfaces, the accounts take no account of her inner depths, of what it was *like* to mother the savior of humanity.

❖

18 In her excelling of all other women, Māyā is like that other enigma of beauty, so far to the west: Helen of Troy, daughter of Zeus in the form of a swan; as glorious as the dawn, and as mysterious. The tales of her are so various, so contradictory, that we may even question whether she existed; but if there was no Helen, how could her face launch a thousand ships? What power did she wield over the destinies of men? What did she think, as she stood on the battlements of Troy, looking at the legions dying to win her back? Was she abducted against her will, staying true in her heart to her husband Menelaus? Or was she a wanton strumpet, forgetting Menelaus in her passion for Paris? Was she acting out of her own will, or was she a mere pawn in the designs of the gods? Aphrodite bribed Paris with the promise of Helen, so that Paris would judge Aphrodite more beautiful than Hera and Athena; and how could Helen resist the impulse of Love Herself? But while Aphrodite's desires were plain, Zeus had his own designs: the age of heroes was coming to an end. Wheels within wheels, turned by the deathless gods, heedless of the mere human lives tossed about below.

19 In the end we must admit we know nothing of her thoughts, of what it was *like* to be Helen. But perhaps being Helen wasn't *like* anything at all. Euripedes has Helen herself claim that the Helen who was seen at Troy was merely an illusion, a magic trick, a *māyā* wrought by Hera, mother of Gods.

> 20 'But Hera, indignant at not defeating the goddesses, brought to naught my marriage with Paris, and gave to Priam's princely son not Helen, but a phantom endowed with life, that she made in my image

> out of the breath of heaven; and Paris thought that I was his, although I never was—an idle fancy! Moreover, the counsels of Zeus added further troubles unto these; for upon the land of Hellas and the hapless Phrygians he brought a war, that he might lighten mother-earth of her myriad hosts of men, and to the bravest of the sons of Hellas bring renown. So I was set up as a prize for all the chivalry of Hellas, to test the might of Phrygia, yet not I, but my name alone; for Hermes caught me up in the embracing air, and veiled me in a cloud; for Zeus was not unmindful of me; and he set me down here in the house of Proteus…'.[9]

21 The 'real' Helen was in Egypt all the time. Herodotus added scholarly *gravitas* to Euripedes' fancies, claiming that the priests of Memphis told him personally that, after the abduction, Paris and Helen were cast by the weather on Egyptian shores. Some of Paris' attendants took advantage of the sanctuary offered by a local shrine to Hercules, and told the priests of Paris' heinous rape of Helen and theft of treasure. The Egyptians, acknowledging Paris' rights as a guest, released him, but kept Helen and the treasure. When the Greeks arrived at Troy, the Trojans told them the truth, but the Greeks did not believe them, and so destroyed the city. Herodotus himself was inclined to accept this rationalizing version of events, for why would the Trojans have fought a war over one woman?[10]

22 In Herodotus we are seeing the emergence of history from myth. For him the 'illusion' of Helen is no more than simple human folly, resulting in a ridiculous, calamitous war that divided Asia from the West, fought over a non-existent Woman of Mass Destruction. But the story of Helen was less historical than Herodotus supposed, and modern interpreters prefer to see the war fought over trade routes rather than a woman.

23 So, were the Egyptians guilty of delusion themselves? Was this fable just another *māyā* that they cast for their own ends? Perhaps. But the etymology suggests a more interesting story.

24 Helen's name has long been a mystery, related by linguists to the moon, or a torch, or Venus. If she is one of the old goddesses, however, she should have a properly dignified Indo-European root. And so she does: **wei2*, with a spectrum of meanings from 'roll, turn', to 'cover, hide'. Helen's Indic equivalent is Saraṇyū, who like Helen was forcibly abducted (or fled of her own will) and was closely related to twins; Helen was the sister of Castor

and Pollux, while Saraṇyū was the mother of their Indic equivalents, the Aśvins, and also Yama and Yamī. The notion of 'twins' is bound up with the idea of 'copies', often human and divine, expressing our dual nature. Saraṇyū is the wife of Sūrya, the Sun, the goddess of the dawn and clouds, the 'shadow' of the sun. She is also known as Saṁjñā (= *sañña*, 'perception', 'idea'), who was born of a reflection. She transformed into a horse, and when the time came for marriage, a copy called Chāyā, or 'Shadow', took her place.

25 If these connections between Helen and Saraṇyū speak the truth, then it is no coincidence that the most beautiful woman in all the world should be so illusory. Illusion is her nature; she is the dawn, the half-light, the reflection, the shadow, the transformation. The beauty is not hers, but sheer 'perception'; it is not in the eye of the beholder, it *is* the eye of the beholder. Helen's inscrutability is her very essence; hence the tendency, developed by Gustave Moreau and Frederic Leighton, to paint her blank-faced, drained of humanity. There is no better way to depict perfect beauty.

❖

26 Far to the East, another story has been told as long as there have been storytellers to tell it.[11] Sītā, the beautiful and virtuous wife of Rāma, was abducted and taken to Laṅkā over the seas. She was forced to live in the court of the demon king Rāvaṇa, who coveted her as his wife. But he had enough self-respect that he would not force his will against her virtue—unless it be that he was afraid to rape her, under the power of a curse incurred by a previous rape. Rāma then assembled an army and fought a terrible war to rescue her. When the enemy was vanquished and the lovers reunited, Rāma did the unthinkable: he rejected Sītā. For how could he know that she had not given herself to her demon lover?[12]

27 Sītā walked into the fire to prove her purity, and still Rāma would not accept her. Sītā's virtue must remain unassailable against any suspicion, however slight, for if Rāvaṇa had forced himself upon her, even though she was unwilling, his demon nature would pollute her body. Besides, who could ever trust the paternity of the children? So many years later Rāma rejected Sītā again, forcing her to live in the wilds, pregnant with his children.

28 The deepest heroes somehow never manage to stay with their True Love: Rāma & Sītā, Odysseus & Penelope, Romeo & Juliet, Jason & Medea, Layla & Majnun, Siddhattha & Bimbā. Small wonder that the most popular flavor of Indian poetry is *viraha*, love in separation. For love, in whatever form it takes, is but a prelude to separation. And who is to say which is the sweeter?

29 Finally Sītā returns, but not for Rāma. In the ultimate vindication, she is embraced by the Earth Goddess and taken down into the earth from which she was born.[13] Still this was not enough! Even the suggestion that she might have been touched by the demon was unthinkable. Eventually the *Adhyātma Rāmāyaṇa* revealed the truth: Rāma, knowing what was to come, told Sītā to create an illusion (*māyāsītā*) and to hide her real self in fire, where she is safe in the custody of Agni.[14] It was the illusion who was abducted by Rāvaṇa. The 'real' Sītā remained hidden in the fire, and only emerged a year later, when the illusory Sītā was made to undergo the ordeal by fire. Only then did the real Sītā re-emerge, like Helen who reappeared only after the war was over. The *Adhyātma Rāmāyaṇa* wants to display Rāma's 'higher self', and retells the story to justify his apparent cruelty to Sītā. The bloody carnage of war was fought over an illusion; and Rāma knew this all along.

30 Or did he? He lies to his brother, grieves for Sītā, and in general acts as though it is the real Sītā who has been abducted. Through all the tellings of the tale, the truth seems hidden from Rāma. The story, indeed, is that of him coming to know his own nature. Like the Bodhisatta in countless Jātakas, the hero of the story knows far less than the truly Omniscient One—the storyteller.

31 'Rāma' is in fact an idea, an illusion, just as much as 'Sītā' is. The humanity lies within us, the audience, not within the characters. We give the lifeless words of the story a beating, trembling heart—our heart. So if the 'real' characters of the story are in essence empty, but are gifted their souls by the reader, why can the shadows not receive the same? And this is exactly what happens. As the tale evolves, Sītā's 'shadow', the illusory Māyāsītā, gradually acquires a subjectivity. She becomes not just a device to be disposed of according to the expediency of the plot, but a person, with her own needs, desires, and destiny.

32 When the 'real' Sītā reappears, Māyāsītā is, understandably enough, distraught. She no longer has any purpose in life. Rāma doesn't want her. Distraught, she begs him for guidance, and Rāma advises her to do ascetic practices. Śiva himself is impressed by her efforts, and appears before her. She begs him five times, 'Give me a husband'; and so in the next life she is reborn as Draupadī, wife to the five Pandava brothers as told in the Mahābhārata.[15]

33 Sītā's purity is ensured by splitting off the shadow, which in this case is a predatory sexuality: implied lover of a demon, and the only woman in Indian myth so insatiable as to need multiple husbands.[16] In the early story the characters behaved rather like actual people—flawed, erratic, narcissistic, and noble. These ambiguities have been extracted, drawn out like blood, leaving idealized puppets whose purpose is explain the ideology of the authors. The result is a work of theology rather than humanity; and the once rich personalities are becoming more like the characters in the Buddha's myth every day.

❖

34 A woman's surface, her beauty, the perception of her skin is inseparable from the idea of a man's gaze. So her *māyā*, that by which she ensnares the world, ends up ensnaring her. Carol Gilligan comments:

35 > Our tendency when we lose something is to hold on to an image of that thing, which often becomes the only thing, what we most wanted or value; or else to disparage what we have lost, seeing it as nothing, nothing of value. The pervasive images of women, idealized and degraded, reflect a pervasive loss of connection with women. Loving an image of woman rather than an actual person becomes a way of fending off the possibility of losing again, because an image can be held apart from relationship, and one woman can take another's place. 'The voice of the Mother is the largest absence in literature,' the writer Tillie Olsen observed in 1976; it is the voice that haunts the tragic love story.[17]

36 Gilligan traces the implications of this absence through the classical myth of Cupid & Psyche. It is another riff on the theme of woman as image, as surface without substance. Psyche is so beautiful she is worshiped, literally, as the living image of Venus. But Venus is, in fact, all image—she

exists in the world only as statue and painting. Psyche is, then, more real than the goddess, just as the girls who model themselves after an image in a magazine are more real than the fantasies they imitate. The irony is that, while they worship a real woman rather than a goddess, it is only the *image* of the woman they worship.

37 And they hate it. Psyche hates being worshiped as an image, not being seen as a person; and Venus hates that someone else gets the worship she deserves. Only the gods have the right to be all surface and no interior. So Venus hates Psyche, and sends her son to dispatch her; but Cupid falls in love with the rival, the image of his mother.

38 Psyche is taken to Cupid's beautiful palace, where they spend their nights in pleasure. Psyche is forbidden to ever see her forbidden lover; while she is all image, he is invisible. By day he disappears and she is alone, waited on by mysterious servants. Eventually it becomes too much. Her sisters maliciously suggest that her husband is really a demon in disguise. She can't resist the temptation to have a peek. She lights a lamp and looks upon his sleeping form at night: and he is revealed as the most beautiful divine youth, Love himself. A drop of hot oil from the lamp falls on his skin; he awakes, realizes what has happened, and disappears. Love flees the light of the Soul.

39 Psyche must endure a series of trials set by Venus if she wants her husband back. In typical masculine quests, the hero must fight, overcome wild beasts and perilous voyages. Psyche's tasks, however, are more domestic: she is given barrels full of seeds all mixed up—wheat, barley, beans. She must sort them all out by morning. It's impossible; but the ants appear in their millions to help. A series of such tasks must be accomplished so she can prove her fitness. She needs to be more than a lover, she must be capable at domestic duties before the mother-in-law will accept her as bride of her son.

40 In the end, Psyche steals the forbidden jar of Beauty—the special make-up secret of the Goddess of Love—but when she opens it she falls into a deep swoon. Only then, after Beauty's betrayal, does Cupid see the real Psyche in the bright daylight; and Love falls in love with the Soul. After all their travails, Jupiter calms the spiteful Venus and arranges a divine

marriage. In the very last line of the story, it is said that Psyche gave birth to a daughter, who they called 'Pleasure'.

41 The key to this story is that we are not formed from conflict, but from love, from the long struggle to build relationship that goes beyond surfaces. The better known classical myths—Oedipus, Agamemnon, Troy—place conflict at the center. Gilligan argues that by emphasizing these stories, Freud and his followers developed a masculinized psychology that depicted breakage and separation as our defining experiences. I think there is something to this. But I also remember that in even the most tragic of Greek myths, the cycle ends with a moment of forgiveness: Achilles sitting quietly with Priam, who had entered alone into his enemy's camp to humbly ask for the remains of his son, Hector; or Orestes, who found forgiveness for the long feud of blood and savagery that had marred his house.

42 Perhaps the most astonishing transformation in all Greek tragedy is that of Oedipus himself. Exiled, blinded, an abomination in the eyes of all, he wandered friendless though the wilderness. Only his daughter, the incomparable Antigone, remained by his side. As the time came for his death, a storm announced the will of the gods: it was time for Oedipus' death. No longer fighting the fates, he was filled with an inexplicable new strength. He promised to Theseus, the Athenian leader, that he would show them a place of safety, 'a great mystery that words should never rouse from the depths'.[18] He leads them to a secret shrine in the heart of the sacred grove. Oedipus the outcast, the despised, slayer of his father, husband of his mother, goes to his death with a blessing to Theseus.

43
> 'Dearest friend, you and your country and your loyal followers,
> may you be filled with greatness, and in your great day remember
> me, the dead, the root of all your greatness, everlasting, ever-new.'[19]

❖

44 The extraordinary Kusa Jātaka twists the theme once again.[20] The Bodhisatta is born as Prince Kusa, as wise as he is ugly. He and his brother were divine gifts; he received wisdom while his brother received beauty, so the premise of the story is the disjunct between inner and outer. He is married to the most beautiful of all women, Princess Pabhāvatī, on the condition that they cannot see each other, but may only consort at night.

45 Eventually, of course, the ruse is uncovered. Unlike Cupid & Psyche, Kusa is genuinely ugly, and so it is Pabhāvatī who flees in horror from her grotesque husband. Elaborate and often comic adventures ensue. It is Kusa, not Pabhāvatī, who undergoes the trials of domestic life, proving his worth as a cook and a potter. He does not hesitate to undertake such demeaning work for the sake of his love.

46 At long last the lovers are reunited; but not until he has humbled himself as a servant and she has destroyed her vanity by literally grovelling in the mud before him. To re-establish his manly credentials, he crowns his courtship by winning a tremendous battle. For his heroism and compassion Kusa is granted a wish-fulfilling gem by Sakka, and by the end of the tale the couple are raised to glorious lordship, each as radiant as the other.

47 The conventions of the fairy tale are playfully undermined. Not until the princess becomes ugly is her true beauty revealed, for in her heart she is a prisoner to her vanity. The adventures of the hero are not primarily the masculine feats of war—although the story is careful to end with Kusa's martial prowess—but humble household work, especially cooking. The author was aware of the clichés of his genre and consciously worked to subvert them. By the end of the story mere image, delusory *māyā*, is transcended, and the outward glory of the couple is a true manifestation of their inner selves.

❖

48 *Māyā* means deceit. It is a magic trick; it is the falseness of the world; it is an ancient name of the goddess; it is the absence of women's inner life from the stories told by men. But India being what it is, *māyā* itself went through a magical transformation, elevated from a mere magic trick to become a central philosophical conception, the creative play by which the Absolute manifests the phenomenal world. Though herself neither real nor unreal, her womb is the source of all things, boundless and imperishable. It brings forth the limited and delusory forms of life, nourishes them with life for a time, then dissolves them back into the nameless, eternal state. She is the protector of the entire universe, which rests like a baby sleeping in her lap.[21] In the period of early Buddhism such philosophical conceptions had not yet been articulated. Yet we cannot deny that a strictly literal reading of our Buddhist sources says that the Buddha is born of the *play of magic*...

CHAPTER 10

LET'S PLAY

AND SO, NOT ENTIRELY UNLIKE the upright German philologist Roth playing with the ragamuffins of Patna, we enter the dream landscape of faerie to play. Playing with myth doesn't undermine it, as the fundamentalists fear; it brings the myth to life. Huizinga's *Homo Ludens* develops this idea, pointing out that in mythology there is always a 'fanciful spirit' that plays on the border between 'jest and earnest'.[1] He argues that ethnologists and anthropologists are well aware of this, agreeing that tribal celebrations and rituals have an 'underlying consciousness of things "not being real".'[2]

2 This playful tone will be familiar to anyone who has read the early Suttas. It emerges in the gentle satires on the pompousness of Brahmā, or in the inevitable humbling of Māra. In the Udāna, a pair of *yakkhas* see Sāriputta in meditation under the full moon, his freshly shaven head offering a sore temptation for a *yakkha's* club. Though warned by his friend, one of the *yakkhas* can't resist giving Sāriputta a blow on the head, powerful enough to fell a great elephant or split a mountain! But, while the *yakkha* falls screaming to hell, Sāriputta sits serenely, his meditation undisturbed. His friend, Mahā Moggallāna, saw the *yakkha* with his psychic powers, and asks Sāriputta if he is alright. Sāriputta says, 'I'm fine, although I do have a slight headache.'[3]

3 The Sagāthāvagga tells of a miraculous reversal in the interminable wars between the *devas* (gods) and the *asuras* (titans).[4] The *asuras* won the battle and were chasing Sakka and his army. But the fleeing gods had to pass through a forest filled with delicate birds' nests. Sakka ordered

his charioteer to turn back: better to sacrifice their lives to the *asuras* than destroy the homes of innocent, defenseless creatures. But when they turned about, the *asuras* assumed that Sakka was about to re-engage in combat. Stricken with fear, they fled. The ferocious war god of the Vedas won the battle by his tender concern for creatures, a compassion that the *asuras* just don't get.

4 This playful spirit is no accident, but flows from the very source of myth and rite in dream, fantasy, and imagination. A life in which dreams are given concrete form is a life that is, literally, the stuff of nightmares. That way lies madness. A true engagement with the spirit of myth emerges through intuition, grace, irony, humor, and creativity, while never forgetting that the game is deadly real, since it is the game of life itself. Myth is illusion, but it is no more illusion than everything else, which is why it is so true. The deeper our appreciation of the dream of myth, the deeper we will become aware of the dreamlike, shadow nature of our own self.[5]

5 When this underlying sense of play wears out it is replaced by a grim literalism that we call 'textual fundamentalism'. A world is imagined that does not creatively interact with the texts, but is subject to them. This world has never existed and can never exist. Fundamentalism is never a 'return to the roots', for those roots were living and adapting to their environment. Fundamentalism is an innovation of modernity, whose theoretical basis is a rejection of the methods and findings of text criticism, and which seeks to recreate the world as a whole based on a text and an interpretation that is narrowly partial, and utterly alien to the people who created the texts in the first place.[6] It is an essentially delusory and destructive reaction to modernity, a dysfunctional postmodernism.

6 The literalism of the fundamentalists grinds the joy out of spiritual life, while play lights it up. Play is, however, not just kids' stuff. It's serious business. J.C. Heesterman shows that Vedic sacrfice, like most other forms, is not 'merely' symbolic. Sacrifice embodies the paradox of life and death, which cannot be separated, and yet which are each other's opposite. Rather than resolve this paradox, it is enacted by the participants in ritual 'play'. But this ritual does not merely symbolize life and death, it actually redistributes wealth, cattle, and food, the very substance of life. While the

ritual plays on the riddle of life-&-death, the outcome of the ritual is the very real partitioning of life and death among the participants.[7]

7 In the Mahābhārata, Yudhiśthira wins a kingdom in a game of dice; and for the Aztecs, a game of ball meant death. The Jātakas are full of people who meet life-changing forces while they 'play'. Play suspends conventional boundaries and allows spontaneous creativity to burst forth. In a study of kingship and sacrifice in ancient Hawai'i, Valeri says that the most attribute of the New Year's fertility festival is play. Since play is an end in itself, it is an expression of that most human of qualities, creativity. This creative play is mirrored in the reneawl of life that takes place during this seasonal festival.[8]

8 In this fluid, creative, playful state, the hierarchies and structures of society are temporarily dissolved, and people become as equal as they were when they were born. How might these things be handled within a literature produced by sober, celibate, hierarchical monks? Buddhist culture, like all others, finds a space somewhere for the relaxation of all bounds, the dissolution into chaos that precedes the inevitable reforming of order. This might be surprising, given the austere, forbidding image of Buddhist monastics. But ritual play, with its semi-serious half-smile, happens all the time in the monasteries. The monks treat rituals much less solemnly than the average devotee. And as the Tibetan story of the Jalno has shown us,[9] when the monks get serious, the fun really starts.

9 In play, we can assume whatever role takes our fancy. Ancient sacred festivities such as the carnival and the saturnalia upturned all social positions. In play, the random and the chaotic find their proper, bounded, and acceptable place.

10 It is still seen today in extreme sports, where the kids, lacking any socially endorsed form of ritual mutilation, prove their manhood. Piercing and tattooing, too, are useful in convincing the mother that she's given birth to some sort of alien being. The similarity between ancient rituals and modern play is no mere analogy, but a genuine historical continuity. One example of this is the history of bungee jumping, which descends directly from the 'Land Diving' or *nagol* practiced by the men of Pentecost Island.[10]

11 Who knows when it all began? Long ago there lived a man called Tamale. His voracious sexual demands proved too much for his wife, and she ran away into the forest. Tamale chased her up a tree. Just as he was about to grab her, she leapt. He leapt after her, not knowing that, as a clever woman, she had tied liana vines to her ankles before jumping and so was saved. Tamale was not so lucky: the foolish man plunged to his death.

12 This story has all the hallmarks of an ancient memory of human sacrifice, with the inevitable substitution. Since the legend has the man dying and the woman living, the original form was probably a sacrifice to the goddess. In such homely, village-level tales, however, the story never strays far from ordinary domestic concerns. The legend offers a way of managing the ever-present threat of male sexual violence. It reminds him that he too can die if his demands become excessive.

13 In the past, the clever woman was saved and her husband died. These days, according to the young men who perform the dive, things are the right way up. The young, brave, strong men leap safely, while the women dance and sing in adoration below.

14 While the origin story had a woman leaping from a natural tree, these days a tower is specially constructed, at great effort, for the men to leap from. The building work is supervised by the male elders, who have survived the leap themselves, and take care that all safety precautions are satisfied. They support the hot-blooded displays of the youths, but the elders must be cool-headed, knowledgeable, and careful.

15 The entire ritual is steeped in sexual symbolism. The tower itself, like the ritual, is called *nagol*, which means 'body'. Each part of it is symbolically identified with parts of the body, including both male and female genitals. The festival is linked to the yam harvest; in the local system, yams are masculine while taro is feminine. As usual in such ritual displays of virile masculinity, while the tower is being built the participants are expected to refrain from sex and women must not approach the tower. The leap itself enhances sexual prowess and strength. In addition, a successful leap, where the man curls his shoulders up to just touch the ground, promotes a vigorous yam crop.

Figure 10.1: *N'gol*

16 The ceremony is a whole. It involves the whole village, each in their appointed role, and is integrated with the seasons and the supply of basic foodstuffs. While the men make speeches and show off their extravagant codpieces, the women dance in their grass skirts, whooping and singing in chorus.

17 Yet even in Pentecost Island, the ritual is not what it used to be. The pressures of colonialism were felt early, during an ill-advised display put on for Queen Elizabeth II in 1972. The elders opposed it, as the vines and woods were not in the right season and would break—and they were right. One of the jumpers broke his back and died soon afterwards. This is the only recorded death from Land Diving.

18 More recently, tourism has had its influence. The spectacle is more staged, more showy than the earliest recorded examples.

19 But the changes have not just come from nefarious outside influences. The warrior culture of former times provided a way for young men to prove themselves in battle. In these more peaceful days, the dive has proven to be an effective substitute, and for this reason is probably more significant for the local people than ever.

20 The decay of the ritual is, of course, taken to extremes in its Western incarnation as bungee jumping. Gone is any symbolic significance, gone is the meaning-creating legend, gone is the connection with the seasons and the harvest. Now it's just a thrill.

21 We could not ask for a clearer example of how cults evolve: from human sacrifice to the goddess (as remembered in the myth); to a ritual re-enactment as fertility rite and initiation from the clutches of the women; to a game, still deeply thrilling, yet commercialized and safe. This watered-down, sanitized version can never recapture the 'power' (*mana, brahman, māyā...*) of the Real Thing. But there is still a moment where one launches off from the tree like a bird; suspended, neither in the sky or on the ground. And for all the 'play' of it, in that moment we confront our most primal fear.

❖

22 Modern Buddhist culture takes itself far too seriously. The myths give the lie to the doctrine that Buddhism is essentially 'rational'. Hence they are as absent from modernist Buddhism as Māyā is absent from the early

texts. The traditional Buddhist is fed sugary, didactic tales for moral edification, which are regarded with disdain by modernists. So overlaid are the stories with later rationalizations that the substance of deep myth is easily overlooked. When discussing Jātakas or other 'children's tales' with Buddhist audiences, there is an constant struggle to explain, justify, or make sense of the 'moral of the story'. But sometimes there is no moral—and that is precisely the point.

23 The denial of myth is a corollary of the rational agenda of modernist Buddhism. Determined to prove that Buddhism is 'scientific', Buddhists and scholars have focused on the rational teachings of the Suttas. That's fine, but it's time to relax now. The rational modernist program has done its job: we have differentiated the Dhamma from the inherited mass of superstition and folly. We know that Buddhism is not a mindless devotional cult. We know that it encourages inquiry and reason. We know that meditation has been 'scientifically' validated. We need not fear that the Dhamma will sink into darkness.

24 Our task, rather, is that of integration: to assimilate the dark side of the Dhamma. 'Buddhism' contains much that by any normal standard is irrational. The denial of this is the unspoken contract of modernist Buddhism. But myth, far from being a footnote to the triumphant march of the pristine Dhamma through the ages, constitutes a major, major factor in Buddhist culture, including monastic culture. The denial of myth means that neither within traditional Buddhism, nor within modern Buddhist studies, do we find much to help understand the mythology.

25 So for inspiration I have turned to cross-cultural examinations of myth, especially those that consider the psychological aspects. This work will frequently reference the writings of Erich Neumann, one of Jung's students. He specialized in psychological interpretations of mythology, with a particular focus on the feminine. I use his work, not because I have a particular theoretical commitment to the Jungian framework as such, but because, after struggling with these issues for years, it has helped me make sense of many apparently intractable problems.

❖

26 One of the key ideas of Jungian theory is that the unconscious speaks in a symbolic language, which is universal across all human cultures, and

which finds expression in the individual primarily through dreams, and in a culture primarily through myth. Buddhism shares this symbolic language with all other religions; but what it says in that language is unique, for myth and symbol derive their meaning from their context. Just because different religions share common symbolic patterns does not prove they are 'all the same in the end': this is the fallacy of reductionism. Nor should we fool ourselves into thinking that 'rational' Buddhism is somehow above myth and other trivial pursuits. Rational dismissal of the power of myth is itself evidence of the hold it has over us, and of the fear of hearing what it may have to say. This is, precisely, the way to guarantee that the grip of the irrational will never loosen.

27 From a Jungian point of view, the rational is like a few low-lying islands, which have strenuously and over a long time emerged from the vast ocean of unconsciousness. Jung's way of talking about the unconscious stems from a different context and set of concerns than the Buddha addressed, and so cannot be directly mapped on to the Buddha's teachings. Nevertheless, such ideas can be compared with the Buddha's description of the 'dark mass of ignorance', of the 'inherent tendencies' which, although we are unaware of them, underlie the development of our conscious psyche.[11] The unconscious is not merely what is repressed, but constitutes almost all of existence, from matter on up. When the rational mind relaxes its defenses and loses its fear that it will be submerged back into the ocean, the whispers of the unconscious may be heard in the restless heaving of the sea.

28 It is not threatening or menacing. It is like a child, not a monster. It just wants to be heard and acknowledged: it is part of us. It speaks in ambiguous or unclear symbolic forms, not because it wishes to hide anything, but because that is the only language it knows. It hasn't learned to speak the language of reason. We can't reason with it, but we can play with it. In the contemplation of myth, dream, and symbol, the rational mind reaches out in response to the call of the unconscious. Like the Buddha taming Nāḷāgiri the elephant, there is no power, no matter how chaotic or malevolent, which will not respond to loving acceptance.

29 And acceptance means more than a historical acknowledgment that myth is the mother of Buddhist culture. It is a recognition of how our lives,

here & now, still embody the forms of myth—still! For while the academics may speak of the 'absence of myth', our children are brought up on the old stories, and the living faith communities still swim in those waters. Popular culture has never lost sight of myth's emotive power. If we are to engage in Buddhism with any depth—not just cherry-picking bits & pieces—we must learn to notice how our Buddhist experience is shaped by mythic presence—and mythic absence.

30 In sympathy with the disappearance of religion from culture, recent psychology has witnessed the gradual disappearance of myth, which was so central for Jung, Freud, and other early theorists. In Jung's day, a classical education was essential. Brought up on the myths, it was only natural to use them in one's thinking. And the issue runs deeper than this. Not only do the myths suggest certain lines of interpretation, but they also shape the psyche in ways both conscious and unconscious; they don't just expose the problems, but contribute to causing them. In secular culture, the myths are treated so playfully we can no longer appreciate the depths of their influence. But for Buddhists the myths still lay down a blueprint for how to live. More frighteningly, as the theoretical basis for fundamentalism, myths threaten the very survival of our world.

31 We live in the belly of the Buddha's myth, it surrounds us like Jonah's whale. As we explore, we can only hope it does not suffer indigestion.

CHAPTER 11

PERCEPTION, SYMBOL, MYTH

IF I AM TO USE JUNGIAN MODES OF ANALYSIS within a Buddhist context, I should offer some indication of where such ideas fit in the Buddhadhamma. Apart from its intrinsic interest, this may help allay the concerns of those who still think of 'psychology' as 'non-Buddhist'. It might also help defuse concerns that this analysis of myth is conceptually 'etic', that is, an outsider's perspective. Of course, for me as a monk it feels anything but etic, but there you go.

2 In the terms of Buddhist psychology, it's useful to analyze myth as a social aspect of *saññā*. The meaning and function of *saññā* are not entirely obvious from a casual perusal of early Buddhism, and the definitions do not help much.[1] So let's investigate this term first, before we go on to draw out its implications for our current problem.

3 The significance of *saññā* is best appreciated in the context it's most commonly found, that is, the five aggregates (*khandhas*). These are one of the most characteristic of Buddhist teachings, used as a summary of 'the stuff of life', and as a scheme for classifying theories of the Self, all of which fail in the light of the true nature of the aggregates. We will briefly survey these, then return to look at *saññā* in more detail.

4 The five aggregates are 'form' (*rūpa*, 'matter', also 'appearance'), 'feeling' (*vedanā*), 'perception' (*saññā*), 'volitional activities' (*saṅkhārā*), and 'awareness' (*viññāṇa*, often rendered as 'consciousness').

5 Form, in the simplest sense, is the physical realm in general. But its root meaning of 'appearance' suggests an 'inside-out' orientation. Form is not objectively conceived stuff in the world, but our lived experience of the physical, the objects of the five external (i.e. physical) senses. It also extends to physical qualities imagined or remembered in the mind, such as mental imagery.

6 Feeling is a very simply-treated category, just the pleasant, painful, or neutral tone of experience. It relates closely to the most primal of gut-instincts and desires. *Vedanā* is characteristic of the animal realm, with its intense suffering and instant gratification.

7 Perception is more subtle, filtering and making sense of experience. While this—like all the aggregates—is also shared with animals, humans develop this faculty much further through the use of symbols and signs, setting up tokens for recognition. These 'signs' are the basis of language and human culture in general. Even today, a sense of identity is evoked through recognition of a common sign: religious icon, flag, football club colors.

8 *Saṅkhāra* is, narrowly, volition, and relates to our sense of ourselves as independent agents exercising our free will. It manifests as thought, concepts, plans, and is future oriented, whereas *saññā* looks to the past. But the most critical aspect of *saṅkhāra* is that it is ethical: one *chooses* to do good or bad. The three previous aggregates are pre-ethical; there is no notion of good or bad suggested in their definitions. Later theorists of the Abhidhamma decided to use *saṅkhāra* as a catch-all category, including a long list of any and all miscellaneous mental factors that didn't fit into the other aggregates. But this lumps all kinds of primitive and sophisticated mental qualities in together, entirely obscuring the developmental structure of the five aggregates.

9 *Viññāṇa* stands in apposition to all of these things; it is the knowing, they are the known.[2] When the stuff of experience is set to one side, *viññāṇa* remains. In everyday experience it is the 'awareness of' the six kinds of sense objects, and is reckoned as sixfold. Refined and cultivated it is the

radiant awareness of 'infinite consciousness'. Historically, this is where the pre-Buddhist Upaniṣadic yogis such as Yajñavālkya found the Self,[3] and today it forms the ultimate reach of countless popular spiritual writers. *Viññāṇa* is normally translated as 'consciousness', but this is meant in the sense of simple awareness, as opposed to its use in psychological discourse, where consciousness is used in a more complex sense as the totality of thoughts and feelings, or even as self-reflective awareness.

10 The aggregates are aspects of our embodied experience, and may be treated as both a hierarchical or 'nested' structure and as an evolving process. While they operate simultaneously and may be discerned in any moment of awareness, nevertheless they have a progressive aspect, moving from the coarse to the refined. What this means is that there is a tendency to identify with each of the aggregates in turn as the process of development unfolds.

11 This evolution of the locus of identity may be traced in both general and individual development. What do I mean by this? If we look in the broadest terms at how our world is structured, at the most basic level we find inorganic matter, from which plant life evolves. In these things form is the most prominent of the aggregates. With the appearance of animals, who rely on pleasure/pain and fight/flight responses, feeling comes to the fore. In human culture, with its language, beliefs, and rituals, perception plays the prominent role. In the great civilizations, rational, ethical, future-building thought is the distinctive feature. Finally there is the highest level of evolution, the development of purified awareness through meditation. At its most general level, then, the structure of our world mirrors the structure of the five aggregates.

12 And what of individual development? Psychologists have come up with any number of schemes to formalize this, and virtually all of them correspond in some way with the five aggregates. As just one example, take Maslow's famous scheme of the hierarchy of needs. The basic needs are physical—food, shelter, sex—which is the form aggregate. The next set of needs revolve around safety, which is less obviously related to the feeling aggregate, but the connection is there, since safety is ultimately about protecting one from suffering and ensuring happiness. When we have safety, our most pressing need is for belonging, our connections with other people,

which corresponds exactly with *saññā*. Next comes esteem; once more it is not so obvious how this correlates with *saṅkhārā*; but esteem, whether self-esteem or the esteem of others, stems from engaging in mature undertakings, in a responsible manner, which is precisely what *saṅkhārā* is about.[4] Finally Maslow describes a person's highest need as 'self-actualization', when a person becomes conscious of who they and of what they can be, which clearly corresponds to *viññāṇa* as the awareness of the other four aggregates.

13 In drawing these parallels I am not saying that these are all the 'same thing'. Obviously there are differences, both in details and in the purpose and function of these frameworks. I am trying to make vivid the notion that the aggregates relate to a development or evolution, and that this process, in its general outlines, is apparent in many different contexts. It is, to me, an astonishing thing that the five things that the Buddha drew attention to, saying that it is here that we tend to locate our sense of self, should so closely parallel what modern psychologists have described as the development of the self.

❖

14 Bearing this general orientation in mind, let's look more closely at *saññā*. The common rendering of *saññā* as 'perception' is justified by definitions of perception as: 'the active psychological process in which stimuli are selected and organized into meaningful patterns.'[5] Or else: 'the process by which we take raw sensations from the environment and interpret them, using our knowledge and understanding of the world, so that they become meaningful experiences.'[6] Such definitions equally apply to *saññā* in Buddhism, if we bear in mind that for Buddhist psychology the mind is treated as a sense organ like any other, albeit more complex and sophisticated.[7]

15 *Saññā* is the mental function whereby present reality is perceived (remembered, re-collected) through familiar associations of past experience. This kind of knowing is inherently collective, in that it associates different events of consciousness. It makes a kind of 'average' of experience: while each of us sees a slightly different image of a 'tree', *saññā* recognizes the similarities between this visual data and previous experiences we have labeled 'tree'. Thus while our specific sense data of 'tree' differs, our general notion of 'tree' is similar enough for us to understand each other. Hence

saññā forms the basis for communication through concepts and language.[8] From there, *saññā* comes to be used in the sense of 'contract'.[9]

16 In everyday speech, it is used to mean a 'mark' or a 'token', such as a rope or a pile of leaves used to mark a place. In this sense, *saññā* lies close to a range of terms such as *nimitta, ākāra, uddesa*, or *liṅga*, all of which mean 'sign, symbol, summary'.

17 In the process of conceptualization, it falls between sense awareness and thinking: *saññā* prepares the raw data of sense experience for conceptual operations. The most elegant formulation of this is in the Madhupiṇḍika Sutta.[10] The sense organ, impacted by sense data, gives rise to sense consciousness. This is just the raw data; so far, the eye just sees 'light', not the conceptually constructed entities we believe we 'see'. This process is fully automatic, and is syntactically expressed with a series of nouns that condition each other, like dominoes falling. Nevertheless, it is a non-linear process, as all conditions have to be present for sense impingement to occur. This sense impingement gives rise to an affective response (*vedanā* = feeling), and perception (*saññā*). The immediate outcome of perception is 'thinking'. These functions are expressed as verbs, rather than the earlier nouns, suggesting a more active process, like streams rushing downhill. But from here on, things really get going. 'Thought' gives rise to 'proliferation', and then there is, not merely an impersonal cognitive process, but a 'person' who is 'swamped' by the rampant 'proliferative perceptions and notions', sweeping them into the past, present, and future: the stream gushes over a waterfall.

18 *Saññā* is not limited to physical sense perception. We have seen how *saññā* emerges from 'contact' (or 'stimulus'). The Suttas describe contact as of two kinds: 'impingement' contact experienced through the five physical senses, and 'linguistic' contact experienced through the mind.[11] The early Abhidhamma theorists framed perception in the same terms.[12]

19 Ethical discussions, in evaluating moral responsibility, constantly emphasize the possibility of perception not equating with reality. For example, one may 'perceive' that a pool of water does not contain living beings, although in reality it does.[13] One can only be held fully responsible if one's perception was accurate. But we should not think of *saññā* as a problem in itself. The averaging-out, good-enough nature of *saññā* is necessary for

cognitive functioning, and so it makes up one of the basic constituents of *nāma* ('name'), the conceptual, affective, and active aspect of the mind, as opposed to awareness itself, *viññāṇa*. Later theorists made this more explicit by listing *saññā* among the mental factors that are present in every event of consciousness.

20 *Saññā* 'puts together' the data of experience in a way that makes sense, and allows us to deal in a world of overwhelming sense impingement. We can think of it as 'recognition', and remember the difficulty in training a computer to recognize a face or a fingerprint, basic tasks that *saññā* performs a million times a day without us noticing. It is *saññā* that we learnt when Sesame Street asked us: 'Which one of these is not like the other one?' Without such cognitive simplification, experience would be a meaningless mess. We only have to read some of the case studies by Oliver Sacks to appreciate how difficult things get when our perception doesn't work straight.[14]

21 In Buddhist psychology, therefore, *saññā* is not intrinsically good or bad. It depends on whether it is used with a good or bad intention (*saṅkhāra*). In meditation we develop *saññā*, which can mean a 'meditation subject': we cultivate the 'perception' of impermanence, or of a part of the body.[15] This gives rise to experiences in meditation such as the 'perception of light'.[16] On the other hand, we guard against the 'perversions of perception'—perceiving the impermanent as permanent, suffering as happiness, not-self as self, or beautiful as ugly.

❖

22 The interpretation I am developing here, based on the early canonical texts, is broadly similar to the understanding found within the later traditions.[17] Buddhaghosa, in his classic Theravādin treatise the Visuddhimagga, says of *saññā*:

23 > Its function is to make a sign as a condition for perceiving again that 'this is the same', as carpenters, etc., do in the case of timber, and so on. It is manifested as the action of interpreting by means of the sign as interpreted, like the blind who 'see' an elephant.[18] Its proximate cause is an objective field in whatever way that appears, like the perception that arises in fawns that see scarecrows as men.[19]

24 Asaṅga, the great commentator of the Yogacāra school of Mahāyāna says in his Abhidharmasamuccaya:

> 25 Recognizing is the characteristic of perception. The nature of perception is to know various things, and to express things seen, heard, conceived, and those that one recalls.[20]

26 Asaṅga's brother Vasubandhu says more laconically that perceptions are 'the grasping of signs (*nimitta*) in a sense-object'.[21] Vasubandhu expresses the difference between *saññā* and *viññāṇa* by a grammatical subtlety: one cognizes blue (*nīlaṁ vijānāti*), but one perceives 'blue' (*nīlaṁ iti saṁjānāti*).[22] In his Abhidharmakośa he explains more fully:

> 27 The aggregate of perception has for its essence the grasping of images, i.e. it seizes hold of the attributes blue or yellow, long or short, male or female, pleasant or unpleasant, antipathetic or sympathetic, etc.[23]

28 Images or signs are especially characteristic of *saññā*, for they are seen all-at-once. An immediate apprehension is made of the overall outline or form, the pattern of data. Such seeing ignores more than it sees, adds to experience more than it derives from it. Underneath that act of recognition lies a fathomless process of training the mind through countless re-experiencings of comparable situations.

29 *Saññā* is this *seeming* aspect of things, what we make of our perceptual data, how we construct them, how we interpret them. This is why the Buddha likened *saññā* to a mirage.[24]

❖

30 The world of myth, symbol, and ritual is largely an external projection of *saññā*. As we have seen, the early texts show *saññā* at work in all contexts, so I am not trying to suggest that it is somehow solely used in that way. But, while all five aggregates are found in all aspects of experience, they are more-or-less characteristic or prominent in different kinds of activities. Mythic identity, symbol, and ritual closely and characteristically involve *saññā*. They are based on the recognition of 'signs' that are repeated over and again, whose meaning is dispersed widely among a community, giving a sense of shared identity, yet always lacking the precision we associate with the logical workings of *saṅkhārā*.

31 Perception is specially developed by humans to form the symbolic culture which is essential in building communal identity. This is what has made all higher achievements of humanity possible. This theory can be derived from Buddhist principles, but has also been recently emphasized by Knight *et al.* arguing from a Darwinian point of view.[25] They propose that the purpose of symbolic culture is to create collective fantasies without direct perceptual counterparts, which nonetheless play a role in sustaining and enabling communities to function.

32 Knight *et al.* point out that we live in a world that has been subjectively constructed. Of course, as materialists they assume, without bothering to argue the point, that this world is constructed by the brain, whereas Buddhism more cautiously and accurately speaks of the mind as the constructive force. While in the 'objective' world we are just an insignificant speck, in the world of experience we are central. Perception distorts the information of the senses to suit our own interest, for example, by noticing opportunities for food or sex. This basic functioning of *saññā* is common to all animals. Humans, however, develop language, ritual, and culture, which creates a whole new layer of interpretation. This new layer is a communally developed map or pattern that gives meaning to the world, negotiated through collective behaviors like storytelling and ritual. Members of a symbolic community—tribe, nation, religion—possess a personal (imperfect) copy of this communal map. This collective web of belief and value serves to expand a person's sphere of concern from themselves to the group. It enables the community to become 'self-sacrificing', for example by laboring on huge buildings that are not one's own, and gives the community power to limit individual behaviors if they are felt to be harmful to the group, using the notions of taboo or law.

33 This collective map entails belief in an entirely new class of things, that is, things that do not exist in sense perception (in Buddhism these are called *paññatti*). Such things include 'concepts' like good and evil; cosmologies and legends; or social realities like nations or the rules of chess.[26] These things are given meaning through a process of social authorization. These days we typically rely a legal process or a governing body to authorize social conventions. In the past, gods and magic were given effective force through the power of ritual. The whole community joins together

to create an illusion that may be fearful or beneficent. It expresses their dreams, and in doing so shapes their waking. Repetition and standardization, the constant little shifts and negotiated modifications, ensure that the communal ritual is an adequate expression of each individual's dreaming. Once the emotional response of ritual has been reinforced over and over, a mere allusion or reference to the deity, magic spell, or legal code is sufficient to grant a sense of authority.

34 Don't get sidetracked here by the emphasis that these symbols refer to illusions that 'don't exist'. This is not an ontological argument about what kinds of things 'really' exist or not, but a social argument about how we create collective beliefs. In this context, 'God' does not exist in exactly the same sense that, say, an 'electron' does not exist. Neither of these terms has a shared direct perceptual basis, so there is no common ground on which a community can create language describing them. It is not enough to suppose that occasional visionaries might in fact see God, just as expert physicists can claim to 'see' an electron in the traces left in a particle accelerator. In neither case is the experience simply 'seeing' something in a normal, concrete sense that can be widely accepted in a community. If I 'see' a saber-tooth tiger about to attack, I can grunt and point, and everyone else in the group can *see* exactly the same thing—and either respond appropriately or be removed from the gene pool. But no-one can point to 'God' or an 'electron' in the same way. Symbolic culture enables us to create a world beyond our senses.

35 The creation of this extra-sensory world is systematically pursued in Brahmanic texts that detail the mystical correspondences between the symbols of the ritual and the cosmos. A man's hand, the back of the horse, or the pouring of ghee; such mundane, observable realities are systematically mapped on to the very shape and nature of the cosmos. These links, performed in ritual, and made conscious through reflective comprehension of the mantras (*ya evaṁ veda...*), evoke the power that was the earliest meaning of *brahman*, the swelling, life-enhancing energy of the spirit.[27]

36 When the correspondence has become complete, there is no separation between the self and the cosmos. This is expressed in the Upaniṣads with the famous phrase 'Thou art that' (*tad tvaṁ asi*), or as the Pali Suttas put it, 'the self is identical with the world' (*so attā so loko*). At its highest level, this

dissolution is a profound meditative realization of infinite consciousness (*viññāṇa*); it may also arise through philosophical reasoning (*saṅkhāra*). Ritual, on the other hand, is concerned with neither reason nor realization, but with correlation (*saññā*). Ritual activity expands awareness from the selfish individual to the group, extended both in space and time, binding a people together and connecting them with their ancestors through cultural continuity. When taken to extremes, this connection does not merely loosen an individual's pre-occupation with themselves, it entirely dissolves it. Through the collective conditioning of ritual an individual becomes nothing in the eyes of the community, and even in the individual's own eyes. They exist purely to serve the welfare of the group.

37 Hence the strangest, most perfect meaning of *saññā*. A *saññā* between two people is a contract, an agreement. They 'know together'. To form such an agreement is to 'persuade'. And according to the Brahmanical texts, the victim must be 'persuaded' to be sacrificed. Only with their 'acquiescence' is the rite truly sacred. The victim is the one who agrees. And as the ritual text so matter-of-factly puts it: 'To persuade means to kill.'[28] Once someone has agreed to be a victim, they are lifted out of their personal reality and have become one with the symbol. Their personal identity is dead already, and the cosmic self can never die, so the sacrifice is not 'killing' in any normal sense.

38 The 'mark' of this persuasion is the wreath of red flowers, the shaven head, ochre robes and other typical adornments of the victim—which, not coincidentally, reveals the very root of the English word 'victim', from the Indo-European **wei*, meaning to twist, wind, or bind, and referring to the 'wreath' with which the victim was 'marked'.

39 The shaman or witch-doctor puts on a mask or covers himself with an animal pelt: magically, he *becomes* what he *seems*. The voodoo doll *seems* like a particular person, and *becomes* that person through mystical participation: seen from 'above' this is just the failure to differentiate, but from 'within' it is an extension of the self. A story picks out and summarizes certain aspects of what happened, so that what *seems* to have happened *becomes* the 'truth'. A young man or woman dons a headdress, puts on makeup, is dressed in feathers and finery, and hence takes on the attributes of the divinity; thus *seeming* to be at one, he or she *becomes* truly at one, and may

be joyously sacrificed, in the certain knowledge that divinity never dies, for it is death itself.

40 Or in Buddhism, one may undergo the ritual of ordination, wrap oneself in the ochre robe, shave one's head and thus, *seeming* to be like the Buddha, one *becomes*... what, exactly? On the outside, a symbol of Buddhism, of purity and the possibility of sacred humanity. On the inside—well, who knows?

CHAPTER 12

ON USING JUNG

IT IS IN THIS REALM, THE EVOCATIVE ASSOCIATIONS OF SYMBOL, that Jung's 'archetypes' have their abode. These are seen as 'primordial determinants', inherent images in the psyche that pre-exist the conscious mind, and which, while simultaneously existent, manifest in more evolved ways as our minds mature. The archetypes themselves are not seen; what we have access to is specific, temporal representations of the universal, timeless archetypes.

2 One philosophical difficulty with the archetypes is their elusive ontological status, which Jung compared with Plato's 'forms'.[1] Jung spoke of the archetypes as memory deposits from countless similar experiences through biological history, which anatomically predispose a tendency to form certain types of psychic expression.[2] Similarly, Neumann spoke of the biological aspect of the archetypal structures,[3] but also denies the 'Lamarkian' idea of inherited characteristics.[4]

3 This interpretation doesn't strike me as particularly plausible, for while it is easy to understand how behavioral instincts can be inherited, it is not at all obvious how or why certain kinds of conscious experience could be passed down through DNA. And, although this speculation is intended to persuade due to its apparently scientific basis, it is even less obvious how such a notion could be scientifically tested.

4 I can better understand the archetypes from a Buddhist point of view as the accumulated patterns re-experienced countless times in the round of rebirth. When we encounter experiences in this life that follow a similar

pattern, *saññā* recognizes what it has known before and the archetype is evoked. Jung himself suggests that the Buddhist meditative experience of rebirth refers to the 'same psychological reality' as the archetypes.[5] For Jung, however, the archetypes are the reality, which are mistakenly believed to be an experience of former lives. I am suggesting that the genuine memories of former lives, while they are still unconscious, form universal patterns in the mind, which is what Jung called 'archetypes'.

5 Jung is a psychologist, and so is not concerned with whether rebirth is *true* or not. His concern is in how this experience affects the mind. The archetype brings with it the power of dawning consciousness and so is surrounded by divine glory. The energy actuated by the archetype is called *libido* by the psychologists; but the Indians called it *māyāśakti*.[6]

6 Perhaps the most dramatic evocation of the archetype is the moment of 'love at first sight'. There she is, there he is, aglow. Buddhists attribute the power of instant love to a long-standing connection from past lives. The Jātakas say that one should trust the person who one loves at first sight, as these are people one has loved in past lives.[7] Jungians would say that it happens when the women recognizes her archetypal male figure, her *animus*, in the man, and the man recognizes his feminine figure, his *anima*, in the woman. Wherever it comes from, in that moment it dissolves history, defies reason, and blithely ignores boundaries. It transcends the mundane reality of the senses and reaches for the divine.

7 The archetypes are not universal because of any presumed 'primordial determinants', but simply because the nature of life follows regular patterns, such as birth, ageing, and death. We have experienced these things countless times in their countless variations. Worn smooth by long handling, the echoes of the reflections of the memories of the long past lose their individual features and appear as timeless universals.

❖

8 The very 'universality' of the archetypes has become the target of postmodern critics such as Marina Warner, who insist that stories and myths can only be understood in their lived context.

9 The historical and social context of the printed versions alters the message and the reception of the lovers' perennial conflict and quest; remembering the changing background in which the tellers move constitutes a

crucial part in understanding the sexual politics of the tale. The theory of archetypes, which is essentially ahistorical, helps to confirm gender inevitability and to imprison male and female in stock definitions.[8]

10 This argument has a certain force, and we would be doing our sources a disservice if we were to claim that archetypal analysis exhausts the meaning of our stories. But we likewise do them a disservice if we insist that they are purely local and contingent, with no relevance to broader questions of humanity.

11 Warner makes a common error, one which is clearly repudiated by Jung and Neumann. 'Archetypal theory' is by no means ahistorical. It is a particular theoretical perspective developed by Jung and his followers, and has a history like any other theory. But presumably Warner means 'the archetypes' are ahistorical. This is equally mistaken, for Neumann's work in particular is concerned precisely with the different ways the archetypes manifest in history. While the archetype is universal and eternal in an abstract sense, it is never seen directly, but remains inferred from historical data, and plays a genuinely diverse role in history. Jung claimed to be an empiricist, who in his long life observed and analyzed thousands of dreams and other psychological aspects of symbolism, and regarded his theories as generalizations inferred from experience.[9] There is an irreducible problem here: history has both change and continuity, both diversity and unity, so we must learn to acknowledge both these aspects. We only fall into error when we fall out of balance.

12 Warner's dismissal of archetypal analysis is mistaken, but her warning remains relevant. She discusses how fairy stories have been subsumed within a corporate culture that standardizes and Disneyfies them. This process of 'canonization' bears much in common with the standard corporate production of the Pali canon, which also exists in constant tension with the diverse and mischievous products of heterodox Buddhist culture.

13 This process of loss has to be resisted: as individual women's voices have become absorbed into the corporate body of male-dominated decision-makers, the misogyny present in many fairy stories—the wicked stepmothers, bad fairies, ogresses, spoiled princesses, ugly sisters and so forth—has lost its connections to the particular web of tensions in which women were enmeshed and come to look dangerously like the way things are. The

historical context of the stories has been sheared away, and figures like the wicked stepmother have grown into archetypes of the human psyche, hallowed, inevitable symbols, while figures like the Beast bridegroom have been granted ever more positive status.[10]

14 This passage summarizes quite neatly a major theme of this work. The individual voices of women have been absorbed into and integrated with the corporate product of the male Sangha's 'canon'. The misogyny that can be discerned in certain Buddhist texts is the product of specific persons working in specific contexts, and yet is 'dangerously' taken to be 'the way thing things are'. However, I don't share Warner's pessimism as to the historical evolution of the male and female symbols, nor the corporatization of the story. In the world generally, and in Buddhism in particular, there are more voices, more diversity, and more challenging of roles, than any time in history; and the future evolution of this global culture will owe not a little to the internet, which enjoys stealing stories from the patriarchs.

❖

15 A further problem with Jungian analysis has been analyzed by Ken Wilber as the 'pre/trans fallacy'. I agree with this aspect of his theorizing, and I think it is crucial to understand his argument here.[11]

16 Wilber takes as his basis the notion of 'pre-rational', 'rational', and 'trans-rational' states of mind. For Wilber, these are genuine stages of psychological development which are a part of normal personal growth: a child is pre-rational; we (ideally) learn how to become rational as we grow up; and if we undertake meditative or other suitable spiritual practices we can experience trans-rational states, for example the unified consciousness of samādhi. These stages can also be straightforwardly mapped onto the five aggregates as we have seen them. The 'rational' is the domain of *saṅkhārā*. 'Pre-rational' is, obviously, anything more primitive than that, in our case especially *saññā*. 'Trans-rational' is the higher states of developed consciousness, i.e. *viññāṇa*.

17 The problem arises when the primitive 'pre-rational' is confused with the evolved 'trans-rational', because 'pre-' and 'trans-' rational always have something in common: that is, they are not rational. The confusion results in either the 'reductionist' or the 'elevationist' fallacy.

18 The reductionist fallacy takes all higher states of consciousness and equates them with pre-rational states. Meditative samādhi, mystical union, or transcendence are explained away as a regression to infantile narcissism, the 'oceanic' experience of the foetus in the womb, etc. Wilber says that this is the path taken by Freud in *The Future of an Illusion*. For the reductionist, rationality is the high point of human development. Transcendent consciousness does not exist, and those who claim to experience such things in fact suffer from regressive neurosis.

19 The elevationist makes the opposite mistake. Primitive, undeveloped pre-rational states are taken to be transcendent and spiritual. Mere blankness and undifferentiation is confused with integration. Wilber argues that this is the route taken by Jung and his followers.[12] For the elevationist, rationality becomes the enemy. It is because of 'reason' that humanity is debased, separated from our true home in the Divine. This tendency is prominent in most forms of modern spirituality, especially New Age, and is commonly found in some schools of Buddhism.

20 The tricky part is that both of these positions are sometimes right. In many cases, so-called 'spiritual' states really are pre-rational and are a genuine regression to narcissism, infantile dependence on an infallible guru/parent, blank unawareness in meditation, and so on. In our current context, the study of attitudes towards the feminine in Buddhism, we frequently find that primitive sexism, which is an unawareness of the suffering caused by discrimination, is claimed to stem from Awakened insight, when really it is a product of unexamined conditioning and/or personal neurosis. Such regression needs to be recognized for what it is, and overcome, at least in part, with the help of reason.

21 On the other hand, there really are genuine states of heightened consciousness that are obviously more 'real', clear, and profound than the truth of mere reason. Someone who has experienced such states can never mistake them for the darkness of infantile slumber.

22 It is, therefore, essential to apply the appropriate form of analysis for the problem at hand. Jungian analysis focusses on the the mythic domain of *saññā*, and in that domain I have not found anything else that makes better sense. This will not tell us anything about higher states of transcendent consciousness; but Buddhist books are full of discussion of such matters.

We understand these things better than any generation in modern times. What we, as Buddhists, do not understand is the effect of the pre-rational on our practice of Dhamma.

23 But we should beware of misusing Jung. If we suggest, as some do, that the mythic archetype of the King is the 'unconditioned', we make a claim that has no foundation in Buddhism, and badly misconstrues the archetype as it appears in myth. The King represents, not the surmounting of all *viññāṇa*, but far more humbly, the attainment of self-conscious individuality, able to make decisions and to accept responsibility for them.[13] In other words, the King is no more—and no less—than a normal, well-adjusted adult. This is why the Buddha rejected the King archetype before he set forth on his quest for Awakening. This is what distinguishes him from other kings on a spiritual quest, such as Rāma, Odysseus, or Gilgamesh, who through all their wanderings still expected to return to the throne—and thereby failed to realize the Deathless. In the evolutionary perspective of the five aggregates, the accession to the throne represents the transformation from *saññā* to *saṅkhārā*, the shift of the locus of identity from the tradition-bound group to the future-building individual.

❖

24 Modernist Buddhism identifies itself almost exclusively with the two highest aggregates, *saṅkhārā* as the locus of reason and intellect, and *viññāṇa* as the locus of awareness itself, especially as experienced in states of refined meditative consciousness.[14] This strategy has its uses, since human conscious development must be oriented towards these qualities. We have had enough of tribalism, and need to enhance both the sense of personal responsibility for our choices (*saṅkhārā*) and on a more refined level to purify and expand our quality of awareness. This development is constantly heard in the Buddhist anti-intellectual critique of 'thinking too much', or 'attachment to views'. In such discourse we hear *viññāṇa* seeking to differentiate from and establish primacy over *saṅkhārā*; which is all very well, except for those of us who have not actually learnt to think properly.

25 The function of this discourse within the Buddhist community is to divorce Buddhist storytelling from that of other religions. *Their* sacred books are full of myths and legends, while *ours* are full of facts. Or—and this is the flip-side of the same attitude—if our sacred books contain things that

are not facts, they are not worth our attention. They become silently edited out as 'not real Buddhism'. The uncomfortable truth is, however, that the myths have been regarded as 'real Buddhism' by countless generations of Buddhists.

26 There is a very real dichotomy in our relationship with our heritage. In traditional Buddhist teachings, Jātaka stories and similar myths are told solely for the sake of illustrating a spiritual or ethical meaning. They are either assumed to be literally true, or else the question of truth is regarded as a bit pedantic, a concern for academics, not practitioners. The actual facts of the story become irrelevant, glossed over. The story is retold to edit out uncomfortable aspects, or to shift the perspective. And in the whole process we can rely on nothing other than the wisdom and the good intentions of the storyteller. But the reality is that the stories themselves contain many ambiguities and contradictions, and can be used for both good and bad purposes. When didactic storytelling is cut off from its roots, it can no longer be held to account. The storyteller can shift blame to the myth, disclaiming any responsibility. It's not my fault if I object to women's ordination—after all, that's what the story says.

27 Academic studies of Buddhism, on the other hand, tend to focus on the 'hard facts' and forget questions of meaning. Academic discourse becomes ever more specialized and the kinds of questions that can be respectably asked become safer. We insist that the only truths are those cast in stone. In their efforts to be scientifically and intellectually rigorous, Buddhist scholars sometimes forget they are in the 'humanities' department.

28 The problem is not either of these tendencies as such, but the inability of these different spheres of concern to communicate meaningfully. The academics produce their studies, clarifying facts and giving new insights into Buddhist texts, history, and so on; these studies are methodically ignored by the Buddhist community (except when they reinforce their own beliefs). Meanwhile, Buddhists continue to live a way of life that leads to Awakening and provides a sense of ultimate meaning, notions that are outside the narrow empirical scope of academic studies.

29 We don't need to buy into this dichotomy. The 'hard facts' of Buddhist studies have a very real relevance in the spiritual search; and questions

of meaning and higher spiritual purpose are indispensable if we want to make sense of the data provided by Buddhist studies.

30 The ideological stance of Buddhist modernism is not a natural or inevitable feature of Buddhism itself, but a historical development that emerged from the threat posed by the colonialists' accusation that Buddhism was just spirit worship, animism, or pagan idolatry. Faced with a promiscuous mix of magical, animist, and brahmanical strands within Buddhist praxis, Buddhists in the 19th century used 'masculine' tools of analysis and purification to identify and establish the Buddhist traits within a culture. The historical outcome of this in places such as 19th century Thailand was the reification of an all male Sangha as the representative of 'real' Buddhism, not coincidentally in alliance with the forces busy constructing a modern Thai national identity. Meanwhile the diverse, syncretistic religious folk culture—formless, archaic, magical—was condemned as 'Other', non-Buddhist and therefore wrong.

31 While some would regret the passing of a more syncretistic native Buddhism,[15] and while we can't agree with all the forms that modernist Buddhism has taken, there is no doubt that this process was essential in allowing Buddhism to survive and thrive in our modern age. We take 'rational' mindfulness practices and test them within a laboratory. They work, and so they find acceptance within modern culture, in hospitals, schools, and corporations. No-one in a secular environment in Australia, to my knowledge, has suggested using amulets to treat depression, or prescribed a diet of holy water for those suffering anxiety. Which is not to say that such things might not work in the proper context; it is just that the modern secular world is not that context.

32 But the dark side is that modernist Buddhism has not yet learnt how to integrate the lower levels of experience. We are embarrassed by the prevalence of mindless superstition and meaningless ritual in traditional Buddhist cultures—refuges for foolishness and greed. But we cannot pretend that the Dhamma can be reduced to a logical philosophy, a morality, or a meditation technique. It must be an integrated practice, which involves, engages with, and develops all of the five aggregates, each in its appropriate way.

❖

33 The Jungian notion of archetypes has withered under postmodern criticism, as it stems from an archaic era of hegemonic discourse. Archetypal theory, along with such notions as Campbell's treatment of the hero legend as the 'monomyth' underlying all stories, impoverish the diversity that is such a vital part of what makes us human. Diversity is replaced by an idealized projection, invented by professors who study 'primitives' but never live among them. Universal 'metanarratives' can't be divorced from the colonial context that gave them birth: just as the West tried to assimilate the rest of the world in its own political and economic systems, it tried to digest world culture in its own belly.

34 A related critique is of the notion of universal stages of development. Theorists such as Frazer assumed that certain societies—i.e. his own—were more advanced, and that other societies were objectively worse. They could develop, but only by becoming more like modern, 'rational' Westerners. Such an idea is seen as patronizing and not supported by the anthropological evidence.

35 This critique has force, and today we can't read Frazer's casual reference to 'primitive savages' without squirming just a little bit. But there is a historical dialectic going on here, a positive evolution that, ironically enough, suggests that the notion of stages of development is not quite dead yet. In Frazer's day, the 19th century, it was common enough for white people to regard non-whites as sub-human. This was certainly the case in Australia, where indigenous people were casually hunted down and murdered like beasts by Englishmen who regarded themselves as civilized.[16] What Frazer did was to show that apparently bizarre and irrational beliefs and practices of indigenous peoples were not as alien and incomprehensible as all that. He went to great lengths to show that Christian beliefs and rituals shared a great deal in common with the 'pagans' and 'primitives' who the Christians so despised. This perspective greatly impressed Jung and others, and contributed to the development of a truly 'human' psychology. The essence of the hegemonic monomyth discourse is to raise the question 'What is humanity?' and then show that different peoples all over the world have given similar answers; that their perception of their humanity is essentially similar to our perception of our humanity.

36 Once we have a handle on the question 'What makes us all similar in our humanity?' we are ready to address a second question: 'What makes us different?' This question would have made no sense in the 19th century, as the differences between 'advanced' and 'primitive' societies were so obvious as to seem insurmountable. Postmodern thinkers, emerging when the intellectual climate was ready, have developed challenging and useful perspectives on diversity. However, while it is true that hegemonic theory doesn't exhaust the possibilities of understanding, postmodernism overestimates its importance in the scheme of things. The questions that Frazer and others were asking have become neglected. We produce an abundance of studies that show what *that* group of people in *that* time and *that* place thought, how they acted, and what they believed. But we can no longer address such profound questions as, 'How does humanity deal with its own mortality?'

37 The Buddha, as usual, bests them all. He said that the idea 'Everything is a unity' is one extreme; the idea 'Everything is a diversity' is another extreme. These extremes are avoided by means of dependent origination. If we were to apply this to the study of mythology, it suggests that we should be looking for connections between local and universal myths; how particular practices work within specific contexts, and how that relates to the findings of grand theories such as Jung's archetypes. We want to know what specific stories and ideas meant, and still mean, to living Buddhist communities in historical context; we also need to understand how this relates to fundamental concerns of the human psyche as expressed in universal mythemes.

38 Using Wilber's concepts of 'reductionism' and 'elevationism', the hegemonic monomyth theory, typified by Jung, Campbell, and so on, is elevationist; postmodern theory, tied down to specific contexts, is reductionist. Both perspectives have their place; neither exhausts the possibilities of understanding. Our choice of emphasis should depend on the kind of question we are interested to answer.

❖

39 This study of Buddhist myth on a comparative basis, seeing significance in the broad similarities of myth and practice in far-flung lands and times, is open to the postmodern critique. But I believe a comparative approach

is essential, as it asks questions that postmodernism cannot. I am a Westerner, and grew up with stories of Jason & the Argonauts or Helen of Troy. They are part of my basic psychological structure. So for me they have a fascination of familiarity that is unlike other mythologies.

40 Some would argue that the study of myths should be done using the perspectives and interpretations that are found within the culture. I disagree. Those living in a faith community vary tremendously in their own experience of their religion, and later generations inevitably read the texts and practices of earlier times from an outsider's perspective. Those who read Jātakas, for example, online or in a modern printed edition experience the tales very differently than those who heard them delivered in a sermon in the evening time, sitting silently in an open hall on a warm tropical night among the village community they had known their entire life. And those devout listeners had a very different relationship with the stories than those who created them in the first place. It is crucial that we try to understand the context that gave these stories such profound meaning; but it is also crucial to recognize that that context has gone forever.

41 All mythology is comparative. The oldest myths describe pantheons of gods. These have been gathered, at least in part, by collating the spiritual experiences of different peoples. Any religious movement on a larger scale than simple village animism must involve a synthesis of various deities. We have already seen that the very ancient myth of Gilgamesh consciously uses comparative mythology. Indic myth takes this to extremes, with countless deities jostling, realigning, competing, melding, loving, and warring. These constantly shifting mythologies are always developed and explained by people other than those who experienced or invented the deities in the first place. Buddhist myth is no exception; witness the stunning Greco-Buddhist artworks, where the very idea of a Buddha image may have originated.

42 The more profound significance of the comparative approach, however, is this. We are witnessing an unprecedented melding of Western and Eastern cultures. While this is itself just a part of the wider impact of globalization, nevertheless it is of crucial significance for those such as myself who live in the nexus between Asia and the West.[17]

Figure 12.1: *Buddha head, Greco-Indian style, Gandhāra*

43 As Buddhism becomes an increasingly global religion and distinctions between 'traditional, Asian' Buddhism and 'modern, Western' Buddhism are left behind in the 20th century where they belong, it becomes more important for Westerners to take an interest in the *mythos* that has been such an integral part of traditional Buddhism; and that traditional Buddhists should take an interest in the approaches to mythology that have had such a meaning and resonance for the West.

44 Studying this material on a comparative basis, then, contributes to the integration of modern and traditional approaches to Buddhism. At a deeper level, it integrates these different aspects of our own psyches.

45 Dhamma is different from new religious movements precisely because of its depth. It has served as a well of meaning and Awakening for millions of people for 2500 years. This historical depth is largely mediated through *saññā*, which provides the sense of continuity. The symbols of Buddhism still evoke a genuine spiritual energy: the image of a yellow-robed, shaven headed nun or monk has become part of our spiritual vocabulary.

46 Such historical continuity inevitably brings its problems. Our age is different, very different, and while the questions we ask are the same as those of sincere aspirants of all time—how are we to best embody the Dhamma here & now?—the answers we give must differ. This is the case even in the internal aspects of Dhamma: the way we relate to meditation, for example, is extensively conditioned by what we have been taught about meditation, and that teaching necessarily involves language, with all its contextual and associative baggage.[18] How much more so in the external aspects of Dhamma, where even the Buddha would freely adopt cultural norms and practice, sometimes changing the details, or else just reminding us of the proper spirit.

47 Continuity in Buddhist culture is not just a textual, ideological, or mystical transmission. It has a substantial institutional basis, the monastic Sangha. All Buddhist cultures have had both lay and monastic wings, and they always will, or else they will stop being recognizable forms of Buddhism.[19] But the monastic Sangha is not just a community of spiritual seekers: it is a screen for the projection of Buddhist dreams.

CHAPTER 13

THE DHAMMA OF GENDER

THE *YAKKHA* IN THE ROOM IS GENDER. Monastic institutions have denigrated, sidelined, or better still, totally eliminated the role of women in monastic life. The result is that women have zero access to or control over the massive resources controlled by the monasteries, despite the fact that it was, very often, women who donated them in the first place. In modern Theravāda, the problem is not merely the disempowerment of nuns, but their total denial: it is not possible for them to exist, so how can they claim any rights?

2 The absence of the feminine is easily overlooked by men, but is a painful, nagging, ever-present reality for women. As absent as Māyā, and as vulnerable to projection, nuns are the great Buddhist unknown; their absence is the great wrong of Buddhist culture.

3 Taboo, prejudice, mythic identity: such matters fall outside the rational self-definition of modernist Buddhism, so they get ignored in almost all modernist tracts. Discussion gets sidetracked into details of ordination procedure or Vinaya niceties; or else women are told to just meditate to realize Nibbana, and not get involved in politics.

4 Such tactics are a painfully transparent attempt to deflect attention from the actual issues. These have to do with, first of all, staying alive. How are women to get food to live and sustain their practice when the monks control the material resources? In original Buddhism, this was accomplished by forming a recognized community of women, the bhikkhuni Sangha, who were supported by the lay community, who found delight

in having the opportunity to nurture the spiritual path of others. But in modern Buddhism of the Theravādin or Tibetan forms, this model has disappeared, and women simply have no accepted social role where they are supported in their practice.

5 The bhikkhuni Sangha is a construction of communal identity. There is, of course, no objectively existing entity that we can point to and define as 'the bhikkhuni Sangha', any more than we can do that for the bhikkhus. Rather, we create in the Buddhist collective psyche an idea of a class or community with a membership defined through certain collectively accepted acts. These acts start with ordination, involving shaving the hair, donning the yellow robes, and undergoing the formal procedure in the midst of other bhikkhunis and bhikkhus. Afterward, the bhikkhuni identity is maintained through such regular rituals as the observance of *uposatha* and other Vinaya requirements.

6 Crucially, all these ritual acts, which require the participation of the bhikkhunis as a group, are authorized in a text which functions as the myth of origins. It is by a collective act of belief in that text that bhikkhunis can be accepted within the Buddhist community. But that myth is itself fractured, broken, and traumatic, and hence it both underlies and is symptomatic of the deeply ambiguous, divided attitude to bhikkhunis in modern Buddhism. A young western monk once said to me, 'The Buddha never even wanted them to ordain *in the first place*.' This '*in the first place*' is what we are concerned with here. That is why the domain of *saññā* is our primary focus. Not because the analysis presented here is better than more familiar Buddhist approaches, but because the problem is mythic identity, and to understand that we must delve into the realm of symbol, association, image, and archetype.

7 The five aggregates describe a process of development. Problems in development need to be addressed at the appropriate level. There is no point in forever debating minutiae of Vinaya legal proceedings, ever calling for 'more research', if at the end of the day we belong to a group of people that believes the Buddha never wanted female monastics 'in the first place'

❖

8 Just as each Jātaka story tells a story of the past, then connects the story with events in the present, so too we draw the parallels between the long

deeps of Buddhist culture with contemporary attitudes and issues among Buddhists today. The *yakkha* of gender haunts every house of the past, with no exceptions. We just can't avoid it. We even have to choose between calling it a *yakkha* or a *yakkhinī*! The values that we use when we think about gender are just so different from those of the past. Any text of the past will, sooner or later, push some kind of gender-sensitive button. If we were to reject all that failed the most stringent test of PC-ness today, we would find ourselves with the impossible task of reconstructing consciousness from the ground up. And that would be rather a shame. After all, only a tiny percentage of authentic Buddhist texts are problematic, while there is a vast ocean of profound scripture inviting us to come in for a swim. The ancient world may have been *always* chauvinist, but it was not *only* chauvinist.

9 So perhaps there is a gentler way. Perhaps we can discern a positive side to the presentation of women, one which has become obscured but remains as the minority report.

10 The idea that human pre-history bears witness to a time that was more balanced and sympathetic to the feminine has a long history of its own. Many theorists have argued that paleolithic (before 10 000 BCE) and/or neolithic culture (in India, roughly 8000 BCE–1500 BCE) reflects a feminine oriented society. Reasons for this are adduced from myth, where older goddesses are raped, dismembered, married, or converted by patriarchal forces; from archaeology, noting the abundance of fertility figures in this period; and from anthropology, where certain tribal systems or social structures, such as matrilinear succession, are claimed to give a stronger role to the feminine. In such culture there was a close connection with nature, mediated through the experience of the feminine divine. This culture was destroyed by the patriarchal societies, for example of the Semites and the Āryans, who built the Axial Age cultures, and whose patriarchal legacies have endured until today.

11 This thread of interpretation may be traced from Bachofen in the mid-19th century up until Gimbutas in the late 20th.[1] Such ideas underlie the 'New Pagan' movement, including New Age spirituality, and spilled over to the mainstream in *The Da Vinci Code*. In academic circles such thought is called

'matrix history', avoiding the use of the term 'matriarchal', which implies that the women merely dominated men, the inverse of patriarchy.

12 There are many issues here, too many to address meaningfully. But from my perspective, it seems that, while such ideas have become rendered in overblown, crass, and inaccurate ways, the evidence in favor of a more feminine belief structure in the Neolithic is too strong to be ignored. The male deities were, of course, always present, but the female usually predominated, or at least had a less subservient place than she did in later times. I do not believe, however, that this should be idealized as a 'Golden Age' of the past.[2] It is true that in certain places, such as the Indus Valley Civilization, the evidence does point to a long enduring society with startlingly little violence.

13 However, it is not so easy to say whether the 'masculine shift' was a good thing or not. We must be wary of projecting our own values and concerns back in history, and we must respect that people of the past faced very different issues than we do today. There is a serious case to be made that in certain contexts either a masculine or a feminine bias is essential, or at least useful, for the evolution of society as a whole. And while there is abundant evidence of societies where women and men live in relatively egalitarian ways, and where the oppression of patriarchy is refreshingly absent,[3] it remains an uncomfortable fact that the few societies that have attained a literate, philosophical, scientific culture have all done so with a masculine bias. The evidence for the universality of male dominance has led some to seek the causes in biology.[4] But regardless of how societies of the past have coped with gender issues, our own task is integration.

14 It is also unclear whether goddess worship means an improved lot for women. It is a plausible notion—if the sacred feminine is honored, surely this will create a 'halo effect' in the lives of real women.[5] The widespread adoption of transgressive goddess worship by modern feminists gives us an obvious example. Given the complexities of history and culture, however, matters are not so straightforward. There are abundant sayings in praise of women within tantric circles: 'Women are heaven; women are dharma; and women are the highest penance. Women are Buddha; women are the Sangha; women are the Perfection of Wisdom'.[6] Yet in Tibetan or Hindu societies where such practices were common women were no

better off than anywhere else—which means, not very well off at all. Such fantasies allow men in power to project their image of the perfect woman onto a remote ideal, while regarding with disdain the real suffering of the all-too-human women who live around them. The woman is valued because *men* praise her, while her voice disappears into silence. Eager to obtain the approval of the powerful, knowledge-bearing patriarchs, she is exposed to a grave risk of abuse and exploitation.[7]

15 There is a further problem in assessing the nature of power, for too often we judge this by male standards.[8] For example, in hunter-gatherer societies it would seem to us that the men have the power: they have weapons, protect the tribe, raid other tribes, and procure valuable meat. But the women have quite distinct sources of power, which are not so obvious. The male children spend most of their days with the women, and only at puberty are they initiated into the circle of the men. The drastic, often violent and terrifying nature of the initiation ceremonies is a testimony to the effort required to detach them from the women's domain. And the conditioning and teaching the men receive from the women will shape their characters through their whole lives.

❖

16 Another nest of theoretical worms is the question of 'essentialism' in gender studies. Essentialism is the focus on biologically determined aspects of gender to identify 'essential' characteristics of male and female.[9] Many feminists reject such an approach, emphasizing the cultural aspect of gender and questioning whether any aspect of gender could be regarded as 'essential'; and whether, indeed, the very idea is a limitation of the humanity of both men and women.[10] Recent theorists have developed a more nuanced theory of typical differences, which emphasize different manners of negotiating similar territory.[11] The battle between 'difference' theorists and 'equality' theorists continues, with unabated casualties on the front line.[12]

17 It seems to me that the mind and body are always interconnected, and it's inherently unlikely that the physical differences between male and female bodies have no effect at all on their psychology. Studies have repeatedly shown that there are some gendered differences in neurology. Still, these differences are trivial. The problem that needs real attention

is not, 'Are men and women different in some ways?', but 'Why are we so obsessed with the differences between men and women?'

18 We should never forget when dealing with Buddhist texts that the whole 'essentialist' thing is utterly alien to the relational perspective of the early teachings. The early texts accept gender change as a fact, and deal with it in a far more pragmatic and non-judgmental way than we do today. Here are some guidelines from the Pali Vinaya on how to deal with spontaneous sex change in the Sangha.

> 19 On that occasion female genitals appeared on a monk. The Buddha said, 'I allow monks, the very same preceptor, the very same ordination, the years of seniority to be accepted by the nuns. Any offenses [they might have committed earlier] that are held in common between the monks and nuns are to be dealt with in the presence of nuns. The offenses that are not held in common between the monks and nuns are no offence.'
>
> 20 On that occasion male genitals appeared on a nun. The Buddha said, 'I allow monks, the very same preceptor, the very same ordination, the years of seniority to be accepted by the monks. Any offenses [they might have committed earlier] that are held in common between the nuns and monks are to be dealt with in the presence of monks. The offenses that are not held in common between the monks and nuns are no offence.'[13]

21 One could hardly imagine a more matter-of-fact response. Sex change is merely a procedural matter as far as management of the Sangha is concerned. Notice that, as well as the sex change being a non-issue, monks and nuns are treated exactly alike. This is the normal state of affairs in the Vinaya, a fact that we are liable to overlook if we focus too much on the occasional discriminatory passages.

22 This case is by no means isolated. There are several passages in Buddhist literature, early and late, that deal with gender transformation.[14] Not until perhaps 500 years after the Buddha do we find any explicit assertions of ontological essentialism.[15] For those who follow early Buddhism, gender changes. We are only man or woman in this life, and in the past or future we will undoubtedly be either, both, neither, or something else. So the dilemma of modern theorists—are gender differences cultural or innate (i.e. biological)?—misses the point. We are born due to the infinitely com-

plex mesh of past kamma.[16] There is no cut and dried formula as to why one is born as a woman or a man.

23 Early Buddhist texts contain no trace of the popular idea that one is born as a woman because of one's bad kamma in past lives.[17] This idea is not merely absent from the early Buddhist theory, but contradicts it, for human birth is always the result of good kamma. In any case, we are in the inconceivable (*acinteyya*) realm of the details of kamma, and shouldn't expect any simplistic conclusions. Research can clarify the nature and degree of gender differences. But even findings that purport to demonstrate 'innate' gender differences, if correct, merely show differences pertaining to this life, not something fixed forever in stone.

❖

24 Regardless of whether gender differences are intrinsic or not, we are dealing with texts and cultures that are, in fact, deeply gendered. This is an irreducible aspect of our data, one which we must see from within, while retaining an outsider's stance. For example, a few pages ago I casually referred to 'analysis' as a 'masculine' quality—did you notice? I was setting you up. Of course, both men and women can analyze equally well, although they might (if one follows the 'difference' approach) tend to go about it in different ways. But within our cultural environment, analysis has been patterned along with an infinitely receding matrix of other things as somehow 'masculine'.[18] We can't choose this matrix of associations, but can choose how to interact with it.

25 The words 'masculinity' and 'femininity' do not refer to any absolute or clearly defined reality. They evoke a set of connotations, those qualities that we have become accustomed to associate with men or women. While some of these associations have a genuine physiological basis—especially the creative power of women to nurture life and give birth—they should never be reduced to biology or sociology. Men cannot give birth in a literal sense, but they 'give birth' to all kinds of other things—ideas, projects, works of art—and so partake of creativity just as women do. 'Femininity' and 'masculinity' are archetypal and hence underlie and inform our awareness of any individuals as 'female' or 'male'. Men and women come to bear the projections of masculinity and femininity, but they do not own them or exhaust them.[19]

26 This kind of 'yin/yang' duality goes a long way down, and can't be lightly ignored. Our job is to understand how these general tendencies work themselves out in these particular Buddhist contexts. So we shall use gendered concepts as relevant for the cultural domain we are in, without making assumptions as to their universality. This is not just a contingent making-do, it is part and parcel of the territory. We want to understand how gender is constructed in modern Buddhism, and to do that we must understand how it has been constructed in the past.

CHAPTER 14

MYTHIC FACT, HISTORIC FICTION

IN THE FORMLESS DOMAINS OF MYTH AND SYMBOL, what could it possibly mean to capture the 'Whole Truth'? How can we expect to tease out the truth from ancient Indian scriptures when 23% of Britons think Winston Churchill was a myth?[1] Myth is always more than we can know, and inquiry is carried forward only by the acknowledgment of our own ignorance.

2 Unknowing is reflective; it knows what it is not. Like the Buddhist logical principle of *apoha*, it accepts only the definition of what is absent. Reading myth is like seeing the image of our own face in the mirror. Both of them present a surface and, as egocentric as we are, we automatically see our 'self' in that surface. We cannot rest content with the reality that is presented to us, and set to work constructing a story with ourself the Hero of our own narrative. We assume that there must be a reality underlying the surface image. But these reflections, echoes, mirages reveal no more than a few coy hints as to what any underlying reality might be. And it is even worse than that. A reflection strictly withholds any information that would allow us to determine, not merely what the underlying reality is, but even whether it actually exists.

3 History proceeds by assembling dated facts and drawing inferences from them, while myth tells of things that 'never happened, but are always'.[2]

Myths are never heard for the first time. Children participate in mythic re-enactment, otherwise known as 'ritual', before they learn to speak. We recognize a Christmas tree long before we understand the theology of Immaculate Conception. Myths are the life-blood of culture, and need no assurance of truth other than their own inevitability.

4 The ancient Indians knew this better than we. One of the greatest of the Indic myths is the Rāmāyaṇa, which is told and retold in countless versions, both literary and colloquial. The pivotal event is Rāma's expulsion from his kingdom to go and live in the forest. He does not want his beloved wife Sītā to come with him, as it is too dangerous and she is unused to the trials of the wild. She argues that she is his wife, she must be with him, her place is at his side, and she should bear his suffering with him. But Rāma resists her ever more desperate pleas. In several later versions, such as the 16th century *Adhyātma Rāmāyaṇa*, she gets so furious she breaks the fourth wall: 'Countless Rāmāyaṇas have been composed before this. Do you know of a single one in which Sītā does not go with Rāma to the forest?'[3]

❖

5 Myth is neither true nor untrue; it is a shattered mirror that reflects the face of our humanity in a million shards. So many stories, so many lives, so many dreams: anthropology, psychology, ritual, dance, art, literature, religion, death, medicine, accounting, the timetable of the Manly ferry: their germs lie dormant within myth, waiting for the season to sprout and send out their tendrils.

6 Myth gleefully transgresses any normal standard of believability, yet it is by no means lacking its own logic. Early anthropological theorists such as Frazer or Max Müller were dismissive to the point of contempt of mythic logic, but Claude Lévi-Strauss made detailed studies in an attempt to prove the opposite. Lévi-Strauss studied how mythic logic tends to create opposing concepts, such as 'sacred' versus 'profane', or 'raw' versus 'cooked'. The most fundamental of these logical systems revolve around kinship rules and incest taboos. Such logical systems, however, can never be fully watertight, and myth plays with the paradoxes and contradictions. For example, 'life' and 'death' are a fundamental contradiction, and yet we can never have one without the other. Or in the case of the incest taboo, this promotes the psychological health of society as individuals learn to

differentiate from their immediate family; and yet most peoples have a remote myth of unilinear descent, where the ultimate founders of the clan were committing incest. Myth plays with such contradictions, sometimes through riddles, but more generally by offering multiple variant perspectives on the same events. Each time the story is told, the weight of emphasis shifts slightly, and so the contradictions are shown to be not as final as they appear.[4]

7 There's an interesting example in the introduction to the Kuṇāla Jātaka, which depicts the clans of the Śākyans and Koliyans (Māyā's clan) abusing each other in a dispute over water rights.[5] The Kolyians accused the founders of the Śākyan clan of having sex with their own sisters, while the Śākyans for their part abused the Koliyans as lepers who slept in the hollow of a tree. Each of these abuses is based on the traditional origin myth for these clans. Things got so bad the clans were on the verge of war before Ānanda intervened. It is not only today, it would seem, that myths of origins can lead to war.

8 In this story the incestuous origins of the Śākyans was used as a rhetorical criticism. Yet the canonical story of this incestuous origin, recounted by the Buddha himself in the Ambaṭṭha Sutta, is turned into a criticism of the conceited brahman Ambaṭṭha, who despite his claims to purity of caste, was forced to admit that his own forebears descended from the Śākyans' slave girl.[6] The Buddha passed over the incest motif, merely remarking that the founding brothers had to do it as they were cast out of their kingdom and had no women—an early example of the rationalizing tendency in Buddhist mythology.

9 Gentle clusters of contradiction, myths multiply and evolve with every telling. The search for the original 'correct' version is doomed to failure, for even at the time, there were many points of view on the same events, and as the story grows it is the divergences that accommodate the deeper reaches of meaning. There are multiple meanings, so we can't insist on one or the other as definitive.

10 Each tale presents one story, one resolution of a problem. The classic Buddhist problem is choice: renunciation or the home life. And while in any one case the answer may be clear, across the spectrum of tellings each tale gives a slightly different answer. Thus while the Great Renunciation

gives an unqualified thumbs up to the renunciate life, the story cannot end there. It must be qualified by hundreds of examples, in the Buddha's time or in past lives, of different ways of negotiating this crisis. No one telling can capture the complexity of the truth. The shades of variation lead to a more nuanced, contextual sense of values.

11 One text may be shallow, simplistic, black & white. But there is always a countertext, another situation, a different way of resolving things. They are all there in the scriptures, like different outfits for the occasion.

12 For every passage condemning women as foolish, there is one praising a wise woman; for each passage that decries their vanity, there is another extolling a beautiful woman; for each passage railing against their sneakiness and duplicity, there is one that exalts faithfulness and devotion. There is, however, one revealing difference: the faults are the faults of 'women', while the virtues are those of a woman.

13 In 'damming' the threat of the bhikkhunis, they are returned to a virginal state. Order is re-asserted. This is the critical issue. For the most part, men have power over women due to their physical strength; and yet for all their apparent frailty, only women can create a child. In the Sangha, the precept of non-violence removes the potential threat of violence that always overshadows male/female relations, and for this reason the men are uneasy, vulnerable. But the threat of violence against women must always been tempered, for without them there is no new generation. The bhikkhunis have lost that hold over men's minds. From this chaotic state, a new order must arise. The story of Mahāpajāpatī and the *garudhammas* is precisely this, the formation of a new order to govern the relations between the genders.

❖

14 Tales of the dominance of the woman, her magic potency, and the need for the men to divest her of her magic may be found in many parts of the world. They are a specific variety of the general theme of the loss of the divine, the death of the god. Taking such myths literally, men have done terrible things, of which we are most familiar with the European witchhunts. It is always difficult to know whether people actually believed in the bizarre fables that spurred these atrocities. Sometimes the most

primitive myths are the most informative, as they express themselves with wonderful directness.

15 Here is the story of the Ona people of Tierra del Fuego. They were a hunter-gatherer people whose lineage can be traced back 9000 years. In 1999 the last full-blood member of the tribe, Virginia Choinquitel, passed away. Before their decimation by measles and other alien diseases, Lucas Bridges, son of an English missionary, gained their trust and wrote of their lives and beliefs. He described their life as 'communistic', with no chiefs. The men owned their wives—usually one old and one young—and spent his time in hunting or feuding while the women fished, cooked, and reared the children. The Ona had no gods in the normal sense, but believed that birds can talk and that some mountains had once been human beings.[7] Like all peoples, the Ona had a myth of origins.

> 16 Once upon a long-lost age, the forest was evergreen, and witchcraft was the speciality of the Ona women. They kept a Lodge, where they practiced their arcane arts, and from which men were strictly forbidden. The girls were taught how to bring sickness, even death, upon any who displeased them. The men were entirely under their thumb, living in abject fear. Their bows and arrows were effective against the beasts of the jungle, but how can one fight disease and other magics? Eventually, the men staged a revolution: they banded together and there was a dreadful killing, in which all the women were murdered. The men had to wait for the young girls to grow up so they could take them to wife. Meanwhile, they wondered, 'How can we keep the ascendancy? What if the women turn back to their magical arts?' So the men formed their own secret Lodge, from which the women were banished.[8]
>
> 17 But this men's club was still under constant threat, and could only be kept up by a systematic falsehood. The Ona men would imitate spirits in their rituals, whose fearsome appearance would terrify the women. Bridges assumed that the men actually believed in these spirits, until he himself won initiation into the men's Lodge. There he heard that, following the massacre of the women, the men 'invented a new branch of Ona demonology: a collection of strange beings ... who would take visible shape'. These demons were invented to prevent the re-formation of the feared women's Lodge of witches in the past. The women never failed to scare, but Bridges believed it 'impossible that [they] were utterly deceived.'[9]

Figure 14.1: *The Ona people of Tierra del Fuego*

18 In his comments on this story, Joseph Campbell does not fail to draw the obvious, if playful, parallels:

19 > The mythological *apologia* offered by the men of the Ona tribe for their outrageous lodge was marvelously close, as the reader may have noted, to that attributed to Adam by the patriarchal Hebrews in their Book of Genesis; namely, that if he had sinned, it was the woman who had done so first. ... This curious mythological idea, and the still more curious fact that for nearly two thousand years it was accepted throughout the Western World as the absolutely dependable account of an event supposed to have taken place about a fortnight after the creation of the universe, poses forcefully the highly interesting question of the influence of consciously contrived, counterfeit mythologies and inflections of mythology upon the structure of human belief and the consequent course of civilization. We have already noted the role of chicanery in shamanism. It may well be that a good deal of what has been advertised as representing the will of 'Old Man' actually is but the heritage of a lot of old men, and that the main idea has been not so much to honor God as to simplify life by keeping woman in the kitchen.[10]

20 The men of the Ona felt so threatened by the women that they resorted to inventing fake magic powers to protect themselves from the women's magic, which was, of course, real. As a student of Buddhist history, I cannot help but wonder at the parallels with the creation myth of the bhikkhuni Sangha. The bhikkhunis, apparently, have the power to cause a flood that will sweep away all of Buddhism, and rules are needed to make sure this flood is dammed. What is this magic power that they hold, that strikes such fear into the hearts of monks? Or more to the point: how can such a patently ridiculous notion have gained the acceptance of so many apparently reasonable people for such a long time?

21 The notion that respected pillars of religious society might make outright fabrications for personal gain is not restricted to far-off Tierra del Fuego, and was not only resorted to by simple tribesmen. It is a standard trope of Buddhist literature. The Buddhist texts repeatedly tell us that the Brahmans did rituals and sacrifices for their own ends, while not believing a word of the mumbo-jumbo that they uttered.[11]

22 But surely Buddhist monks could never have consciously created a false story. They have vows of truthfulness, and are devoted to mental devel-

opment, not construction of fanciful myths. Except we know that this is exactly what they do. The modern Dhammakāya movement, as just one example, is validated by the invention of a preposterous mythology, which in crude Manichean terms tells of the 'White Dhammakāya' and the 'Black Dhammakāya', cosmic forces in battle since the creation of the world.[12]

23 Now, modern fabrications like this can, and should, be interpreted in the light of modern values. When we turn to the past, however, it becomes much less clear how we should apply our categories of right and wrong. The origin story for bhikkhunis, for example, is just one of countless tales in the Vinayas that purports to tell of how particular monastic rules came to be established. It has long been recognized that these origin stories cannot be a sober record of the facts. Hermann Oldenberg, the first translator of the Pali Vinaya into English, wrote in 1879 that the origin stories were 'undoubtedly pure inventions'.[13] This conclusion was made on the basis of the Pali text, which, despite its claim to represent the purest tradition, contains countless stories that are improbable, incoherent, and downright farcical. I am not aware of any serious attempt to refute Oldenberg's claim.

24 Quite the opposite: since then, several different recensions of the Vinayas have been studied, and it is a striking feature that, while the rules are held in common, the origin stories are usually different. One example is a rule that restricts nuns from crossing a river alone: in one version, she swims across the river, is taken by a strong current and drowns; another version says that she is raped by the ferryman; another says she was raped by a bystander after hitching up her skirts to wade across; another says she was trapped overnight on the far shore after the river rose in flood; while yet another castigates her for stripping naked, swimming across the river, and sunbathing in a public place![14]

25 Clearly, Buddhist monastics have not let mere historicity get in the way of a good story. Not only is there indisputable evidence of invention throughout the monastic codes, there are even instructions, in at least two Vinaya texts, that mandate the invention of stories, and give detailed instructions in how it should be done.[15]

26 It's somewhat disturbing that Buddhist monastics should be caught lying, right there in their sacred texts, on matters of grave importance. But are they really guilty of lying? There is no doubt that they are telling

deliberate falsehoods. But a deliberate falsehood is not always a lie. To be a lie, there also has to be the intention to create a false belief in the listener.

27 We have a word for stories where speaker is telling falsehood, and the listener knows it is falsehood, and the very falseness of it is the point. We call this 'fiction'. We understand that fiction can be, in its own way, as meaningful as mere documented facts. If the compilers of the Vinaya texts were playing with fictions, and they all knew it, then it is not they who should be chastised, but we, for taking their play all too seriously.

28 It is, then, far from radical to suggest that the bhikkhuni origin story is a fiction, not a sober record of events. As a tale, it becomes a part of the great myth of Buddhism, the life of the Buddha himself. In the denial of bhikkhunis, we are hearing that great mythic theme, sounded in all the world's sacred texts: the disappearance of the divine feminine.

❖

29 Yet myth cannot be reduced to fiction any more than it can be reduced to history. The difference lies in the fragmenting self of modernity. In the past, we were satisfied to share our stories in common, perhaps adding a detail here and there for color. But now we insist that each of us has her own story. Fiction is created by an individual who is conscious of her own individuality. The author knows she speaks Untruth, and her audience knows she speaks Untruth, and she knows that her audience knows, and her audience knows that she knows. An infinite unspoken contract.

30 An author pours her soul into her work, so if we criticize the fiction we criticize her soul. But a myth is the product of a community. It was not created by one person, but by countless retellings. Over time it is purified and honed to perfection, worn down like a *mathom*, a birthday present handed down from generation to generation, bereft of individual personality, its meaning and context forgotten, but evocative of a depth and a glory that redeems this sordid life.

31 For that very reason it comes to embody the dreams of a people in a way mere historical facts never can. A myth is their life-story, but it is more than that: it is literally their life. If we destroy the myth, we also destroy the sense of communal identity. We destroy values, language, imagery, ideas. We destroy that sense of continuity with the past that enables them to make sense of the present. And, in the end, we destroy them.

CHAPTER 15

THE OTHER FIRST BHIKKHUNI

ENOUGH THEORY! LET'S HAVE ANOTHER STORY, a tale of the first Buddhist nun. In this account of events, it is not Mahāpajāpatī who is the first nun, but the little-known Bhaddā Kuṇḍalakesā. I want to rescue Bhaddā's extraordinary story from the obscurity to which it has been unjustly consigned. Bhaddā does not fit easily into conventional ideas of what a nun *should* be, and tends to be overlooked in favor of more amenable female figures.

2 When we read the endless repetitions of the claim that Mahāpajāpatī was the 'first bhikkhuni', we gradually lose any critical perspective and come to accept it as the unquestioned truth, regardless of the thin, unreliable facts on which this 'truth' is based. As Lewis Carroll's Bellman says, 'What I tell you three times is true'[1]—a principle rigorously followed by religions and politicians everywhere. There is an implicit contract whereby the listener suspends disbelief so as to make the story come alive. This can be, and often is, taken advantage of by less scrupulous tellers of tales. In the *Odysseus*, Homer makes a sly joke of it, referring to himself as much as to his character.

> 3 'Odysseus', said Alcinous, 'we are far from regarding you as one of those imposters and humbugs whom this dark world brings forth in such profusion to spin their lying yarns which nobody can test...'.[2]

4 This, to the inventor of the Trojan horse, the man who raised cunning to the greatest of arts!

5 So sacred is this truth in story that the Buddhist tradition, while allowing that the Bodhisatta might break precepts in his past lives, claims that in all the hundreds of Jātakas, he never told a lie.[3] This is, ironically enough, untrue, for there are several Jātakas, including some of the best known, where the Bodhisatta lies.[4] The motive behind this claim, however, is not to describe the facts, but to persuade ourselves that the texts are infallible. The real irony is that *all* the Jātakas are based on the fiction that they record genuine past life experiences.[5]

6 As I hope to have shown, the power of the Jātakas remains undimmed by their fictional settings. Fiction has its place; but so do facts. We learn one kind of wisdom from the myths, and a different kind of wisdom from the real story of real people. So let's see what we can glean about the facts of Bhaddā's extraordinary life.

❖

> 7 The occasion was this. The Blessed One was staying at Rājagaha in the Bamboo Grove, together with 500 bhikkhus. Then, having stayed in the Bamboo Grove as long as he wished, the Blessed One went to stay on the Vulture's Peak. Then, in the morning, the Blessed One dressed, and taking his bowl and outer robe, he descended from the Vulture's Peak, followed by the 500 bhikkhus.
>
> 8 At that time, Bhaddā Kuṇḍalakesā, the Jain nun, had gone to the Vulture's Peak for the day's abiding. She was wise, clever, learned, and wandered about Jambudīpa refuting the doctrines of the sectarians with the sharp sword of her tongue. Then Bhaddā Kuṇḍalakesā, seeing the Blessed One descending from the Vulture's Peak followed by the 500 bhikkhus, came on to the path and stood there leaning on a staff, facing the Blessed One and obstructing his progress.
>
> 9 The Blessed One looked at Bhaddā Kuṇḍalakesā, the Jain nun, and said: 'Bhaddā, do not obstruct the path of the Tathāgata and the Sangha of bhikkhus. It is not good to obstruct the path of the Tathāgata and the Sangha of bhikkhus.'
>
> 10 Bhaddā Kuṇḍalakesā replied to the Blessed One: 'So it seems that the Great Monk, while himself obstructing the path of many, cannot stand to have his own path obstructed! It seems that the Great Monk, having obstructed the path of the group of five ascetics, having ob-

structed the path of the fire-worshiping Kassapa brothers and their retinue, having obstructed the paths of Sāriputta and Moggallāna and the followers of Sañjāya, cannot stand having his own path obstructed by a lone woman!'

11 When this was said, the Blessed One said to Bhaddā Kuṇḍalakesā: 'There is a sense, Bhaddā, in which you could say that the paths of all those people have been obstructed by me. For after hearing the Dhamma of the Tathāgata the path to hell has been obstructed for all those people, the path to the animal realm has been obstructed, the path to the ghost realm has been obstructed, the path to rebirth in a future state of existence has been obstructed, and the path to suffering has been obstructed. But perhaps that is not what you meant?'

12 'If what you say is true, Great Monk, then it seems that you teach a Dhamma leading to the end of all suffering—for men!'[6]

13 'Do not say so, Bhaddā! Do not say so, Bhaddā! It is for one who feels that the Tathāgata declares: "This is suffering"—"This is the origin of suffering"—"This is the end of suffering"—"This is the way of practice leading to the end of suffering". The Tathāgata teaches the Dhamma out of compassion for the world with its devas, its Māras, and its Brahmās, this generation with its ascetics and priests, its nobility and its people.

14 'If any son or daughter of family should go forth in such a well-proclaimed Dhamma and Vinaya, and should they practice in accordance with that Dhamma, then it may be expected that in no long time they shall realize for themselves with their own direct knowledge the unexcelled supreme culmination of the holy life.

15 'If, Bhaddā, women go forth from the home life into homelessness in this Dhamma and Vinaya, then they are capable of realizing the fruit of arahantship, of non-return, of once return, or of stream entry.'

16 When this was said, Bhaddā Kuṇḍalakesā said to the Blessed One: 'So it seems, Blessed One, that you teach a Dhamma that leads to liberation for all beings, not just for men alone. Forgive me, Blessed One! A transgression overcame me in that like a fool, blundering and confused, motivated by pride I tried to obstruct the Blessed One's path, and to trap him with words like daggers. May the Blessed One accept my confession out of compassion so that I may restrain myself in the future.'

17 'Indeed, Bhaddā, your conduct was rude and disrespectful, in that motivated by pride you tried to obstruct the Blessed One's path and

to trap him with words like daggers. But we forgive you, since you see your fault as a fault, so that you may restrain yourself in the future.'

18 Then the Blessed One gave Bhaddā Kuṇḍalakesā a talk on Dhamma: 'Bhaddā, form is not self...'. And while this discourse was being given, the stainless immaculate vision of the Dhamma arose within Bhaddā Kuṇḍalakesā: 'Whatever is of the nature to arise, all that is of the nature to cease.'

19 Then Bhaddā Kuṇḍalakesā, having seen and reached and found and penetrated the Dhamma, having left behind uncertainty, having crossed over doubt, having gained perfect confidence and become independent of others in the Teacher's Dispensation, bowed down to the Blessed One and said to him: 'I wish to receive the going forth under the Blessed One, I wish to receive the full ordination into the state of a bhikkhuni!'

20 Then the Blessed One said: 'Come, Bhaddā! The Dhamma is well proclaimed. Live the holy life for the complete ending of suffering!' That was Bhaddā Kuṇḍalakesā's full ordination. And so at that time there was one bhikkhuni in the world.

21 Then, having received full ordination from the Blessed One, Bhaddā Kuṇḍalakesā returned to her hermitage. Having returned to her hermitage, before entering her dwelling, she washed her feet. As she watched the stream of water disappear into the ground, the mind of Bhaddā Kuṇḍalakesā was freed from defilements without grasping. Then she became the first female arahant.

22 At that time there were five other Jain nuns living in that hermitage, engaged in painful and difficult ascetic practices. When they saw Bhaddā Kuṇḍalakesā, they said to her: 'Your faculties are serene, sister, the color of your skin is bright and clear. Can it be that you have seen the Deathless?'

23 And Bhaddā Kuṇḍalakesā replied to them in verse:

24 'Formerly I wandered in a single cloth,
With plucked hair, covered in mud,
Imagining flaws in the flawless,
And seeing no flaws in the flawed.[7]

25 'I came out from my day's abiding
On the mountain Vulture's Peak.
I saw the spotless Enlightened One
Accompanied by the Bhikkhu Sangha.[8]

26 'He then taught me the Dhamma;
The aggregates, sense bases, and elements.
The Leader told me about the ugliness [of the body],
Impermanence, suffering, and not-self.[9]

27 'Having heard the Dhamma from him,
I purified the Vision of Dhamma.
When I had understood the true Dhamma,
I asked for the going forth and full ordination.[10]

28 'Then I humbly bowed down on my knees
And in his presence bowed to him.
"Come, Bhaddā!" he said to me—
That was my full ordination.[11]

29 'When I was fully ordained,
I saw a little stream of foot-washing water disappear.
I understood the process of rise and fall, and reflected
That all conditions were of the same nature.
Right on the spot my mind was released—
Totally freed through the end of grasping.'[12]

30 While Bhaddā Kuṇḍalakesā was speaking, the stainless, immaculate vision of the Dhamma arose in those nuns: 'Whatever is of the nature to arise, all that is of the nature to cease.'

31 And those nuns said to Bhaddā Kuṇḍalakesā: 'We also wish to receive the going forth and the full ordination in the Dhamma and Vinaya proclaimed by the Tathāgata.'

32 Then Bhaddā Kuṇḍalakesā together with those five nuns went to where the Blessed One was staying. Having bowed down to the Blessed One, standing to one side, Bhaddā Kuṇḍalakesā said to the Blessed One: 'Blessed One, these nuns also wish to receive the going forth and the full ordination in the Dhamma and Vinaya proclaimed by the Tathāgata.'

33 Then the Blessed One said: 'Come, bhikkhunis! The Dhamma is well proclaimed. Live the holy life for the complete ending of suffering!' That was those five nuns' full ordination. And so at that time there were six bhikkhunis in the world.

34 Then the Blessed One said to those bhikkhunis: 'Sisters, form is not self.' ... And the hearts of those five bhikkhunis were released from defilements without grasping.

> 35 Then Bhaddā Kuṇḍalakesā said to the Blessed One: 'Blessed One, when women seek the going forth and the full ordination, how should we proceed?'
>
> 36 And the Blessed One replied: 'Bhaddā, I am free from all fetters, whether human or divine. You, too, are free from all fetters, whether human or divine. Well then, Bhaddā, you yourselves should give the going forth and the full ordination to women in this Dhamma and Vinaya. And this is how it should be done...'.

❖

37 Bhaddā was a real nun, a living example for the bhikkhuni movement. Her fearlessness and bold challenge to male authority stand in striking contrast to the 'meek and mild' behavior expected of nuns today. Little wonder that her story remains largely untold: nice girls don't do it like that.[13]

38 Buddhist nuns must deal with abundant negative stereotypes, few positive representations, and a male hierarchy that wields power over them but will not listen to them or take them seriously. Bhaddā is an outstanding example of how rebellion can be a sign, not of stubbornness and conceit, but of resolution and confidence.

39 Most likely you have never heard this story of Bhaddā before. It is not part of the traditional storytelling repertoire. It sits uneasily with the standard account of Mahāpajāpatī as the first nun. Nevertheless, the authenticity of this account is, generally speaking, not contested. To see why, we should first consider the available sources in authentic texts. There are six main sources of textual information on bhikkhunis in the time of the Buddha.

40 **The Therīgāthā**, a collection of verses mainly attributed to awakened nuns.

41 **The Bhikkhunī Saṁyutta**, which includes several of the same verses as the Therīgāthā (with occasional variations), but places them within a specific narrative context: Māra comes to disturb the bhikkhunis while they meditate alone in the 'Blind Man's Grove'.

42 **Occasional suttas found in the main Nikāya/Āgama collections** that feature bhikkhunis, such as the Cūḷavedalla Sutta. In these three sources we come closest to the voices of the historical bhikkhunis.

43 **The Bhikkhunī Vibhaṅga and Bhikkhunī Khandhaka of the Vinayas** were compiled at a somewhat later stage, and contain many additions by the monks, yet probably retain some traces of the bhikkhunis' own oral literature.

44 **The Therī-Apadāna** of the late canonical period. This has expanded versions of the lives of the bhikkhunis from the Therīgāthā, detailing episodes from their past lives. This post-dates the Buddha by several centuries, but stands as a record of nuns' hagiography in the developing Buddhism of the time.

45 **Commentaries and later legends**, giving information as understood 500–1000 years after the Buddha, though in part stemming from earlier traditions.

46 Now, if we consider the story of Bhaddā, the verses are found in the Therīgāthā or the Therī-Apadāna. The Therīgāthā verses are likely to represent Bhaddā's own words, while the Therī-Apadāna stems from a later phase of development.

47 The prose background stands firmly in the style of the Vinaya Khandhakas. The references to Sāriputta and Moggallāna, the Kassapa ascetics, and so on, the setting in Rājagaha (confirmed within the early verses themselves), and the well-attested stylistic idioms all confirm this affinity. The teachings attributed to the Buddha are all found, close or exactly, in other places in the canon.

48 Comparative study of Buddhist texts reveals, time and time again, that the details of narrative, character, setting, and structure often differ, while the content of the teaching remains identical. But we know, without a shadow of doubt, that much of what is found even in the early texts is sheer invention and cannot be literally historical. It is therefore axiomatic that nothing can be accepted blindly, without reflection; nor can we ignore the perspectives of the redactors.

❖

49 Any realistic account of Bhaddā must start with her own verses, which are probably the only genuine record of her life. But the commentarial story (which is given in the next chapter) totally contradicts Bhaddā's verses: it is set in Sāvatthī rather than Rājagaha,[14] and makes Sāriputta the main teacher, bringing in the Buddha only at the last moment.[15]

50 The commentary also changes the mode of ordination: instead of the Buddha ordaining by saying 'Come, Bhaddā', it has the Buddha say: 'Go over to the bhikkhuni quarters and receive the going forth and full ordination in the presence of the bhikkhunis!'[16] The Buddha says 'Come!', the tradition says 'Go!' Despite the fact that the Pali Vinaya[17] mentions the 'Come, bhikkhuni!' ordination in its basic definition of a bhikkhuni,[18] the commentator Dhammapāla goes to painful lengths to prove that there never was such a thing, arguing that women do not have enough merit.[19]

51 Elsewhere, too, the 'Come bhikkhuni' ordination was remembered by the traditions. The Puggalavāda Vinaya treatise Lu Er Shi Er Ming Liao Lun mentions it.[20] The Avadānaśātaka has seven 'Come bhikkhuni' ordinations: Suprabhā, Supriyā, Śuklā, Somā, Kuvalayā, Kāṣikasundarī, and Muktā.[21] The Dharmaguptaka Vinaya mentions it in its standard passage defining a bhikkhuni, much as the Theravāda.[22] This mention is repeated in a shorter Vinaya document of the same school.[23] The Vinaya Mātṛkā Sūtra of the Haimavata school (one of the northern branches of the old Theravāda) describes 'Come bhikkhuni' ordination like this: the Buddha says 'Now listen! Rightly live the holy life in my Dhamma for the complete ending of suffering!'[24] A similar passage is in a Ni Jie-mo (*Bhikkhunī Saṅghakamma).[25] In the Dharmapāda Avadāna Sūtra the precise words 'Come, bhikkhuni' are not used, but two stories depict the women saying they wish to ordain; the Buddha simply responds by saying 'Excellent!', and with that their hair falls off and they become bhikkhunis.[26]

52 Despite the denials of the tradition, and the omission from the 'official' account of bhikkhuni ordination, both the Vinayas and the voices of the nuns themselves tell us there was a going forth by the joyous calling out to live the holy life for the ending of suffering. It will never be possible to 'prove' that this was the original ordination. Yet the account of Mahāpajāpatī's ordination is full of problems. Since the mainstream account is unacceptable, perhaps the 'minority report' preserves a memory of better things. And regardless of whether 'Come bhikkhuni!' was the first ordination or not, these accounts remain as evidence of the enthusiasm with which bhikkhuni ordination can be received. Someone, sometime, said these things!

CHAPTER 16

A BUDDHIST FEMME FATALE

THE STORY OF BHADDĀ IN THE LAST CHAPTER: I MADE IT UP. Bhaddā's verses are accurate translations, and some details were drawn from traditional commentaries, but much of it was sheer invention. I played you, deliberately using style and form to create an impression of authority where none existed. Sorry about that. I hope you're not upset. We've got a long way to journey together, and we might as well trust each other. Because, like any other redactor or commentator, I am not immune to the temptations of the artist: to stand in God's shoes and think, 'What would I have done *better*?'

2 Which implies a certain dissatisfaction with the traditional account. There is no doubt the commentary felt uncomfortable with Bhaddā and her verses, and made considerable efforts to reconstruct an alternative history. My own version may be sheer fiction, but at least it is a fiction that does not fly in the face of the few facts at our disposal.

3 I even admit to a lingering suspicion that my fiction might be closer to the truth than the official version. The act of ordaining a monk using the 'Come, bhikkhu' formula is highly characteristic of the earliest phase of the Buddha's ministry. The fact, recorded in her verses, that the Buddha used a similar formula to Bhaddā is no proof that this was in the same period, but it is suggestive. The setting at Rājagaha is characteristic of this period; and Bhaddā was formerly a Jain nun, just as most of the earliest bhikkhu disciples were formerly ascetics in other religions.

4 If our suspicions are on the right track, how have our texts let us down? The story of the first bhikkhu ordinations is found in the early conversion narrative, the Catuṣpariṣat Sūtra.[1] But this text breaks off and disintegrates towards the end in all the versions I have seen. I think the text originally told the story of the first bhikkhuni ordination, as its Sanskrit title implies: the Discourse on [the Establishing of] the Four Assemblies. The broken character of the existing texts could be a remnant of the removal of the bhikkhuni ordination section, as it was reshaped and constructed into the story that became known to history. We can never know how the text was formed 'in the beginning', and perhaps the sheer brokenness is ultimately the most telling thing.

❖

5 The image of Bhaddā standing obstructing the Buddha on the road up to the Vulture's Peak is sheer invention, but nevertheless Bhaddā was an impressive figure, and the background story as imagined in the commentaries shows that she was not a woman to be messed with.

> 6 Bhaddā Kuṇḍalakesā was born in the family of a treasurer of Rājagaha. On the same day, a son was born to the king's chaplain under a constellation favorable to highwaymen, and was therefore called Sattuka—the Enemy.
>
> 7 When Bhaddā was sixteen, she was beautiful, gorgeous, and charming. Now at that age, women burn with lust for men. So her parents kept her safe in a splendid chamber atop a seven storied palace, with only a single woman to wait on her.
>
> 8 One day, however, Bhaddā heard a great noise from below. She peered through the latticework of her window. Sattuka had been arrested for thuggery and was being led to his death, his hands tied behind his back, having been whipped in all squares of the town.
>
> 9 She fell at once in love with him and lay face down on her bed.
>
> 10 Her mother asked: 'What is it, dearest?'[2]
>
> 11 'If I get that thief,' she said, 'I shall live; if not, I shall die right here.'
>
> 12 'Dearest, don't do this!' her mother begged. 'With a family rich and wellknown such as ours, we can surely find another husband for you.'
>
> 13 'I'll have nothing to do with another,' said Bhaddā. 'If I don't get him, I shall die!'
>
> 14 Unable to persuade her daughter, the mother told the father; but he was equally unsuccessful. Out of his great love for his only daughter,

he bribed the guard to release Sattuka, and arranged for another man to be put to death in his place. He had Sattuka bathed in perfumed water, brought him home, and presented him to his daughter. Bhaddā, bedecked in jewels, waited upon him, serving his every need.

15 Very soon, however, Sattuka began to covet Bhaddā's jewels. He told her that he had made a vow to the deity of the Robbers' Cliff that, should he escape execution, he would bring an offering. She trusted him and on his request made ready an offering of rich rice porridge, flavored with honey, and adorned with the five kinds of flower. He said to her:

16 'Let us go, with your family and friends. Put on all your ornaments, we will laugh and play and enjoy ourselves.'

17 They climbed to the peak of Robber's Cliff; but nearing the top Sattuka had the others wait behind as he and Bhaddā went on to the peak alone. Now, this place was called the 'Robbers' Cliff' because they would take condemned criminals up there and toss them off to their death.

18 On arriving at the top of the cliff, Bhaddā said: 'My husband, let us make our offering.' He said nothing.

19 'But my husband,' she said, 'why are you silent?'

20 'I have not come here to make an offering,' he said. 'I have come here to kill you.'

21 'But what fault have I committed, my husband?' she said.

22 'You fool!' he said. 'I'm after your jewels!'

23 Shaken by the fear of death, she said: 'But my husband, whose ornaments are these? Whose am I?'

24 'That makes no difference!' he said. And though she begged again and again, he would not relent.

25 'So be it, my husband,' she replied. 'But grant me one request. Allow me, while still arrayed in my finery, to embrace you, my beloved, on all sides.'

26 He agreed to this. She embraced him from in front, then the sides, then making to embrace him from behind, she pushed him over the cliff! Falling in the belly of the mountain, he was smashed to pieces.

27 The deity of the mountain uttered these verses in her praise:

28 'A man is not wise on all occasions.
A woman is also wise, being skilful here and there.
A man is not wise on all occasions.
A woman is also wise, thinking quickly of what is useful.'[3]

29 An unwise robber, indeed; and in the spirit of our inquiry we cannot help but notice the archetypal nature of many of the images. The maiden trapped in her tower is well-known to readers of fairy tales; the criminal 'victim' who is honored with perfume and decoration while a substitute is killed reminds us of Frazer's King of the Wood. The connection between the robber and a sacrificial offering is made in the text itself, which says that he initially tricked Bhaddā into going to the mountain to make an offering to the deity; and the deity's response at the end shows that he accepted the gift, which was the robber himself. But if you are not convinced of the archetypal nature of this story, consider the Sulasā Jātaka.

> 30 Once in Benares there lived a courtesan, Sulasā, whose price was one thousand a night. In Benares also lived a robber, Sattuka.
>
> 31 One day he was taken by the king's men, and, as he was being led to execution, Sulasā saw him from a window and fell in love with him. She thought that if she were only to have such a consummate warrior as her husband, she would give up her profession and be his wife. She bribed the chief guard to free him and lived with him.[4]
>
> 32 After a few months Sattuka tired of her, and, wishing to kill her, took her to a lonely mountain top, saying that he had made a vow to the deity dwelling there. When Sulasā discovered his real intention, she begged leave to pay obeisance to him before her death. She circumnambulated him thrice, paid homage at his feet, and going behind him she shoved him down the cliff with the force of an elephant. Crushed and mangled, he died. The deity uttered verses in her praise.
>
> 33 Returning to her home, her attendants asked, 'Where is your husband?'
>
> 34 'Do not ask,' she replied, and went into the city.[5]

35 The same story, stripped back in detail. This story was told as the paradigm for the following events, which occurred in the time of the Buddha and involved the same characters under different names.

> 36 Puññalakkhaṇā was a slave girl of Anāthapiṇḍika's wife. The girl borrowed a costly jewel belonging to her mistress[6] and went to the pleasure garden to play. There a bandit became friendly with her and plied her with alcohol, fish, and meat. They withdrew to privacy, but when he insisted on going even further away from the crowd, she knew he was intent on violence, not love. She asked him to draw some

> water for her from a well near by, and as he did so, she pushed him into the well and threw a stone down on to his head.

37 The archetypal motifs have receded. We no longer have the girl in the tower or the condemned criminal. The events have become more everyday, more believable. Myth is becoming journalism.

38 In some tellings the woman lacks the wisdom of Bhaddā. In the next version, the Bodhisatta, supposedly the ultimate exemplar of virtue, is a murderous brigand and traitor. The story is called the Kaṇavera Jātaka, for the red flowers which wind around the story: they are the wreath of the condemned criminal, but also the brilliant promise of spring love.

> 39 Once the Bodhisatta was born under the star of a robber in a village of Kāsi and became notorious for his banditry. The people complained of him to the king, and so the king ordered the City Guard to arrest the thief. Contingents were placed around the city; the thief was caught and brought to the king, who ordered that his head be cut off.
>
> 40 A wreath of red *kaṇavera*-flowers was placed around his neck, red brickdust was sprinkled on his head, and he was scourged in every square of the city. On his way to execution Sāmā, the chief courtesan of the city, looked out from an upper palace window and saw him, so handsome and strong. She immediately fell in love, and conceived a plan to have him as her husband.
>
> 41 Sāmā sent one of her women with a thousand coins to bribe the City Guard, telling him that the robber was her brother. But the City Guard said they must have a substitute. That night, a young man who was infatuated with her came to see her as usual. She sat weeping, and told him that she needed to free her brother, but had no-one to take the money for her. He bravely volunteered to help her; but the City Guard threw him in a cell, then had him killed after dark, when no-one could see that it was not the robber. The robber was brought to Sāmā, and from then on she spurned the hand of all others, taking her pleasure with him alone.
>
> 42 But the robber reflected that Sāmā, having betrayed her former lover, might do the same to him.
>
> 43 'My dear,'[7] he said. 'We spend all our time cooped up here, like two cockatoos in a cage! Some day we must go to play in the park.'
>
> 44 Taking all good things for a picnic, they amused themselves with play in the park. With a show of lustful desire, he took her into a bush of *kaṇavera* flowers and in a pretense of embrace, squeezed her until

she fell unconscious.[8] Then taking all her ornaments, he made good his escape.

45 Sāmā, all unsuspecting, imagined him to have run away from fear of having killed her by his too violent embraces. She was so distressed she declared that she would not lie on a comfortable bed until she saw him again, and would sleep only on the ground; nor did she adorn herself with scents and finery.

46 She called some wandering minstrels to her and taught them a song. She asked them to travel the breadth of India, singing of her love. One day the minstrels arrived in Benares where the robber was living. A crowd gathered to hear them sing:

47 'In that springtime,
Bright with the *kaṇavera* blossoms,
Sāmā was squeezed with strong arms:
She declares her life to him.'

48 The robber replied to them with this verse:

49 'As if one could believe that the winds could shake a mountain,
And if they could shake a mountain, then even the whole earth!
How could Sāmā who has died, declare that Sāmā lives?'

50 The minstrels replied:

51 'She has not died, she does not wish for another.
Living on one daily meal, Sāmā longs just for you.'

52 But the robber replied:

53 'For me who was unknown, Sāmā left her long-time lover,
Betraying the steady for the unsteady.
Me too she would betray for another,
So I will flee still further from here!'

54 The minstrels returned bearing her lover's message. In regret, Sāmā returned to her former means of livelihood.[9]

❖

55 The story tells of the transition from girl to woman, from the sphere of the parents, an unchosen biological destiny, to that of the husband, a conscious, adult partnership. It bears comparison with such western stories as Beauty and the Beast, or more precisely, Bluebeard: the man

appears desirable, but he is a murderer, who hides the bodies of his former wives in his dungeon. In Bluebeard, the violence is hidden, but in our story she wants the man precisely because he is dangerous.

56 Her voice is carried to her lover in a song; and in a song, too, her story has been told in countless forms in lands to the west. The story of Bhaddā, with more prominent Bluebeard-ish parallels, was sung on the Carrick coast of Scotland in the ballad of May Colven.[10]

57 False Sir John a wooing came
To a maid of beauty fair;
May Colven was this lady's name,
Her father's only heir.

58 He's got on [his steed] and she's got on,
As fast as they could flee,
Until they came to a lonesome part,
A rock by the side of the sea.

59 'Loup off the steed,' says false Sir John,
'Your bridal bed you see;
For I have drowned seven young ladies,
The eighth one you shall be.

60 'Cast off, cast off, my May Colven,
All and your silken gown,
For it's oer good and oer costly
To rot in the salt sea foam.'

61 'A turn you about, O false Sir John,
And look to the leaf of the tree,
For it never became a gentleman
A naked woman to see.'

62 He turned himself straight round about,
To look to the leaf of the tree,
So swift as May Colven was
To throw him in the sea.

63 'O help, O help, my May Colven,
O help, or else I'll drown;
I'll take you home to your father's bower,
And set you down safe and sound.'

64 'No help, no help, O false Sir John,
No help, nor pity thee;

Tho' seven kings' daughters you have drowned,
But the eighth shall not be me!'

65 The beautiful maiden, the bad man, the rescue from the home, the adornments, the cliff, the trick, the push; and the triumph of the wily, self-made woman.[11] Bhaddā's sisters are still doing their thing.

❖

66 The bad man is the Beast, the frog who must be kissed if he is to become a handsome prince. But the transformation sometimes fails, despite all the prince's promises. In these stories, the degenerate man, despite undergoing the transformative initiation of sacrifice and redemption, fails to achieve a responsible adulthood and cannot enter into a mature relationship with a woman. And her story is similarly uncertain: sometimes she fails the test and remains in thrall to the evil man; sometimes she succeeds in killing him, but without further development; and in Bhaddā's case the killing is a spur to a higher spiritual plane. All these gradated variants of the story show the uncertain, dangerous course of spiritual development, with new and terrible challenges at every turn.

67 As a woman's story, this legend codes information about the life expected of women. Her coming of age is fraught with the awakening of her sexuality. Her parents want to control this, protect their child from her own willful desires. The conflict between arranged marriages and partnerships of desire is one of the major dramas of women's lives through history, and remains so in India today.[12] Daddy knows best—or so he thinks—and he just wants to arrange a safe marriage with a nice, respectable boy. But she has her own ideas.

68 She is hidden away in her 'splendid chamber'—*sirigabbha*; the word *gabbha* means both 'inner chamber' and 'womb'. Carol Gilligan quotes Edith Wharton on this symbol:

69 I have sometimes thought that a woman's nature is like a great house full of rooms: there is the hall, through which everyone passes in going in and out; the drawing room where one receives formal visits; the sitting room where the members of the family come and go as they list; but beyond that, far beyond, are other rooms the handles of whose doors are never turned; no one knows the way to them, no

> one knows whither they lead; and in the innermost room, the holy of holies, the soul sits alone and waits for a footstep that never comes.[13]

70 She knows that sanctuary, while others, bedazzled by surfaces, do not even suspect it exists. But not all women are content to wait for the footstep to come. Bhaddā peers outward, like the soul peeking through the eyes. Her desires are inflamed by the dirty, sweaty, violent man; naked, muscular, covered in blood, despised by respectable society, yet bearing within himself a fascinating strength. Daddy's nightmare. The love of a cloistered virgin for such a man is Darwinian (the warrior is the best protector of the women in the tribe), Freudian (Sattuka evokes the irresistible power of her first memory of her father), Jungian (the adolescent girl's acceptance of her *animus*), but most of all, fun. And that is the real tragedy. The Beast, for all his danger, is deeply arousing, while Prince Charming is a boring nerd, who can promise nothing but the stultifying safety of a conventional marriage. Fairy stories end with a fantasy marriage 'happily ever after'; but they start with the agony of banal family life.

71 Social tensions are pulling our heroes to and fro. For the patriarchs, the lesson is: Daddy is right after all, look where a woman's desires will lead her! But in some tellings the woman is redeemed, and there we find another message: follow your bliss, though it leads you to peril, for only that will lead to fullness of life.

72 Such different perspectives have played themselves out in how these texts have been repeated, shaped, listened to, and discussed through the ages. The texts as we have them were put together by men, and we are unsurprised to find patriarchal motifs. Yet notice this curious detail: the verses around which the stories coalesce are attributed to women, and the stories themselves may well have spent some time as 'old wives' tales'. Marina Warner shows that folk tales are often passed down among women before being collected and shaped into a literary format by men. Often enough, storytellers claim that their tale stems from an old grandmother, which serves as a stamp of authenticity.[14] In Sāmā's story, she teaches her verses to some wandering bards; the male minstrels are telling a woman's tale.[15] This bears comparison with the story of Bhaddā, where her own verses have become embedded in a much later tale composed and/or commented on by men; or indeed the Bhikkhuni Vinaya, where the rules that

were originally part of the women's own oral tradition became clouded by so much commentary and additions by the monks that the women' own voices become obscured.

73 Other fears may be encoded here, too. Warner argues that the Bluebeard motif, with the succession of former wives hanging dead in the husband's dungeon, betrays the very real fear of women that they may die in or because of childbirth. Such, it would seem, was the sad fate of Māyā. This was so prevalent that it was not uncommon for husbands to have several wives in succession. Women knew that the longed for union with the husband could very well be their death. Thus Bhaddā's choice: to remain forever a child within the safety of Daddy's walls, or to risk death in the arms of a stranger.

74 Our story tells us that Bhaddā, before she became a nun, was a killer, even if she had a good justification in self-defense. In the conventional ethics of Buddhism, killing is *ethically* wrong, against the first precept. But our story blithely sails over this crucial juncture. Despite many other tales where the Bodhisatta is praised for sacrificing his life, here the act of killing in self-defense is accepted without a murmur, indeed praised by the gods. I am not at all suggesting that Bhaddā's actions were wrong, merely that there is a genuine ethical issue that would seem to warrant attention, but which is simply passed over. To me, this is just another indication that the ethics are not the point of the story. Bhaddā's 'cleverness' here is not the universal wisdom of the Buddha, but more akin to Odysseus' wiliness, an ability to lie, trick, or deceive to get out of any scrape. The story is pre-ethical. This is why the Bodhisatta can play the ambiguous role of the condemned thief, who was originally, it seems, the glorified victim of the sacrifice. In myth, killing may signify a positive transformation just as well as a negative degeneration.

❖

75 We are left to wonder what might have been going on inside Bhaddā. Her first, unrepeatable flush of infatuation, the manipulation of the family, the thrill of love, the awfulness of betrayal, the terrifying exaltation of the kill. What shame did she feel? How did her limbs tremble as she watched Sattuka tumble and rend himself on the rocks? Was she afraid that she would not be accepted back into her family, who had committed a serious

crime to assuage her outrageous desires? Was she disillusioned with the conventional aspirations of marriage and family? How did she make the decision to never return home?

76 The verses do not speak of shame, but of wisdom: knowing the right time to act with decision. Tricking and killing her husband show her 'swiftness of intuitive knowledge', a quality in which the Buddha later declared her to be the foremost of all the bhikkhunis. The killing was, so the story tells us, the spur for her spiritual career. And in that career, we see the development of her understanding, from the naïvety of the girl, to the cunning of the adult, to the intelligence of the philosopher, and culminating in the wisdom of the sage. Leaving the enclosed chamber of women's destiny, she goes forth as a wanderer. And we can only imagine, projecting our own pride and vulnerability onto her, why she felt the need to prove her wits again and again against those of men.

❖

77 The traditional account continues after the killing of Sattuka. Bhaddā could not return home—being a murderess and widow would bring devastating shame on her family. She asked for ordination among the Jains, and they pulled out her hair with tweezers. When it grew back it came in curls, so they called her 'Kuṇḍalakesā', 'Curly-hair'.

78 Finding the Jain teachings inadequate, she traveled widely, learning from wise men wherever she could. Soon, however, she couldn't find anyone who could teach her, so in town after town she set up a branch of a rose-apple tree at the gates, challenging all comers to a debate. If no-one trampled the branch within seven days, she went away.

79 When Sāriputta saw the branch, he had it trampled by some boys, and challenged Bhaddā to a debate. Bhaddā gathered a great crowd to watch the fun.

80 Sāriputta answered all her questions without hesitation. When it was time for him to ask, he said: 'What is the one?' Bhaddā had no answer. She asked to take refuge in Sāriputta, but he told her to go to the Buddha. She ordained and attained arahantship immediately.[16]

81 She meets her match! The violent brigand can't keep her down, but the Buddha's disciple stumps her with the simplest question.[17]

82 This entire story, however, is stock, and is found point for point in the Cūḷakāliṅga Jātaka,[18] including the Jain nuns, the rose-apple branch trampled by boys, Sāriputta's question, and so on. The stereotyped nature of the story is apparent in the commentarial story of the nun Nanduttarā, which merely says she wandered over India disputing 'like Bhaddā Kuṇḍalakesā'.[19] I may be guilty of falsifying Bhaddā's story, but at least I had the good grace to use my imagination.

83 The entire subplot of Bhaddā's debating career and encounter with Sāriputta is absent from both her own verses and the Therī-Apadāna. This instead depicts her being agitated by the sign of repulsiveness in a decaying human hand. Her fellow Jains were unable to help her, and told her to go to the Buddhists. She was taken directly to the Buddha. As usual, the tradition is comfortable to preserve several mutually contradictory but equally authoritative accounts.

84 The motif of the rose-apple branch planted in the pile of sand is a curious one, which I have not seen explained anywhere. Presumably it was a recognized custom, a way of asserting that one was ready for a debate. It is the setting up of a temporary ritual tree, which we might compare with the traditional May-pole in English culture, or even the Christmas tree. It served as a symbolic substitute for the sacred tree under which the sages sat, and where the offerings of the people were given daily. Like all sacred trees, it was a local representative of the *axis mundi*, the backbone of the world. It was an outward gesture to signify that some act of inner significance was about to unfold.

❖

85 This story gained enough prominence that a full book *Kuṇḍalakesī* was written by a Tamil monk called Nāgasena, using Bhaddā's story as a vehicle to criticize the Jains. The book is now lost, but it prodded the Jains into writing the *Nīlakesī* in the 10th century as a rebuttal.[20] Somehow I think that Bhaddā would be dead chuffed to know that she was at the center of debate for over a thousand years.

86 Bhaddā was a disturbing and ambiguous figure: a woman who beat men at their own game, tough and independent. Her verses boldly celebrate her spiritual confidence.

87 I wandered over Aṅga and Magadha,
Vajjī, Kāsi, and Kosala.
For fifty years without debt,
I have enjoyed the alms of the kingdoms.

88 Truly he produced much merit.
Truly wise was that lay follower
who gave a robe to Bhaddā,
who is now completely free from all bonds.[21]

89 By praising the layman who offered her a robe, she dares to reverse the gender roles around offerings of cloth. There are plenty of reasons why such a character would be marginalized in the official Buddhist history in favor of one whose claim to fame was not her own accomplishments, but her relationship to the Buddha; and one for whom the offering of cloth was a sign of emotional entanglement.

CHAPTER 17

THE WEAVING OF THE WEB

ROBES ARE THE MOST RECOGNIZABLE SIGN OF A BUDDHIST MONASTIC. They cover our body, protect us from the elements. They make a very public statement about who we are and what we hold most valuable. They are the skin, the surface, that a monastic presents for the world to see. As the verses of Bhaddā take for granted, the offering of robes is one of the basic duties of Buddhist lay followers, symbolizing a monastic's dependence on kindness and material support. Cloth is one of the four basic monastic requisites,[1] and it was normal for lay supporters to offer cloth to the Buddha or disciples.[2] While Bhaddā makes a point of praising the one who offered her the robe, Mahāpajāpatī's story features her offering a robe; and receiving a very ambiguous response.

2 Before she was ordained, Mahāpajāpatī approached the Buddha to offer him him two beautiful robes, woven with her own hand.[3] There was nothing unusual about this, yet the Buddha refused her kind offer. Or rather, he deflects it, encouraging her to offer the cloth to the Sangha as a whole, not just to him personally. But she persisted, wishing to offer the robe to him alone. Again, the Buddha deflected the offering. He said that offerings made to the Sangha are of greater merit than those offered to him personally. Ānanda intervened, encouraging the Buddha to accept the offering, and reminding him of the great mutual gratitude that these two share. The Buddha was raised since he was a baby by Mahāpajāpatī, who suckled him with her own milk; and through the Buddha, Mahāpajāpatī gained faith and realized the four noble truths.

3 So far had Mahāpajāpatī developed in her spiritual journey. She had seen four noble truths—she was a Stream-enterer, endowed with the first stage of Awakening. She was on the path, understood dependent origination, and was independent from others in her comprehension of the truth. Her insight was so stable it had permanently uprooted some of the deepest of all defiling forces in the mind, and she had only a tiny amount of time left in *saṁsāra*—seven lives at most, although as it turned out she finished her work in this very life.

4 And yet she still loves her son. Since she was a young woman, she suckled, nurtured, nursed, and doted on this man. Now he was a grown man and she was in the final decades of her life. Still she wants to care for him; if not for the strictures of the ascetic rule, what would have stopped her from embracing him like she had all her life? To see him there, adored by all, refusing to treat her as someone special. She knew him better than anyone. Surely it was not unreasonable to expect him to simply accept the robes? Wouldn't any of us do as much? The Buddha suggests she would make more merit by offering to the Sangha. But isn't that her choice? If she wants to offer to the Buddha specifically, why not? And anyway, what does she need merit for—she's already freed from all bad destiny, and she goes on to realize arahantship in this very life.

5 Although the Sutta segues into a discussion of the best way of making merit, the emotional issue has nothing to do with merit, and everything to do with relationship. These two have to establish a new way of being together, which turns their former relationship upside down. Now he is the senior, and she is to expect spiritual support and help from him. The Buddha wants to relate to his stepmother as part of a community. His primary identification now is as the leader of the Sangha, not the son of the Śākyans. His deflection of the offering is not to refuse or harm Mahāpajāpatī, but to encourage her to a more mature relationship.

6 In the Mahīśāsaka version of Mahāpajāpatī's story, which we have translated in Chapter 2, the offering of robes happens immediately before she requests ordination.[4] These two episodes are normally presented as distinct texts, with no immediate connection. Indeed, they usually appear in different collections, the ordination episode in the Vinaya Piṭaka,[5] the robe offering episode in the Suttas.[6] To my knowledge this passage from

the Mahīśāsaka Vinaya is the only text that explicitly links them.[7] But there is no reason why they need be separated, for they have the same characters (the Buddha, Ānanda, Mahāpajāpatī) in the same place (the Nigrodhārāma near Kapilavatthu).

7 Linking the robe offering and the ordination request makes sense, as it reflects the universal psychology of supplicatory prayer: first praise the god (or teacher or other superior being), then ask for what you want. This pattern appears in the Vedic tradition as the *dakṣiṇa*, an offering of robes from student to teacher at the end of the period of studentship. Here's a typical example from a Hindu Dharmaśāstra.

> 8 Now when returning (home from his teacher) he should get the following things, viz. a jewel (to be tied round the neck), two ear-rings, a pair of garments, a parasol, a pair of shoes, a staff, a wreath, (pounded seed of the Karañga fruit) for rubbing with, ointment, eye salve, a turban; (all that) for himself and for the teacher.[8]

9 It seems that this Brahmanical practice was also followed in Buddhist circles. One of the nuns' rules says that if a student presents a robe to a teacher on the understanding that she will receive ordination, but if the teacher subsequently makes no effort to carry out the ordination, then the teacher falls into an offence.[9] Thus this practice of offering a robe before ordination was known in the Sangha, especially among the nuns, which further reinforces the plausibility of the Mahīśāsaka here.

10 From this point of view, the purpose of the offering is not so much the merit of giving, but as a gesture of respect for the teacher. By deferring to the Sangha, the Buddha is not ensuring the maximum return on merit for Mahāpajāpatī, but ensuring that the Sangha receives its due respect.[10]

11 We can never know whether the robe offering and the ordination request did in fact happen on the same occasion (or if they happened at all), but placing the two episodes together emphasizes the shared pattern: Mahāpajāpatī's request and the Buddha's resistance. The Buddha in both cases encourages his stepmother to respect the Sangha as a whole, rather than him as an individual; first by giving gifts, then by requiring that she bow to even junior monks. The implication is that Mahāpajāpatī is so attached to the Buddha that she neglects to think of the Sangha.

12 The personal dimension is a recurring theme in the delicate process of accepting the Buddha's family members within the Sangha. The pride of the Śākyans is notorious in the Buddhist tradition. When the Śākyan princes, Bhaddiya, Anuruddha, Ānanda, Bhagu, Kimbila, and Devadatta sought ordination, they asked that their barber, Upāli, be ordained first, so that in the future they will have to bow down, make *añjali*, and respect him in order to reduce their 'Śākyan pride'.[11] These gestures of respect are the same ones that Mahāpajāpatī is required by the *garudhammas* to perform for the monks. Channa, the Buddha's charioteer, due to his incorrigible bad behavior, had the 'Supreme Punishment' imposed on him by the Buddha at his deathbed. The 'Supreme Punishment' is not as bad as it sounds: he is given the silent treatment by the monks, but is so shamed that he rapidly reforms and realizes arahantship, upon which the punishment lapsed.[12] Devadatta, the Buddha's cousin, wished to usurp the Buddha and tried to murder him. Once, when walking for alms, the Buddha's son Rāhula was given a sharp admonition by the Buddha.[13] The commentary explains that Rāhula admired the Buddha's physical perfection, thinking that he too was handsome like the Buddha.[14] Upananda the Śākyan was notorious for annoying donors by constantly nagging them for cloth requisites.[15]

13 Since in all these cases problems arose because of the pride and greed of the Buddha's relatives, it is plausible that Mahāpajāpatī might have suffered similar problems. The robe offering episode is not an isolated case, merely a feminine version of the problems with the Śākyans generally. I suggest that the response to the robe offering—the laying down of the *garudhammas*—was intended for Mahāpajāpatī personally. That is, in fact, what the Pali text says: 'If Mahāpajāpatī accepts these eight *garudhammas*, that will be her full ordination.'[16] It would seem, then, that the *garudhammas* were not imposed by the Buddha on all women for all time for no good cause, but on Mahāpajāpatī to counter her personal problems, just like Rāhula, Channa, and the rest. Of course, the texts as we have them assume that the *garudhammas* apply to all bhikkhunis, but this is a later extension of the rules.

❖

14 When Ānanda tries to persuade the Buddha to accept the robes, he says that the Buddha should be grateful to Mahāpajāpatī because as an infant

he suckled her milk. Ānanda invokes the positive side of Mahāpajāpatī's association with fluids, the mother's milk that is so revered in India. Yet as positive as it is, it's infantile. And so when the Buddha repeats Ānanda's words he makes two changes; he omits the infantile reference, and he removes names, depersonalizing the example. This detail is no accident: in the dialogue about the Buddha's mother passing away after his birth, the Buddha depersonalizes Ānanda's words in the same way.[17]

15 Maternal attachment is right on the surface of this passage, and is strengthened in the symbolic associations of cloth. Cloth was precious in those times, so its use is governed by a series of Vinaya rules, whose complexity is only rivaled by two other topics in the Vinaya—food and sex. It was an object of desire for monastics, a tactile reminder of the softness and comfort of family life. Cloth is what we feel on our skin; it defines the boundaries of our physical self. The soft touch of cloth surrounds us always, murmuring.

16 All over the world, weavers are women, and the development of cloth was one of the central cultural achievements sustained down to the present day primarily by women. And, like all great technologies, the weaving of cloth became surrounded with a complex web of symbolic and sacred allusions. The weaving is not just the cloth that a woman makes for a man, but the very body he 'wears' was woven by her, which is why 'Clother' is one of the names of the Goddess.[18] The sacralized women, the goddesses, are the Fates, the only power feared by Zeus, who weave life as they weave the cloth. The great Goddesses are weavers, whether in Egypt or Greece, among the Germans or the Mayans, and in their constant plaiting and knotting they bind us all to the patterns of Fate.[19]

17 In this sense the cloth is also a net, a web, within which the spider traps the unwary and gobbles them up. If she weaves life, she can also unravel it, as Penelope wove for her suitors, and each night unraveled what she had done in the day. The Buddhist texts speak of the 'Net of Illusion' (*māyājāla*[20]), and say that 'craving is the seamstress'.[21] The greatest female sage of the Upaniṣads, Gargī, raises the weaving analogy to new spiritual heights: she challenged Yājñavalkya to explain in what space was 'woven'.[22]

18 Like all great mythemes, the imagery of weaving is pre-ethical, and so it can erupt in its negative form as a loathing of women, the source of death

and entrapment. The following is from 'The Tale of King Udayana of Vatsa' in the central Mahāyāna collection, the Mahāratnakuṭa.

19 The dead snake and dog are detestable,
But women are even worse.
Women are like fishermen; their flattery is a net.
Men are like fish caught by the net.[23]

20 Here the issue is female sexuality, which as always is the trap for unsuspecting and innocent men. Sex does not just trap a man for life, however, it binds him to death and beyond. The whole complex web of allusions is woven together as early as this funeral invocation from the Ṛg Veda:

21 As a mother covers her son with the hem of her cloak,
so cover him thou, O earth.[24]

22 Mother earth covers us over after we die. She does not stop caring for us. On the contrary; she has loved us our whole lives and resents the separation that has, for a time, taken us from her. At death our bodies return to the elements, to the matrix from which we were formed.

23 Within this symbolic context, the Buddha's refusal of the robes takes on a new aspect. Woman as weaver of Fate harks back to the primordial, chthonic Goddess; implacable, inescapable Necessity. The Buddha refuses to be caught in the net. By deflecting the offering to the Sangha as a whole he is setting a paradigm, one which the Sangha still lives by today: the material resources belong to the community and so do not give rise to a sense of personal attachment and entrapment.

24 Nevertheless, the imagery of destruction haunts this episode. The prediction of Buddhism's demise is irrational, and should be read as a sign of lateness. When Mahāpajāpatī asked for ordination it was only five years or so after the Buddha's Awakening. He had just converted the kings and leaders of the most powerful nations to his following, had set up a thriving and energetic new order, and was endowed with limitless energy for spreading the Dhamma. You don't agonize about the disappearance of your religion when it is only a few years old; you do it when the leader is dead or dying. The prophecy is an expression of the fear within the Buddhist community after his passing away. The flood and the disease are profound symbols of time and decay.

CHAPTER 18

FEARS OF THE FUTURE

NOW, THE MAHĀPAJĀPATĪ STORY MIGHT HAVE SAID that when women enter a celibate monastic community, this will give rise to issues regarding sexual misconduct, and these problems have to be sensitively managed so that the aspirations of those who wish to lead the monastic life may be fulfilled. But it says nothing of this.

2 It might have said that the male Sangha has a defined decision-making structure, and the role of women will have to be carefully integrated into this so as to preserve the harmonious functioning of the community. But it doesn't.

3 These things—sex and power—are addressed elsewhere. They are real issues and are treated in a rational manner. We can sensibly inquire as to the relevance or accuracy of any statements that might be made. But here at the end of the narrative, sex and power are not the issue. The issue is death.

4 Nuns will destroy Buddhism. This is irrational in a deep sense: there is no 'ratio' between cause and effect, they don't 'fit together',[1] they are unrelated, disproportional. Nor is any evidence thought necessary to make the argument persuasive. It persuades, not by reason or evidence, but by invoking deeply unconscious associations.

5 The Mahāpajāpatī story claims that the Buddha prophesied the ending of Buddhism in 500 years. But it is now five times 500 years, and the holy life doesn't look like failing any time soon. Nor is it tenable to argue that the statement was meant to apply only if the *garudhammas* had not been laid

down, for the text states twice that now (*dāni*), even after the *garudhammas*, the true Dhamma will last only 500 years. Rather than try to justify the prediction, we should consider the motivations behind the passage. It sounds like the author thought Buddhism was in terminal decline and needed someone to blame.

❖

6 In the early texts there is no substantial evidence that the Buddha made this kind of calender prediction for the future, nor did he claim to be able to.[2] In his standard list of powers, the only knowledge of the future he claimed was to predict rebirth based on kamma, and to ascertain that this is the last birth.[3] The only truly prophetic text in the early canon is the Cakkavattisīhanāda Sutta, which famously predicts the arising of Metteyya, the future Buddha. But this text is clearly mythic, and does not deal with historical time. Another case is when, in the Mahāparinibbāna Sutta, the Buddha predicts the future greatness of Pāṭaliputta. This did not really require psychic powers, given the evident ascendancy of Magadha at the time. His predictions of the threats to the city are equally mundane: fire (which history tells us was a constant danger to the largely wooden buildings of ancient India), water (Pāṭaliputta was built on the Gangetic flood-plain, and Aśoka's palace is still flooded today), and internal dissension.

7 The Buddha's more important statements about the future, such as the 'Future Dangers' discourses, do not contain any crude calender predictions.[4] What he pointed out was the nature of cause and effect: the future of Buddhism is what we choose to make it. This is entirely in keeping with the notion of choice, *kamma*. The idea of destiny or fate is explicitly rejected by the Buddha.[5]

8 So-called 'predictions' of the ending of Buddhism, like prophecies in any religion, tell us nothing about the future. They tell us of the fears and hopes of the people who made the statements, at the time they made them. The prediction that nuns will destroy Buddhism is patently false as history, but deeply revealing as mythology. It must have been made at a time when the future of Buddhism was unclear, but when the apocalyptic ending could be ascribed to a far-distant future. In other words, the passage must

have been composed in the centuries following the Buddha's death, when 'five hundred years' meant 'way in the future'.

9 On many occasions the Buddha commented on the factors leading to the decline and disappearance of Buddhism.[6] In various contexts he points to the preservation of the scriptures; or keeping the *pāṭimokkha*; or respect for training; or respect for meditation; or energetic leadership from the Elders of the Sangha. In each of these cases we recognize the sweet voice of reason. Here is one example. The Buddha, speaking to Mahākassapa, denies that any external force will destroy the Dhamma:

> 10 '... the true Dhamma does not disappear as long as the counterfeit of the true Dhamma has not arisen, but when a counterfeit of the true Dhamma arises in the world, then the true Dhamma disappears.
>
> 11 'It is not the earth element, Kassapa, that causes the true Dhamma to disappear, nor the water, fire, or air elements.[7] It is the senseless people who arise right here who cause the true Dhamma to disappear.
>
> 12 'The true Dhamma does not disappear all at once the way a ship sinks. There are, Kassapa, five detrimental things that lead to the decay and disappearance of the true Dhamma. What five? Here, the bhikkhus, bhikkhunis, male, and female lay followers live without reverence and deference to the Buddha ... the Dhamma ... the Sangha ... the training ... *samādhi*.
>
> 13 'There are, Kassapa, five things that lead to the longevity, non-decay, and non-disappearance of the true Dhamma. What five? Here, the bhikkhus, bhikkhunis, male, and female lay followers live with reverence and deference to the Buddha ... the Dhamma ... the Sangha ... the training ... *samādhi*.'[8]

14 So the presence of a healthy, well practicing bhikkhuni Sangha is one of the conditions for the longevity of Buddhism, not the decline. And the source of danger comes through neglect of the sincere practice of the teachings. Those who oppose bhikkhunis are hastening the growth of the false Dhamma and the disappearance of the true Dhamma. But this is merely the authentic early text, and so has little importance in actual Buddhist culture.

15 The idea that bhikkhunis are essential to sustain the *sāsana* is no isolated, chance statement, but is a regular, recurring theme. In the Mahāparinibbāna Sutta it is recorded that the Buddha said to Māra:

16 I shall not come to my final passing away, Evil One, until my bhikkhus and bhikkhunis, laymen and laywomen, have become true disciples—wise, well disciplined, apt and learned, preservers of the Dhamma, living according to the Dhamma, abiding by the appropriate conduct, and having learned the Master's word, are able to expound it, preach it, proclaim it, establish it, reveal it, explain it in detail, and make it clear; until, when adverse opinions arise, they shall be able to refute them thoroughly and well, and to preach this convincing and liberating Dhamma.[9]

17 This statement, found widely in the different versions of this text, was said to have been made by the Buddha shortly after his Awakening.[10] It was his aspiration, right from the start of his teaching, to establish the bhikkhunis.

18 A little later the same sutta refers to bhikkhunis again as a positive and essential sector of his dispensation:

19 But, Ānanda, whatever bhikkhu or bhikkhuni, layman or laywoman, abides by the Dhamma, lives uprightly in the Dhamma, walks in the way of the Dhamma, it is by such a one that the Tathāgata is respected, venerated, esteemed, worshiped, and honored in the highest degree. Therefore, Ānanda, thus should you train yourselves: 'We shall abide by the Dhamma, live uprightly in the Dhamma, walk in the way of the Dhamma.'[11]

20 Or again, the Vacchagotta Sutta says:

21 If in this teaching the venerable Gotama were to be accomplished ... bhikkhus were to be accomplished ... but no bhikkhunis were to be accomplished, then this holy life would be incomplete...[12]

22 Similarly, the Pāsādika Sutta discusses the conditions for the longevity of a religion after the death of its founder. It states that, were the Buddha to pass away while there were senior and accomplished bhikkhus, but no bhikkhunis who were skilled, disciplined, confident, and attained to freedom, able to teach the Dhamma and refute wrong interpretations, then Buddhism would be incomplete in that respect.[13]

23 In a mythic context, the *dhammatā* of the fourfold assembly is implied in the Lakkhaṇa Sutta. This text describes in detail the kammic conditions for various qualities of the Buddha, and correlates each of these with the so-called '32 Marks of a Great Man'. These marks are a curious feature

of early Buddhism, which the texts say stemmed from an ancient Brahmanical tradition. One who is born with such marks will attain worldly supremacy as a Universal Emperor or spiritual pre-eminence as a Buddha. Most of the marks are straightforward signs of physical perfection—gold skin, black hair, white teeth—while others range from the odd (40 teeth), to the bizarre (his penis is enclosed in a sheath),[14] to the impossible.[15] They are listed several times in the early texts, but the Lakkhaṇa Sutta is the only place that goes into detail.[16] It says that the Buddha lived for the happiness of the many-folk in his past lives, and was the provider of shelter and necessities; and the kammic fruit in this life is that the Buddha has a great retinue of bhikkhus, bhikkhunis, laymen, and laywomen.[17] The text continually reinforces the message that bhikkhunis are an essential part of Buddhism.[18] For the author of this text, Buddhism is unthinkable without bhikkhunis.

24 All these passages, and many others, treat bhikkhunis with dignity, as part of the fundamental structure of the Buddhist community. They speak with that balance and reasonableness that is the hallmark of the Buddha. But when the texts say that women are the cause of decay and disease, I can no longer recognize the Buddha's voice. It is the voice of Māra, the Apostle of Unreason.

25 The process of de-rationalizing the texts starts within the Mahāpajāpatī story itself. The first danger of ordaining women is that a village with few men and many women is weak and at risk from thieves and bandits.[19] What this has to do with bhikkhuni ordination is left to the imagination. But this image is taken from the Saṁyutta Nikāya, where it is said that a monk who does not develop his mind through loving-kindness may be assailed by non-human beings, just as a village with few men and many women may be assailed by robbers.[20] There is no suggestion of any moral or spiritual failing of women; it was a tragic fact of life that robbers would prey on women. But in the Mahāpajāpatī story it has become a sermon on the weakness of women.

26 To seek a rational explanation for the irrational is to miss the point. If, my dear friend, we have learnt nothing else after our time together, at least we must acknowledge this. If sense is absent, let us then see what meaning might be found in non-sense.

❖

27 The dominant fear, expressed constantly, like a mantra through these texts, is of the disappearance of the Dhamma-Vinaya. Disappearance, ending, passing away: the inexorable tide of impermanence has been so keenly seen by these yogis in meditation, it's as if that's all they can see—not a vigorous new growth, but the inevitability of decay. The arahants have dispelled the fear of death, but the community behaves as if that fear has been, not transcended, but transferred from the person to the religion. Whereas the Buddha serenely passed away in the knowledge that, do as he may, his religion would not last forever, now there is a feverish effort to stem the tide. Individually they know that it must end, but as a community they still fear it: the rational voice and the emotional voice are singing different tunes.

28 Towards the end of the Buddha's life, he faced an unprecedented series of challenges. His two chief disciples, Sāriputta and Moggallāna, died, and the Buddha said the Sangha appears as if empty without them. The great lay supporter Anāthapiṇḍika had also passed away, as indeed had Mahāpajāpatī herself. Kings Pasenadi and Bimbisāra, the Buddha's greatest supporters, also died, their thrones usurped by violent and aggressive sons. The fragile peace that had held for most of the Buddha's life was breaking down. Kosala and Magadha fought over Benares; Viḍūḍabha led Kosala towards the annihilation of the Buddha's people; and Ajātasattu was scheming to invade the democratic Vajjians. All this added to the climate of uncertainty as the Buddha died, leaving his Sangha to face the future.

29 The Buddha's death scene is remembered and celebrated in story and artwork: the arahants reflect on impermanence, while the unenlightened weep and wail, tear out their hair, beat their breasts, and roll about on the ground as they cry in despair: 'All too soon the Eye of the World has vanished!' If looked at as individual behavior, this scene acknowledges the simple reality that people are at very different stages along the path, but all are accepted within Buddhism. And that is a sane and healthy perspective. But looking at it as a collective act, it is as if the collective consciousness is divided against itself. There is a strange dissonance between the enlight-

ened behavior of individuals, and a collective mind that is dis-integrated, dis-associated.

30 The resulting tension spurred many of the developments in later Buddhism, as the community attempted to come to terms with this root trauma. Just as the history of Christianity can be read as an attempt to resurrect Jesus, make him real again for his followers, the history of Buddhism evidences an unquenchable thirst to bring back the Buddha. We must remember that, at this stage in Buddhist history, the texts are corporate products, produced and authorized by the Sangha as a body, not by individuals. And in these collective scriptures we can read the fractures in the collective consciousness.

31 This dichotomy is not immediately apparent in the history. On the surface, the efforts taken to preserve Buddhism are entirely sensible and admirable. Establish a strong sense of communal unity, agree on a substantial, consistent, and broad-ranging set of scriptures, attempt to practice these as sincerely as possible, and teach the Dhamma to others in order to help them with Dhamma. No problem here, just what we would expect of an enlightened religion.

32 But something else is going on, something barely suppressed behind the traditions. In the Mūlasarvāstivāda Vinaya, when the Dhammacakkappavattana Sutta is recited at the First Council, Aññā Koṇḍañña falls to the floor, struck senseless, almost as if dead himself.[21] The Aśokarājasūtra has Upagupta, the greatest Buddhist leader of his times, fall prostrate before the form of the Buddha—but he knows it's not really the Buddha, it's Māra, the King of Death, in disguise.[22]

33 In these stories, the fear of death is inscribed into the Buddha's passing away. This is a standard religious motif: for human gods from Osiris to Jesus, their own deaths (and resurrection) become the paradigm for their followers to find salvation from death. The Buddhist representative of this ambiguous tradition is Ānanda, who cannot hold back his tears when faced with the passing of the Buddha. And Ānanda, the champion of the bhikkhunis, is the suspect, the one who must be held outside the assembly until he can prove his worthiness.

34 Since the Buddha's passing away was a matter of great, perhaps final, concern for the Buddhist community, it is only natural to look for a scape-

goat. Who are we to blame—who is it that has brought disease and corruption into the Sangha? Scapegoating is a time-honored human custom. It allows us to escape the burden of responsibility, by 'sacrificing'—literally, 'making sacred'—someone who can carry away sins, like a lamb of God. When bhikkhunis were likened to a disease and flood, they become the scapegoat for the ending of Buddhism.

❖

35 So what are these diseases that Mahāpajāpatī introduces that evoke such fear and disgust? 'White bones' (*setaṭṭhika*) and 'red rot' (*mañjiṭṭhikā*) are genuine crop diseases and are to this day a serious threat to livelihood for people in the region. 'White bones' is perhaps bacterial leaf blight, described thus: 'Lesions begin as water-soaked stripes on the leaf blades and eventually would increase in length and width becoming yellow to grayish-white until the entire leaf dries up.'[23]

36 'Red rot' is positively identified in Needham's authoritative volume on the science of ancient China.[24] The Indic word *mañjiṭṭhikā* means 'color of madder', a deep red dye still used today in India. This is the color that the sugar-cane becomes when afflicted by the most widespread cane disease, 'red rot'. This disease, which is still prevalent in the area the Buddha taught, often manifests only as the cane is ripe for harvest. It particularly affects the node and internode of the cane, hence it is translated in some Chinese sources as 'red internode disease (*chih-chieh-ping*)'. The Pali commentary says that the disease turns the inside of the sugarcane red, which also agrees exactly with the symptoms of 'red rot'.

❖

37 Thus far the facts. But notice how the mere act of considering the details directs our attention away from the enormity of what the Buddha is said to have done here. It is simply abnormal to compare your beloved stepmother in her spiritual aspiration with a *disease*. It is almost impossible to take this account seriously. The mind just slides off it, wanting to look but not look, like the gory bits in a horror movie.

38 While most analysts of the Mahāpajāpatī story have focused on the nature of the eight *garudhammas*, for me those rules are not the issue. I

discuss them more fully elsewhere,[25] but to be honest, I think that too much attention to the *garudhammas* is a rationalist avoidance tactic. The real killer is the similes at the end. The modernist mind wants to dismiss such things. It would prefer not to know, prefer to stick on the label 'chauvinist', and rest content in the belief that this explains everything. For me, on the other hand, they are the most intriguing part of the whole thing, for they announce the presence of the Prince of Unreason, the King of Fools, wandering astray and appearing like an alien imposter in the calm, reasoned environment of a Buddhist disciplinary text. But appearances are *māyā*, their very essence is illusion. Could it be that our story, so apparent in its misogyny, hides a deeper truth beneath its patchwork surface?

❖

39 We have seen earlier how Hārītī, goddess of smallpox, at once devourer and protector of children, has been adopted within the Buddhist context. Disease is not the property of Mahāpajāpatī alone; nor is it just here that sickness is red. Red is, of course, blood; the blood of violence, wounding, menses, anger; the bleeding flesh of a slain beast; the everyday glory of the death and rebirth of the day and night.

40 The paleolithic 'Venus' figures of Old Europe are often daubed with red ochre, or in red surroundings. But by then—20 000 BCE—ochre was already old school. Carved ochre has been dated back as far as 100 000 BCE in the Blomos caves in South Africa, which is believed to be the earliest form of human symbolic culture.[26]

41 In many ways red stands out for its magical usefulness. Here are a few examples from Frazer.

> 42 In the Central Provinces of India, when cholera breaks out in a village, every one retires after sunset to his house. The priests then parade the streets, taking from the roof of each house a straw, which is burnt with an offering of rice, ghee, and turmeric, at some shrine to the east of the village. Chickens daubed with vermilion are driven away in the direction of the smoke, and are believed to carry the disease with them. If they fail, goats are tried, and last of all pigs. When cholera rages among the Bhars, Mallans, and Kurmis of India, they take a goat or a buffalo—in either case the animal must be a female, and as black as possible—then having tied some grain, cloves,

and red lead in a yellow cloth on its back they turn it out of the village. The animal is conducted beyond the boundary and not allowed to return. Sometimes the buffalo is marked with a red pigment and driven to the next village, where he carries the plague with him.[27]

43 But the best known case of human sacrifices, systematically offered to ensure good crops, is supplied by the Khonds or Kandhs, another Dravidian race in Bengal. Our knowledge of them is derived from the accounts written by British officers who, about the middle of the nineteenth century, were engaged in putting them down. The sacrifices were offered to the Earth Goddess, Tari Pennu or Bera Pennu, and were believed to ensure good crops and immunity from all disease and accidents. In particular, they were considered necessary in the cultivation of turmeric, the Khonds arguing that the turmeric could not have a deep red color without the shedding of blood.... He was then anointed with oil, ghee, and turmeric, and adorned with flowers; and 'a species of reverence, which it is not easy to distinguish from adoration,' was paid to him throughout the day. A great struggle now arose to obtain the smallest relic from his person; a particle of the turmeric paste with which he was smeared, or a drop of his spittle, was esteemed of sovereign virtue, especially by the women.[28]

44 Similarly the woman who died in the character of the Corn-mother at the Mexican midsummer sacrifice had her face painted red and yellow in token of the colors of the corn, and she wore a pasteboard mitre surmounted by waving plumes in imitation of the tassel of the maize. On the other hand, at the festival of the Goddess of the White Maize the Mexicans sacrificed lepers. The Romans sacrificed red-haired puppies in spring to avert the supposed blighting influence of the Dog-star, believing that the crops would thus grow ripe and ruddy. The heathen of Harran offered to the sun, moon, and planets human victims who were chosen on the ground of their supposed resemblance to the heavenly bodies to which they were sacrificed; for example, the priests, clothed in red and smeared with blood, offered a red-haired, red-cheeked man to 'the red planet Mars' in a temple which was painted red and draped with red hangings. These and the like cases of assimilating the victim to the god, or to the natural phenomenon which he represents, are based ultimately on the principle of homeopathic or imitative magic, the notion being that the object aimed at will be most readily attained by means of a sacrifice which resembles the effect that it is designed to bring about.[29]

45 The Indian culture in which the Buddha lived was dependent on the crops of grain, and so the fertility of the grain was a central concern. While we naturally think of the conditions for fertility of crops as the quality of the soil, the timely falling of rain, and so on, ancient people saw this as only part of the story. Everywhere in the ancient world we witness the placation of deities with offerings to ensure a good crop. This we can understand. And it has been well documented that the image of the Sangha as 'field of merit' was consciously developed as a rational transference of the old offering system.

46 More remote, more primitive, is the practice of sacrifice, even human sacrifice, for the growth of crops. This is not an offering to a deity, but is an act of sympathetic magic. Unlike, say, fruit trees, the grain must be destroyed each harvest. If the grain is embodied as a spirit or deity, this becomes expressed as the ritual murder of the deity, essential for their future health and regrowth. That is, we must kill in order to ensure new life. 'Blood & bone': we still use that as fertilizer today.

CHAPTER 19

THE FLOOD

FLOOD IS A FEARFUL THING, a threat not merely to personal life, but to the very existence of a people. The flood is the primordial image of relentless destruction.[1] The story of Mahāpajāpatī's ordination, after comparing bhikkhunis to a disease, declares that the Buddha is making these eight *garudhammas* like a man would build a dyke to hold back a flood of water. But what kind of flood, and what kind of water?

2 Mahāpajāpatī first appeared in her son's teachings when he recalled how, when he went forth from the home, his unnamed parents wept with tears running down their faces. After the Buddha rejects her request for ordination, Mahāpajāpatī leaves weeping. Following him to Vesālī, she weeps again. Ānanda, her champion, weeps for the Buddha's death. So there is this almost constant association of Mahāpajāpatī with tears, a salty liquid flowing out due to her womanly weakness. This was one of the allegations brought against Ānanda in some versions of the First Council—he allowed the tears of women to soil the Buddha's body.

3 But a few tears hardly constitute a flood of death—or do they? In one of his most unforgettable images, the Buddha said:

> 4 The stream of tears that you have shed as you roamed and wandered through this long course, weeping and wailing through being united with the disagreeable and separated from the agreeable—this alone is more than the water in the four great oceans.[2]

5 Tears of grief are a fatal sign of human frailty, proof that Awakening is incomplete. That little leak in the dyke, that inconsequential trickle, is

the ominous sign of the breaking down of the walls, and the flooding in of endless births and deaths.

6 And not just in the past, but also in the present, Buddhists are divided over the spiritual implications of the shedding of tears. Luang Ta Bua has long been one of the most charismatic and powerful figures in Thai Buddhism, a fiery forest monk in the austere Mahākassapa style, who in recent years has aroused terrific controversy by publicly claiming to be an arahant. These claims are not the done thing for Buddhist monks, but such is Luang Ta Bua's spiritual authority that, for many, he gets away with it. In one talk, he spontaneously burst into tears as he recollected the amazing power of the Dhamma that he realized at the time of his enlightenment. This was very controversial in Thailand, with many people saying that it was impossible for an arahant to shed tears. Luang Ta Bua was undaunted. He spoke in defense of his tears, saying that those who criticize do not comprehend the power of the Dhamma.[3]

❖

7 Tears are not the only bodily fluid that is compared with a flood.

> 8 The mother's milk that you have drunk as you roamed and wandered through this long course—this alone is more than the water in the four great oceans.[4]

9 Mother's milk also forms the flood of *saṁsāra*. And in the Buddha's life story, Mahāpajāpatī is pre-eminently the source of this flood as well, since the Buddha is grateful to his stepmother for her irreplaceable gift of life-sustaining milk.

10 Taking the imagery one step further, the Buddha identifies another bodily fluid with the flood of *saṁsāra*.

> 11 The stream of blood that you have shed as you roamed and wandered through this long course—this alone is more than the water in the four great oceans.[5]

12 Now, there is no explicit textual connection between Mahāpajāpatī and blood. But the Buddha elsewhere made a provocative statement equating blood and mother's milk. The Mahātaṇhāsaṅkhaya Sutta speaks of the difficulty and burden with which a mother must carry her child, and 'When

[the baby] is born, she rears it with her own blood; for mother's milk is called "blood" in the noble discipline.'[6] This text challenges us to identify the milk of life with the blood of death.[7] This is good science, for the composition of milk and blood are very similar. But the point here is that the mother must give of her very essence, must sacrifice her own blood, for the life of the child.

13 Ancient Indic belief held that mother's milk was a purified form of blood. Such beliefs were also prevalent, in a very literal form, in Europe.[8] Medical writers in the early modern period believed that the breast-milk originated as the blood that nourished the foetus in the womb, which was later drawn up to the breasts through a vein and there purified into milk, with the impurities expelled as lochia. This belief is found as far back as Aristotle. In his *Generation of Animals* Isidore writes that 'whatever blood has not yet been spent in the nourishing of the womb flows by a natural passage to the breasts, and whitening by their virtue, receives the quantity of milk.'[9] Guillimeau likewise opines that 'The milk is nothing else but blood whitened, being new brought to perfection and maturity.'[10] He compares refusal to breastfeed with abortion, refusal to nourish with blood.

> 14 The transformation of blood into milk is just one step in the far greater process of the transformation of the waters. The waters circulate in the bodies of all living creatures, as they circulate through the cosmos itself. The dew and rain descend from heaven under the control of the gods and form the oceans, rivers, and groundwater. In this way the nectar of heaven, the Amṛta or Ambrosia, becomes our everyday drinking water. The waters enter the plants as sap; from sap they become cow's milk, which becomes our blood. When we die our body dries out and the nectar moves on. The heat of the sun evaporates the waters, where they ascend to the sky to continue the cycle. The heavenly vessel of this immortal fluid is the moon.[11]

15 Mahāpajāpatī is explicitly said to be leaking the floods of tears and of milk, and I think we are not stretching the texts too far in thinking that her blood is also implied. The following story, told with the dry humor characteristic of Pali, further adds to her polluting image:

Figure 19.1: *Witch*

16 Now on that occasion the Buddha, the Blessed One, was dwelling among the Śākyans at Kapilavatthu, in the Banyan Park. And then Mahāpajāpatī Gotamī, having approached the Blessed One, bowed, stood upwind, [and said]: 'Blessed One, women stink.' And then the Blessed One said: 'Well, let the bhikkhunis wash [their vaginas][12] with water'.[13]

17 Can we imagine Sāriputta or Moggallāna being ridiculed like this? Surely the entirely unnecessary, if colorful, addition of 'upwind' serves only to make Mahāpajāpatī (and hence all the bhikkhunis) an object of fun, if not repulsion?

18 And this miasma of impurity, spreading like a fog from her body, may well have been conceived as a cause of disease in a literal sense. Hélène Cixous remarks that: 'In the witch's case, contagion spreads through bits of bodily waste and through odors.'[14] Such ideas were popular in early modern Europe. For example, a tract called *Occulta naturae miraculai* (*Occult Marvels and Secrets of Nature*) published by the learned Dutch doctor Levinus Lemnius in 1559 says that woman 'is full of excrement, and because of her flowers [periods], she exudes a bad odor; also, she worsens all things and destroys their strength and natural faculties.' On the other hand, the 'natural heat of man is vaporous, mild, and smooth, almost like being showered by an aromatic odor.' The female body is itself sinful and venomous, infecting all that is pure.[15]

19 Such images of women as a dangerous source of leaking fluids, transgressing the boundaries of society as their fluids transgress the boundaries of their own bodies, emerge in male fantasies of the hag or crone. The lack of concern for political correctness allows the psychological objectification to shine through with disarming clarity. While it is true that everything we say is contingent on our own personal conditioning, biases, and so on, this applies with even greater force to statements on the opposite sex.[16]

20 Projection plays freely in the wilds and the unknown. The imagined Woman of Power—the witch or the bhikkhuni—allows men to define their own heroic virtue through their disdain and rejection of the Other. He is the Man of Reason, straight-thinking and upright, while she is fluid, magical, dangerous.[17] Elizabeth Grosz comments:

21 > Can it be that in the West ... the female body has been constructed not only as a lack or absence, but with more complexity, as a leaking, uncontrollable, seeping liquid; as formless flow; as viscosity, entrapping, secreting, as lacking not so much or simply the phallus but self-containment—not a cracked or porous vessel, like a leaking ship, but a formlessness that engulfs all form, a disorder that threatens all order?[18]

22 Diane Purkiss, discussing the above passage in the context of the European early modern witch, argues that the female body as 'formless spillage' arises from the infant's perception of their mother's body, which is still not separate from its own. As the child grows, it beomes conscious of itself as a distinct entity; yet its separation is a precarious achievement, and even the adult retains the unconscious fear of being absorbed back into the infinite, undefined body of the dream-mother of infancy. Freudians say that this fear is stronger in the girl than the boy, as she is always less distinct from the mother. This unconscious fear reappears in dreams, imagination, and emotional response to fluids, pollution, engulfing, or drowning.[19] When it surfaces in the rational mind it becomes fear of magic and magic's servants: witches.

23 Magic, at its heart, is the denial of boundaries, the refusal to accept that my body ends at my skin, so that the same power I exert over my limbs I can also exert outside my body. It is the formlessness of the woman, the 'un-clear-cut-ness'[20] of her body that makes her the magician *par excellence*. The witch's capacity to effortlessly flow across the boundaries of the Self and society must therefore be 'bottled up', just as a dam must be made to control the bhikkhunis.

24 Purkiss describes a typical remedy for witchcraft, the magic bottle or 'bellarmine', which contained the witch's own waters. One must place a piece of her hair or clothing, and if possible her urine, and then seal the bottle. This sealed the witch's body in a literal sense, making her unable to urinate. More importantly, it contained her body, making her unable to extend her polluting power and thus disabling her magic.[21]

25 This 'bottled-up' state is a deeply problematic denial of the woman's body. For it is in the very breaching of her body's boundaries that she can fulfill her unique capacity for creation. Just as the rains overflow the vessel of the moon and nourish the earth, the woman's waters break to signal

the singular magic of birth; and her breast overflows to nurture the infant. So a virgin is called a closed well, or a 'fountain sealed'.[22]

26 The vessel is the central symbol for the woman as container and protector, giver of birth and source of nourishment.[23] It enters Buddhist symbolism as the monastics' alms-bowl. It features in countless images of the Buddha, and is present in many of our contemporary images of monks and nuns. Each day monastics walk silently through the village collecting food for the day's meal. There is no need to beg or advertise their presence; the empty bowls exert a seemingly magnetic force that calls to be filled. This is the power of the open vessel, a source of limitless abundance each day. In damming up the nuns, this fertility is denied; and the very practical result is that in those Buddhist countries where the alms tradition is mantained it is difficult or impossible for nuns to support themselves through alms. Their source of sustenance is dried up.

27 When she is dammed up, there is drought; when she is unleashed, there is flood. When the Creatrix gives life, there is always a subtext: one day, just maybe, she might not. Demeter is the cause of drought and devastation just as she is of bounty and fruitfulness. Our nine months bathing in the womb leave perhaps the most profound of all unconscious impressions. It is impossible to separate fully the notions of femininity and that of water. And so mythology the world over is replete with sirens, mermaids, naiads, and the like, which are by turns seductive and deadly.[24]

❖

28 This imagery occurs in the Ṛg Veda, with all its exuberance and its penetration to the essential mythic themes. The pre-eminent goddess of the waters was Sarasvatī, she who 'swells with rivers', whose worship was inspired by the rush of life-giving waters from the Himalayas.[25]

29 She with her might, like one who digs for lotus-stems,
has burst with her strong waves the ridges of the hills.
Let us invite with songs and holy hymns for help
Sarasvatī who slays the Paravatas.

30 You cast down, Sarasvatī, those who scorned the Gods,
the brood of every Bṛsaya skilled in illusion (*māyā*).
You have discovered rivers for the tribes of men,
and, rich in wealth! made poison flow away from them.

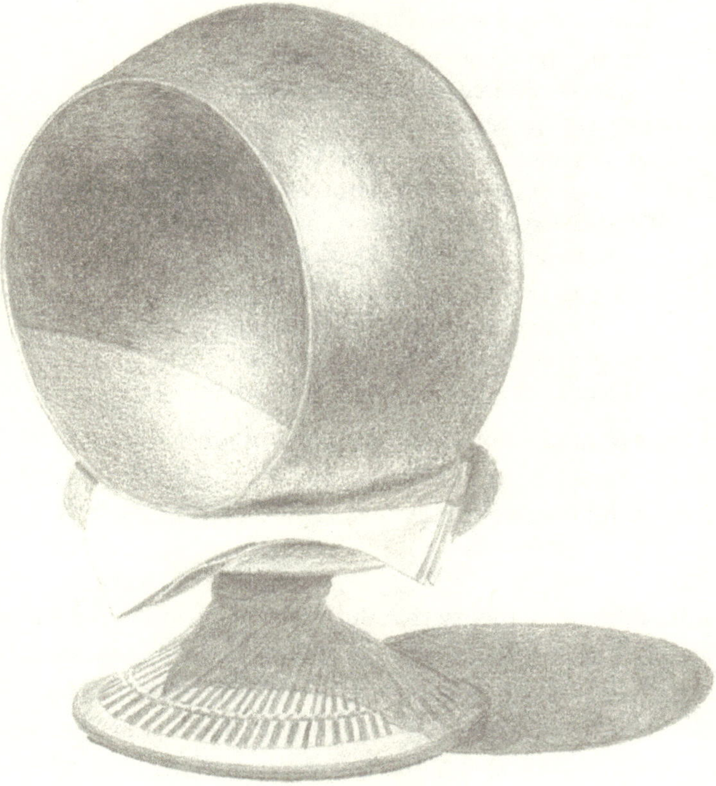

Figure 19.2: *Monastic bowl, Thai style*

31 May the goddess Sarasvatī, rich in her wealth, protect us well,
Furthering all our illumined awareness (*dhī*) with might.

32 Yes, this divine Sarasvatī, terrible,
with her golden path,
Dragon-slayer[26]

33 Whose limitless unbroken flood,
swift-moving with a rapid rush,
Comes onward with tempestuous roar.

34 Yes, she the stream most dear of all,
Seven-sistered, graciously inclined,
Sarasvatī has earned our praise.

35 Marked out by majesty among the Mighty Ones,
in glory swifter than the other rapid Streams,
Created vast for victory like a chariot,
Sarasvatī must be extolled by every sage.

36 Guide us, Sarasvatī, to glorious treasure:
do not refuse us your milk, nor spurn us from you.
Gladly accept our friendship and obedience:
let us not go from you to distant countries.

37 She is the essential, inexhaustible bringer of life, and yet the danger of flood is ever-present. She must be invoked, placated, entreated so her gifts are neither withdrawn nor unleashed in their destructive frenzy.

❖

38 It is this ambiguous quality that defines the powers of the water. And so the creature of the deeps is the Serpent, the formless emanation of the waters, shape-shifter, indefinable and powerful. It lurks hidden in the abyss, allied with the powers of the twilight. As Calasso points out: 'In every story, if you go back, as far back as you can, to the point where every horizon disappears, you find a snake, the tree, water.'[27] She brings tears just as she brings life, for the Aztecs:

39 Our mother, the goddess with the girdle of snakes,
is taking me with her as her child.
I weep.[28]

40 As also for the Egyptians, the Serpent lurks as the fundamental threat to the Being which it has brought forth.

41 And I shall destroy everything I created. The earth will again appear as primordial ocean [*nun*], as endlessness [*hut*], as in the beginning. I am everything that remains ... after I have turned myself back into the snake that no man knows.[29]

42 A fundamental Egyptian myth of the primordial combat tells of the dark, cave-dwelling serpent Apep, who attacks the sun-boat of Ra as it draws near the western horizon. All night long they battle, until Apep is killed by sword, spear, and magic might, dismembered and buried far beneath the earth so that Ra might rise again in triumph at the dawn.[30] In far off America, the Cora Indians told of a mighty snake, the very night itself, who lived in the west of the world. Each morning it is slain by the morning star and devoured by the daytime sky, a great eagle. If this battle is lost, the world would be filled with flood.[31]

43 There is only one ultimate outcome to the dragon fight: the waters must be controlled so that the ordered land may rise above the watery chaos; the serpent must be slain so that limbs and hands might grow; and the tree must sprout in the rotting corpse.

44 And there is only one person who can accomplish this task: the Sky Hero. In India the archetype is Indra, the King of Gods, whose vehicle is the eagle.[32] He slew Vṛtra the Dragon, a famous feat that underlies the entire mythos of the Ṛg Veda. Here is just one version of this battle. In these verses, 'Maghavan' is one of Indra's many epithets, while 'Tvaṣṭar' is the Indic Hephaestus, smith of the gods.[33]

45 I will declare the heroic deeds of Indra,
the first that he achieved, the Thunder-wielder.
He slew the Dragon, then unleashed the waters,
and cleft the channels of the mountain torrents.

46 He slew the Dragon lying on the mountain:
Tvaṣṭar fashioned his heavenly bolt of thunder.
Like lowing cattle descending in rapid flow,
the waters glided downward to the ocean.

47 Impetuous as a bull, he chose the Soma
and in three sacred beakers drank the juices.
Maghavan grasped the thunder for his weapon,
and smote to death this firstborn of the dragons.

48 When, Indra, you have slain the dragon's firstborn,
and overcome the charms (*māyā*) of the enchanters,
Then, giving life to Sun and Dawn and Heaven,
you found not one foe to stand against you.

49 He, like a mad weak warrior, challenged Indra,
the great impetuous many-slaying Hero.
Not able to endure the clashing of the weapons,
Indra's foe crushed the shattered forts in falling.

50 There as he lies like a bank-bursting river,
the waters taking courage flow above him.
The Dragon lies beneath the feet of torrents
which Vṛtra with his greatness had encompassed.

51 Then the strength of Vṛtra's mother was humbled:
Indra has cast his deadly bolt against her.
The mother was above, the son was under
and like a cow beside her calf lay Danu.

52 Rolled in the midst of never-ceasing currents
flowing without a rest for ever onward.
The waters bear off Vṛtra's nameless body:
the foe of Indra sank to enduring darkness.

53 Guarded by the Dragon stood the thralls of Dāsas,
the waters captured like cattle held by the robber.
But he, when he had smitten Vṛtra,
opened the cave where the floods had been imprisoned.

54 A horse's tail were you when he, O Indra,
smote on your thunderbolt; you, God without a second,
You have won back the cattle, have won the Soma;
you have let loose to flow the Seven Rivers.

55 Neither lightning, thunder, hailstorm, or mist
which had spread around him could help him:
When Indra and the Dragon strove in battle,
Maghavan gained the victory for ever.

56 Who did you see to avenge the Dragon, Indra,
that fear possessed your heart when you had slain him;
That, like a hawk frightened through the regions,
you crossed nine-and-ninety flowing rivers?[34]

57 In this primal form of the myth, the victory was one of un-damming the waters, freeing them from their rocky homes. The rivers are sent 'like

cattle' down to the fertile plains. But whether the waters are to be freed or locked up, the essential issue remains the same: the control must be wrested out of the feminine and given to the hands of the thunderbolt-wielding, sky-flying male.

58 In this telling, of course, Vṛtra the Dragon is a man, not a woman. However this does not change the essence of the conflict. It is, rather, an example of what Jung calls 'secondary personalization'. Vṛtra, the cosmic Serpent, is personified as male, and so the explicit narrative is a contest between two men. But Vṛtra, for all his pretended might, in the end is just a Mother's boy; and so Indra kills Vṛtra the serpent, then dispatches his mother Danu. They die lying together, becoming one again, just as when he lay in her womb. This is confirmed in the following retelling, where, while the surface of the narrative tells us that Vṛtra is male, the imagery—the emptied bag, the Soma-moon with its swelling belly—is that of the woman's body. Such tensions between the conscious and unconscious are no oversight: for those with eyes to see, they are the key to unlocking the depths.

> 59 Now [the Serpent] Vṛtra, on being struck [by Indra's thunderbolt], lay contracted like a leather bottle drained of its contents, like a skin bag with the barley-meal shaken out. Indra rushed at him, meaning to slay him.
>
> 60 He said, 'Do not hurl (your thunderbolt) at me! You are now what I (was before). Only cut me in two; but do not let me be annihilated!'
>
> 61 Indra said, 'You shall be my food!'
>
> 62 He replied, 'So be it!'
>
> 63 Indra accordingly cut Vṛtra in two; and from that (part) of his which was of the Soma nature, he made the moon. And that which was demoniacal (*asurya*) he made enter these creatures as their belly. Hence people say, 'Vṛtra was then a consumer of food, and Vṛtra is so now.' For even now, whenever that one (the moon) waxes fuller, it fills itself out of this world; and whenever these creatures crave for food, they pay tribute to this Vṛtra, the belly. Whosoever knows that Vṛtra as a consumer of food, becomes himself a consumer of food.[35]

64 Killed-but-not-killed, the mysterious destiny of the sacrificed. Vṛtra feeds our belly's needs, but is also the ambrosial Soma, secret nectar of immortality. He completes the circle: for Indra gained his power to defeat

Vṛtra only by consuming that same Soma (just as Tvaṣṭar created Indra's weapon, the *vajra* or thunderbolt, but he also created Vṛtra himself, as revenge for a former killing by Indra.[36]) Despite his ignominious defeat, Vṛtra retains the power to bargain with Indra, and comes to an agreement, or covenant (*saññā*), just as the Hebrew flood story ends with a covenant. He willingly gives up his personal existence to assume his cosmic destiny, which is 'proven' by the undeniable fact that the belly, swelling with the 'offerings' of food, imitates the waxing moon. In essence, then, Vṛtra is no malignant demon but the source of bounty.

65 Again and again the Vedas retell this primeval conflict, as the freeing of the waters or the sundering of the rocky cavern to reveal the treasure within, which might be the sparks of fire from the flint, or the metal burnt from ore, or the sun rising from the earth, or the summer born of winter. Vṛtra, the 'Constrictor' is the undivided, the unawakened (*abudhyam*), sunk in deepest sleep. His opposition to awakening is remembered in the Buddhist 'hindrances' (*nīvaraṇas*), from the same root and equally on the side of darkness. Vṛtra obscures the world-mountain,[37] preventing the cattle from running free or the rivers from flowing.[38] Vṛtra is defeated by the thunderbolt; but this is no mere meteorological allegory, for he may also be defeated by prayer, the divine words of knowledge.[39] Mounting the radiant chariot of truth,[40] the thunderbolt is sharpened by insight.[41] And while in a cosmic sense the victory is eternal,[42] it must be repeated by each of us if we are to attain the radiance of the heavens.[43]

❖

66 The story of the control of the waters by the male continued in the Śaivite myths. When the mighty Gaṅgā descended from the heavens onto Śiva's head, she thought: 'I will carry Śiva into the underworld with the force of my streams!' But Śiva knew her thoughts, and in a rage decided to make her disappear, lost among his endless dreadlocks. As a triumphant hero, Śiva may not be dragged back down into the 'underworld': he represses the unconscious forces, but only as long as he wishes. Later he releases them, sanctified and full of vitality, so that they might flow over the whole earth bringing life.[44]

67 From her descend in streams the seas of water;
Thereby the world's four regions have their being,
Thence flows the imperishable flood,
And thence the universe has life.[45]

68 The conflict, terrible as it is, results in fruitfulness and bounty. Such stories embrace the complexities and ambiguities of existence, not whitewashing life's pain, nor sinking into hopelessness and cynicism. But they also make available a wealth of imagery which can be stolen by shallower storytellers and used for less benign purposes.

CHAPTER 20

THE SERPENT

INDIAN LITERATURE ENJOYS DENIGRATING WOMEN, and likening them to snakes works splendidly.[1] In Indic imagination, the snake lurks in the dark and the wilds, malignant, slimy, and venomous, master of shape-shifting.[2] Like a woman.

2 A snake is also the bearer of poison, which is a concentrated form of the pollution that leaks death from womens' bodies. And so women are often depicted as dealing death by poison.[3]

3 Similarly, the notion that women 'poison' by means of their gossip and unrestrained tongues is widespread. In folklore women's seductive words of honeyed poison cause mischief, debasing language itself.[4] The words of women pollute culture just as their fluids pollute the body.

4 The woman, as objectified gender, is identified with the primitive sensuality of the animal. The closer we are in our own minds to that state, the more we will fear it and attack it. A text in the Aṅguttara Nikāya depicts the Buddha declaring that women are 'utterly a snare of Māra', and that it would be better to associate with a demon or a deadly snake than to converse alone with a woman.[5] Another text has the Buddha declare five ways that women are like black snakes.[6]

> 5 Monks, there are these five dangers of a black snake. What five? It is filthy, stinking, cowardly, terrifying, and betrays friends.
>
> 6 Just so, monks, there are five dangers of a woman. What five? She is filthy, stinking, cowardly, terrifying, and betrays friends.

7 And a variation on the theme:

8 Monks, there are these five dangers of a black snake. What five? It is aggressive, bears grudges, has terrible poison, is fork-tongued, and betrays friends.

9 Just so, monks, there are five dangers of a woman. What five? She is aggressive, bears grudges, has terrible poison, is fork-tongued, and betrays friends. Herein, monks, a woman's terrible poison is this—generally, a woman has keen lust. A woman's forked tongue is this—generally, a woman uses back-biting speech. A woman's betrayal of friends is this—generally, a woman commits adultery.[7]

10 This is the all-wise, all-compassionate Buddha speaking, the spiritual exemplar of humankind, the World Teacher? After breaking open the very bounds of reality, his profound insight into the utterness of Truth revealed—what?—that the cruel, unthinking prejudices of his fellow men are right after all? My faith falters before this leap.

11 These passages we have quoted, while they should not be ignored, are very rare and unusual, found within a massive corpus of thousands of texts. Most Suttas present positive and negative qualities of women and men in balanced terms.[8] And the passages that do talk about the differences between men and women almost exclusively refer to social roles, which is just where cultural influences have the greatest influence. In the few places where gender is addressed in the context of higher spiritual development, it is emphatically denied that it makes any difference.[9] Given the balance and reasonable approach shown by the Buddha on countless occasions, it is both disrespectful and implausible to assume without examination that he could have said such hurtful, unkind things.

12 The usual justification for such passages is that they aim to detach the celibate monks from their sexual desires. But the imagery of the snake is clearly intended to evoke fear, disgust, and aversion. In Buddhist psychology, these emotions are not the opposite of lust, but its partners. After all, who do we get angriest at—a stranger or a family member? The suttas typically encourage detachment in much gentler terms: a monk is taught to be like the moon, or like the lotus to which water doesn't cling, or aloof like the wild deer. To deal with sexual desire, the Bhāradvāja Sutta suggests that a monk think of younger women as a daughter, older women as a mother, and women of the same age as a sister.[10]

13 So the Black Snake Suttas are not typical of early Buddhist attitudes to women. But are they *true*? Perhaps they stem from the Buddha's insight into the reality of femininity, which we are simply too blind to see. If so, then the texts should be amenable to empirical study. As Buddhists, we are proud when modern psychological studies confirm the benefits of Buddhist meditation. Are we ready to face the evidence when it comes to other things found in our sacred texts? Of course it is probably impossible to find clear cut answers to these things, but at least we should follow the Buddha's advice and try. Let's take each of these qualities in turn and examine them in the light of research.

14 **Aggression.** Behaviorally, men are generally more aggressive than women and are responsible for far more physical violence. However, a few studies go against this conclusion, suggesting that there may be little or no innate gender difference in aggression.[11]

15 **Holding grudges.** I haven't found any studies dealing with this. As a little survey, then, let's consider a discussion thread on a social anxiety support website. Men and women alike share their experiences, and it seems pretty much balanced: both men and women sometimes have problems bearing grudges, sometimes not.[12] More importantly, some men and women show a reflective capacity to understand the problem and move on—and some don't.

16 **Sexual Lust.** A detailed study of research findings concluded that: 'All the evidence we have reviewed points toward the conclusion that men desire sex more than women... We did not find a single study, on any of nearly a dozen different measures, that found women had a stronger sex drive than men.'[13]

17 **Backbiting.** Studies show little gendered difference in the quantity or ethical quality of gossip.[14] One study concludes that 'women spent more time gossiping than men and that women were much more likely than men to gossip about close friends and family members. However, no significant sex differences were uncovered regarding the derogatory tone of gossip and men and women were found to gossip about many of the same topics.'[15] What may be relevant, however, is that some studies claim that, while there is little overall difference in aggression between men and women, men tend to express aggression physically while women

do so verbally.[16] This could give rise to the impression that women love back-biting.

18 **Adultery.** Studies consistently put men in the lead.[17] Sources quoted on a men's rights website say that 45–55% of married women and 50–60% of married men engage in extramarital sex at some time during their relationship.[18] The same site quotes research that 86% of men and 81% of women admit they routinely flirt, while 75% of men and 65% of women admit to having sex with people they work with.

19 This little survey yields the admittedly unspectacular conclusion that the stereotypes stated so boldly in the Black Snake Suttas are unfounded. At the very least, they do not stand up as a universal and verifiable truth, such as we expect from the Buddha's teachings. So, did the Buddha get it wrong? Are we justified in thinking that, despite his undeniable insight in so many other areas, the Buddha fell back on conventional bias when it comes to gender?

20 This is one case where text-critical work saves the day, like a knight riding on his white horse to save the maiden. Anālayo discusses the Bahudhātuka Sutta, where it is said that a woman can never become a Buddha.[19] This makes some sense within the context of Indian society at the time, since it would be difficult for a female Buddha to be accepted as the teacher of all strata of society. A parallel statement claims that the Buddha must be born in the highest class of society, presumably for the same reason. Nevertheless these are curious things to say—what use could they be? The Buddha taught that words should be beneficial, leading to the goal, pleasing to the ear, concerning the Dhamma and Vinaya, reconciling those who are divided; but these words fulfill none of these standards. However, while several versions of this text contain such a statement, one variant, in the Sarvāstivādin Madhyama Āgama, does not mention this or other statements about women at all, raising the question as to whether these were all later additions to the text.[20]

21 Anālayo suggests that the tendency to discriminate against women becomes more pronounced in the Aṅguttara Nikāya, citing, in addition to the Black Snake Suttas, a passage saying that women never tire of sex and giving birth.[21] The Kamboja Sutta arguably exceeds all of these in its misogyny. It not only repeats the claims the women are angry, envious, greedy,

and stupid, but the Buddha, in response to a question by Ānanda, uses these traits to justify social injustice. It is because of these bad qualities that women do not take part in political or judicial proceedings, undertake business, or travel to foreign lands.[22]

22 Anālayo points out that these Pali discourses do not have as much as a single counterpart in all the Chinese Āgamas. Moreover, the Suttas elsewhere speak in praise of fully Awakened bhikkhunis such as Dhammadinnā and Khemā,[23] or wise, devoted lay women such as Visākhā or Sāmāvatī who had reached various stages of Awakening.[24] These were not isolated cases; the Buddha said that many hundreds of his female disciples had reached spiritual heights up to arahantship.[25] Given these frequent cases of women of extraordinary wisdom and spiritual development, it is absurd to think the Buddha would make such unthinking, blanket condemnations of womankind as are attributed to him in the Aṅguttara Nikāya. This negative attitude to women in the Pali Aṅguttara Nikāya appears, according to Anālayo, to have also influenced the account of the formation of the bhikkhuni order.[26]

23 Anālayo's method is sound: he relies on comparative textual studies, together with the criterion of internal consistency, both of which point to the same result. If these criteria are accepted, it is hard to escape the inference that these texts are later additions.

24 Yet the problem is not so clear cut. We have already encountered cases where the women in the story warn of the wickedness of women. Such apparent contradictions frequently appear even in the same short text. The *Rāmāyaṇa*, for example, exalts Sītā as the ideal wife, and constantly praises her virtue, gentleness, loyalty, and so on. Yet in the next breath it speaks of the 'essential nature of women' as fickle, cruel, and treacherous, a nature even Sītā cannot fully escape.[27]

25 Indeed, contradiction is our trusty companion in Indian literature. We hear, for example, of the city that is impregnable and invincible, so that the attacking warriors tremble in fear; yet they too are invincible and allmighty and attack without fear. Many are the gods who are 'like Brahmā', while Brahmā himself is 'without compare'. This contradiction is also found in Buddhism, for Sāriputta is the disciple who is 'like the Teacher',

yet the Buddha is 'without a counterpart'. The Indic mind is simply less concerned with contradiction than the European.

26 Not to speak of mythology, this is true even in the sphere of logic. For Aristotle, any proposition was either true (A) or false (not-A). It's either day or it's night. Nice, clear cut, as definite as the outlines on a Greek vase. But the Indians had a four-fold scheme: A; not-A; A & not-A; neither A nor not-A. Just trying to think about it, our head starts to curl, our world becomes populated by ambiguous creatures that belong neither to the day nor the night...

27 We would like to believe that the Buddha was more rational than this, and he often obliges us. I agree that the inconsistency in how women are presented is likely just common-or-garden variety misogyny sneaking in the back door of the Buddhist texts. But consistency is a hard thing to measure, and what is true in the daytime may become something else in the twilight.

28 There is a genuine diversity of attitudes towards women in the early texts. Everyone agrees on this, but the question is, where does this diversity arise from, and what does it mean? Sponberg has studied the topic, and suggests two sources of diversity in attitudes: ambivalence and multivocality. Ambivalence suggests that there is one speaker, who has conflicting or unresolved attitudes towards women. Sponberg prefers to think in terms of a 'rich multivocality', different voices recording different attitudes. I would suggest that, as well as these options, we can locate the diversity not in the subject, but in the object. Femininity itself is diverse, and a diversity of responses is entirely appropriate.

❖

29 In likening women to the black snake, men have revealed much of themselves and little of women. Yet their chosen symbol, while readable as simple chauvinism, is more suitable than they themselves suspected, for the snake, far from being all-black, is ambiguity embodied; shapeless and hence susceptible of forming any shape—the line, the circle, the spiral, the wave—the snake is a matchless analogue for the formless woman's body, and yet retains its phallic associations.[28]

30 The serpent coils at the very roots of human civilization, and is already present in ancient Sumer and far-off Egypt. The serpent rising up beside

the yogi is depicted in the Indus Valley Civilization. Obviously it is there that we must look for the roots of the Hindu yogic teaching of *kuṇḍalinī*, the psychic energy depicted as a serpent that, rooted at the base of the spine, rises and falls in a series of seven coils. While this doctrine must derive from ancient roots, it is one of those curiousities of Indian history that this specific image occurs in a Buddhist text long before any Hindu texts. For it is the image of the *nāga* king Muñcalinda rising in seven coils around the triumphant Buddha as he meditates after Awakening.

31 With its miraculous ability to shed its skin and be reborn, the snake is more than a metaphor for reincarnation: it shows us how to shed our skin *in this very life*. Sex, death, dirt, power, danger, the formless abyss, the capacity for transcendence; there is hardly an idea that cannot be read into the snake, imposed on a common animal who really just wants to get on with catching that frog.

32 The Jātakas tell how the serpent became, not the embodiment of poisonous death, but the voice of redemption.[29] This could only happen in the moment of deepest despair, when the very survival of their species was under threat. The sky-bird of fire, the Garuḍa, loved to eat the earth & water dwelling Nāga serpent. The Nāgas would cling to a tree for safety, but sometimes the Garuḍa even ripped the whole tree out of the ground.[30] The Nāgas had only one defense: eat rocks. Then they're too heavy for the Garuḍas to lift. But the Garuḍa king found out their secret. He grabbed the Nāga king by the tail so that the rocks tumbled out of his open mouth. All seemed lost, until the Nāga appealed to the Garuḍa to show him the same love that a mother has for her child. And that is how there came to be peace between these ancient enemies.

CHAPTER 21

THE DEEPEST TABOO

DEATH IS BLOOD, THE JUICE OF LIFE FLOWING OUT and leaving only a dried-up husk. All the world over, this association manifests as a taboo on menstruation, one of humanity's deepest secrets.[1] It is passed down through millennia; the underlying fears remain, while the surface forms adapt to suit time and place. Advertisers get it: to show how effective the latest 'sanitary product' is, they pour *blue* liquid on it.

2 To get in the mood, let's have a few of Frazer's examples of menstruation taboos. Before reading (and judging) these examples, remember that anthropologists since Frazer's day have come a long way in understanding such apparently irrational customs.[2] Through modern eyes, they are cruel and unjust. However, within the original culture they frequently have a more balanced effect. For example, the sequestering of women during their menses appears like a form of imprisonment; but it may be a welcome relief from backbreaking labor. What is disturbing is not that we find what are, to us, inexplicable taboos within indigenous societies, but that such taboos persist today long after any possible reason has been left behind.

> 3 Thus, in the Encounter Bay tribe of South Australia, there is, or used to be, a 'superstition which obliges a woman to separate herself from her camp at the time of her monthly illness, when, if a young man or boy should approach, she calls out, and he immediately makes a circuit to avoid her. If she is neglectful on this point, she exposes herself to severe beating by her husband or nearest relation, because

> the boys are told from their infancy that if they see the blood they will early become grey-headed, and their strength will fail prematurely'. The Dieri of Central Australia believe that if women at these times were to eat fish or to bathe in a river the fish would all die and the water would dry up. The Arunta of the same region forbid menstruous women to gather the *irriakura* bulbs, which form a staple article of diet for both men and women. They think that were a woman to break this rule, the supply of bulbs would fail....
>
> 4 ... 'There is a regulation relating to camps in the Wakelbura tribe which forbids the women coming into the encampment by the same path as the men. Any violation of this rule would in a large camp be punished with death. The reason for this is the dread with which they regard the menstrual period of women. During such a time, a woman is kept entirely away from the camp, half a mile at least. A woman in such a condition has boughs of some tree of her totem tied round her loins, and is constantly watched and guarded, for it is thought that should any male be so unfortunate as to see a woman in such a condition, he would die....
>
> 5 In Muralug, one of the Torres Straits islands, a menstruous woman may not eat anything that lives in the sea, else the natives believe that the fisheries would fail. In Galela, to the west of New Guinea, women at their monthly periods may not enter a tobacco-field, or the plants would be attacked by disease. The Minangkabauers of Sumatra are persuaded that if a woman in her unclean state were to go near a rice-field the crop would be spoiled....
>
> 6 Amongst the civilized nations of Europe the superstitions which cluster round this mysterious aspect of woman's nature are not less extravagant than those which prevail among savages. In the oldest existing cyclopedia—the Natural History of Pliny—the list of dangers apprehended from menstruation is longer than any furnished by mere barbarians.[3]

7 Frazer continues by summarizing the statement of Pliny, but I think it's worth reading in full:

> 8 Contact with the monthly flux of women turns new wine sour, makes crops wither, kills grafts, dries seeds in gardens, causes the fruit of trees to fall off, dims the bright surface of mirrors, dulls the edge of steel and the gleam of ivory, kills bees, rusts iron and bronze, and causes a horrible smell to fill the air. Dogs who taste the blood become mad, and their bite becomes poisonous as in rabies. The Dead

> Sea, thick with salt, cannot be drawn asunder except by a thread soaked in the poisonous fluid of the menstruous blood. A thread from an infected dress is sufficient. Linen, touched by the woman while boiling and washing it in water, turns black. So magical is the power of women during their monthly periods that they say that hailstorms and whirlwinds are driven away if menstrual fluid is exposed to the flashes of lightning.[4]

9 Frazer details a vast array of similar beliefs, which are found all over the world.

10 The parallels with the story of Mahāpajāpatī are clear and strong. Women are to be feared because of their 'outflows'. Men are not to look at them.[5] Women must be isolated, kept outside the community. The sight or touch of them would bring decay and death to the men. And if they were to enter a field, they would bring with them a ruinous disease.

11 In Christianity, while there was debate and variation among the traditions, menstrual taboos clearly formed an obstacle for women. The medieval theologian Paucapalea asserted that:

> 12 Women are not allowed to visit a church during menstruation or after the birth of a child. For a woman is an animal that menstruates. Through touching her blood fruits will fail to get ripe. Mustard degenerates, grass dries up and trees lose their fruit before time. Iron gets rusted and the air becomes dark. When dogs eat it, they acquire rabies.[6]

13 In early modern Europe there are cases that are strikingly reminiscent of Mahāpajāpatī and the Śākyan women standing outside the monastery gates. The parish records of Deckenpfronn, a German village in the Black Forest, recorded in 1684 that menstruating women 'lingered outside the church door and do not go in, but stand there as though in the pillory.'[7]

14 We tend to be a little conceited in our thinking about Buddhism, and believe that such superstitions have been left behind. And this is true as far as the orthodox teachings are concerned—there are no taboos against menstruation in the early Buddhist texts. The Vinaya discusses menstruation in its usual rational tone. A problem arose when bhikkhunis who were menstruating sat on seats and they were soiled with blood. An allowance was made for a cloth, and the usual kinds of adjustments and extensions

were made as the rule evolved.[8] The problem was simple hygiene, and no hint of taboo or fear of magic power is present.

15 But deep fears are not so easily overcome. A little googling reveals plenty of menstruation taboos in modern Buddhist cultures. In the next few pages I quote some examples, some from nuns, some from academics, others from random blog entries.

THAILAND

16 > Many temples do not allow women to circumnambulate around the stupas. There is clear evidence of it particularly in the north of Thailand. This practice cannot find any support in the actual Buddhist teaching but is commonly believed and handed down as custom. This belief in fact found its root in Hinduism[9] where women are seen as religiously unclean because of their menstruation. Taking an opposite standpoint, one could say that women possess natural power. They are capable of nullifying sacred mantras long practiced by Hindu men and priests. Because of this, Brahmin priests had to keep women outside their sacred sanctuary. Men, with their superior position in society, must control women who possess the natural power and declare them unclean during the menstruation period. This practice and belief is carried into Thai custom unknowingly. Just to give an example, while fermenting rice, menstruating women are not allowed near the area or the rice will be spoilt. They believe that menstruation holds secret power that can actually overcome magical spell. This is all Hindu belief and practice carried over into Thai culture and most Thais would think that prohibiting menstruating women is correct Buddhist practice, but is far from it.[10]

17 > For me personally, it's hard to understand the cruelty coming from many Thai Buddhist monks when it comes to the female body. Such men who cling to the belief that women are impure because of their menstruation and thereby impose unfair restrictions on them, I've concluded, must be doing so either out of insecurity or out of stupidity, or both.[11]

JAPAN

18 > The title of this article [A Mirror for Women?] is taken from a popular religious tract written in 1300 by Muju Ichien, a Rinzai Zen monk....

19 ... Muju accepted the belief, prevalent in popular Buddhism of the time that women were by nature unclean. This understanding has significant implications for women's spiritual practice because of the great emphasis placed upon ritual purity in Japanese religion, both Buddhist and Shinto. Since women were at all times unclean, it was not possible for them to enter the holiest parts of monastery or temple compounds, or in extreme cases, to even set foot on the mountains where these retreats were built. More importantly, according to the Menstruation Sutra (Ketsubon kyo), which was widely read in Japan from the time of Muju until the end of the nineteenth century, every time a woman bled, she polluted the ground and the waters that were used to make offerings to the Buddhas and severely offended them. As a result she was constantly accruing negative karma, the result of which was rebirth in the 'Bloodpond Hell'.[12]

20 This is a startling claim and is clearly in conflict with fundamental Mahāyāna principles such as emptiness and non-duality. How can a woman's body be 'inherently' defiling? This paradox was addressed by certain male exegetes of this sutra such as the author of the early 19th century work, 'Random Stories about the Buddhist Ceremonies—The Origin and Transmission of the Ketsubon kyo', who reasoned that:

21 'Because they were born as women, their aspirations to Buddhahood are weak, and their jealousy and evil character are strong. These sins compounded become menstrual blood, which flows in two streams each month, polluting not only the earth god but all the other deities as well.' (cited in TAKEMI 1983:235)

22 In this analysis of women's 'sins', their lack of spiritual aspiration, jealousy and evil nature are the volitional characteristics that result in negative karmic effects or *saṁskāras*. Women's menstrual blood is here not seen so much as a symbol of these negative volitions but a physical effect of them just as obesity might be the result of greed. Despite the fact that this position can be undermined using basic Mahāyāna principles, it does not seem to have been criticized by Buddhist teachers in any systematic way. Indeed, the 'defilement' of women became the paradigmatic Japanese Buddhist view.[13]

TIBET

23 [Ven Tenzin] Palmo strongly identified with Buddhism after reading her first book on the subject at the age of eighteen. At the age of twenty, she left England for India to join a Buddhist monastery where she soon found her spiritual mentor, or Lama, Kantral Rinpoche. She

was the only woman among hundreds of men and realized that males dominated the spiritual tradition in Tibet. Women were forbidden to participate in certain Tibetan Buddhist traditions and rituals as they were considered subordinate to men. Based on a myth, women were considered unclean due to menstruation and were prohibited from holy places and ceremonies. These restrictions, as Palmo elaborates, had been practiced for centuries despite being in stark contrast to the true teachings of the Buddha who is considered to be the first spiritual leader to emphasize the importance of women in society, and stress the equality of spiritual liberation in the female form.[14]

MYANMAR

24 I faced a similar encounter when I accompanied some Westerners to the Inle Phaung-daw Oo Pagoda. Women are not allowed to enter the close quarters of the five Buddha images. The foreign ladies asked me why it was so. When I replied carelessly, 'It's because we are the weaker sex', the ladies exclaimed, 'Weaker sex!' wide-eyed. So there! I had to say some comforting words to them. I said, 'Now, now. Please don't feel dejected. We can venerate it from a close distance, as it is only a small surrounding, to our satisfaction. I understand how I would feel if I were in your shoes. Women are referred to as the weaker sex, only because of their femininity. They are not regarded as inferior to men. Women have to undergo natural suffering like menstruation, pregnancy, and giving birth. That is why it is considered not proper for women to climb up, or tread on some places where Buddha's relics are enshrined.' On hearing this, the ladies looked convinced but they asked, 'What happens if some women disobey?' I replied, 'Well, I haven't seen it with own eyes but I have learnt about sudden occurrence of storms, earthquakes, and disasters when women go there.'[15]

SRI LANKA

25 With some *kems* [spells], women are prohibited from entering the field altogether, while other kems have to be performed by women only or even by pregnant women only. The effectiveness of a *kem* can be nullified if the person is exposed to a *killa* or impurity caused by eating certain food (especially meat). Attending a funeral also causes impurities. Another major impurity is associated with women's menstruation.[16]

> 26 She should not frequent religious places and temples during her menses, nor attend religious ceremonies. During menstruation, farm women in the North Central Province have to ritually purify themselves before starting work in the field. Moreover women are never allowed to touch the threshing floor, as their uncleanliness might seriously reduce the yield. In contrast men are not in any way unclean during their lives.[17]

27 It is easy to find examples of menstruation taboos in most Buddhist countries today. These are just the same as those in other religions. The rationalizing tendency of Buddhist thought, it would seem, is far less influential in Buddhist lands than we like to imagine.

❖

28 Given that menstrual taboos are common in Buddhist countries, it is inevitable that such beliefs play a role in the treatment of Buddhist nuns. While the nature of the topic makes it difficult to document, I have heard of women objecting to bhikkhunis, as they might bleed on the robe. Bhikkhuni Dhammanandā reports that menstruation taboos have been invoked to prevent bhikkhuni ordination in Thailand:

> 29 When Ven. Bhikkhuni Voramai Kabilsingh was fully ordained in the 1970s, people who were unhappy with her ordination blamed her and suspected that she would soil the robe (with menstruation) and hence make the sacred robe unclean. The association of menstruation to impurity has no place in Buddhist belief and practice. Menstruation is only a monthly flow of blood for women who are in fertile age. Should the robe get soiled, it needs to be washed. Unlike Hinduism, there is neither stigma nor taboo around menstruation in Buddhism.[18]

30 In the bright light of consciousness, ancient taboos lose their power and become a mere sanitation issue. This is the position, as we have seen, of the Vinaya, and it is certainly the position of modernist Buddhism. But the beliefs and practices of the Buddhist community are rife with taboo. And such things are not just a quaint folk belief, like kissing under the mistletoe. In all seriousness, the hero may be instantly disempowered by a woman's blood.

31 This is a popular theme in Northern Thai literature. Queen Cāmdevī was a culture heroine who battled barbarian tribes led by an apparently invin-

cible warrior-chief. She could only win by means of a trick. She offered the chieftain a hat; little did he know that she had daubed the hat with her menstrual blood. As soon as the chieftain placed the hat on his head, his fighting prowess was lost forever.[19] The politics of menstruation are alive and kicking in Thailand today. In 2008, the ultra-modern Suvarnabhumi airport was taken over by the People's Alliance for Democracy (PAD). Their leader Sondhi Limthongkul boasted how he used magic to counteract the evil powers who had attacked the source of Thailand's security as embodied in certain national monuments.[20] He said that 'The [base of the] Equestrian Statue is like this [draws hexagon with his hands] with the statue inside. Tacks had been inserted at the six corners so that the statue of the revered king could not emit its power.[21] We drew out the tacks from all six places.' He went on to describe the means used by the masters of magic to prevent such nefarious attacks in the future.

> 32 'I must thank the women of the PAD because after [the tacks] were pulled out, to ensure they would not be replaced, they took sanitary napkins from menstruating women and placed them on the six points.[22] Experts said the spirit adepts were furious because they couldn't send their spirits back; their magic was rendered ineffective.'

33 The struggle for the political control of a large modern nation was carried out using the power of the most ancient taboo, menstrual blood. Chang Noi, writing in the Thai newspaper *The Nation*, correctly sees this act, not as an eccentric aberration, but as inherent in patriarchy.

> 34 Ideas about the fearful power of female sexuality are fundamental to a structure of male supremacy. In both Buddhism and supernaturalism, males are privileged in acquiring superior spiritual status. Only men can become Buddhist monks. Only men can draw *yantra* diagrams, activate amulets, utter incantations and use all the other techniques of *saiyasat* [magic].
>
> 35 But female sexuality poses a terrifying threat to these powers. Thus monks have to remain celibate and avoid contact with women. Serious adherents of *saiyasat* also practice celibacy. Casual users remove their amulets before lovemaking to prevent their efficacy from getting annulled.
>
> 36 Menstrual blood is the most powerful symbol of this terrible, destructive power. There are rules and conventions about avoiding contact with this fearful force. In the past there were many restrictions

> involving women's underwear. But Sondhi is possibly breaking new ground by making active use of this substance as a weapon.[23]

37 Monks are the quintessential spiritual heroes of Buddhism, and their power, though great, may be destroyed as easily as that of a great warrior or an evil political force, as observed by Terwiel in central Thailand.

> 38 Women are associated with a type of magical power which is believed to be diametrically opposed to that of the monks because of the feminine capacity to menstruate. Menstrual blood is considered highly charged with dangerous magical power and even a casual contact may destroy some of the beneficial force of members of the Sangha.[24]

39 The taboo on menstruation *per se* is a part of a much wider set of taboos that govern the relationship between monks and women. In the Vinaya, for example, there is no prohibition for a monk to touch a woman. The offence falls if a monk sexually gropes a woman, with 'mind perverted by lust'.[25] This protects women from sexual harassment in the monastery, a place where they should be free of fear. But in some Buddhist countries the very idea of a monk touching a woman, even brushing her hand by accident, is viewed with horror.

40 This goes so far that in Thailand monks have to use a 'receiving cloth' when accepting offerings from a woman. We have already seen how this practice makes literal the idea of the 'insulating horse' that isolates the sacred from the profane. The use of the 'receiving cloth', unknown in the Vinaya or any other Buddhist land, is sternly insisted upon. It is certainly a convenient way for monks to be able to accept gifts from women while remaining ritually isolated from their impurity. Even bhikkhus from other Theravāda countries regard this practice with disdain; K. Sri Dhammananda, the late Chief Monk of Malaysia, told me the use of the receiving cloth was a 'Brahmanical' custom.

41 Once again, there is a Christian parallel to the Thai 'receiving cloth'. Here are some rules that were decided at a diocesan synod in Auxerre, France, in 585 or 588 CE:

> 42 Canon 36. 'No woman may receive the holy eucharist with bare hands.'
>
> 43 Canon 37. 'Also she may not touch the pall.'

44 Canon 42. 'Every woman must have her *dominicale* (= a linen cloth to cover her hand) at communion.'[26]

45 Similarly, in some Buddhist regions, women are forbidden to touch a Buddha image, even to clean it. They may also not touch a monk's requisites, such as his bowl. None of these customs have anything to do with the Vinaya, nor with a rational practice of sense restraint. They are taboos, plain and simple.

❖

46 In Christianity, while some of the acts of Jesus are read as challenging the received notion of the polluting nature of menstruation, menstrual taboos are a decisive factor in the continued opposition to women's ordination. The Encyclopedia of Religion states that menstrual taboo is still influential in disqualifying women from ordination. In the Orthodox and Catholic Churches especially, it is still the belief, even if rarely stated, that the presence of women's blood pollutes that sacred altar.[27] The 12th century Greek Orthodox patriarch Theodore of Balsamon wrote: 'The order of deaconesses was once known and had access to the altar. In consequence of their monthly pollution, however, their order was ousted from the ritual domain and the sacred altar.'[28]

47 Although the link between menstruation and holding holy office is usually not made explicit, the logic is straightforward. Many of the Church Fathers and other leaders of Church believed that menstruation made women ritually unclean. This resulted in a wide variety of taboos on women: they were not allowed to approach the altar, touch the sacred cloth or vessels on the altar, or even enter the church during menstruation or after childbirth. How then could they possibly ordain and preside over the Eucharist at the altar itself?[29]

48 In just the same way, in Buddhist cultures that refuse to let a woman approach a shrine, or clean a Buddha image, or wear a sacred amulet, or take part in rituals, or offer food directly into a monk's hand, how can she presume to put on the yellow robe and enter the holy Sangha?[30]

❖

49 The menstruation taboo, like all magical conceptions, is by no means unambiguous. Although condemned as 'impurity', menstruation is a vivid

reminder of woman's creative power, a power that no man can ever share. In the famous dreams of King Pasenadi, trees sprout from the ground and bear flowers and fruit, which the Buddha identifies with the menses and children of young girls.[31] The initiation rites by which girls become women are blood-transformation mysteries. The long periods of confinement and other drastic measures are a sign of the unfathomable power of the creative energies she is manifesting, a power that cannot fail to evoke awe in men.[32]

50 In tantric practice, the menses is adopted, precisely because of its magical taboo power, as a potent force for spiritual transformation. The Hindu Mātrikabheda Tantra lists five kinds of 'auspicious menses', and many of the Kaula tantras treat the ritual consumption of mixed menses and semen as the source of the highest blessing.[33]

❖

51 Perhaps the deepest of all magic is a woman's ability to bleed each month, in mysterious sympathy with the moon, and yet not die. While she is with child she does not bleed, but she magically produces a new person, as if curdled from her own blood. The traditional Buddhist view was that the embryo arose with the fusion of the father's semen and the mother's blood (the ovum is of course a modern discovery).[34] Neumann suggests that menstruation taboos originated among women as an expression of their creative power, and became the paradigm for all taboo.[35]

52 A recent paper goes even further, arguing on Darwinian grounds that menstruation was not merely the first taboo, but was the origin of all symbolic culture.[36] The very visible menstruation of human women evolved as a means of sexual politics, controlling the men's access to sex by synchronizing the women's fertility with the moon. This ensured greater investment by the men in child-rearing, necessitated by our large and biologically expensive brains. In this model, menstruation was part of a cluster of phenomena that not merely enabled us to become so intelligent, but was itself the earliest form of human symbolic activity, as the women daubed themselves with blood and/or ochre to create the illusion of menstruation and hence sexual unavailability. In so doing, changing their nature and enhancing their power, they became, quite literally, the first gods.

53 I'm not persuaded by this theory. It reduces a wide and rich variety of phenomena to a simplistic mechanism, which itself is based on an extended chain of reasoning. It seems to me that symbolic culture would likely have emerged in complex ways in response to a whole range of primal human motivations: hunger, sex, lust for power, fear of the dark, fear of wild beasts; and a growing sense of confusion and unease in the face of death. And I would not ignore the role of genius—exceptional individuals who make an intuitive leap that makes a real difference, and catches on. Nevertheless, the fact remains that fear of menstruation is a potent provocation for male fear of women and the consequent compulsion to control them. Their power over life and death can undo male magic.

54 Fertility religions celebrate this cycle, embracing and affirming the gory necessity for blood sacrifice as the price for new birth. But such beliefs, while serving a valuable role in some societies, expose the inadequacy of the fertility religions as feminist icons. In celebrating women for their nurturing, fertile attributes we forget that women are not baby-machines. Some women never give birth, some choose not to, some are unable. Many are now either too young or too old to give birth. Even while pregnant or nursing, a woman is far more than just a system for supporting a child. Women are people: sentient, conscious beings, whose ability to bear children, when they have it, is a special capacity unshared by men, but is not emblematic of their being as a whole. The predominance of fertility motifs in ancient religions tells how needs, desires, and perceptions were projected on to women, not of women's nature or spiritual destiny.

CHAPTER 22

HOW TO KILL A DEAD NUN

WHEN WE SEE HOW PERVASIVE MENSTRUATION AND OTHER TABOOS are in Buddhism, and how they influence the very real lives of women, we can but wonder at how they have such a hold on the minds of so many good men. Monks do not, leaving occasional neurotic behavior aside, bear women any ill-will. In fact, the opposite is true: a woman is usually received kindly in a monastery, treated well, and offered teachings and support for her spiritual practice. There is a startling dichotomy between compassionate, rational individual behavior, and collective, institutional neurosis. Because of this very apparent service offered to women by monks, monks themselves cannot see any problem. They are acting with kindness, to the best that they can within the institutional framework.

2 But, I am suggesting, that institutional framework is structured upon unexamined fears, confusion, and incomprehension about women and their possible role in the holy life. This institutional sexism does not make all monks individually sexist; but it does allow sexist tendencies to flourish without check, and often reinforces them. A significant minority of monks have joined the Sangha to escape from women, out of fear or incomprehension; and there is no culture of participation within the Sangha that offers help towards reconciling these problems. Misogyny as a psychological problem does not mean a hatred of all women. It is a hatred of women who are out of their place, who transgress the boundaries that men place around them.

3 The institutional policy of the male Sangha in Theravādin countries utterly denies the existence of bhikkhunis. They are, quite literally, legislated out of being. The monastic Sangha is legally defined, in bald contradiction with the texts, as consisting of monks-only. Not content with paltry discrimination or exploitation of the bhikkhunis, the male institutions deny their very right to exist. In so doing they cannot avoid drawing sustenance from the shared belief that the Buddha never wanted bhikkhunis to exist *in the first place.*

4 At the minimum the monastic culture is indifferent to the broader questions of women's participation, and resistant to any dialogue. Such dialogue as exists is dominated and diverted towards the male agenda, the legitimacy of ordination lineages. The suggestion that powerful unconscious forces are at play is dismissed with scorn. It would be even more outrageous to suggest that the repression of nuns shows not the macho strength of monks, but their weakness, their fear of female power and need to control this in a system of rules of their own devising.

5 The ritual denial of the existence of bhikkhunis occurs as part of the central rite of Theravādin bhikkhus. Each fortnight we monks perform our central mystery: the recitation of the disciplinary code (*pātimokkha*). Gathered in solemn conclave, we reaffirm our communal identity, our shared way of life, and our continuity with the Sangha of the past. If we do this according to the Thai style, we preface the recitation with a description of the 'preliminary duties', one of which is supposed to be the teaching of the bhikkhunis. But, so the monks ritually intone, this duty is no longer performed, since the bhikkhunis 'do not exist now'.[1]

6 This existential denial is the inverse of the existential threat that the bhikkhunis pose. Since the presence of bhikkhunis is a flood or a disease that can destroy Buddhism, best if they can be completely eliminated. The *garudhammas* were set up as a dyke to contain the flood, especially by making the ordination of women dependent on the co-operation of men. Control of ordination takes away from women their most fearful power: procreation. Just as men try to control women's bodies with technology, culture, and ritual, male control over female ordination renders the women's community infertile. But the ever-present anxiety among monks that bhikkhunis actually keep the *garudhammas* is a sure sign of

how flimsy such a safeguard is. Rules may be negotiated, interpreted, or rejected. Only annihilation promises safety.

7 In a religious system such as Buddhism, such annihilation is not the mere non-existence of bhikkhunis in the flesh, but must also involve a symbolic destruction. They must be deprived of the enduring symbols that express a community's honor, and which enable their memory to be passed down through the ages. In traditional forms of Buddhism, the pre-eminent symbol of eternity was the stupa. And the destruction of nuns' stupas is a recurring story in the canonical Vinayas.

❖

8 We can appreciate that the destruction of a sacred shrine, a stupa built for the honored departed, is distasteful, but it is hard for us moderns to really appreciate how transgressive this is in ancient thought. For example, in several Greek myths the crux of the drama is the refusal to pay proper funeral rites, an act that was felt to be far worse than mere killing, for it deprived the soul of peace in the beyond.[2]

9 In the Pali bhikkhuni *pācittiya* 52, set at Vesālī, an elder nun of the notorious troublemakers the 'group of six nuns', dies. They make a stupa for her and hold a noisy mourning ritual. Venerable Upāli's preceptor, Kappitaka, who was living in the cemetery, was annoyed at the sound, and smashed the stupa to bits—somewhat of a distasteful overreaction, one might think. Anyway, the group of six nuns say: 'He destroyed our stupa—let's kill him!' Kappitaka escapes with Upāli's help, and the nuns abuse Upāli, thus prompting a rule, not against noisy funerals, or smashing stupas, or attempted murder, but against abusing monks.[3]

10 Another example is found in the Mūlasarvāstivāda Vinaya.[4] This occurs in part of a story, found in various forms in other Vinayas, about the destruction of nuns' stupas by monks. The Mūlasarvāstivāda version says that the group of twelve nuns built a stupa for Venerable Phalguna, despite the fact that Phalguna had been far from an exemplary monk, being scolded by the Buddha for his conduct with the nuns.[5]

11 The Dharmaguptaka version is quite similar, although it is found split over two rules.[6] If we edit these narratives together, leaving out the specifically legal sections, we get the following account.

12 At that time, the Bhagavat was staying in the Jetavana in Anāthapiṇḍada's park in the country of Śravastī. At that time, in the city of Śravastī, a very wise *bhikṣuṇī* died. There were *bhikṣuṇīs* who erected for her a pagoda in a monastery where *bhikṣus* were staying. The *bhikṣuṇīs* came to the monastery in large numbers. They stood there, talked and enjoyed themselves. Some chanted, some lamented. Some adorned themselves. Consequently they disturbed the *bhikṣus* who were sitting in meditation. At that time there was the honorable Kapila. He was always happy when he sat in meditation. On the day that the *bhikṣuṇīs* went away, he immediately destroyed their pagoda. He removed it and put it out of the *saṁghārāma*. When the *bhikṣuṇīs* heard that Kapila had destroyed and removed their pagoda, they all took knives, sticks, tiles, and stones and they wanted to beat him. Thereupon, Kapila ascended in the air by means of his supernatural power....

13 ... At daybreak, when the night had passed, the honorable *bhikṣu* Kapila put on his robe, took the alms bowl and went to beg in Śravastī. When the *bhikṣuṇīs* saw Kapila, they reviled him: 'That corrupt and mean kin of smiths![7] He destroyed our pagoda and removed it out of the *saṁghārāma*.'[8]

14 The Mahīśāsaka Vinaya tells the story like this.

15 At that time, *Samā bhikkhuni came to the end of her life. The bhikkhunis made a stupa for the bones in the bhikkhus' monastery. The women in the daytime went three times around, crying and wailing: 'She who gave me Dhamma! She who gave me robes, food, dwelling, and medicines! How can, in one day, such a benefactor to me be gone forever?' The bhikkhus were annoyed and their meditation disturbed. At that time Upāli came and entered the Sangha monastery. He questioned the resident bhikkhus: 'What is that noise?' They told him what was the matter. Upāli sent a man to destroy [the stupa]. The bhikkhunis heard, and they had the idea: 'We should all take sticks and beat that bhikkhu! If we do not go together, we shall not return to live together.' Having had this idea, they all took sticks and went to the Sangha's monastery. Seeing a bhikkhu, they thereupon surrounded [him] wishing to beat [him]. Realising this was not [the right bhikkhu] they desisted, and went further on until they confronted Upāli on the path. They surrounded him and raised their sticks to beat him. Upāli used his psychic powers to fly to where the Buddha was. He told the Buddha what had happened.[9]

16 Since it's such a memorable moment in Buddhist history, let's have the Sarvāstivāda account.

> 17 The Buddha was living at Kosambi. At that time *Kalulatissa bhikkhu came to the end of his life. He had seven bhikkhunis who were his sisters, who were called: Thullanandā bhikkhuni, *Śoṇanandā bhikkhuni, Tissā bhikkhuni, Upatissā bhikkhuni, *Tissayuttā bhikkhuni, *Tissapālanā bhikkhuni, and *Tissacattā bhikkhuni. Those bhikkhunis were very influential. They gathered firewood, burnt that bhikkhu's body, gathered the bones, and made a stupa.
>
> 18 At that time there was one bhikkhu called *Kata. From the *He-qi country he approached *Wei-ye-li. On the way he saw that stupa. He asked: 'Whose stupa is that?' He was told: 'The stupa of *Kalulatissa bhikkhu.' He said: 'How can they make a stupa for such a foolish person?' Then he destroyed that stupa, and made his bed and seat on top of it.
>
> 19 Thullanandā bhikkhuni heard that *Kata bhikkhu had destroyed their elder brother's stupa and made his bed and seat on top of it. When she heard this, she was very angry. She said to her younger sisters: 'All of you, bring needles and thread. We'll sew that bhikkhu onto his bed!' They took a short-cut to that Sangha monastery.
>
> 20 At that time Upāli arrived. He heard of this matter, and immediately went to tell that bhikkhu: 'This place where you are sitting—the bhikkhunis are coming straightaway to sew you onto the bed!' He said: 'If they sew me onto the bed, I will then escape from this stinking body!' Upāli said: 'Even if you escape from this stinking body, the bhikkhunis will perform a terrible misdeed.'
>
> 21 That bhikkhu entered into jhana so that his body should not be visible. Upāli then went away. The bhikkhunis came in, and they all said thus: 'That bhikkhu is not here, for we look but cannot see him.' They touched the bed with their hands and realized that it was warm. They said: 'It must have been because that barber Upāli told him and then went away!'[10]

22 The variations in these texts are too complex to analyze in detail here, but there are some general affinities along sectarian lines. The Vibhajjavāda schools (Dharmaguptaka, Mahīśāsaka, Mahāvihāravāsin) all preserve a story about a dead senior bhikkhuni, and the resulting problem is the noise of the lamentation; while the Sarvāstivāda and Mūlasarvāstivāda speak of a dead bhikkhu who was dear to the nuns, and the problem is the

erection of a stupa for a 'false idol'. The Sarvāstivāda adds the delightful detail that the bhikkhunis who are out for revenge take their needles and aim to sew the bhikkhu on to his bed—a fitting manner of murder, given the universal connections between the goddess, weaving, and death. But all these Vinayas, which represent most of the Sthavira group of schools, preserve an account of bhikkhus destroying a stupa built by bhikkhunis. There is no trace of our story in these rules in the Mahāsaṅghika[11] or Lokuttaravāda[12] Vinayas, which suggests the story is a post-Aśokan one. This would fit the devotional emphasis of post-Aśokan Buddhism and the emergence of the stupa cult.

❖

23 The fact is there: the story exists. But the meaning is elusive—what are we to make of such tales? I think Gregory Schopen's argument in this case is brilliant, and although the conclusions may seem strange, they are no stranger than the evidence warrants. He argues that a stupa was more than a memorial. It was a symbol of a deceased person, especially a religious teacher. More than a symbol even, it was their very life. When Nigaṇṭha Nātaputta, the leader of the Jains, passed away, his followers were so distraught they cried their 'stupa was broken' (*bhinnathūpa*).[13] So when the group of six bhikkhus, or the group of twelve nuns, made a symbolic stupa out of food(!), named it after the non-Buddhist teacher Pūraṇa, and with a flourish and a rousing incantation 'Nandopananda!' demolished it, they and the followers of Pūraṇa believed that by this act the teacher became truly dead.[14] Thus to destroy a stupa would amount to murder; at the very least, this would account for the vengeful rage that gripped the aggrieved nuns.

24 Frazer discusses at length the concept of an 'external soul', some physical thing that embodies a person's life.[15] As long as that physical thing, which may be a tree, a bird, or anything near or far, survives, the person cannot die. But when the external 'soul' is destroyed, the person must die. The 'external soul' survives in the popular mythos as Sauron's ring or Voldemort's horcruxes. The creation of a stupa as memorial, containing the physical relics of a saint—which throughout the Buddhist world are fervently believed to possess wondrous powers—would be a fitting form for an external soul.

25 Schopen notices that, while the accounts of the deaths of the bhikkhus are regularly accompanied by stories of their stupas, such accounts are conspicuously absent from the nuns' stories. Perhaps even more telling is the well known mention by Xuan-zang of how the different sections of the Buddhist community offer worship to the appropriate stupa. Thus the Abhidhamma scholars worship the stupa of Sāriputta, the *samādhi* specialists worship the stupa of Moggallāna, the Sutta students worship Puṇṇa Mantāniputta, while the Vinaya experts worship Upāli. Uniquely, the bhikkhunis do not worship the stupa of one of their own kind, but that of Ānanda.[16]

26 Our stories from the Vinaya are unusual in preserving accounts of stupas built by or for nuns. In each case, they are destroyed by monks who seemingly get away with it, even though destruction of a stupa is normally regarded as a terrible deed, such that even the symbolic destruction of the stupa of non-Buddhist teachers is forbidden. Destroying the nuns' stupas is more than just a symbolic violation, however. As always, symbols have a very real impact on the basic stuff of life. The nuns would have lost a devotional and organizational center and a potent source of funds and support. Schopen describes such actions as 'not just ritual murder but something more akin to the political assassination of a group's special dead'.[17] In the face of such determined and destructive opposition, it is little wonder, argues Schopen, that the Indian epigraphic record lacks all evidence for stupas built for nuns.

27 I don't know enough about the archaeology to test Schopen's claim that there is no epigraphic evidence of nun's stupas in India. However, I have come across several references to stupas for nuns in the written sources. The following is from the Sri Lankan Mahāvaṁsa.

28 When the great Elder Nun Saṅghamittā, gifted with the great supernormal powers and with great wisdom had fulfilled the duties of the doctrine and had brought much blessing to the people, she, being fifty-nine years old, in the ninth year of this same king Uttiya, while she dwelt in the peaceful Hatthalhaka-convent passed into nibbana. And for her also, as for the Elder [Mahinda], the king commanded supreme honors of burial a week through, and the whole of Lanka was adorned as for the Elder.

29 The body of the Elder Nun laid upon a bier did he cause to be brought when the week was gone by, out of the city; and to the east of the Thūpārāma, near the Cittisala (of later times) in sight of the great Bodhi-tree, on the spot pointed out by the Elder Nun (herself), he caused the burning to take place. And the most wise Uttiya also had a stupa built there.[18]

30 Also, Fa-xian mentions a stupa built on the spot where Uppalavaṇṇā greeted the Buddha when he descended from Tāvatiṁsa heaven after preaching the Abhidhamma,[19] and another at Mahāpajāpatī's monastery in Sāvatthī,[20] which was also seen by Xuan-zang.[21] Xuang-zang also notes a stupa at Vesālī at Ambapālī's land, commemorating the *parinirvāna* of Mahāpajāpatī and other bhikkhunis.[22]

31 Though few, these references do show that stupas for nuns existed in ancient India, and played their legitimate role in religious life. This does not disprove Schopen's argument, it merely reminds us that reality is complex. It remains an uncomfortable fact that the traditions accept that monks may destroy nuns' stupas with impunity. It is not unreasonable to connect this with the relative paucity of mentions of nuns' stupas in later years, and further, with the decline of nuns in India. At the very least, the canonical Vinayas show monks destroying the sacred space of nuns.

CHAPTER 23

A VERY GRIEVOUS TEXT

We are getting a certain image of Buddhism here, one which is far from serenity and enlightened compassion. A Buddhism where women are treated, not as humans of equal dignity and spiritual capacity, but as the other, a threat to be feared and quashed whenever possible. Such attitudes were not uncommon in traditional Buddhist circles, and may be found in Buddhist teachings for ages past. I would like to crave your indulgence and wander, like the Prince of Unreason, into some of the less popular—in modern times—corners of Buddhist lore. Let us play around with another Jātaka story.

2 Jātakas are the bread-&-butter of Buddhist sermons. Children are brought up on these tales, and they remain the main source of Buddhist teachings for many adults. They are an immeasurably important treasury of folk wisdom, preserving many hundreds, perhaps thousands, of tales from the vast ocean of Indian story. The best known collection is found in the Pali canon, but there are hundreds more in the northern collections and in later extra-canonical sources. Most of them are not originally Buddhist, but were legends and fables current within the Indian folk tradition, which were adopted within a Buddhist context by the literary device of identifying the Bodhisatta (here meaning Siddhattha Gotama in his past lives) with the hero. Frequently the Buddha's associates in 'this' life are assigned parallel roles in these past lives as well: for example, Ānanda would be the devoted student, Bimbā would be the wife, Māyā the mother, Devadatta the enemy, and so on.

3 According to the official doctrine of the schools, the Bodhisatta was supposed to have been diligently and consciously pursuing his heroic task of developing his spiritual perfections bit by bit in each life, for the ultimate attainment of Buddhahood. In point of fact, however, the hero of the story rarely appears to be aware of his spiritual destiny. As the narrative is presented to us, the Bodhisatta is unaware of his true destiny, a 'consciousness hidden from itself'.[1]

4 Each Jātaka story is made up of three main sections. The oldest layer is the verse, which formed the memorized kernel of the story. Next was the 'Story of the Past', the prose framework that provides the narrative context for the verse. Finally there is the 'Story of the Present', which gives the events in the life of the Buddha that prompted the tellings of the story. Typically, the 'Story of the Present' begins the Jātaka, where the events unfold in a pattern or with a moral that evoke the association with a traditional tale. The tale is then told by the Buddha as the 'Story of the Past'. The verse typically forms the emotional and dramatic climax of the story: at the moment of greatest emotional tension, the rational, linear prose breaks down, and the story reverts to the older, deeper language of rhythmic verse. Then the Jātaka returns to the 'Story of the Present', rounding off the narrative by locating the events in relation to the characters familiar from the Buddha's life.

5 In the Pali tradition the verse is the only strictly 'canonical' part, the prose sections being officially a commentary; but such distinctions are rarely if ever made within the tradition, and in practice the verse and prose are almost always found together. Indeed, as shown long ago by T.W. Rhys Davids, the verses in many cases must have been passed down together with their accompanying story, which is sometimes the only way to make sense of the riddling verse.[2] I am not aware that the distinction between canonical and non-canonical parts of the Jātakas is recognized in the northern traditions.

6 Due to their non-Buddhist origins, it is easy to find Jātakas where the ethics are, to say the least, not Buddhist.[3] This is, of course, not a fatal criticism of such stories, for they are by their very nature episodes of the Buddha before Awakening, and thus are part of his learning process. Nevertheless, they are traditionally assumed to depict straightforward

moral lessons, and are used as such in Buddhist contexts. The unethical stories are the most interesting, as they betray the persistence of primitive, pre-ethical remnants, dating from long before the Buddha—which is, of course, just what the stories claim.

7 The Jātakas preserve plenty of gloriously incorrect sayings about women. To get us in the mood, here are a few sample verses. Let's edify ourselves as to the real nature of women.

> 8 Every river is twisted,
> All forests are made of wood,
> And whenever they get a chance,
> All women do what is wicked.[4]

> 9 Clever thieves never reveal the truth,
> And so womankind is unknowable,
> like the path of fish in the water,
> Holding truth for falsehood,
> falsehood for the truth!
> As a cow with much grass thinks more is better
> These female rogues are cruel
> as a beast of prey, like quicksand.
> There's nothing that men speak of that they don't know.[5]

> 10 Women are wrathful, ungrateful, slanderous, and divisive.
> Live the holy life, monk, then you will dwell happily.[6]

11 We get the message. A few basic points are hopefully obvious, but should be mentioned anyway. First, such passages express unbridled misogyny; that is, not merely androcentrism (seeing things from a male point of view), but active hate of women.

12 Second, these verses, chosen from many in the Jātaka books, both express an attitude already present within the Buddhist community, and also condition future attitudes. Such 'moral' lessons were imbibed by the children and must have informed the future shaping of views of the monastics, unless there was a vigorous counter-current of critique and deconstruction, of which there is, to my knowledge, no evidence in the Pali tradition.

13 A third point, which must seem obvious to most of us, is that such stories make a mockery of the Buddhist ideals of compassionate understanding. Although this is rarely stated as such in the traditions, there is at least one exception. Dōgen Zenji (1200–1253), the founder of the Sōtō Zen sect of

Japanese Buddhism, claimed that, on the level of enlightenment, men and women are completely equal, going so far as to say that one should not even discuss 'man' or 'woman' when dealing with an Awakened person.[7] Men who refused to recognize that women could attain Buddhahood are 'stupid people who insult the Dharma'.

14

> Furthermore, nowadays extremely stupid people look at women without having corrected the prejudice that women are objects of sexual greed. Disciples of the Buddha must not be like this. If whatever may become the object of sexual greed is to be hated, do not all men deserve to be hated too? [...] if we hate whatever might become the object of sexual greed, all men and women will hate each other, and we will never have any chance to attain salvation.[8]

15 And fourthly, as we have already shown for the Black Snake Suttas, the psychological traits attributed to women are objectively false.

16 Given that 'teachings' such as these Jātaka verses are not true, one might be forgiven for wondering how they gained traction in Buddhist circles. It is conventional to dismiss unpleasant aspects of Buddhism as 'Hindu' influences, but such rhetoric avoids answering the question as to why and how such supposedly foreign elements became accepted as a part of Buddhist doctrine. Of course misogynist attitudes are available in Indian culture, as they were in all other cultures. But the Buddha, and subsequent generations of Buddhists, did not simply accept willy-nilly everything that was around them. They used their discernment to adopt only those things that were compatible with Buddhism. Why, then, did no-one ever notice this un-Buddhist misogyny, which seems so obvious?

17 The images of women in such verses are a staple of monastic fare, warning monks against the dangers and treacheries of married life. We must be clear about what we are actually saying here: such dangers are very real. It is the case that many, perhaps most, women do betray their husband. The romantic fantasy of 'they lived happily ever after' is a fairy tale, not a description of real marriages. And as a warning about the dangers of married life, this is an unpleasant truth which we should be aware of before making such a decision. But it is equally true that at least as many men betray their wives. The problem is not the warning of the dangers of adultery, it is that only the women are blamed. The issue is externalized,

objectified, projected outside of the male arena and made, not a problem with human culture and expectations and emotions, but a moral failing of women.

18 Such texts are by no means rare, nor restricted to a certain place or period. Many Jātakas express similar views, such as the whole arsenal of misogyny marshaled in the Kunāla Jātaka.[9] These stories feed into perceptions of women in popular culture in Buddhist lands. Woman is depicted as of excessive, unbridled sexuality, 'as wide as the ocean and as intense as a roaring fire', with desires eight times as strong as mens'.[10] To solve the question, 'Who has greater pleasure in sex?' they consulted the seer Tiresias, who had spent time as both man and woman. He confirmed that, if love's pleasure were divided in ten, women receive nine parts, men only one. Understandably, Hera blinded him for his trouble. His Buddhist counterpart is Soreyya, whose story is told in the Dhammapada commentary. Despite being married with children, he was attracted to Venerable Mahākaccāyana's body and immediately turned into a woman. He left his family, remarried, and had more children as a woman. Later, he confessed to Mahākaccāyana, became a man again, and ordained as a monk. When asked which children he loved more, he said it was the ones he had as a woman.[11] Within a Buddhist soteriology that sees the ending of all desires as the spiritual goal, this means that women are intrinsically hindered in their spiritual path. It should go without saying that the belief in women's insatiability is a projection of male desire; and the belief that women are thereby obstructed from Nibbana betrays the unconscious fear in men that their own spiritual progress is undercut by their sexual drives.

19 Let us look in a little more detail at how misogynist attitudes are constructed through recasting mythic motifs. The Asātamanta Jātaka will do nicely. It deals with a peculiar form of arcane knowledge, rendered in our translation as the 'Grievous Text' (*asātamanta*). In the 'Story of the Present' there is a monk beset by lust, for whom the Buddha tells the following 'Story of the Past'.[12]

❖

> 20 Once upon a time, while Brahmadatta was reigning in Benares, a son was born to a brahman family in that same Benares. On the day of his birth his parents took the Sacred Fire and kept it burning until

he turned sixteen. Then they offered him a choice: either retire into the forest and worship the Sacred Fire, seeking for communion with Brahmā; or else travel to Takkasilā to study with a renowned teacher so that he could manage the estate. Reflecting that the ascetic's way was hard, he chose to go for study. He traveled to Takkasilā, completed his studies, then returned to Benares.

21 But his parents really wished him to go into the forest to worship the Sacred Fire. So his mother, believing that the renowned teacher would be able to explain the faults of women to her son, asked him whether he had *quite* finished his studies.

22 'O, yes, mother!' he replied.

23 'But have you learnt the "Grievous Text"?'

24 'Well, no, mother.'

25 'Then how can you have finished your studies? Go, and return when you have learnt it!'

26 Saying 'Very well, then,' the son returned to Takkasilā.

27 Now, the teacher had a blind old mother, 120 years of age, who he would bathe, feed, and look after with his own hands. When neighbors criticized him for this, he decided to move into a private place in the forest. He built a little hut in a delightful grove with water flowing by, carried his mother there, then spent his time in service to her.

28 The student, having asked for his teacher's whereabouts, went to him and presented himself. The teacher asked:

29 'But, my boy, why have you returned so soon?'

30 'Did I not fail to learn the "Grievous Text" from you?' he replied.

31 'But who told you to learn the "Grievous Text"?'

32 'My mother, master.'

33 The teacher reflected, 'There is in fact no "Grievous Text". His mother must want me to teach her son about the Faults of Women.'

34 So he said, 'Good, I will show you the "Grievous Text". From today on you must take my place in service of my mother: washing, feeding, and looking after her. As you massage her hands, feet, head, and back, say, "O lady! If your body is so lovely even though old, how must you have been in your youth?" And as you perfume her hands, feet, and so on, lavish praise on them. And whatever my mother tells you, repeat them exactly to me. So doing, you will master the "Grievous Text"; but if you fail, you cannot master it.'

35 Saying 'Very well!' the student did all as instructed.

Figure 23.1: *Baba Yaga*

36 When the student so assiduously praised her beauty, the old woman thought that he had fallen in love with her. Blind and decrepit as she was, lust was kindled within her heart. So one day she said to the student:

37 'Are you in love with me?'

38 'I am,' he said. 'But I respect my teacher.'

39 'If you want me, kill my son!' she said.

40 'But how can I kill my teacher who has taught me so much, out of mere lust?'

41 'If you will not do the deed, then I will kill him myself!' she said.

42 The student repeated this to his teacher, who reflected on his mother's term of life and saw that she was fated to die that very day. Wishing to test her, he cut down a fig tree and hewed from it a figure his own size, which he wrapped in a cloth and laid upon his bed with a string tied to it. He told the student to take an axe for his mother and give her the string as her guide.

43 He did so, and the hag, with trembling limbs, groped her way along the string until she thought she could feel her son. Pulling the cloth back from the head, she thought, 'I will kill him with a single blow!' and whacked the neck with the axe! But by the 'thud' she knew it was wood.

44 The teacher, standing by the door, said, 'Careful with that axe, mother.'

45 Crying out: 'I am betrayed!' she fell down dead. For, it seems, she was destined to die in that hut and at that very moment.

46 The son cremated her body and offered flowers for her ashes. Then, sitting with the student, he said:

47 'My boy, there is no specific text called the "Grievous Text". But it is women who are grievous. When your mother sent you back here, she wished you to learn of the Faults of Women. And now you know how women are grievous, wicked, and depraved.'

48 The student took leave of his teacher and returned to his parents. On his return, his mother asked him how he wished to spend his life. He replied:

49 'Desire is called "woman" in this world.
They know no limit. Lustful, insatiable,
Devouring all like the crested flame:
Having left them I will go forth to develop seclusion.'

50 After hearing these stirring words from the Buddha, the lust-bedevilled monk he was addressing realized the fruit of stream-entry. The Buddha revealed the links between that life and this: 'The mother was Bhaddākāpilānī; the father was Mahākassapa; the student was Ānanda; and I myself was the teacher.'

❖

51 Now, it is a difficult task, but a necessary one, to refrain from either laughing at or being revolted by such 'teachings'. Deep matters are at hand here, for this nasty little fable compresses within it many of the classic motifs of ancient myth.

52 To start with, let us notice the motif of the doubled parents. First, there are the 'natural' parents. In our story the father is absent and the mother is actively 'all for the male'.[13] The teacher and his mother take the role of the substitute parents. The natural parents, in this story, are the spiritual parents, while the teacher and his mother are the worldly parents. This, of course, parallels Siddhattha's final birth, where Mahāpajāpatī and Suddhodana figure as the worldly parents, while Māyā and Siddhattha himself (in his divine aspect as six-tusked white elephant) are the spiritual parents.

53 This is made quite explicit in the choice offered to the student, which parallels exactly the choice offered to the Bodhisatta in his last life as Siddhattha: to live the life of worldly good, or to renounce and seek peace in the forest. The only difference is that the scale of the motifs is adjusted for the each story. Whereas Siddhattha chooses between becoming a Universal Monarch or a World Savior, our student makes the more humble choice between looking after the family estate and retiring to worship the Sacred Fire.

54 The worship of fire is one of the chief mystical aspects of the Ṛg Veda, harking back to the very origins of human culture, the hearth-fires that allowed humans to dwell in cold climates and to cook their food. Fire is power, and is the most apparent link between the physical world and the mystical play of magic, transforming cloddish matter into dancing energy. In the Indic imagination, fire is a gendered entity, for 'water is female and fire is male'.[14] The Taittirīya Brāhmaṇa says:

55 You, Agni, are our cord and our bridge; You are the path which conducts to the gods. By you we may ascend to the summit (of heaven) and there live in joyful fellowship with the gods.[15]

56 The parents, by keeping the fire kindled for him his whole life, have already announced their spiritual aspiration for their son. This is reinforced when his natural mother instructs him to learn the 'Grievous Text' (*asātamanta*). *Asāta* is a synonym of *dukkha*, and so the mother's role is to introduce him to the Dhamma: the first Noble Truth. In this respect, the text mirrors Siddhattha's story, for there his natural father traps him in the home, resisting his spiritual vocation, while his mother, Māyā, reveals the nature of suffering to her son through her own death.

57 In our Jātaka, the student fails to respond to the call, which is declared to him by his parents as a coming-of-age test. He is then sent to the teacher, whose job is to teach those skills of the world that he will need to run the estate.

58 Another mythic motif is the repeated substitution. First the student is explicitly instructed to 'take the place' of the master (*mama ṭhāne ṭhatvā*). Thus the son substitutes for the father in the preparation for the killing. But next the wooden log substitutes for the father again, precisely at the moment of the killing. This motif recalls the historical institution of substitute sacrifices. The wooden log makes the connection specific: it is a *kaṭṭha* that the old hag attacks with an axe, just as Kaṭṭhahārī was gathering sticks.

59 The situation is straightforwardly Oedipal. The son aims to kill the father in order to have sex with the mother. But where *Oedipus Rex* transforms this terrible conflict into a profound meditation on choice and fate, the Asātamanta Jātaka is a kind of mythic pornography, pulling raw images out of deep time for sheer shock value. The ethics of killing have been inverted to make the 'moral' of the tale. The blame has been shifted from the hero entirely on to the mother. What remains is without depth or drama, and merely appalls in its crassness. Since the son is imbued with civilized values, it is the mother, as embodiment of blind, primeval, animal lust, who seduces the son and kills the father.

60 And most crucially, the hag dies. Her death is a natural one, which our cunning teacher merely takes advantage of.[16] She is too old, a relic of

archaic pre-consciousness, and will not be missed. Her death is not brought about through physical violence; all that is required is for him to know her. As soon as he sees her, that is, brings her into awareness, she passes away. The teacher is a 'Hero of Consciousness'; like Oedipus, he destroys the female monster through the sheer power of awareness.

61 From now on, only the bright, spiritualized aspect of the feminine—who in our story is represented by the natural mother—lives on. And we know that she can be trusted, for she is the secret teacher, the helper for the student to attain the Jewel of Knowledge. Thus, while the story's surface is straightforwardly misogynist, it contains a curious ambiguity, for it is the spiritualized female who provides the crucial assistance for the son. It is she who shapes the final outcome: renunciation, the breaking of the cycle, rebirth in the purified spiritual domain of Brahmā.

62 The conscious 'ethics' of the story depict women negatively, while the narrative pattern offers a distinct duality. On the one hand woman is the hideous devourer, while at the same time she is the helpmeet. This narrative dimension is not ethical, but existential. It does not pass value judgments on 'women', but depicts the creative and destructive aspects of femininity in the life of the hero.

63 Finally, we note the identifications of the characters at the end. This aspect is crucial, since it is the means by which the Buddhist redactors brought this un-Buddhist story within a Buddhist context. The identifications in the Jātaka stories relate the characters in the story with particular personality traits or roles of individuals living at the time of the Buddha, the aim being to demonstrate how the events of the present day echo patterns that have taken place countless times before. Often there is a causal link, as the same characters do the same things under the sway of kamma; but in our present story this is not so, as the lust-bedevilled monk is not identified with anyone in the Story of the Past.

64 The Buddha is the teacher. The student is Ānanda, echoing his role as a junior student, eager and intelligent, but a little backwards in the ascetic practices; this story is just one of Ānanda's many adventures with women.

65 Crucially, the natural mother and father are Bhaddākāpilānī and Mahākassapa. They were husband and wife in 'our' Buddha's day as well until they went forth and attained arahantship. Mahākassapa is, of course,

well-known as the foremost in ascetic practices. He took leadership of the Sangha after the death of the Buddha, and came into conflict with Ānanda, even referring to Ānanda—then a middle-aged man—as 'boy'. Since Bhaddākāpilānī and Mahākassapa are together in both lives, they may be seen as acting 'as one' in admonishing the student about the dangers of women, even though only the wife speaks. If anything, this emphasizes even more the distant, paternal aspect of the Mahākassapa figure.[17]

CHAPTER 24

THE HERO DEPARTS

BUDDHA. THE AWAKENED ONE, THE LION, THE BULL AMONG MEN. The story of Buddhism is, to begin with, the story of the Buddha. It is a man's story, and women figure in it as extras. They are defined by their difference. The Buddha is Self-Awakened: he stands magnificently alone; women appear in relationship to him. If we are to understand the role of women, we must understand his story. How is it put together? What are its values? And what is its message?

2 The Buddha is no ordinary man, and so his story can be no ordinary story. He has stood as the supreme spiritual embodiment of humanity for half the civilized world for half the age of human civilization. Far heavier than the burden of Atlas, he must carry the accumulated projections of billions of people. Little wonder that he must buckle and strain to do so. Little wonder that the resources of story-telling and art have been stretched beyond their limits for over 2000 years, and still he eludes us.

3 This process of projection is a normal, indeed essential, feature of the human mind. As children, we all experience our parents through the projection of the archetypes of 'mother' and 'father', the vague yet potent echo of our memories of countless 'mothers' and 'fathers' in the past. In society this archetypal projection is amplified, as Great Individuals, whether geniuses, saints, warriors, or leaders, bear the projection of an entire people. In the past this amplified projection was experienced as divinity, pure and simple. The king or hero was a god. Now we cannot think of actual humans as divine, and yet the quality of our projections has not changed

all that much. If such projections remain moderate they are a healthy force, uniting a people behind a leader or in a common cause. When they become extreme, however, the Great Individual arrogates to themselves godlike qualities, such as omniscience or infallibility, and the culture is placed in great danger. This trajectory is all too familiar in the world's dictators; and sadly enough, also in its religious leaders.[1]

4 The story of such Great Individuals is the myth of the hero. It is scarcely possible to overestimate the importance of the hero myth in the formation of culture and our modern identity. The hero is the one who unifies life in this world with the transcendent: humanity in its fullest sense. A hero has a unique destiny, and is imbued with 'superhuman' qualities of strength, courage, resourcefulness, or wisdom. A hero stands out from the herd. They glow; they are drawn in more vivid colors.

5 But the great secret of the hero's story is this: it is their very 'specialness' that makes the hero ordinary. They are special because they are 'I'. In each individual's experience, they themselves form the center of the Universe. The world spreads out around one, and the meaning of the world is the meaning it has 'for me'. Each 'One' has a special destiny and special powers. I can make the world go away by closing my eyes; I can change my world by turning my head. Each one of us has, in our own world, special powers that are shared with no-one else. We can create all kinds of magic in our heads, defy the laws of physics, rewrite history, ignore time. We are all Superman or Wonderwoman. The hero in myth mimics in an external setting the world as experienced in each subjective consciousness. This is why myth is not unreal, it is hyperreal.

6 In the hands of Joseph Campbell the hero myth took on a definite, if complex and shifting, structure in all cultures, with endless variations played out on a few basic themes. The fundamental structure is threefold, described by Campbell thus:

> 7 **[Departure]** A hero ventures forth from the world of common day into a region of supernatural wonder; **[Initiation]** fabulous forces are encountered and a decisive victory is won; **[Return]** the hero comes back from this mysterious adventure with the power to bestow boons on his fellow man.[2]

8 Campbell's analysis has remained one of the most influential treatises of the 20th century. It was a general survey; and so while he frequently spoke of the life of the Buddha as one of the most magnificent incarnations of the hero myth, both sumptuously ornate and deeply spiritual, he did not enter into questions of the formation of this myth in its historical context.[3] In particular, he relied on later developed tellings of the story, such as the Jātaka Nidāna, the Lalitavistara, and Aśvaghoṣa's Buddhacarita. These tell us how the Buddha's life was conceived by the followers living 500 years or more after the Buddha himself. We wish to learn more about the attitudes of those who formulated the Buddha's life story in the generations following his death.

9 To do this we must rely on the early scriptures, of which we possess a complete set from the Theravādins of the Sri Lankan Mahāvihāra in Pali, and abundant materials from other schools such as the Sarvāstivāda, Dharmaguptaka, Mūlasarvāstivāda, Mahīśāsaka, and Mahāsaṅghika, in Chinese, Sanskrit, and Tibetan. Examining all this material for different perspectives on the Buddha's story is a daunting task.

10 The main story is told, however, with remarkable unity, only varying in details. So for simplicity's sake, I will restrict myself primarily to one source book: Bhikkhu Ñāṇamoḷi's *The Life of the Buddha*. This classic modern compilation assembles the crucial episodes from throughout the Pali canon, found both in Sutta and Vinaya, arranged chronologically as far as possible to tell the story of the Buddha's life. Interpolations from the later legends are kept to a minimum and are carefully separated from the canonical sources. One advantage of using this source book is that it is widely available: get yourself a copy and keep it by your bedside. As we go on, I will give the relevant pages from Ñāṇamoḷi's book for each stage of the hero's journey. I hope the inquiring reader will study in detail the episodes which I must present in summary. I will also mention elements from later retellings or alternative sources where I feel these are significant, but I make no attempt to be comprehensive.

11 Campbell's classic formulation uses a scheme of seventeen stages of the hero's journey. But this focuses on the actual journey of the hero, and hence only starts with the 'Call to Adventure'. It leaves out the fuller details of the hero's life story, such as the virgin birth, although these

are discussed elsewhere in his book. The Buddha is one of the earliest heroes for whom we have a life story from birth to death, albeit with major gaps in between. To complete the picture, then, we shall have to preface Campbell's seventeen stages with the Buddha's early life, and extend it to his passing away.[4] Obviously, we will pay special attention to the depiction of women in the story.

12 Myth is not constructed out of fixed formulas, it is a fluid and creative expression. So the 'stages' described by Campbell and other theorists are mere generalizations. Few if any myths have all stages; frequently the stages appear in different orders, or they are repeated, separated, or combined. Each stage is a metaphor, and hence may be represented in countless ways. The same stage may be represented both as external events and as internal psychological process. If one aspect of a myth is missing within a given story, it is often supplied from elsewhere in the culture. In the stories we are dealing with, which inhabit that twilight zone between faerie and the real world, the final composition of the myth will exhibit a creative tension between the 'hard facts' imposed on the author(s) and the archetypal pattern that informs the narrative structure.

13 To show something of this variability, from time to time I refer to the *Rāmāyaṇa*, which tells itself as a kind of inversion of the Buddha's story, sharing multiple layers of commonalities, but at crucial points turning the story inside out.[5] While the Buddha's father strives to keep him at home, Rāma's father, tricked by the wicked stepmother, forces Rāma out into the forest. While Siddhattha leaves all behind him, Rāma goes with his brother and wife. And of course, while Siddhattha's victory is entirely spiritual, Rāma's involves a deadly massacre. But for both, the period spent in the wilderness is a key part of the spiritual journey, an essential initiation that leads to their final maturity.

❖

14 It would be imprudent, given the delicate nature of our inquiry, to embark upon our adventure without a few remarks on gender. The hero's quest as analyzed by Campbell, displays definite gender bias. The temptation, for example, is by a woman. This is not a problem for us, for we are not saying that the mythic cycle is a universal psychological process, but merely showing how it is actually presented in the Buddha's case; and that

is very definitely gendered. It is the story of a man, told by and for men; and analyzed now by a man. If women had been in charge of the redaction process, we would be dealing with a very different story.

15 It is sometimes argued that the hero myth speaks from the masculine psyche, neglecting the 'feminine' and exalting the 'masculine' virtue of self-willed independence. Hence the 'hero' is almost always male. Gilligan remarks that:

16
> '... men's histories frequently chronicle a sacrifice of relationship made earlier in childhood, often in the name of love and for the sake of manhood. We know this story; it is the quest story, the hero with a thousand faces. It is the quintessential story of patriarchy, the story of the man's introduction into the battle between the good and the bad guys.'[6]

17 Corresponding 'feminine' myths are of the 'Bluebeard' or 'Beauty and the Beast' type, as we have already encountered in the story of Bhaddā, and will consider in more detail later. Where the male hero goes out, leaving family and relationship behind to discover his destiny, she finds her destiny through staying put, completing relationships. But the matter is not so simple. There is no sheer separation or opposition between women's stories and men's stories. The connection between these two story-cycles must be ancient, as it harks back to the roots of the word 'hero'.

18 The etymology of the word hero is unclear. However, a series of scholars have argued for a link between 'hero' and the very ancient Greek goddess Hera.[7] The root carries the sense of 'timely, seasonable, ripe' and even 'marriagable'. The etymologists argue that the 'hero' was the divine consort of the Goddess, who was 'ripe' for marriage.[8] In addition, he was often united with her in a 'seasonal' ceremony: the periodic sacrifice of the fertility rites.[9] This connection, it is argued, is not merely a matter of etymology, but is felt within the very language of the epics.[10]

19 If this etymology is correct, the very word hero stems from the ancient concept of the young divine consort for the goddess. The hypothesized Primitive Indo-European root is **ye-ro*, which appears in Pali as *hora* 'hour', and in English also as 'hour', 'year', 'horoscope', etc. The goddess was the embodiment of the seasons: in the spring she brought life, and with the coming of winter, death. The 'King of the Years' was married and conse-

crated to the goddess before being sacrificed; and indeed, Hera spends an inordinate amount of time persecuting Herakles.

20 From its very roots, then, the story of the hero is the story of a man. Which raises a problem: if the hero myth is masculine, and if it tells the story of the attaining of consciousness, could consciousness itself be a 'masculine' symbol? This was one of Jung's basic theses, framed by his student Neumann thus '... in both sexes the active ego consciousness is characterized by a male symbolism, the unconscious as a whole by a female symbolism.'[11] This does not mean, of course, that men are conscious and women are unconscious; it means that consciousness is associated with stereotypically 'masculine' qualities, such as light, the sun, analysis, etc., while unconsciousness is associated with qualities regarded as 'feminine', such as darkness, the moon, intuition, etc. We have already noted that in Jungian theory, the unconscious is not a twisted realm of suppressed desires, but is the entire ocean of life, from which consciousness emerges as fragile, low-lying atolls, always under threat from the rising tide. Neumann remarks that men tend to identify primarily with consciousness and see the unconscious as alien, while women tend to identify primarily with the unconscious and see the conscious as alien.

21 Obviously such attitudes are problematic, for while we may assert that the conscious and unconscious are equally real, equally essential aspects of our selves, we can hardly escape making a value-judgment: consciousness is *better* than unconsciousness. We don't need to solve such problems here, but simply be aware that they are present in both our primary sources and secondary analyses. It could be the case that this pattern represents a fundamental truth of human nature; or it could be merely a contingent aspect of the cultures we are studying. Our aim is not to construct a post-gendered psychology, but to better understand the way such gender stereotypes are depicted within these ancient texts.

MIRACULOUS BIRTH

22 *In an inconspicuous village the maid is born who will maintain herself undefiled of the fashionable errors of her generation: a miniature in the midst of men of the cosmic woman who was the bride of the wind. Her womb, remaining fallow as the primordial abyss, summons to itself by its very readiness the original power that fertilized the void.*[12]

23 Campbell describes four types of heroic birth, reflecting the stages of evolution of the *mythos*: the cosmological emergence from the World Mother; the individualized, often anthropomorphic goddess; the perfect, spiritualized, human mother; and the virgin mother, human or animal, of folk-tales. Although Campbell here just mentions the Buddha in passing under the fourth category, it would seem rather that his birth should be considered under the third, which I have quoted above.[13]

24 As we have seen, the birth is told in the context of the Buddhas of the past in the Dīgha Nikāya; by Ānanda in reference to Siddhattha in the Majjhima Nikāya; and is referred to in the Aṅguttara. Even in these early sources, the event is accompanied by miracles: light radiates across the vasty cosmos; divine beings attend on the Buddha; the mother is a 'virgin'. The birth confirms most of the standard elements of the hero's birth. There are two sets of parents, human and divine.[14] These two sets are mirrored in two sets of attendants at the birth: 'first deities receive him, then humans'. The use of water symbolizes the emergence from the womb (comparable to the common motif of the baby rescued from the waters). The gem resting on the cloth symbolizes the baby in the womb (comparable to the more common motif of the rebirth from a box or chest).

25 The birth is on a journey, neither in the paternal nor maternal home, but returned to the original home, nature.[15] The true hero is an outsider, an exception, and loneliness is the heritage of his singularity.

26 Māyā is a miracle on the bleeding edge of reality. Just as she vanished from Siddhattha's vision after seven days, still today she dissolves when we look at her directly. Her passing, the separation from the natural mother, is yet another classic item of the hero's story. Māyā's absence is her most essential attribute. Calasso says:

> 27 We are born old, of an age that dates back to the beginning of time. Every life is a segment in which certain actions fade and others blossom. More than anyone else, the Buddha appreciated the mass of pain stored up in time by the accumulation of one act after another. Perfection is achieved when someone is about to put an end to the long series of actions. Then that person is surrounded by a sudden lightness, an emptiness.
>
> 28 When the Buddha was born, he was close to that perfection. He just had to finish 'doing what had to be done', as one common for-

> mula among his disciples put it. Hence his whole life was a gesture of farewell. Hence it was overlaid with a patina of melancholy and absence. The loves of his youth—his father, his mother, his wife—these figures are barely sketched in. They have no features. They perform their functions and disappear.[16]

PROPHECY

29 This is not depicted in the prose Suttas or Vinaya, but is found in the Sutta Nipāta verses, poetic rapture being the appropriate literary form for prophecy.[17] The sage Asita, seeing the rejoicing of the Gods at the birth of Siddhattha, visited Siddhattha's family. In vivid narrative verse we are shown the splendor of the child, like 'beams of brilliant gold', with divine beings holding parasols over his head. Asita discerned the marks that showed Siddhattha's future spiritual prowess, and promptly burst into tears: he himself would die without hearing the Dhamma.[18]

30 This story is not part of the earliest records of the Buddha's life. Quite apart from the subject matter, the metre betrays it as a late addition to the Sutta Nipāta.[19] Still, it represents an earlier version of the tradition than the final form we are used to, for here we find no mention of the two paths open to the Bodhisatta, to become a Buddha or a Universal Monarch. Later tellings of this story rationalized this discrepancy by the simple device of multiplying the number of sages who made prophecies: the lesser figures asserted that the Bodhisatta faced a genuine dilemma, while only Asita saw the inevitability of Awakening.

31 The idea that Siddhattha was destined for Awakening from the time of his birth was already implied in the birth narrative and is made explicit here. Yet it stands in direct contradiction to the doctrine of choice which was the hallmark of the conscious aspect of the Buddha's teaching. Remember: the Buddha explicitly rejected doctrines of destiny, and made it quite plain that his Awakening was dependent, not on his destiny from birth, but on his efforts in meditation during his period of striving.[20] Once the story is adopted within a mythic framework, however, it must take on the aura of inevitability, for that is what myths do. For Buddhists, telling and retelling the story countless times, the idea that Siddhattha might not get Awakened would be as preposterous as Sītā not following Rāma into the forest.

MARVELOUS CHILDHOOD

32 The hero may be either of humble or of royal birth. The Buddha was a member of the Śākyan clan, the ruling class of an aristocratic republic.[21] It should be noted that the Śākyan republic was not a 'kingdom', and despite later tradition, the Buddha's father was not a king. In the early texts, all we are told directly is that the Bodhisatta was brought up in luxurious style, in marked contrast to his later ascetic lifestyle. These two phases of his life formed the nexus that inspired his first sermon, where he warned against following the extremes of sensual indulgence and self-mortification.

33 The most important event of his childhood was his spontaneous entry into the first jhana while he was sitting under the cool shade of a rose-apple tree, his father away working.[22] The later memory of this celebrated event, recorded by all the traditions, marked the turning point in the Buddha's journey towards Awakening. The absence of the father at this crucial juncture signifies Siddhattha's independence. But when the father returned, we are told in later sources, he bowed to his son.

34 These meager details are just about all we know with any surety of Siddhattha's early life. Of course, the later stories are eager to fill this gap with all manner of fancies, which I will pass over for now. But even the few details we do have conform to the 'wonderful childhood' pattern. The general pattern tells us the general truth: we are dealing with someone with an extraordinary future. And the specifics, the peculiarities, give a hint as to the nature of Siddhattha's particular brand of hero: the transcendent meditator, explorer of the outer reaches of consciousness.

❖

35 From here we embark on Campbell's seventeen stages, summarizing the general description of each stage from the relevant sections of Campbell.

DEPARTURE

1. THE CALL TO ADVENTURE

36 *A blunder—apparently the merest chance—reveals an unexpected world, and the individual is drawn into a relationship with forces that are not rightly*

> *understood ... there is an atmosphere of irresistible fascination about the figure that appears suddenly as a guide, marking a new period, a new stage, in the biography. That which has to be faced, and is somehow profoundly familiar to the unconscious—though unknown, surprising, and even frightening to the conscious personality—makes itself known; and what formerly was meaningful may become strangely emptied of value ... destiny has summoned the hero and transferred his spiritual center of gravity from within the pale of his society to a zone unknown.*

37 The early prose texts simply say that Siddhattha reflected on the suffering of worldly life and decided to go forth in search of the deathless.[23]

38 There is a quite different account of the call in the Attadaṇḍa Sutta. And just as the verses of Asita's prophecy are late, metrically artificial, inauthentic, and are regarded without question as literal history by the Buddhist tradition; so the Attadaṇḍa Sutta is found in the perhaps the earliest section of the canon (the Aṭṭhakavagga), is realistic, formally archaic, and authentic, and is utterly ignored by all Buddhists. Here is a translation of the relevant passage:

39 Fear is born from taking up arms—
See the people fight!
I'll describe the motivation
By which I was inspired [to go forth].

40 I saw people flapping about,
Hostile to each other—
Like fish in too little water.
Seeing this, fear came upon me.

41 All around, the world is without essence,
Every direction is trembling.
I longed to find a place for myself,
But I could see nowhere that was unoccupied.

42 Hostility until the very end:
Seeing this, I became dispassionate.
But then I made out a dart,
Hard to see, stuck in the heart.

43 One who is overcome by this dart
runs about in all directions.
But if the dart is removed,
one doesn't run, one settles down.[24]

44 In these verses, the call stems not from any divine intervention, but from an existential crisis triggered by the universal prevalence of conflict and violence. The psychology of the process is breathtakingly normal, and will be familiar to anyone who has been seriously moved to undertake the spiritual quest.

45 For Buddhists everywhere, however, the call occurs, not in an ordinary response to stress and conflict, but in the story of the four 'signs'. This story, like the birth, was originally told of Vipassī in the Mahāpadāna Sutta; so the life of our Buddha is derived from legends of previous world systems, as if the tradition itself were telling us that these are archetypes, not personal history. The Bodhisatta's father kept him caged within the house so that he would not know suffering. Inevitably, he went out and encountered the four signs: the old man, the sick man, the corpse, and the sage.

46 Earlier I suggested that the Jungian notion of archetypes may be understood through the Buddhist perspective on rebirth. This allows a straightforward reading of this episode. In each life, we are nurtured and protected by our parents, who shield us as best they can from the harsh realities of the world. As we mature, however, the power of our parents to control the world diminishes, and inevitably we step outside their protective realm. We see the signs, uncomfortable visions of death, disease, and suffering, and we realize that this is our nature. All this is simply part of the process of growing up. It is not a fantasy, but simply a mythic projection of a universalized human experience, experienced as numinous, magical, and exalted because our own experience in this life resonates in some uncanny, unconscious way with our experiences in countless past lives. What is not so universal, however, is the encounter with the sage. Many of us might go our whole lives without this rare blessing. Nevertheless, the sage is a standard trope of the hero myth, and meeting a wise old person who helps direct our life in the right way is, if not universal, perhaps not so unusual.

47 Later tradition claims that these signs were manifested by the gods specifically for the Bodhisatta. The four 'signs' become the four 'Divine Messengers'. Thus the mythographers elevate the episode further and further from the personal.

48 They also tell us why the Bodhisatta went out to the park in the first place: to play.[25] Thus the Bodhisatta returns to the (symbolic) place of his birth, for the same reason his mother entered the grove. It is there that he brings to consciousness the same pattern that had been imprinted unconsciously by his mother in her self-sacrifice. The encounter with these archetypes, resonating with the infant's most powerful early experience, and beyond that to the wisdom of the endless stream of past lives, triggers the unleashing of psychic energy that propels Siddhattha from his home and into his spiritual quest.

49 The resistance and caging by the father represents Freud's superego: the constraining dictates of conventional authority. The hero must, by his very nature, transcend the limitations of ordinary life, breaking out of the cycle. If the mother represents the instinctual world of nature, the father represents the conventional rules of culture. She is the 'is', he is the 'ought'. This role is not played by Suddhodana in 'this' life alone. In the past, too, he has been the obstructive father, as we have already seen in the Kaṭṭhahāri Jātaka. At this stage the relation with the father as the primary male figure is adversarial, and demands a later resolution.

2. REFUSAL OF THE CALL

50 *Often in actual life, and not infrequently in the myths and popular tales, we encounter the dull case of the call unanswered; for it is always possible to turn the ear to other interests ... One is bound in by the walls of childhood; the father and mother stand as threshold guardians, and the timorous soul, fearful of some punishment, fails to make the passage through the door and come to birth in the world without.*

51 This is not apparent in Siddhattha's story in the canon, but is found in the Mahāpadāna Sutta. Bodhisatta Vipassī, having seen the four Divine Messengers, returns to the palace and broods over the meaning of what he has seen before making the fateful decision. In later retellings this was made into an intrinsic part of Siddhattha's experience.

3. SUPERNATURAL AID

52 *For those who have not refused the call, the first encounter of the hero-journey is with a protective figure (often a little old crone or old man) who provides the adventurer with amulets against the dragon forces he is about to*

pass. This stage is interpreted psychologically as the voice from the depths of the unconscious: an inner assurance that the hero possesses abilities beyond what he considers normally possible, which he can call upon at the time of crisis.

53 The supernatural aid has appeared twice in the late canonical texts, as Asita and as the Divine Messengers. Later texts elaborately develop this theme; the gods hold the hoofs of the Bodhisatta's horse, so that the noise does not disturb anyone and prevent his escape; the Bodhisatta meets a hunter in the woods who supplies him with the ascetics' robes (but the hunter is really a deity in disguise); and so on. Such motifs, in the Bodhisatta's case, appear more as embellishments rather than essential guides, for the thrust of the story concerns Siddhattha's resolute individual achievements.

54 Nevertheless, divinity is a tricky thing. Gods don't like to show their true face. They prefer to work undercover. We should be careful lest the most unlikely stranger turns out to be a divinity in disguise.[26] The early texts speak of Yasa, one of the first disciples, leaving his home in disgust at seeing the women of the harem lying sprawled, naked, and drooling. The scene, with its evocative imagery, inevitably made its way into the Buddha's life story. Eventually Aśvaghoṣa in his Buddhacarita revealed that, like the four Divine Messengers, the whole thing was the plan of a deity, conceived when they saw that the Bodhisatta took no delight in the beauty of the women.[27] Here are a selection of verses describing the scene.

> 55 Thereupon the Akaniṣṭha devas, supreme in austerities, taking cognizance of his resolve, all at once brought sleep there over the women and distorted the gestures of their limbs.
>
> 56 So one, as she lay there, supported her cheek on an unsteady hand, and, as if angry, abandoned the flute in her lap, dear though it was to her, with its decoration of gold leaf.
>
> 57 Another, lying with her bamboo pipe in her hands and her white robe slipping off her breasts, resembled a river with lotuses being enjoyed by a straight row of bees and with banks laughing with the foam of the water.
>
> 58 Another lay, leaning against the side of a window with her beautiful necklaces dangling, and seemed with her slender body bent like a bow as if turned into the statue of a *śāla*-plucker on a gateway.[28]

59 Another again had her lotus-face bowed down, thereby causing the jewelled earrings to eat into the lines of paint, so that it took the likeness of a lotus with its stalk half-curved, as it is shaken by a *kāraṇḍava* bird standing on it.

60 Others lay in the position in which they had sat down, and, embracing each other with intertwined arms decorated with golden bracelets, appeared to have their bodies bent down under the load of their breasts.

61 Yet another clasped her mighty *parivādinī*, as if it were her friend, and rolled about in her sleep, so that her golden threads shook and her face had the pendant strings on her ears all disordered.

62 Another too had her hair loose and dishevelled, and with the ornaments and clothes fallen from her hips and her necklaces scattered she lay like an image of a woman broken by an elephant.

63 But others, helplessly lost to shame despite their natural decorum and endowment of excellent beauty, lay in immodest attitudes, snoring, and stretched their limbs, all distorted and tossing their arms about.

64 Others looked ugly, lying unconscious like corpses, with their ornaments and garlands cast aside, the fastening knots of their dresses undone, and eyes moveless with the whites showing.

65 Another lay as if spawled in intoxication, with her mouth gaping wide, so that the saliva oozed forth, and with her lims spread out so as to show what should have been hid. Her beauty was gone, her form distorted.

66 When the king's son saw the young women lying in these different ways and looking so loathesome with their uncontrolled movements, though ordinarily their forms were beautiful, their speech agreeable, he was moved to disgust:

67 'Such is the real nature of women in the world of the living, impure and loathesome; yet man, deceived by dress and ornaments, succumbs to passion for women.'

68 Thus he recognized the difference and there arose in him a desire to escape that night. Then the gods, understanding his purpose, caused the doors of the palace to fly open.

69 An irresistible scene, on which the poets loved to linger. Aśvaghoṣa outdoes himself to evoke the opposing aesthetic flavours of lust and revulsion. He plays with his audience; the verses start with erotic imagery that is cunningly calculated to arouse a conflicted response in his audience, who

would have been primarily Buddhist men. They would know that they shouldn't be turned on by these 'loose women', yet the poet does his best to do so. Almost imperceptibly, the imagery moves from arousal to disgust, with imagery that is at first ambiguous—the dishevelled, bent, and broken—before revealing his final artistic purpose: to show the sleeping women as a charnel ground of vile corpses.

70 We experience in ourselves the poignant ambiguity of the Bodhisatta's situation. The ambiguity is an emotional response, but is also part of the playful narrative structure. The reality is a god of a very high order, whose being is radiant and pure. He creates the false appearance of women, who are intrinsically impure but try to fake purity. So, being himself pure, he is faking impurity to show the reality of impurity; while the women, themselves impure, are faking purity. And the god who reveals this truth is a fake; for the whole hall of mirrors is nothing but a *māyā* from the imagination of the poet, Aśvaghoṣa.

71 This is not mere literary play. It is a genuine, heartfelt struggle in the poet's mind, as it is for us. For how tenuous is the line between desire and disgust! The same scene might appear in quite a different light when illumined with a different imagination. When Hanumān snuck at night into the citadel of Rāvaṇa, demon king of Laṅkā, in search of the noble Sītā, he saw thousands of lovely women sleeping after a night of love.

> 72 Their thick garlands and lovely ornaments had fallen into disarray as the women had played their games of love drunkenly before falling asleep. The vermillion on the foreheads of some of these women had smeared and spread, others had lost an anklet, yet others had their pearls over to one side where they had slipped. The necklaces of some women had broken, the girdles of others had snapped, some even lay there totally naked like mares who, with their burdens removed, were free to roll in the grass. Pearl necklaces gleaming like soft moonlight lay between their breasts like sleeping swans. Even the marks left by their ornaments on their bodies were as lovely as the ornaments themselves. Stirred by their soft breathing, their upper garments fluttered over their mouths and their earrings quivered gently. Their naturally sweet breath mingled with the fragrance of wine and liquor and fanned Rāvaṇa gently. Some of his wives kissed their companions again and again, imagining they were kissing Rāvaṇa. One slept with her arms thrown over another's breasts. Overcome with love and

> alcohol, they slept happily, their limbs entwined, breasts, hips, and thighs pressed to each others'. Even when their ornaments, garlands, and limbs were in the right places, it was not possible to tell which belonged to whom.[29]

73 The same scene, but how different the eyes! The Rāmāyaṇa is simpler, its emotions more straightforward, less disturbing. But in both cases the dancing girls are a distraction from the quest and must be left behind. The Rāmāyaṇa, a worldly epic, sees the dancing girls through the eyes of desire. In the Buddhist story they are cast in shadow; but, like the four Divine Messengers, their very negativity is ultimately positive, for it is the spur to Awakening. So, while the Rāmāyaṇa version seems to depict the women more positively, they are more or less irrelevant distractions from the main quest, whereas they are essential in the Buddhist version.

74 Which is why the dancing girls are messengers from the Gods.

4. THE CROSSING OF THE FIRST THRESHOLD

75 *With the personification of his destiny to guide and aid him, the hero goes forward in his adventure until he comes to the 'threshold guardian' at the entrance to the zone of magnified power. Such custodians bound the world in the four directions—also up and down—standing for the limits of the hero's present sphere, or life horizon. Beyond them is darkness, the unknown, and danger; just as beyond the parental watch is danger to the infant and beyond the protection of his society danger to the member of the tribe ... The regions of the unknown (desert, jungle, deep sea, alien land, etc.) are free fields for the projections of unconscious content.*

76 This first threshold is represented by the Buddha's family.[30] His father Suddhodana's resistance is not explicitly depicted in the earliest tradition, and his imprisonment of Siddhattha in the palace is a later melodrama. Still, an early passage says that when he went forth, Siddhattha's 'mother and father wished otherwise and grieved with tearful faces'.[31] Later on, when the Buddha returns home, his father spoke to him of the pain that he suffered seeing so many of his family go forth as monks.

77 When the Blessed One went forth, I experienced no little suffering; similarly with Nanda, and even more so with Rāhula. Love of one's children, Bhante, pierces the surface; having pierced the surface it pierces the skin; having pierced the skin it pierces the flesh; having

> pierced the flesh it pierces the sinews; having pierced the sinews it pierces the bones; having pierced the bones it enters the marrow and stays there. It would be good, Bhante, if the venerables did not give the going forth without the parent's permission.[32]

78 So this emotional conflict is there from the start, before the mythic elaborations. The Buddha, acquiescing to his fathers' wishes, lays down a rule requiring that a candidate get the permission of their parents before taking ordination. But this was a later concession to conventions, not Siddhattha's own journey. For ignoring the wishes of his family and the cultural expectations on him to fulfill his political destiny, Siddhattha abandoned all to face the wilderness alone.

79 The most moving and emotionally troubling aspect of his going forth was the abandoning of his wife and child. This is not directly mentioned in the earliest versions, but the developed tellings lingered over the scene, wringing the maximum emotional impact from the pathos of the poor wife, left behind; and Siddhattha's inner turmoil as he surmounted his attachment in his heroic struggle. Typically it is said that he glanced in at his wife and child sleeping just as he was about to leave. Sometimes she is said to wake up; knowing that he is leaving her, she says, 'Take me to the place you are going.' He replies, 'I will.' And of course, many years later, he took both wife and child to the place he was going: Nibbana.

80 The traditions cannot leave such points of conflict alone, but worry them with their interpretations. Was Siddhattha a callous deserter? Was it somehow okay because he knew she would be looked after in their extended family? Does his higher spiritual purpose justify inflicting such suffering? Each new telling presents this crisis afresh, offering a slightly revised perspective. And that is very purpose of such conflicts. They can never be resolved once and for all. If they were, they would leave behind a dead myth. The life of the story comes from the irreconcilable contradiction between the values of the world and the values of the renunciate. Rather than trying to ethically justify Siddhattha's choice, the narrative serves to highlight this basic conflict in a moment of unforgettable agony.

81 The story is gendered: it is the man who leaves, while the woman stays at home. The same tale is played out countless times in Indian stories. Yet occasionally we encounter a woman who treats her man the same. The

Kumbhakāra Jātaka tells of a time when the Bodhisatta was a potter in Bārāṇasī. He met four Pacceka Buddhas who inspired him with stories of their own renunciation.[33] Hearing those stories, both he and his wife—who was of course Bimbā, his wife in this life, too—had the desire to leave the world immediately. His wife said she wanted to be free, 'like a bird released from the hand'. But there was the delicate problem of what to do with the children. She told her husband that she wanted to collect water, and taking a water pot, she ran off and took ordination. He stayed behind until the children were able to look after themselves, and then he too became an ascetic. Later when he met his former wife, she accused him of killing the children, but he denied this, and in turn accused her of abandoning her duties, merely following her own pleasure in ordaining. So not only is the women as a home-leaver and husband-deserter far rarer than the reverse, when she does she is subject to a specific ethical critique that men largely escape. Of course we could question her ethics in leaving in such a deceitful manner; but Siddhattha's going forth was, in most tellings, no less deceitful.

82 Leaving family behind means leaving order behind. The rules of kinship, bonds of love and duty, settled urban life, a mapped-out career; all these things give a structure to life, a reassurance of safety amid the chaos of the wilds. The essence of the renunciate's journey is to leave this conventional safety, exposing oneself to the primitive elements, the course of nature, the vagaries of the wind and weather. In such an environment, one returns to the roots of the mind, encountering the same forces met daily by our evolutionary ancestors. The assumptions and comfortable dilemmas of settled life fade away, replaced by more raw and primal fears. While nature is beautiful, hers is a ragged and demanding beauty. The dangers were very real: the forests were haunted by tigers, lions, elephants, bears, and snakes. Disease, thirst, and hunger were never far away. Siddhattha was by no means immune to these fears. In the discourse titled 'Fear & Dread', he told how he deliberately sought out the most terrifying and powerful of locations to sit in during the night. He felt the fear coming on, even at the mere sound of the wind or a bird rustling a twig. He determined to practice until he could overcome all such fears as they arose.[34]

5. THE BELLY OF THE WHALE

83 *The hero, instead of conquering or conciliating the power of the threshold, is swallowed into the unknown, and would appear to have died ... the physical body of the hero may be actually slain, dismembered, and scattered over the land or sea ... the hero whose attachment to ego is already annihilate passes back and forth across the horizons of the world, in and out of the dragon, as readily as a king through all the rooms of his house. And therein lies his power to save....*

84 The Bodhisatta 'dies' to his family and to civilization as he disappears into the raw jungle.[35] Like countless other seekers, he surrenders to the powers of nature, and there finds his inner strength. He adopts the timeless symbols of the outsider: the shaven head—as a baby, an old man, a sacrificial victim,[36] or a condemned criminal[37]—and the ascetic's robes. These robes are the red of sacrificial blood, and are worn by the hunter,[38] the executioner,[39] the mourner,[40] and the criminal in exile.[41]

85 The ceremony of going forth is an initiation rite which significantly parallels funeral rituals. The ascetic to this day in India is thought to have died to his parents, and will not so much as greet them if he passes them in the street. Gilligan remarks that 'the sacrifice of relationship is the ritual of initiation into patriarchy.'[42] But ordination is not just a 'rising out of' (*vuṭṭhāpana*) the conventional family, but the 'entering into' (*upasampadā*) the spiritual family of the Sangha.

86 The same motif is repeated a little later in the story in the dramatic accounts of the Bodhisatta's ascetic practices. With vivid imagery the Buddha describes how he tortured himself until even the gods could not tell whether he was alive or dead.[43] But, as always in the journey of the hero, this stage of virtual death is not an ending, but a sign of the great transformation to come.

87 Buddhist traditions have always been uncomfortable with this stage of the Buddha's life. The Buddha condemned severe austerities, this being the burden of his first discourse. Yet within the structure of the Buddha's life, the severity of his efforts functions as a badge of authenticity, used by the Buddha himself to contest the claims of rivals who asserted that his 'middle way' was merely indulgence.

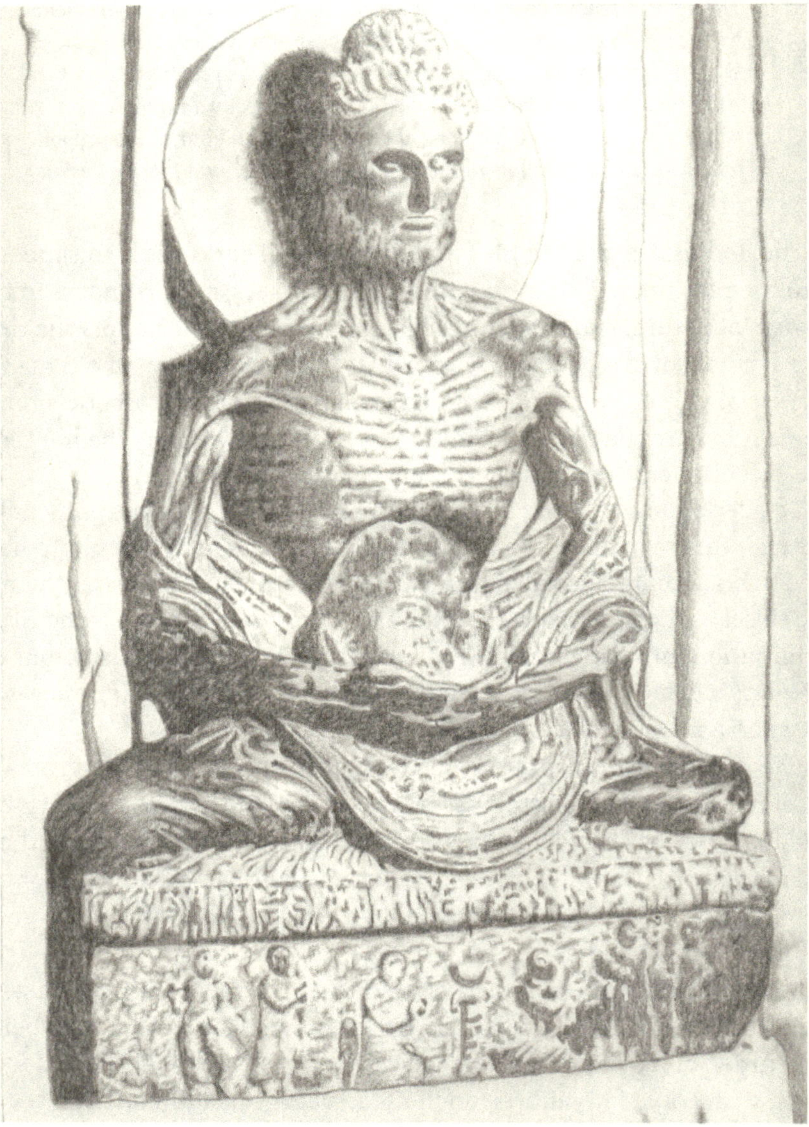

***Figure 24.1:** Starving Bodhisatta*

88 Later traditions attempted in diverse ways to rationalize this ambiguity: the Bodhisatta did the austerities because of his past kamma (but he denied that the pain of austerities was born of past kamma); or he was setting an example of unflagging effort (but he stated that others were not to follow this example); and so on. Furthermore, it is ridiculous to say, as does the later tradition, that the Bodhisatta, having practiced a conscious program of spiritual development for countless lifetimes, should at this last moment completely forget what he is supposed to do and waste time in useless penance.[44] All attempts to explain this away falter before the Buddha's assertion that he practiced in this way because of his own wrong view: he falsely believed that the way to pleasure was through pain.[45] But the period of self-torment, while incongruous in the 'official' version of the Buddha's career, makes perfect sense as an episode in the hero's journey.

CHAPTER 25

THE HERO WAKES

CAMPBELL CALLS THE NEXT STAGE 'INITIATION'. It marks the climax of the heroic quest; in Buddhist terms, Awakening. The hero has escaped the stultifying safety of family and friends. Ahead lies his greatest test.

THE INITIATION

6. THE ROAD OF TRIALS

2 *Once having traversed the threshold, the hero moves in a dream landscape of curiously fluid, ambiguous forms, where he must survive a succession of trials.... The ordeal is a deepening of the first threshold and the question is still in balance: Can the ego put itself to death?... The original departure into the land of trials represented only the beginning of the long and really perilous path of initiatory conquests and moments of illumination. Dragons have now to be slain and surprising barriers passed—again, again, and again. Meanwhile there will be a multitude of preliminary victories, unretainable ecstasies, and momentary glimpses of the wonderful land.*

3 The Bodhisatta studied with the foremost mystics of his day, Āḷāra Kālāma and Udaka Rāmaputta.[1] There he learnt to enter into the deepest levels of formless *samādhi*, a purified and expanded world of the mind. This meditation attainment was taught within a theoretical framework where *samādhi* led to an afterlife of purity and bliss. Intent on transcending all forms of rebirth, no matter how wonderful, Siddhattha left his teachers behind. Following this was the years of terrible ordeal as he tortured his body beyond endurance.

Figure 25.1: *The assault of Māra*

4 The assault of Māra also comes under this heading. In its earliest forms the struggle with Māra is depicted solely in psychological terms: the ten 'armies' of Māra are desire, hunger, sloth, and so forth.[2] This, however, was too abstract for the storytellers, and soon enough we find legends and art depicting the nightmare forms of Death and Desire trying to forcibly smash the Bodhisatta from his seat. The utter hopelessness of the attack is conveyed in some of the oldest representations, which show the furious army raging around a Buddha who is not there. Since he is only symbols—the tree and the empty seat—he offers no target for their wrath.

7. THE MEETING WITH THE GODDESS

5 *The ultimate adventure, when all barriers and ogres have been overcome, is commonly presented as a mystical marriage of the triumphant hero-soul with the Queen Goddess of the World. This is the crisis at the nadir, the zenith, or at the uttermost edge of the earth, at the central point of the cosmos, in the tabernacle of the temple, or within the darkness of the deepest chamber of the heart.... Woman, in the picture language of mythology, represents the totality of what can be known. The hero is the one who comes to know.*

6 The meeting with the goddess is made literal only in the later legends.[3] She is evoked with the startling image of the earth-goddess, who appears in her full sensual glory beneath the Buddha on the very cusp of his Awakening, bearing witness to the power of the virtues Siddhattha had accumulated in countless past lives. These accumulated virtues (*pāramī*) made his victory over Māra possible, even inevitable. As so often, the goddess is associated with the notions of fate, of destiny, of the cyclic repetitions of events. Sometimes she is imagined as letting loose a flood from her hair, drowning Māra's army while the Buddha remains high and dry: an inversion of Mahāpajāpatī's flood, but one which cannot be understood outside the wider context of Indic myth. The rush of the Ganges unleashed upon the earth from the heavens is caught by Śiva in his massive ascetic's dreadlocks. He checks the mighty rush, and releases it gently so that the transformed waters become a source of bounty for all.[4]

7 Her appearance here is even more apt. We have read several of the Jātakas so as to emphasize the divine nature of the female characters. So we agree with the mythographers: the goddess was present in the Bodhisatta's past lives and did indeed witness his acts.

Figure 25.2: *The Goddess washes away the host of Māra*

8 The earth-goddess appears on the cosmic plane. Her more homely counterpart is Sujātā,[5] who fed him the milk-rice that rescued him from the self-imposed starvation of his self-torment. Sujātā is not found in the early texts, and this episode is only alluded to by the bare mention that the Bodhisatta decided to eat some rice and bread.

9 The Sinhalese say that Sujātā had prepared a special offering for the god of the tree in gratitude for having given birth to a son. She took the milk from a thousand cows and fed it to five hundred; then took their milk and fed it to half as many, until it got down to sixteen cows, whose milk was fed to eight cows. Their milk was sweet and full of goodness. Finding the Bodhisatta sitting under the tree she took him for the god and offered the milk-rice to him. The gods came and sheltered the Bodhisattva for his meal.[6]

10 This story makes the fertility motifs quite explicit, right down to the actual food offered. The grain is the paradigmatic fertility fruit of Mother Earth; historically, the achievement of grain cultivation made civilization possible, with its massive increase in human population; while the milk is, obviously, the offering of the mother, the animal embodiment of the same spirit of nurturing. This is made even more explicit in the Abhiniṣkramaṇa Sūtra, where, on seeing the Bodhisattva, Sujātā's breasts spontaneously give forth milk.[7] Just like Māyā. The repeated feeding of the milk back to the cows suggests the 'purification' theory of milk-production: milk is purified blood, so if the cows consume it again and again, it will become even more purified.

11 But the way the Mahāsaṅghikas tell the story, Sujātā's involvement with the Bodhisattva is a little more direct. The Bodhisattva was seen walking for alms by Sujātā, who 'was stirred by the passion of love'. Weeping, she stood before him and begged him to stay, for 'my eyes can never have enough of gazing upon thee ... my heart is blinded with unrequited love.' As he left the village, she ran after him with a crowd of women all weeping. She lamented that such a delicate one could never survive the rigors of the wilds, and wished 'May the ogres, spirits, and serpents guard thy body, the delicate body of the offspring of devas, which delights heart and mind more than sun and moon.'[8] Thus, despite her longings, she would not cling

or obstruct his spiritual path, but would only urge him to practice in peace and joy.

12 Before this, the Bodhisatta was pursuing the path of destroying his body to free his mind. Accepting the milk-rice, to the disgust of his more ascetically-minded companions, signified the acceptance of his whole humanity, both body and mind. It was then that his companions abandoned him: the extreme ascetic mind is in unconscious thrall to the temptress, and so rejects the nourishing aspect of the feminine.

13 After eating, the Bodhisatta proceeded to Uruvelā, where he saw a delightful grove near a clear stream, with a resort for alms nearby. He found a place to sit. And it does not seem improbable that his chosen place was well cleaned and beautiful because of the special attentions paid to it by the locals. In India even today, there is one tree that is accorded special worship. Calasso says:

14 What happened in India, from the Vedas to the Buddha, belonged to the trunk of a single tree, the immense *aśvattha* rooted in the sky, that spread its branches everywhere, covering the earth. What was inside that trunk? *Brahman*. And what was *brahman*? The 'unique that awakes' says the Maitri Upaniṣad. The *brahman* was consciousness and what brings consciousness to birth: the Awakening One. In the end, a solitary monk came to sit at the foot of the tree, which on this occasion was a common fig tree, in Bihar.[9]

15 The tree is a feminine symbol not merely because it is the bearer of fruit. It is also a 'container' which shelters birds and their nests, and all manner of other creatures. Moreover, it is a conduit, a locus of transformation between the Mother Earth in whom its roots are so deeply embedded, and the sky whose denizens it offers a home to in its branches.[10]

16 The sheltering aspect of the tree is brought forth in the Pali word for 'plant', *bhūtagāma*, which means 'home of a being'. It was quite literally believed that the tree was home, not just for the animals, birds, and bugs, but for deities. As the world tree, the fig known to Buddhists as the 'Bodhi Tree' was revered by the Brahmans as the home of all.

17 With the root above and the branches below stands the eternal fig tree. That truly is the pure, that is Holy Power, that alone is called the deathless. In it all the worlds rest and no one ever goes beyond it. This, truly, is that.[11]

18 Inverted, its roots in heaven, the tree of the all-mother is the roosting place of the soul, which rests in its shelter, and feeds upon its bounty.[12] The sight of birds roosting in the tree like the soul roosts in the body, coming and going as they will, inspired one of the most enduring of spiritual images, repeated throughout Indic literature, starting with the Ṛg Veda itself.

> 19 Two Birds with fair wings, knit with bonds of friendship,
> have found a refuge in the same sheltering tree.
> One of the two eats the sweet Fig-tree's fruit;
> the other does not eat, but only watches over.
>
> 20 Where those fine Birds hymn unblinking their portion
> of the deathless, and the sacred synods,
> There is the Universe's mighty Keeper, who, wise,
> has entered into me the simple.
>
> 21 The tree on which the fine Birds eat the sweetness,
> where they all rest and procreate their offspring—
> Upon its top they say the fig is luscious:
> none gains it who does not know the Father.[13]

22 This image, with its clear differentiation between the 'knower' and the 'doer', is one of the earliest passages anywhere to speak so vividly of the reflexive nature of consciousness. We can still feel the 'two birds' within us, each flighty and flittery, one acting within the world, feeding on the senses, while the other stands back and watches, impassive. The image is reassuring, for the two birds are 'constant companions' peacefully sharing the fruit of the tree, so abundant in fertility, while they sing the sacred mantras. But the tree is also home to the Father of Knowing, who brings wisdom. And those who plucked the highest fruit: who might they have been?

8. WOMAN AS THE TEMPTRESS

23 *Generally we refuse to admit within ourselves, or within our friends, the fullness of that pushing, self-protective, malodorous, carnivorous, lecherous fever which is the very nature of the organic cell. Rather, we tend to perfume, white-wash, and re-interpret; meanwhile imagining that all the flies in the ointment, all the hairs in the soup, are the faults of some unpleasant someone else. But when it suddenly dawns on us, or is forced to our attention, that*

> *everything we think or do is necessarily tainted with the odor of the flesh, then, not uncommonly, there is experienced a moment of revulsion: life, the acts of life, the organs of life, woman in particular as the great symbol of life, become intolerable to the pure, the pure, pure soul.*

24 Campbell has been criticized for speaking of the woman as temptress. Of course, the woman is just one form that temptation takes in story. Although she is especially relevant for a man intent on an ascetic path, in other contexts the temptation is presented in very different forms. However, in Buddhism, as in Indic tradition generally, the tempter is, indeed, typically a woman,[14] although a man might also fulfill this role, as in the confrontations between the bhikkhunis and Māra or various would-be suitors.[15]

25 This part of the story is taken up in the Sutta Nipāta. As with the tale of Asita, it seems that here we have the first occurrence of some of the more colorful episodes that fleshed out the dry prose statements.[16]

26 The Bodhisatta strives in meditation and vanquishes the hordes of Māra, which this earliest account depicts in purely psychological terms. Shattered by his defeat, the despondent demon allows his daughters to enter the fray. Craving, Lust, and Desire appear before the Bodhisatta with all their manifold delights, but he ignores them, so that even Māra dismisses them as 'trying to split a rock with a lily stem, dig a hill with your nails, chew iron with your teeth, or cling to a cliff face with a boulder on your head...'.

27 Here is the negative depiction of the feminine. The temptation of the sage by a woman is one of the most well-worn tropes of Indian myth, a standard means to undermine the ascetic fervor of one who is becoming so powerful as to threaten even the gods. But here the women are acting in support of Māra, and their sensuality plays out the female stereotype just as his violence plays out the male. Thus there is a two-dimensional symmetry: as bad women they provide the gender balance for Māra the bad man; while in moral terms they balance Sujātā and the earth-goddess, the good women.

28 The pattern requires a 'good man', who in one sense is obviously the Buddha. And yet the myths show the Buddha as someone who transcends gender, even though he may play the male role in a conventional sense. If

the Buddha is the one beyond gender, then the positive male archetype is represented by Brahmā, who acts as Māra's opposite number.

9. ATONEMENT WITH THE FATHER

29 *Atonement (at-one-ment) consists in no more than the abandonment of that self-generated double monster—the dragon thought to be God (superego) and the dragon thought to be sin (repressed id). But this requires an abandonment of the attachment to ego itself, and that is what is difficult. One must have a faith that the father is merciful, and then a reliance on that mercy.*

30 This motif appears explicitly in the second half of the myth, on the return to Kapilavatthu, when the Buddha met his father and converted him.[17] We have seen above that the Mahīśāsaka tradition carried this further by having Suddhodana request ordination. Since the Buddha is the perfect hero the atonement must also be perfect: thus it is believed that Suddhodana attained arahantship on his deathbed.

31 Suddhodana is the Buddha's mortal father, but he also reaches an atonement with Brahmā, the World-Father. The Buddha rejected the texts, social customs, rituals, and philosophy of the brahmans; but after his Awakening, Brahmā himself, the very embodiment of that world-view, comes to the Buddha, declares himself a follower, and asks the Buddha to teach, establish the Dhamma, and refute those of wrong view, i.e. the brahmans. Rather than taking revenge on his rebellious son, Brahmā shows forgiveness and compassion.

10. APOTHEOSIS

32 *Having surpassed the delusions of his formerly self-assertive, self-defensive, self-concerned ego, he knows without and within the same repose. What he beholds without is the visual aspect of the magnitudinous, thought-transcending emptiness on which his own experience of ego, form, perceptions, speech, conceptions, and knowledge ride. And he is filled with compassion for the self-terrorized beings who live in fright of their own nightmare. He rises, returns to them, and dwells with them as an egoless center, through whom the principle of emptiness is made manifest in its own simplicity.*

33 In these culminating stages of the path, the journey becomes more overtly spiritual and hence less transparent to clear formulation.[18] One aspect that Campbell emphasizes here is that the apotheosis—where the

individual transcends the normal state of mortality—involves a dissolution of the boundaries separating the individual from the rest of the world. The Buddha realizes the 'deathless', not in the sense of endless life, but in the sense of freedom from the cycle of birth and death. This freedom is not a matter of chance or destiny or the will of a deity, but is the product of mere humanity in its fullest. Hence it is available to all.

34 So it is here, in the culminating moments of his practice, that the Buddha has a series of momentous dreams, symbolic predictions of his Awakening that emphasize the universal significance of his achievement. Not only will he gain the supreme Awakening, but the reverberations of that event will cover the whole world, with countless beings following the Buddha to liberation. One of the dreams, for example, showed four birds of different colors alighting upon him, foretelling that the four castes would achieve liberation under his teaching. Here the ancient symbolism of the bird as the liberated being is neatly combined with the quasi-racial idea of 'caste', which is the same word as 'color' (*vaṇṇa*).

35 This dream sequence is possibly the earliest passage that hints that the Buddha's awakening would be of such momentous significance for the whole world. To appreciate this, we must free ourselves from the expectations that we have been conditioned into by the traditions. The idea of the 'Bodhisatta' developing their *pāramī* (spiritual perfections) over countless lifetimes is entirely absent from the early scriptures. The Buddha's own followers, and the early centuries of the Buddhist community, knew nothing of such matters. If we follow the story as told in the early texts, there has been scarcely any hint, until now, that Siddhattha was concerned for anything other than making an end of the round of rebirth. It is only now that he reaches beyond the mere human to become a larger-than-life spiritual figure, which is what 'apotheosis' means.

36 The true significance of this dream emerges in a remarkable parallel with the circumstances of Jung's final book, *Man and His Symbols.*[19] These days, Jung has a reputation as a star-gazing irrationalist; but anyone familiar with his writings would know they are in fact dense, difficult, and demanding. He consciously wrote for a specialized audience, for doctors and academics. When he was approached in his old age by the publisher Wolfgang Foges to write a summary of his work for a general readership,

he politely refused. However, he shortly afterwards had a dream of momentous importance to him. He was standing and delivering an address. The audience was not specialists and academics, but a large crowd of ordinary people who listened carefully and understood what he had to say. When Foges returned a few weeks later and repeated his request, Jung agreed.

37 For Siddhattha and for Jung, the first intimation that their wisdom could and should be shared among humanity at large came, not from rational thought, but from a dream. A mere coincidence, perhaps, if such a thing exists.

38 Such imagery could easily be taken as narcissistic. Who sees themselves as the world-liberator? But it is not narcissistic if it is the truth: the Buddha was in fact to become one of the great religious figures of humanity, so the dream simply reflects his genuine capacity. And, like the Buddha, Jung's message has made a deep impression on the minds of many. Because they listened to these dreams and brought their message to the world, their experiences transcended their own mere mortality and took on a significance for us all. They both live within us as conveyors of essential wisdom. But the difference between the scale of their dreams is just as significant: while Jung spoke to a mere crowd, the Buddha became the refuge of humanity.

11. THE ULTIMATE BOON

39 *The agony of breaking through personal limitations is the agony of spiritual growth.... As he crosses threshold after threshold, conquering dragon after dragon, the stature of the divinity that he summons to his highest wish increases, until it subsumes the cosmos. Finally the mind breaks the bounding sphere of the cosmos to a realization transcending all experiences of form—all symbolizations, all divinities: a realization of the ineluctable void.*

40 This is presented from many angles.[20] Sometimes the radiant solar aspect of the Buddha's universal wisdom is stressed:

41 When Dhammas are fully manifest
to the ardent brahman in jhana
There, like the sun that lights the sky,
He stands repelling Māra's hordes.[21]

42 Equally important is the tremendous embrace in the coils of the dragon Muñcalinda. The primeval serpent, chthonic attendant to the Great Mother,

emerges to rise above the ground and wrap the Buddha in its seven coils, a figure of awe-inspiring protection. We have met the number seven many times already; here it carries its usual meaning of the 'whole cycle of life, creation, birth and death'. The dragon here is totally unified with the Buddha, and appears in its aspect of transformation and transcendence. The Buddha is called a *nāga* or dragon, and the iconography depicting this favorite episode is virtually identical with the very common depiction of *nāgas* throughout India. Having encompassed the complete cosmic cycle, as suggested by the number seven, the *nāga* spreads its hood over the Buddha, like wings of freedom or like the parasol of royalty. The completion of the seven stages signifies the perfection of the Self, while the spread hood indicates transcendence. Hence the verse uttered by the Buddha concerns happiness, specifically that the greatest happiness of all is the absence of the idea 'I am'.

CHAPTER 26

THE HERO RETURNS

THE RETURN PIVOTS AROUND THE NIGHT OF THE AWAKENING. The events prior to this are essentially solitary: the Bodhisatta leaves all behind, his family, teachers, and even his spiritual companions. From here on, however, the adventure becomes a social one: how to bring the gift of Awakening back to the community. For all the Buddha's emphasis on his lonely striving in solitude, the depictions of his life in the old Indic inscriptions are crowded with people. Every corner of the frame is stuffed with as many beings as possible; even the skies are full of deities. Those who created these images were not trying to show what 'really happened'. They show themselves in wondering relationship with the Buddha's life. They show what it means to them.

2 Thus the prime source text here is called the Catuṣpariṣat Sutra, the 'Discourse on the [Establishment of the] Four-fold Assembly'.[1] While the Sarvāstivādins preserved this account in the Sutra collection (the Dīrgha Āgama), most other schools included a parallel account in their Vinaya. In fact, from here on the narrative structure is found primarily in the Vinayas, which is appropriate, as the Vinaya is about how to manage a disciplined spiritual community; that is, how to create in many people the Awakening that Buddha found in his solitary adventure.

3 It is crucial to distinguish between the events involved in the 'return' cycle of the Buddha's myth from those of the outward journey. We know that for Buddhists the individual spiritual quest is the most important thing. This the Buddha has already accomplished; and this he shares in

common with Paccekabuddhas or even with 'ordinary' arahants. But his specific function as Fully Awakened One manifests in this return phase, for only such a one can establish the four-fold community. Thus, while the Buddha's personal victory is unshakeable, it was not at all certain that the return would be successful. The community, after the Buddha's demise, could all too readily be re-absorbed in the great swamp of Indic spirituality, like the Nāga King that emerges from the earth to cover the Buddha for seven days, only to sink back into its chthonic slumber.

4 Male law-givers everywhere, from Moses to Manu, prevent this dire fate by a simple means: keep the rules! The very idea of natural laws can be traced as far back as Sumerian observations of the immutable workings of the heavens, which are like a pure, distilled reflection of the chaotic rhythms of Mother Nature as experienced in the rain, the seasons, the growth of plants, or the behavior of animals. Buddhism was swamped in the goddess cults—Kuntī, Hārītī, and the rest—with their child sacrifice, cannibalism, and steamy sexuality. Buddhist monks lived literally side by side with such cults; they had shrines in the monasteries and, it seems, some early Buddhist monks were 'sons' of such goddesses. Small wonder that the Mūlasarvāstivāda Vinaya developed a set of rules to govern the conduct of her sons.

5 The appearance of a legal system within a divine/heroic biography is no accident, but follows the most ancient precedents we have. We are all familiar with the Bible, which sets the rules of the Torah within the majestic Creation myth invented by the Hebrews while in exile in Babylon. But this text, which was redacted not long before the Buddha, followed much older precedents.

6 The earliest examples we possess for the idea of 'Law' stem from Mesopotamia, starting around 2100 BCE. The most famous example—and one which appears to directly presage Aśoka's famous pillars, which were probably carved by Babylonian craftsmen—is the so-called Code of Hammurabi. Hammurabi, acting as the steward of his god Marduk of Babylon, ruled Mesopotamia during one of the high periods of its culture, from 1792 BCE to 1750 BCE, which saw him pull together most of the city-states of the region. Hammurabi made abundant use of written directives, and was perhaps the first literate king. His famous 'code' was carved in Akkadian

cuneiform on a 2.25 meter high black basalt stele. This was placed next to a statue of Hammurabi, reinforcing the sense of personal authority for one who comes to 'hear my words', as the stele puts it. The stele depicts Hammurabi gazing directly into his god Marduk's eyes as he receives the symbols of royal power. There is a sense, not only of divine authority, but of direct communion with the god. The Code consists of a series of 282 coolly reasoned judgments of the 'eye-for-an-eye' variety, which in some sections allow for presumption of innocence and the reliance on evidence. Rule three, for example, says, 'If any one bring an accusation of any crime before the elders, and does not prove what he has charged, he shall, if it be a capital offense charged, be put to death.'[2]

7 The rules are contextualized within an prologue and epilogue of a very different nature. Hammurabi boasts of his accomplishments: he 'conquered the four quarters of the world', 'made great the name of Babylon', 'made all glorious in E-shidlam', 'beloved of the god Nebo'[3] and so on. The boasts are, inevitably, accompanied by equally lurid and lengthy threats. Kings who come afterward are to preserve and enforce the Laws without change, and one who damages the Laws is cursed: 'May Bel, the lord... ordain the years of his rule in groaning, years of scarcity, years of famine, darkness without light, death with seeing eyes be fated to him; may he (Bel) order with his potent mouth the destruction of his city, the dispersion of his subjects, the cutting off of his rule, the removal of his name and memory from the land.'

8 There could hardly be a greater contrast between the cool, economical phrasing of the Laws, and the inflated bluster of the prologue and epilogue. They are two different modes of communication, speaking to, and presumably from, two very different parts of the mind. The prologue and epilogue, together with the impressive statues and ritual setting, are calculated to create an emotional response, a sense of awe, respect, veneration, fear. The rules themselves appeal solely to reason.[4]

9 One cannot help but be struck by the very close parallels between the formal construction of this text and the Khandhakas. In the middle of the Buddha's hero myth, with all its magic and its miracles, its exalted spirituality and sincerity of devotion, is a seemingly endless listing of mundane rules, prescribing every conceivable detail of monastic life right down

to the color of the shoes. It is the Buddha himself who laid down those rules, just as the god promulgates the laws. The narrative background was made by the tradition who 'heard' the rules from the Buddha, just as the framework for the Code is supplied by Hammurabi, who 'heard' the rules from his god. It goes without saying that the Vinaya is incomparably more sophisticated as a legal system, and is entirely gentle and humane throughout, lacking any taint of violence, threat, or vengeance. Nevertheless, it relies on the time-honored method of supporting and authorizing its legal judgments through its mythic trappings with their overwhelming emotional response.

10 This book is not a study of Vinaya, so we are not looking closely at the prosaic legal passages. It is crucial, though, to bear in mind that the events from now on appear, for the most part, as an authorizing narrative for Vinaya rules. These stories are not just for inspiration, they frame rules that create and sustain a community.

THE RETURN

12. REFUSAL OF THE RETURN

11 *Having found bliss and enlightenment in the other world, the hero may not want to return to the ordinary world to bestow the boon onto his fellow man.*

12 The refusal to return is represented in the famous episode of the Buddha's Hesitation.[5] After expending such tremendous effort to gain the Deathless, he pondered that there are two things that are very hard to see for a generation wrapped in defilements: dependent origination and Nibbana. He therefore inclined to inaction, living a life of solitary meditative bliss. But Brahmā Sahampati knew his mind; vanishing from the Brahmā realm he appeared before the Buddha, went down on his bended knee, and begged the Buddha to throw open the Doors to the Deathless. The Buddha reflected, and used his Eye of Awakening to survey the spiritual potential of beings. He realized that there were, indeed, some who have 'little dust in their eyes', and so he consented to teach: not an easy decision, for it meant a lifetime's work.

13. THE MAGIC FLIGHT

13 *If the hero in his triumph wins the blessing of the goddess or the god and is then explicitly commissioned to return to the world with some elixir for the restoration of society, the final stage of his adventure is supported by all the powers of his supernatural patron. On the other hand, if the trophy has been attained against the opposition of its guardian, or if the hero's wish to return to the world has been resented by the gods or demons, then the last stage of the mythological round becomes a lively, often comical, pursuit.*

14 The flight motif does not appear as such, since the Buddha is a fully accomplished hero with nothing to fear.[6] However this does not stop Māra from trying, even after his defeat on the night of the Awakening. He reappears throughout the Buddha's life trying to obstruct Buddha's return. He serves as comic relief in Buddhist texts, his bold challenges all too predictably followed by a humiliating defeat: 'his lute slipping from under his arm', he sits 'silent, dismayed, with shoulders drooping and head down, glum, with nothing to say, scraping the ground with a stick.'[7]

15 There is only one occasion where Māra gets his way. As Lord of Death, it is only appropriate that this is when he requests the Buddha to pass away. Feigning compassion, he suggests that the Buddha attain final Nibbana; he should rest content with accomplishing his solitary quest and not share his teaching with others. The Buddha declares that he will not pass away until he has fully established the fourfold assembly: bhikkhus, bhikkhunis, laymen, and laywomen.[8] The Pali includes this episode only as a remembrance, looking back from near the Buddha's death, when Māra visits the Buddha one last time and repeats his request. But the text refers back to when the Buddha was newly Awakened, and the Sarvāstivādin version does indeed have the episode in the early section as well.[9] Although the Buddha refuses Māra's initial request, when he repeats it near the end of the Buddha's life the Buddha agrees, telling Māra not to worry, as his time is near.

16 The Buddha's statement that he will not pass away until the bhikkhuni order is well established, a forceful assertion at a critical juncture in the Buddha's career, stands in bold contradiction to the idea that the Buddha was reluctant to set up a bhikkhuni order. The traditions do not try to resolve this contradiction, preferring to ignore it. But it is irreducible and

may not be explained away. Why is this passage ignored, along with many similar statements, while the Mahāpajāpatī story is trotted out again and again to justify the exclusion of women? The texts are ambiguous; this is obvious to any fair-minded reader. To insist on one interpretation among many possibilities is called by the Buddha a 'body-knot'.[10] It ties us 'bodily' to our views, so that we can never see past our own limiting perspective. Faced with a range of possibilities, it is the reader's duty to read the text with compassion.

14. RESCUE FROM WITHOUT

17 *The hero may have to be brought back from his supernatural adventure by assistance from without. That is to say, the world may have to come and get him.... Whether rescued from without, driven from within, or gently carried along by the guiding divinities, he has yet to re-enter with his boon the long-forgotten atmosphere where men who are fractions imagine themselves to be complete. He has yet to confront society with his ego-shattering, life-redeeming elixir, and take the return blow of reasonable queries, hard resentment, and good people at a loss to comprehend.*

18 We have already noted this stage, with the intervention of Brahmā to prompt the Buddha to begin his teaching mission, thus adopting the supreme deity of the predominant Brahmanical world view as a devout supporter of the Buddha. This episode echoes the themes of the 'call refused' and the 'supernatural help'. The later traditions develop the idea that the Buddha's family, obsessed with the disappearance of their favorite son, continually sent delegates to beg the Buddha to return to Kapilavatthu, which he did in his own good time.

15. THE CROSSING OF THE RETURN THRESHOLD

19 *The two worlds, the divine and the human, can be pictured only as distinct from each other—different as life and death, as day and night. The hero adventures out of the land we know into darkness ... and his return is described as a coming back out of that yonder zone. Nevertheless—and here is a great key to the understanding of myth and symbol—the two kingdoms are actually one. The realm of the gods is a forgotten dimension of the world we know. And the exploration of that dimension, either willingly or unwillingly, is the whole sense of the deed of the hero.... There must always remain, however, from the standpoint of normal waking consciousness, a certain baffling inconsistency*

> *between the wisdom brought back from the deep, and the prudence usually found to be effective in the light world.... The first problem of the returning hero is to accept as real, after an experience of the soul-satisfying vision of fulfillment, the passing joys and sorrows, banalities and noisy obscenities of life.... The idea of the insulating horse, to keep the hero out of immediate touch with the earth and yet permit him to promenade among the peoples of the world, is a vivid example of a basic precaution taken generally by the carriers of supernormal power.*

20 Having decided to teach, the Buddha reflected about who he should approach first.[11] Realizing that his two former teachers had passed away, he decided to go to see his former companions, the group of five ascetics, who were then staying in Benares. On his way he encountered the Ājīvaka Upaka ('Nearly there'), who noted the Buddha's serenity and asked about his teacher. The Buddha said that he had no teacher, but was Awakened by himself. Upaka shook his head, muttered 'May it be so, friend,' and departed by 'another road'.

21 Arriving in Benares, the group of five at first agreed to not receive the Buddha; but when he arrived they were strangely moved and could not help themselves. Even so, the Buddha had to repeatedly persuade them before they were willing to listen to the Dhamma. Such problems were to persist: the father of Yasa, one of the early converts, came trying to drag his son back; the Kassapa ascetics required long and patient coaxing, including display of many miracles, before they could be persuaded; and so on. Māra appears again and again obstructing the Buddha's mission. All this is a reminder of how hard it is to adapt the transcendent wisdom to the 'real world'. In fact, the entire Vinaya may be seen as an extended development of this theme.

22 The 'insulating horse' in the above quote by Campbell refers to the Irish hero Oisin, who met and married the princess of the Land of Youth. They lived in divine joy for many years; but when he wished to return to see his father, his princess warned that 300 years had gone by in the land of men. If he touched the ground, he would immediately become a blind old man. She gave him a white horse, warning him to on no account allow any limb of his to contact the earth. But, in retrieving his ancestral horn from underneath a stone, his foot inadvertently touched the earth....

23 Campbell quotes Frazer on this topic.

24 Apparently holiness, magical virtue, taboo, or whatever we may call that mysterious quality which is supposed to pervade sacred or tabooed persons, is conceived by the primitive philosopher as a physical substance or fluid, with which the sacred man is charged just as a Leyden jar is charged with electricity; and exactly as the electricity in the jar can be discharged by contact with a good conductor, so the holiness or magical virtue in the man can be discharged and drained away by contact with the earth, which on this theory serves as an excellent conductor for the magical fluid. Hence in order to preserve the charge from running to waste, the sacred or tabooed personage must be carefully prevented from touching the ground; in electrical language he must be insulated, if he is not to be emptied of the precious substance or fluid with which he, as a vial, is filled to the brim. And in many cases apparently the insulation of the tabooed person is recommended as a precaution not merely for his own sake but for the sake of others; for since the virtue of holiness or taboo is, so to say, a powerful explosive which the smallest touch may detonate, it is necessary in the interest of the general safety to keep it within narrow bounds, lest breaking out it should blast, blight, and destroy whatever it comes into contact with.[12]

25 For the Buddha, and monastics generally, this 'insulation' is provided in a quite literal way by the secluded lifestyle, outwardly symbolized by the robe, bowl, and shaven head, contained within a disciplinary code, and lived in a separated monastery, with interaction with lay folk carefully limited and controlled.

26 The magical energy that is contained by taboo is, of itself, ethically neutral: this is a crucial and commonly misunderstood point. Frazer's passage illuminates this aspect vividly by comparing magic energy with electricity. Electricity is a force of nature, neither good nor bad, which can be used for good or bad purposes; but in either case it is still dangerous and one must be careful to insulate the power. Magic too is a force of nature, neither good nor bad, which can be used for good or bad; but in either case it is still dangerous, and one must be careful to insulate the power.

27 This non-ethical quality of magic stems from its primitive place within the psyche. Magical thinking has not learned the separateness of things, but proceeds as if 'similar' (e.g. a person and a 'voodoo doll' made in their image) means 'identical'; or one cannot distinguish between one's body

and the outside world, and imagines one can operate on the world in the same way as one does on one's own body. As the mind develops, it learns to distinguish, and concepts like 'good' and 'bad' become possible. These labels are then applied to magic, which becomes 'white' or 'black', as a higher level of consciousness reads its ethical categories into a lower; but really the magic is the same, all that differs is the ends to which the magic is put, i.e. the intention of the magician. In terms of the progressive analysis of the five aggregates that we made earlier, magic and taboo are a function of *saññā*, how the mind 'perceives' or 'recognizes' things as separate or identical, while ethical choice is the function of *saṅkhārā*.

28 This failure to differentiate is sometimes called 'mystical participation'. This term, however, invites confusion between the pre-rational consciousness of magic, which is simply unable to properly distinguish between separate things, and the trans-rational consciousness of *samādhi*, which is a state of transcendental wholeness.

29 It will be obvious to anyone who has observed Buddhist communities that monks are wrapped around in elaborate taboos; and that the most powerful taboos occur at the juncture of greatest potential energy—the monk and the woman. Perhaps the most tabooed Buddhist society today is Thailand. When receiving an offering from a woman, monks must use a 'receiving cloth' to provide the necessary 'insulation'. Once, while receiving alms in a remote Thai village, my fingers accidentally brushed against the woman donor's; she literally jumped, like she had been shocked. More recently, stopping over in Bangkok's shiny new Suvarnabhumi airport I sat down at one end of a row of chairs: a lady at the other end of the row leapt up, again as if shocked. I had become used to such things when staying among the simple villagers of the rural north-east, but it was made newly strange in such modern surroundings. At such moments Frazer's image of magic or taboo energy as a kind of electrical discharge comes vividly to life.

16. MASTER OF THE TWO WORLDS

30 *Freedom to pass back and forth across the world division, from the perspective of the apparitions of time to that of the causal deep and back—not contaminating the principles of the one with those of the other, yet permitting the mind to know the one by virtue of the other—is the talent of the master....*

> *His personal ambitions being totally dissolved, he no longer tries to live but willingly relaxes to whatever may come to pass in him; he becomes, that is to say, an anonymity. The Law lives in him with his unreserved consent.*

31 We have already remarked on the repeated appearance of divine beings, both in evil guise, as Māra to be vanquished, and in good guise, as the supportive Brahmā.[13] Upon the completion of the first teaching, the gods took up the cry of the Rolling Forth of the Wheel of the Dhamma until it resounded as far as the Brahmā realm. The Buddha's mastery of both the human and divine is further emphasized when he claims to be free from all fetters, both human and divine. This is repeated through the Buddha's life as a concrete symbol of his supremacy. He travels at will to whatever realm he wishes, and demonstrates his mastery even of the exalted deities of the Brahmā realms.

32 But the Buddha also recognizes that he will not live at ease without something to revere: this, he decides, must be the Dhamma, the transpersonal principle of which he is merely a temporary embodiment. And so he states that 'who sees the Dhamma sees me, who sees me sees the Dhamma.'[14]

33 A celebrated aspect of this 'at-one-ment' with the Dhamma is the Buddha's unsurpassed ability to adjust his teachings to time and place, to respond with effortless poise to every circumstance, and to speak directly to the needs of the person before him.

17. FREEDOM TO LIVE

34 *Powerful in this insight, calm and free in action ... the hero is the conscious vehicle of the terrible, wonderful Law, whether his work be that of a butcher, jockey, or king.*

35 The Buddha commences his wandering across the breadth of India, teaching and serving, making his quiet yet forceful presence felt wherever he goes. While giving the first sermon, Aññā Koṇḍañña realized the first stage of Awakening; soon afterward, all five ascetics realized full arahantship. Thus the Buddha's confidence, inspired by Brahmā, that others could indeed understand the Dhamma was confirmed. This motif is extended throughout the remainder of the Buddha's life, right up to his deathbed teaching to Subhadda.

36 But an even more momentous theme is announcing itself here. The Buddha does not merely teach and allow others to taste the same nectar that he has drunk; he does not merely embody the Dhamma in its glorious fullness: he encourages his followers to teach and to ordain disciples as well. Thus the story of Awakening continues in the lives of many nuns, monks, laymen, and laywomen, all of whom echo in a lesser way the stages of the hero's journey perfected by the Buddha.

THE RETURN CONTINUES

37 Thus end Campbell's seventeen stages. But the Buddha's career is just beginning. And the 'return' continues to be fraught with difficulties. Many of these are addressed within the Khandhaka narrative. These include the dispute with Devadatta; the betrayal by a close associate or family member is one of the deepest mythic motifs (Osiris and Set, Jesus and Judas, and so on). It is closely related to the myth of the sacrifice of the divine king, who is ritually slaughtered in favor of a younger relative. There was also the episode at Kosambi, where the Sangha was split by a dispute over whether it was allowable to leave water in the dipper in the bathroom. The Buddha, unable to heal the problem, disappeared into the jungle, where he was waited upon by a monkey and an elephant. On top of this are the frequent challenges, often belligerent, by members of other sects. Indeed, each Vinaya rule, responding to a particular problem that had arisen with the Sangha, overcomes in ways big or small the threat of the profane world that wants to invade the sacred realm of the Sangha. It is within this context, as a threat to the 'return', that the story of Mahāpajāpatī is placed.

❖

38 It should be obvious by now that the Buddha's life story has been constructed, from the very earliest times, under the influence of the ancient mythic archetype of the hero. Of course, this does not mean that all details of his story are 'just a myth'. It is entirely normal for the lives of real-life heroes echo the myths in certain respects. But there is a universal tendency for the biographers of heroes to bring the individual hero more and more in line with the primordial myth. As time goes on, any elements of

the hero myth that were missing become filled in, and the supernatural elements inevitably become exaggerated as the person disappears behind his halo. The parallels between the Buddha's life and the hero cycle are just too close, even in the early texts. The archetype presses through in the many gaps that exist in between the recorded events of the Buddha's life.[15]

39 This mythologizing process is the exact reverse of the great river of time, which flows from the mythic towards the historical. This is no accident. The growing elaborations of the Buddha's myth do not show the growing naïvety of the Buddhist community, but the reverse. Indian culture was growing ever more rational and skeptical. The work of the logicians was proceeding apace. Vasubandhu, writing around 400 CE, assumes that the demons of hell are merely projections of the mind, which he apparently thought was so obvious that it forms, not a conclusion, but an axiom of his argument.[16] The flowering of Buddhist myth compensates for this tendency, holding on to the ever-more improbable miracles of the past in a secularizing present. The florid elaborations have something desperate about them, an insistence, a loss of lightness and humor. In this we read the distant precursors of that modern disease, fundamentalism.

40 The later developments of the Buddha's myth contain virtually every motif of the hero myth. These are a 'leaking in' of old story-telling motifs, which often appear to trivialize rather than enhance the myth. When we hear of the Bodhisattva taking part in the classic contest to win the hand of his bride, excelling not only in the archery contest (as Odysseus, etc., etc.), but also in mathematics and so on, we find nothing of spiritual inspiration.[17] Similarly, when we are told that the Bodhisatta's birth was from his mother's side, we are more likely to think of this as a weird denial of the realities of birth than to imagine it of any spiritual worth. And, rather than painfully attempting to rationalize the fable as the 'first cesarean birth', we should not be surprised to find that this motif, among others, is directly copied from the birth of Indra in the Ṛg Veda.[18]

41 Because of these misguided and misinterpreted elements, which are very many, most modernists dismiss Buddhist myth out of hand. But other aspects of later mythologizing represent genuine insights. I would mention

here the image of Indra's net, the sparkling web of interconnectedness that renders in vivid imagery a key philosophical insight.

42 The Buddhist traditions rarely articulate the difference between primitive folk tales and sophisticated symbol-play; which is not helped by the fact that the myths themselves mix these different kinds of mythologizing promiscuously. While certain kinds of myth are clearly intended as symbolic representations of the highest truth, we are just as likely to be told that thousands of deities got Awakened from hearing a simple morality tale. All this is just Ken Wilber's 'pre/trans fallacy'.

CHAPTER 27

BUILDING THE LEGEND

LET US CONSIDER HOW THIS GREAT MYTH CAME TO BE CONSTRUCTED. Even within the early texts most of the hero myth tropes are found in the Buddha's story. But these are scattered here and there throughout the texts, with no coherent chronological narrative. I suggest that this scattering of episodes represents a time when the archetypal aspect of the Buddha was primarily unconscious, while his personality was vivid.

2 During the life of the Buddha, and for perhaps a generation or two after, the Buddhist community's primary experience of the Buddha was as a living person. As such, what would be remembered would be *episodes*. Individuals would recall occasions when they had met the Buddha, times when he had given a particular teaching, or met a certain person. This is marked in the Suttas by the stereotyped formula, 'On one occasion the Blessed was staying…'. Such episodes clearly had a profound impact on many people, and would be remembered with clarity for long afterward. The particular episodes would be recalled within a less articulate sense of the Buddha's wider significance as an Awakened being.

3 But time goes on as it will; memory grows dim and the archetype grows bright. The conscious arrangement of the episodes of the Buddha's life into a formally conceived narrative biography marks the transition: from then on the Buddha will be experienced through the nimbus of archetypal associations. This literary process reflects the posture of the Buddha's myth, like all axial mythology, standing on the cusp of reason: looking

forward to the rational future, but being informed 'from behind' by the ageless images of the human heritage.

4 The 'scattered' pieces of the Buddha's life occur in three main kinds of early canonical sources:

5 **Prose discourses attributed to the Buddha himself,** where he describes in the first person an aspect of his early life. Here we include especially such passages as the account of the going forth, the period under the two teachers, the period of ascetic practices, and other miscellaneous references to his practice and attainment. In the Pali tradition these are primarily found in the Majjhima Nikāya, although the Sarvāstivāda tradition places several of these texts in their Dīrgha Āgama.[1] Such accounts are generally vivid and realistic, and must count as our earliest sources.

6 **Prose narrative, not directly placed in the Buddha's mouth,** telling in discursive third-person form of events in the Buddha's life, and including within itself episodes of direct teaching by the Buddha. The most important elements here are the Catuṣpariṣat, Mahāparinibbāna, and Mahāpadāna Suttas, all found in the Dīgha Nikāya (as well as the corresponding Dīrgha Āgamas of the Dharmaguptaka and Sarvāstivāda) or else in the Vinayas. These texts no doubt reflect a general knowledge of the Buddha's life that was current from the earliest days of the community; but they have reached the form we find them in today only after considerable development.

7 **Verse episodes, found mainly in the Sutta Nipāta.** These include the story of Asita, the defeat of Māra and his daughters, and the first meeting with King Bimbisāra. While all these are later than the early prose texts, the Attadaṇḍa Sutta stands in a class of its own as referring to the critical juncture of the going forth from a unique early perspective.

8 These sources are welded together, not by formal literary construct, but only in the memory and imagination of the listener. Within a community which is bound together by a particular story, a myth is heard many times; it soaks into the consciousness and frames the perspective of the community. When we hear one episode, we are not learning new facts, but are being reassured that the old truths are still valid. Thus the fact that there is no single chronological account of the Buddha's life in the early texts

does not mean that it was irrelevant; rather, it had not been consciously expressed.

9 Even though explicitly mythic episodes only occur in a minority of early texts, each Sutta or Vinaya passage is preceded by the formula saying that at that time the Buddha was staying at such & such a place. This little tag embeds each text, no matter how simple or prosaic, in the story of the Buddha, and imbues it with the authority, the aura, the glory, of the Supreme Awakened One. In this use of literary form to unify the texts, we discern how the redactors moved towards framing the entire scriptural collection as one story.

10 It is no easy matter to pin down the sense in which a text such as this 'exists'. During recitation, only one sound at a time is heard; the rest of the story is assimilated through memory, both the immediate memory of what has just been recited, and the longer term collective cultural memory of the story as a whole.

11 This problem of the sense in which the Dhamma 'exists' is interwoven with the foremost philosophical debate of early Buddhism, the question of the ontological status of the *dhammas*, the phenomena of existence that are categorized in the Abhidhammas. The Sarvāstivādins famously asserted that the *dhammas* 'exist' in the past, future, and present; while other schools, including the Theravādins of the Mahāvihāra, said that only the present moment 'exists'. But *dhamma* in its philosophical sense of 'phenomenon of reality' is never entirely separate from the ordinary use of *dhamma* as 'teaching on reality'. For this reason the debate on the reality of the *dhammas* in the three times parallels the change in medium of textual transmission that was occurring around this time. Originally the texts were recited orally, in which case the 'present' nature of each phoneme is most apparent. But from about 400 years after the Buddha writing came to be used more extensively. We read only one word or phrase at a time, but the 'existence' of the whole text cannot be doubted, since, well, there it is on the table. So from this time the *dhamma* came to be seen as existing all-at-once, just like the words in a book.

12 In the early period, with its oral recitation, the scope for individual, personalized interpretation is huge; each person will remember the texts in a different way, and they will therefore 'exist' differently for each. Notice

that this is a psychological reality, entirely independent of the question of whether there was a standardized canon at this stage: even if there was a standardized group of texts, each person would remember different texts, with different order, different emphasis, and so on.

❖

13 It is no great puzzle to work out who was the key figure in developing the Buddha's biography. For it was Ānanda who became the Buddha's attendant twenty years after the Awakening, followed him like a shadow for the rest of his life, and appeared in almost every important event of the latter part of the Buddha's life. He outlived the Buddha, according to the plausible testimony of both Southern and Northern traditions, by some 40 years.[2] And he is universally regarded as the founder of the entire canonical Sutta tradition.

14 In the decades following the death of his dear Teacher, is it to be doubted that he would devote himself to the creation of the great literary works in which his Teacher is immortalized, and in which he himself plays such a prominent part? It is in this period, and to this man, that we should ascribe the beginnings of the Buddhist biographical tradition. And while the texts were finalized later, the essential outlines, and many of the details (especially of the second group of texts mentioned above, the extended prose narratives such as the Mahāparinibbāna Sutta and its counterpart the Catuṣpariṣat Sutra) were established by Ānanda himself, with the work being continued by his 'school'. This is suggested in the Pali commentary when it says, for example, that the verses accompanying the Lakkhaṇa Sutta were composed by Ānanda.[3]

15 Despite the massive preparatory work done by Ānanda, this period did not see the emergence of a fully realized Buddha epic. It has been famously demonstrated by Frauwallner that the first such formal construct of the Buddha's life is the narrative framework of the section of the Vinayas called the Khandhakas.[4] This framework appears in all traditions—although greatly varying in clarity, extent, and detail—and typically tells the events we have described as the return; that is, from the Awakening until the Parinibbana, and afterward to the First and Second Councils that continued the Buddha's work.

16 Frauwallner argued that the basic structure of the Khandhakas was discernible in all Vinayas, but had been subject to varying levels of decay, obscuring the earlier structure. This part of his thesis is not generally accepted as being a sufficient explanation of the variations in the Khandhakas. Nevertheless, the idea that Buddhist scripture tends towards bloated, inclusive forms that subsequently break down as the outlines become lost is a very persuasive one.

17 Scholars have criticized this and other aspects of Frauwallner's theory, but I believe such criticism, while correcting certain aspects of Frauwallner's thesis, misses the essential point. Frauwallner is surely correct to say that the Khandhaka narrative—however it may have been originally shaped, and regardless of whether it is truly pan-sectarian or even presectarian—constitutes the first real attempt to frame the Buddha's teaching as a heroic story. Frauwallner emphasizes the crucial point.

> 18 '... the core of the work, the exposition of Buddhist monastic rules, was enclosed by a biography of the Buddha. Nor was this framework a mere embellishment. It is well known that the Skandhakas do not give the monastic rules as a collection of precepts, but in the form of a historical account. They narrate the events which gave occasion to the single rules, and we are told how the Buddha thereupon promulgated these rules. The exposition of the rules appears thus in the form of a current narrative of the activity of the Buddha. This character is still more strengthened by the insertion, at shorter or larger intervals, of legends that give more life to the narrative. Thus the core of the work melts together with the framework into a great unity.'[5]

19 Rather than criticizing Frauwallner for pushing his thesis too far, I would suggest that it can be taken much, much further. For the literary unity that Frauwallner describes does not just apply to the Khandhakas, but to the entire Suttas and Vinaya. Each passage begins by saying, 'At that time the Blessed One was staying at...'. In other words, each Sutta and each Vinaya rule is presented as an episode in the life of the hero. Thus *the entire canon is an extended hero epic.*[6] The earliest stages of the development of this myth are, as we noted above, primarily unconscious; but soon enough the need was felt to make the structure of the hero myth explicit, that is, conscious.

20 The elements from which the overall narrative was constructed are present in all schools; and I am suggesting here that, while the 'official'

organization of this into the Khandhaka structure was significant, the background narrative would have been assumed in memory, regardless of whether it had been made into a coherent 'text'. This is merely to say that the Buddha's early followers would have had an idea of his life story, and when hearing the various episodes, these would naturally be understood as part of that story. The various episodes would have been seen together (synoptic), even when remembered as separate 'texts'.

21 This can be amply proven by the massive parallelism between quite separate elements in the narrative. As just one example, take the well-known story of the Buddha becoming ill after eating his last meal, which is told in the Mahāparinibbāna Sutta. The Sarvāstivādins in their Catuṣpariṣat Sutra paralleled this by having him become ill after eating his first meal following Awakening. Clearly, these ideas evolved as a pair, even though neither of these texts are included in the Khandhaka narrative. Such features could be multiplied indefinitely.[7]

❖

22 The Khandhaka narrative usually starts immediately after the Buddha's Awakening, tells the story of his hesitation to teach, etc., then the first teaching, conversion of disciples, and leads up to the time of the ordination of the great disciples Sāriputta and Moggallāna. Then the text diverges into more legalistic concerns, firstly for ordination procedure. Then each chapter deals with a different topic, sometimes melded with mythic aspects, such as the rebellion of Devadatta. The story resumes in the final chapters. Khandhaka 20 tells of the bhikkhunis, starting off with the story of Mahāpajāpatī. In Khandhaka 21 the narrative leads to the Buddha's passing away, followed immediately by the First Council, where the scriptures were collected. And 100 years later Khandhaka 22 tells of the Second Council, which dealt with certain disciplinary laxities that led to a serious conflict in the Sangha.

23 When we reflect on the matter in this way, two things immediately become apparent. First is that the story of women's ordination appears now, not as a startling, singular event, but as an episode in a hero myth.

24 The second thing is that the conscious construction of this heroic cycle was, in all likelihood, achieved by those who most directly benefited from it. While the hero cycle has typically been seen as a healthy assertion of

the individual's development, the myth also has a political dimension. As Buddhists, we focus on the individual evolution of consciousness, and tend to marginalize the social and institutional aspects of our texts. We're happy to see the Buddha myth as a of spiritual growth; but we avoid noticing how this same story is used to justify institutional authority.

25 In this case, the authority that is justified is that of the victorious party at the Second Council. This group of monks hail from diverse parts of India, but are known as the Pāveyyakas ('The ones from Pāvā'). They upheld the rigorous, hardliner position of Vinaya, and refused to allow even the tiniest relaxation of rules that had been laid down. It would be only human for them to shape the textual material they inherited to enhance their own perspective.

26 This highlights the curious ambiguity in how Ānanda appears in this literature. On the one hand, he is the Buddha's closest disciple, revered and beloved. On the other hand he is in conflict with Mahākassapa, who assumed the leadership of the Sangha. We have suggested that Ānanda was responsible for the early construction of the Buddha's legend, and that this includes the main narrative of the Mahāparinibbāna Sutta, where he is a major character throughout. The inclusion of episodes strongly critical of Ānanda could have occurred in a number of ways: they could have been actual events, too well known to be ignored; they could be an expression of Ānanda's unconscious guilt, a feeling that as the Buddha's carer he was somehow responsible for his death; or they could be an attempt by parties opposed to Ānanda to denigrate his role in the Sangha in order to bolster a particular sectarian posture.

27 As far as the political aspects of the textual changes are concerned, the first principle is that authors like to make themselves look good. It is unlikely that Ānanda would insert texts that denigrated himself, such as the trashing of Ānanda by Mahākassapa in the First Council. This is so implausible as a straight historical record that we are well justified in seeking a political angle. To explain these things, then, we should look to the period after Ānanda's death. Ānanda lived on for about 40 years after the Buddha, so the text was redacted some time after that, when the personal memories of these monks were becoming dim: again, we approach the Second Council.

28 The Second Council is the historical end-point of the Vinayas. It was said to have been concluded by a recitation of the Vinaya, and some accounts add that the Dhamma was also recited. The traditions assert that these recitations were a re-affirmation in all respects of the original recitation, 100 years previous at the First Council of Rājagaha. But this is a standard piece of rhetoric and need not be taken seriously. In fact the scriptures were in flux for many years following the First Council. The agenda of the Second Council must have left its imprints on the scriptures, and not just in their account of the Second Council itself.

29 This is not a radical theory, but is the most conservative hypothesis in the circumstances. The radical hypothesis is that of the tradition, which asserts that the redactors left no marks, or only trivial ones, on the texts that were in their care. This hypothesis runs so counter to what we know of human nature and the nature of textual transmission that it would require detailed and specific evidence to be acceptable. As David Hume said, 'A wise man proportions his belief to the evidence'.[8] But such evidence is, alas, not forthcoming. This is not to criticize the work of the redactors, who have passed down to us a most remarkable spiritual literature. It is simply to accept that they are human.

❖

30 When reading the Vinaya as a guide for monastic conduct, we are always reminded of the role of the narrative structure of the Vinaya in giving an emotive context to the bare rules. The Vinaya delineates the ritual wholeness and identity of the bhikkhu Sangha, a wholeness that is authorized and given concrete form through narrative.

31 Each rule in the Vinaya is prefaced by a story which purports to tell the historical circumstances that led to the laying down of the rule. And each of these stories begins with: 'At that time, the Buddha was staying at...'. These stories only make sense as part of the master-narrative of the Buddha's life story. It is the record of his unparalleled spiritual attainments that imbues all the prosaic, sometimes comical or absurd, origin stories with unimpeachable authority. The Buddha's presence and personal voice is felt through the entire Vinaya, providing the final authority for all rules and procedures, despite the fact that most of the Vinaya, as generally agreed by scholars, post-dates the Buddha's life.[9]

32 We are starting to appreciate the complexity of the problem here. The bhikkhuni origin story, is not an isolated passage, to be explained away by reference to vague 'cultural' or 'chauvinist' attitudes. The entire compilation of the Buddhist scriptures is being drawn within our web: and this is as it must be, for we have been warned that the entry of bhikkhunis is a disease that will destroy all of Buddhism. The very size of the problem renders all attempts at solution partial and inadequate.

❖

33 The account of the Second Council is fairly vivid and realistic, rather more like journalism than mythology. It has detailed accounts of the monks' comings and goings, their discussions and reflections about the crisis. The Mahāparinibbāna/First Council narrative is still fairly vivid, but less so, and with more miraculous and mythic elements. The Catuṣpariṣat Sutra, telling of the start of the Buddha's life, is less realistic still. For example, in the Mahāparinibbāna Sutta, we hear such touching scenes as the Buddha sitting in the sun to warm his back; or Ānanda, unable to contain himself, going off to cry. Such personal details are absent from the Catuṣpariṣat Sūtra narrative. And by the time we get to the birth narratives all pretense at realistic history has been forgotten.

34 This shifting focus makes sense from the perspective of a narrator speaking shortly after the Second Council. The Council itself was fresh in his memory. The Mahāparinibbāna/First Council still has life, due to the work passed down by Ānanda, but also room for embellishment, for shining the Buddha's halo and making certain other adjustments. The Catuṣpariṣat is receding into the mists, partly because Ānanda was not present at the events; and the birth is lost from all realistic sight. This pattern only applies to those portions of the Buddha's life told by others. The Buddha's own accounts, chiefly preserved in the Majjhima, have the freshness of direct experience.

35 In reading these texts we are listening to different voices who are saying different kinds of things. The stronger the journalistic element, the more we can look to establish historical 'facts' and details about what 'really happened'. And the stronger the mythic element, the deeper the insight into the unconscious dynamics of the Buddhist community. The Buddha's story stands in the half-light, its back to the unconscious, mythic past, its face to

the rational, sunny future. When images of the past force themselves into the future, our fears and hopes manifest not as rational philosophy, but in dream and symbol. The surface narrative of Buddhism tries to clean up its act as best as possible, to dry out the stormy, fetid anxieties and paradoxes of old myth in the antiseptic rays of the sun. But they will not be denied, and invade the story in the edges and margins.

CHAPTER 28

THE WICKED STEPMOTHER

THE AMBIGUITY OF THE TWILIGHT IS RESOLVED most easily by splitting off the dark and the light into two contrasting pairs. And this is exactly what has happened to the Buddha's mother. If Māyā is the crystalline fantasy of pure, virginal motherhood, Mahāpajāpatī is the mother of blood, tears, and milk. She is as present in Siddhattha's life as Māyā is absent. Hers is the reality of nurturing and day to day caring. It was she who had to get up in the middle of the night to hold the child, wipe his bottom clean, and gently rock him to sleep. While basking in her gaze the tiny Siddhattha came to know unconditional love. And yet for all that she is a fake mother: who has ever heard of a stepmother who was not wicked?

2 The wicked stepmother of fairytales is, as so often, just a stage in the process of trivializing a theme, which traces its arc from the primal leviathan of creation to the nagging stepmother of sitcoms. The classical parallel is Hera, forever persecuting Zeus' sons and the nymphs whose charms bewitched her husband far more than she ever could. In Greek and Roman literature the stepmother is almost always the incarnation of evil: murderous, seductive, cunning, and treacherous.[1] We noted above that Aśoka's second wife Tissarakkhita played the wicked step-mother to perfection. And in Jātakas, too, the role appears. Kṛṣṇa's wet nurse was really the demon Putanā in disguise: she smeared her breasts with poison. Never do we find the wicked stepfather, although the evidence shows that stepfathers pose a greater danger to their wards, with greater tendency towards sexual abuse and violence.[2] As always, the disjunct between the mythic

claims and the empirical facts is our truest sign of the unconscious at play. Neumann has this to say:

> 3 The growth of self-consciousness and the strengthening of masculinity thrust the image of the Great Mother into the background; the patriarchal society splits it up, and while only the picture of the good Mother is retained in consciousness, her terrible aspect is relegated to the unconscious.
>
> 4 (Footnote:) The splitting of the Great Mother into a conscious 'good' mother and an unconscious 'evil' one is a basic phenomenon in the psychology of neurosis. The situation then is that consciously the neurotic has a 'good relation' to the mother, but in the gingerbread house of this love there is hidden the witch, who gobbles up little children and grants them, as a reward, a passive, irresponsible existence without an ego. Analysis then uncovers the companion picture of the Terrible Mother, an awe-inspiring figure who with threats and intimidation puts a ban on sexuality.[3]

5 This splitting, and its representation in childrens' stories, has been seen as a therapeutic, even necessary, way for children to resolve the conflicts they feel about their real mothers. Bruno Bettelheim used this Freudian approach in his *The Uses of Enchantment*.[4] He argued that when a child splits the mother into a good (usually dead) mother and an evil stepmother, it enables them to preserve a mother who for them is free of any flaws when the real mother is all too flawed. It also allows the child to feel angry at the wicked 'stepmother' without endangering the love of the true mother, who is seen as a different 'person'.[5]

6 Bettelheim has been criticized for ignoring the social conditions that inform the creation of tales. The dead mother was a simple reality of life in a world where the mother often died in childbirth.[6] The gradual 'psychologizing' of myth and story is an inevitability of history, as the circumstances of the story become dim to us; this exactly parallels the modernist vogue for psychologizing Buddhist figures such as Māra. However, a rediscovery of the social context does not undo the psychological import, for social conditions are one of the great influences on the mind. If the real mother is in fact dead, the deprecation of the 'false' mother in the mind of the child could be even greater, as, in addition to the usual conflicts of growing up, there lurks the unknowing fear of what really happened to the 'real'

mother. It is important to remember, however, that the demonization of the stepmother is only a storytelling caricature. It does not mean that the child would simply hate her. On the contrary, his love for her gift of milk, of touch, of time, would forge even greater bonds of love. But this love has the complexity of emerging adulthood, not the fantasies of the vanished, and hence perfect, mother.

❖

7 Mahāpajāpatī's name, like that of Māyā, suggests her mythic ancestry. Pajāpati is one of the chief creator deities of the Brahmanical tradition, the name itself meaning 'Lord of Creation'. The Bṛhadāraṇyaka Upaniṣad describes Pajāpati as 'this person who is "son-made"' (*ya evāyam putramayaḥ puruṣaḥ*).[7] That is, Pajāpati is defined, even created, by his offspring: if nothing is created, how can there be a creator?

8 In the same way, Mahāpajāpatī only enters the story of Buddhism because of her role in bringing up the young Siddhattha. If he had not gone on to become a Buddha, she would have vanished in the mists of time. Her existence in the Buddhist consciousness is due to her son, thus she is 'son-made'. Traditional explanations agree that Mahāpajāpatī is an epithet, based on the prognostications of the palm-readers, who saw that she was to be the mother of a Wheel-turning Emperor or Empress.[8] In Pali, when used of a woman *pajāpatī* usually means 'wife'. Here, it is probably corrupted from *pajāvatī*, 'rich in progeny'; another functional title, expressing her essential attribute: children. But the suffix *-patī* conveys something more potent than mere possession; it means literally 'ruler', so associates her with the domineering Mother of infancy.

❖

9 We have seen the central canonical texts that show how Mahāpajāpatī requested ordination, with such a disturbingly ambiguous response from the Buddha. Despite her questionable beginnings, or perhaps because of them, the later traditions imagined Mahāpajāpatī to have ended her life on an extravagantly positive note. Her biography, found in the Therī-Apadāna and the commentary on the Therīgāthā, might as well have been purposefully designed to undo the negativity surrounding her ordination.[9]

10 The story starts in an age long past when she hears Padumuttara Buddha praising his aunt as the foremost of all bhikkhunis in longstanding. She expresses her aspiration to fulfill the same position, which the Buddha freely confirms for her, predicting that she would fulfill that goal in the time of Gotama Buddha. As always, historical establishment of the bhikkhuni order under Gotama is *dhammatā*, a part of the natural and inevitable order of things.

11 She spends several lifetimes waiting on Buddhas and encouraging the other women to do the same, or experiencing celestial bliss as a result of such good kamma. She is closely associated with cloth; in one life, she organizes for 500 robes to be offered to some Paccekabuddhas, and in the next life she is born in a village of weavers.

12 In 'this' life, after ordaining and living as an arahant bhikkhuni for an unspecified number of years, she reflected that her span of life was coming to an end, and resolved tell the Buddha that she would attain final Nibbana. The 500 bhikkhunis—who had been her companions in past lives, and had taken the going forth with her—approached Mahāpajāpatī, as the deities meanwhile were lamenting, their tears sprinkling the bhikkhunis below. Thus the gods show their emotional weakness, which Mahāpajāpatī shared before she ordained, but has now left far behind. The 500 bhikkhunis determined to all attain final Nibbana together. People not freed from desire lamented and begged her to remain, just as they did when the Buddha passed away. Mahāpajāpatī admonished them gently, saying, 'Enough of crying, children!'

13 When she meets the Buddha, she says, 'I am your mother, and you are my father'—thus giving a typically Buddhist spiritual twist to the mythic concern with kinship and taboo and the riddles that result from transgression. She presses the point, saying that just as his body was raised with her milk, so her body of Dhamma was raised with the milk of Dhamma that her gave her. She wishes that all mothers could have a son like hers. Praising him repeatedly as a 'Hero', she bows down with the 500 bhikkhunis at the Buddha's feet. She requests forgiveness, since women are thought to perform all sorts of bad deeds; and again if there was any fault in her repeated requests for ordination. She asks permission from the Sangha of bhikkhus, then bows to the senior monks Rāhula, Ānanda, and Nanda,

before explaining her decision to pass away: 'I am disgusted with the body, which is like a snake hole, abode of disease, a mass of misery…'.

14 Ānanda was struck by grief and wept, only to be admonished by Mahāpajāpatī: 'Do not grieve. A time of joy is here, my son. Through you I reached Nibbana…. You begged our father and thereby got permission for us to go forth…. now [Nibbana] has been realized even by seven year old girls.'

15 Extraordinarily, the Buddha asks Mahāpajāpatī to make a display of her psychic powers, which she does in grand style. She displays all the normal abilities—flying through the air, walking on water, and so on—and then added some new ones apparently of her own invention. She turned Mount Sineru into a stick, turned the earth over with its roots and made it into a sunshade; carrying it, she walked up and down in the sky. Then she filled the world with smoke and fire like the six suns at the end of the æon; she wore a thousand suns and moons as a garland; she carried the waters of the four oceans in her hands; and many more besides.

16 Returning to the bhikkhuni monastery with the 500 bhikkhunis, they sat in meditation as the lay followers wept. She entered all the meditation attainments in sequence, just as the Buddha did before his passing away. Rising from the fourth jhāna, she attained final Nibbana, with great earthquakes, drum rolls, a rain of flowers from the sky, and other marvels.

17 The gods conveyed the news to the Buddha, who instructed Ānanda to assemble the bhikkhus. He did so, calling the monks from all directions to come and honor the Buddha's mother. They placed her couch in a golden, pinnacled building made by Vissakamma, the builder for the gods. Similar buildings were made for each of the 500 bhikkhunis, and the surface of the sky was covered with a golden canopy decorated with the sun and stars. All the gods, men, and bhikkhus assembled to honor them. The Apadāna says that the occasion was far more splendid even than the death of the Buddha himself.

18 The funeral pyre was built with perfumes, and when the body was cremated the Buddha was presented with the relics by Ānanda. The Buddha then gave some stirring verses in praise of Mahāpajāpatī: she has crossed the ocean of existence, was of great wisdom, a master of supernormal powers, of purified knowledge, and her destiny cannot be traced, like a spark that has become quenched.

❖

19 This astonishing hagiography presents one side of the story, offering a welcome positive icon for women's spirituality. But is it, perhaps, a little *too* enthusiastic? Does the very extravagance of the miracles, as compared to the relatively subdued canonical account of the Buddha's own passing away, suggest the authors were trying too hard? I wonder whether this text, which to all appearances is consciously designed as propaganda for the bhikkhunis, might in its excesses compensate for a darker reality.

20 This undercurrent breaks through to the surface in Mahāpajāpatī's rare Jātaka appearances. Despite her pivotal role in Buddhist history, Mahāpajāpatī is mentioned in only two Jātakas,[10] while Māyā appears again and again. These Jātakas are ignored in the Apadāna and the commentary, as if the the tradition is preserving two quite different, isolated attitudes towards Mahāpajāpatī. On the conscious level she is celebrated as the founder of the great spiritual order of bhikkhunis, as well as being a great Awakened being in her own right. Unconsciously, perhaps, she still poses the threat of destroying Buddhism.

21 In considering these stories, we must bear in mind the lessons we have learnt from earlier Jātakas. The forms we have them in are those of the fable, the folk tale; that is, watered down and trivialized, with the primordial themes disguised behind ethical rationalizations. Of course, not all Jātakas contain ancient material; many of them are no more than they seem, simple moral fables. But where there is a marked tension between the surface moral and the underlying imagery, and where that imagery is inadequately explained in the story, we are fully justified in seeking beneath the surface.

22 The essential thing is the hiddenness of the deep truth. Once the facts are made plain they evaporate in the skeptical, if not scornful, light of reason. Like dreams, like monsters under the bed, like terrorists lurking to blow up the bus, they derive their power only from our imagination, the limitless power of our own mind that projects onto them the deepest of our unconscious images of fear. And these archetypes inform the Mahāpajāpatī Jātakas in full, unedited force.

❖

23 The Culladhammapāla Jātaka concerns the evil deeds of a certain King Mahāpatāpa (Great Fall) of Benares.[11]

> 24 When his son Dhammapāla was seven months old, his mother, Queen Candā (Moon), bathed him in scented water and sat playing with him. So absorbed was she in her mother's love that she failed to rise when the king entered the room.
>
> 25 Incensed by her disrespect, he thought, 'Even now this woman is filled with pride on account of her son, and does not value me a straw.... I will put him to death at once!'
>
> 26 He summoned the executioner, who put on his ochre robe,[12] took up a crimson wreath, and on the king's instruction, fetched the boy from his mother. The king ordered that the boy's hands be cut off, though the queen wept and begged that her hands be severed instead, as it was she who was at fault. But the king ordered that the hands be cut off straight away, 'without complicating things'.[13]
>
> 27 The boy endured without weeping or wailing, with love and acceptance in his heart; but the mother gathered the severed, bloody hands into her lap and wailed.
>
> 28 The king ordered that the feet be cut off next, and though the queen again offered herself, there was no relenting and the deed was done. Again the queen gathered the severed feet into her stained and bloody lap as she wailed.
>
> 29 The king then ordered that the boy's head be cut off, and despite the mother's offer of her own life in place of the boy, the executioner did his duty. But still the king was not sated: he ordered the executioner to toss the boy into the air, catch him on the end of his sword, and slice him into pieces, like a 'sword-garland'. This he did, so that the pieces of the corpse were scattered over the dais.
>
> 30 Queen Candā gathered the dismembered flesh into her lap and cried out in agony as her heart burst, like bamboo exploding in a flaming bamboo grove. She died right there; but the ground swallowed the king as the flames of Avīci hell wrapped around him like a blanket.
>
> 31 The Buddha revealed the connection between that lifetime and this: 'The king was Devadatta; Queen Candā was Mahāpajāpatī Gotamī; but I myself was Prince Dhammapāla.'

32 What a disturbing story! Fables for children, indeed; we could expect a few nightmares arising out of this one, if the story is not itself a nightmare thinly veiled.[14] The Wonderful Boy, like so many victims of the sacrifice,

endured unspeakable torment without flinching. But mere death was not enough: he must be tossed into the air—yet again!—and shredded in a gratuitous display of swordsmanship, a flamboyant demonstration of masculine violence. While in the Kaṭṭhahāri Jātaka he chose the father over the mother, and in the Vessantara Jātaka he declared himself beyond both, here the father as ogre emerges in full fury. Once more the conflict is Oedipal, the father's jealousy of the son for the affections of the mother. The agent of his wrath is the executioner wrapped in the robes of a monk. And Mahāpajāpatī is married to Devadatta!

33 The actions of the king are scarcely to be accounted for by the mild provocation. All the queen did was not rise for him. But this is a cliché of old myth, for the gods of old were always jealous. Countless times we hear of death and devastation following on from the neglect of tribute; think of Artemis' fury towards Agamemnon, which would only be sated by the sacrifice of his daughter Iphigenia; or the vengeance wreaked by Jehovah in his fury at the faithless Hebrews.

34 This reluctance to pay formal respect is precisely the problem with Mahāpajāpatī in 'this' life. She wanted to not bow to the monks, and so a special rule had to be made for her. And the reason is the same: pride in her son, the Buddha.

35 Her motherliness is presented as an ideal of ethical virtue, a radical embodiment of the Buddha's injunction that true love was like that of a mother who would sacrifice her life for that of her child.

36 While the surface narrative is ethical, the imagistic associations reveal the primitive roots of the myth, forcing themselves through the veil: Candādevī, the 'Moon Goddess', howling as she bathes in the flesh and blood of her own dismembered child. She gathers the scattered parts together (like Isis 're-membering' Osiris or Kaṭṭhahāri gathering sticks) and holds them in her lap, drawing back to her womb the fruit of life. Mother Kāḷī in her ferocious aspect lurks only just beneath the skin of this tale.

37 Dismemberment is a common aspect of devotion to Her; and the dismembered 'victim'—who is little short of a god himself—is gathered by the devotees and buried in the 'lap' of Mother Earth. A few Indian examples from Frazer.

38 > Among the Lhota Naga, one of the many savage tribes who inhabit the deep labyrinthine glens which wind into the mountains from the rich valley of Brahmapootra, it used to be a common custom to chop off the heads, hands, and feet of people they met with, and then to stick up the severed extremities in their fields to ensure a good crop of grain.... Once they flayed a boy alive, carved him into pieces, and distributed the flesh among all the villagers, who put it into their corn-bins to avert bad luck and to ensure plentiful crops of grain. The Gonds of India, a Dravidian race, kidnapped Brahman boys, and kept them as victims to be sacrificed on various occasions. At sowing and reaping, after a triumphal procession, one of the lads was slain by being punctured with a poisoned arrow. His blood was then sprinkled over the ploughed field or the ripe crop, and his flesh was devoured.[15]

39 Frazer continues, as usual, detailing such ceremonies for many pages. He interprets them as displaying both an aspect of offering for the god or, more usually, goddess; and also as an act of sympathetic magic, where the vital energy of the sacrificed victim infuses the fields with life.

40 It is interesting that the Dravidians mentioned prefer a Brahman child. This suggests a racial revenge motif; but it also suggests that such children were in some way more potent, more highly charged with that magical force which, since the earliest times, has been called *brahman*. According to the Hindus, killing a brahman is the ultimate crime; but that power, being magical and hence pre-ethical, works both ways. In the same way the Bodhisatta is the Buddhist representative of the boy with 'super-powers', and it is only proper that stories which originally harked back to sacrifice should feature him as the victim. Hence the many times he found it necessary to offer his body in the pursuit, so they say, of Awakening, although such a doctrine is alien to the historical Buddha. The victim is regarded, so Frazer's informants say, as 'something more than mortal', and 'A species of reverence, which is not easy to distinguish from adoration, is paid to him.'[16]

41 The moon is a fittingly ambiguous image for this Queen. The Pali *candā* is, it seems, descended from a root meaning of 'glowing'. The Sanskrit is *candrā*; and the *r*, although lost from the Pali, makes itself felt in the retroflex syllables of the cognate *caṇḍa*, 'ferocious', i.e. burning with fury. The moon with her cycles is the beguiling face of death, an ever present

reminder of mortality. Her gracious mien gently hints at what the goddess Black Fury (Caṇḍakāḷī) makes all too explicit.

42 The image of the earth opening up to receive the villain—a staple of Buddhist dramatics—is a standard mythic re-invention. The earth is the womb of all life, the fertile domain of the goddess, bringing forth fruit and flowers, and demanding the return of the dead to ensure future fertility. As we become alienated from the goddess, she must be demonized. This happens to all the 'Older Gods'. In Buddhism these are the Asuras, who are explicitly called the 'older gods', and are kicked out of their ancestral heaven to live in the swamps and the seas.[17] In the same way the devil's attributes—horns, cloven hoofs and so on—belong to the pagan fertility gods (hence his undeniable sex appeal). Thus in the image of Buddhist hell, the bountiful aspect of the earth is ignored, and she becomes a gaping maw, a devouring cavern of limitless agony.

43 Her flaming mouth reminds us of the fire of the dragon. The flame here is a clue to the 'glowing' of the moon (*candā*) and the fury (*caṇḍa*). Fire in its aspect of consuming is feminine, while in purifying it is masculine. On return to the earth, the dead are 'digested' in the warmth of the earth, digestion being a function of the heat element according to Indic medicine.

44 So this little Jātaka presents Mahāpajāpatī as standing all too close to the ancient ferocious goddess; as close as she may stand without bursting through the veil and showing herself in her true colors. And yet she remains complex, for her love and concern for her son are still to the fore. She unites two aspects of femininity: her conscious aspect, in the surface events of the tale, is beneficent and nurturing, while the images reveal the Kālī aspect.

❖

45 Equally gruesome, the other mention of Mahāpajāpatī in the Cūḷanandiya Jātaka deals with the difficulties faced by a group of monkeys when confronted by a fierce hunter.[18]

> 46 Big Nandiya and his brother Little Nandiya lived in the Himalayas overseeing a company of 80 000 monkeys. They looked after their blind old mother, seeking out the sweetest fruit to send back for her. But the messengers were unreliable and not enough food made it back home, so the mother grew thin, just skin and bones.

47 The brothers consulted together and resolved to abandon their great company in order to look after their mother together. They took their mother from the mountains down into the wilderness, where they set up home in a banyan tree.

48 Now, there was a hunter in that region who was no ordinary low-caste peasant, but was a graduate of the Brahmanical studies at Takkasilā. His world-famous teacher had discerned by the peculiar marks of his limbs that he was of rough nature, and warned him that this would lead to his downfall. But after his graduation he was unable to make a living by other means, so resorted to the bow and arrow. He withdrew to a borderland forest and lived by slaughtering many animals and selling their meat.

49 One day he was particularly unlucky, and was returning home with empty hands, when he spied the banyan tree and approached it. The brothers, leaving their mother visible on the ground, hid in the tree, thinking that no hunter would be so cruel as to take such a wretched old monkey; but the hunter made to shoot her. Big Nandiya leapt out of the tree, stood before his mother, and offered his life to the hunter in her stead. Accordingly, the hunter shot Big Nandiya; but then drew his second bow on the mother. At this, Little Nandiya also dropped down and offered his life to save his mother, even if she should live but a day. Pitiless, the hunter shot him, and then shot the mother.

50 Stringing the three monkeys on a pole, he set off; but at that moment lightning struck his home. His wife and two children were consumed in the flames, and nothing was left of his house but the roof held up by bamboo supports.

51 A man standing at the village gate saw the hunter and told him what had occurred. Overcome with anguish for his wife and children, he threw down the pole with his game, together with his bow; stripping his clothes he went naked, wailing with his hands outstretched. Entering his home, the bamboo uprights snapped, and the roof collapsed on his head: and the ground gaped open as the flames of Avīci hell rose to take him. As he was being swallowed by the earth he remembered his teacher's warning, and uttered the following verses:

52 'I call to mind my teacher's words—Pārāsariya said:
"Be careful you should do nothing which you may regret!
What's done by a man, that he sees in himself.
Doing good one finds good; doing bad, bad one finds.
Our deeds are like seeds, bringing forth fruit in kind."'

53 Making the connection, the Buddha said: 'The hunter was Devadatta; Sāriputta was the brahman teacher Pārāsariya; Ānanda was Little Nandiya; Mahāpajāpatī Gotamī was the mother; while I myself was Big Nandiya.'

54 The surface dialogue teaches conventional Buddhist values: not harming, care of others, the fruits of kamma. But the primitive roots force themselves through the foundations. The brahman teacher does not assess his student by living with him and observing his character—as the Buddha recommended[19]—but by recognizing certain inauspicious marks. Omenology, though against the Vinaya,[20] here is an infallible science, a revelation of fate. Having heard this warning we know, as the characters within the story do not, that the hunter is doomed.

55 Such omens appear long before the Buddha. They are very common in Mesopotamian cuneiform writings from the second millennium BCE. Thousands of clay tablets tediously record connections between unrelated phenomena: if a fox runs into a public square, the town will be devastated; if a man treads on a lizard and kills it, he will prevail over his adversary. Omens were recorded in every conceivable domain: the marks on an abnormal foetus; facial and bodily characteristics; favorable or unfavorable months or times; the phenomena of the stars, sun, and planets; thunder and rain; earthquakes; dreams, portents; and on and on and on....[21]

56 Such things will be immediately familiar to anyone who has read the 'Great Section on Ethics' found in each Sutta in the first chapter of the Dīgha Nikāya, which elaborates many such 'low arts', regarding them all as unfit for monastics. Certainly the Mesopotamian evidence for such things is prior to that of the Indian; and given that the Indus Valley Civilization was trading with the Mesopotamians 1500 years before the Buddha, it seems inevitable that there is an interchange here, probably mainly into India.

57 The best known Buddhist examples of such omenology are the '32 marks of the Great Man' which are said to be an ancient Brahmanical teaching, supposedly signifying that one is to become either a Buddha or a Universal Monarch. Perhaps the earliest teacher of these marks was Bāvari, whose name, as the Pali Text Society Dictionary long ago pointed out, is just the Pali spelling of 'Babylonian'.[22]

58 A further primitive feature of the Jātaka is the incoherency of the presentation of kamma. The verses present the orthodox Buddhist view: one inherits one's own kamma. But these verses have been rather superficially attached to the story. In many cases the verses are intrinsic to the story, such that the verses only make sense in the context given by the story; hence they must have been passed down together from the first. The difference would be that the verses are relatively fixed at an early stage, while the story would remain open to the elaborations of the storyteller's art.

59 Our current text has a different character. Notice that the brahman teacher's name is not mentioned in the early part of the story, and only appears suddenly just before the verses. And Pārāsariya's words in the verses do not relate very closely to what the teacher said to his student earlier; true, they are both about kamma, but this is so common as to be unremarkable. The specific feature of the unnamed teacher's warning was of the rough character of his student, while the specific feature of Pārāsariya's teaching was the individual ownership of kamma. And that is contradicted in the story itself, for the hunter's wife and children are punished for the deeds done by the hunter. It seems that Pārāsariya's verses on the ownership of kamma were tacked on to the story of the monkeys, which was originally a story of vicarious atonement.

60 The story is constructed around the mirroring of the hunter's family and the monkey family. In both cases a mother and two children perish due to the wicked deeds of the hunter. And in both cases the mother is a burden, a passive figure who relies totally on the livelihood procured by the male. For the monkeys, the mother is a caricature of the crone, a blind decrepit old thing. She does nothing for herself, but, like the crone in the 'Grievous Text' Jātaka, her sons think nothing of devoting their lives to her, giving up all worldly power and ambition, and sacrificing their lives without regret. She is, yet again, identified with the tree; and the son, yet again, is at the crucial moment suspended in the air.

61 In this story, as in the previous, the action revolves totally around the woman, who herself does nothing. The male is the agent of violence, the deliberate outward expression of the mind that wills its presence in the world. In both stories, this evil character is played by Devadatta, who is constellated relative to Mahāpajāpatī. She remains passive as the carnage

he unleashes unfolds around her. This is the difference between the ethical and the existential dimension of suffering: from an ethical perspective, the choice to do good or bad is up to the individual, who must bear responsibility for those choices. But from the existential perspective, death is as natural as birth. We need do nothing; in fact we can do nothing, for the fates woven by the goddess enfold us all. In this sense, the primitive, violent masculinity is not opposed to the Old Mother, but is her servant, manifesting her will in the world.

62 The connections between Mahāpajāpatī and Devadatta cannot be coincidental. Certain traditions maintain that they were brother and sister in 'this' life, and that Devadatta's jealousy for their sister Māyā was the motivation for his hatred of Siddhattha.

❖

63 What a startling thing this is! There are only two Jātakas that mention Mahāpajāpatī; and in both she is identified with a mother whose sons suffer a violent death, due entirely to her own presence, even though unintended by her, with the violence perpetrated by Devadatta. Why, we might wonder, would the compilers of the tradition bear with them these particular associations for Mahāpajāpatī?

64 In the origin story for bhikkhuni ordination, Mahāpajāpatī is depicted as the opposite of the ideal ascetic. While the ideal monk is clean, restrained, collected, pure, she is dirty, emotional, weeping outside the gate. Her unrestrained demeanour reveals her for what she really is, a fake ascetic, who has donned the robe as a fraud, but who does not have the toughness that it takes to be a 'real monk'. Her tears are the external manifestation of the *āsavas*, the defilements or 'outflows' that keep us trapped in *saṁsāra*. In crying she is like like Ānanda and the other weak monks who, in the very next episode of the Khandhakas, break down in tears at the Buddha's passing away. Thus it is her tears that attract Ānanda's compassion.

65 To modern eyes, she looks pitiful rather than disgusting or defiled. Yet there is no doubt that the traditions saw her behaviour as seriously troubled. While the Pali version is quite brief, the Mūlasarvāstivāda version draws out the implications.

> 66 She stood barefooted outside the door, feeling defeated, and with tears pouring out like rain. Her face was filthy with dirt and her

> expression was one of despair. Her garments were dirty and her body was tired. She was sobbing sorrowfully and uncontrollably. Indulging in self-remorse and without restraint, (she exhibits) the eighty-four faults (of women); thus a deluded and confused person loses moral restraint. The Buddha knows the profound truth and is careful. Men on earth, all without exception, will become defiled because of women. (It's) extremely disastrous, extremely disastrous.[23]

67 The imagery around dirt, tears, and defilements is central to the notion of purity which is so important in descriptions of the Buddha's path. Mahāpajāpatī's appearance is explicitly constructed to subvert these perceptions of the proper, 'pure', state of a renunciate. And yet she is dressed as a bhikkhuni, even though she has not taken formal ordination. She is 'leaking', threatening to breach the carefully constructed and maintained boundaries of the Sangha. She stands 'outside the gate' of the monastery: she knows she cannot come in, but is on the verge of doing so anyway. By disobeying the Buddha she is making a subversive challenge to his power, like a flooding river that eats away at the structure of cultivated land.[24]

68 Thus far a political analysis. Authority and power, always crucial issues. But these cannot be divorced from spiritual matters, since the Sangha's source of power is its spiritual authenticity. Ideally this stems from the practice of its members, who emulate their Teacher and realize the same wisdom and freedom that he did. Practically, though, much of the institutional authority comes from the successful leveraging of the Buddha's own second-to-none spiritual charisma.

69 When the Buddha refuses Mahāpajāpatī, he sets up a boundary. He will not be swayed by her will. In this way he demonstrates his strength and independence. Myths are full of dreadful tales of what happens if the man is not strong enough to withstand the pull of the Great Mother. One of the great classical examples was Laocoön on the shores before Troy. He tried to defy necessity, arguing that the Trojans should not bring the wooden horse, votive offering the Athena, back to their city; a serpent emerged from the ocean and dragged him under. The Ṛg Veda speaks of the same crisis: 'He, yet enveloped in the mother's womb, source of much life, has sunk into destruction.'[25]

Figure 28.1: *Laocoön & sons dragged under by the serpent*

70 Neumann cites a number of examples from classical mythology. King Pentheus, proud of his rationality, wished to resist the chaotic orgies of Dionysus. But his mother was Dionysus' kin, so eventually both mother and son were overwhelmed by the frenzy. Pentheus put on women's clothing and joined the orgies, and his maddened mother ripped him to shreds and carried his head home on a pike. Her repressed unconscious does exactly what her conscious mind is most repelled by. Hippolytus likewise tried to scorn his step-mother Pheadra, out of devotion to the chaste Artemis instead of the seductive Aphrodite. He was dragged to death by his own horses. We have already seen how Gilgamesh avoids the same fate, by his wisdom born of understanding the archetypal situation—but even he cannot save his brother. Neumann makes explicit the psychological implications of this crisis.

71 Hippolytus is at the stage of critical resistance to the Great Mother, already conscious of himself as a young man struggling for autonomy and independence. This is evident from his repudiation of the Great Mother's advances and of her phallic, orgiastic sexuality. His 'chastity', however, means far more than a rejection of sex; it signifies the coming to consciousness of the 'higher' masculinity as opposed to the 'lower' phallic variety.[26]

72 Again, the issue here is not the Buddha's own surmounting of this crisis: this is already accomplished. It is the ability of the male Sangha to maintain its independence that is at question. And here we see the need for strict control measures.

73 In myth the parting of the World Parents, the sundering of heaven and earth, the differentiation of consciousness from the unconscious, is commonly represented as the rebellion of the son against his mother. Rebelling, he defines his Self by what he rejects. Yet this new process of differentiation, while crucial, was present before and will continue to evolve long after. For while babies learn to respond and imitate their mothers in the minutest of details, modeling their behavior and in doing so, internalizing the motivations that determine the behavior; yet at the same time, they already have the rudiments of a core sense of identity, a centering and coordinating of experience that in time will become what we are conscious of as our 'Self'.[27] We exist in relationship and in isolation, and this ambiguity is the glory and the tragedy of being. Stages such as the rebellion

of the son mark nodes of crisis within this context, not the creation of unprecedented realities. They are dramatized in myth, made vivid to the mind. This mythic truth is projected on to actual living women, as though they exist merely to serve as a screen for male fears and fantasies.

74 When the separation is still tender and the individual is not yet fully confident, one finds strength in numbers. Having budded off from the mother, the youth gangs together with other youths. Associating with others of a similar age reinforces the distinction from the mother. On a social level, this tendency appears as Men's Clubs, which are the ultimate basis of virtually all our central social institutions—military, educational, government, judicial, and religious.

75 According to Neumann, Men's Clubs stem from the networks among members of the various age groups in a tribe or clan.[28] The members are relatively equal within the group, but there is a hierarchical relationship between the groups, so induction from one age group to another requires a rite of initiation, which is often brutal, or at least difficult.

76 Such clubs act as a safety valve to redirect personal conflicts between the generations. The potential for father/son conflict, which is so real that it has become institutionalized as the widespread cultural practice of ritual regicide, is formalized in the initiation rituals. Conflict is contained within an archetype expressed through social and religious conventions, rather than in potentially devastating personal combat. Facing, overcoming, and resolving intergenerational conflict, the youth enters the circle of Men, and through his bravery and suffering escapes the domain of the mother, which has become stifling and limiting.

77 Entering the Men's Club the youth comes closer to his mature nature. He becomes conscious of himself as a Man, as an actor and agent who takes responsible choices.[29] This is reflected in the 'mysteries' of ascension to the Men's Club, which, since they are a ritualized reenactment of the primordial Hero's Journey, invariably grant a secret knowledge, the Pearl of Great Price, the consciousness of the Self. The young man is called to transcend the hot-blooded, violent, or coarsely sexual drives of his youth, and to redirect his energy to self-awareness, wisdom, and responsible action. This is what Neumann calls the Higher Masculinity. It is not sexual, and in fact it is often hostile to sexuality, requiring periods of celibacy

or isolation from women. Its symbolic canon is light, the sun, the head, and the eye. This implies that, while the initiation itself is primarily a ritual and hence archetypal act, the future course of development for the man will move beyond ritual to a more reflective, independent sense of self-determination.

78 Neumann's analysis of the Men's Club is point by point applicable to the Sangha. The monastic culture offers the support and solidarity that allows monks to find themselves, outside of the conditions and expectations of family and society. Even today, Men's Clubs, whether formal or informal, help men to find their own masculine identity so that they may enter into a mature relationship with women. Men always resist the entry of women into their clubs. This is why the bhikkhuni Sangha was set up mostly independent of the bhikkhu Sangha. For practical purposes, the monastery could remain a Men's Club, but the women had their club, too.

CHAPTER 29

THE PRINCESS & THE DRAGON

WE ARE NOW READY TO BEGIN WEAVING the disparate strands of our inquiry together. Up until now I have been mainly interested in deconstruction, in pulling apart the expectations and ideologies that cluster so thickly. Now I would like to weave the threads back together again, and I need a frame to rely on. That frame is the distinction, used throughout Neumann's work, between the 'higher' and 'lower' aspects of masculinity and femininity.

2 We have seen how the Buddha's life follows the pattern of the hero cycle, and that within that cycle there is a contrast between the outward leg, the individual attainment of Awakening, and the return, where the insights are brought back to society. And we have seen that in the Buddha's personal journey, he met two distinct aspects of the feminine. The encounter with Māra's daughters shows him heroically surmounting the animalistic, sexual feminine; but at the same time the Buddha is crucially supported by Sujātā on a personal level, and the earth goddess in the cosmic dimension, both of whom represent positive aspects of femininity. These two aspects are the 'Lower Femininity' and the 'Higher Femininity'. These, in turn, have their counterparts in the Lower and Higher Masculinity: the violence of Māra and the radiant consciousness of Brahmā.

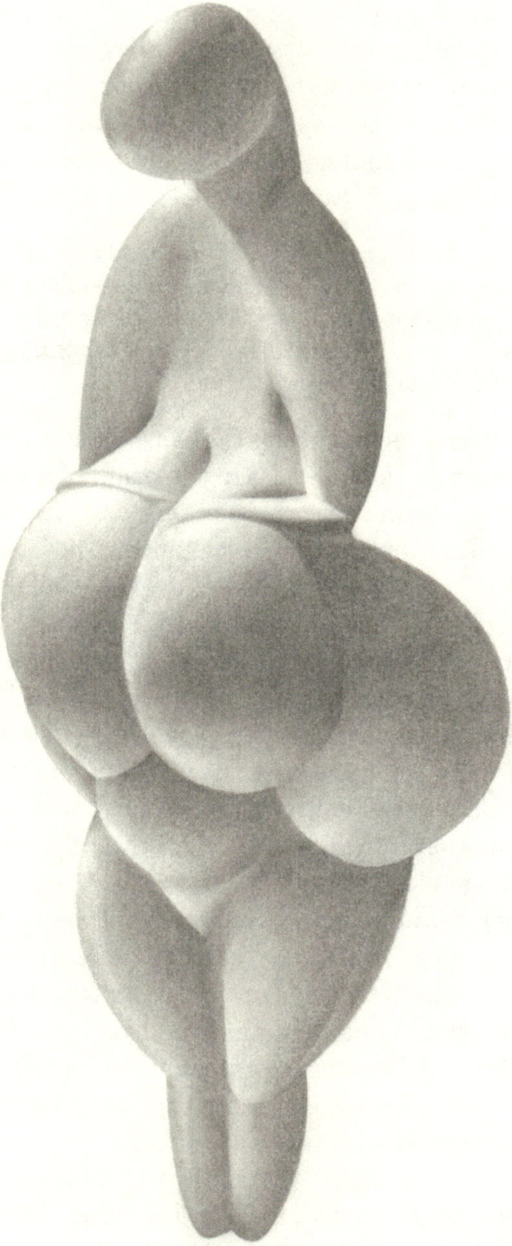

Figure 29.1: *Venus of Lespugue*

3 The terms 'lower' and 'higher' should not be taken literally. They are just another metaphor. Nevertheless, they are frequently figured in literal terms, where the lower parts of the body, for example, are associated with excrement and darkness, while the upper parts are associated with consciousness and light. A stunning example of this is the 'Venus of Lespugue', a paleolithic goddess figure. Neumann interprets it thus:

> 4 The delicate upper part and the virginal head are bent over a luxuriant body bursting with the elementary fullness of motherhood, so stressing by purely stylistic means the contrast between the static elementary character of the mother and the dynamic transformative character of the young woman.[1]

5 'Higher' and 'lower' do not mean the same thing as 'good' and 'bad'. As we have insisted all along, we are in the realm of the existential, not the ethical. The higher and lower have no absolute meaning, but refer to stages of psychological or spiritual development. The lower is what must be let go of (*pahātabbaṁ*), while the higher is what should be developed or attained (*bhāvetabbaṁ*). This will change as development proceeds. When an infant is born, he must adjust to the emergence from the womb and learn to develop attachment to the mother as breast-feeder and nurturer. Here, the womb experience is the Lower Feminine and the breast-feeding mother is the Higher Feminine. Later he is weaned from the breast, and must learn to relate to the mother as an independent person. Now the breast-feeding mother is the Lower Femininity. The process goes on and on, never stopping as long as life breathes.

6 Such metaphors are ultimately grounded in our experience as biological entities. They have a physicality to them, a spatial and 'massive' aspect. And yet biology does not determine spirituality, so we agree with Neumann that 'neither [masculinity nor femininity] exhaust the ultimate possibilities of transformation.'[2] Describing psychological processes in gendered language is merely for teasing out certain kinds of problems and illuminating particular aspects of being; no more, no less.

7 Neumann and other psychologists speak of these stages with a lurid vocabulary: the 'Devouring Mother', the 'Terrible Father', 'castration', 'death', 'uroboric incest', and so on. The violence implied in such imagery derives ultimately from the images found in myth itself, especially Greek myth.

But it is not a matter of perversion or sickness; it is just growing up, with all its everyday tragedies and challenges. Only if the process goes wrong do we speak of neurosis. The 'Terrible Mother' is not really terrible, she is just the 'Mother Who Won't Let Go'. The myths depict her as a devouring monster. But if we consider myth from the 'inside', she is nothing more than the image of the mother in the mind of the one who cannot let go.

8 We have encountered these Higher and Lower pairs not just in the Buddha's heroic Awakening, but in the contrast between Māyā and Mahāpajāpatī; in the pairs of parents in the 'Grievous Text' Jātaka; in the pre- and post- conversion Hārītī; in the twofold aspect of Queen Candādevī; in Kaṭṭhahāri the stick-gatherer raised to become queen; in the spiritual career of Bhaddā Kuṇḍalakesā; and so on.

❖

9 The distinction between the Lower and Higher Feminine is classically illustrated in the story of the rescue of the princess from the jaws of the dragon. The Jungian interpretation is that the feminine image as anima crystallizes out from the more pervasive, less differentiated archetype of the mother. In doing so she retains many of the positive, nurturing, helpful qualities of the mother, but leaves behind the devouring Lower aspects.[3]

10 The 'dragon' is the physical incarnation of the primeval Waters, and the hero always risks being 'swallowed by the whale'. The time in the womb is the only irreducibly gendered, universal event in human experience. Thus the 'Monster of the Waters' is always archetypally feminine. Of course, the uterine experience precedes gender differentiation, and so contains the germs of what the developed consciousness will later call 'masculine' and 'feminine'. This is why it is not uncommon for the Dragon to appear as a male in the surface narrative of myth;[4] but the underlying archetype is always feminine. Not only does the Monster contain the germs of the masculine and feminine, it contains all possibilities, good and bad.[5]

11 Here is a typical tale of the Higher Feminine being saved from the clutches of the Dragon: Perseus and Andromeda.[6] I will dwell on this story at some length, as it draws together many of the themes I have touched on through this book.

> 12 Acrisius, King of Argos, was warned by the the oracle at Delphi that he would one day be killed by his daughter's son. His only daughter

Danaë was childless, and to keep her so, he shut her up in a bronze chamber.[7] The workings of fate are not so easily foiled, however: Zeus came to her as a shower of gold.[8] She called their child Perseus.

13 Acrisius cast the mother and child into the sea in a wooden chest. They washed ashore on the island of Seriphos, where they were taken in by the fisherman Dictys, who raised the boy to manhood.

14 The brother of Dictys was Polydectes, the king of the island. Polydectes fell in love with Danaë, but Perseus stood in the way. To get rid of him, Polydectes announced a banquet where each guest would be expected to bring a horse. Perseus had no horse, so he offered to bring some other gift instead. Polydectes demanded the head of Medusa, whose very expression turns people to stone. Medusa was the only mortal of the three Gorgon sisters, whose heads of snaky hair recall their origins: they were the daughters of primordial sea monsters Phorcys and Ceto.

15 With Hermes and Athena as his guides Perseus sought out the three Grey Ladies.[9] They lived on a round island somewhere beyond India.[10] The Grey Ladies had only one lidless eye among them, which they took turns using. Perseus crept up on tiptoe, keeping his footfall noiseless, and with hollowed hand and robber's fist he stole the eye as it was passed from one sister to another. He said he would return it only if the Grey Ladies directed him to certain Nymphs, who had in their possession winged sandals, a magic knapsack, and the helmet of Hades that conferred invisibility.[11] The Grey Ladies agreed to his request, so he went to the Nymphs, received these gifts and put them on, ready to start his quest proper.

16 Perseus took flight to remote lands, through rocky pathless crags, over wild hills that bristled with great woods. Along the way, in fields and by the roads, he saw on all sides men and animals like statues, turned to flinty stone at the sight of Medusa's face. He came to Okeanos, where night in the far west meets the setting sun. There he found the Gorgons sleeping in their cave. Their heads were entwined with the horny scales of serpents, and they had big tusks like hogs, bronze hands, and wings of gold on which they flew.

17 Perseus rushed into the cave like a wild boar. With Athena guiding his hand, he kept his eyes on the reflection in his bronze shield as he stood over the sleeping Gorgons. When he saw the image of Medusa, he reaped the hissing hair, sliced her teeming throat, and stained his sickle red! As soon as her head was severed there leaped from her body the winged horse Pegasus, and Chrysaor, the boy with a

golden sword. Perseus lifted the lifeless token of victory: the head of Medusa, with its snaky hair dripping blood, wheezing a half-heard hiss through the severed throat.

18 Perseus placed the severed head in the knapsack and fled with the speed of thought on his winged feet, trembling at the shrill lamenting cries from the fierce Gorgons' ravening jaws. After him rushed the two remaining Gorgons, Medusa's sisters, unapproachable and unspeakable, longing to seize him. Two serpents hung down at their girdles with heads curved forward; their tongues flickered, their teeth gnashed with fury, and their eyes glared fiercely. But the helmet kept him hidden, and they could not find him.

19 Arriving in Ethiopia, Perseus came upon King Cepheus' daughter Andromeda tied to a rock in the ocean as a meal for a sea monster. The king's wife Cassiopeia had boasted that her beauty outshone even the Nereides, the nymphs of the sea. As a result the Nereides were in a rage, and Poseidon in sympathetic anger sent a flood-tide upon the land and a sea monster, the goddess Cetos, as well. The oracle of Ammon prophesied an end to the trouble if Cassiopeia's daughter Andromeda were served up to the monster as a sacrifice, so Cepheus tied his daughter out on a rock. When Perseus saw her he thought she was an image carved of marble, so perfect was her beauty; but the breeze moved in her hair, and from her eyes warm tears fell. She so amazed his heart that his swift wings almost forgot to wave.[12] He promised to kill the sea monster and rescue the girl in return for her hand in marriage.

20 As the swift eagle of Zeus, when he beholds a basking serpent in an open field, fixes his grasping talons in the scaly neck for fear it should turn to strike with venomed fang; so did the winged youth Perseus press down on the great monster's back, and thrust his sword to the hilt in its right shoulder. Wild with the grievous wound, the monster reared high in the air, or plunged in the waves, or wheeled around. The hero on his active wings dodged the monster's jaws, and with his curved sword tortured its back wherever he could pierce its mail of hollow shell, or struck between the ribs each side, or wounded its lashing tail. The monster spouted forth streams of blood that sprayed upon the hero's wings. Finding purchase on a rock, Perseus thrust his sword, unswerving in his aim, sheer through the monster's entrails.[13]

21 Celebrations ensued. Perseus made offerings to the gods, and there was a magnificent wedding feast. But Cepheus' brother Phineus, who

was previously engaged to Andromeda, conspired against Perseus. Perseus, however, learned of the plot and defeated the conspirators.

22 When Perseus returned to Seriphos with his new bride, he found that his mother Danaë along with Dictys had sought refuge at the altars from the violence of Polydectes. So he entered the royal palace where Polydectes was entertaining his friends, and with his own face turned aside he displayed Medusa's head. When they looked at it, each one turned to stone, holding the pose he happened to have been striking at that moment. Perseus made Dictys king of Seriphos. He gave the sandals, knapsack, and helmet back to Hermes, who returned them to the Nymphs. Medusa's head, however, he gave to Athena, who placed it in the center of her shield.

23 Hearing of Perseus' return, Acrisius fled Argos, still fearful of the prophecy that he would die at the hand of his daughter's son. Despite this, he ran into Perseus at Larissa, where athletic games were being held to honor the king's dead father.[14] Perseus was competing with the discus, but it accidentally struck Acrisius on the foot and killed him dead: thus the oracle was fulfilled. What Perseus would not do of his own will was accomplished by the gods. Perseus took his rightful place on the throne of Argos, with Andromeda as his queen.

❖

24 Let's reflect on the mythic significance of each item in this story. It starts with the prophecy, alerting us that the story's events are inevitable, hence archetypal: the events are under the dictates of the Fates. The real-world reason for this, as always, is the inevitability of death. Acrisius, the old king, must give way to the new. But he is an emerging historical figure; his person is struggling to differentiate from his archetype. Not ready to accept his fate, he tries to subvert the prophecy by rendering his daughter Danaë infertile. His death will come at the hands of his own descendant, so if she does not give birth he will not die. This is brutal but realistic: immortality requires the freezing of the cycle of life and death. Like so many fairytale fathers he locks his daughter in a sealed room, a symbol of her virginity and a memory of the practice of isolating girls at their first menstruation. This naturally has the effect of making her more desperate and more attractive, so she is fertilized, both by Zeus as a shower of gold, and by Acrisius' brother, the betrayer. These are the standard motifs of the virgin birth and the twin human and divine parentage. The shower

of gold, however, is specific and encodes Perseus' special destiny: it is the Divine Sun, and announces that Perseus will be a hero of light, the air, and consciousness.

25 The mother and son are cut off from the forms and structures of their conventional inheritance, cast afloat on shipless oceans, to be reborn from the universal waters. They come into the circle of another pair, the brothers with such similar names, Dictys and Polydectes. They are the same person, split in two; Dictys is the good twin, Polydectes the evil. The reason for Perseus' opposition to his mother's marriage to Polydectes is not made clear by the mythographers, but is hinted at in Polydectes' name, the 'Host of All'. This is a title of Hades, Lord of Death, who is the only host who will make all creatures his guest.[15]

26 Thus the quest is not simply Perseus', but also his mother's: how to surmount the Lower Masculine so she can unite with the Higher, her own animus figure, Dictys, freed from the tyranny of his Lower twin. Neither mother nor son can accomplish their task alone. So, while the narrative says that Perseus was sent on his quest by Polydectes as a trick, in reality he is helping his mother.

27 Like all heroes, Perseus, for all his masculine strength, needs help. Hermes is the messenger of Zeus, whose winged feet are the divine archetype for Perseus' own. By taking to the skies, Perseus becomes as a bird, free, detached from the earth, close to the sun and the heavens. Athena, born from Zeus' brow, is the updated, masculinized incarnation of the goddess. She is a virgin warrior, renowned for wisdom, the normal aid for heroes of consciousness, such as Odysseus and Theseus. In Jungian terms, she is the anima, the sisterly companion and helper.

28 Perseus' quest is perhaps the most feminine of all the great heroes. With the exception of Hermes, all the main characters he meets are women. Many of them are generic groups of divine women. The Nymphs are helpful anima figures. The 'Grey Ladies' are ambiguous hags, who, despite having only one eye, possess the secret knowledge he needs. It is a knowledge of the old things, magical powers that will imbue him with the strength of mythic heroes to accomplish his impossible task. They are not hostile, but there is no question of him simply persuading them to help; he succeeds, like Odysseus, through trickery and stealth.

29 The gifts of the Nymphs further underline Perseus' solar nature as a hero of consciousness. Not only can he fly 'swift as thought', he can vanish like thin air. The knapsack, however, is a little different. It is a container for the Medusa's perverse, snaky head. A gift from the anima, it bounds and renders powerless the monstrous feminine. It is the inverse of Athena's shield, or aegis. When the head is given to Athena—in other words, when the tamed Lower Feminine is incorporated in the Higher Feminine—she places it in her shield. This is crucial: the Lower Feminine is not destroyed, but is retained within the structure of the Higher forms.

30 Medusa's power, as a primordial serpent goddess, is to turn men to stone. She undoes evolution and draws all back to the earth. She is evil incarnate, dissociated from civilization, separate from other divinities, living at the utter end of the night. Her cave, like those of the dragons Apep or Vṛtra, is a sign of her primitive nature.

31 Perseus is the only one who can penetrate her darkness, bringing light into her cave. He cannot look at her directly; the darkest reaches of the unconscious make themselves known only through dream, reflection, or echo. The real Medusa is simply too horrible. He is not yet differentiated enough to withstand her gaze, and if she were to look upon him she would draw him back to her chthonic state. He cannot look upon the monster's true form, but only her *māyā*. Athena is there to guide his hand, however; the anima knows the Lower Feminine far better than the male hero ever can. The Medusa slumbers, as hers is the realm of darkness, unconscious, dreaming.

32 When the Medusa is slain, there spring from her body two divine beings, the flying horse Pegasus and the boy-hero Chrysaor. Pegasus is sometimes identified with Perseus himself, as a variation on the winged feet; while Chrysaor, whose name means 'Goldsword', became the father of heroes, and is a divinity of the gently waving leafs of golden wheat. Both of these show the emergence of the Higher Masculine from the death of the lower feminine, prefiguring Perseus' own victory. They remind us that the Lower Feminine is not an enemy to be annihilated: she is their mother, and without her there could be no higher development.

33 Medusa's sisters, however, still live. Perseus' task is not finished, as he has succeeded in bounding the Lower Feminine, but not yet in incorporat-

ing her as part of his own heroic arsenal. This is because, although he has been receptive to and helped by anima figures on his journey, they remain as distant, elevated, divine figures. Athena is above him, drawing him up. He is yet to enter into a relationship with the anima as equal.

34 For this he must face his ultimate challenge: to rescue Andromeda, the human anima, from the grips of Ceto, the mother of the Gorgons. When he first sees her, she appears so beautiful it is as if she were an image; as in so many stories, the masculine gaze first objectifies the woman, and only later sees her humanity, as her tears flow. He wins her in battle, and is finally united with the anima. Later we will see how this scene is depicted by very different images.

35 Next the story moves to the return phase. There is another hostile brother to be dispatched at the wedding before he can return to redeem his mother. Having fully conquered his infantile fears, he is now ready to return the assistance he has received from the Divine Feminine. It is his turn to save her from the grips of the Lower Masculine: Polydectes, the evil brother, Lord of Death. For Perseus this is now a trivial task. He merely needs to expose the Polydectes to the Medusa's head; the Lower Masculine, being reliant only on force, has none of the intelligence that would enable him to withstand the pull of the Lower Feminine. Polydectes becomes stone, his destiny reversing that of Andromeda, who was as if stone brought to life. From now on, Polydectes is only an image; he has found immortality as a statue of himself.

36 This stage of the journey, however, occurs twice. For the story began with another figure of the Lower Masculine, Acrisius. Both he and Polydectes play the role of the violent, imprisoning father who would destroy all he loves in a vain attempt to escape death. Acrisius, however, lies closer to the archetype; he is the 'grandfather', whose means are even less humane. Polydectes merely keeps Danaë in a palace, while Acrisius locks her inside a bronze cell 'like a grave'. Polydectes knows nothing of his fate; but Acrisius listens to the oracle and takes her very seriously, even as he struggles to escape. Both these figures are the king sacrificed, as a memory of a custom of ritual regicide, or as acknowledgment that even the greatest of human glory comes under the sway of death.

37 Acrisius' death is mythically precise. It occurs at the funeral games for a dead king. In truth, Acrisius is that dead king, and the games are a watered-down memory of the ceremony of sacrificial regicide. He dies at the hands of Perseus, who throws a discus. The discus is an obvious symbol for the solar disk, and so is fit for the solar hero, Perseus.[16] And just as Polydectes is turned to rock, Acrisius' death lies precisely at the point where he rests on the earth: his feet.[17]

❖

38 The story of Perseus and Andromeda finds its closest Buddhist parallel in the Ghata Jātaka.[18] King Mahākaṁsa reigned in the north, with his daughter Devagabbha—'Divine Womb'.[19] The prophecy of the brahmans was that she would destroy the lineage and the kingdom. Unable to bear it, the king retired in favor of his sons, who promptly locked their sister in a tower. There are the usual duplications—sons, mothers, children, all exist in copies—and the existence of such copies provides the shadow of *māyā* under cover of which there is the inevitable betrayal, and the equally inevitable pregnancy that results.

39 Devagabbha's ten sons were brought up in secret. The foremost was Vāsudeva, who these days is better known as Kṛṣṇa.[20] His closest brother is Baladeva, and the rest are also well-known deities or heroes. When their existence became known, the king decided to get rid of them by means of a wrestling match. However, the ten brothers won the fights, and in addition Vāsudeva threw a discus that lopped off the heads of his uncles, the king and his brother. The brothers took over the kingship and proceeded to conquer all India, slaying all 63 000 kings with a discus. They decided to share the kingdom, and divided it to ten parts, but they had forgotten their sister Añjanā. So one of the brothers gave up his share, and the nine brothers ruled with the sister, thus showing the incorporation of the anima within the structure of the mature masculine psyche.[21]

40 Much later, there was another prophecy that the ten brethren would die and the line would disappear utterly. It came to pass, once more from a slaughter at what appeared to be harmless games.[22] Only Vāsudeva, Baladeva, Añjanā, and a priest escaped. But Baladeva succumbed shortly after at yet another wrestling match. They went on. One night, while Vāsudeva slept behind a bush, a hunter called Jarā ('Old Age'), threw a spear

that accidentally pierced Vāsudeva in the foot. Thus all the brothers died, leaving only the lady Añjanā.

41 The parallels with the Perseus cycle are too obvious to need spelling out. The story has all the signs of a truly ancient legend. The prominent role of the discus, which is mentioned as a weapon in the Ṛg Veda, suggests the story has its roots in the primitive Indo-European mythos.[23]

42 The crux of Perseus' quest is that he had to kill the monstrous woman, the Medusa, before he could win the anima princess. When we read of the maiden trapped and rescued by the hero, it is tempting to see the female as weak, and needing rescue by the male. But these details are on the surface. Only by seeing through the personal details into the timeless patterns can we discern the resonant meaning. Throughout his journey, Perseus has accomplished his task only with the help of anima figures. It is hardly possible that she will desert him when his need is greatest.

43 The oldest image I have found, from a Corinthian urn of perhaps 600 BCE, depicts the scene with uncanny plainness. Perseus, the hero (i.e. the ego consciousness) takes the center in a pose of aggressive action, featuring his divine attributes, including the bag containing the Medusa's head. He is surrounded by the twin feminine: on the left is the monster, emerging from the darkness like a nightmare. On the right, Andromeda stands strong at the same height as Perseus. She is a very human helper, holding a rock with which to join Perseus in attacking the monster. The rock stands for the chthonic nature of the primeval Earth Goddess/Monster. Andromeda has mastered the Lower Feminine so that she can use it as a weapon, just as Athena uses the Medusa's head. Together they face the monster. The developed myth tells us Perseus could not see the Medusa directly, but only as a reflection. Here, however, his strength is in its fullness: his princess at his side, he need not fear the monster's gaze.

Figure 29.2: *Perseus and Andromeda attacking monster*

44 The next image comes from Pompeii, a few centuries later. It shows a slightly later stage in the adventure. The monster is already slain. Perseus, naked and dark-skinned as in the earlier image, stands with his winged ankles, a short sword, and the Medusa's head in his left hand.[24] Andromeda is on a rock above him, fair and serene, slightly receding in a numinous glow. She is beatific, and raises her arm in blessing, while Perseus responds with a humbly bowed head. Their arms reach out to each other, forming a circle, in a manner reminiscent of the joined arms of Māyā.

45 From the early modern period, the scene became a favorite of artists, but the depictions became strikingly different.[25] Andromeda is naked and chained to the rock. Utterly passive, it's hard to imagine this girl-child picking up a rock to throw at the monster. She seems more like a bondage fetish than the warrior or beatific woman of the earlier images. While the first image depicted Andromeda, Perseus and the monster at the same level, eye to eye, now Andromeda is lifted well above the sea, not just separate but radically sundered from her primeval home. To compensate, the aggressive masculinity of Perseus is even further emphasized. While in the classical images he was naked and she was clothed, now he is clothed and she is naked; many images depict her chained and helpless body with thinly-disguised relish.

Figure 29.3: *Andromeda blessing Perseus, Pompeii*

46 In all these re-imaginings we see how the perspective of the teller shapes the tale, even though the archetypal elements remain constant. The crucial point is that the female appears twice: in monstrous form she is the Dragon of the Deep, while in human form she is the princess, the wakening woman of the same age as the hero. Neumann describes the process as the 'freeing of the anima from the power of the uroboric dragon'. Henceforth, the feminine component is consciously integrated in the hero's own psyche. The masculine ego relates to this feminine element as equal, and this relationship bears fruit in the founding of a kingdom, the establishment of a family, in creative accomplishments, or in higher spiritual development. This conscious relationship with the feminine as equal, sister, and partner, is fundamentally different from the infantile relation to the mother, who can never be the equal of her child. Nevertheless, the anima and the Mother archetype are by no means completely separate. The Mother is like an ocean, the totality of all, while the anima is characterized by a specific set of qualities that have been fragmented from the Old Mother archetype and made conscious in the hero. The Mother, however, continues to play her role in the unconscious; and the link back to her goes through the anima.

47 While the union with the anima is seen as an essential process in healthy development, this does not mean that the anima is purely good. Like any aspect of the psyche, the anima has dangerous aspects, which is why the hero must know her fully.

> 48 The anima is a symbolic and archetypal figure, being made up of magical, alluring, and dangerously fascinating elements which bring madness as well as wisdom. She has human, animal, and divine features, and can assume corresponding shapes when enchanted or disenchanted. As the soul, she can no more be defined than man can define woman; yet, although exceeding the heights and depths of a man, she has finally entered the human sphere, a 'you' with whom 'I' can commune, and not a mere idol to be worshiped.[26]

Figure 29.4: *Perseus rescuing Andromeda*

49 It is through the help of the anima as warrior woman, the wild unpredictable virgin huntress so common in myth, that the hero can overcome the destructive aspect of the Old Mother, while at the same time preserving his connection with her. Perseus retains the head of Medusa, and can even use it as a weapon. His rivals—Polydectes and Phineus—have not vanquished the dragon, and hence succumb to its gaze. Perseus has not merely conquered, he has also incorporated. Just as the ferocious demonesses Hārītī and Kuntī are given shrines in the monasteries, Athena later takes the Medusa's head as part of her Aegis. This kind of thing happens everywhere. The old mother goddesses are not disposed of entirely, but are civilized, tamed, and incorporated within more evolved religious forms with the help of the anima. The vicious Erinyes ('Furies'), for example, are transformed into the Eumenides ('Kindlies') and a cult in their honor is established by Athena.[27] In the same way, only with the help of Sujātā and the Earth goddess could Buddha fulfill his quest, and they are honored to this day in Buddhist myth and iconography.

50 Sujātā and the Earth goddess are dramatically contrasted with Māra's daughters, a reminder that the Higher Feminine is not sexual. The rescue of the Maiden is, to be sure, often crowned with the marriage of the man and woman. But the wedding is the bounding of sexuality, not its licensing. As in our tale of Kaṭṭhahārī the Stick-collector, promiscuity is the freedom of nature, while marriage is the restrictions of culture. This was the decree of the Father in the greatest love of all: Cupid & Psyche. After long and arduous adventures, a love only consummated in the dark and in anonymity, Cupid is permitted to marry his beloved Psyche by his father, Jupiter the King of Gods, who declared:

> 51 'I have decided that the hot-blooded impulses of his first youth must be somehow bridled; his name has been besmirched for long enough in common report for adultery and all kinds of wantonness. We must take away all opportunity for this and fetter his youthful excess in the bonds of marriage. He has chosen a girl and had her virginity: let him hold her, have her, and embracing Psyche for ever enjoy his beloved.'[28]

52 This is why it is also possible, indeed quite common, for the liberated feminine to be a virgin. In classical myth, Medea, Ariadne, Athene, or Artemis

are helpful, sisterly types who do battle with the devouring dragon. At the least such figures are a beloved helpmate, but in the higher forms they call the hero towards the divine. Such figures are actively supportive of the growing self-awareness that is the hallmark of the Higher Masculinity, and do not tempt a man to revert to his Lower sexuality.[29]

53 This is still true in modern myths: Luke relies on Leia, Frodo on Galadriel, Harry on Hermione, and there's nothing sexual about it. In the *Rāmāyaṇa*, Sītā is Rāma's bride. She not just a sexual partner, but Rāma's constant companion and his friend in adversity; and so the Buddhist retelling of the story makes Sītā the sister of Rāma.[30] In the past, the Bodhisatta himself went forth together with his own sister.[31] Sexuality as such belongs to the Lower stages of development. Thus the Buddha's defeat of Māra's daughters is not a rejection of femininity as such. The hero kills only the destructive aspect of the feminine, and in doing so he sets free the fruitful and joyous aspect.[32] Having accomplished this feat, 'The autocratic rule of the mother over her offspring is now ended.'[33] This victory is essential for the maturity, wholeness, and spiritual integration of the hero.

54

> All redeemer and savior figures whose victory stops short without rescuing the captive, without sacramentally uniting themselves with her, and therefore without having founded a kingdom, have something dubious about them from the psychological point of view. Their manifest lack of feminine relationship is compensated by an excessively strong unconscious tie to the Great Mother. The nonliberation of the captive expresses itself in the continued dominance of the Great Mother under her deadly aspect, and the final result is alienation from the body and from the earth, hatred of life, and world negation.[34]

55 This is the extreme of bodily mortification which the Buddha rejected. He alienated his male ascetic companions in accepting the milk-rice from Sujātā. Hence this distinction between the Lower and Higher Femininity is essential. Without it, a man will let the princess fall into the Dragon's maw, and, failing to integrate the feminine in his own psyche, develops a neurotic aversion to womankind as a whole.

56 Neumann says that the patriarchal motto of the ego is 'away from the unconscious, away from the mother'.[35] To attain a healthy adult conscious sense of self, one must differentiate oneself from one's mother in home

life, and from the unconscious in psychic life. In liberating the anima from the grasp of the unconscious, the male hero realizes the strength and wisdom to be gained from a healthy relationship with his own feminine side. He becomes conscious of his own femininity, which is a great victory in the Hero's Quest. Until he establishes such a relationship, the feminine remains identified with the archaic, infantile unconscious as the Medusa, the Gorgon, the Dragon: the dread enemy to be feared, shunned, and if possible killed. Once the relationship with the anima is well-established, moreoever, she provides the conduit whereby the adult male can come to understand his own unconscious and develop a healthy, mature relationship with the mother archetype.

CHAPTER 30

THE SACRED STEPMOTHER

AT THIS POINT WE MUST TAKE A DEEP BREATH and get ready to plunge into the deeps. It is time to revisit the bhikkhuni origin story, equipped with all the knowledge we have gained, and redeem it. Yes, even now, with all we have learnt, I believe we can reclaim this story on behalf of the nuns.

2 Let us take up the story of Mahāpajāpatī once more from where we left off. Remember, she requested ordination three times and was refused. Then, donning robes and shaving her hair, she followed, with the Śākyan ladies, behind the Buddha and his Sangha. Weeping and dirty, covered in dust, she stood outside the gates, where Ānanda came to her help. Taking her case to the Buddha, he persuaded him to accept Mahāpajāpatī, on condition that she accept the eight *garudhammas*, the first of which stipulates that a bhikkhuni ordained 100 years must bow to a bhikkhu ordained that very day. The Buddha likened the ordination of women to diseases that destroy the Sangha, and said he had laid down the *garudhammas* as a dyke to hold back the flood.

3 Traditional retellings of the story, focusing on the Buddha, break off here. Most of the ancient Vinaya accounts, also, go little further with Mahāpajāpatī's story, concerning themselves with legal details of Vinaya procedures. The Pali Vinaya is alone in continuing the story with a short but highly suggestive series of events.[1] These are placed straight after the ordination in consecutive order. There is no indication of the time lapse between the episodes, but we may assume that in at least some cases this was substantial.[2]

4 In these few passages, quietly and unassumingly sitting there in the Vinaya, we find a different way of reading Mahāpajāpatī's request for going forth. It is not presented with a crash of thunder and a rumble of doom as the destruction of Buddhism. Instead, it appears as a series of very human and realistic snapshots from the life of an actual practitioner, one with difficulties and limitations, who nevertheless continues her struggle and overcomes her difficulties. As well as recording the deeds of a specific person, it has a universal significance for followers of the Dhamma.

❖

> 5 And then Mahāpajāpatī Gotamī approached the Blessed One, bowed, stood to one side, and said: 'Bhante, how should I proceed regarding these Śākyan ladies?'
>
> 6 ... [The Buddha said:] 'I allow, monks, bhikkhunis to be fully ordained by bhikkhus.'
>
> 7 And then those bhikkhunis said this to Mahāpajāpatī Gotamī: 'Venerable, you are not fully ordained, we are fully ordained. For it was laid down by the Blessed One: "Bhikkhunis should be fully ordained by bhikkhus." '
>
> 8 And then Mahāpajāpatī Gotamī [told this to Venerable Ānanda, who told it to the Buddha.]
>
> 9 ... [The Buddha said:] 'Ānanda, when Mahāpajāpatī Gotamī accepted the eight *garudhammas*, that was her full ordination.'
>
> 10 And then Mahāpajāpatī Gotamī said to Venerable Ānanda: 'I ask one favor of the Blessed One. It would be good, Bhante, if the Blessed One would allow bhikkhus and bhikkhunis to bow down, rise up, make *añjali*, and proper conduct in accordance with seniority.'
>
> 11 [Venerable Ānanda told this to the Buddha, who said:]
>
> 12 'It is impossible, Ānanda, it cannot happen that the Tathāgata should allow bowing down, rising up, making *añjali*, and proper conduct to women. Even, Ānanda, the followers of other sects, of badly-expounded doctrines, do not allow this, so how could the Tathāgata? Monks, you should not bow down, rise up, make *añjali*, or perform proper conduct for women. Whoever should do so incurs an offence of wrong-doing.'
>
> 13 And then Mahāpajāpatī Gotamī approached the Blessed One, bowed, stood to one side, and said: 'Bhante, how should the bhikkhunis proceed regarding the training rules held by the bhikkhunis in common with the bhikkhus?'

14 'Gotamī, regarding the training rules that are held by the bhikkhunis in common with the bhikkhus: you should train in them as the bhikkhus train.'

15 'Bhante, how should the bhikkhunis proceed regarding the training rules that are not held by the bhikkhunis in common with the bhikkhus?'

16 'Gotamī, regarding the training rules that are not held by the bhikkhunis in common with the bhikkhus: you should train in them as they are laid down.'

17 And then Mahāpajāpatī Gotamī approached the Blessed One, bowed, stood to one side, and said: 'It would be good, Bhante, if the Blessed One would teach me the Dhamma in brief, having heard which I will dwell alone, withdrawn, diligent, ardent, and resolute.'

18 'Gotamī, those qualities of which you know: "These qualities lead to dispassion, not passion; to being unfettered, not fettered; to getting rid of, not heaping up; to few wishes, not many wishes; to contentment, not discontentment; to seclusion, not socializing; to arousal of energy, not laziness; to being easy to support, not hard to support." You may definitely hold: this is Dhamma, this is Vinaya, this is the Teaching of the Buddha.'[3]

❖

19 We have found, again and again, that the deep meaning of myth may only be entered when the surface details are not allowed to obscure the archetypal forms. Let us, then, consider the situation first of all in the most general terms, seeing the characters in terms of the Higher or Lower Masculinity or Femininity.

20 The two main characters are the Buddha and Mahāpajāpatī, and they are initially in an adversarial relation. The Buddha, while in the ultimate sense transcending gender, here plays the role of the Higher Masculine. We have adduced abundant evidence to demonstrate that Mahāpajāpatī is the Lower Feminine. Her entire imagistic association confirms this, her association with dirt, leaking fluids, floods, and disease characterize her perfectly as the Mother Who Just Won't Let Go, who wants to keep her baby forever dependent on her milk. Ānanda is her champion, and just as clearly stands for the Lower Masculine. He is a more immature form of the Buddha, still in the thrall of the Great Mother, repeatedly reminding us of her milk.

21 Both Ānanda and Mahāpajāpatī are at this stage stream-enterers. That is, they are firmly standing on the path to Awakening, but are still subject to the pulls of the world. In this peculiar 'Janus-faced' posture of the stream-enterer, their acts are inescapably ambiguous, aspiring for the highest, yet not quite able to let go. But their faith is absolute, so in some cases a stern jolt can be just the ticket.[4]

22 And the picture is completed by the other bhikkhunis. It is crucial that they are *adversaries* to Mahāpajāpatī. Just as the Buddha's refusal is an existential denial of the possibility of her becoming a bhikkhuni, not an ethical criticism, the bhikkhunis deny that Mahāpajāpatī is fully ordained. And just as the Buddha accepts her only on the condition of the eight *garudhammas*, so too the other bhikkhunis only accept her on the strength of these rules.[5] The other bhikkhunis stand on the side of the Buddha, against Mahāpajāpatī, and hence represent the Higher Femininity. This posture is almost invisible in the text. They are a nameless group of '500', without character or background, and exist only as images to contrast with Mahāpajāpatī. This blankness, devoid of personal details, devoid of individuality, renders them virtually pure archetypal projections within the narrative, with little need to see them as historical.

23 With the other bhikkhunis in the picture we have a perfect pattern: the Buddha and the bhikkhunis as the Higher Masculine and Feminine; and Ānanda and Mahāpajāpatī as the Lower Masculine and Feminine. Suddenly, the myth is transformed. It is no longer a conflict between masculine and feminine, but between higher and lower stages of spiritual development. The misogynist aspect is merely an overlay of detail that does not affect the overall pattern. Like the images of Andromeda and Perseus the same scene, with the same archetypal meaning, may present very different surface details. These tell us about the person or persons who created that particular telling, but not about the events portrayed.

24 I have struggled with this story for many years, and this is the only satisfying explanation I have found. Why else would the other nuns have criticized their own leader, by whose efforts they have gained the ordination? If we try to read the story historically, we come up against an insuperable obstacle: they must have known that the Buddha accepted Mahāpajāpatī for ordination, so why bring the question up? When the

texts cannot be read rationally, this is a sign that they are leveraging us out of our comfort zone into a new way of seeing. Depending on the context, this might drag us down into the depths—as in the supposed threats of 'disease' and 'floods' posed by the bhikkhunis—or elevate us into a new spiritual plane.

25 The whole scenario now makes sense. Mahāpajāpatī as the Lower Feminine is threatening the Sangha, representing the ever-present pull of the unconscious, threatening to swallow consciousness as the dark earth swallows the sun each evening. This manifests specifically as attachment for her son. The Buddha bars her from entering, repeatedly, to prove his imperviousness, as Perseus must prove himself repeatedly against the Hags and Crones. Ānanda takes the side of the immature male, still dominated by the overpowering Mother of infancy. The hero myth here is at the Return cycle, which requires the integration of the transcendent message in the community at large, so Ānanda represents the immature Sangha, whose fledgling consciousness is still unproven in the dragon fight, and which risks re-immersion in the unconsciousness of the unexamined life. The other bhikkhunis are paradigmatically a spiritual community, and they may well have been significantly younger than Mahāpajāpatī, suitable for playing the sisterly role of the anima.

26 This is the critical thing: the Buddha is not a partial hero. He is no sacrificial king, who is permitted to reign and wield power for a time, only to be drawn back into the mire of inevitability; for his deliverance is unshakeable. And so he does not get stuck in the defensive tactic of denying the Attaching Mother totally: on the contrary, he accepts her with conditions. The *garudhammas* are explicitly said to be a dyke holding back the flood. They contain the infantile mother-son attachment within bounds, by requiring that Mahāpajāpatī bow to the bhikkhus; that is, the Lower Femininity must respect the Higher Masculinity. Having held back the Devouring Flood, the Buddha accepts her into the Sangha, just as Perseus takes the head of Medusa, contains it in the knapsack gifted by the Nymphs, and can even use it as a weapon. And as Athena uses the Medusa's head, the other bhikkhunis accept Mahāpajāpatī on the basis of the *garudhammas*. Whereas before they followed her, now they have been set free and may question her authority.

27 The following episodes tell a concise but clear spiritual history. First Mahāpajāpatī asks for the abolition of the rule that the bhikkhunis must bow to the monks. Having just avowed that she will adhere to this rule like a precious garland for the rest of her life, this is a classic slander on the changeableness of women. She shows that she has not yet mastered the defilements which had prompted the Buddha to lay down the rule in the first place, and so the Buddha denies her.

28 In the next question she asks about Vinaya. No longer trying to escape the power of the Higher Masculinity, she asks how best to manage the relationship between the monks and nuns, that is, how to integrate and harmonize the Higher Masculinity and Femininity. And so the Buddha's response is no longer a refusal, but a rational, straightforward guideline. Since the bhikkhus' discipline was already well-developed, the bhikkhunis could in many cases simply adopt their training and follow that. However, in certain cases rules were laid down specifically for the bhikkhunis, and these should also be incorporated as they are laid down.

29 Finally, she indicates her spiritual readiness by saying that she wishes to go on retreat. This is a stock passage indicating that a monk or nun wishes to strive unrelentingly for Nibbana, and is used several times in the context of monks who had previously misbehaved, but who now wished to devote themselves to practice. And so the Buddha responds with a powerful and beautiful teaching, emphasizing the letting go and dispassion which is just what Mahāpajāpatī needs. We are no longer concerned with rules, but with Higher spiritual development.

30 The sequel is truncated, which may be a result of the generally poor condition of the bhikkhuni Vinaya texts; but such passages normally end with the monk or nun practicing until they realize arahantship.[6] In any case, we know what happens in the end: Mahāpajāpatī overcomes her problems and realizes her ultimate goal.

❖

31 Unlike Māyā we have the chance to see into the 'inside' of Mahāpajāpatī, for several verses ascribed to her are preserved in the Therīgāthā. This collection is almost unique in maintaining in authentic early form the verses of the enlightened nuns. Here, as near as we are ever likely to come, are the words of Mahāpajāpatī herself.

32 'Buddha, my hero, homage to you!
Supreme among all beings,
You have released me from suffering,
As you have done for so many other people.

33 'All suffering has been fully understood,
And its source, craving, has been dried up.
The eightfold path has been developed,
And I have touched cessation.

34 'Mother, son, father, brother,
And grandmother—all these I've been before.
Not knowing how things come to be,
I wandered in *saṁsāra* without finding a home.

35 'But now I've seen the Blessed One!
This is my last body,
Wandering in *saṁsāra* is now truly ended,
Now there's no further existence.

36 'Energy aroused, resolute,
Always strong in effort,
See the disciples practicing in harmony—
This is how to worship the Buddhas![7]

37 'Truly, for the benefit of many
Māyā gave birth to Gotama.
For those overcome with affliction and death,
He has annihilated the mass of suffering.[8]

38 In these verses we can see the echo of her tremendous love for her son, the Buddha, her 'hero'. Praising the true practice of the followers, she makes a pointed comment on the *garudhammas*: real homage is dedicated practice, not rules about hierarchies of bowing.

39 She reminds us of her role as mother, yet she relativizes this with the startling claim that she has played all family roles, including male ones, in her countless rebirths. Here she undermines any attempt at reifying gender in absolute terms. Gender, like everything else, changes. There is no hint of a value judgment here, no attachment to an ideal of malehood or femalehood, just a straightforward acknowledgment that this is how it has been for her. She knows what the past has been, and, like Tiresias the blind seer of Thebes who spent seven years as a woman, she could speak authoritatively about the state of both women and men.

40 While the first and second-last verses speak of homage for the Buddha, the second through fourth verses here are suggestive of her spiritual biography. The second verse refers to her vision of the four noble truths. This implies stream entry, an attainment which the tradition ascribes to her as a laywoman, before she ordained. The next verse shows she has attained the 'recollection of past lives', one of the higher knowledges which is typically realized shortly before arahantship. Then she claims to have made an end to all birth, escaping from all bodies, both male and female.

41 This progression shows that, in trying to make sense of Mahāpajāpatī and her problematic body, we must take into account her spiritual development. Only after her attainment of stream entry does the text speak of surmounting gender roles. This suggests, as clearly as we could hope from such scarce sources, that only after her ordination did she resolve her problematic attachment for her son.

42 Finally, she ends up by remembering Māyā, one of the very few to do so. Here she dispels any suggestion that, as the potentially 'wicked stepmother', she harbored jealousy or ill-will towards the Buddha's birth mother. They were sisters, and as sisters should be, they were different people, not enemies. I have maintained all along that these two women form a complementary pair, with Māyā as the spiritual mother, and Mahāpajāpatī as the earthly mother. The presence of this pattern is beyond doubt, the problem is interpretation. Is the relationship between them conflictive? Could we suspect—as melodramas so often do—that the stepmother may have got rid of her rival?[9] Or could the very stuff of Mahāpajāpatī's milk have infiltrated Siddhattha's being, making him something other than the child of his mother?[10] Could Mahāpajāpatī's fluid bodily identity, literally flowing from herself into Siddhattha, have diluted or polluted the holy being himself? Such worries, inarticulate and unconscious, appear in the images of flood, tears, milk, and disease, with which Mahāpajāpatī is associated in the Vinaya texts. Here, however, all such fears are put to rest. And so, while the imagistic flows between Mahāpajāpatī and witches may not be denied, the tales of the witch, the hag, or the Old Mother found in mythology nowhere contain the idea of transcendence of all identity itself, a transcendence that Mahāpajāpatī explicitly, emphatically asserts.

❖

43 There is another Sutta, not found in the Pali collections, which features Mahāpajāpatī. This short exchange is set in Kapilavatthu. The collection from which this Sutta is taken, the Ekottara Āgama found in Chinese translation, is of an unknown school (possibly Mahāsaṅghika), and is highly erratic, including many later elements. Sometimes it presents even basic teachings inconsistently. This makes it hard to assess the authenticity of isolated passages such as this. It might be a later interpolation, but could just as well be a relic of an earlier tradition that was squeezed out of the more uniform traditions.

44 Thus have I heard. At one time the Buddha was staying, together with a large number of bhikkhus, five hundred persons altogether, among the Śākyans at Kapilavastu, in the Nyagrodha Park.

45 Then Mahāprajāpatī Gautamī went to the Exalted One. She bowed her head at his feet and said to him: 'I hope for a long time the Exalted One will bring the ignorant and deluded to their senses, and may his life never be endangered!'

46 'Gautamī', responded the Exalted One, 'such words in regard to the Tathāgata are not appropriate. The Tathāgata can prolong his life-span which will not be short, and his life will never be in danger.'[11]

47 Now Mahāprajāpatī Gautamī improvised the following verses:

48 'How [can one] revere him who is foremost,
Who is unparalleled in the world?
Capable of removing all doubts; that is why
These words [of veneration] are uttered.'

49 The Exalted One in turn responded to Gautamī with these verses:

50 'Reverence for the Tathāgata implies
This effort and steadfastness
A mind that is ever more courageous
And which looks upon Disciples as equals.'

51 In reply to the Exalted One Mahāprajāpatī declared: 'Hence-forth the Exalted One, the Tathāgata, should be revered [for his] insisting on regarding all sentient beings with a mind free from [the discriminatory concepts of] upper and lower. Among the heavenly beings, men ... and Asuras, the Tathāgata is supreme.'

52 The Exalted One acknowledged what Mahāprajāpatī had said, and [she] rose from her seat, bowed down ... and left.

53 The Exalted One said to the bhikṣus: 'Among my disciples it is Mahāprajāpatī who is foremost in respect of great knowledge.'

54 Having heard the Buddha's words, the bhikkhus were pleased and respectfully applied themselves to practice.[12]

55 Long life: a conventional wish, but the Buddha, as usual, rebukes Mahāpajāpatī. Perhaps the refusal of Mahāpajāpatī had become such a trope that the exchange could not be imagined any other way. But the refusal masks a deeper affirmation. The life of the Buddha is not dependent on her; he is his own man, and his destiny has led him beyond her. She is no longer the bringer of life; and in the usual mythic inversion, she is no longer the dealer in death. There is, accordingly, no mention of the 'floods' or 'disease' that stain Mahāpajāpatī's image elsewhere.

56 Since her mother's role is over, Mahāpajāpatī wonders how she is to revere the Buddha. The Buddha answers that it is by sincere practice that one can express devotion. This is the very same answer that her own Therīgāthā verses have given.

57 The Buddha raises another theme: even-mindedness. The Buddha tells Mahāpajāpatī that one who worships him properly will treat all disciples impartially. This, of course, relates directly to the theme of Mahāpajāpatī and her relationship with the bhikkhu Sangha, as in the robe-offering story and in the *garudhammas*. She is not to show special favor to the Buddha, or to any of the bhikkhus, for example because of family pride. On the one hand, the Buddha is teaching her what she needs to know; on the other hand, she upholds this virtue and praises the Buddha for his lack of discrimination. This is highly suggestive: how are we to reconcile the emphasis on this particular quality with the Buddha's supposed refusal of permission to ordain? Could it be possible that this text celebrates a time when there really was no discrimination, a time before Mahāpajāpatī became associated with the subservience of the nuns? At the very least this is a record of the value of equality as expressed in the Buddhist community.

58 This much might be implied in the ending, where the Buddha says that Mahāpajāpatī is the foremost in great understanding.[13] This is unusual, and I haven't come across any parallels. If her personal devotion to the Buddha had been a serious obstruction for her, which she had overcome through developing a universal, unbiased mind, it would explain why she

should be singled out in this way. And she is not merely the foremost bhikkhuni, but the foremost of all disciples, surpassing even the bhikkhus in this quality. For women in search of a non-discriminating approach to Dhamma today, such an honor must have a special resonance.

❖

59 This developmental perspective makes perfect sense of the two aspects of Mahāpajāpatī that we have already seen. The imagery of tears, milk, flood, and disease is associated with her Lower phase, while her Higher development appears in her personal testimony in the Therīgāthā, the continuation of the ordination story in the Pali Vinaya, and is mythically exalted in the Apadāna.

60 Mahāpajāpatī reduces by half the duration of Buddhism; hence she is Time Herself, Kālī incarnate. But she is not turned away; she is brought within the Sangha. The unconscious is allowed to remain, and is simply given boundaries: it must respect the higher consciousness. She is not truly threatening, for, as a Jātaka verse says, Time is the biggest eater in the world, consuming all, even itself; but there is one person who eats Time: the arahant.[14]

61 In my analysis, the fact that Mahāpajāpatī is challenged by the 500 bhikkhunis is of central importance. Yet it is a minor detail in the text, and I have not found it in any parallel versions. Nevertheless, the disappearance of the 500 bhikkhunis is simply another instance of the disappearance and marginalization of bhikkhunis in Buddhist history. The consequent responsibility is that we must listen carefully and with respect to the occasional voices that do survive.

62 The development of the myth shows a trend towards disparaging the bhikkhunis, as evidenced by the growing list of 'dangers' that would accrue because of bhikkhuni ordination. Tellingly, the 'dangers' in the later lists are more numerous, but are not mythic in a deep sense.[15] They say the entry of the bhikkhunis would lead to the gains and fame of the monks declining; such trivia is nothing more than a reflection of the decadence in the Sangha, a major theme in the time of Aśoka. But this kind of childish whingeing is an implicit acknowledgment that the dire existential threat did not come true. Buddhism lasts, and still does today.

❖

63 The fourfold matrix of high/low, male/female conforms to the Jungian concept of the quaternity as the symbol of balance and harmony of the Self. Closer to home, four is the most common number used in Buddhism, where it suggests a 'balanced completion'. This is embodied in the fourfold assembly, where the bhikkhus and bhikkhunis represent the Higher, and the laymen and laywomen, the Lower aspect. That this division is purely conventional, relating to the social roles of these groups, rather than the spiritual development of individuals within the groups, is shown by the fact that within each sector, the Higher and Lower may once again be discerned. In the story of Mahāpajāpatī's ordination, all four of these are found within the ordained Sangha. Similarly, all four are found within the lay community, where many disciples have high spiritual achievements.

64 On a conventional social level, one belongs to one or other of these groups. Psychically, however, one does not belong to them, one *orientates oneself among them*. The four assemblies do not really exist in the outside world; they are just conventions for classifying groups of people. They exist only in the mind. We have an inner representation of these ideas as part of our spiritual imagination. Denying one of these groups, one denies part of oneself.

65 The fourfold pattern is fundamental in how the Dhamma is structured as a whole. In an earlier work, *A History of Mindfulness*, I showed that the Saṁyutta Nikāya/Āgama is patterned after the four noble truths, and that this 'matrix' formed the template for the earliest Buddhist canonical scriptural collection, at least the prose part. But the verse section of the Saṁyutta, the Sagāthāvagga, is modelled after, not the four noble truths, but the 'eightfold assembly': Warrior-nobles, Brahmans, Householders, Ascetics, Gods of the Four Great Kings, Gods of the Tāvatiṁsa, Māras, Brahmās.[16] This eightfold pattern is of course a doubling of the more fundamental four-fold assembly.

66 And the existing texts addressing the monastic community as such are clearly modelled after the four-fold pattern. The Bhikkhu- and Bhikkhuni-Saṁyuttas, together with the Thera- and Therī-gāthās display the unparalleled spiritual achievements of the Awakened disciples. In these collections the women are strong, independent, and undaunted by male challenges.

The Vinaya presents the dark side, with a Bhikkhu- and Bhikkhuni-Vinaya that tell endless stories of the bad conduct of the monks and nuns. Thus, in those collections that speak to or from the ordained Sangha, the four-fold pattern applies. This is perfectly balanced. The imbalance of Buddhist scriptures stems from the fact that the vast majority of texts are by default addressed to the monks. This is evidence of 'androcentricism' (seeing things from a male point of view) but not of 'misogyny' (hatred of women).

67 In the early collections of texts, the principles in which the texts were organized always followed a four-fold pattern. The initial division was between the philosophical texts, patterned after the four noble truths, and the personal ones, which used the four-fold assembly. In each case, archetypal patterns became embodied in the very shape of the canonical scriptures, in terms of their overall structure. Such large-scale structures are not easy to spot. They only become apparent when we withdraw from the details of the individual texts and focus of the big picture, in the same way that the archetypal patterns of the myths only become apparent when we don't get distracted by personal detail.

CHAPTER 31

RESCUING THE HERO

WE HAVE RESCUED THE MAIDEN FROM THE JAWS OF THE MONSTER. But how are we to save the hero? If we can't redeem the masculine, our process will be incomplete and our Higher Feminine will always be under threat, be it explicit or implicit, from men's violence.

2 As always, we maintain several perspectives on our material. The stories are telling of the growth of individual men, but also of the growth of male institutions: patriarchy. Carol Gilligan cuts to the heart.

3 Patriarchy, although frequently misinterpreted to mean the oppression of women by men, literally means a hierarchy—a rule of priests—in which the priest, the *hieros*, is a father. It describes an order of living that elevates fathers, separating fathers from sons (the men from the boys) and men from women, and placing both children and women under a father's authority.[1]

4 Such a state of affairs is so common we take it for granted. It takes a leap of imagination to envisage how things could be different. The 'priest', the 'father', heads the social order and thinks he always will. This is problematic in Buddhism, given that the Vinayas allow no power of command or duty of obedience. Nevertheless, the Buddhist Sangha remains as one of the last pure patriarchies. Its sense of self-identity stems from separation, holding itself sundered and aloof from women and non-ordained men.

5 The process of transforming masculinity is just as rife with conflicts and dangers as the development of the Higher Femininity. The same principle applies: as the new stage is becoming established, it must differentiate

from the earlier stages. This is represented in myth as the 'demonization' of the Lower Masculinity and that which the Lower Masculinity desires: the Lower Femininity, the fascination that binds. The Higher Masculinity evolves in concert with the Higher Femininity. So while the process is incomplete, the individual can't discern between the Lower and Higher Femininity, and will demonize all women along with the Lower Feminine, tendency found in both men and women. Integration can only happen when differentiation is complete and consolidated.

6 Neumann speaks of the infantile 'phallic-chthonic' masculinity, which is succeeded by the Higher Masculinity, characterized by the ego's growing awareness of itself and the power of its own consciousness and rationality. This is focussed on the head, which wants to prove that the mind dominates the body. In teenagers this manifests as recklessness, disregard for health and safety, extreme sports, experiments with drugs, and so on. In spiritual circles it becomes nihilism, world-negation, bodily mortification, and misogyny. These are all regular parts of male adolescent initiation rituals. Such tests prove the will's victory over the body. The ego rises in triumph over the fears, pains, and desires which are so all-powerful in childhood. The superiority of the mind over the body is reinforced in initiation ceremonies by the transmission of secret wisdom, arcane knowledge, or through trance and visions, whether attained through ritual, drugs, contemplations, and the like. These bestow on the initiate the knowledge of how the world is dependent on and bends to his awareness.[2]

7 For ascetics this testing of the will is essential. It gives strength, the burning *tapas* of spiritual power, the heroic capacity to transcend the body. But, like all aspects of development, it carries its own dangers. The ascetic triumphs over the lower instincts through strength and resolve, and feels pleasure as his ego is reinforced. Yet the drives he rejects are part of him, and so the process is depicted in myth as a desperate struggle. Only gradually, as the ego becomes more confident in its own nature, is the conflict between the Higher and Lower masculinity resolved.[3] This task is no simple one, and may not be taken for granted. Monks tell countless stories of their struggles to overcome the temptations of the flesh. For many, there is a long period of trial before the mind is confident within itself. While this is not consolidated a dour attitude to women is common.

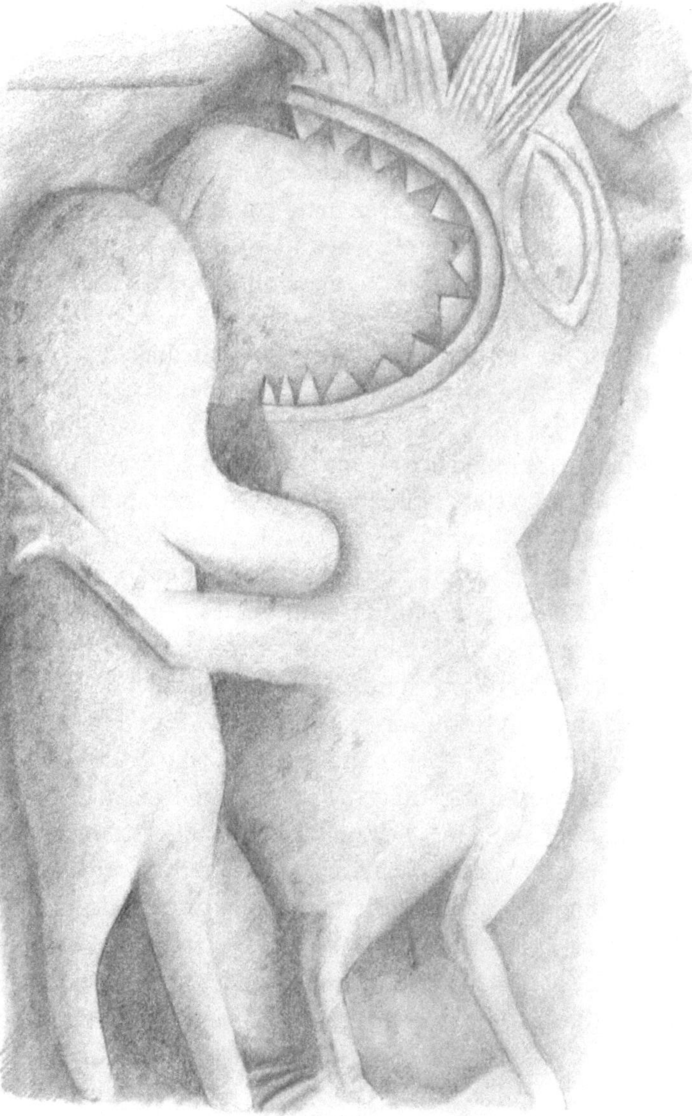

***Figure* 31.1:** *Demon devouring a man's head*

8 But the task does not end there. In addition to the ascetic aspect, Buddhist monks also represent the Ancient Law. These two things need not go together, and in fact they are often separate. The mystics follow the call of their inner voice wherever it may lead, contemptuous of the system that imprisons minds; while the Judges, Lords, and Rājas maintain that same system, which is justified by a sense of duty to society at large, and which conveniently affords them luxuries. Thus the developmental process for Buddhist monastics is even more complex, reflecting the dual role of Buddhist monks as contemplatives and as ethical exemplars. And just as the Terrible Mother represents the symbolic power of the unconscious to undermine the Hero's Quest for self-awareness, there is a Terrible Father who appears as the spiritual system that, acting from above, imprisons the son's consciousness. This manifests as the ancient law, religion, morality, convention, or tradition, which binds a man into a conventional, limited role and will not let him discover his own truth.[4]

9 As the son escapes the dominance of the father at puberty, the father's role as guardian of conventions and laws is taken over by the Men's Club. Both the father and the Men's Club are greatly helpful in guiding the boy to an awareness of his own masculinity. And yet if the man is to be in any way extraordinary or creative, he cannot merely remain within these confines. He must break out and forge a new path for himself.[5]

10 In the Buddha's myth this crisis is primarily found in the struggle between Siddhattha and his father Suddhodana, who wanted his son to live the lesser destiny of a king—in other words, Suddhodana wanted the son to fulfill the father's dream. The Buddha could only attain his true destiny of spiritual awakening by disobeying his father. By destroying the dream of the family lineage, Siddhattha created a far greater dream. Siddhattha, following exactly the classic process, left the father and entered into a Men's Club: the ascetic communities in which he practiced before Awakening. When these, too, were too limiting, he left them all to find his own path.

Figure 31.2: *Kronos devouring son*

11 Just as the differentiation from the mother accompanies a deeper relationship with the sister, so too the differentiation from the father precedes the emergence of the brother. And just as establishing relationship with the anima is fraught with danger, the brother becomes a new locus for conflict for one who is escaping the domain of the parental archetypes. The ego wants to establish its fledgling identity, but feels threatened by absorption into the mere group. The Men's Club accepts and shelters a young man, but can also make him into no more than an interchangeable number. He sees the other young men around him as potential threats, and must assert his differentiation from them, while at the same time preserving the connection that has elevated him above childish things. In myth this sets in motion the long tradition of fraternal conflict between twins: Cain and Abel, Baal and Mot, Osiris and Set, Gilgamesh and Enkidu.

12 In place of the undifferentiated wholeness that is so predominant in the maternal unconscious, the son gains a heightened awareness of 'difference'. He wants to be one of the crowd, and yet furiously resents any implication that he is a conformist. His 'self' is split and he only forges strong friendships with those he has done battle with and found to be a worthy adversary. Rather than being threatened by difference, he comes to see the affinity and value in opposites. This is especially significant in the many sets of twins who are one divine and one mortal. Each sees the other as alien, yet curiously fascinating. At first each believes he is clearly superior and is surprised when events prove otherwise. In battle or adventure both of the twins prove their value, and each ultimately accepts the other.[6]

13 The early history of Buddhism, specifically the dynamics of the community immediately following the death of the Buddha as 'father', follows exactly this pattern. There is an initial period of tension between unequal 'brothers', which gradually resolves itself as each establishes their confident, though quite different, masculinity. Their relationship is then characterized by respect and appreciation rather than conflict. The turbulence in the community is a natural effect of the highly charged situation.

***Figure* 31.3:** *Cain kills Abel*

❖

14 For monks, letting go the Lower Feminine liberates tremendous energy, which empowers the formation of his own masculine character, while at the same time permitting the emergence of the Higher Feminine. The force of this energy is felt in the conflict between the twins, or more generally in the riotous chaos of adolescence. Like any energy it must be harnessed and directed if it is to do any meaningful work. Neumann captures the essential dynamic in this brief passage, which I will unpack over the next few pages.

15 > ... spiritualization always means the retention of a certain amount of libido, which would otherwise be immediately squandered in sexuality. Experience shows that when the libido is retained, one part of it flows into the spiritualized expression, while the remainder sinks into the unconscious and activates images that correspond to it...[7]

16 When a person desires an object, there is a movement of psychic energy (libido) towards it.[8] They become invested in that thing, consumed with a need to possess it, and fixated upon it. This happens with any object of desire—chocolate, beer, gambling, cars, whatever. If a person is not able to restrain that desire, they are doomed. This is what we call addiction. The object becomes, not just one among many things that might provide some passing pleasure to leaven life's struggles, but the purpose of living itself. So it is essential, regarding any object of desire whatsoever, that restraint and moderation be found. We learn this from the cradle. It is not an exclusively ascetic or monastic principle, but something that everyone must develop.

17 If there is sufficient restraint regarding the object of desire, one's psychic energy is not so completely bound up with that, and there is excess energy for higher things. This may be a work ethic, or time with family, or any relatively refined and selfless activity. Or it may be spiritual activities, such as meditation.

18 Such development is never simple. While on the one hand there is a genuine growth, this never really uses 100% of the available energy. Some of that is cut off where it sinks down and remains in potential form in the unconscious. It's like squeezing a balloon in the middle—it bulges out at both ends.

19 Actually, any energetic transformation is similar. When we burn a log, the potential energy that has previously been fixed in the wood is liberated and can be used for a variety of good purposes. But there's always ashes left behind and these have to be dealt with.

20 This process happens in monks in more-or-less the same way it happens for anyone else. The difference is not of kind but of degree. We undertake our vows of celibacy and so on, requiring a huge redirection of our psychic energies, far more drastic than most of life's experiences. The restraint of monastic life liberates a tremendous energy, which I felt very strongly as a young monk. There is a burning enthusiasm, sense of certainty, dedication to the task, willingness to undertake ever more ascetic practices to free up even more energy. This *tapas*, the burning fervor of asceticism, has such potency that it can unseat the very gods.

21 Let us consider the process more carefully. A young man feels desire for women, who are perceived as an object external to him. Normally that desire leads him to an intimate relationship, with sexual, emotional, intellectual, and other dimensions. Before entering into such a relationship, however, he already has an image of woman in his mind, the anima. He projects this image onto the women he meets; while it is true that our encounters with all people are colored by our subjective projections, this is even more strong in the case of members of the opposite sex, who are perceived as 'other'. In the relationship itself, he encounters the gap between his ideal woman and the actual woman he experiences, and his ability to negotiate this, together with the woman's corresponding process, determines the outcome of the relationship. In other words, not only is there an external relationship between two people, there is an inner relationship in each person, between the feminine (or masculine) as imagined (the anima/animus) and as experienced in the other person.

22 This relationship moderates the man's experience of the feminine; his fantasies, whether sexual or spiritual, become more mature and moderate as his love grows and he understands more of what she is in herself, rather than his projections.

23 Then there is the decision to go forth. This comes, it may be, when the development that a sexual relationship formerly supported becomes stuck. Instead of leading him upwards to greater love and empathy, it

has become restrictive and binding. He withdraws from intimate sexual and emotional connection with women. The energy that formerly was invested in this external relationship is strongly restrained and directed upwards. No longer loving just one woman, he loves 'all sentient beings'. A variety of spiritual teachings and practices are employed to enable this transformation. The Sangha provides a supportive community in which his choice is valorized and his development applauded.

24 During this process, notice how the specific objects and activities of the mind change, but the common factor is energy. In relationship, one brings tremendous energy to another person in thought, speech, deed, and emotion. When one ordains, or undertakes a similar spiritual transformation, this energy is redirected to ones' spiritual practices. And the result is an energy of consciousness, a realization of purified, bright states of mind. This preservation of energy is a general feature of spiritual transformation, not just the specific case of monasticism that I am considering here. However, as monasticism is such a powerful crucible, the energies unleashed are highly amplified. This is experienced in the young monk as a very real energy, a faith and enthusiasm that enables him to endure pain and physical hardship, and sparks an unprecedented radiance in awareness.

25 This transformed spiritual energy invariably leads to a magnification of the ego. This is especially the case since, before entering the monastery, most of us were lost—we were looking for something, that's why we ended up in the monastery in the first place. The act of renouncing one's former life is explicitly articulated as a shift in identity, letting go who one was before, and creating a new person. This is powerfully reinforced by the community in which one lives, where the other monks are solely interested in monks and their doings; and the lay community literally places you on a pedestal and bows down in worship to you, the living embodiment of their most profound spiritual aspirations.

26 There are very potent and dangerous energies at work here, which the tradition is well aware of. There are many teachings and practices that are designed to minimize ego-inflation and cultivate humility. These work, more-or-less, much of the time; when they fail, monks either become egotistical and arrogant, in extreme cases convinced of their own Awakening;

or if they cannot deal with the new position, they feel unworthy, become depressed, and often disrobe.

27 And then there are the ashes. What is left behind? In general, all one's negative thoughts, experience, or emotions regarding the feminine. As I have said before, any development leaves something behind—the *sesa*—and this is not a problem as long as we deal with it. Empty out the trash every so often, no worries. Nevertheless, there often are problems, depending on the situation. And the monastic situation is no different.

28 It seems to me that there are a number of potentially problematic areas here. The most general is simply the size of the transformation. It's a big shift, and the energies involved can simply overwhelm our coping mechanisms—which one can see in many of the monastics who choose to disrobe.

29 More specific to this context, however, is that as monks we see ourselves as Heroes of Consciousness. We're on the cutting edge, battling defilements, getting into those cool states of altered consciousness, not like those defiled laypeople still blindly trapped in their attachments. We've let go a lot, and to compensate we identify strongly with our new situation, our communities, our Awakened teachers. It is hard for us to think that the painful and difficult practices we do may, in fact, have a cost. So we excessively focus on the higher development which we are so heavily invested in, and strongly disidentify with the rubbish that has been left behind. We really don't want to know. This strengthens the tendency to see ones' own feminine side, or at least its shadow, as 'other' and hence to project it from the unconscious onto actual women.

30 This is further exaggerated due to another factor, that is, the lack of meaningful relationship with real women. When entering the monks' life, one does not merely stop having sex with women, one hardly even sees or talks to them at all. This is especially true in the first few years of monastic life, when restraint of sexuality is a central force in shaping the lifestyle. For this reason ones' ability to empathize with and understand real women remains largely frozen at the point when one ordains. After that, ones' anima is essentially split off from relationship with real women, and takes its own course, free to idealize or demonize 'women' without the complicated business of dealing with this woman here.

31 If ones' anima was essentially healthy and balanced before this, there should be no problem. Obviously, however, this is often not the case. In any group of men there will be some whose relationship with the feminine is troubled and unhealthy; this is also true of monks. Perhaps among monks this may be even higher than the general population, as men come to monastic life seeking a refuge from women, but I don't know whether this is actually the case.

32 So, as a result of the spiritual transformation of ordination, monks often inherit a residue of negative attitudes around women. This will presumably last until Awakening. In many cases it is expressed through simple, normal means: dreams, negative emotions, crude locker-room chat, and the like. When it is recognized for what it is, the monk understands it is unwholesome and lets go. No big deal. In some cases, however, either because of the strength of the problem or the inadequacy of the means of dealing with it, it is not recognized and will form unhealthy patterns of thought, emotion, and ideology.

33 If that is the case, how does it affect the spiritual development of our woman-challenged monk? Jung says that when psychic energy is detached from women as experienced in relationship it is transferred to the subject, becoming internalized as a magnification of his own feminine.[9] The shadow side sinks into the unconscious, where, for one using (or misusing) Buddhist contemplations, it becomes 'not mine'.

34 This is a not uncommon phenomenon in Buddhist meditators: dissociation pretending to be disidentification. It is important to understand the difference between these. Disidentification is a profound realization of not-self, reached through full comprehension, which enables a genuine letting go. Dissociation, on the other hand, is a failure of communication; a part of ourselves lives in internal exile, with no connection to the rest of our psyche.

35 As long as the rejected shadow of the feminine lies undisturbed, he can comfortably avoid the issue, since the development of the higher feminine—through, say, loving-kindness meditation and the like—is proceeding quite well at the same time. Since the negative attributes of the feminine are rejected and dissociated However, with the proper stimulus, his unwholesome attitudes are expelled from his unconscious and their energy,

which may be very great, is experienced in the external object, that is, a real woman or women.

36 This projection is not formless—for example, it is not sheer emotion—but is shaped by the symbols or images that characterize the feminine. These images lie very deep in the psyche and appear in countless forms, given specific meaning in context. Perhaps the most basic feminine image is the vessel. In medieval thought this appears as the Holy Grail—which may be identified with Mary's virginal womb—but at the same time it is the witch's cauldron. Jung argues that the late medieval scourge of the witch hunt was an outcome of the excessive idealizing of Mary, which was accompanied by the proliferation of stories of the quest for the Holy Grail. These pervasive images of idealized Woman accompanied a loss of connection with real women, in particular the archaic and infantile aspects of the Terrible Mother. These remained dormant in the unconscious, not integrated or understood. When they were stimulated, they expressed themselves as a projection of daemonic traits on real women. In a massive collective fantasy, ordinary housewives or mothers were experienced as evil, Satan-loving witches.[10]

37 One might expect that a man's confusion regarding women would be primarily sexual, and that the bad woman would therefore be imagined as the whore—which of course does happen a lot; think of the voluptuous man-eating *yakkhinīs* of Indian legend. Here, however, it is not the enticing, beautiful whore on whom the daemonic feminine is projected, but the repulsive witch. She is not sexy, despite her unnatural congress with the devil. The witch is loathed by spiritual man, since she operates within the same sphere. She has a source of spiritual authority that competes with his, and has powers of healing and salvation that he would claim for himself alone.

❖

38 So for young monks the task is to differentiate themselves from the Lower Feminine, subduing their intoxication with their own bodies, and liberating energies that have been tied to sex. Achieving this is no mean feat, and constitutes his heroic quest. However, Jung says that the crucial task for one who is in the mature years of their life is to 'let go the hero'. The achievements and triumphs of our youth must be renounced if we

are to live a fruitful and wise old age. If we cling on, we end up retelling endless stories of 'when I was a young man'.

39 After the middle of life, however, permanent loss of the anima means a diminution of vitality, of flexibility, and of human kindness. The result, as a rule, is premature rigidity, crustiness, stereotypy, fanatical one-sidedness, obstinacy, pedantry, or else resignation, weariness, sloppiness....[11]

40 Jung gives a lovely image for the development process through life. He compares it to the sun, which rises out of the waters of the unconscious in the morning. In the first half of life, the sun is oriented to the zenith. It is climbing towards ever higher consciousness, illuminating ever more widely and more brightly. And every passing hour is a further revelation of splendor. From noon, however, things change. Each hour signifies a diminishing of light. One is no longer looking up, but down towards the horizon. One is approaching, once more, the darkness of the twilight. But the twilight of the dusk is very different than the twilight of the dawn, which is full of such excitement and hope. The dusk has the peace of familiar memory and mature reflection as one draws to completion.

41 This is a point of difference between Jung and Freud. While Freud located the cause of neurosis in early childhood, Jung realized that often neurosis is caused by what we do as adults, especially when we carry into our mature years the values and patterns of our youth.[12]

42 But we cannot live the afternoon of life according to the programme of life's morning; for what was great in the morning will be little at evening, and what in the morning was true will at evening have become a lie.[13]

43 As a man ages, the concern is not so much to establish his masculinity and form a stable sense of himself independent of the body. The body is now in decline, and the problem is not intoxication, but acceptance. The teachings on impermanence, the 'breaking of the teeth, the greying of the hair', which were recited as Dhamma lessons in youth, are now the palpable reality. One no longer imagines that one can find happiness in sexuality.

44 In the years of maturity there is no longer such a pressing need to define one's gender. Rather than differentiating from the feminine, the monk

engages and incorporates the Higher Feminine more deeply. Older monks often have closer relationships with women than younger monks, as a teacher or adviser, but also as friend. Jung comments:

45 What must be regarded as regression in a young person—feminization of the man (partial identity with the mother) and masculinizaton of the woman (partial identification with the father)—acquires a different meaning in the second half of life. The assimilation of contrasexual tendencies then becomes a task that must be fulfilled in order to keep the libido in a state of progression.[14]

46 In middle-age the monk must learn how to make mature decisions. As a young monk he was encouraged to let go his opinions and views—which was another aspect of his heroic quest. Now he can no longer simply 'let go' whenever a problem arises, he must know how to deal with it in practice, and to accept the consequences. To do this well he must learn to work with people, compromise, and listen, all of which are qualities of the Higher Feminine.

47 The stages of life and their importance has not, it seems to me, been considered carefully in Buddhism. Perhaps this is because in the prime story of Buddhism, the Buddha himself seems to transcend such development, reaching a completion of his journey while still a young man. Most of us have a slower and more uncertain path. Such lesser lives as ours are recounted throughout the Jātakas, and these often tell of spiritual progress through the stages of life. We find that the young man is a student, a prince, or a warrior; defeating his dragon he ascends to the mature stage, a teacher, king, or family leader; in the last stage of life he continues his growth, finally becoming a sage, an embodiment of wisdom for all.

CHAPTER 32

THE HARD TWIN

IF YOU LOOK AT MANY BUDDHIST SHRINES, you will see a tableau of the central Buddha, with a pair of monks standing in attendance on either side. In the Theravāda tradition these monks are Sāriputta and Moggallāna, the two chief disciples. They were faithful friends, and even though they had distinct spiritual talents (Sāriputta was foremost in wisdom, Moggallāna was foremost in psychic powers), they are depicted like identical twins.[1] Their individual personalities have been subsumed within the archetype of the 'perfect monk'.

2 Shrines in the northern traditions, however, often depict two other monks: Mahākassapa and Ānanda. While Sāriputta and Moggallāna are indistinguishable, Mahākassapa and Ānanda are unmistakably differentiated. Mahākassapa scowls down from under ancient bushy eyebrows, while Ānanda seems boyish and tender, even slightly camp.

3 These two sets of pairs are manifestations of one of the basic archetypes, the twins. From an original unity, the world starts to diversify, a process which might unfold in many ways. Sometimes it is relatively painless, as the two principles harmoniously complement each other, which we see in the case of Sāriputta and Moggallāna. The outcome is a complex integrated whole, which maintains the unity of the original, but enriches it with diversity. In other cases the harmony breaks down; the differentiation goes too fast, or without maturity, and the result is conflict and disintegration. Neumann locates the conflict exactly where we found it in Mahāpajāpatī's story: in the emergence from the ocean.

***Figure* 32.1:** *Mahākassapa*

***Figure* 32.2:** *Ānanda*

> 4 The motif of hostile twin brothers belongs to the symbolism of the Great Mother. It appears when the male attains to self-consciousness by dividing himself into two opposing elements, one destructive and the other creative.
>
> 5 The stage of the strugglers marks the separation of the conscious ego from the unconscious, but the ego is not yet stable enough to push on to the separation of the First Parents and the victorious struggle of the hero.[2]

6 It might seem a little strange that different Buddhist traditions have chosen these different sets of monks, with such distinct symbolic possibilities, to represent on their shrines. I think the difference pivots on two different attitudes to time. Sāriputta and Moggallāna died before the Buddha. Their memory will always be associated with the pure, unsullied original dispensation. But Mahākassapa and Ānanda survived the Buddha, and so they represent something quite different: they were the first in the lineages of the patriarchs. The Theravādin shrine longs for and identifies with the idealized pristine origin, while the northern shrines are orientated to the lineage, the networks of continuity that bind us today with the Buddha in the past. And that memory is bittersweet: both the joy and gratitude for the fact that the teachings have come down to us; and the pain to think of the conflict, divorce, and schism that have fractured the Buddhist community. We are an old family, with many memories, some of which are better left untouched.

❖

7 All we can *know* about Ānanda and Mahākassapa is that they appear as characters in ancient texts. Anything else is imagination, tempered by our own sense of what seems reasonable. The characters in Buddhist stories, including the Buddha himself, are as much products of Buddhist imagination as they are 'historical' figures. They spring into consciousness as archetypes that create and sustain Buddhist identity. Their enduring continuing power is bled off the unconscious. This unconscious force underlies the continual process of imagination and re-imagination of these figures and their meaning, a dialogue that continues unabated within the Buddhist community.

8 Mahākassapa and Ānanda are shifting from history to legend, losing their individuality and becoming representatives of wings within the Sangha, the rigorists and the laxists. Of course, such legend-making must have fuel to burn on; rarely is it sheer invention. No doubt the personalities of these two great monks were different, and there may have been tension. But here these differences are used in the service of sectarian polarization. Dialogue on disciplinary matters is unending, and must have been a significant part of Buddhist discourse since the beginning. Such a debate would naturally be framed as a discussion between two of the great patriarchs, for such was the literary style.

9 Much later the form was still being used. Mahāyāna sutras such as the Vimalakīrtinirdeśa treat the great disciples as characters in a play. The author(s) of this sophisticated text would not have thought that anyone would be so naïve as to take the fun literally. Notoriously, it depicts Sāriputta as a literal-minded chauvinist, needing a lesson in the illusory nature of gender. This is taught by Vimalakīrti's maid, really a high-level goddess/Bodhisattva in disguise.

> 10 Sāriputta: 'Goddess, what prevents you from transforming yourself out of your female state?'
>
> 11 Goddess: 'Although I have sought my "female state" for these twelve years, I have not yet found it. Reverend Sāriputta, if a magician were to incarnate a woman by magic, would you ask her, "What prevents you from transforming yourself out of your female state?"'
>
> 12 Sāriputta: 'No! Such a woman would not really exist, so what would there be to transform?'
>
> 13 Goddess: 'Just so, reverend Sāriputta, all things do not really exist. Now, would you think, "What prevents one whose nature is that of a magical incarnation from transforming herself out of her female state?"'
>
> 14 Thereupon, the goddess employed her magical power to cause the elder Sāriputta to appear in her form and to cause herself to appear in his form. Then the goddess, transformed into Sāriputta, said to Sāriputta, transformed into a goddess: 'Reverend Sāriputta, what prevents you from transforming yourself out of your female state?'
>
> 15 And Sāriputta, transformed into the goddess, replied: 'I no longer appear in the form of a male! My body has changed into the body of a woman! I do not know what to transform!'

> 16 The goddess continued: 'If the elder could again change out of the female state, then all women could also change out of their female states. All women appear in the form of women in just the same way as the elder appears in the form of a woman. While they are not women in reality, they appear in the form of women. With this in mind, the Buddha said, "In all things, there is neither male nor female."'
>
> 17 Then, the goddess released her magical power and each returned to his ordinary form. She then said to him: 'Reverend Sāriputta, what have you done with your female form?'
>
> 18 Sāriputta: 'I neither made it nor did I change it.'
>
> 19 Goddess: 'Just so, all things are neither made nor changed, and that they are not made and not changed, that is the teaching of the Buddha.'[3]

20 'Sāriputta' in his folly is locked into a naïve realist worldview, trapped by narrow conventions, unable to comprehend a greater vision. Here 'Sāriputta' is a trope for the realist Abhidhamma scholasticism, which insisted on the 'inherent existence' (*svabhāva*) of things such as gender. The connection between this 'Sāriputta' character and the historical disciple exists only in the imagination: but this is precisely the same sense in which, according to our text, everything else exists! Modern Theravādins who object to the text as unhistorical are falling right into the trap. They just prove that they are adherents of the narrow, literal doctrine of 'Sāriputta'. For suffering itself arises in the mind, and as long as we take the stuff of our minds to be real, we are projecting fantasies as history, and locate our suffering in objective existence. Gender—like chairs, houses, or flowers—appears in the text as part of social discourse, not as inherent reality. Femininity itself is *māyā*, and only a modern-day academic 'Sāriputta' would not allow Vimalakīrti's' divine housemaid to play with the Buddha's mother. The same point is made elsewhere in the Mahāyāna texts.

> 21 'Suppose a certain man goes to a magic show. The magician creates a magic woman, and, seeing her, desire arises in the man. Due to the mind of desire he becomes anxious and fretful, and, rising from his seat, he leaves. He leaves and contemplates the impurity of that woman.... Now what do you think, O Son of Good Family, has that man done the right thing, or has he done the wrong thing?'
>
> 22 'Lord, anyone who contemplates the impurity of a nonexistent woman ... has done the wrong thing.'

23 The Lord spoke, 'O Son of Good Family, in this [same way] whatever monk or nun, or lay man or lay woman contemplates the impurity of an entity that has never arisen and never existed ... has made a similar [mistake]. I would not say that such a foolish person is practicing the path.'[4]

24 Such logic, the inescapable spiral of the Prajñāpāramitā, relentlessly undermines the philosophy of the Abhidhamma. But we must beware of criticizing the literalist abhidhammic 'Sāriputtas' of the Buddhist imagination. It is all too easy to fall into the same literalist trap. For 'Sāriputta' and the other early Buddhist saints themselves appear to us as *māyā*. Migot comments:

25 What is striking is their lack of personality: each is stereotyped and represents not a live individual but an image of the Buddha conceived in the mind of a particular community, the figuration of a peculiar tendency, crystallized around a historical character who is in a way 'depersonalized'. The same sentences recur word for word in the mouth of divers characters, the same clichés are used indifferently for the Buddha and his disciples, depriving the characters of their vitality, transforming them into interchangeable mannikins.[5]

26 It's time we played around with our ideas of Mahākassapa. Locked into the idea that he was an arahant and hence 'perfect', we forget that what we confront in the texts is no arahant, but a character in a story. Like all the characters we have met so far, his persona is informed by the aura of his archetype, no less than by the reality of his historical presence.

❖

27 Kassapa is an ancient clan name. The mythic progenitor of the clan was the greatest of the 'Seven Sages', archetypal fathers looming in the distant past.[6] The very name of Kassapa is imbued with mythic resonance in the Indic culture. Since the texts we are interested in have a prominent mythic dimension, it would be unprecedented, if not actually impossible, for this resonance to be absent.

28 Kassapa is Old Man Turtle, wrapped in the flame of Agni as the first sacrifice. Kassapa was the 'mind produced' son of Brahmā; just like Siddhattha or like Athena sprung from the brow of Zeus, his birth escapes the natural defilements of birth from the womb. He is an emanation of the pure, bright,

consciousness of the Higher Masculinity, but he is still remembered for taking care of his mother.[7] The seven sages are masculine heroes of light and consciousness, yet the Ṛg Veda records the curious notion that their gender is a trick: 'They told me these were males, though truly females.'[8]

29 Kassapa became the husband of Aditi, both mother and daughter of Dakṣa (intelligence). Aditi, the nurturing cow, the 'thousand-syllabled', the boundless light of highest heaven,[9] was the mother of the seven solar Ādityas. Thus was started the most ancient and greatest of all Indian lineages, the Solar Dynasty. Kassapa's name appears in close conjunction with fire; the *Rāmāyaṇa* refers to 'Kassapa, radiant as Fire, together with Aditi...'.[10]

30 This is a close point of contact between the old mythos and the Buddha's story, for the Kassapa clan as depicted in the narrative stream of the Buddha's life is incessantly associated with fire. After his Awakening, the Buddha first went to Benares to teach the five ascetics; then he returned to Magadha, where his first major assignment was to convert the 1000 matted-hair ascetics led by three Kassapa brothers, who were orthodox Brahmanical fire-worshipers. The Buddha, uniquely, had to rely on an extensive series of miracles to convert them. The first was the Buddha's taming of the fierce fire-breathing dragon; then he showed his ability to re-light the fires that the worshipers were unable to ignite. Other miracles were on display, also, prominently the Buddha's mastery over fire's opposite, water.

31 Then, having converted the 1000 ascetics, came the renowned Fire Sermon: 'All is burning! ... Burning with what? Burning with the fire of greed, hatred, and delusion...'. The mythic patterns in this text are quite explicit, and were clearly intended by the authors. The Buddha plays with Vedic vocabulary, radically shifting the meaning. The fire god may no longer be placated by means of ritual and invocation, for even these small fires are under control of the Buddha, not the ascetics. And now fire itself is revealed to be merely a metaphor for a universal existential situation. Suddenly the world is a less tame place.

32 Less explicit, closer to the unconscious, the theme of fire continues in the person of Mahākassapa. He was no relation to the Kassapa brothers mentioned above. Yet his role in the narrative arc of the Buddha's life

echoes theirs, as it were, completing the circle. The story of the Fire Sermon is told in the canonical account of the beginning of the Buddha's ministry, the Catuṣpariṣat Sūtra. The complement to this is the Mahāparinibbāna Sutta, telling of the Buddha's last days, which segues into the First Council, where Mahākassapa was presiding.

33 Now, Mahākassapa does not feature in the account of the Buddha's early ministry, since his ordination was later.[11] Nor does he feature in the main portion of the Mahāparinibbāna Sutta. He appears abruptly in the narrative after the Buddha has passed away. He learns of the Buddha's demise from an apparently chance encounter on the road.

34 Right then the corrupt monk Subhadda rejoices, saying: 'Now we're not going to be hassled by the Buddha, we can get rid of all those bothersome rules and do as we please!' This prompted Mahākassapa to hold the First Council to preserve the Dhamma. He goes to Kusinārā to see the Buddha, whose cremation had been delayed for a week, as the devas had refused to allow the fire to light until Mahākassapa arrived. As soon as he bowed with his head on the Buddha's feet (thus noticing the smears left by the women's tears) the cremation fires ignite.

35 We thus have a direct *physical* transmission to Mahākassapa, and Mahākassapa alone; and this transmission is christened by fire. The mere touch of the Buddha's body by Mahākassapa completes an circuit of magic power. This power, beyond the capacity of the gods, erupts in a crown or a halo as Mahākassapa's head touches the Buddha's feet. In a spiritual domain such as Buddhism, this magical power instantly converts to a more tangible political force. Hence Mahākassapa, after this event, finds no problem in organizing the First Council to his pleasure, with the avowed purpose of burning away the impurities from the Sangha. And further, Mahākassapa's name stands at the head of the lists of the patriarchs of all schools. It is through him that the sense of a 'lineage of Elders' is passed down.

❖

36 This parallels very closely the situation in Christendom. In both Buddhism and Christianity, the Founder's message of compassionate morality was formed into an institution after the Founder's death, based on a pre-moral transmission of magic power. The ordination of priests in the

Catholic Church ultimately stems from the disciples who met Jesus after the resurrection:

> 37 'He breathed on them; and he said to them: "Receive ye the Holy Ghost. Whose sins you shall forgive, they are forgiven them: and whose sins you shall retain, they are retained."'[12]

38 The power to forgive sins is unlike anything taught by Jesus during his life.[13] And while the canonical text says that Jesus conferred this power on the immediate disciples, the comment by the editors of the New Advent Bible shows how easily this special grace may be extended to the officers of the Church in general.

> 39 See here the commission, stamped by the broad seal of heaven, by virtue of which the pastors of Christ's church absolve repenting sinners upon their confession.[14]

40 The physicality of this encounter is insisted on, echoed in the 'laying on of hands' that forms a crucial aspect of priestly ordination.[15] This rite descends from the ancient Hebrews, and may be used to transfer *sin* (as when, in ancient times, the priest laid the sins of the people upon the sacrificial animal or 'scapegoat'[16]) or *grace* (as when the priest at his ordination is authorized to forgive sins[17]). The transmission of grace with a physical ritual is essential, since Original Sin itself is transmitted, according to Thomas Aquinas, through semen.[18] This conflation of positive and negative power, mediated by physical contact, is unmistakable evidence of primitive magical conceptions at work.

41 This ordination empowers the priest to perform the communion, a ritual that imitates the words and gestures of Jesus at the Last Supper,[19] and imbues the bread and wine with the 'Real Presence' of Christ, a rite 'whose literal meaning [the Roman Church] has uninterruptedly adhered to from the earliest times.'[20]

42 The ordination of priests, then, conforms with the two principle aspects of 'sympathetic' magic as defined by Frazer: connective magic and imitative magic.[21] Connective magic derives power from a physical medium of contact, like a relic, the touch of a saint, or the fire that crowns Mahākassapa. Imitative magic transmits power through resemblance, for example by repeating a ritual such as the last supper.

43 This insistence on a personal and physical transmission serves the monopolization of institutional power. The Catholic Encyclopedia tells us that: 'The doctrine of the Church is that Holy Communion is morally necessary for salvation...'.[22] Magical conceptions, even if spiritualized and refined, underlie this dogma, a belief in the actual transference of spiritual energy through the correct performance of ritual under the authority of the temporal institution of the Church of Rome.

44 The Buddhist ordination procedure also reflects these two forms of magic. The ordination is performed by bhikkhus who themselves are fully ordained, in a lineage that stems in unbroken line of connection back to the ordinations performed by the Buddha himself. The grave significance of this lineage is not bothered by the lack of historical evidence. All that is necessary is that it is believed to have been maintained. And the procedure follows the words and gestures used in those first ordinations, carefully imitated down to the last detail.

45 This similarity with magic rituals cannot be arbitrary. The Buddha, as so often, was making use of forms and customs that were familiar to his followers. The resemblance to magic adds an emotional resonance to the whole procedure. This emotional resonance still pervades our modern secular culture, as, despite the relentless onslaught of reason, we still cling to our mistletoe, our crossed fingers, our touching wood, bereft though they are of all that once gave them meaning.

46 But the resemblance to magic is only that, a resemblance. There is no place for magic in authentic Buddhist practice. There is nothing in the description of ordination procedure that implies it had anything to do with a magical transference of spiritual power. The aims are all quite rational: to ensure the applicant is appropriate, healthy, accepted by the Sangha; and that they should have a mentor who will look after them, teach the Dhamma & Vinaya, and ensure they are supplied with the necessary requisites and supports for the monastic life.

47 The resemblance to magic, innocuous in itself, gives the impression that the *upasampadā* is a magical rite involving a mysterious transmission of spiritual authority. One cannot escape this impression in traditional Buddhist cultures. For example, in Thailand the act of ordination is often not the means to enter a vocation of disciplined spiritual practice, but is an

end in itself, an elevation into an exalted spiritual status that need merely be sustained for a short period, but does not involve study or practice of Dhamma-Vinaya.

48 And while the ordination may be conferred by any group of monks, the burden of the transmission by fire to Mahākassapa is that the real, central lineage must come through him. The narrative is cunningly constructed, for the whole dignified process of the Buddha's passing away is imbued with such an aura of sanctity that it would seem highly irregular, heretical even, to question the political dimensions of the text. But political it is, and we who live inside the Buddhist community cannot afford to ignore the implications.

❖

49 One of the key elements in Mahākassapa's mythic status is that he was the only disciple who exchanged robes with the Buddha. In fact, the Buddha openly remarked that he quite liked Mahākassapa's robes, which is perhaps the only time where the Buddha is recorded as dropping hints for the sake of material things.[23] This created a physical link between the two; and later traditions imagine Mahākassapa, ensconced in deepest meditation within the Kukkuṭapadagiri, holding the Buddha's robes in wait for Maitreya. But when Mahāpajāpatī offered robes, these were openly rejected. The two appear as opposite sides of the same symbol. Later sources resolve the tension by saying that Mahāpajāpatī's robes were eventually accepted by none other than Maitreya himself.[24]

50 If a physical transmission of virtuous power can be transmitted from the Buddha's body to Mahākassapa's, is it not possible that a physical transmission of corruption and disease might also take place? It is hard for us to take these concepts seriously, conditioned as we are by millennia of philosophies that have asserted that good and evil are non-material qualities. But the physicality of sin is a universal belief, and in axial myth we are witnessing the shift, still incomplete, from a physical to a mental understanding of ethics. The *Rāmāyaṇa* tells of how after Indra had slayed Vṛtra, who was a brahman, the sin was so great the gods and *ṛṣis* had to bathe him with water. The sin fell from his body onto the ground.[25] In the Dasabrāhmaṇa Jātaka, a (very entertaining) list of bad brāhmans includes those who lie down under the king's gorgeous couch at the soma sacrifice;

the king bathes, washing off his sins onto the brahman, who then receives the couch as payment.[26] The notion that sin is washed away by water is criticized by the Buddha in the Vatthūpama Sutta, where he says that a fool may constantly bathe in a holy river but never wash away his bad deeds.[27]

51 There is one other monk who was accused of soiling the Buddha's robes; who, following a lifetime of devoted service to the Buddha, got a stern rebuke for stepping on the Buddha's bathing cloth, a physical soiling that became an ethical transgression. That monk was Ānanda; the rebuker, Mahākassapa; the occasion, the First Council.

❖

52 Patterns, associations, webs of meaning, insinuations of implication: they are all pointing to a certain image of Mahākassapa, an image that feminist eyes are sorely tempted to see as misogynist.[28] But he has another side, a side barely hinted at above. The transmission from the Buddha to Mahākassapa happens not only through fire, but through the gift of a heavenly blossom. Mahākassapa is with a group of monks on the road to Pāvā when they encounter a wandering ascetic. He is carrying a coral tree flower.[29] He tells Mahākassapa that the Buddha had passed away seven days ago, and he had taken the flower from there.

53 This image has had a lasting impact on the Buddhist mythos, for it prefigures a famous Chan/Zen koan that forms an integral part of the myth of lineage for the Chan/Zen school.[30] Instead of teaching by words, the Buddha held up a flower, at which the disciples were confused. Mahākassapa alone smiled, indicating he was worthy of the Dhamma transmission 'outside the scriptures'. We are quite justified, then, in seeing the transmission of a flower as not merely a random incident, but a meaningful association, as significant in its own way as Mahākassapa's crown of flames. The divine flower is a perfect symbol for the Higher Feminine, and invites us to consider how the divine She figures within the mythos of such a hard-core ascetic.

54 In Mahākassapa's case, we are lucky to have preserved a selection of around forty verses in the Theragāthā which are attributed to him. We thus gain a glimpse, as direct as could be wished for, into his own attitudes. And we find, somewhat to our surprise, that his verses shine with some of

the earliest verses anywhere that express an undiluted, glorious love of nature's beauty and bounty.

55 We've looked at the lives of some of the bhikkhunis, and agreed that their spiritual journey must be primarily assessed from their own words rather than from third party sources. We should grant Mahākassapa the same grace. If we stereotype him as a grizzled, rigid, woman-hating ascetic, we are not witnessing his sensitivity and love of nature's beauty.

56 These regions delight my heart
Where the Kareri creeper spreads its flower wreaths,
When sound the trumpet-calls of elephants.
These rocky heights delight my heart.

57 These rocks with hue of dark-blue clouds
Where streams are flowing, cool and crystal-clear,
With glow-worms covered (shining bright),
These rocky heights delight my heart.

58 Like towering peaks of dark-blue clouds,
Like splendid edifices are these rocks,
Where the birds' sweet voices fill the air,
These rocky heights delight my heart.

59 With glades refreshed by (cooling) rain,
Resounding with the calls of crested birds,
The cliffs resorted to by seers,
These rocky heights delight my heart.

60 Here is enough for me who, resolute,
Desires to meditate (in solitude).
Here is enough for me, a monk determined,
Who seeks to dwell in the highest goal's attainment.

61 Here is enough for me who, resolute,
Desires to live in happy ease (and free).
Here is enough for me who is on effort bent,
(Devoted to the practice) as a monk determined.

62 Like dark-blue blooms of flax they are,
Like autumn sky with dark-blue clouds,
With flocks of many kinds of birds,
These rocky heights delight my heart.

63 No crowds of lay folk have these rocks,
But visited by herds of deer.

With flocks of many kinds of birds,
    These rocky heights delight my heart.

64 Wide gorges are there where clear water flows,
    Haunted by monkeys and by deer,
With mossy carpets covered, moist,
    These rocky heights delight my heart.

65 No music with five instruments
    Can gladden me so much
As when, with mind collected well,
    Right insight into Dhamma dawns.[31]

CHAPTER 33

THE SAGE & THE GOLDEN MAIDEN

VERSES INSPIRED BY NATURE'S WONDER—NOT WHAT WE EXPECT from the crusty old Mahākassapa. Perhaps under the tough exterior we might find some tenderness after all. And the surprises don't stop here. Despite his apparent opposition to the nuns, Mahākassapa's traditional life story is one of the great love stories of Buddhism. Throughout Mahākassapa's past lives, he is linked with the woman who, in our Buddha's time, became the arahant bhikkhuni Bhaddā Kāpilānī.[1] She was foremost of all the bhikkhunis in her recollection of past lives; this detail alone hints at the significance of her past with Mahākassapa.

2 In the Jātaka and Avadāna literature, their backstory is recorded in some detail. Kāpilānī was already Mahākassapa's wife in the far distant past, during the time of Padumuttara Buddha. It was then that Mahākassapa made the dedication to be born in the future as the disciple foremost in ascetic practices. In life after life, she speaks of the joy they had together: 'I went with him to a happy existence. We enjoyed both divine and human bliss…';[2] 'Happy and joyous, we journeyed on in many lives…';[3] 'I was very dear to him, because of my husband's love in former lives.';[4] 'I was his wife, happy, joyous, and beloved.'[5] This joy was the result of the many meritorious deeds they undertook and shared together.[6] In their last life together, they surpassed the conventional merit-making they had performed previously.

Born as a great king and queen, they honored the *paccekabuddhas*, then gave up their realm and went forth. They developed the four measureless states of mind (*brahmavihāras*) and were reborn in the Brahma realm.[7] Their final birth in the time of 'our' Buddha was the culmination of a long spiritual evolution, a path that they walked together since before our universe was born.

3 In the time of 'our' Buddha, the relationship between Pippali Mahākassapa and Bhaddā Kāpilānī was celebrated with a long tale, adorned with flowers and a golden maiden.

❖

> 4 Pippali the brahman youth was born in the country of Magadha in the brahman village of Mahātittha, in the womb of Kapila the brahman's chief queen. Bhaddā Kāpilānī was born in the Madda country in the city of Sāgala, in the womb of Kosiyagotta the brahman's chief queen.
>
> 5 When they had grown up, and Pippali was 20 and Kāpilānī was 16, his parents said to him, 'My dear, you are of age. Come, we will set you up in a good family.'
>
> 6 He was very depressed by this, and said, 'Do not say such things within my hearing. As long as you are alive, I will support you, but when you have passed away I will leave and go forth.' They repeatedly remonstrated with him to no avail. But his mother would not give up, and so he made a plan, thinking, 'My mother will agree to this.'
>
> 7 He had the form of a woman made (*itthirūpaṁ*) of gold, of outstanding beauty, bedecked with flowers and ornaments. He showed it to his mother, saying, 'Mother, if I can get such an thing (*ārammaṇa*) as this, I will stay in the house, if not I will not stay.'
>
> 8 Being wise, she thought, 'My son is of great merit, for sure there will be a golden one like this for him.' She called eight brahmans, fitted them out with all they needed, and gave them a wagon on which she placed the golden figure. She instructed them to seek among families of the same social standing for a daughter like the golden statue.
>
> 9 Leaving, they thought to start looking in Madda, as it was famous for beautiful women. They placed the golden statue beside a bathing place and sat nearby.
>
> 10 In the palace, Kāpilānī's nurse washed and adorned her and settled her in her chamber. Then she came to that ford to bathe herself.

11 She thought, 'My lady's daughter has come here.' Thinking it was Kāpilānī, she scolded, 'You naughty girl, why have you come here?' Raising her hand, she said, 'Hurry back!' and gave her a smack. But her hand hurt as if hitting stone! She stepped back in shock, realizing how foolish she'd been to mistake her girl for a statue.

12 The brahmans asked, 'Does your master's daughter look like the statue?'

13 She replied, 'Why not? In fact, my lady's daughter has a hundred, no, a thousand times this beauty. When she sits in her chamber, there is no need for a lamp for 12 spans about her, such is the radiance of her body.'

14 'Then take us to her,' they said. They went with the cripple to the house of the brahman Kosiyagotta.

15 Arriving at the house, the brahman greeted them and asked the reason for their visit. The brahman said, 'It is good, my daughter, for he is of the same caste.' He wrote a letter to Kapila the brahman which said, 'You have my daughter, do the necessary rituals.'

16 Having heard this message, Pippali announced, 'It seems I have the girl.' He thought to himself, 'This is truly no good, I should write to her.' In private he wrote, 'Please enter the house of a suitable family, I will go forth, do not sorrow.'

17 Meanwhile, Kāpilānī was thinking to herself, 'It seems they want to give me away in marriage.' She too wrote a letter, expressing exactly the same sentiments, and saying her wish was also to go forth.

18 The messengers bearing the two letters passed each other in the middle of the journey. When the bearers found that the letters were being exchanged between the two betrothed, they opened them and, having discovered the plot, threw the letters away in the forest. They wrote similar-looking letters for each and delivered them. Thus the wedding came about despite the lack of desire from each party.

19 Now, on that very wedding day Pippali tied together a bunch of flowers, and so did Kāpilānī. They placed the flowers in the middle of the bed. Pippali ascended the right side of the bed, Kāpilānī the left. Kāpilānī said, 'Who sees these flowers decay, we shall know that lust has arisen in their mind; may this garland not be defiled.' For fear of their bodies touching, they spent the whole night without falling asleep, and without bending. By day, they did not so much as laugh. Unsullied by worldly things, as long as their parents supported them, they did not even have to look after the family estate. However, after the parents died, they took over the duties.

20 One day Pippali, surrounded by a large following, rode a horse to work the fields. Standing to one side he saw the crows and other birds eating the worms that were ploughed up in the field. He asked an attendant, 'What are they eating?'

21 'Worms and so on.'

22 'But who do that kamma belong to?'

23 'It is yours, master.'

24 He thought to himself, 'If if receive bad kamma from this, what use is all my wealth? What use is my lands, my fine chariots, or my villages? I will make them all over to Kāpilānī and go forth.'

25 Meanwhile, Kāpilānī was inside the house. She laid out some sesame seeds to dry, and saw the crows come to eat the insects in the seeds. She asked the maid, 'My dear, what are they eating?'

26 'The insects, my lady.'

27 'But who receives the unwholesome kamma?'

28 'You do, my lady.'

29 She thought, 'If by even this much I do evil, then I shall never lift my head above even in a thousand lives. When my husband returns I shall turn all over to him and go forth.'

30 Pippali returned to the palace, bathed, and sat down, and they ate a meal fit for a king. After, they dismissed the servants and sat together in private.

31 Pippali said, 'Kāpilānī, when you came to this house, how much wealth did you bring?'

32 '55 000 wagon loads, my husband.'

33 'All this, plus 87 myriads and much else besides, I give to you alone.'

34 'But what of you, my husband?'

35 'I will go forth.'

36 'But I have sat here with you looking to say the very same thing! I too will go forth.'

37 The whole of the three worlds appeared to them like a burning hut of leaves. Thinking to go forth, they obtained ochre robes and small bowls and shaved each other's hair.

38 They declared, 'We go forth in dedication to those who are arahants in this world!'

39 They slung their bowls over their shoulders and left the palace, unnoticed by the servants and workers. But after they left the brahman village, they were recognized at the gate of the nearby servant's village. The servants wept and fell at their feet, saying, 'How can you leave us with no protector?'

40 They said: 'Seeing the three worlds like a burning hut of leaves, we are going forth. If we were to free each one of you individually, 100 years would not be enough, so you should wash each other's head, be free, and live.' They left, the servants still weeping.

41 Mahākassapa walking in front turned to look at Kāpilānī and thought, 'This Bhaddā is the most extraordinarily beautiful woman in all the land, and she walks behind me. Maybe someone might think that we, having gone forth are not able to remain chaste, that we do what is inappropriate. If they corrupt their minds with such thoughts, they may go to hell. We should go our separate ways.'

42 Going ahead, he came to a fork in the road, where he waited for Kāpilānī. She arrived, saluted him, and stood there. He said, 'Kāpilānī, with a woman such as you following me, people may think we are not proper ascetics, and with such corrupt thoughts many people may go to hell. I will take one of these paths, you take the other.'

43 'Yes, venerable, womankind (*mātugāma*) is indeed a stain for those gone forth. There are some who would suspect misbehavior between us, but if we take separate roads this will not happen.'

44 She circled him three times in respect, and in four places made the five-point prostration. Placing her ten fingers together she raised them to her head, saying, 'Our relationship that has been built over 100 000 æons is ended today.'

45 She continued, 'You are born on the "right side", as it were, you should go on the right-hand path; we women are born on the "left side", so I will proceed along the left-hand path.' Having paid respects she walked down the road.

46 At the time those two went their two separate ways, it was as if this great earth said, 'I am able to bear the mighty mount Sineru, but I cannot bear the virtues of this pair!' And there was a rumble and a quaking; the sky cracked like thunder, and the world-encircling mountains roared.

47 The Buddha was seated in the fragrant hut in the Bamboo Grove Monastery when he heard the sound of the earthquake. He thought, 'For who is the earth quaking?' Turning his mind, he knew, 'Pippali the young brahman and Bhaddā Kāpilānī in dedication to me, having abandoned measureless wealth, have gone forth.'[8]

48 This story is retold from the Pali commentary. It reflects popular understanding as accepted many centuries after the Buddha's passing away, and so we should not be surprised to find mistakes in basic Buddhist doctrines.

When Mahākassapa and Kāpilānī observe the suffering that is inevitable even in innocent activities, they echo a well-known event in the story of Siddhattha as a young child, observing the insects and creatures that were exposed and eaten by the birds during the plowing of the fields. But whereas Siddhattha used the image to reflect on the suffering inherent in existence, Mahākassapa and Kāpilānī worry who will experience the kammic result. The Buddha said kamma is intention, and by this standard neither of them would suffer any kammic result from such unintentional harm. The conception of kamma in this story is more reminiscent of the Jain teaching, where intention is not a critical factor. But doctrinal correctness is not our concern here, for the point of the story is to express the community's image of Mahākassapa.

❖

49 Virtually all of this story has been derived from other tales well known in the Buddhist tradition. The Cullabodhi Jātaka tells of a time when the Bodhisatta and his wife had descended from the Brahma realm, were born in our realm, got married, and lived side by side without desire until the time came that their parents died.[9] The husband offered to make over all his wealth to the wife so that he could go forth. She asks, 'Is going forth for men only, or for women also?' He answers, 'It is for women to live as well.'[10] They go forth together. While in the Mahākassapa/Kāpilānī version it becomes necessary for them to part, the Cullabodhi has them living together even as ascetics.

50 The Kusa Jātaka has the Bodhisatta, King Kusa, create a golden image; the likeness is found in Princess Pabhāvatī of the city of Sāgala in the Madda country, who glows in the darkness; and the nurse finds the statue by the bathing place. Many of the very same phrases are common with the Mahākassapa/Kāpilānī story, and it is clear that in the Pali version at least, these two stories influenced each other.[11] And it is not just Pabhāvatī and Kāpilānī who were discovered as images like a golden statue in the city of Sāgala in the Madda country, for similar matches are told in the Anitthigandhakumāravatthu[12] and the commentary to a verse in the Khaggavisāna Sutta.[13]

51 In the Udaya Jātaka the perfectly matched couple are once more descended from the Brahma realm. They are born from the same king of

different mothers and given the same name, Udayabhadda for the boy, Udayabhaddā for the girl.[14] The golden image is made, and only Udayabhaddā the Bodhisatta's half-sister matches it, so they are married. The motif of close family members marrying in the royal clans is a common one; even in the present day royal families tend to marry among a limited circle of relatives. But here, they are so close they're almost like mirror images of each other, barely keeping their separate identities. After their marriage they remain chaste. They made a promise that if one of them were to die, they would return and visit the other to tell them where they were reborn. As it happens, the Bodhisatta was the first to die, after only 700 years, and was reborn as Sakka, the King of gods. Meanwhile, Queen Udayabhaddā ruled the kingdom. Sakka returned to her in accordance with their vow, and tested her virtue and faithfulness. Eventually he revealed his identity, and encouraged her in the Dhamma. Inspired, she renounced the kingdom and went forth as a nun.

52 Yet another version occurs in the Ananusociya Jātaka.[15] Again, the Bodhisatta is reluctant to marry, the image is sent out, and a sixteen year old maiden newly descended from the Brahma realm is the perfect match. They marry and live chastely until the parents die. He wants to make over the family estate to her, but she wishes to go forth too. They live together, until she is stricken with illness and dies. People are amazed that he shows no grief at the passing of one so fair and so dear to him.

53 And finally, it would not be a Buddhist tale if it had not happened before.[16] In the Sāma Jātaka, Mahākassapa and Kāpilānī are born as pure, radiantly beautiful beings who have descended from the Brahmā realm into a hunters' village, but will harm no creature. When their marriage is arranged, they secretly send each other letters saying they have no desire to consummate their union. As soon as they have permission from their parents they go forth and live as ascetics together. No less than Sakka himself supplies them with the requisites.

54 Foreseeing danger, Sakka instructs them to have a child; but this is not by normal means. The male ascetic touches the female on the navel, and she becomes pregnant. The child, who is the Bodhisatta, is raised by the ascetics, helped by the local nymphs (*kinnarī*). Later, Sakka's prophecy

comes true: the parents are blinded by the poisonous breath of a snake, and the son looks after them.

55 It is not long before tragedy strikes again. A king is out hunting, he spies the Bodhisatta and shoots him with a poisoned arrow. He is horrified when he speaks to him and finds out what he has done. He goes to the parents, admits his crime, and offers to take care of them. To the king's astonishment, neither the dying son nor the parents harbor even a thought of ill-will against the king. The story has a happy ending: a local goddess, who had been the Bodhisatta's mother in a previous life, intervenes, and through her grace, and the power of an Asseveration of Truth, the Bodhisatta is restored to health.

❖

56 Since the main features of the romance of Mahākassapa and Kāpilānī are commonly found in Buddhist literature, there is no question of their story being a historical one. In all likelihood, apart from a few incidental details, it is only the texts in the early canon that preserve any realistic historical sensibility; and from these we can infer little beyond the likelihood that these two were in fact formerly married. The legendary story tells us how the Buddhist community imagined the ideal marriage; and how they wanted Mahākassapa, as the great lineage holder, to be remembered.

57 The story tells of the Divine Marriage (*hieros gamos*). Kāpilānī appears as a golden image, a goddess projected from Mahākassapa's fantasy. She is the princess rescued from the dragon of the family (although such violent imagery is out of place in this tender tale).

58 Their 'romance' is throughout gentle and respectful, a true spiritual partnership. Every detail is carefully mirrored, as they perform a perfectly matched dance about each other. Their sexual restraint is symbolized, not with the grim fervor of ascetic denial, but with garlands of flowers, each partner offering one. It expresses in pure form the notion that the true nature of marriage is the restraining of sexuality within a context of spiritual partnership, which elevates each partner. Such a perfect harmony is the context within which Mahākassapa's stern demeanor should be understood. The audience already knows that his character arises from a perfect, idealized union of the Higher Masculine with the Higher Femi-

nine. More than that: the very toughness of his reputation demanded an appropriately feminine rebalancing.

59 While the perfect mirroring of the relationship is the overall theme of this set of narratives, there is no doubt that the man is the first among equals. The story emerges as a reflection of the Buddhist community's interest in his life, and she appears as his anima figure. It is he who shows agency—although prompted by his mother—while she remains passive at home in her chamber, waiting to be chosen. Each time the paired actions are described, his acts are presented first.

60 And he is identified with the 'right' side, she with the 'left'. These sides are no less value-laden in Pali than their English equivalents. 'Right' is *dakkhiṇa*, related to the English 'dextrous', and meaning both skilful and auspicious. 'Left', as one might suspect, is far more ambiguous. The Pali is *vāma*, which seems to start out meaning 'good, beautiful, fair', and is closely associated with desire; its absence, according to one possible etymology, is what the word *nirvāṇa* means. It became closely associated with femininity, whether animals or even the goddess of love, whose name is still remembered today: Venus. But the connotations of beauty and nobility receded, and *vāma* came to mean crooked, adverse, out of line. It was adopted by the tantrics, who provocatively called their transgressive practices the 'left hand path'. So identifying herself as 'left hand' and Mahākassapa as 'right' our text is subtly reinforcing the normalcy of masculinity, and the transgressive otherness of the female. In the Cullabodhi Jātaka, it was she who asked her husband whether women could go forth; there was no need for him to ask her.

61 Mahākassapa does not express any misogynistic views in our story. His wish to part from Kāpilānī was prompted by his fears of the gossip of others; a trait of Mahākassapa's character that may well have been inferred from the First Council, where he argues against abolishing any Vinaya rules because the lay people might criticize it. It is Kāpilānī who expresses the misogyny, just as she did in the 'Grievous Text' Jātaka. This could be read a number of ways. Perhaps it is a device of the redactors, to authenticate their sexism by having women agree to it. Nevertheless, it is normal for women in patriarchies to internalize their inferiority in this way. Mahākassapa's silence on the question could be read as implying that he did not

espouse such views; or perhaps he is the ultimate patriarch, so confident that his women know their place that he leaves it to them to maintain their subservience. Whatever we read into this motif, however, is our voice, not Mahākassapa's.

62 Kāpilānī's formalized honoring of Mahākassapa at their parting was the normal relationship of wife to husband in that culture. It is the same as the worship that our other Bhaddā, Kuṇḍalakesā, pays to her husband before shoving him off the cliff, showing the cultural norms that underlay the *garudhamma* requiring nuns to bow to monks. It is hard for us to accept such a way of relating between the sexes, but in a tender story like this, the intention is to convey love and respect, not subservience. Throughout the story, Kāpilānī acts with discretion and decision. She was an equal partner for Mahākassapa, no mean feat for anyone.

63 Even harder to accept is that Kapilānī herself states that women are an obstacle for the ascetic. This misogynist opinion is found also in her past life in the 'Grievous Text' Jātaka. The irony is uncomfortable, and reminds us of the many women in Buddhist countries today who oppose the presence of nuns, especially bhikkhunis, in the monastery. We have come far enough to not be surprised at such statements in a Buddhist text, passed by as something normal. We can interpret this saying within the pattern of Higher/Lower Femininity, although this is not explicit in the context, as Bhaddā here (as in the 'Grievous Text' Jātaka) refers to 'women' in general.

64 There is little reason to think that Bhaddā Kapilānī actually said these things. The Pali story is a fairy-tale in the commentaries, told centuries after the events. The Tibetan version says nothing about women being an obstacle for the ascetic, nor does it have her bowing to Mahākassapa, but merely says they parted, since it was not allowable for them to live together as ascetics.

65 The story presents us with two aspects. On the one hand it is a fairy tale of the perfect union of spiritual partners, while on the other hand it implicitly endorses the inferiority and otherness of women. My own feeling is that the fairy tale perfection expresses the tale's profound, universal meaning, while the sexism is a local and limited counterpoint to the main theme.

❖

66 Bhaddā Kāpilānī's verses in the Apadāna and other late sources fill out her journey from the few details available in the old texts. She lived with the non-Buddhist wanderers for five years. When the bhikkhuni Sangha was established she ordained as a bhikkhuni. This detail is a retcon to solve the problem that Mahākassapa is reckoned to have ordained very soon after the Buddha's Awakening, but the bhikkhuni order was not believed to have been established until five years later.

67 The Pali story has Kāpilānī tell Mahākassapa that their relationship is now over. But this does not mean that they never had any dealings after this time, for the traditions record several points of contact.

68 The Tibetan sources allege that while living among the ascetics, the non-Buddhist monks thought Kāpilānī looked as beautiful as a divine maiden, and they wished to discover whether she was the giver of divine love as well. They obtained special permission from their teacher Pūraṇa to spend all day with her.[17] Later, Mahākassapa saw Kāpilānī when she visited Rājagaha along with many ascetics for a Nāga festival. Noticing she looked different, he asked her whether she had kept her chastity. She told him what had been going on, and he encouraged her to the Buddha's teaching. She hesitated, but he reassured her that the Buddha's Dhamma had nothing harmful in it, since its followers had no desire for the love even of gods, what to speak of human love. She went to Mahāpajāpatī, who arranged for her ordination.

69 The next time she met Mahākassapa was when they encountered each other while collecting alms. She complained that, like a fat sheep, she attracted too much attention because of her appearance. Mahākassapa said that there was no need for her to endure such abuse; he would offer her every day half of what he received on alms round. This he did, even though the group of six monks—the archetypal 'bad boys' of the Sangha—scoffed at them. After Kāpilānī attained arahantship, she resumed alms round, she would no longer be affected by the stares of others.

70 These little episodes show Mahākassapa continuing to provide care and support for Kāpilānī when she was in need, even after ordination. It's striking how far he went to make sure she could eat without having to put up with catcalls and stares, giving her half of what would have

been a meager meal (Mahākasspa was well known for frequenting the poorest districts for alms). It's not Mahākassapa that criticizes excessive fraternizing with nuns, but the group of six. Mahākassapa is the protector of women in these stories, which depict the Buddhist Sangha as a refuge from the leering stares of the male public, and the scurrilous motivations of the other ascetics.[18] Far from being an unreconstructed misogynist, Mahākassapa was a pioneer in protecting women from harrassment.

❖

71 Soon after her ordination Kāpilānī attained arahantship. The following verses from the Therīgāthā record her own voice.

72 He is the son and the heir of the Buddha.
Kassapa the well-concentrated
Who knows his past lives,
And sees heaven and hell.

73 He has attained the end of rebirth,
A sage possessed of higher knowledge.
By means of these three realizations
He is a brahman of threefold knowledge.

74 Just so, Bhaddā the Kapilānī
Has the threefold knowledge, vanquisher of death.
Having defeated Māra and his host,
She bears her final body.

75 Having seen the danger in the world,
We both went forth.
We have ended defilements, and are tamed,
Become cool, extinguished.[19]

76 Just as the commentarial story emphasized the harmonious mirroring of the lives and aspirations of Kāpilānī and Mahākassapa, Kāpilānī's verses treat their lives and attainments as essentially complementary. No clearer expression of the spiritual harmony between masculine and feminine could be wished for.

❖

77 In her later life, Kāpilānī became well known as a teacher, and trained many nuns as students. This success did not come without its pitfalls.

Her renown in teaching Dhamma earned her the jealousy of Thullanandā. She was the baddest nun in the whole Sangha, but a woman of wit and intelligence nevertheless, who was rather attached to her own reputation as a teacher, and would not put up with a rival. One of the background stories in the Pali Vinaya depicts Thullanandā and her students walking up and down, reciting loudly, in front of Kāpilānī, purely to annoy her.[20]

78 Another time, Kāpilānī needed to travel to where Thullanandā was, and Thullanandā promised her that there would be a dwelling place for her when she arrived. But once Kāpilānī was settled in her place, Thullanandā had her thrown out.[21] These incidents may be nothing more than a reminder of how silly supposedly religious people can behave. The details are probably not historical, but they may well represent some of the typical conflicts present within the bhikkhuni Sangha. But they are of interest to us in that they show us Kāpilānī in conflict with Thullanandā, a nun who is rather more famous for arguing with—you guessed it—Mahākassapa.

79 Soon after the Buddha passed away, Ānanda approached Mahākassapa and asked him if he would come to the bhikkhuni monastery to teach the nuns.[22] The two monks were greeted with respect by the bhikkhunis and Mahākassapa gave a lengthy Dhamma teaching, which the nuns found inspiring. But after the talk one nun complained loudly. She is called Thullatissā in the Pali, but Thullanandā in the Chinese versions.[23] She said that for Mahākassapa to be teaching in front of Ānanda was like a needle-pedlar selling needles to the needlemaker.[24] Mahākassapa didn't take kindly to this, and Ānanda asked him to forgive, as she was only being foolish.[25]

80 Mahākassapa responded, according to the Sarvāstivāda versions of the text, by reminding Ānanda that the Buddha compared Mahākassapa, not Ānanda, to the waxing moon that was always growing in brightness. All versions continue with Mahākassapa recounting the occasion when the Buddha praised Mahākassapa in front of the Sangha for his attainment of the four jhanas and the higher knowledges.

81 Such is the story that is more or less common to the three extant versions of this text. But the Pali version adds several details. First, Mahākassapa initially declines the invitation to teach, slightingly remarking that Ānanda is the 'busy one with many duties'. The commentary explains that since the Buddha passed away the fourfold assembly had been constantly

coming to Ānanda for teachings. Only after repeated encouragement—or nagging—by Ānanda does he consent. The Chinese versions mention no reluctance on the part of Mahākassapa, merely saying that they had gone for alms together in Rājagaha, and as the time was still early they visited the nuns' monastery. The Pali shows Ānanda responding to the bhikkhuni's criticism by saying 'the woman is foolish' (or perhaps 'women are foolish'), whereas the Chinese texts don't mention gender here at all. After Ānanda's call for Mahākassapa to show kindness, the Pali depicts him as threatening Ānanda, saying that if he is not careful, the Sangha will investigate him further. This is apparently an allusion to the events of the First Council; but it is not found in the Chinese. Finally, the Pali version declares that Thullatissā disrobed, while the Chinese versions omit this.

82 In a closely related Sutta, Mahākassapa was staying in Rājagaha after the Buddha's passing away.[26] Ānanda arrives with a large following of mostly young monks, several of whom disrobe. Mahākassapa criticizes Ānanda, calling him a 'boy'.[27] When a bhikkhuni heard this, she criticized Mahākassapa, saying that he had formerly been a follower of a different religion. Mahākassapa refutes this, saying that he had gone forth in dedication to the 'arahants in the world', and had taken the Buddha as his teacher. He goes on to recount their first meeting, and the exchange of robes. The Pali version again ends by remarking that the bhikkhuni disrobed, which is not mentioned in the Chinese versions.

83 It's hard to ignore this systematic difference. The Pali consistently plays up the conflict between Mahākassapa and Ānanda, emphasizing the failure of the nuns who oppose Mahākassapa. Mahākassapa is meant to appear tough and uncompromising, but he comes across as arrogant and defensive, especially in his hypersensitivity when women are involved.

84 If we were to consider only the Pali Suttas, we would be tempted to interpret these episodes as evidence of Mahākassapa's misogyny, and would be liable to draw from that conclusions about the nature of the hard core ascetic's attitude to women. If we take the Chinese versions into account, however, the conflict in these tales is softened, and the harshness in Mahākassapa's character is revealed to be largely an illusion of the redactors. When we take Mahākassapa's relationship with Kāpilānī into consideration, the archetypal pattern of the conflict reveals itself with

clarity. Mahākassapa and Kāpilānī represent the Higher Masculine and the Higher Feminine, and as such are adversaries to Thullanandā/Thullatissā as the Lower Feminine, and Ānanda as the Lower Masculine. Their fates are different, for Ānanda at this stage is a stream-enterer, and his existential situation is thus ambiguous, Janus-faced: he clings behind to the Lower, while knowing that his destiny is the Higher. The two nuns, unlike Mahāpajāpatī, fail. Whether or not they depart the Sangha, they depart our texts, and their spiritual career ends just as surely.

85 These incidents took place near Rājagaha, where the First Council was held, and it seems plausible that they happened between the *parinibbāna* and the First Council. They record the Sangha's concern for the future of Buddhism. Are all the young monks going to disrobe? Sāriputta and Moggallāna have already gone; after the first generation of disciples, such as Mahākassapa, pass away completely, will the young generation led by Ānanda be up to the task? Will favoritism and jealousies among the nuns divide the monks? In this troubled period the evident tensions between these two monks are more understandable, more human. What family hasn't argued after the death of a parent?

86 Mahākassapa plays the curmudgeonly old monk who jumps sternly on any misdemeanor in the Sangha. In these passages he criticizes the bhikkhunis, but only a little earlier he has been just as critical of a bad monk like Subhadda, who rejoiced at the Buddha's passing away. Thullanandā as the Lower Feminine is the counterpart of Subhadda as the Lower Masculine. At no time did Mahākassapa make derogatory remarks about bhikkhunis or women in general. He criticized a bad nun on valid grounds. If we interpret these passages as misogynistic, this is our projection onto Mahākassapa, not Mahākassapa's projection on to the bhikkhunis.

87 So many of these conflicts stem from a basic lack of understanding. We don't know how Mahākassapa felt, why he made the choices he did. We don't know why the nuns wanted to side with Ānanda. We can only imagine what the dynamics of these relationships were. And yet they are still so influential. We forget how difficult it is for us to understand even those closest to us, who we live with every day, sharing our hopes and dreams. How much harder it is to know those who *are* our dreams.

CHAPTER 34

THE SOFT TWIN

ĀNANDA IS BUILT INTO THE BUDDHIST CONSCIOUSNESS as opposite to Mahākassapa. Mahākassapa is old, Ānanda is young; Mahākassapa is grouchy, Ānanda is tender; Mahākassapa is aloof, Ānanda is involved; Mahākassapa is fire, Ānanda is water. And—need it be said?—Mahākassapa is male, Ānanda is female.

2 Ānanda is remembered in the traditions for his touching faith and devotion to the Buddha. He attended the Buddha with love and care for 25 years. In many ways he played the role of the devoted wife. So it should come as little surprise that in the Mahāparinibbāna Sutta, shortly before the Buddha passed away, he told a story that, ever so subtly, associated Ānanda with a devoted wife who was still attached to her husband when he was passing away.

3 The Buddha has made his way to his final resting place in Kusināra, with Ānanda by his side every step of the way. When the Buddha was lying between the twin *sāl* trees, with the devas sprinkling flowers upon him, Ānanda was overcome with emotion. He withdrew to a dwelling and stood leaning against the doorpost, weeping and lamenting: his beloved teacher, who had been so kind to him, was about to pass away. He is like Mahāpajāpatī standing outside the monastery gates, weeping after her encounter with the Buddha; both events happened near Vesālī and both at the end of a long journey. In both cases the weeping protagonist is situated in a liminal space, nearly inside, but not quite. Like the two-faced Janus,

Roman guardian god of doorways, they face into the monastery but cannot yet fully enter.

4 The Buddha called Ānanda back, gently reminded him that all things were impermanent, and spoke words of praise and encouragement. Ānanda had great wisdom, he knew the right time for people to come to see the Buddha, and he was beloved by the four assemblies of bhikkhus, bhikkhunis, laymen, and laywomen, just as the citizens loved a Wheel-turning Monarch. They all loved to hear him speak Dhamma, and when he finished they were left wanting more.[1]

5 Ānanda responded by begging the Buddha to not pass away in this 'little wattle-and-daub town' of Kusināra, but in one of the great cities. Ānanda is associated with the urban, popular spread of Dhamma that came to the fore under Aśoka. Here, too, we see a contrast with the everlonely forest dweller Mahākassapa.

6 Why does Ānanda bring this up here? What does the location of the Buddha's passing away have to do with Ānanda's emotional distress? Well, nothing, on the surface of it. And yet the narrative goes on to weave a whole web of subtle connections.

7 The Buddha said that this place had indeed been a great city in ages past, and was the capital of the Wheel-turning King Mahāsudassana. The Buddha then told the story of that king.[2]

8 Mahāsudassana ruled over the splendid, vast city that had once stood on the site of Kusināra. He was possessed of the seven treasures of the Wheel-turning Monarch, and was beloved by the people, just as Ānanda was. After a long time the king reflected that his glory arose from his past practice of giving, self-control, and abstinence. He determined to retire in meditation. He stayed alone in a palace, where he developed the four Divine Abidings. After a long time, when the king's life was drawing to a close, Queen Subhaddā decided to visit him.

9 There are several significant details in this visit that are found in the Pali version, but not in the corresponding Sanskrit passage. She came and stood leaning against the door-post—just like Ānanda. The king told her to stay there and not enter. Then he lay down on a couch in the lion's posture, on the right side with one foot on the other, mindful and clearly aware—just like the Buddha. The queen exclaims that the king's complex-

ion has become exceedingly bright and pure[3]—a concern for his physical appearance that is echoed by Ānanda in his description of the Buddha.[4] All these details seem to have been added at a later date in the Pali text. From here on the two versions are similar.

10 Reminding him of the glory of his chief city and other royal possessions, she exhorted him to stay alive—just as Ānanda asked the Buddha to prolong his life. The king responded that the queen was now treating him like an enemy, not a friend, and told her to reflect on impermanence.

11 Unable to bear it, the queen cried out and burst into tears—just like Ānanda. But she accepted the king's admonition, and from then kept reminding him of the truth of impermanence and the need to let go. The king passed away in peace, like someone falling asleep after a good meal. The Buddha went on to identify himself with the king. He had the good taste to avoid drawing the obvious inference that Ānanda had been the queen.

12 The essence of the story concerns the withdrawal of the king; the approach of his wife to encourage him to live on by reminding him of the good things of the world; the king's rebuttal; the queen's tears and acquiescence; and the king's peaceful death. These themes are enough to draw a general parallel between the queen and Ānanda. The extra details that make this parallel conclusive, and which make it clear that it was deliberate, are mostly found in the Pali version, not the Sanskrit. It seems they were added as part of the process of expanding the Sutta in the Pali tradition, making the connection with Ānanda even closer. Curiously, the result is that in the Pali narrative the story is more tightly interwoven with the Mahāparinibbāna Sutta, despite the fact that it is a separate text, whereas the Sanskrit version, though it is contained within the Mahāparinibbāna Sutta, is less tightly connected.

13 So Ānanda is emotionally like a woman—and the force of this would have been even stronger in those days than it is for us. This emotive spirit is expressed in the devotional tradition. We know Ānanda had a great personal love for the Buddha, and that this resulted in the creation of the classic devotional scriptures. In addition, the later tradition links him with the worship of the Bodhi tree and thus with bhikkhuni Saṅghamittā, and far earlier, with goddess worship, as we have already seen.[5]

14 The people of Sāvatthi were used to having the Buddha stay nearby at the Jetavana. When he went traveling they felt lost. They missed his guiding presence. So they approached Ānanda, asking whether it would be possible to establish a shrine of some kind where they could offer flowers and perfumes in the name of the Buddha while he was away. Ānanda consulted with the Buddha, and they decided to plant a Bodhi tree, a sapling of the original tree under which the Buddha sat in Bodhgaya on the night of his Awakening. Moggallāna fetched the fruit with his psychic powers; rather than damage the tree in any way, he waited until a fruit was dropping and caught it as it fell. It was planted amid a great festival, attended by the great and good of Sāvatthi: King Pasenadi, Anāthapiṇḍika, Visākhā. Vessels full of lotuses were placed around it, scented water was poured, gold dust was sprinkled. The Buddha consecrated the place by sitting the whole night experiencing the bliss of Awakening. In this way the Buddha's personal spiritual achievement is co-opted as a blessing for the populace.

15 Ānanda is associated with the devotional tradition, and specifically with the worship of the Bodhi tree, with its deep goddess connection. His connection with the feminine was not always so positive, however. Ānanda was, it seems, very handsome and the ladies had a way of falling for him.[6] The Suttas tell the story of a nun who pretended she was ill, lying down on a couch with her head covered so that Ānanda would visit her.[7] But Ānanda saw through her ploy. He taught her the Dhamma, and rather than accusing her of trying to seduce him, he spoke of detachment from sensual desires. The nun got the point and begged forgiveness.

16 The stories of Ānanda and women become reduced to satire, even within the canon itself. One time there was an excess of cakes donated to the monks.[8] The Buddha suggested to Ānanda that he dispose of them by distributing them to those in need. To ensure they would be distributed fairly, Ānanda asked the recipients to line up. He went down the line and gave one cake to each in turn. Some of those receiving the food were non-Buddhist nuns from a nearby community. When Ānanda came to one nun, however, two cakes stuck together and he gave them both without noticing. The nuns to each side glanced at each other and one of them whispered, 'He's your lover!' 'He's not my lover,' she retorted. When he came to the end of the line, there were some cakes left over, so Ānanda went

down the line once more giving each nun a single cake. Except—would you believe it?—when he came to that same nun, two cakes stuck together. And a third time... Well, I think you get the idea. The nuns ended up arguing, and the Buddha laid down a rule forbidding handing out food in this way.

17 It's natural to think that Ānanda himself must have provoked this type of story. We know that he was generous and caring for women's welfare;[9] but perhaps there is more to it? Was Ānanda himself, being not yet fully Awakened, prey to sensual desires, which unconsciously constellated such situations? His own verses deny this: he states that in the twenty five years that he was a stream-enterer—from the year of his ordination until the eve of the First Council—not so much as a sensual perception had arisen in him.[10]

18 While Ānanda did not suffer the pangs of sexual frustration in his life as a monk, his kammic background depicts a past that was less restrained. In the past he had been born as a woman, a rare case of gender change in Buddhist past life stories. His adventures with gender identity were the result of his having been a serial adulterer.

19 Ānanda was born as the wise and beautiful princess Rujā.[11] She was the faithful and honest Cordelia, who dared to speak the truth to her father the king when he had strayed from the path and there was no-one to show him the dangers of his choices. King Aṅgati wisely ruled the kingdom of Videha from his capital Mithila for many years, until he received evil counsel from an ignorant ascetic. He fell under the view that there was no fruit or result of good or bad deeds, since there was nothing after this life. Accordingly, he neglected his former careful and charitable governance and gave himself over to pleasure. No-one could bring him back to the path of righteousness except his only daughter, Rujā, who told her father of her own past lives and her strange kammic inheritance.

> 20 I remember seven past lives through which I have fared on, and after passing from here there will be a further seven.
>
> 21 In my seventh previous life I was born as the son of a smith in the city of Rājagaha in Magadha. I had a bad friend and did much evil. We went about sleeping with other men's wives as if we were immortals. These actions remained laid up as fire covered with ashes.
>
> 22 By means of other kammas I was born in the land of Vaṁsa in a wealthy family of Kosambi, great and prosperous with much riches. I

> was their only son, and was always honored. There I followed a friend who was devoted to good works, wise and learned, and he established me in good purpose. On many nights I observed the 14th and 15th day *uposatha*. Those good kammas remained like a treasure hidden in water.
>
> 23 But the fruit of the evil deeds I had done in Magadha came around afterward like a noxious poison.
>
> 24 From there, O king, I passed to the Roruva hell for a long time, where I was tormented by my kamma: when I think of it I cannot be happy. After experiencing wretched suffering there for many years I was born as a castrated goat in Bheṇṇākata. I carried the sons of the wealthy on my back and in a carriage; this was the specific result of the kamma of going after other men's wives.
>
> 25 After that I took rebirth in the womb of a monkey in the wilds. On the day of my birth they took me to the leader of the herd, who cried out, 'Bring my son!' Grabbing me with force, he ripped off my testicles with his teeth, despite all my cries. Then I was born as a castrated ox among the Dasaṇṇas; though swift and fair, for a long time I pulled a carriage. Next I was born among the Vajjians, but was neither men nor woman, even though born in this human state, so hard to attain. All of these births were the result of my going after other men's wives.
>
> 26 Then I was born as a gorgeous nymph in the Nandana Grove in Tāvatiṁsa heaven, adorned in bright colors and flashing jewels, singing and dancing in attendance on Sakka. While I was there I remembered the seven previous births, as well as the next seven. The former good deeds I did while at Kosambi have come around in their turn, and from now I will only be born as a human or deity. For seven births I shall be honored, but not until the sixth will I be free of my female gender. At that time I will be born as a supreme male deity in heaven.

27 In identifying Ānanda with this complex tale of moral ambiguity and gender transgression, the Buddhist tradition records its uncomfortable acceptance of the liberal tendencies that Ānanda demonstrated. The basic character is powerful and brave: she stands beside her father when all others had failed, just as Ānanda stood by the Buddha when the drunk elephant Nāḷāgiri charged him, while all the arahants fled.[12] Standing up to the patriarchy she is, or could be, a great female role model. This is undermined by her identification with Ānanda, and more so due to the dubious gender ambiguity of her past. She is not standing up because

of her true 'feminine' strength, but because she is, quite literally, a man trapped in a woman's body. Her crime—or rather, the crime of the man who she once was—was adultery; that is, transgressing on another man's property. The role of the women in the relationship is not considered.

28 The specific nature of the kammic reprisal is interesting: adultery is punished by gender confusion. It seems the point is that he in some way destroyed or attacked the masculinity of the husbands, which is shown by their rule and control over their wives. If the women stray, this sends the message that the husband is not man enough for them. The transgressor is, accordingly, punished by having his genitals attacked, ripped off, missing, or replaced by female genitals. The severity of the punishment is gradually attenuated, until with the ripening of good kamma he takes a positive female form where he can be happy. The image of a good female life is entirely a product of the male imagination: a happy woman is sexy and beautiful, dancing and singing for his pleasure. This text, unlike the early Suttas, takes it for granted that the male form is desirable and normative.

29 Rujā's eloquent and moving testimony, however, is not enough to persuade her father, for 'while parents naturally love their children's words, they do not thereby give up their old opinions.' She did not give up, but made worship to the deities and begged for divine help. No less a being than the Bodhisatta in the form of a Great Brahmā answered her call. He appeared to the king in the form of an ascetic and engaged him in a debate on virtue and its results. The king, wittily enough, challenged the ascetic, saying, 'If you are so convinced of the truth of the next life, how about you lend me $500 now, and I'll pay you back $1000 in the next life!' This incipient Marxist critique, however, was refuted, as the ascetic said that no wise man makes a loan to an unreliable person—thus showing that ethics are as relevant to our prosperity in this life as the beyond.

30 Reason was not enough, however, for this obdurate king, so the ascetic used his psychic powers to show him in detail the horrors of hells, seeing which the king broke down and begged for redemption. Thus Rujā's quest was successful in the end, but she needed the help of the ultimate patriarchal authority to succeed.

❖

31 Ānanda's womanly associations emerge further in his connection with cloth. He was the world's first and most successful fashion designer: on the Buddha's request he designed the basic pattern for Buddhist monastic robes, based on the pattern of the dykes in the rice fields of Magadha. The same design is still used today.

32 Perhaps his skill in fashion stems from his past life as a tailor. He offered a small piece of cloth, only the size of a hand, and a needle to a Paccekabuddha. Because of the gift of a needle he became wise—a needle penetrates through the surface of things, and weaves the hidden links. Here emerges the meaning of the simile of the needlemaker that Mahākassapa uses against Ānanda. In addition because of the gift of cloth he got 500 robes.[13] This motif is found repeatedly: the women of King Udena's harem gave him 500 robes, and the king himself another 500.[14] When the ladies of King Pasenadi's harem desired to receive the Dhamma, they unanimously selected Ānanda as their teacher,[15] although the Vinaya says it was the Buddha himself who appointed Ānanda to this task.[16] In gratitude they gave Ānanda 500 robes, which had been a gift of the king for them to wear. The king was initially upset, but then his heart softened and he gave Ānanda another 500 robes. Ānanda distributed the robes among the Sangha for those in need. What the monks looked like when they were wearing robes intended for the king's harem women is, sadly, not recorded.[17]

33 Ānanda repeatedly finds himself in the role of donor to the Sangha, giving robes, or as we saw above food, a role that is normally the preserve of lay people, and especially lay women.[18] The accumulation of costly materials by the Sangha is a deeply corrupting influence. Ānanda's association with this is yet another point of difference from the austere Mahākassapa.

❖

34 Despite Ānanda's closeness to the Buddha, his intimate knowledge of the Sangha and lay communities, and his mastery of the texts, Mahākassapa appears after the Buddha dies and in a burst of flame claims the authority. It is he who determines what happens next, not Ānanda. How did Ānanda feel about this? Here is one of his own verses, which is very suggestive of his state of mind in the later years.[19]

35 The old ones have gone,
I don't fit in with the new;
So today I'll do jhanas, alone,
Like a bird that's withdrawn to its roost.

36 Mahākassapa decided to hold a Council in order to recite the Buddha's words so that the holy life can last. He set it up in Rājagaha, inviting 500 arahant bhikkhus and excluding all others, including bhikkhunis and laypeople, despite the fact that the Buddha's instruction for holding a Council clearly included them.[20]

37 Ānanda is a problem. He is acknowledged as the master of the texts, but he is not yet an arahant. Mahākassapa's treatment is ambivalent. The other, unnamed, monks invite him to select 500 monks for the Council. But he chooses only 499; Ānanda is the unnamed space, the chink of imperfection in the perfect round number. This could be read as a veiled criticism of Ānanda's limited spiritual attainment; or else as a special provision for an esteemed colleague. The other monks ask Mahākassapa to include Ānanda, citing his good character, knowledge of the texts, and attainment as a stream-enterer. Mahākassapa consents.

38 Thus, despite the question mark over Ānanda, Mahākassapa agreed without objection to his inclusion in the Council. It was Ānanda himself who felt unworthy to attend such a gathering while still a learner. On the eve of the Council, after great striving, Ānanda rested his head on the pillow, and in that moment of letting go with mindfulness, he realized full arahantship. The traditions emphasize this little detail, saying that if anyone should be remembered for attaining enlightenment in-between the four postures, with his feet having left the floor and his head not yet reached the pillow, it is Ānanda who should be so remembered. His in-between posture recalls his leaning on the door-post weeping, his support for Mahāpajāpatī when she was in a similar liminal position, and also the poise of the Bodhisatta suspended, hovering in the air between mother and father.

39 So Ānanda comes to the Council as an arahant.[21] But he is not asked to speak first. Mahākassapa decides to start with the Vinaya, in contrast with the normal sequence, which prioritizes Dhamma over Vinaya. It seems that it was this emphasis on the Council as a Vinaya event that meant the bhikkhunis and laypeople were excluded. Normally, of course, at a

teaching event anyone may attend, whereas the disciplinary proceedings for monastics are done in private.

40 After Upāli recited the Vinaya, Mahākassapa interrogated Ānanda regarding the Suttas. At the end of this, Ananda announced, as if it had only just occurred to him, that shortly before he passed away the Buddha said that the Sangha could abolish the lesser and minor rules if it wished. There was some discussion of this, and, somewhat implausibly, after the greatest experts in Buddhist history had just finished compiling the entire Vinaya, they could not agree on which rules were 'lesser and minor'. In the end, Mahākassapa, true to his rigorist outlook, proposed that no rules be abolished, and that the Sangha should train as when the Buddha was alive. His conservative position won the day over Ānanda's more liberal proposal.

41 Despite this favorable outcome, Mahākassapa still saw fit to rebuke Ānanda for not asking what these rules are. Ānanda admitted, rather humbly, that he was not being mindful at the time. But Mahākassapa was not finished. He proceeded to level a series of charges against Ānanda, charges which are neither Vinaya offenses nor have anything to do with the business of the Council. In each case, Ānanda gave a reasonable explanation for his conduct, and then said: 'I do not see that as a wrongdoing, but out of faith in the Venerables I say it is a wrong-doing.' Let us look at each of these charges.

42 The first was that Ānanda stepped on the Buddha's bathing cloth. This is so trivial one wonders how it ever made it into such august scripture. But it makes perfect sense within the narrative play of robe-offering: the Buddha authorized Mahākassapa by suggesting they swap robes; he marginalized Mahāpajāpatī by refusing her offering; and now Ānanda is scolded for defiling the Buddha's robe with his foot. Mahākassapa plays the pedantic rigorist to perfection.[22]

43 Mahākassapa next accuses Ānanda of allowing women to first worship the Buddha's body. This refers to the events of the Mahāparinibbāna Sutta, where Ānanda had been entrusted by the Buddha with making arrangements for this event. In the text itself, the Buddha praises Ānanda for knowing the right time for monks, nuns, male & female devotees, kings, ministers, and sectarian teachers with their pupils to visit the Buddha. Thus Mahākassapa is criticizing Ānanda in a sphere in which the Buddha

praised him; and this criticism was specifically to do with women. The Mūlasarvāstivāda version adds to this the revealing accusation that, when Ānanda allowed the women to worship the Buddha, their tears soiled his body.[23]

44 The next criticism was that Ānanda did not, despite the Buddha's hint, beg the Buddha to live on for an æon. This concerns the curious episode, also in the Mahāparinibbāna Sutta, where the Buddha claims that he could, if he wished, live on for the rest of the æon. This claim is made many times, and each time Ānanda misses the point. Eventually the Buddha relinquishes his will to live, and Ānanda begs him to stay on, but too late. His excuse is that his mind was possessed by Māra. The whole episode is bizarre, and reeks of the later supernatural Buddha.[24] Only a little before this episode, the Buddha had been commenting, in an all-too-human way, on the pains of his old, worn-out body. One wonders what it would have been like to carry such a thing around for millions of years. The point, of course, is not whether the Buddha could have lived such a span, but to associate Ānanda, weak, emotional, prone to possession, with the premature ending of Buddhism, just as when he supported women's ordination.

45 Which brings us to the last, and presumably the worst, of Ānanda's offenses: the ordination of women. Mahākassapa offers no explanation for why this should be a bad thing. This omission assumes knowledge of the 500 year doom pronounced by the Buddha to Mahāpajāpatī, which, as I do not tire of repeating, occurred in the previous chapter of the Khandhakas. Thus the text only makes sense within the broader narrative context. It assumes that you, the reader, are familiar with this, and will know why Mahākassapa objected to the ordination of women. Ānanda's reply is not based on the spiritual benefits that women will receive, but rather on familial gratitude for Mahāpajāpatī as she who fed the Buddha with her own milk. Here he stills harks back to the infantile imagery associated with the Lower Masculinity

46 But this whole episode may be read as a test for Ānanda. Remember that he has only just attained arahantship, and it is not unreasonable that Mahākassapa should wish to prove this, to himself, perhaps, or to the wider community. It is no coincidence that Ānanda, the subject of the test, was a relative of the Buddha. Early Buddhism was, to a greater extent than

is normally realized, a family affair, a soap opera where hidden tensions among the Śākyans are imported into the Sangha. Part of the maturing of Buddhism is to escape from the personal family sphere, following Siddhattha's example. However, Siddhattha's return to the family must also be followed; that is, Buddhism must integrate those aspects of worldly nature which are renounced at the point of departure, assimilate them, and transform them into a positive force within Buddhist culture. Hence the test. Mahākassapa is insinuating that Ānanda is still Mummy's Boy.

47 Ānanda's response shows his triumph. First he asserts himself, stating that he did not see that his actions were blameworthy. Here he exhibits the Higher Masculinity to perfection, standing up to the intimidating figure of Mahākassapa, stating his case calmly and reasonably. But such an attitude, if it is unchecked, could lead to endless legal wrangling. So next he humbly apologizes, showing his gentleness and flexibility, his ability to let trivial legal disputes go. Here Ānanda's embodiment of the Higher Feminine defuses the situation. By itself, this would have been just wimpy, but coming after his assertion of strength, it is grace and humility.

48 Equally important, this grace comes in a context of a bending and acceptance from the other party, Mahākassapa. So far we have read the surface of the text in emphasizing his masculine qualities of control and dominance over the proceedings, and his sometimes harsh rebukes. But these surface details risk hiding a far more fundamental dynamic, one which is, so far as I know, not explicitly stated in the traditions, but which underlies the entire series of events.

49 And that is that Mahākassapa, the tough ascetic loner, is now lending his considerable charisma and prestige to support Ānanda's specialty, the preservation of texts. Despite resisting the Buddha's invitation, even late in life, to come and live in the Sangha and give up his more austere practices, now he is devoting himself to preserving the texts and working together with community.[25] He is showing that his acts are genuinely motivated by a broad and deep sense of communion and compassion. Indeed, some texts go so far as to say that when the Buddha passed away, all the other arahants decided there was no point in living and that they would follow the Buddha immediately, and they were only persuaded from this by Mahākassapa,

who spoke eloquently of the need to preserve the texts out of compassion for future generations.

50 There is no mistaking Mahākassapa's curmudgeonly character. Yet there is even less mistaking his sincerity and strength when it counted. Even though it meant giving up his life of simplicity in the forest, he worked with the community so that all could access the same liberating teachings that he himself had benefited from so much. In this caring for community and relationship, his concern to nurture the tender young religion, his willingness to set aside his wishes for the welfare of others, he shows his mastery of the Higher Feminine.

CHAPTER 35

WHAT A WOMAN WANTS

What does a woman want? A question so simple, yet so puzzling to men—and perhaps to women too. Even married men, living intimately with their wife for years, find her a mystery—is it any wonder that celibate monks, with only superficial contact with women for much of their adult life, should be confused? Sigmund Freud did not know:

> 2 The great question that has never been answered, and which I have not yet been able to answer, despite my thirty years of research into the feminine soul, is 'What does a woman want?'[1]

3 Where Freud hesitated, the Buddha spoke with confidence.[2] He was asked of the desire, quest, resolve, need, and ultimate goal of various types of people, ranging from a *khattiya* to a thief to an ascetic. One of the kinds of people was a woman, and the Buddha gave the following response.

> 4 A woman's desire is for a man; her quest is for adornment; her resolve is for a son; her need is to be without a rival; and her ultimate goal is for sovereignty.

5 Most of these are pretty straightforward. Most women, by and large, like to have a man, adornments, children, and to not have a rival for their husband's affections. Worldly aims, neither better nor worse than the aims the Buddha described for the other types of people.

6 The curious one is 'sovereignty'. Why is this something that a woman, in particular, wants? And why is it her 'final goal'? She shares this goal in common with the *khattiyas*, the ruling noble class. It is fairly obvious why

a *khattiya* should be intent on overlordship. But we are left to wonder just what this sovereignty means for women.

❖

7 The Mahājanaka Jātaka contains an episode where the hero returns to claim the throne that is rightly his.[3] The kingship stands vacant, and one who aspires to the throne must pass a series of tests, the hardest of which is to please the daughter of the former king and thereby win her hand in marriage. The royal retainers, searching for a suitable candidate, invited a great general to make the attempt.

8 He came at once to the royal gate and signaled to the princess that he was standing there. She wished to test whether he had the wisdom to carry the standard of royalty, and so she gave a command for him to come. He quickly ran up from the foot of the staircase and stood beside her.

> 9 'Now,' she said, 'run quickly on the level ground.'
>
> 10 Thinking to please her, he sprang swiftly into action.
>
> 11 'Come here,' she said.
>
> 12 He hurried to her side.
>
> 13 Knowing that he was nothing, she said, 'Come and massage my feet.'
>
> 14 Thinking only to please her, he sat before her and started massaging her feet. She kicked him on his chest, knocking the general clean over on his back. She signaled to her serving-maids, saying, 'This blind fool of a man is such a loser. Give him a drubbing, then toss him out by his neck.'
>
> 15 When they saw him outside, the retainers said to the general, 'So, how did it go?'
>
> 16 'Don't ask,' he said. 'The woman is inhuman.'
>
> 17 In the same way, she put to shame the treasurer, the accountant, the bearer of the royal standard, and the sword-bearer.
>
> 18 Then it was time for the Bodhisatta.[4] They found him lying asleep on a stone in the park. Nevertheless, the royal retinue immediately recognized his qualities. They brought him to the palace, where he immediately began organizing matters to his own liking.
>
> 19 The princess sent a message to invite him to see her, but he just ignored it. The messenger reported back to the princess, who thought to herself, 'Ahh, he must be a man of great character.' She sent a second, and a third messenger, which he continued to ignore.

> 20 Finally he ascended the palace, walking at his own leisure like a lion yawning. As he drew near, such was his majestic bearing that the princess could not remain still. She went to him and gave him her hand to lean on. He took her hand and ascended the throne. The retainers told him that the throne was for the one who could please the princess.
>
> 21 'Princess Sīvalī gave me her hand as I came near,' he said. 'and so I have pleased her already. Tell me something else.'

22 She wants sovereignty, and at the same time she wants her male to be alpha. The whole performance was a trick, a *māyā*. She did not boss the men around because she was bossy, but because she wanted to test their mettle. If they can't stand up to her, how could they have the resolve and strength to rule a kingdom?

23 The other candidates had the outer form of palace initiates. They had the status, the clothes, the roles, the *māyā*. But they didn't have the guts. The Bodhisatta was a nobody, but he was the rightful heir. He had no need to woo the princess. She was drawn by the sheer force of his charisma. And when she knew that he was not fooled by her *māyā*, she became a devoted wife, and he a loving husband and great king.

24 They lived happily after that, until he felt the urge to renounce and live the life of an ascetic in the Himalayas. Unable to bear such a parting, Queen Sīvalī staged an elaborate hoax, pretending that the city was burning, or under attack, and that the desperate people, all running about or being carried as if wounded, needed their king. The Bodhisatta saw through her trick and kept walking. The parting scene is perhaps the longest in the Buddhist texts, as she repeatedly refuses to leave his side. Eventually, with great grief, he disappears into the forest, while she returned to the palace. Queen Sīvalī, who is identified with Bimbā, built a little hut in the palace grounds, anointed their son as the new king, and spent the rest of her life in meditation.

25 They were two characters, each as strong as the other, and each headed for the same high destiny in the Brahmā realms. The game of marital conflict was just that, a game, and it was in the very act of playing it that they showed their true colors.

❖

26 In the Mahājanaka Jātaka, the woman appears to be a terror, but this is just an illusion, which she deliberately adopts to test her man. The story of the horrific bride-to-be is another story-telling standard, the complement to the Beauty & the Beast. It was especially popular in western Europe, where it is found in Chaucer's *Wife of Bath*, and a variety of ancient Celtic myths. Here is a retelling from the King Arthur cycle, as told in the 15th century *The Wedding of Sir Gawen and Dame Ragnell.*[5]

> 27 King Arthur was a-hunting in Inglewood forest with a small company of young knights. The king sped ahead of the others in pursuit of a deer. As he dismounted after the kill, he was confronted with a strange knight, full dressed in mighty armor, alone in the wild woods.
>
> 28 'Well met, King Arthur!' growled the weird knight. 'You have done me wrong this many a year. You took my lands and gave them to Sir Gawain!'
>
> 29 'Sir,' said the king, 'what is your name?'
>
> 30 'My name,' said he, 'is Sir Grim Summerday.'[6]
>
> 31 'Well, Sir Grim,' said the king, 'here I stand in my hunting greens, while you are full dressed in armor. If you were to slay me in such a state, the shame would follow you wherever you went.'
>
> 32 The king had cleverly touched on the knight's most precious possession, his honor. But the strange knight was not finished yet.
>
> 33 'In that case,' he said, 'I will grant you a reprieve, King Arthur. But there is a condition. For one year you shall be free, then you shall return here to this exact spot, wearing the same hunter's green, where you will tell me the answer to the question I give you. If you fail I shall have your head.' The king, lacking useful alternatives, gave his word that he would honor the deal.
>
> 34 'The question is,' said Sir Grim: 'What does a woman want?'
>
> 35 Loathe as he was to accept such a strange quest, the king gave his word. He returned dejected to his knights and told them of his situation. Sir Gawain, his nephew, suggested that they each travel in different directions and enquire of as many people as they meet, whether man or woman, and compile all the answers in a great book. Surely someone will get the answer right.
>
> 36 So off they went and sought their answer. Some said that women like to be well adorned. Others said women love to be wooed. Others said women like nothing better than a lusty man to embrace and kiss. Many and diverse answers they received, and all were recorded in

the book. But the king was still nervous, wondering whether any of them was the true answer.

37 In his travels he returned to the Inglewood forest, where he had met the weird knight. This time he encountered another strange figure: an old hag, the ugliest woman man had ever seen. Her face was red, her nose full of snot. Yellow teeth hung over her gaping, bleary mouth, with its cheeks as wide as other women's hips. Her neck was thick and long, her clotted hair piled in a heap, her drooping dugs fit to feed a horse. Truly, words cannot express her loathsomeness. Curiously enough, however, she was riding on a brightly decorated, well-bred horse, all set with gold and gems, and on her back was a lute.

38 She rode up to the king and, without ado, told him that none of the answers he had were any good.

39 'I can help you,' she said. 'If you grant me one wish. If you refuse, you are as good as dead.'

40 'What does all this mean?' said the king. 'Tell me what you wish, and why you know this answer, and I shall give you what you ask.'

41 'You must grant me a knight to wed,' said the hag. 'His name is Sir Gawain.'

42 'Mercy!' cried the king. 'I cannot make such a promise for Sir Gawain.'

43 'Well then,' she said, 'return and speak fair words to him and see what he shall say. For I may yet save your life. I may be ugly, yet I am full of grace.'

44 'And what, lady,' said the king, 'shall I say is your name?'

45 'My name,' said she, 'is Dame Ragnell.'

46 'Then fare well, Dame Ragnell,' said the king, and left with a heavy heart.

47 He returned to the palace, and told Sir Gawain of the dreadful turn of events. Gentle Sir Gawain, however, rose to the challenge, and said he would marry her, even if she was as foul as Beelzebub.

48 'Ahh, Gawain,' said Arthur, 'of all knights that I have known, you bear the flower.' He rode back to meet Dame Ragnell in the woods once more. He told her that her wish and been granted, and bid her tell him the answer without delay.

49 'Sire,' she said, 'now you shall know what women desire most of all. Some men say that we desire to be beautiful; or to have the pleasure of many men in our bed; or to be considered always young and fresh. But there is one other thing that we all fancy: our desire, above all, is

for *sovereignty*. For when we have sovereignty, all is ours; we win the mastery of the manliest knight, though he be ever so fierce.'

50 The king galloped forth at great speed, through mire and moor and bog, to reach the appointed place and meet for the last time with the weird knight, Sir Grim Summerday.

51 Sir Grim was waiting. He demanded the answer, and was ready to chop off the king's head if he failed. The king began by pulling out the book of answers that he compiled with Sir Gawain. He went through each answer one by one, but Sir Grim dismissed them all, saying, 'No, king, you are a dead man—prepare to bleed.'

52 'Wait one moment, sir,' said the king. 'There is another answer. Above all, women desire sovereignty; to rule over the manliest man.'

53 Grim was furious. 'Curse she who told you that!' he said. 'May she burn on a fire! For you have met my sister, Dame Ragnell, the old scott.[7] Go where you will, King Arthur! From this day on, you are my enemy, and woe befall you if I ever come across you in such a plight again.'

54 Arthur returned, and arrangements were made for the wedding. Dame Ragnell would accept no private engagement, insisting on a full public ceremony. The ladies of the court wept to think of Sir Gawain wedding such a creature, with her mouth full of bristly hairs, and great teeth like boar's tusks, one going up and the other down. But Sir Gawain did not falter: he stepped forward manfully and pledged his troth.

55 'God have mercy!' said Dame Ragnell, 'I wish I were a fair maid, for you are of such good heart.'

56 At the wedding feast, she sat and ate without waiting, ripping open the meat with her three-inch nails, and devouring as much as six men. Sir Kay, who was Gawain's companion, shook his head.

57 'Whoever kisses this lady,' he said, 'stands in fear of his own kiss.'[8]

58 That evening, Sir Gawain at first could not bring himself to face that snout.

59 'Sir Gawain,' she said, 'since we have wed, it is only right that you show me courtesy in bed. At least give me a kiss.'

60 'By God,' said Gawain, mustering his courage, 'I shall do more than just kiss!' He turned to her; only to see the fairest creature that he had ever seen!

61 'What is your desire?' she said.

62 'Jesus!' he cried out. 'What are you?'

63 'I am your wife,' she said. 'Why be so unkind?'

64 'Lady,' he said, 'I am to blame. I ask for your mercy, fair madam, I did not know. Until now you were the foulest wight that I ever saw, but now you are beautiful in my sight!' He took her in his arms and kissed her, and they made great joy.

65 'Sir,' she said, 'my beauty will not hold. You may choose: whether to have me fair at night and foul by day; or fair by day and foul at night.'

66 'Alas!' said Gawain, 'The choice is hard. I would like to choose the best, but I do not know. So, then, my lady, let it be as you will. The choice is yours. For I am bound to you; body and heart is all yours, I avow by God.'

67 'Mercy, gentle knight,' she said. 'Of all knights on earth you are the most blessed, for now I am honored properly. You shall have me fair both day and night, fair and bright as long as I shall live. So do not grieve. For I was transformed by my stepmother's necromancy, God have mercy upon her. Her enchantment was that I should take such a loathsome form until I should wed the best knight in all England, and he should give me sovereignty, body and goods. Kiss me, Sir Knight! Be glad and have good cheer, for I am well again.'

68 They made joy out of mind. And when the sun rose, and even until midday, they had not reappeared from their bridal room. King Arthur began to fear for his friend, and they went to his room. But Sir Gawain arose and took his lady by the hand. She stood in her dress by the fire, with her hair falling to her knees shining red as gold.

69 'Lo!' said Sir Gawain, 'See my comfort. This is my wife, Dame Ragnell, who saved your life.'

70 They told the story to the court. And when they had told of Sir Gawain's pledge of sovereignty, Dame Ragnell said, 'God thank him for his kindness. He saved me from evil foul and grim. Therefore, gracious Gawain, I shall never harm you. As long as I live I shall be obedient, and never think to argue.'

71 From that day, Gawain never left her side, day or night. But her time was not long; only five years were they together, then Dame Ragnell died, to Sir Gawain's eternal grief.

❖

72 The gift of sovereignty, freely offered with all kindness, transforms the woman from a loathly object of fear to a beautiful bride. And when the gift is so gracious, she cannot help but reciprocate, pledging to be meek.

This is the dynamic of oppression everywhere. People are not naturally violent or rebellious, but they will not put up with suppression. It breeds resentment, and the result is always ugly.

73 The nature of sovereignty in these tales is curiously ambivalent. It is, on the surface at least, something to do with domestic arrangements. In practice, it probably meant that a husband would give autonomy to the wife in managing the household. But the stories connect it with a greater question, that of sovereignty over the land. The Bodhisatta wins his throne, and Sir Gawain's problems stem from the claim by Sir Grim Summerday that his lands had been taken from him and given unjustly to Gawain.

74 The magical and mysterious elements of the story, however, suggest that the roots of this ambiguity may lie deep. The antagonist is himself a mysterious figure with a paradoxical name, which might connect him with the ancient pagan deities of the summer. He is not unlike the Green Knight, appearing at random and making outrageous demands, yet for all that he is honorable. He is found in the wilds, after leaving behind the civilized domain of the court. And, most significant of all, he is the hag's estranged brother. The story starts from the disconnect of Sir Grim Summerday with his revolting sister, and moves to the union of Gawain with his transformed bride.

75 In Irish and Germanic legend, the woman represents the sovereignty of the land. By embracing and marrying her, he wins the crown. Niall Noígíallach was an Irish king of legend, who may have lived around the 5th century. When his father died, there was a quarrel among the sons as to who would succeed the throne. It was settled when they were out hunting. They met a hag by a well, and only Niall had the courage to kiss her properly. She granted him and his descendants lordship over all Ireland.[9]

76 In some cases she is a goddess who presents the king with a chalice filled with mead; he drinks, and the ritual seals his throne. She is sometimes a horse deity, which perhaps explains her loathsome appearance in the later tales.[10] This divine old woman approaches the archetype of the oldest woman of all, Mother Earth. She is the land, and only the ancient powers have the right to grant true sovereignty.

77 Our story, even in its developed, romanticized version, may retain a link with ancient pagan traditions: the knight's name, 'Summerday', together

with his appearance at yearly intervals in the wilds, suggests a celebration of the yearly cycles, a suggestion confirmed by his sister's death after a five year cycle. The wicked stepmother, as so often, lurks in the background; but if it had not been for her curse, Sir Gawain would never have met his beloved.

78 Now, it is a strange thing that our sources, both east and west, not only agree that a woman's truest desire is sovereignty, but that this has a dual nature: a woman's sovereignty over her man, and the ruler's sovereignty over the land. According to the Buddhist version, the *khattiya*'s desire is sovereignty, but according to the western tales this can only be granted with the blessing of the local goddess. Mastery flows easily from a person to the land as a whole, and from the man to the woman and back. And this is, in the end, the moral of the story.

79 Sir Gawain, like the Bodhisatta, sees through the horrific exterior, and wins true love. A real relationship comes from trust freely offered, not from rules that bind and control. The contrast with the *garudhammas* imposed on bhikkhunis is all too plain. The *garudhammas* are built on distrust. Their aim is to enforce submission of women. While the main thrust of the Vinaya is, indeed, to grant nuns sovereignty, by granting them autonomy in all things, the *garudhammas* undermine this trust. As long as the basis of relationship remains unequal, the nuns will feel resentment, the monks will see them as fearful, and the conflict will never be resolved.

80 These stories say something important about the relationship between women and men, and about the real nature of a woman's wishes. They start with the prosaic and move towards something more profound and less sayable. In their mystery and magic they spill over their boundaries, taking a deeper significance than first appears. And yet there is another cycle of stories that deal with a woman's desires on a still more profound level.

CHAPTER 36

THE HEROINE

THE BUDDHA IS THE ULTIMATE HERO. His quest encompasses the stories of just about any hero you might care to mention, whether the locals like Kṛṣṇa,[1] Rāma,[2] Arjuna,[3] and Yudhiṣṭhira,[4] or international heroes like Noah,[5] Jonah,[6] Prometheus,[7] Jesus,[8] Odysseus,[9] Daedalus,[10] and the rest. It is perhaps the greatest, most complete, and most spiritual version of the universal tale. And it arises from the 'play of Māyā'.

2 Heroes tend to be men. It's a whole bloke thing—leaving home, seeking adventure in the wilderness, battling opponents, finding one's individual truth and standing firm in that. Establishing relationship is a matter of secondary concern, which is relegated to the 'return' leg of the cycle.

3 I've wondered about the women's hero story, and searched for it. It's not obvious, not exalted as the central story of a people, but lives quietly away in the nooks of culture, told by nannies to the children, or by adults for whom the playfulness of the thing lets you not take it all too seriously. It's found in *Sleeping Beauty*, in *Bluebeard*, in *Beauty & the Beast*, in *Cinderella*. It's the story of a woman who finds her truth by staying home. Her realization does not come alone in a forest, but by establishing domestic relationships. It is the story of the princess who waits in her tower, yearning, for the prince who will come one day.

4 So what is the connection between these story cycles, which have expressed the experience of masculinity and femininity so often in so many cultures? The feminine stories are sidelined, marginalized, their quest and

their realization seen as immature, feeble, as the male hero is exalted. Yet there is always another story, another way of seeing.

5 And that other story starts with the irrational desire of a woman.

❖

6 Once upon a time, it seems, there were two crocodiles, who lived together happily in the Ganges. One day a *yearning* arose in the wife, and she said to her husband, 'Darling, there is something I must have.'

7 'What is that, my dear?' answered the genial husband.

8 'The heart of the monkey king,' she said.

9 'But my dear, monkeys are not our natural prey! They are too clever by far to allow me to catch one.'

10 'I don't care how you do it,' she replied, 'but caught he must be. If I don't get the monkey's heart, I shall die right here.'

11 'Never mind, dear,' said the crocodile. 'I shall get it for you at once.'

12 He swam downstream until he saw the monkey king eating a fig by the bank. He said to him, 'Good day, dear monkey. I say, why are you eating such poor fruit? The other side of the river is full of the most luscious mangoes!'

13 'Well, my good friend,' said the monkey, 'I can't swim so far.'

14 'Hmm,' said the crocodile, 'I see your problem. I tell you what: how about you jump on my back, and I'll take you over to the far shore?'

15 'Terrific,' said the trusting monkey, 'let's go!'

16 So he clambered on the back of the crocodile and they set out. But when they were in midstream, the crocodile sank down, plunging the monkey under water.

17 'What?' said the monkey between splutterings. 'What are you doing?'

18 'You fool,' said the crocodile. 'Did you really think I wanted to take you to get some more fruits? Not a bit of it. My wife wants to eat your heart.'

19 'Really?' said the monkey, thinking fast. 'Well, I'd be happy to oblige, but I'm afraid there's a bit of a problem. You see, we monkeys spend all day leaping about the trees. If we were to keep our hearts inside us, they'd get all shaken up and useless. So we take them out in the morning and hang them in a tree for the day. See, over there?' And he pointed to a fig tree that was hanging clusters of fruit. 'If you want my heart, just pop me over there and I'll get it for you, no problems.'

20 'All right, then,' said the crocodile. 'But no funny business!'

21 The crocodile took the monkey to the shore, where he leapt off and scampered up the bank. Then he turned and laughed at the crocodile. 'You silly crocodile! When have you ever heard of a beast hanging their heart on a tree? I've outwitted you—your body may be big, but your mind is tiny!'

22 Sad and miserable, the crocodile returned home—to face his wife.[11]

23 A witty tale, full of observations about animal nature, and plenty of fun for the kids. Like many popular tales, variants are widely distributed.[12] The most obvious 'moral' of the story is that greed is bad, especially when it involves violence. The female crocodile's whim is entirely selfish, and she cares not for the harm done to the monkey—or indeed, the difficulties that will be faced by her husband. The ruse is undone, in good Buddhist style, through cleverness rather than force. Such tales help to show kids how to deal with schoolyard bullies; and their lessons are not irrelevant for adult bullies either.

24 The deeper implications of the story emerge from the monkey's laugh: how could the crocodile be so silly as to think monkeys keep their hearts in a tree? Who would imagine such a thing?

25 Well, for a start, anyone who's read *The Golden Bough*. Frazer documents at length the notion of an external soul: a physical object that is preserved independent from the body, and on which life depends.[13] The monkey's heart is clearly such an object, but our Jātaka has reduced the external soul to an object of superstitious nonsense, fit only for the mindless credulity of the crocodile. The persistence of the motif, however, suggests that the story may have deeper roots than appear at first. What, after all, is the wife longing for? Just a piece of flesh? Why, then, it is the heart of the monkey, the cleverest of beasts; and why, of all monkeys, the king (who the Buddhist version makes out to be the Bodhisatta)? Is it too much to wonder that her wish was not just an irrational longing for taste, but something that the monkey's heart symbolized on a deeper level—like wisdom?

❖

26 It might seem far-fetched to read a little fable like this as a parable of the search for wisdom. But our story is far from unique. The theme of a woman's *yearning* is the defining element in a cycle of about nineteen stories in the Pali Jātaka collection.[14] Each of these stories tells of a kind

of desire, known by the special term *dohaḷa*, or *dohada* in Sanskrit, which is found among women alone.

27 One of these is the Vidhurapaṇḍita Jātaka, one of the most complex and rewarding of all the Jātaka tales.[15] I can only offer a brief summary here. It is the story of the great sage Vidhura. His fame reaches even to the *nāga* realm, where there is a queen called Vimalā. When Vimalā hears of Vidhura, she lies on her couch pretending to be ill. The king came to see her, worried that she was so thin and pale.

> 28 'O king,' she said, 'there is a *yearning* in women that will not abate. I must have the heart of Vidhura the sage.'
>
> 29 'My dear,' said the *nāga* king, 'ask for the moon or the sun or the wind and I will bring them to you. But how I am to bring you the heart of the sage?'
>
> 30 When he spoke she turned away from him, covering her face with her robe, and lay there saying, 'If I do not get it, I will die right here.'
>
> 31 The *nāga* queen's daughter undertook the quest. Using all her wiles she ensnared a powerful *yakkha*, who went in disguise to the land in the human realm where the sage lived and challenged the king to a game of dice. To entice the king he staked a great price: a magic gem in which one could see everything. The *yakkha* won, and for his prize he demanded the sage Vidhura; thus in aiming for knowledge of all things, the king lost his wisdom. After many adventures the sage learnt of the quest for his heart. Unafraid, he asked to be brought before the princess, even if it meant his life, thinking, 'Vimalā has no need for my heart.'
>
> 32 He was taken to the *nāga* realm and brought before the king. The sage taught the Dhamma, and all were delighted. The *nāga* king exclaimed, 'The heart of sages is their wisdom!'
>
> 33 That morning the human king had a dream. At the door of the palace was a great tree, whose trunk was wisdom, whose branches were virtues and which was covered in all riches and auspicious signs. A black man dressed in red came bearing weapons. He cut down the tree and took it away, although all the people lamented. Soon after, though, he returned and planted the tree once more in its old place. The king immediately understood the dream: the sage Vidhura was to be returned to him unharmed. And so it came to pass.

34 The search for wisdom, which was so faintly suggested in the fable of the crocodile and the monkey, has in this high myth been brought to the

surface, made entirely conscious. The desire of the woman, though still mysterious, is not irrational or harmful, but leads only to benefit. Her action manifests as inaction. She lies as if dead, while the whole story revolves around her in her absence.

35 In the coda of the story, the human king interprets events with the help of a dream. His unconscious mind is telling the same story through symbols that his waking life experiences as facts. Through this symbolic truth he understands the deeper reaches of the events which he has been a part of: the removal of the tree (of life and wisdom) by the man dressed as Death is not the end, but is merely part of the normal cycle of birth and death. The destruction of the tree is always followed by renewal. This timeless truth, the heart of all myth, is revealed to him in a dream. It appears as a prophecy, but is nothing more than the understanding of the cycles of nature. Once he understands this he knows that renewal must happen; it is simply a matter of waiting for the inevitable.

❖

36 These two stories stem from the same scenario, the quest by a man to achieve the thing yearned for by a woman. In the 'lower' form of the myth the quest fails, while in the 'higher' form it succeeds. But this is not always the case. Sometimes the story appears in base form, and yet still succeeds.

> 37 One time there was a jackal called Māyāvī. His wife conceived a *yearning* for redfish. The husband agreed to find one, although he had no idea how a jackal could catch such a thing. The jackal had somehow to figure out how a land animal could catch a fish. But as it turned out, the answer was simple. He came across two otters who had just caught a nice juicy redfish, and were arguing about which one would get to eat which part. When they saw the jackal coming, they entreated him.
>
> 38 'O Lord of the grey grass-color, would you be so kind as divide this fish fairly between us?'
>
> 39 'That is a simple matter,' said the wily jackal. 'I have decided many such cases. Let it be thus. For you, friend otter, the head; and for you, friend otter, the tail. I myself will take the middle as legal fee!' Leaving the otters downcast and depressed, he ran off with the best part and presented it to his wife.[16]

40 This is a popular and widely-distributed folk parable. Jokes about lawyers, it seems, never go out of fashion.

41 The jackal is just about the lowest character in Indic myth. Here, however, he is becoming rather more like the 'wily coyote', who in Native American Okanogan myth is given the job of Trickster precisely because he is universally despised. The Trickster's chief power is transformation. He is a true master of illusion: Māyāvī.

42 Who's the hero in this story? The dumb otters or the tricksy jackal? Actually, no-one; the editors distance the story from Buddhism by saying the Bodhisatta was a deity who observed the events from a nearby tree.

❖

43 While Māyāvī the jackal succeeds in his very limited quest, in other cases the quest is far more difficult. The hero may fail, even in the most exalted tellings. Such is the Chaddanta Jātaka, which is another of those extraordinary long Jātakas, full of unexpected detail, of which we can only present an impoverished summary.[17]

> 44 The Bodhisatta was born as a magnificent royal white elephant with six tusks. He was the head of eight thousand elephants, all of whom could fly through the air with their psychic powers. They lived at lake Chaddanta in the remotest Himalayas, in a golden cave.
>
> 45 The Bodhisatta had two wives. Due to some trivial incidents, one wife conceived a jealousy of the other and a hatred for the Bodhisatta. She died and was reborn as the maiden Subhaddā in the Madda country, and became the chief queen of the king of Benares.
>
> 46 Finally she was in a position to take revenge. She anointed her body with oil, put on a soiled cloth, and lay down as if sick. The king sat by her side and asked what was wrong. She replied that she had a *yearning*, as it were in a dream, for that which she could not obtain. The king promised her anything she wanted, so she asked for all the hunters in the realm to be assembled.
>
> 47 She told the hunters of her yearning. But they were skeptical, wondering where on earth they could find this beast who appeared only in a dream. But she spotted one of the hunters: broad of foot, calf swollen like a basket, big in the knee and ribs, thick-bearded, with yellow teeth, disfigured with scars. His name was Soṇuttara, and in his past life he had been an enemy of the Bodhisatta. The queen took him to the roof of the palace, and pointed to the north.

48 'There!' she said, 'Past seven vast mountains there is the golden cave. There dwells the elephant with his six tusks and his vast company of huge, grim tuskers. They wait and watch, ready to grind to death any human who comes to their secret place.'

49 Though terrified, he accepted the task. The queen made elaborate preparations, ordering all manner of mountaineering and wilderness gear. He set off on the impossible journey. He ascended the mountains by hammering in pegs and tying ropes to them, and he descended like a spider at the end of a rope; but on the greatest cliffs he cast himself to the wind, and flew down with his leather parachute—or so they say.[18]

50 The hunter appeared before the elephant. The great beast asked the hunter what he was seeking, and he explained how he had been sent by Subhaddā for the tusks. Realizing that this was his former wife, the Bodhisatta knew that she wanted him dead.

51 The elephant allowed the hunter to cut off his tusks, although he knew it meant his life. But the beast was too large and the hunter could not reach. So the Bodhisatta lay down before the hunter, who climbed his trunk and stood upon his head. He stood with his foot in the Bodhisatta's mouth, thrust in the saw, and cut the tusk at the root. The elephant's mouth was filled with blood. But despite the agony, the hunter was still not strong enough to cut the tusks fully. So the Bodhisatta asked the hunter to raise the tip of his weakened trunk and place it on the saw; then he sawed his own tusks off.

52 Giving them to the hunter, he said, 'It is not because I do not value these tusks that I give them to you, but because the tusks of Awakening are far more valuable.' He gave the hunter leave to go. But the Bodhisatta died before his wife returned with the herd.

53 By the magic of the tusks the hunter returned to Benares in just seven days. He presented the tusks to the queen, saying, 'The elephant, against whom you had a grudge for a slight offence, has been slain by me.'

54 The queen placed the tusks in her lap, and realized that she had killed her husband, who she had loved so dearly. Remembering his nobility, she was filled with sorrow beyond enduring; her heart broke and she died that very day.

55 This story, with its betrayal by the beloved, its noble being who goes to a sordid death of his own volition, glad to sacrifice his own life for the sake of all creation, is perhaps the closest that the Buddhist scriptures

come to the story of the Gospels. It is one of the few Jātakas that dwells at length on vivid details, giving extraordinarily detailed descriptions of his mountaineering and abseiling abilities; in this story technology and human ingenuity, rather than magic, enables the hero's superhuman feats. The hunter, who remains unredeemed, is Devadatta, while the wife is a bhikkhuni in this life. The story is easily recognized as a variant on the same tale we have heard before, the tale of the crocodile, the jackal, or the *nāga* queen.

CHAPTER 37

THAT INDEFINABLE YEARNING

DOHAḶA ARISES, AND THE MAN SPRINGS INTO ACTION. He might briefly hesitate or question, but soon he is given over to the woman's will. She is entirely passive; often she complains of illness or lies down, threatening to not move until she dies. Sometimes she gets what she wants, sometimes not. Any manner of means may be used to obtain her ends, but in the highest forms of the myth the goal is achieved through compassion.

2 The object of her longing is essentially mysterious. It may be a rare food, a treasure, or the gift of Dhamma. It is something outside the norm, something difficult or impossible to get. Some stories hint that the true prize is no less than immortality itself. Our jackals or crocodiles had to leave their normal domains; the hunter had to leave civilization entirely. In a twist on the usual heroic theme of the ordinary man leaving the human realm to venture into the weird, the *nāgas* left their realm to enter the human realm, which was weird enough for them. In whatever form it takes, the quest for the prize is full of twists & turns.

❖

3 One time the Bodhisatta and his wife were outcasts. She conceived a *yearning* for the taste of mango.

4 'But my dear,' said the husband ineffectually, 'this is not the season. There are no mangoes. Here, let me get for you some other fruit.'

> 5 'I must have a mango,' she replied, 'or I will die right here.'
>
> 6 In desperation, the husband brooded until he remembered that in the king's garden there stood a mango tree that, according to reputation, fruited all year. It would, of course, be death to steal the king's mangoes, yet in thrall to his wife's wishes he set out nonetheless.
>
> 7 He crept into the palace garden by night, and climbed the mango tree, clambering from limb to limb in search of fruit. But his search took so long that the day began to break, and he thought he must stay up the tree until the next evening, or he would be caught as a thief.
>
> 8 At that time the king was learning the sacred texts from his chaplain under the mango tree. The king sat on a high seat, while his teacher sat on a low seat.
>
> 9 The outcast thought to himself, 'That's not right. The king should respect his teacher by sitting below him to receive the lesson. But am I not the same, taking orders like this from my wife?'
>
> 10 He jumped from the tree before the king and his chaplain, and said, 'Your Highness! I'm ruined, you're a fool, and this priest is dead!'
>
> 11 The king was so astounded that rather than have him arrested straight away, he asked the outcast to explain his extraordinary behavior. He was pleased with what the man said, and asked what caste he belonged to.
>
> 12 'I am an outcast, Your Highness,' he said.
>
> 13 'If you were from a good family,' said the king, 'I would have made you king in my stead. But be that as it may: I shall remain king by daytime, and you shall be the king of night.'
>
> 14 With that the king laid a wreath of red flowers upon his breast, making him the City Guardian. From this, so it seems, is derived the custom for the City Guardian to wear a wreath of red flowers. And from that day on, the king never failed to take a low seat when learning his lessons.[1]

15 The 'moral' of the story, as reflected in the framing narrative, is that one should never teach Dhamma to one who shows the wrong attitude by taking a high seat. A perfectly decent lesson in etiquette, no doubt. Yet the story cannot be read without thinking of darker things. The 'king of the night'—what a title! We are in the realm of the periodic regicide, the outcast who substitutes for the king, but in the end is redeemed as well. He gains his title by stealing fruit from the grove—which is proven to be

sacred by the fact that it fruits all year round—just as the challenger to Frazer's King of the Wood in Nemi must first steal the Golden Bough from the sacred grove. The outcast's role as a sacrificial victim is confirmed by the wreath of red flowers. It is not at all implausible that a post such as City Guardian might have been enjoyed, for a short or longer time, by the outcast marked as sacrificial victim in the king's stead. Enjoying his position too much to relinquish it, a means was found, so it seems, to make his post a permanent one. Perhaps another victim was found.

16 The wife is not mentioned at the end, but no doubt she would have been well pleased, and could have enjoyed mangoes all year round. She had sent her husband out on a perilous mission at the mysterious behest of her own unconscious urges; and in accomplishing his mission, he became the lord of the darkness, the governor of those same mysterious forces. He could accomplish this only through transgression, breaking into the perilous garden of the king and then, while hung in his tree, suspended between the earth and the sky, he shifted to a new level of values. The original quest was, it seems, forgotten, as he discovered something infinitely more valuable.

17 His conscious mind resented the fact that he was running around at the whim of a woman, and the overt moral of the story is to reassert traditional values of hierarchy. Yet this only happened because he risked all in violating the hierarchy. An outcast in the king's garden, perched over the heads of both the king and his priest, who dared criticize them for not maintaining the accepted customs of respect! It is the very daring, the outrageousness of his acts that guarantee his safety. If he had not risked all, if he had refused his wife's call and kept to the narrow confines of his predictable life, none of this would have happened. There would be no story for us to read.

❖

18 The motif of *dohaḷa* is not restricted to Buddhist stories, as it is a major trope of Indian literature generally. It usually refers to the mysterious desires of a pregnant woman, although in the Jātaka versions the women are usually not pregnant. It is believed that the physical and/or kammic influence of the child manifests in the mother. Her desires, no matter how outrageous, must be fulfilled, or else the child may be harmed. This is not

merely a literary device, but is still a belief in Indic societies. In the West, a pregnant woman's desires would, by and large, be indulged if possible, but in Indian culture this becomes a sacred duty. The husband must do whatever he can. There are plenty of stories of how this license is misused. In Sri Lanka it is said that a woman who wants to meet her lover can simply mention to her husband her need for a distant object of desire, knowing he'll be safely out of the way while the lover's tryst took place.

19 As an example of a non-Buddhist *dohaḷa*, here is the Jaina tale of King Dadhivahana, who reigned in Campā.[2] A *yearning* arose in his pregnant Queen, Padmavatī. She wished to sport through the parks and groves on the back of a noble elephant, arrayed in the royal regalia, with the parasol of sovereignty held over her by the king himself. The King could not resist her wish, so they mounted the great royal elephant. Now, at that time it was the beginning of the rainy season, and the air was full of fragrance. When the elephant got wind of the enticing odors of the fertile earth, he galloped away in abandon, leaving all behind him. The royal couple was swept away in his mad rush, so when the king saw that the elephant was to pass under a banyan tree, he told his wife to grab hold of it. But though she tried her best, she could not, and the king was left clinging on to the banyan tree as she was carried into the deep forest. She could only dismount when the elephant, weary from its running, plunged into a great lake. She had escaped, but was lost, on the verge of despair. However, she encountered some kind nuns at a nearby Jaina convent. The nuns were sympathetic to her situation, yet when the child was born she exposed it to perish in a cemetery. But he was found and survived. He grew up to become the Paccekabuddha Karakandu. In this story the ritual and fertility motifs lie close to the surface; from the intoxicated sensual rush through the swelling forest was born a supreme ascetic.

20 The word itself is explained with three possible etymologies. *Dur-hadaya*, or 'ill-heart', expresses a sadness and possible malevolence. *Dve-hadaya*, or 'two-heart', says something quite different: the woman 'with child', who possesses her child's heart as well as her own. *Doha-da*, on the other hand, means 'giver of milk'.

21 The classic western study of the topic was by Bloomfield, who classified *dohaḷa* stories into six types. The various types of *dohaḷa*: #1 injure or en-

danger the husband; #2 prompt the husband to heroism; #3 form a pious aspiration;[3] #4 are a mere literary ornament; #5 are feigned by the woman; or #6 are settled by tricking the woman.[4]

22 This classification, though cited favorably,[5] is messy and incomplete. #1 and #2 are little different, since any act of true heroism involves danger and often death. #5 and #6 refer to the means, not to the adventure itself. Obviously, a feigned *dohaḷa* may lead the husband to heroism and danger; and satisfying it with a trick is merely the husband's failure to rise to true heroism. #3 and #4 are something quite different again; they refer to decadent styles that adopt the trope for either moral edification or entertainment.

23 More importantly than the classificatory jumble, Bloomfield's study, as well as the later works on the subject, ignore the higher dimensions of our story. Durt's relatively recent study, noting that most previous work on the topic was in the early 20th century, expresses surprise that it has not been noticed more recently in the age of 'Gender Studies'. What is more surprising to me is that he does not consider how the treatment of the motif may have been conditioned by patriarchal perspectives, which inevitably see a woman's desires as problematic.

24 This problematic is not resolved by the Freudian approach taken by Gilbert. She relates the *dohaḷa* with the actual experiences of women, noting that what for the Indic tradition is a spiritual concern is treated as irrational, and hence irrelevant, whims by modern medicine. Only when the cravings involve forms of food do the doctors take any interest in the nutritional implications. Gilbert, however, sees the cravings as a symbolic projection of the mother's psychological state. As the Indic tradition sees the mother influenced by her child's 'heart', Gilbert sees the mother's neediness as an infantile regression that corresponds to the state of the child within her. The mother feels ambivalent about the new presence within her, and wishes to either expel it (through vomiting) or assuage her guilt by re-assimilating (through eating).

25 The mother's behavior frequently shows a rejection of her female role, since she demands foods rather than preparing them, taking advantage of what in some cultures would be a rare relief from domestic servitude. Although her wishes are normally ignored or marginalized, while in the

state of *dohaḷa* she becomes the master, a situation that is endorsed in literature, custom, and even law. Since she is in the unique position of wielding power over her husband, the *dohaḷa* story can easily be seen as a revenge motif. The wife can finally harm or get rid of the husband who she unconsciously resents because of how he controls, and often enough, punishes her. In the context of pregnancy, as the mother's body adjusts to the new presence within her, she experiences confusion and resistance, and projects this on to the husband who put this thing inside her.

26 Gilbert argues that the oral literature on *dohaḷa* can be explained in terms of the rejection of the fetus and male envy. This approach works in such stories as the conception of Ajātasattu. The mother conceived a *dohaḷa* to drink blood from the right knee of her husband, the good king Bimbisāra. Bimbisāra asked the astrologers about this, and they told him that his son would kill him and seize the throne. True to character, Bimbisāra thought nothing of his own life. He went to his wife, cut open his knee and allowed the blood to flow into a golden dish for her to drink. In this kind of bizarre and morbid fantasy an Oedipal interpretation is invited; however, unlike Oedipus, Ajātasattu is not rejected by his parents, but was brought up with love and accepted even in his worst moments. The flow of blood from the husband's knee is a reproduction of the menstrual flow, which for the wife has ceased during pregnancy. Her blood is being held within and curdled to make new life, and she needs him to experience just what this means.

27 Such an approach, however, is inadequate to account for the *dohaḷa* motif as it appears in the Buddhist tales. For a start it is rarely to do with with actual pregnancy. But more fundamentally, this treatment ignores the woman's actual role in producing life. She is the creatrix, not he, and it is perverse to read such stories as envy of the male and need for revenge. The highest forms of the myth have nothing to do with revenge and cannot be read as neurosis. They do not tell of a woman satisfying an infantile, irrational whim, but the flowering of the whole world.

CHAPTER 38

THE FLOWERING OF THE WORLD

THE *DOHAḶA* STORY-TYPE STEMS FROM A VERY OLD MYTHIC FORM. This is best preserved in the folk/fairy-tale/mythic stylings of the Jātakas, and so I will leave out of consideration the decadent edificatory or literary use of the trope. Basic features include the expression of yearning by a woman; she is often lying or in a dream; she wants a specific and apparently irrational object; a man searches for that object; he may succeed or not, but if he does succeed there is often an unexpected bounty; and the means he uses varies, sometimes tricksy, sometimes violent.

2 The different tellings of this story can be classified as 'lower', 'middle' or 'higher'. In each case the goal that is sought, and the means by which it is sought, is appropriate for the characters. The 'lower' forms tell of jackals or crocodiles. The object of desire is limited and so the degree of transformation is limited. The 'middle' forms of the story feature human beings and, as for example the story of the outcast and the mango, move towards a more profound transformation, a genuine transcendence of limitations.

3 The most common form, however, is an exalted quest for a mythical animal, where the means of success is compassion. The myth, which is broken and partial in lesser tellings, here approaches its own truth; the archetype lies close to the surface, straining to break through the veneer of

contingent fact and reveal the timeless truth. As one of the finest examples of this type, here is the magnificent Mahāmora Jātaka.[1]

4 Once upon a time, while Brahmadatta was king in Benares, the Bodhisatta was conceived as the son of a peahen in a border region. She laid a golden egg; and when the time was right, it cracked open to reveal a tiny golden peachick, with eyes bright red as a *guñja* fruit, a beak like coral, and three red stripes that ran around his throat and down the middle of his back. When he grew, his became very large and all the other peafowl took him as their king.

5 One day he saw his own reflection in the water. He thought to himself, 'My body is very beautiful. As long as I stay with others among the paths of men, I shall be a danger to them. I should go away to a secret place in the Himalaya.'

6 He left in the dead of night while the other peafowl were asleep, and crossing three ranges of mountains, he settled in the fourth. There he found a great lake in the forest, covered with lotus, and nearby a hill shaded by a huge banyan tree. The peacock alighted in the branches of the tree, and there he looked to the hill, where saw a delightful cave which he made his home. This place was impossible to climb to from above or below; it was free from predatory birds, wildcats, snakes, or men, and was altogether delightful.

7 The next morning he emerged from the cave and as he watched the sun rise he sang Brahma-verses of protection.

8 'He rises, the One King who sees all
Of golden hue, shedding light over the earth
I pay homage to Him!
May you guard me safe through this day!'

9 Then the Bodhisatta, having worshiped the sun, sang in homage to the Buddhas of the past and their greatness.

10 'Those saints, knowers of all truth,
I worship, may they protect me!
I pay homage to the Awakened ones,
And homage to Awakening!
Homage to the freed,
And homage to freedom!'

11 After singing these hymns of protection the peacock went in search of food. When he returned in the evening, he perched at the top of the

hill facing west, and as the night fell he sang once more in homage to the sun, and the Buddhas. Thus his life passed in safety and peace.

12 Now at that time the chief queen of Benares was Khemā. As the dawn broke she lay dreaming, and a golden peacock came to her. The glorious bird taught her the Dhamma and she listened with delight. But when he finished his teaching he flew away, and she awoke as she cried out, 'The king of peacocks is leaving—catch him!'

13 The queen reflected that if she told the king of her dream, he would not believe her. So she lay down as if ill.

14 The king came and asked, 'My dear, what is wrong?'

15 'I have a *yearning*,' she said.

16 'What is your desire, my dear?' said the king.

17 'I wish to hear the Dhamma from a golden peacock,' she said.

18 'But my dear, where are we to find such a peacock?'

19 'My king, if I do not get it, I shall die.'

20 'Do not worry, my dear,' said the king. 'If one exists anywhere we shall find it.'

21 The king asked for advice from his Brahman councilors, who told him that a golden peacock was indeed spoken of in their texts. But they did not know where one could be found, so they had the king summon the hunters from all the realm.

22 Only one man knew where he may be found. This hunter had not seen the golden peacock himself, but his father had spied it one day as he sat on the hilltop. He told nobody of this until he lay on his death bed, and with his last words he revealed his secret to his son.

23 The king gave money to the hunter and instructed him to catch the bird for his queen. The hunter climbed the mountains and found the bird. He lay traps all around, but each day, due to the power of the protective chants, the peacock eluded the snares. The hunter persisted, but he died without success. Queen Khemā, too, pined away and died before the peacock was caught.

24 The king was furious. To ensure the peacock's capture, he had the story inscribed on a golden plate, guaranteeing that whoever would eat the peacock's flesh would be forever young and never die.

25 The king passed away, and the next king read the inscription. Wishing to live forever, he sent another hunter in search of the golden peacock, but he too died without success. In this way six kings died.

26 The seventh king sent a seventh hunter, who pursued the bird for seven years without success. Then he reflected why the bird was able to escape the snares, and thought it must be due to the power of

the protection mantras. The hunter then determined to destroy the bird's holy power. He captured a peahen and brought her to the golden peacock's hill. As he was about to sing his mantra in the morning, the peahen uttered her cry; and the lust that had laid hidden for seven thousand years reared up like a cobra spreading its hood. Forgetting his mantra, he went to the peahen blind with lust, and put his foot right in the snare.

27 The hunter looked at the peacock dangling upside down in the trap, and thought, 'Such a mighty and virtuous being has been brought so low by the power of lust. It is not proper to hand him over for the sake of a bribe. What are the king's honors to me? I will let him go.'

28 Thinking that it would be dangerous to approach the beast too close, he readied an arrow to cut the bonds of the snare. The peacock thought his end was near, and he said to the hunter, 'If you take me to the king alive, he will give you a great reward.'

29 But the hunter reassured the peacock that he did not mean to harm him, but to release him. The peacock asked why he had such a change of heart.

30 The hunter asked, 'O king of peacocks, what happiness is gained by one who abstains from killing, who gives to all beings the gift of fearlessness?'

31 'One is praised in this life,' said the peacock, 'and after death one goes to heaven.'

32 'But some say there is no such thing as gods,' said the hunter. 'After this life, one passes into non-existence. Good and evil deeds, giving and so on, are declared to be useless. This is what the perfected ones say, and because I trust them, this is why I trap birds.'

33 Wishing to convince him of the existence of other worlds, the peacock said, 'You can see this sun and moon, evident to anyone as they proceed through the sky. Do men say they belong to this world or another?'

34 'They belong to another world, for men say they are gods,' said the hunter.

35 'Then those who teach that good and evil are without cause are refuted,' said the peacock.

36 The hunter pondered and said, 'What you say is true. It cannot be that good and evil have no result. But how then are we to act? How is one to live? What should I practice, and what ascetic vows should I pursue if I am to escape from hell?'

37 The peacock thought to himself that if he revealed the full truth of the Dhamma to the man, the world would become as if hollow and meaningless to him, so he resolved to teach him the doctrine accepted by the eternalists.[2] 'You should go to see the good ascetics,' he said, 'clad in ochre robes, who walk for alms and eat only in the morning. They will explain about the good for this life and the next, in accord with their own understanding.'

38 When he heard this the hunter was overcome with fear of hell. But this was no ordinary man; he was filled with the perfections of a Paccekabuddha. His knowledge was on the point of ripening, like a lotus that stands looking for the touch of the sun's rays. As he heard the peacock's teaching he investigated the three characteristics and penetrated the knowledge of a Paccekabuddha. At the same instant, the peacock was released from the snare.

39 The hunter thought of the many birds that he held captive at his home, and asked the peacock what he should do about this; for omniscient Bodhisattas have greater understanding of means than Paccekabuddhas.

40 The peacock answered, 'You have overcome all defilements and realized Awakening! Make an Act of Truth, and there shall be no creature left in bonds in the whole of India.'

41 So the hunter declared, 'All those birds I have bound, in their hundreds and thousands—today I give them life! They are free, may they fly away to their own homes.'

42 When this was said, not only were the birds in his home released, but all creatures were released. Not one was left in bondage, even a single cat.

43 The Paccekabuddha rubbed his head, and immediately the features of a householder disappeared and he looked just like one gone forth, an Elder of sixty years, with the eight requisites. He paid homage to the peacock and departed keeping him on his right. Then he flew in the air and went to live in a cave on the side of Mount Nanda. Meanwhile, the peacock arose from the snare, took his food, and returned home.

❖

44 The story starts with the golden egg: a little piece of wonder. It is a perfect shape, made of the perfect, untarnishable material; eternal and yet of the nature of fire. It is a little avatar of the great golden egg in the

sky, the *hiraṇyagarbha* that is Pajāpati the lord of creation, whose shadow is eternal life and death, the One King of the breathing and the seeing, the Lord of man and bird and beast. In the Ṛg Veda's *Hiraṇyagarbha śūkta*, Pajāpati is invoked with the repeated question 'Who is the god we should worship?'[3] The Vedic for 'who' is *ka*, the first syllable of Indic languages, created in the back of the throat, and a fitting question for the first creator of all.

45 Like any divine birth, we know that the being to be born is something special. He is already eternal, oldest and yet youngest—as was Siddhattha in his final birth. His pre-eminence is readily acknowledged by the other birds. He does not have to struggle for power, but is freely granted it as his natural right. He rules wisely and well, but he sees deeply into men's hearts, and he knows that their greed would pursue him. Maybe he has heard too many stories about the geese who laid golden eggs; but in any case he decides to make for the hills. The mythic is, as it must be, in flight from the prosaic. Its magic guarantees its downfall.

46 In the remotest Himalaya the peacock king finds his refuge. It is a sanctuary of nature. Even 2000 years ago, humanity brought about the diminishing of nature's wonder. This is a story of safety; the peacock flees his flock fearing their safety; he lives in the remotest sanctuary; he sings mantras for protection; and the outcome is safety for all beasts.

47 The sanctuary is perfect, an idyll that is only just of this world. The material perfection is mirrored in the spiritual harmony that the peacock finds. Each day he sings his mantra to the sun, which on one level is a conventional prayer: praise followed by a call for help. But the peacock himself is more than just an animal, he is no less than an avatar of the sun itself. We see this in his birth from a golden egg; in his golden hue, surrounded by a glorious halo of peacock feathers; and most of all since eating his flesh is said to bestow immortality. The fact that this started as an insincere ruse on the part of the vengeful king makes no difference. The identification of the magical beast's flesh as the source of immortality is an ancient motif; gold would have been seen as immortal as long as it was known to humanity. Our story is a Buddhist adaption of a much older Brahmanical myth, and it is entirely normal for Buddhists to depict the origin of Brahmanical beliefs and customs as sheer trickery.

48 The mixed origins of the story emerge with perfect clarity in the prayers of homage. The first prayer, offered to the sun, the 'One King' *ekarāja*, is suggestively Vedic in its style and form. It is reminiscent of the *Hiraṇya-garbha śūkta*, where Pajāpati, in a rare suggestion of Vedic monotheism, is called the 'One King'.[4] Our Jātaka even goes so far as to call this prayer a *brahmamanta*. It is unusual to find the Buddhist texts so blatantly adopting Brahmanical prayers. Perhaps the story was so tightly woven with solar imagery that it could not be easily removed; and at the same time, it could be well adapted for a Buddhist purpose.

49 Be that as it may, the text does not attempt to disguise its origins, but merely places a Buddhist verse after the Brahmanical one. The Buddhist verse is harmonized with the Brahmanical by use of quasi-Brahmanical terms (*brāhmaṇa, vedagū*), but these are used in Buddhist senses ('holy one', 'accomplished in knowledge'), and the verse is pure Buddhism, just as the previous is pure monotheistic Brahmanism.

50 Such adoption allowed Buddhist devotees to continue with their accustomed rituals, as long as these did not offend Buddhist precepts. But it also suggests a more interesting notion, that Buddhist spiritual development is an evolution past the Brahmanical. The more polemical of the Buddhist texts simply dismiss Brahmanism as hocus-pocus, as our text suggests in the lie that the peacock's flesh grants immortality. Yet this solar deity is the Bodhisatta, on the verge of Buddhahood; and although he is fallible, his wisdom is greater than even a Paccekabuddha.

51 After the introduction giving the backstory of the peacock king, we are introduced to Khemā, queen of Benares. Like all the female 'heroes' of the *dohaḷa* cycle, she is passive, yet inexorable as death itself. She dreams, lies as if ill, and makes impossible demands. Her dream is a genuine prophecy: the peacock teaches the Dhamma. Except she does not see the prophecy fulfilled. In the world of the story, it is the hunter who is taught the Dhamma. But in the 'real' world, the peacock teaches the Dhamma to us, the readers. Khemā's dream is a prophecy of our future, not hers. The entire story springs from her unconscious. She is the wellspring of creative energy that sets all events in motion, while she remains still, unchanged.

52 Her passivity might not sit well with modern notions that women should excel in the male field of activity. Yet in ancient times, passivity was not

regarded as a negative thing. In fact, a king in China or Japan was expected to maintain an extraordinary stillness, since the stability of the realm depended on it. According to Frazer:

> 53 At a certain stage of early society the king or priest is often thought to be endowed with supernatural powers or to be an incarnation of a deity, and consistently with this belief the course of nature is supposed to be more or less under his control, and he is held responsible for bad weather, failure of the crops, and similar calamities. To some extent it appears to be assumed that the king's power over nature, like that over his subjects and slaves, is exerted through definite acts of will; and therefore if drought, famine, pestilence, or storms arise, the people attribute the misfortune to the negligence or guilt of their king, and punish him accordingly with stripes and bonds, or, if he remains obdurate, with deposition and death. Sometimes, however, the course of nature, while regarded as dependent on the king, is supposed to be partly independent of his will. His person is considered, if we may express it so, as the dynamical center of the universe, from which lines of force radiate to all quarters of the heaven; so that any motion of his—the turning of his head, the lifting of his hand—instantaneously affects and may seriously disturb some part of nature. He is the point of support on which hangs the balance of the world, and the slightest irregularity on his part may overthrow the delicate equipoise. The greatest care must, therefore, be taken both by and of him; and his whole life, down to its minutest details, must be so regulated that no act of his, voluntary or involuntary, may disarrange or upset the established order of nature. Of this class of monarchs the Mikado or Dairi, the spiritual emperor of Japan, is or rather used to be a typical example. He is an incarnation of the sun goddess, the deity who rules the universe, gods and men included; once a year all the gods wait upon him and spend a month at his court.

54 The notion that a king controls the weather and other natural forces through his virtue—or lack thereof—is a standard one in the Jātakas.[5] Less common is the degree of stillness that was required of the Mikado:

> 55 In ancient times, he was obliged to sit on the throne for some hours every morning, with the imperial crown on his head, but to sit altogether like a statue, without stirring either hands or feet, head or eyes, nor indeed any part of his body, because, by this means, it was thought that he could preserve peace and tranquility in his empire;

> for if, unfortunately, he turned himself on one side or the other, or if he looked a good while towards any part of his dominions, it was apprehended that war, famine, fire, or some other great misfortune was near at hand to desolate the country. But it having been afterward discovered, that the imperial crown was the palladium, which by its immobility could preserve peace in the empire, it was thought expedient to deliver his imperial person, consecrated only to idleness and pleasures, from this burdensome duty, and therefore the crown is at present placed on the throne for some hours every morning.

56 In the Dasaratha Jātaka, which tells the Buddhist version of Rāma's story, while Rāma is in exile in the forest he sends his shoes to rule the country in his absence. It sounds like a ridiculous fabrication; but the existence of a close parallel in historical times makes me wonder whether there may not, in fact, have been kingdoms in ancient India that were ruled for a time by a pair of slippers.[6]

57 In any case, such stories allow us to evaluate Khemā's stillness in a very different light. She is not still because she is ineffectual and incapable, but because she is the source from which all activity springs. Just as the later Hindu philosophy claimed that the whole world was but a dream of Viṣṇu, the world of our story is a dream of Khemā. She sets all in motion, upsetting the balance and harmony of the land, and moving us all to a higher ethical and spiritual plane. Her dream is just a dream in a story; yet it creates the story, and as we read the story helps to create us and our world. The spiritual evolution that the story imagines is not just a game, but a very serious program to change the world for the better. Khemā's passivity is meant to create a real peace in the world, just as the stillness of a sacred king brings stability to the realm.

58 And if stillness is a supreme virtue even in a ruler, how much more so from the perspective of a contemplative religion like Buddhism? In her quietness, immobile while the world revolves around her, Khemā approaches the ideal of an Awakened One.

59 Khemā's role as an archetype of peace is confirmed when we glance at the related stories in this cycle. Of the nineteen Pali Jātakas in the *dohaḷa* cycle, there are six that deal with golden peacocks, deer, or geese. In all of these, Khemā plays the same role. Her name reveals her true nature: Khemā means 'safety', and it is a synonym for Nibbana. The men in these

stories search for Khemā. In the stories of the golden geese, this motif is duplicated, in that the geese are offered a place of refuge, a beautiful lake called 'Lake Khemā'.

60 When Khemā expresses her yearning, she knows she cannot appeal to the king in a normal way. If she just tells the king she had a dream and wants to see the golden peacock, the king would dismiss her, treat her like a silly woman. In order to bend him to her will, she must enter her archetype. It is not a matter of reasoning or persuading the king; Khemā's body must assume the classic posture. Lying down as if ill, turning her back to him, she becomes one with the other Khemās, with all the whose tales spring from their *dohaḷa*, and with creator deities everywhere. Once she has become one with her archetypal form, the king can put up no resistance. Ostensibly the commanding ruler of all, he is in fact a mere instrument of her will.

61 To satisfy her feminine demands, he turns to his masculine helpers. First the brahman advisers, who are the intelligentsia of the court. They are the custodians and interpreters of the wisdom of the ages as passed down in the patriarchal brahmanical system. Like all patriarchies, they preserve a memory of older things. Their scholastic texts tell stories of the beast of wonder, but for them it is only a legend. They have no contact with the living reality, and so are useless in the quest.

62 The king turns next to the hunters. These are a despised yet necessary caste. Hunting is one of the oldest tasks of humanity, harking back to the most primeval instincts of the mind. Hunters wore the ochre robe which we know as the symbol of the Sangha, which is why Siddhattha swapped his royal robes for a hunter's rags soon after he left the palace. Hunters live a lonely and brutal life. They deal out death, and endure all manner of dangers and hardships. Their career has been on the decline for thousands of years already, as agriculture continues its march of efficiency. By the time of our story, the hunter was already archaic, a memory of more brutal times.[7]

63 So it is no chance that the Chaddanta Jātaka depicts the hunter as the ugliest and crudest of men.[8] He is the Beast to Khemā's Beauty. This gives us a clue as to the true nature of the hunter: he is Khemā's animus. She has had a vision in a dream of the golden peacock, the glorious solar image of the

perfect Higher Masculine. But the 'real man' she encounters is the violent, crude hunter. Our story tells of the hunter's awakening to compassion through his encounter with the golden peacock; this reveals Khemā's inner transformation in her relation to her own masculine.

64 The hunter sets out on his task, but is foiled by the mantras recited by the peacock. The Buddhist tradition, while criticizing Brahmanical superstitions, generally accepts the efficacy of such acts, although it regards them as inessential for higher development. The hunter fails in his task, and both he and Khemā die. Seven generations are caught up in this quest; the quest is eternal, hence timeless.[9] It applies to everyone, all the time, and is not bound to a specific historical context.

65 The first king has become blinded with grief and anger. Khemā's original quest was for the Dhamma. She wanted to learn wisdom from the magical bird, not to kill it. The wisdom she would learn is the Dhamma that leads to the Deathless (*amata*), another Brahmanical notion adapted by the Buddhists. For Buddhists, of course, this means the escape from the cycle of birth and death for one who makes an end of greed, hatred, and delusion. Such a spiritual interpretation is found in higher Brahmanical philosophy as well, yet on the popular level this idea becomes the literal search for some substance that will guarantee immortality. The king has corrupted the spiritual quest, turned away from the true path, and diverted men's energies to the material source of immortality, which ironically leads them to their own deaths.

66 The final hunter accomplishes his task, not through strength and perseverance, but through guile. This is a critical juncture in the hero's evolution. The earliest heroes—Gilgamesh, Hercules, Achilles—are known for their strength and bravery rather than their intellect. This changed with 'wily Odysseus', who conquered Troy with his wooden horse where conventional warriors failed. Our hunter has just made this leap. Instead of sheer force, he observes and understands the peacock's behavior.

67 The peacock is a Brahmanical solar symbol of the Higher Masculinity. He embodies the aloofness and independence of the ideal Man, and finds his security through leaving relationship and finding the remotest of caves. But as far as he goes, the hunter will always find him. No matter how secure he thinks he is, the world is always encroaching; his safety can never be

more than temporary. Which is not to say that it's wrong. It still last a good few thousand years, so it's not a foolish strategy. It's just that it cannot last forever, as it is still in the circle of the world. Eventually, the hunter will climb that last mountain.

68 The hunter and the peacock are locked in conflict. Their needs can never be reconciled. The hunter is full of violence and death, and seeks fame and wealth through his exploits on behalf of the royal family. His energy and persistence are fueled by this need. The peacock, on the other hand, is content and aloof. He wants nothing more than to be left alone. And it is this one thing that the hunter cannot give him.

69 The hunter succeeds by capturing a peahen and having her seduce the peacock. A moment's lust is enough to distract his mind from his mantras of safety, and he is lost. On so tenuous a thread is hung his safety! Here, the Lower Masculine is violence and the Lower Feminine is sensuality. They ally themselves to bring down the Higher Masculine; and of course they indirectly threaten the Higher Feminine as well. For if the hunter kills the peacock, the quest is lost and the woman's transformation fails, just as in the Chaddanta Jātaka. The wish of the queen, whether she consciously realizes it or not, is for unification with the Higher Masculine, not for its destruction. Her original wish has become corrupted by the anger of the first king. With the entrapment of the peacock our story enters its most dangerous point. The quest balances on a knife's edge.

70 We arrived at this point due to one specific thing. The hunter knew that the sound of the peahen would distract the peacock. He knew this because the peacock, like himself, was a male. He saw through the *māyā* of surfaces and recognized an underlying similarity. The peacock had suppressed his sensual lust for ages; but it was still there, still connecting him to this Lower plane. It is this recognition of similarity that is the basis for compassion. Unrestrained lust broke through the peacock's purity and, for just a moment, brought him down to the hunter's level. They were so very different, but they shared this much in common.

71 Once the connection is made, the hunter is able to empathize with the peacock. No longer a remote icon, he is now trapped, mortal, on the same existential plane as the hunter. And it is through this recognition that the crucial change comes: compassion. Though covered for long years by the

hunter's cruel vocation—as the peacock's lust was covered for years by his purity—compassion arises at the peacock's plight. The hunter, emblem of all that is brute and violent in the male, is beginning to transform. Before, the peacock and hunter were two opposite poles of masculinity; but now they see a seed of each in the other, like the little dots of black and white in the *taijitu*, the classic *yin/yang* symbol.[10]

72 Rejecting worldly honors and the fear of punishment, the hunter determines to release the bird. When the peacock shows surprise, they engage in a dialogue, while the peacock is still hanging upside down; a fitting symbol for the reversal of values that is going on. The hunter is willing enough to take the peacock as his teacher, and asks about the benefit of doing good—a crucial question in Indian religions. The peacock answers conventionally enough that practicing harmlessness brings benefits both in this life and the next. In this way he follows the normal Buddhist approach to ethics. Moral conduct is primarily situated in the benefits that are observable in this very life; but this does not mean that the afterlife is ignored or denied. It is relevant to a discussion of ethics, since our choices do determine our course after death, and knowing this will influence some people to behave better here and now. But it is not necessary to believe in an afterlife in order to be ethical, as anyone can observe the benefits of ethical conduct for themselves.

73 Here, the note of skepticism that is sounded by the hunter prompts the peacock's refutation. Like most of us, the hunter is attracted to an ethical reasoning that justifies his own choices. The peacock refutes his suggestion that there is no afterlife. He points to the very visible sun and moon, and asks whether these belong to this world or the world beyond. The hunter gives the reply that must have been obvious to most people in the ancient world—they belong to another realm.[11] 'Our world' is full of mess and decay, constantly changing, fermenting; while the world above is static, serenely rotating, precise—and things don't fall down. That the stars are eternal, not tiring in their motion like earthly things, is taken as axiomatic by Aristotle.[12]

74 This very empirical contrast between the heavenly worlds and earthly life is one of the major influences on the development of ideas of life after death. Faced with the universality of decay and corruption, people coped

with the fear of death by looking to the skys. Early theories of rebirth took this all quite literally; the Upaniṣads speak of rebirth in the moon.[13] The heavens are the very meaning of 'divinity'; and even today words like *deva*, divine, and deity recognizably share the same Indo-European root, **déyw-o-* ('shining one'). It is rare, however, to find the connection between the 'heavens' and 'Heaven' put so clearly.

75 The argument sounds completely unconvincing to us: the sun and moon are gods? Of course, there's been 2000 years of science between then and now, and we all know the sun and moon are simply physical objects. Yet so many cultures have seen divinity in the celestial bodies that this argument must have had an overwhelming force. Religions such as Christianity or Islam are a later stage of development, since for them God cannot be a mere object, not matter how brilliant and ethereal. The reality of the celestial divine has become a worn-out metaphor.

76 The very fact that such an argument exists is testament to the waning power of the divine. Divinity flourishes when it overwhelms the mind, when rapture and awe are dominating powers. When reason enters, divinity diminishes. An argument about whether the sun and moon are divine is quite a different thing from our peacock's dawn song in praise of the universal Lord. Now they are reduced to squabbling over provable reality, and as the Buddha so laconically pointed out, rational argument can end up one way or the other.[14]

77 Our text makes another great leap, from the fact that there are other worlds, to the inference that our ethical conduct is crucial. This is, of course, the basic Buddhist position, shared in common with most developed religions: our conduct in this life shapes our life to come.

78 When the hunter asks for teaching, the peacock is cautious. He knows that a direct revelation of the deep truth will be too much for the hunter's tender consciousness, so he merely encouraged the hunter to frequent good teachers to learn about this life and the next. But it seems he underestimated his student, for just this much was enough for the hunter to realize full awakening as a Paccekabuddha. The hunter scrutinizes the 'three characteristics' of impermanence, suffering, and not-self, even though the peacock doesn't actually mention them.

79 This point, which is exclusively Buddhist, is an unusual feature of this particular text. How readily can a purely Buddhist Awakening be fastened on the end of a Brahmanical tale! In all the other versions of this fable, the hunter brings the golden beast to the king, where he preaches for the benefit of the king & queen. But in our current version, the hunter becomes a Paccekabuddha. The Paccekabuddha is a curious feature of Buddhology. They are rishis, sages of old, who become Awakened through their own insight, without the need for a Buddha to teach them. The element *pacceka* is usually interpreted to mean 'solitary', and as in our current case they are said to live in caves and retreats. Strictly speaking they were not always solitary—the Isigili Sutta, for example, speaks of many Paccekabuddhas living on the same hill—but they are distinguished from 'proper' Buddhas in that they do not set up a Sangha and establish a lasting dispensation. They may teach, but this is only a limited personal affair, not a systematic presentation of the Dhamma. The Paccekabuddha fulfills the need, found in all Indic religions, to acknowledge the sages of old. India has always had sages, and memories of sages older still. The Buddhist texts claim that, while many of these were practicing primitive austerities, rituals, or meditations, in some cases individuals have actually penetrated to the same truth as the Buddha.

80 The Paccekabuddha motif is a late adaptation of the text to Buddhism. This is revealed in the curious textual detail that all the beasts of the land are freed. This outcome only happens due to the intervention of the peacock; as a Bodhisatta, he had dedicated himself for countless æons for the welfare of all sentient beings. The Paccekabuddha, although free, has no aspiration to help others. Hence it is up to the Bodhisatta to liberate the animals. With the compassion that was aroused in the hunter, and led to his Awakening, he is empowered to save all beings.

CHAPTER 39

HER DREAMING

OTHER VERSIONS OF THIS STORY REVEAL YET MORE ASPECTS of the archetypal situation. In the Ruru Jātaka the Bodhisatta is a Golden Deer, and the hunter is a dissolute merchant's son.[1] He is rescued by the golden deer after he tried to drown himself, and pledged to keep the deer's existence a secret. But Queen Khemā had her dream, and the king promised a rich reward, so he betrayed the deer to the king. When the king found the deer, however, from pity he was unable to kill him. When the merchant's son's betrayal was revealed, the king wanted to punish him, but the Bodhisatta persuaded him to have mercy. The deer went to the palace, where he spoke Dhamma to the queen, 'in a human voice sweet as honey'. After the admonition to harmlessness, the king declared an amnesty on killing, saying 'I give protection to all creatures'. However, herds of deer took advantage of this, and devoured men's crops. The Bodhisatta intervened and told his herd not to eat the crops of men; and he asked the men to put a sign on their fields, 'and at that sign even to this day the deer do not devour the crops'.

2 In this version there is no specifically Buddhist details; and we have the significant appearance of a covenant between man and beast. Rather than the magical release that we saw earlier, this is a simple contract, acknowledging mutual rights, and guaranteed by the sincerity of the two leaders.

3 The Rohantamiga Jātaka[2] also concerns deer, but in some ways is more similar to the peacock stories.[3] The Bodhisatta is a deer king, who flees

with his herd to the inner reaches of the Himalayas for safety. Together with his younger brother (Ānanda) and sister (Uppalavaṇṇā) he looks after his blind, aged parents. Khemā has her dream, and the hunter sets out. The Bodhisatta is snared, but his younger brother and sister stand by him. Seeing this, compassion arises in the hunter, he rejects royal favors, and releases the deer. The deer offers to go to the king, but the hunters says this would be too dangerous, so instead the deer gives the hunter a few hairs from his body. With these as his talisman, the hunter is able to go to the royal court and teach the Dhamma to the satisfaction of the king and his Queen Khemā. The king offers a great reward; but the hunter rejects it and goes to live as an acetic in the Himalayas. The king kept to the Dhamma his whole life; but there is no mention of a universal amnesty or covenant.

4 The Haṁsa Jātaka[4] tells of a golden goose, while the Mahāhaṁsa Jātaka[5] tells essentially the same story in much more detail. After Khemā's dream, the king builds a beautiful lake called 'Khemā' to attract the golden goose. He arrives and gets caught; the hunter frees him out of compassion and brings him to the king, who listens to the Dhamma and releases him to safety. Here, too, while the goose flock finds safety, and the king and queen learn and practice Dhamma, there is no mention of an amnesty.

❖

5 Like most of the Jātakas, these tales are told on a small scale. They have not been developed to the stature of the great myths. But to me this cycle, especially those featuring the mythical 'golden beasts', represents one of the keys to understanding all mythology.

6 Following Campbell, we have emphasized the centrality of the Hero's Journey, which is the pre-eminent story for all ancient civilizations, and which formed the template for the Buddha's life. We have also seen how the Buddha's birth, which is part of that cycle, suggests a mysterious birth full of illusion, play, and dream. This story is the woman's story, just as the heroic epic is the man's. Our cycle of *dohaḷa* tales achieves nothing less than the integration of these two aspects. The hero's journey emerges from the woman's dream. Her passivity is the essential pre-condition for his activity. It is she who provides meaning, while he accomplishes tasks. If it were just she, the story would go nowhere, and our heroine would pine away in the darkness. And if it were just he, there would be no story, no

heroism, just mindless violence. Only with the precarious coming together of the two is there safety.

7 And it is indeed precarious; time and time again, our story falls short of the final goal, or remains limited in its perspective. Only in the 'golden beast' forms, where the tale expresses the underlying archetypes with most clarity, is the unity achieved with perfection. At each stage in the journey, success is achieved through relationship. The king must listen to his wife; the hunter must obey the king. Even though the hunter goes far into the wilderness, he always bears in mind the purpose for which he was sent. His royal connection is broken only at the moment when true compassion arises. At that critical moment, all values are overturned; the need for worldly status, wealth, and renown, are tossed aside as a genuine connection is made that is far more meaningful.

8 Why is it meaningful? This is a matter of archetypal completion. The whole journey of the man is a projection of Khemā's dream; in other words, the hunter is her animus. The Lower Masculine, the hunter, meets with, takes on a part of, and is transformed into the Higher Masculine, the man of wisdom and peace. The king's own journey, which plays a larger role in the stories of the golden deer and goose, mirrors this in a less dramatic form. Like the hunter, he is, to start with, not averse to using violence, but by the end has been converted to the teaching on harmlessness. In a way, the hunter and the peacock are the two aspects of kinghood that compete in every ruler: is he to be a vicious tyrant who rules by fear, or a righteous beacon of justice for the land?

9 While the golden peacock (and the rest) are fitting symbols for the Higher Masculinity, there is something wrong. Their lives, though serene and idyllic, are shaped by fear. The encroachment of humanity in nature drives them far away. The Higher Masculine still fears the hunter, the Lower Masculine. And the Lower Masculine allies himself with the Lower Feminine to bring about the downfall of the Higher Masculine. There are countless Indian myths that tell of the fall of the sage as he comes under the sway of a beautiful woman.[6] Sometimes she comes to him in the wilderness, while in others he visits the town or palace only to meet his doom. This is, of course, an everyday reality in a culture with so many ascetics; and

while the woman is the typical temptress, sometimes the gender roles are reversed.[7]

10 Just as the hunter overcomes his cruelty, the peacock overcomes his fear. He offers to return to the king's palace, despite the likelihood of his own death at the hands of the king. And it is when this happens that the magic circle is completed. Khemā's dream comes true: she meets and is taught by the golden beast. In Jungian terms, the animal is typically a symbol for intuition or instinct. Khemā has finally opened up to her own intuitive wisdom. She is no longer afraid of masculinity, since she knows that the influence of her own great compassion can soften the cruelest heart.

11 And the peacock is no longer afraid of femininity. He has survived so long because of his seclusion, and the swiftness with which he fell when the peahen appeared is a sign of the fragility of his resolve, even after such a long time. Yet with the integration and acceptance of the Lower Masculine, the Lower Feminine also loses its power over him. He can, with ease and dignity, return to the palace to meet the Queen. His is the daytime, the clarity and brilliance; while hers is the languor of dreams. Their coming together is like the story of the outcast who tried to steal a mango from the king, only to be annointed as 'King of Night'.

12 With the integration of the Higher Masculine and Feminine, which only became possible through the Lower Masculine and Feminine, our heroes finally achieve safety, 'Queen Khemā'. Before, safety was just an uneasy truce, an interval between conflict. Now there is a covenant. And just as a social contract creates peace through accepting the mutual rights and interests of different parties, psychological integration happens through mutual acceptance and understanding of different aspects of the psyche.

13 No longer does the ascetic have to live in fear, alert for the tread of the hunter, or the wiles of a passing maiden. And no longer does the queen have to live in ignorance, trapped within her stifling walls, knowing nothing of the wider world. Her love and compassion for her family becomes transcendent, spreads to the whole world.

14 In this sense, the third meaning of *dohaḷa* is most relevant: giver of milk (*doha-da*). She is no longer the depressed, pining woman (*dohaḷa* = bad-heart), nor is she dominated by her ambivalent child within (*dohaḷa* = two-heart), but wishes to give bounty to all. Mother's milk is purified blood, and the

spontaneous spurt of milk from the breasts, as when the goddess Māyā heard of her son the Buddha, is a miraculous expression of this overflowing, a giving of oneself to the whole world.

15 When the woman achieves her ultimate wish, the world bursts forth in joy and fruitfulness. And here we have the answer to our question: what does a woman want? What she really wants, in the fullness of her being, is nothing less than universal happiness. And our *dohada* stories suggest that maybe, just maybe, if men were to listen and respond to a woman's wishes, listen with their intuition rather than their reason, we might all be a little closer to this happiness.

❖

16 We began our journey with Māyā, the Buddha's mother, in her classic pose as a *sālabhañjikā*, holding the tree as she gave birth. We noted that this was only one instance of a widespread motif in Indian art, and that the artistic motif was reflected in religious texts and even in children's games. Like all the imagery of women in myth, it is ambivalent: the *sālabhañjikā* is giver of beauty and bounty, but she is also the 'breaker', the bringer of death.

17 The bountiful aspect of the *sālabhañjikā* is known throughout India as the *dohada*.[8] The poets and artists capture it in the moment when the *sālabhañjikā* gives the tree a playful kick or stroke, which stimulates the sudden blossoming of flowers in the springtime. The bursting fertility of nature must, like all creation in Indian thought, be preceded by desire. It is the desire of the trees themselves that calls out to the *sālabhañjikā* girls.

> 18 '(Came spring) when the *kuruvaka* trees bloom, as they are embraced by young maids; when the *asoka* trees burst into bloom, as they are struck by the feet of young women; when the *bakula* trees bloom, if sprayed with wine from the mouths of gazelle-eyed maidens; when the *campaka* trees burst as they are sprinkled with perfumed water.'[9]

> 19 'Came spring, that makes *bakula* trees horripilate from sprinkling with rum in mouthfuls by amorous maids, merry with drink; that has hundreds of *asoka* trees delighted by the slow stroke of the tremulous lotus feet, beautiful with anklets, of wanton damsels, enslaved by amorous delights.'

> 20 'In spring, by its fresh shoots the *asoka*, because of its longing to be touched by a maiden's ankleted foot, red with the dye of new lac, seemed to have assumed that color. The *bakula* shone as if, thru sprinkling with mouthfuls from amorous girls' lotus lips, completely filled with sweet wine, it had assumed its (the wine's) color in its own flowers.'[10]

21 The poets fancy an intoxicating, swelling, world of sensual delights. According to Buddhist thought, this realm is nothing but the 'play of illusion'; but as we have seen, the birth of the Buddha himself springs from the same 'play of illusion'. Just as the bounty of the world springs from the *dohada* of the woman, the birth of the Buddha depends on the *dohada* of Māyā.

❖

22 The *dohada* of Māyā is discussed in the account of the Buddha's life found in the Mūlasarvāstivāda Vinaya.[11] Durt remarks that:

> 23 '... it was difficult for Buddhists to consider positively the woman's instinctive impulse that is *dohada*. It thus becomes interesting that the Mūlasarvāstivāda Vinaya uses the term *dohada* to describe the purified impulses of the exalted mother of the Buddha.'

24 As I have shown, this should not be surprising at all, for the Buddhist literature preserves many positive expressions of *dohada*. Arguing that the Buddhist texts depict *dohada* negatively, Durt cites the Vidhurapaṇḍita Jātaka, saying that the *nāga* queen longed for the heart of the sage, but her desire was converted to longing for teachings. But this is a misreading of the text. In fact, her *dohada* right from the start was to listen to a discourse on the Dhamma from the sage, and she merely feigned desire to eat his heart. She intuited that only by this expedient could she obtain her wish, and as events turned out, her intuition was spot on. It is Durt who has been fooled by her *māyā* into seeing the *dohada* as negative.

25 Māyā's five *dohadas* are among the higher forms of *dohada*, and serve to unite Māyā's inner desires with her symbolic canon. They are: #1 to drink the water of the four oceans; #2 that all bonds be undone; #3 that gifts be given and merits made; #4 that she might see beautiful parks; and #5 that she might stay in those parks.

26 In wishing to drink of the four oceans, Māyā pre-empts the much later dream of the Bodhisatta immediately before his awakening, when he saw

himself lying on the land of India, with his limbs reaching to the four oceans. Both symbols are interpreted in a similar way; Māyā's *dohada* is said by the readers of signs to mean that her son will comprehend the entire ocean of knowledge, while the Bodhisatta's dream is said to mean that his teachings will be universal. In each case, the oceans evoke a universal dimension to the Buddha's realization.

27 In those times, Māyā's wish would have been impossible to fulfill by normal means. So it is satisfied by having a magician called Raktākṣa, or Red-eye, take her to the top of a tower where he magically produces the water of the four oceans for her to drink. Now, red eyes are one of the distinctive features of a *yakkha*, and while this person is said to be a *parivrājaka*, or non-Buddhist wanderer, he is behaving much more like a witch-doctor or shaman. I wonder whether the association of magic with red eyes is related to the ingestion of entheogens, which had been a part of Indic religion from Vedic times. In any case, he takes her to the tower, the classic location of the bounded female as she waits for her lover to liberate her. In that virtual prison, that tiny woman's world, she imbibes the universal flavor of the oceans. This is the same salt water that is bounded by the *garudhammas*, the menstrual flow, the waters of the womb, the mother's milk. In this moment she dissolves all boundaries and fully enters her archetype.

28 It is surely no coincidence that the ocean is said by the Buddha to have but one taste, the taste of freedom; and that the next wish of Māyā is for the liberation of all from their bonds. She has seen the universality of knowledge, how she partakes of the same waters as women everywhere. In that realization she cannot abide the separation of beings, the setting of one against the other. Her compassion has become universal, and she creates, with the magic of her feminine desires, a state of freedom and equality for all persons.

29 When all have the capacity to choose, the critical thing is to choose wisely. It would not do to free all slaves and prisoners, only to have them go about wreaking havoc, or perhaps taking revenge for their former imprisonment. Freedom must go along with responsibility, and so her next wish is for gifts and offerings to be made by all. The rich, those who can afford to, must share with the poor, and the poor must help each other.

In this way Māyā's universal compassion spreads through all people, and freedom leads not to chaos, but to blessings for all in this life and the next.

30 The next two wishes are more personal. They relate to Māyā's journey to Lumbini to give birth. She is traveling even closer to her archetypal home, the grove, where she can become one with the *sāl* tree and give it a little kick. If she doesn't, there'll be terrible confusion; the artists would all be wrong for a start.

CHAPTER 40

THINGS HIDDEN SINCE THE BEGINNING

SECRETS. THEY'RE SO SEDUCTIVE. We've been seeking meaning in images, symbols, and stories, searching for what lies hidden. But the real secret is this: the things hidden since the beginning are not hidden at all. They are plain to see, the very stuff of our lives, a lesson we have been taught since the cradle.

2 The Buddha sits upon a lotus. He sits under a tree. He wears the robe, and carries the bowl. In the earliest images, he is represented by his absence, imagined not as a person but as symbol: the seat, the footprints, the stupa, the tree, the wheel. All of these have been used by Buddhists as long as they have been using symbols.[1] In archetypal terms, all these symbols belong to the Higher Feminine. We have visited them in our long journey together, but let us now bring them together.

Figure 40.1: *Buddha head in tree, Ayutthaya*

3 The lotus is the most feminine of all images and has been the emblem of the goddess since before history. The lotus rises unsmeared from the mud, just as the Bodhisattva emerged unsmeared from Māyā's womb. The lotus is the Higher Feminine emerging from the Lower, a little piece of everyday magic to bring brightness to the heart.

4
> The psyche as flower, as lotus, lily, and rose, the virgin as flower in Eleusis, symbolize the flowerlike unfolding of the highest psychic and spiritual developments. Thus birth from the female blossom is an archetypal form of divine birth, whether we think of Ra or Nefertem in Egypt, of the Buddhist 'divine treasure in the lotus', or, in China and the modern West, of the birth of the self in the Golden Flower.[2]

5 The tree is one of the primordial feminine symbols: home and shelter, source of fruits, connected with the earth, support of life.

6 The stupa was originally a funeral mound. It is the sacred mountain, the cave of return to the all-consuming Mother Earth.[3] In worshiping a mound of earth, Buddhists connect with a strand of spirituality that stretches back long before the Śākyan Sage appeared in the world.

7 The footprints, gentle impressions on the earth, are the visible signs of the absent presence of the Buddha: we know he was here because of a hollow. The earth witnesses the passing of the Buddha, exactly as the earth goddess witnessed the Bodhisattva's past deeds on the eve of his Awakening.

8 The wheel is an abstract representation of the 'round', the wholeness, the all-encompassing. Primordially it echoes of the time in the womb, enclosed and encircled. But it turns and evolves—as wheels do—appearing as the *maṇḍala*, the round of *saṁsāra*, and a thousand other 'world-circles'. Within it, contained as a vessel, is everything. But while the wheel of existence carries within it all suffering, the wheel of the Dhamma carries within it the eightfold path, the all-embracing spiritual qualities that lead to Awakening.

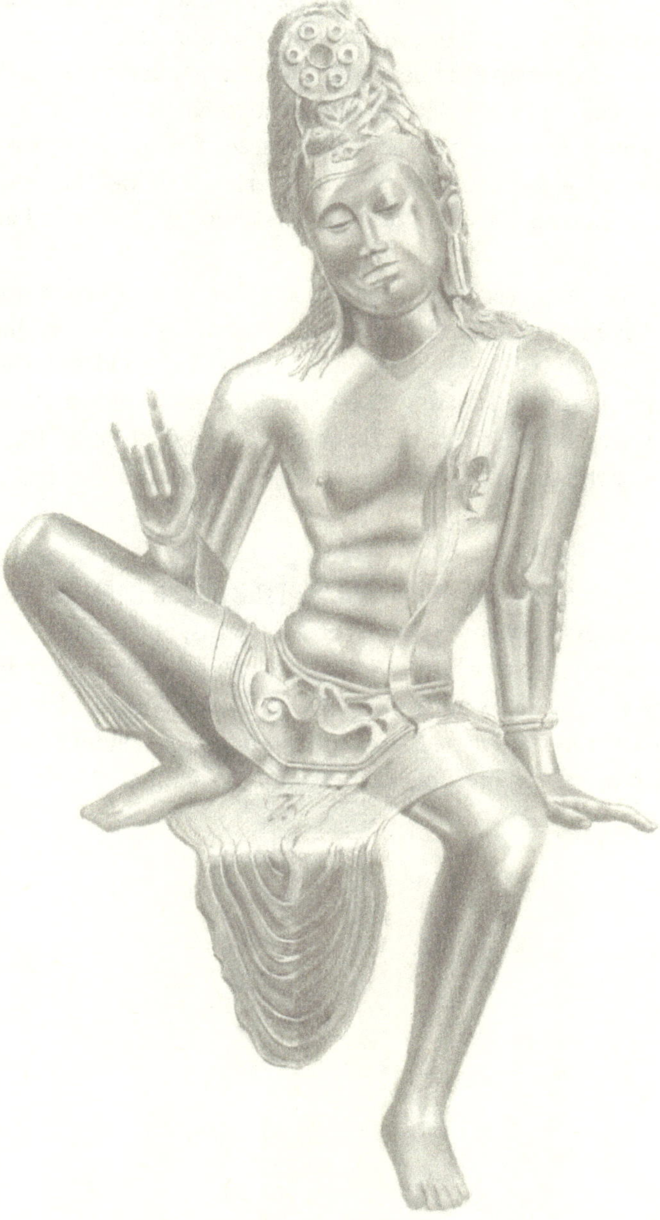

Figure 40.2: *Bodhisatta, Sri Lanka*

9 The bowl is the vessel, and hence always evokes that earliest vessel within which we all spent the first months of our life. The bowl is not merely a passive container or bearer. It exerts a magnetic power, through its emptiness calling to be filled. As the cornucopia, the Grail, the begging bowl, or the humble cooking pot, it is the source of magical, life-sustaining food.[4] It echoes the second most primal experience of life, the breast, and hence the Greek tradition held that the first bowl was modeled after Helen's breast.[5]

10 The seat: enclosing, receptive, bearing the man in his passive state. The first seat is the mother's lap, the suckling infant in his secure resting place. Like Mother Isis who served as the throne of the king,[6] goddesses the world over hold the Divine Child safe in their lap. Such enclosures are echoed in the caves, in which we find so much of our most ancient Buddhist art, and the interior of the stupa or temple, known as the 'womb' (*gabbha*).[7]

❖

11 Surrounding, embracing, and protecting the Buddha, the images reveal a man in utterness of harmony with the tree, lotus, and the rest, a perfect symbol of male/female balance. So confident is the Buddha in his own masculinity that he rests within in total stillness. We see him as a man only within the feminine. The male aspect is conscious, explicit, while the feminine lies in the unconscious, evoked only as symbols.[8]

Figure 40.3: *Quan Yin Bodhisattva*

12 And the Buddha image itself, the vision of idealized humanity, is itself androgynous. This is a more subtle matter; while it is easy enough to follow conventions and place the Buddha in a lotus, capturing the fluid quiescence of his form is a different matter. The crude, stiff depictions are many, but those that embody the grace of mindfulness are few. Yet whether in the remnants of Gupta images, or the sensuous walking Buddhas of Sukhothai, we recognize when the artist comes close to the true form of the Buddha.

13 The androgyny of the Buddha extends further in the form of the Bodhisatta. Unconstrained by a historical memory of the Buddha as male, Buddhists drift towards feminine depictions of the aspiring Buddhas-to-be. The male forms show a relaxed ease within the body; and Bodhisattvas like Avalokiteśvara are content with nothing less than incarnation in female form.

14 Just as the male form of the Buddha loses its aggressiveness and tends towards the feminine, so too the female images lose their flamboyant sexuality. The Mahāyāna developed a mythology around Prajñāpāramitā, the 'Perfection of Wisdom'. In theory, this is a corpus of texts which teach of the highest, intuitive wisdom. But it was not just a philosophy, for it embraced a devotion for wisdom, the 'Mother of All Buddhas'. Inverting the expected gender stereotyping, wisdom was seen as feminine, while compassion was masculine. But this makes perfect sense, for the wisdom of Prajñāpāramitā is precisely that wisdom that sees beyond analysis of particulars into the essential emptiness of all things. And compassion is not just a soft feeling, but is the readiness to leap up from one's seat at any moment to go forth in the world and act to help others.

Figure 40.4: *Prajñāpāramitā, Java*

15 And so, in good mythic style, we come full circle. From Māyā, the magical maid in the grove at Lumbini, to the Perfection of Wisdom as the ground and matrix of Awakening. In the process, down the long and winding road, I hope we have gained a little appreciation for Mahāpajāpatī, whose difficulties are so crucial for our generation.

16 If we have answered certain questions about gender as portrayed in Buddhist myth & image, we have raised many more. Our time together is just an illusion, just another play of magic; close this book and it disappears. But, inadequate as our method has been, might we nevertheless be excused in seeking some sort of 'moral' in our story, some general picture which, oversimplified as it must be, might serve to orient us as we perch on the thin present, between the ambiguous past and the intimidating future?

17 Imagine three threads—white, red, and black. White is the masculine, red is the feminine, and black is Nibbana the Unconditioned, the emptiness that lies beyond all form. The Buddha wove a single strong rope with a black core, and entwined and en-twinned around it the white and the red.

18 But as we trace the rope into the future, with hard use it unravels. Lesser lines spin off into a complex web, as the sects emerge from the original Buddhist community. Each of these strands contains the white, the red, and the black, yet in varying proportions; and the black core becomes thinner. In many strands, also, the red diminishes, and the remaining ropes become more and more white. Thus weakened and fragmented, many fail; they snap off or wear out and become lost.

19 Only three ropes survive into our times. In these, the black core has been replaced by white, while the black itself is relegated to a few flimsy strands on the outside. The red, too, is hardly to be seen, except in the thread that winds through East Asia, where it remains strong. It seems as if the tides of history are against us, that the outcome is inevitable.

20 But behold! The ropes that have been separated for so long are starting to rejoin; and the red is leading the way. Slowly, the plain white is infiltrated with strands of vivid crimson, and the divided ropes are binding themselves together in a subtle, intricate pattern.

21 And as the red slowly regains strength, a strange thing may be seen. For the black, long neglected, is starting to reappear, to regain the center. The white, rather than trying to hold the core, patterns itself with the red,

protecting and supporting the black. A shift is happening, a return to the source—a new hope.

❖

22 Once more we take the road to Lumbini. It is evening, the sky aflame with sunset, its golden glory like the halo of the living Buddha. In the grove the lake is broad and deep, the tree vast and strong. In our imagination the place has changed but little since Māyā grasped the *sāl* branch in the sacred grove. The gods may not be seen, and the Bodhisatta's astonishing birth is only a memory, fading like the sun. Yet the Aśokan pillar stands firm, its Mauryan shine proof against the ages as it proclaims, in its vernacular Magadhī: '*hida budhe jāte sakyamuni!*'—'Here the Buddha, Sage of the Śākyans, was born!' The grove is quiet, and there comes, borne on the swell of the silence, a lingering melancholy, sweet and solemn. All must dissipate, all must disappear; all is vanity, all is illusion. And yet:

ciraṁ tiṭṭhatu saddhammaṁ!

THANKS

First is love and gratitude for my mother, father, and sister: the perfect family for a prodigal son. And for my great friends Thisbe, Lisa, Peggy, Jodie, and Maryella, who shared with me my first faltering steps towards 'Eastern' spirituality. In my Dhamma life, there have been so many expressions of kindness to me that I am afraid of drowning in gratitude: but I must at least mention Ajahn Pasanno, Ajahn Jayasāro, and Ajahn Brahmavaṁso, who shared so much of their time and wisdom with me, and who gave me role models of monks with genuine compassion for women; and also Pra Ajahn Maha Chatchai, who taught me how to meditate on kindness. In the long preparation of this book, I give thanks to Ven. Anālayo, Allison Goodwin, Bhikkhuni Dhammanandā, Ayyā Tathāālokā, Bhante Tapassī, Jacquelyn Miller, Kester Ratcliff, Ayyā Mahācittā, Ayyā Adhimuttā, Ayyā Jagarīyā (Chong Peng), Justine McGill, Dustin Cheah, Ayyā Nirodhā, Ayyā Upekkhā, Chandra Kumarasinghe, Venerable Nandiya, and Alex Sebby. Special thanks are due to Darryl Gradwell for his extraordinary pencil drawings, done in a time of great illness. I also acknowledge the work that has been done by so many scholars, on whose broad shoulders I rely so often. And finally, for all those who have supported my holy life with offerings of food and all the other essentials by which I live: without you, I could not survive in this life. May you all rejoice in all the blessings of the Triple Gem.

Sadhu! Sadhu! Sadhu!

BIBLIOGRAPHY

Pali texts are sourced from www.tipitakastudies.net. For the Dīgha and Majjhima Nikāyas, I refer to the sutta and section number of the *Long Discourses of the Buddha* (trans. WALSHE) and *Middle-length Discourses of the Buddha* (trans. BODHI, ÑĀṆAMOḶI) respectively; for the Saṁyutta Nikāya to the *saṁyutta* and sutta numbers of the Connected Discourses; for the Aṅguttara Nikāya to the *nipāta* and sutta number. Text, translations, and parallels for these may be found through www.suttacentral.net. For the Vinaya and Jātakas I give the volume and page of the PTS edition of the Pali; I also include the Jātaka number. Chinese texts are from the CBETA digital edition of the Taishō canon.

MAHĀPAJĀPATĪ'S ORDINATION

Pali Vinaya 2.253–259 (Cūḷavagga 10.1 Bhikkhunikkhandhaka).

Dharmaguptaka Vinaya T22, № 1428, p. 922, c6.

Mahīśāsaka Vinaya T22, № 1421, p. 186, a.14.

Mahāsaṅghika Vinaya T22, № 1425, p. 471, a25.

Lokuttaravāda Bhikṣuṇī Vinaya (Gustav ROTH, *Bhikṣuṇī Vinaya—Manual of Discipline for Buddhist Nuns*, K.P. Jayaswal Research Institute, Patna, 1970), pp. 1–21*ff.*

Mūlasarvāstivāda Vinaya T24, № 1451, p. 350, b10; Dulva 11 f. 326b-338 (translated in ROCKHILL, pp. 58–62).

Bhikṣuṇī-Karmavācanā (Mūlasarvāstivāda). Michael SCHMIDT (ed.) Indica et Tibetica, Band 22, 1993, pp. 239–288. (Translated as 'The Stating of the Matter' by Frances WILSON in PAUL, pp. 82–94.)

Aṅguttara Nikāya 8.51 (VOL 4.274).

Sarvāstivāda Gautamī Sūtra (Madhyama Āgama 116) T1, № 26, p. 605, a10–p. 607, b15.

Gautamī Sūtra T1, № 60, p. 856, a7–p. 858, a6 (Note: this sutra is virtually identical with the previous.)

Bhikṣunī Mahāprajāpatī Sūtra T24, № 1478, p. 945, b25–947, a9.

OTHER PRIMARY SOURCES & SECONDARY LITERATURE

AGRAWALA, Prithvi Kumar. *Goddessess* [sic] *in Ancient India.* Abhinav Publications, 1984

AESCHYLUS (trans. Robert FAGLES) *The Orestia.* Penguin Books, 1966.

ALLCHIN, F.R. *The Archaeology of Early Historic South Asia.* Cambridge University Press, 1995.

ALLEN, Terry J., Donald M. DOUGHERTY, Howard M. RHOADES, Don R. CHEREK. 'A Study of Male and Female Aggressive Responding Under Conditions Providing an Escape Response.' The Psychological Record, Fall 1996.
http://findarticles.com/p/articles/mi_hb3538/is_n4_v46/ai_n28676715

ALLON, Mark. *The Mahāparinirvāṇa Sūtra*. Unpublished Honors submission, Australian National University, 1987.

AN Ok-Sun. 'A Critique of the Early Buddhist Texts: The Doctrine of Woman's Incapability of Becoming an Enlightened One.' Asian Journal of Women's Studies, Vol 8, № 3, 2002, pp. 7–34.

AN, Yang-Gyu (trans.) *The Buddha's Last Days*. Pali Text Society, 2003.

ANĀLAYO, Bhikkhu. *A Comparative Study of the Majjhima Nikāya*. (Unpublished draft.)

———. 'The Four Assemblies and the Foundation of the Order of Nuns.' Abstract for the International Congress on Buddhist Women's Role in the Sangha, Hamburg University, 2007.
http://www.congress-on-buddhist-women.org/45.0.html

———. 'The Arahant Ideal in Early Buddhism—the case of Bakkula.' The Indian International Journal of Buddhist Studies 8, 2007.

———. 'The Buddha and Omniscience.' The Indian International Journal of Buddhist Studies 7, 2006.

———. 'The Bahudhātuka-sutta and its Parallels On Women's Inabilities.' Journal of Buddhist Ethics, Vol 16, 2009.

———. 'The Vicissitudes of Memory and Early Buddhist Oral Transmission.' Canadian Journal of Buddhist Studies, № 5, 2009, pp. 5–19.

ANDAYA, Barbara Watson. 'Studying Women and Gender in Southeast Asia.' International Journal of Asian Studies, 4.1. Cambridge University Press, 2007, pp. 113–136.

APULEIUS, Lucius (trans. E.J. KENNEY.) *Cupid & Psyche*. Cambridge University Press, 1990.

ARMSTRONG, Karen. *A History of God*. Random House, 1993.

———. *The Battle for God*. Knopf, 2000.

———. *Through the Narrow Gate*. St. Martin's Griffin, 2005.

———. *A Short History of Myth*. Canongate, 2005.

———. *The Great Transformation*. Vintage Canada, 2007.

ĀRYASŪRA (trans. J.S. SPEYER.) Gātakamālā. Motilal Barnasidass, 1990. (First published 1895.)
http://www.ancient-buddhist-texts.net/English-Texts/Garland-of-Birth-Stories

ASAṄGA (trans. Walpola RAHULA & Sara BOIN-WEBB). *Abhidharmasamuccaya*. Asian Humanities Press, 2001.

BACHOFEN, J.J. *Myth, Religion, and Mother Right*. Princeton University Press, 1992.

BAMSHAD, Michael, *et al*. 'Genetic Evidence on the Origins of Indian Caste Populations'. *Genome Research*, 11, 2001, pp. 994–1004.
http://www.ebc.ee/EVOLUTSIOON/publications/Bamshad2001.pdf

BANERJEE, Priyatosh. 'Birth of Buddha and its Vedic Parallel.'
www.ignca.nic.in/pb0014.htm

BARTHOLOMEUSZ, Tessa J. *Women Under the Bo Tree*. Cambridge University Press, 1994.

BAUER, Jerome. 'Dohada (Pregnancy cravings)'. *Indian Folklife.* V^OL 2, issue 4, № 13. National Folklore Support Center, April-June 2003.
www.indianfolklore.org/journals/index.php/IFL/article/viewArticle/432

BAUMEISTER, Roy F., Kathleen R. CATANESE, and Kathleen D. VOHS. 'Is There a Gender Difference in Strength of Sex Drive? Theoretical Views, Conceptual Distinctions, and a Review of Relevant Evidence.' Personality and Social Psychology Review 2001, V^OL 5, № 3, 242–273.
http://www.csom.umn.edu/assets/71520.pdf

BEAL, Samuel. *Buddhist Records of the Western World*, 1884. Reprinted Munshiram Manoharlal, 1983.

———. *Romantic Legends of Śākya Buddha: A translation of the Chinese version of the Abhiniskramana Sutra.* Kessinger, 2003. (First published Trubner & Co., 1875.)

BECHERT, Heinz & Petra KIEFFER-PÜLZ, eds. *Indian Studies.* Bibliotheca Indo Buddhica № 32. Sri Satguru Publications, 1986.

BJÖRKQVIST, Kaj. 'Sex Differences in Physical, Verbal, and Indirect Aggression: A Review of Recent Research.' Sex Roles, V^OL 30, № 3/4, 1994.
http://www.vasa.abo.fi/svf/up/articles/sexdiff_a_review.pdf

BLACKBURN, Anne M. *Buddhist Learning and Textual Practice in Eighteenth-Century Lankan Monastic Culture.* Princeton University Press, 2001.

BLACKSTONE, Katherine R. 'Damming the Dhamma: Problems with Bhikkhunīs in the Pali Vinaya.'
http://www.buddhanet.net/budsas/ebud/ebsut066.htm

———. *Women in the Footsteps of the Buddha.* Curzon Press, 1998.

BLOK, Josine. *The Early Amazons: Modern and Ancient Perspectives on a Persistent Myth.* Brill, 1995.

BLOOMFIELD, M. 'The Dohada or Craving of Pregnant Women: A Motif of Hindu Fiction.' *Journal of the American Oriental Society*, V^OL 40, Yale University Press, 1920.
http://archive.org/details/journalofamerica40ameruoft

BODHI, Bhikkhu. *The Connected Discourses of the Buddha.* Wisdom Publications, 2000.

———. *Discourse on the Root of Existence: The Mūlapariyāya Sutta and Its Commentaries.* Buddhist Publication Society, 1992.

BOISVERT, Mathieu. *The Five Aggregates: Understanding Theravāda Psychology and Soteriology.* Canadian Corporation for Studies in Religion, Wilfrid Laurier University Press, 1995.

BRAUNER, Sigrid & Robert H. BROWN. *Fearless Wives and Frightened Shrews: The Construction of the Witch in Early Modern Germany.* University of Massachusetts Press, 2001.

BREKKE, Torkel. *Religious Motivation and the Origins of Buddhism.* RoutledgeCurzon, 2002.

BRIGHENTI, Francesco. 'The Ritual Stealing of the Sacrificial Buffalo's Flesh among the Kondhs of Orissa.'
www.svabhinava.org/friends/FrancescoBrighenti/BuffaloFleshKondhs-frame.php

BRONKHORST, Johannes, Ellen M. RAVEN, K.R. van KOOIJ. *Indian Art and Archaeology* (V^OL 10 of Panels of the VIIth World Sanskrit Conference, Kern Institute, Leiden, August 23–29, 1987). Brill, 1992.

BROWN, Sid. *The Journey of One Buddhist Nun: Even Against the Wind*. State University of New York Press, 2001.

BRYANT, Edwin. *The Quest for the Origins of Vedic Culture: The Indo-Aryan Migration Debate.* Oxford University Press, 2001.

BRYANT, Edwin and Laurie L. PATTON. *The Indo-Aryan Controversy: evidence and inference in Indian history.* Routledge, 2005.

BUCKNELL, Rod. 'The Structure of the *Sagātha-Vagga* of the *Saṁyutta-Nikāya*', Buddhist Studies Review, Vol 24, № 1, 2007.

BUDDHAGHOSA (trans. Bhikkhu ÑĀṆAMOḶI). *The Path of Purification*. A. Semage, Colombo, 1964.

BYRNE, Jean. 'Who am I? A response to the koan "woman".' Woman-Church: A Journal of Feminist Studies in Religion, 2004.
http://www.yogaspace.com.au/resources/pdf/writing_research/Who_am_I.pdf

CABEZÓN, José Ignacio (ed.) *Buddhism, Sexuality, and Gender.* SUNY Press, 1992.

CALASSO, Roberto (trans. Kim PARKS) *Ka*. Vintage, 1999.

———. *The Marriage of Cadmus and Harmony.* Knopf, 1993.

———. *Literature and the Gods.* Knopf, 2000.

CAMPBELL, Joseph. *The Hero With a Thousand Faces*. Princeton University Press, 1973 (First edition 1949).

———. *The Masks of God: Primitive Mythology.* Penguin Arkana, 1991.

———. *The Masks of God: Oriental Mythology.* Penguin Arkana, 1991.

———. *The Masks of God: Occidental Mythology.* Penguin Arkana, 1991.

———. *The Masks of God: Creative Mythology.* Penguin Arkana, 1991.

CAMPBELL, June. *Traveller in Space: In Search of Female Identity in Tibetan Buddhism*. George Braziller Incorporated, 1996.

CHENG, Jianhua. *A Critical Translation of Fan Dong Jing, the Chinese Version of Brahmajala Sutra.*
http://www.library.websangha.org/earlybuddhism/trs.%20from%20Agamas.zip

CHON, Hae-ju. 'An Examination on the Foundation of the Nun's Order.' Korean Buddhist Studies, Vol 11, 1986.

CHOONG Mun-keat. *The Fundamental Teachings of Early Buddhism*, Harrassowitz Verlag, Wiesbaden, 2000.

COUTURE, André (trans. Robert JOLLET). 'A Survey of French Literature on Ancient Indian Buddhist Hagiography.' In GRANOFF, pp. 9–44.

CHUNG, In Young. 'A Buddhist View of Women: A Comparative Study of the Rules for *Bhikṣuṇīs* and *Bhikṣus* Based on the Chinese *Prātimokṣa*.' Journal of Buddhist Ethics, 6, 1999, pp. 29–105.
www.buddhistethics.org/6/chung991.pdf

COLEMAN, Charles. *Mythology of the Hindus.* Asian Educational Services, 1995. (First published Parbury, Allen, 1832.)

CLARKE, Shayne. 'Monks Who have Sex.' Journal of Indian Philosophy, 37:1–43, 2009.

COWELL, E.B., *et al.* (trans.) *The Jātaka, or Stories of the Buddha's Former Births.* Pali Text Society, 2005.

COZAD, Laurie. *Sacred Snakes: Orthodox Images of Indian Snake Worship*. The Davies Group, 2004.

CROSBY, Kate. 'Gendered Symbols in Theravāda Buddhism: Missed Positives in the Representation of the Female', in *Religious Culture and Gender Ethics (Conference Proceedings)*, Hongshi Buddhist Cultural and Educational Foundation, Tau-Yuan, 2007, pp. D1–D15.

DASHU, Max. 'Knocking Down Straw Dolls: A Critique of Cynthia Eller's The Myth of Matriarchal Prehistory: Why an Invented Past Won't Give Women a Future.' Beacon Press, 2000.
http://www.suppressedhistories.net/articles/eller.html

DAVIS, Patricia H. *Beyond Nice*. Augsburg Fortress, 2001.

DAVIS, Richard B. *Muang Metaphysics*. Pandora, Bangkok, 1984.

DEWARAJA, Dr. L.S. *The Position of Women in Buddhism*. The Wheel Publication № 280. Buddhist Publication Society, 1981.
http://www.accesstoinsight.org/lib/authors/dewaraja/wheel280.html

DHAMMANANDA, Bhikshuni. 'Ordination: Sakyadhita's Heritage from the Buddha.' Paper presented at the International Conference on Buddhism in Asia: Challenges and Prospects, at the Central Institute of Higher Tibetan Studies in Sarnath, India, February 10–12, 20, 2006.

DONIGER, Wendy. *Splitting the Difference: Gender and Myth in Ancient Greece and India*. University of Chicago Press, 1999.

DOUGLAS, Mary. *Purity and Danger: An Analysis of Concept of Pollution and Taboo*. Routledge, 2002.

DURT, Hubert. 'The Meeting of the Buddha with Māyā in the Trāyastriṁsa Heaven.' Journal of the International College for Postgraduate Buddhist Studies, Vol 11, March 2007, pp. 45–66.

DUTT, Nalinaksha. *Buddhist Sects in India*. Motilal Banarsidass, 1978.

ELLER, Cynthia. *The Myth of Matriarchal Prehistory: Why An Invented Past Won't Give Women a Future*. Beacon Press, 2001.

FALK, Monica Lindberg. *Making Fields of Merit: Buddhist Female Ascetics and Gendered Orders in Thailand*. NIAS Press, 2007.

FARMER, Steve, Richard SPROAT, and Michael WITZEL. 'The Collapse of the Indus-Script Thesis: The Myth of a Literate Harappan Civilization.' Electronic Journal of Vedic Studies, Vol 11 (2004), Issue 2 (Dec).

FAURE, Bernard. *The Power of Denial: Buddhism, Purity, and Gender*. Princeton University Press, 2003.

FINE, Cordelia. *Delusions of Gender: How Our Minds, Society, and Neurosexism Create Difference*. W.W. Norton & Co. Inc., 2010.

FONTENROSE, Joseph EDDY. *Python: a study of Delphic myth and its origins*. University of California Press, 1980.

FORD, Dennis. *The Search for Meaning*. Berkeley: University of California Press, 2007.

FOX, Kate. 'Evolution, Alienation and Gossip: The role of mobile telecommunications in the 21st century.'
http://www.sirc.org/publik/gossip.shtml

FRAUWALLNER, Erich. *The Earliest Vinaya and the Beginnings of Buddhist Literature.* Rome, Istituto Italiano per il Medio ed Estremo Oriente, 1956.

———. *Studies in Abhidharma Literature and the Origins of Buddhist Philosophical Systems.* SUNY Press, 1995.

FRAZER, J.G. *The Golden Bough.* First published 1922, reprinted Papermac, 1994.

FREDERICK, Jenn. 'The First Taboo: How Menstrual Taboos Reflect and Sustain Women's Internalized Oppression.'
http://home.comcast.net/~theennead/bean/taboo.htm

GADKARI, Jayant. *Society and Religion: From Rigveda to Puranas.* Popular Prakashan, 1996.

GARDNER, Gerald Brosseau. *The Meaning of Witchcraft.* Red Wheel, 2004.

GILBERT, Helen. Pregnancy Cravings as a Motif in Folktales. St. Cloud, Minnesota. Folklore Forum 5(4), 1972, pp.129–142.
http://hdl.handle.net/2022/1214

GILLIGAN, Carol. *In a Different Voice.* Harvard University Press, 1982.

———. *The Birth of Pleasure.* Vintage Books, 2003.

GILMOR, David D. *Misogyny: The Male Malady.* University of Pennsylvania Press, 2001.

GIMBUTAS, Marija, Miriam R. DEXTER. *The Living Goddesses.* University of California Press, 2001.

GIRARD, René, Jean-Michel OUGHOURLIAN, Guy LEFORT, Stephen BANN, M. METTEER; translated by Stephen BANN, M. METTEER. *Things Hidden Since the Foundation of the World.* Continuum International Publishing Group, 2003.

GLASGOW, Rupert D.V. *Madness, Masks, and Laughter: An Essay on Comedy.* Fairleigh Dickinson University Press, 1995.

GOLDBERG, Steven. *Why Men Rule: A Theory of Male Dominance.* Open Court, 1993.

GOLDHILL, Simon. *Reading Greek Tragedy.* Cambridge University Press, 1986.

GOODWIN, Allison. 'Right Views, Red Rust, and Rice Worms: The Eight Heavy Duties and Buddhist Teachings on Female Inferiority Re-examined.' In *Religious Culture and Gender Ethics (Conference Proceedings).* Hongshi Buddhist Cultural and Educational Foundation, Tau-Yuan, 2007, pp. E1–E19.

GOONATILLEKE, Hema. 'The Forgotten Women of Anuradhapura: "Herstory" replaced by "History".' In *(En) Gendering the Spirit.* Durre S. AHMED, ed. pp. 194–218.
http://www.boell-pakistan.org/pics/images_pk/Gendering_the_spirit_final.pdf

GNANARAMA, Pategama. *The Mission Accomplished.* Ti-Sarana Buddhist Association, 1997.

GRANOFF, Phyllis and Koichi SHINOHARA. *Monks and Magicians.* Motilal Banarsidass, 1994.

GRAVES, Robert. *The Greek Myths.* Folio Society, 2002. (Originally published Penguin, 1955.)

———. *The White Goddess.* Farrar, Straus, and Giroux, 1966.

GRIFFIN, Wendy. 'The Embodied Goddess: Feminist Witchcraft and Female Divinity.' Sociology of Religion, Vol 56, № 1, Spring 1995, pp. 35–49.

GRIFFITH, Ralph T.H. (trans.) *Hymns of the Rig Veda.* London, 1889–1892.
http://www.sacredtexts.com/hin/rigveda/index.htm

GREGOR, Thomas and Donald F. TUZIN. *Gender in Amazonia and Melanesia: An Exploration of the Comparative Method.* University of California Press, 2001.

GREEN, Ronald. 'Development of the Bhikkhuni Sangha.'
http://ww2.coastal.edu/rgreen/Bhikkhuni%20Sangha.pdf

GREENEBAUME, Steven E. 'Vṛtrahan-Vərəthragna: India and Iran.' In LARSON, pp. 93–97.

GROSS, Rita. 'Is the Glass Half-empty or Half-full? A Feminist Assessment of Buddhism at the Beginning of the Twenty-first Century.' In *Religious Culture and Gender Ethics (Conference Proceedings)*, Hongshi Buddhist Cultural and Educational Foundation, Tau-Yuan, 2007, pp. F1–F26.

———. *Buddhism after Patriarchy*. SUNY Press, 1992.

GUTERMAN, M.A., P. MEHTA & M.S. GIBBS. 'Menstrual Taboos Among Major Religions.' *The Internet Journal of World Health and Societal Politics* Vol 5, № 2, 2008.
http://www.ispub.com/ostia/index.php?xmlFilePath=journals/ijwh/

GUTSCHOW, Kim. *Being a Buddhist Nun: The Struggle for Enlightenment in the Himalayas*. Harvard University Press, 2004.

GYATSO, Janet and Hanna HAVNEVIK. *Women in Tibet*. C. Hurst & Co. Publishers, 2005.

HACKIN, J. *Asiatic Mythology: A Detailed Description and Explanation of the Mythologies*. Asian Educational Services, 1994. (First published: George G. Harrap & Co., 1932.)

HALLISEY, Charles. 'Councils as Ideas and Events in the Theravāda.' *Buddhism: Critical Concepts in Religious Studies*. Paul WILLIAMS (ed.) Vol II. Routledge, 2005, pp. 171–185.

HARRIS, Ian. 'Cambodian Buddhism: History and Practice.' University of Hawai'i Press, 2005.

HARRIS, Marvin. *Cows, Pigs, Wars, and Witches*. Vintage Books, 1974.

HARTMANN, Jens-Uwe. 'Contents and Structure of the Dīrghāgama of the (Mūla) Sarvāstivādins.' Annual Report of The International Research Institute for Advanced Buddhology at Soka University 7, 2004, pp. 119–137.

HECKER, Hellmuth. 'Man and Woman in the Teachings of the Buddha.'
www.geocities.com/zennun12_8/woman_man.html

———. (trans. and revised by NYANAPONIKA Thera). 'Mahā Kassapa: Father of the Sangha.' The Wheel Publication № 345. Buddhist Publication Society, 1987.
www.accesstoinsight.org/lib/authors/hecker/wheel345.html

HEESTERMAN, J.C. *The Broken World of Sacrifice: An Essay in Ancient Indian Ritual*. University of Chicago Press, 1993.

———. *The Inner Conflict of Tradition: essays in Indian ritual, kingship, and society*. University of Chicago Press, 1985.

HEIRMANN, Ann. *The Discipline in Four Parts: Rules for Nuns According to the Dharmaguptaka Vinaya*. Motilal Barnasidass, 2002.

———. 'Chinese Nuns and their Ordination in Fifth Century China.' Journal of the International Association of Buddhist Studies, Vol 24, № 2, pp. 275–304.

HELLER, Sophia. *The Absence of Myth*. SUNY Press, 2005.

HENSHILWOODA, Christopher S., Francesco D'ERRICOC & Ian WATTS. 'Engraved Ochres from the Middle Stone Age levels at Blombos Cave, South Africa.' *Journal of Human Evolution*, Vol 57, Issue 1, July 2009.

HERCUS, L.A. *et al*. *Indological and Buddhist Studies*. ANU Faculty of Asian Studies, 1982.

HOCART, A.M. 'Buddha and Devadatta.' Indian Antiquary, Vol 52, Oct. 1923, pp. 267–72; Vol 54, Oct. 1925, pp. 98–99.

HOFSTADER, Douglas R., and Daniel C. DENNETT. *The Mind's I*. Penguin, 1981.

HORNER, I.B. *Women Under Primitive Buddhism*. Motilal Banarsidass, 1975.

HOUBEN, J.E.M. 'The Soma-Haoma problem: Introductory overview and observations on the discussion.' Electronic Journal of Vedic Studies, V^{OL} 9 (2003), Issue 1a (May 4).

HOUSEHOLDER, Fred W. and Gregory NAGY. *Greek: A Survey of Recent Work* The Hague, 1972.

HTUN, Rawe. *The Modern Buddhist Nun*. U Tin Shein, 2001.

HU, Hsiao-Lan. 'A Feminist Exegesis of Non-Self.' Metanexus Institute Conference, 2008.

HUIZINGA, J. (trans. R.F.C. HULL). *Homo Ludens*. Routledge and Kegan Paul, London, 1949.

HUME, David. *An Enquiry Concerning Human Understanding*. First Published 1748. Harvard Classics V^{OL} 37, P.F. Collier & Son, 1910.
http://rbjones.com/rbjpub/philos/classics/hume/index.htm

HÜSKEN, Ute. 'Saṅghabheda as Depicted in the Vinaya of the Mahāvihāra School.' In Petra KIEFFER-PÜLZ and Jens-Uwe HARTMANN (ed.) *Bauddhavidyāsudhākaraḥ*, pp. 319–331.

INDEN, Ronald, Jonathon WALTERS, Daud ALI. *Querying the Medieval*. Oxford University Press, 2000.

JACKSON, Peter A. 'Male Homosexuality and Transgenderism in the Thai Buddhist Tradition.' In Winston LEYLAND, ed. *Queer Dharma*. Gay Sunshine Press, 1998.
http://www.enabling.org/ia/vipassana/Archive/J/Jackson/homoBuddhaJackson.html

JAINI, Padmanabh S. *Gender and Salvation: Jaina Debates on the Spiritual Liberation of Women*. Berkeley: University of California Press, 1991.
http://ark.cdlib.org/ark:/13030/ft138nb0wk/

JAMANADAS, Dr. K. 'Rise and Fall of Buddhist Nuns.'
http://www.ambedkar.org/jamanadas/RiseAnd.htm

JAYNES, Julian. *The Origin of Consciousness in the Breakdown of the Bicameral Mind*. Houghton Mifflin, 1976.

JOLLY, Margaret (1994). '*Kastom* as Commodity: The Land Dive as Indigenous Rite and Tourist Spectacle in Vanuatu.' In L. LINDSTROM and G. WHITE, (eds). *Culture, Kastom, Tradition: Cultural Policy in Melanesia*. Institute of Pacific Studies, 1994. pp. 131–146.

JONES, J.J. (trans.) *The Mahavastu*. Pali Text Society, 1976.

JUNG, Carl G. *On the Nature of the Psyche*. Ark Paperbacks, 1991.

———. (trans. R.F.C. HULL) *Aspects of the Masculine/Aspects of the Feminine*. Fine Communications, 1997.

JUNG, Carl G. *et al. Man and his Symbols*. Picador, 1978.

JUO-HSÜEH Shih. *Controversies Over Buddhist Nuns*. Pali Text Society, 2000.

JUSCHKA, Darlene M. (ed.) *Feminism in the Study of Religion—A Reader*. Continuum, 2001.

KABILSINGH, Chatsuman. *The Bhikkhunī Pāṭimokkha of the Six Schools*. Sri Satguru, 1998.

———. *Thai Women in Buddhism*. Parallax Press, 1991.

———. 'The History of the Bhikkhuni Sangha.'
http://tinyurl.com/cuvdgzm

KAPUR, Alexandra R. *Thailand: Buddhism, Society and Women*. Abhinav Publications, 1998.

KARLSSON, Klemens. *Face to Face with the Absent Buddha: the formation of Buddhist Aniconic Art*. Acta Universitatis Upsalsiensis, Historia Religionum, 15, 2000.

KARVE, Irawati. 'The Cultural Process in India.' Man, V^{OL} 51, Oct. 1951, pp. 135–138.

KENOYER, Jonathon M. 'Early Developments of Art, Symbol, and Technology in the Indus Valley Tradition.' Indo-Koko-Kenkyu, Indian Archaeological Studies, 2000, Vol 22. www.harappa.com/indus3/e1.html

KERBER, L.K., Catherine G. GREENE, Eleanor E. MACCOBY, Zella LURIA, Carol B. STACK, and Carol GILLIGAN. 'On *In a Different Voice*: an Interdisciplinary Forum', in JUSCHKA, pp. 106–133.

KHUANKAEW, Ouyporn. 'Buddhism and Domestic Violence.' www.bpf.org/tsangha/tsm03report/Karma%20Book/khuankaew.html

KIEFFER-PÜLZ, Petra and Jens-Uwe HARTMANN, ed. *Bauddhavidyāsudhākaraḥ*. Indica et Tibetica 30. Swisttal-Odendorf, 1997.

KING, Winston L. 'Myth in Buddhism: Essential or Peripheral?' *Journal of Bible and Religion*, Vol 29.3, July 1961, pp. 211–218.

KINSLEY, David R. *Hindu Goddesses: Visions of the Divine Feminine in the Hindu Religious Tradition.* University of California Press, 1988.

KLEIN, Anne Carolyn. 'Finding a Self: Buddhist and Feminist Perspectives.' In Charles TALIAFERRO, Paul J. GRIFFITHS. *Philosophy of Religion: An Anthology.* Blackwell Publishing, 2003.

KLOPPENBORG, Ria. *The Sūtra on the Foundation of the Buddhist Order (Catuṣpariṣatsūtra).* Brill, 1973.

KLOPPENBORG, Ria & Wouter J. HANEGRAAF. *Female Stereotypes in Religious Traditions.* Brill 1995.

KOSAMBI, D.D. 'The Culture and Civilisation of Ancient India in Historical Outline.' www.vidyaonline.net/arvindgupta/cultddk.pdf

KNIGHT, Chris, Camilla POWER & Ian WATTS. 'The Human Symbolic Revolution: A Darwinian Account.' Cambridge Archaeological Journal 5:1 (1995), pp. 75–114.

KREY, Gisela. 'The Acceptance of Women in Early Buddhism.' Abstract for the International Congress on Buddhist Women's Role in the Sangha, Hamburg University, 2007. http://www.congress-on-buddhist-women.org/34.0.html

KRISHNA MURTHY, K. *Glimpses of Art, Architecture and Buddhist Literature in Ancient India.* Abhinav Publications, 1987.

KUSUMĀ, Bhikkhunī. 'Inaccuracies in Buddhist Women's History.' http://bhikkhunicommittee.googlepages.com/Kusuma.doc

LAKOFF, Robin & Sachiko IDE. *Broadening the Horizon of Linguistic Politeness.* John Benjamins Publishing Company, 2005.

LAMOTTE, Étienne. *History of Indian Buddhism.* Peeters Press, 1976.

LARSON, Gerald James (ed.) *Myth in Indo-European Antiquity.* University of California Press, 1974.

LEFKOWITZ, Mary. *Greek Gods, Human Lives.* Yale University Press, 2003.

LESLIE, Julia. *Myth and Mythmaking: Continuous Evolution in Indian Tradition.* Routledge, 1996.

LEVIN, Jack, Arnold ARLUKE. 'An Exploratory Analysis of Sex Differences in Gossip.' Sex Roles. Vol 12, Numbers 3–4, 281–286. http://www.springerlink.com/content/l052833960021636/fulltext.pdf

LI Rongxi (trans.) *The Biographical Scripture of King Aśoka* (T 2043 Aśokarājasūtra). Numata, 1993.

LONG, Asphodel P. 'Challenge or Inspiration?: The White Goddess in contemporary feminism and women's studies.'
http://www.asphodel-long.com/html/white_goddess.html

LOPEZ, Carlos. 'Food and Immortality in the Veda: A Gastronomic Theology?' Electronic Journal of Vedic Studies, V^OL 3 (1997), Issue 3 (Oct).

LYONS, Deborah. *Gender and Immortality: Heroines in Ancient Greek Myth and Cult.* Princeton University Press, 1996.

MCCARGO, Duncan. 'Buddhism, Democracy and Identity in Thailand.' In John ANDERSON (ed.), *Religion, Democracy and Democratization.* Routledge, 2006, pp. 155–170.

MCDANIEL, Justin. 'Buddhism in Thailand: Negotiating the Modern Age'. In Stephen C. BERKWITZ, *Buddhism in world cultures: comparative perspectives*, ABC-CLIO, 2006.

———. *Gathering Leaves & Lifting Words: histories of Buddhist monastic education in Laos and Thailand.* University of Washington Press, 2008.

MCEVILLEY, Thomas. *The Shape of Ancient Thought.* Allworth Press, 2002.

MCGOVERN, William Montgomery. *A Manual of Buddhist Philosophy.* Routledge, 2000.

MCMAHON, David. 'Orality, Writing, and Authority in South Asian Buddhism: Visionary Literature and the Struggle for Legitimacy in the Mahāyāna.' History of Religions, V ^OL 37, № 3, Feb 1998, pp. 249–274.

MACQUEEN, Graeme. *A Study of the Ṣrāmaṇyaphala Sūtra.* Otto Harrassowitz, 1988.

MAGEE, Michael. 'The Yoni Tantra.'
www.religiousworlds.com/mandalam/ftp/yoni.pdf

MALALASEKERA, G.P. *Dictionary of Pali Proper Names.* London, 1937, 1938.
http://www.palikanon.com/english/pali_names/dic_idx.html

MALINOWSKI, Bronislaw. *The Sexual Life of Savages.* Kessinger Publishing, 2005. First published New York, 1929.

MARLER, Joan. 'The Myth of Universal Patriarchy: A Critical Response to Cynthia Eller's Myth of Matriarchal Prehistory.' 2003.
http://www.belili.org/marija/eller_response.html

MEISIG, Konrad. *Das Śrāmaṇyaphala-Sūtra.* Otto Harrassowitz Wiesbaden, 1987.

MELETINSKIĬ, Eleazar MOISEEVICH, Guy LANOUE & Alexandre SADETSKY. *The Poetics of Myth.* Routledge, 2000.

METTANANDO, Mano Laohavanich, 'The First Council and Suppression of the Nuns.' Xuan Zang Buddhist Studies, 2008.03, pp. 49-120.
http://tinyurl.com/8j8mjt8

MIGOT, André. 'Un grand disciple du Buddha: Śāriputra.' *Bulletin de l'École Française d'Extrême-Orient*, 46, fasc. 2, 1954, pp. 405–554.

MILLER, Jeanine. *The Vedas: Harmony, Meditation, and Fulfillment.* Rider & Company, 1974.

MINGUN Sayadaw, *The Great Chronicle of Buddhas.* Singapore, 2008.

MINH CHÂU, Bhikkhu Thích. 'Milindapañha and Nāgasenabhikṣusūtra—A Comparative Study.'
http://www.budsas.org/ebud/milinda/ml-00.htm

———. *The Chinese Madhyama Āgama and the Pāli Majjhima Nikāya*. Motilal Barnasidass, 1991.
MITCHELL, Stephen (trans.) *Gilgamesh*. Free Press, 2004.
MITRA, Kalipada. 'Cross-cousin Relation Between Buddha and Devadatta.' http://www.wuys.com/news/article_show.asp?ArticleID=6859
MITRA, R.L. (trans.) *The Lalita Vistara*. Sri Satguru Publications, 1998.
MONIER-WILLIAMS, M. *A Sanskrit-English Dictionary*. Motilal Barnasidass, 2002.
MUCHEMBLED, Robert. *Damned: An Illustrated History of the Devil*. Chronicle Books, 2002.
MUIR, J. *Original Sanskrit Texts on the Origin and History of the People of India*. Trubner & Co., 1863.
MUKHERJEE, Biswadeb. 'The Riddle of the First Buddhist Council—A Retrospection.' Chung-Hwa Buddhist Journal, № 7, 1994. 452–473. http://enlight.lib.ntu.edu.tw/FULLTEXT/JR-BJ001/07_15.htm
MURCOTT, Susan. *The First Buddhist Women: translations and commentaries on the Therīgāthā*. Parallax Press, 1991.
MURTHY, S.S.N. 'Number Symbolism in the Vedas.' Electronic Journal of Vedic Studies, V OL 12 (2005), Issue 3 (Sep) .
———. 'A Note on the Rāmāyaṇa.' Electronic Journal of Vedic Studies, VOL 10 (2003), Issue 6 (Nov).
———. 'The Questionable Historicity of the Mahābhārata.' Electronic Journal of Vedic Studies, VOL 10 (2003), Issue 5 (Sep).
NAKAMURA, Hajime. *Indian Buddhism*. Delhi: Motilal Barnasidass, 1996.
ÑĀṆAMOḶI, Bhikkhu and Bhikkhu BODHI (trans.) *The Middle Length Discourses of the Buddha*. Somerville: Wisdom Publications, 2005.
ÑĀṆANANDA, Bhikkhu. *Concept and Reality in Early Buddhist Thought*. Buddhist Publication Society, 1971.
NĀRADA, Thera (trans.) *Abhidhammattha Saṅgaha of Anuruddhācariya: A Manual of Abhidhamma*. http://www.buddhanet.net/pdf_file/abhidhamma.pdf
NARAYAN, R.K. *The Indian Epics Retold*. Penguin, 1995.
NATTIER, Jan. *Once Upon a Future Time—Studies in a Buddhist Prophecy of Decline*. Asian Humanities Press, 1991.
NEEDHAM, Joseph *et al*. *Science and Civilisation in China*. Cambridge University Press, 1954.
NEUMANN, Erich. *The Origins and History of Consciousness*. Bollingen Series XLII, Princeton Universtity Press, Princeton N.J., 1973 (original German publication 1949).
———. *The Great Mother*. Bollingen Series XLVII, Princeton University Press, Princeton N.J., 1974
NICHOLSON, Philip T. 'The Soma Code.' Electronic Journal of Vedic Studies, VOL 8 (2002), Issue 3 (March).
NUGTEREN, Albertina. *Belief, Bounty, and Beauty: rituals around sacred trees in India*. Brill, 2005.
NYANAPONIKA Thera & Hellmuth HECKER (edited by Bhikkhu BODHI). *Great Disciples of the Buddha*. Wisdom Publications, 2003.
NYANAPONIKA Thera & Bhikkhu BODHI (trans.) *Numerical Discourses of the Buddha*. AltaMira Press, 1999.

OBEYESEKERE, Gananath. *The Cult of the Goddess Pattini*. University of Chicago Press, 1984.
O'BRIEN, Joan V. *The Transformation of Hera: A Study of Ritual, Hero, and the Goddess of the 'Iliad.'* Lanham, Md., 1993.
PACHOW, W. *A Comparative Study of the Prātimokṣa.* Motilal Banarsidass, 2000.
PARTRIDGE, Eric. *Origins: A Short Etymological Dictionary of Modern English*. Routledge, 1977.
PATTON, Laurie L., & Wendy DONIGER. *Myth and Method*. University of Virginia Press, 1996.
PAUL, Diana Y. *Women in Buddhism*. University of California Press, 1985.
PAUL, Robert A. *The Sherpas of Nepal in the Tibetan Cultural Context*. Motilal Banarsidass, 1989. (Originally published as *The Tibetan Symbolic World : a Psychoanalytic Exploration*, University of Chicago Press, 1982.)
PAW, Maung, 'The Revival of Bhikkhuni Sasana.' California, 2005.
PENZER, N.M. *The Ocean of Story*, V^OL 1. Read Books, 2006.
PEREGRINE, Peter Neal & Melvin EMBER. *Encyclopedia of Prehistory: South and Southwest Asia.* V^OL 8, Springer, 2003.
PIAGET, Jean. *The Construction of Reality in the Child.* Routledge, 1999.
PINTCHMAN, Tracy. *The Rise of the Goddess in the Hindu Tradition*. SUNY Press, 1994.
PIVEN, Jerry S. 'Buddhism, Death, and the Feminine'. *Psychoanalytic Review* 2003, 90:498–536.
———. *The Psychology of Death in Fantasy and History*. Greenwood Publishing Group, 2004.
POTTER, Karl H. & Harold G. COWARD. *Encyclopedia of Indian Philosophies.* Motilal Barnasidass, 1995.
POWERS, John. *A Bull of a Man: Images of Masculinity, Sex, and the Body in Indian Buddhism.* Harvard University Press, 2009.
PREBISH, Charles S. Buddhist Monastic Discipline. Delhi: Motilal, 2002.
———. 'Review of Scholarship on Buddhist Councils.' *Buddhism: Critical Concepts in Religious Studies.* Ed. Paul WILLIAMS. V^OL I. Routledge, 2005. pp 224–243.
———. *Buddhist Monastic Discipline.* Motilal Barnasidass, 2002.
PREECE, Rob. *The Wisdom of Imperfection*. Snow Lion Publications, 2006.
PRUITT, William (trans.) *The Commentary on the Verses of the Therīs (Therī-gāthā-Atthakathā Paramatthadīpanī VI)* by Ācarya Dhammapāla. Pali Text Society, 1998.
PRUITT, William & K.R. NORMAN (trans.) *The Pātimokkha.* Pali Text Society, 2003.
PURI, Jyoti. *Woman, Body, Desire in Post-Colonial India: Narratives of Gender and Sexuality.* Routledge, 1999.
PURKISS, Diane. *The Witch in History.* Routledge, 1996.
RADICE, William. *Myths and Legends of India.* The Folio Society, 2001.
RANK, Otto. 'The Myth of the Birth of the Hero.' (Trans. by Drs. F. ROBBINS and Smith Ely JELLIFFE of *Der Mythus von der Geburt des Helden: Versuch einer Psychologischen Mythendeutung.* Leipzig, Deuticke, 1909). Originally published: Nervous and Mental Disease Monograph Series, № 18. The Journal of Nervous and Mental Disease Publishing Company, 1914.
http://www.sacred-texts.com/neu/mbh/index.htm
RANKE-HEINEMANN, Uta. 'Female Blood.' *Eunuchs for Heaven*. German publication Hoffmann and Campe Verlag, Hamburg 1988; English publication by André Deutsch, London 1990, pp. 12–17.
www.womenpriests.org/body/ranke.asp

RAY, Reginald. 'A Condemned Saint: Devadatta.'
www.dharmaocean.org/Portals/0/documents/pubs/Devadatta.pdf

———. *Buddhist Saints in India: A Study in Buddhist Values and Orientations.* Oxford University Press, 1994.

RAYA, Udaya Narayana. *Salabhanjika in Art, Philosophy, and Literature*. Rajkamal Prakashan Pvt. Ltd. First edition: Lokbharti Publications, 1979.

REARDON, B.P. *Collected Ancient Greek Novels.* University of California Press, 1989.

RHYS DAVIDS, T.W. New & revised edition by C.A.F. RHYS DAVIDS. *Buddhist Birth Stories (Jataka Tales). The commentarial introduction entitled Nidāna Kathā (The Story of the Lineage).* Routledge, 1878. (Sic! This is the date given by the Uni. of Toronto, but the introduction by C.A.F. RHYS DAVIDS refers to dates as late as 1913, and states the original publication as 1880. So much for scholarly attempts to determine the age of ancient texts.)
www.archive.org/details/buddhistbirth00daviuoft

RHYS DAVIDS, T.W. *Buddhist India.* Fisher Unwin, 1903.

RICHTER-USHANAS, Egbert. *The Indus Script and the Ṛg Veda.* Motilal Barnasidass, 1997.

ROCKHILL, W. Woodville. *The Life of the Buddha.* First published London, 1884; reprinted Asian Education Services, 1992.

ROMBERG, Claudia . 'Women in Engaged Buddhism.' Contemporary Buddhism, Vol 3, № 2. Routledge, 2002 .

ROZARIO, Santi and Geoffrey SAMUEL. *Daughters of Hariti: Childbirth and Female Healers in South and Southeast Asia.* Routledge, 2002.

ROTH, Gustav. *Bhikṣuṇī-Vinaya.* K.P. Jayaswal Research Institute, 1970.

———. 'The Woman and Tree Motif', included in BECHERT and KIEFFER-PÜLZ, pp. 19–44; originally published in Journal of Asian Studies, 223.1, 1957, pp. 91–116.

SACCAVADI, Bhikkhuni (Daw Thissawady). 'Heir I Inherited.'
www.usamyanmar.net/Buddha/Article/BhikkhuniOrdinationHeirIInherited.pdf

———. 'My Experience as a Female Buddhist Monk in Burma (Myanmar).' (Privately circulated).

SACKS, Oliver. *A Leg to Stand On.* Touchstone, 1998.

SALOKOSKI, Märta. 'Ritual regicide versus succession strife: On divine kingship as an order-creating element in the political life of two Owambo kingdoms. A re-evaluation of the political significance of sacred kingship.' Paper presented at a seminar for the Research Project 'State and Everyday Life in Africa' in Tvärminne, Finland on May 4–6 2001.
www.valt.helsinki.fi/kmi/Tutkimus/Sal/Salokoski.htm

SANDAY, Peggy Reeves. *Female Power and Male Dominance: On the Origins of Sexual Inequality.* Cambridge University Press, 1981.

———. 'Matriarchy as a Sociocultural Form: An old debate in a new light.' Paper presented at the 16th Congress of the Indo-Pacific Prehistory Association, Melaka, Malaysia, 1–7 July, 1998.
http://www.sas.upenn.edu/~{}psanday/matri.html

SARAO, K.T.S. 'In-laws of the Buddha as Depicted in Pāli Sources.' Chung-Hwa Buddhist Journal, № 17. Taipei: The Chung-Hwa Institute of Buddhist Studies, 2004, pp. 243–265.
www.chibs.edu.tw/publication/chbj/17/chbj1709.htm

SCHERER, Burkhard. 'Gender transformed and meta-gendered enlightenment: Reading Buddhist narratives as paradigms of inclusiveness.' Programa de Pos-Graduacao em Ciencias da Religiao da Pontificia Universidade Catolica. REVER—Revista de Estudos da Religião, 2006.
http://www.pucsp.br/rever/rv3_2006/t_scherer.htm

SCHMITHAUSEN, Lambert. *Ālayavijñāna*. Studia Philologica Buddhica Monograph Series IVa. The International Institute for Buddhist Studies, 1987.

SCHOPEN, Gregory. *Buddhist Monks and Business Matters*. University of Hawai'i Press, 2004.

SCHREMPP, Gregory ALLEN & William F. HANSEN. *Myth: A New Symposium*. Indiana University Press, 2002.

SCHULTZ, Celia E. 'The Romans and Ritual Murder.' *Journal of the American Academy of Religion*, June 2010, Vol 78, № 2, pp. 516–541.

SCHUSTER, Nancy. 'Changing the Female Body.' In *Buddhism: Critical Concepts in Religious Studies*, Routledge, 2005, Vol 1, pp. 344–382.

SENEVIRATNE, Thalatha, and Jan CURRIE. 'Religion and Feminism: A Consideration of Cultural Constraints on Sri Lankan Women.' In JUSCHKA, pp. 198–226.

SHAW, Miranda. *Buddhist Goddesses of India*. Princeton University Press, 2006.

SHARF, Robert H. 'Buddhist Modernism and the Rhetoric of Meditative Experience.' Numen, Vol 42, № 3 (Oct. 1995), pp. 228–283.

SINGH, Iqbal. *Gautama Buddha*. Oxford Universtity Press, 1997 (first published 1937).

SINGH, Narendra. *Encyclopaedia of Jainism*, Vol 1 (Indo-European Jain Research Foundation). Anmol Publications, 2001.

SKILLING, Peter. *Mahāsūtras, vols. I and II*. Pali Text Society, 1997.

SNODGRASS, Adrian and Craig J. REYNOLDS. *The Symbolism of the Stupa*. SEAP Publications, 1985.

SOPHOCLES (trans. Robert FAGLES) *The Three Theban Plays: Antigone, Oedipus the King, Oedipus at Colonus*. Penguin Books, 1982.

SPONBERG, Alan. 'Attitudes toward Women and the Feminine in Early Buddhism.' In *Buddhism, Sexuality, and Gender*, José Ignacio CABEZÓN, ed. SUNY Press, 1992.

STENUDD, Stefan. 'Psychoanalysis of Myth.'
www.stenudd.com/myth/freudjung/index.htm

STEVENSON, Ian. *Children Who Remember Previous Lives: a question of reincarnation*. McFarland, 2000.

———. *Twenty Cases Suggestive of Reincarnation*. University of Virginia Press, 1980.

STRONG, John S. *The Legend and Cult of Upagupta*. Motilal Barnasidass, 1994.

———. *The Legend of King Aśoka*. Motilal Barnasidass, 2002.

SUCIU, Giulia. 'Stereotyped Perceptions of Gender Differences in Male-Female Communication—re-visiting the stereotype of the female chatterbox and the silent man.' University of Oradea.
http://tinyurl.com/7thcukr

SUJATO, Bhikkhu. *A Swift Pair of Messengers*. Santipada, 2010. (Originally published, Inward Path, 2001.)

———. *A History of Mindfulness*. Santipada, 2005. (originally published, Corporate Body of the Buddha Educational Foundation, 2003.

———. *Sects & Sectarianism*. Santipada, 2006.

———. *Bhikkhuni Vinaya Studies*. Santipada, 2009.

SUZUKI, Teitaro. 'The First Buddhist Council, 1904.
http://www.sacred-texts.com/journals/mon/1stbudcn.htm

TAN, Piya. Sutta Discovery 1.9: 'Who *Really* was the First Nun?' (privately distributed).

———. Sutta Discovery 1.10: 'The Dharma-ending Age.'
http://dharmafarer.googlepages.com/1.10TheDharma-endingagepiya.pdf

TATAR, Maria. *The Hard Facts of the Grimms' Fairy Tales*. Princeton University Press, 2003.

TAYLOR, Phillip. *Goddess on the Rise: Pilgrimage and Popular Religion in Vietnam*. University of Hawai'i Press, 2004.

TERWIEL, B.J. *Monks and Magic*. White Lotus, 1994.

THOMAS, E.J. 'The Lalitavistara and Sarvāstivāda.' Indian Historical Quarterly 16:2 1940.06, pp. 239–245.
http://ccbs.ntu.edu.tw/FULLTEXT/JR-ENG/tho_1.htm

———. *The Life of the Buddha as Legend and History*. Asian Educational Services, 2000.

TIYAVANICH, Kamala. *Forest Recollections: Wandering Monks in Twentieth-century Thailand*. University of Hawai'i Press, 1997.

TORTCHINOV, Evgueni A. 'Cybele, Attis, and the Mysteries of the "Suffering Gods": a Transpersonalistic Interpretation.' The International Journal of Transpersonal Studies, 1998. Vol 17.2, pp. 149–159.
http://etor.h1.ru/torpaper.html

TRIBLE, Phyllis. 'The Genesis of Gender.' In *Religious Culture and Gender Ethics (Conference Proceedings)*, Hongshi Buddhist Cultural and Educational Foundation, Tau-Yuan, 2007, pp. R1–R20.

TSOMO, Karma Lekshe. *Sisters in Solitude*. SUNY Press, 1996.

———. *Buddhist Women and Social Justice: Ideals, Challenges, and Achievements*. SUNY Press, 2004.

———. (ed.) *Buddhist Women Across Cultures*. SUNY Press, 1999.

UPRETI, Kalpana. *Position of Women as Reflected in Avadānaśātaka and its Ideological Ramifications*. Delhi University.

URBAN, Hugh B. *Tantra: Sex, Secrecy, Politics, and Power in the Study of Religion*. University of California Press, 2003.

VAJRACHARYA, Gautama V. 'The Adaptation of Monsoonal Culture by Rgvedic Aryans: A Further Study of the Frog Hymn.' Electronic Journal of Vedic Studies, Vol 3 (1997), issue 2 (May).

VALERI, Valerio (trans. Paula WISSING). *Kingship and Sacrifice: Ritual and Society in Ancient Hawai'i*. University of Chicago Press, 1985.

VĀLMĪKI (trans. Arshia SATTAR). *The Rāmāyaṇa*. Penguin, 2000.

VARADPANDE, Manohar Laxman. *History of Indian Theatre*. Vol 3, Abhinav Publications, 1987.

———. *Woman in Indian Sculpture*. Abhinav Publications, 2006.

VASUBANDHU (trans. Stefan ANACKER) *Seven Works of Vasubandhu.* Motilal Banarsidass, 1998.

VOGEL, J.P. *Indian Serpent-Lore of the Nagas in Hindu Legend and Art.* Asian Educational Services, 1995.

VON HINÜBER, Oskar. 'The Foundation of the Bhikkhunīsaṁgha.' Annual Report of The International Research Institute for Advanced Buddhology. Soka University, 2008, pp. 3–29.

VON SCHIEFNER, F. Anton (trans. from Tibetan to German; trans. from German to English, W.E.S. EALSTON). *Tibetan Tales.* Kegan, Paul, Teench, Teubnee & Co., 1906. http://archive.org/details/tibetantalesderi00schirich

VYAS, R.T. and Umakant Premanand SHAH. *Studies in Jaina Art and Iconography and Allied Subjects in Honour of Dr. U.P. Shah.* Abhinav Publications, 1995.

WAGLE, Narendra K. *Society at the Time of the Buddha.* Popular Prakashan, 1995.

WALDSCHMIDT, Ernst. *Das Catuṣpariṣatsūtra.* Abhandlungen der Deutschen Akademie der Wissenschaften zu Berlin, Klasse für Sprachen, Literatur und Kunst, 1960/1.

WALTERS, Jonathan S. 'A Voice from the Silence: the Buddha's Mother's Story.' *History of Religions* 33/4, 1994, pp. 358–379.

———. 'Suttas as History: Four Approaches to the Sermon on the Noble Quest (Ariyapariyesana Sutta).' History of Religions, V^OL 38, № 3, Feb 1999, pp. 247–284.

WALSHE, Maurice (trans.) *The Long Discourses of the Buddha.* Wisdom Publications, 1995.

WARDER, A.K. *Indian Buddhism.* Motilal Barnasidass, 2004.

WARNER, Marina. *From the Beast to the Blonde.* Vintage, 1995.

WATSON, Gay. 'Buddhism and the Feminine Voice.' Contemporary Buddhism, V^OL 4, № 1, 2003. www.wlu.ca/documents/6505/Buddhism_and_the_feminine.pdf

WATSON, Katherine D. *Poisoned Lives: English Poisoners and Their Victims.* Continuum International Publishing Group, 2006.

WICKRAMASINGHE, Martin. *The Buddhist Jātaka Stories and the Russian Novel.* Associated Newspapers of Colombo, Ltd., 1956.

WIEDERMAN, Michael W. 'Extramarital Sex: Prevalence and Correlates in a National Survey.' Journal of Sex Research, Spring, 1997. http://findarticles.com/p/articles/mi_m2372/is_n2_v34/ai_19551967/

WIJESEKERA, O.H. de A. *Buddhist and Vedic Studies.* Motilal Barnasidass, 1994.

WILLEMEN, Charles (trans.) *The Scriptural Text: Verses of the Doctrine, with Parables* (T № 211 Dhammapāda-avadāna Sūtra). Numata, 1999.

WILLEMEN, Charles, Bart DESSEIN, and Collett COX. *Sarvāstivāda Buddhist Scholasticism.* Brill, 1998.

WILLIAMS, Liz. 'A Whisper in the Silence: Nuns Before Mahāpajāpatī?' Buddhist Studies Review 17.2, 2000, pp. 167–173.

———. 'Red Rust, Robbers, and Rice Fields: Women's Part in the Precipitation of the Decline of the Dhamma.' Buddhist Studies Review 19.1, 2002, pp. 41–47.

WILLIAMS, Louise. *Wives, Mistresses & Matriarchs.* Phoenix Press, 2001.

WILSON, Liz. *Charming Cadavers: Horrific Figurations of the Feminine in Indian Buddhist Hagiographic Literature.* University of Chicago Press, 1996.

WINTERNITZ, M. 'Jataka Gathas and Jataka Commentary.' The Indian Historical Quarterly, V^OL IV, № 1, March 1928.
http://ccbs.ntu.edu.tw/FULLTEXT/JR-ENG/win.htm

WITZEL, Michael. 'Substrate Languages in Old Indo-Aryan (Rgvedic, Middle and Late Vedic).' Electronic Journal of Vedic Studies, V^OL 5 (1999), issue 1 (Sept.)
www.ejvs.laurasianacademy.com/ejvs0501/ejvs0501a.txt

WONG, Ling-ling. 'The Concept of Female Pollution in Buddhism and Taoism', in *Religious Culture and Gender Ethics (Conference Proceedings)*, Hongshi Buddhist Cultural and Educational Foundation, Tau-Yuan, 2007, pp. X1–X16.

YEH, Pao-Kuei. 'Breaking the Taboo of Women's Blood Pollution in Religions and Culture: A Christian Perspective', in *Religious Culture and Gender Ethics (Conference Proceedings)*, Hongshi Buddhist Cultural and Educational Foundation, Tau-Yuan, 2007, pp. U1–U28.

YEO-KWANG Sunim (Bhikkhuni Tathāālokā), *A Brief History of Bhiksuni Ordination*. Unpublished notes.

YOUNG, Dudley. *Origins of the Sacred*. Abacus, 1991.

YOUNG, Serinity. *Courtesans and Tantric Consorts: Sexualities in Buddhist Narrative, Iconography and Ritual*. Routledge, 2004.

———. 'Female Mutability and Male Anxiety in an Early Buddhist Legend.' Journal of the History of Sexuality, V^OL 16, № 1, January 2007, pp. 14–39.
http://tinyurl.com/73h9jnx

ZIMMER, Heinrich. *Philosophies of India*. Meridian Books, 1956.

———. *Myths and Symbols in India Art and Civilization*. Bollingen Series VI, Princeton University Press, 1974.

———. *The King and the Corpse*. Princeton University Press, 1971.

ZIPES, Jack David. *Breaking the Magic Spell: Radical Theories of Folk and Fairy Tales*. University Press of Kentucky, 2002.

FIGURES

The images used in this book, with a few exceptions, are specially commissioned pencil drawings by Darryl Gradwell in 2008–9. They were begun in the lengthy period that Darryl stayed at Santi Forest Monastery, and completed before his tragic death in 2010. They are used by kind permission of his family, and are a testimony to his extraordinary talent. The drawings were prepared for publication by Alex Sebby. The exceptions to this are Figure 19, which is a pencil drawing by Alex Sebby, and the photographs at Figures 5, 21, and 26. Where possible, I supply URLs for the images that were the basis for the drawings.

Figure 1, Frontispiece: The Birth of the Bodhisatta: Māyā clinging to the *sāl* tree in Lumbini. Nepalese school; 9th century.
http://www.myartprints.com/a/nepalese-school/queen-maya-giving-birth-t.html

Figure 1.1, p. 2: Sālabhañjikā. Sanchi; after 70 BCE. British Museum.
http://commons.wikimedia.org/wiki/Image:SanchiBracketFigure.jpg

Figure 1.2, p. 4: Sālabhañjikā. Karnataka, India; *circa* 1100 CE. National Museum, New Delhi, India.
http://images.asc.ohio-state.edu/is/image/ha/0000300_c.JPG?size=668,668&qlt=30&fmt=jpeg

Figure 1.3, p. 9: Female deity in Bodhi tree. Mohenjo Daro; *circa* 2000 BCE. Mohenjo-daro DK 6847, Islamabad Museum, NMP 50.295.
http://www.harappa.com/indus/34.html

Figure 1.4, p. 11: Saṅghamittā greeted by King Devanampiyatissa as she arrives in Sri Lankā with the Bodhi Tree. Solius Mendis. Kelaniya Vihara; *circa* 1800 CE.
http://www.dailynews.lk/2008/12/12/z_p11-a-grant1.jpg

Figure 2.1, p. 19: Nun being shaved before ordination.

Figure 3.1, p. 32: Minoan snake goddess. Knossos, Crete; *circa* 1600 BCE. Boston Museum.
http://www.uned.es/geo-1-historia-antigua-universal/SERPIENTES/GIMBUTAS_1_3.htm

Figure 3.2, p. 34: Adam, Eve, and the female serpent. Notre Dame Cathedral.
http://en.wikipedia.org/wiki/File:France_Paris_Notre-Dame-Adam_and_Eve.jpg

Figure 4.1, p. 54: Wedding couple of Māli (flower-growing) caste in India with marriage crowns. *The Tribes and Castes of the Central Provinces of India, Vol IV.*
http://www.gutenberg.org/files/20668/20668-h/20668-h.htm

Figure 5.1, p. 63: Māyā's dream: the conception of the Bodhisatta. Peshawar, India; Kusana period, 50 CE–250 CE. Indian Museum, Calcutta.
http://en.wikipedia.org/wiki/File:MayaDream.jpg

Figure 7.1, p. 74: Hārītī with her husband Pañcika, holding a cornucopia. Takht-i Bahi, Gandhārā; 3rd century CE. British Museum.
http://en.wikipedia.org/wiki/File:PanchalaAndHariti.jpg

Figure 8.1, p. 90: *The Sacrifice of Domalde.* Halfdan Egedius (May 5, 1877–February 2, 1899).
http://en.wikipedia.org/wiki/Image:Domalde.jpg

Figure 10.1, p. 120: N'gol, the origin of bungee jumping. From a photograph by Michael Craig.
http://www.michael-craig.com/home.html

Figure 12.1, p. 147: Buddha head, Greco-Indian style. Gandhārā, *circa* 2nd century CE.

Figure 14.1, p. 162: The Ona people of Tierra del Fuego.
http://www.victory-cruises.com/ona_indian.html

Figure 19.1, p. 207: *The Witch.* Niklaus Manuel Deutsch (1484–1530). Kupferstichkabinett, Berlin. MUCHEMBLED, *Damned*, p. 100.

Figure 19.2, p. 211: Monastic bowl with stand, Thai style.

Figure 23.1, p. 251: Baba Yaga. From a still from the film *Bartok the Magnificent*, 1999.
http://en.wikipedia.org/wiki/File:Bartok_Baba_Yaga.jpg

Figure 24.1, p. 276: The Bodhisatta's austerities. Sikri Stupa, Gandhārā, 2nd–3rd century CE. Lahore Museum. Pencil drawing by Alex Sebby.
http://www.edepot.com/graphics/bud3.jpg

Figure 25.1, p. 279: The Assault of Māra. Amaravati, India; 2nd century CE.
http://en.wikipedia.org/wiki/File:MaraAssault.jpg

Figure 25.2, p. 281: The Earth Goddess bears witness to the Buddha's Awakening. Doi Suthep, Chieng Mai, Thailand. Photo by Neil Banas, licensed as Creative Commons Attribution-NonCommercial 2.0 Generic.
http://www.flickr.com/photos/neilbanas/437741454/sizes/o/in/photostream/

Figure 28.1, p. 328: Laocoön and his sons being dragged into the ocean by a serpent. Attributed to Agesander, Athenodoros and Polydorus. Rome; *circa* 40 BCE. Vatican Museums.
http://en.wikipedia.org/wiki/File:Laocoon_Pio-Clementino_Inv1059-1064-1067.jpg

Figure 29.1, p. 333: The Venus of Lespugue. Lespugue (Haute-Garonne); *circa* 22 000 BCE. Musée de l'Homme.
http://en.wikipedia.org/wiki/Image:Venus_de_Lespugue_(replica).jpg

Figure 29.2, p. 344: Perseus and Andromeda attacking monster, Greek vase, Corinth; *circa* 600 BCE.
http://tinyurl.com/6oluk27

Figure 29.3, p. 346: Andromeda blessing Perseus, Pompeii.
http://tinyurl.com/7p8uauw

Figure 29.4, p. 348: Perseus rescuing Andromeda. Hogarth William (1697–1764), Figure for 'Perseus and Andromeda' by Lewis Theobald. British Museum.
http://www.posterrevolution.com/gallery/item.cfm?ID=595738

Figure 31.1, p. 367: Devil devouring a man's head. Archstone, Église Saint-Brice, Saint Mandé-sur-Brédoire, Charente Maritime, France; 12th century. MUCHEMBLED, *Damned*, p. 20.

Figure 31.2, p. 369: Kronos devouring his son. Goya, 1888. http://www.stenudd.com/myth/freudjung/freud-mosesmonotheism.htm

Figure 31.3, p. 371: *Cain kills Abel*. Gustave Doré. http://commons.wikimedia.org/wiki/File:Cain_kills_Abel.png

Figure 32.1, p. 381: Ānanda. Luminary Buddhist Institute, Taiwan.

Figure 32.2, p. 381: Mahākassapa. Luminary Buddhist Institute, Taiwan.

Figure 40.1, p. 469: Buddha head in tree. Wat Mahathat, Ayutthaya, Thailand; Ayutthaya period (*circa* 1500–1700 CE). http://en.wikipedia.org/wiki/File:The_head_of_Buddha_in_Wat_Mahathat.jpg

Figure 40.2, p. 472: Bodhisattva. Veragala Sirisangabo Vihara, Allavava, Anuradhapura district, Sri Lanka; Late Anuradhapura Period, 8th–9th century. National Museum, Colombo. http://lakdiva.org/avalokitesvara/avalokitesvara.html

Figure 40.3, p. 473: Quan Yin Bodhisattva. Shanxi Province, China; Liao Dynasty, *circa* 1100 CE. Nelson-Atkins Museum Collection, Kansas City, Missouri. http://en.wikipedia.org/wiki/File:Liao_Dynasty_-_Guan_Yin_statue.jpg

Figure 40.4, p. 475: Prajñāpāramitā. Singhasari, East Java, Indonesia, *circa* 1250 CE. http://commons.wikimedia.org/wiki/Image:Prajnaparamita_Java.jpg

NOTES

Chapter 1 The Lady & the Tree

1. http://www.metmuseum.org/toah/works-of-art/2002.416a,b
2. See CAMPBELL, *Oriental Mythology*, pp. 301–2.
3. YOUNG, pp. 113–4.
4. ROTH, 'The Woman and Tree Motif'. See also ZIMMER, *Myths and Symbols*, p. 69.
5. Jātakanidāna Avidūrenidānakathā: *Deviyā taṁ disvā sālavanakīḷaṁ kīḷitukāmatācittaṁ udapādi.* (Also see Paṭhamasambodhi p. 15.17); Mahāvastu 1.99; Lalitavistara ch. 7 verse 1: *kṣipramahu vrajeyā krīḍaudyānabhūmim.* www.uwest.edu/sanskritcanon/Sutra/roman/Sutra%2022/Chapter7a.html
6. AVŚ_53 sālaḥ: *sālapuṣpāṇy ādāya krīḍanti.* www.sub.uni-goettingen.de/ebene_1/fiindolo/gretil/1_sanskr/4_rellit/buddh/avsata_u.htm
7. The Buddha is depicted as the abolisher of child sacrifice. In a story from a Chinese Dhammapada, the king's mother is ill, and to cure her the brahmans advise sacrificing animals and a boy. The Buddha taught the Dhamma of non-killing, whereupon the mother was cured, the brahmans converted, and the land flourished. (T4, № 211, p. 581c-582a; WILLEMEN, pp. 47–9.)
8. *Aeneid*, 6.1–263.
9. Captured beautifully at http://en.wikipedia.org/wiki/File:Mistleltoe_in_Lebanon.jpg.
10. The first element most obviously stands for the *sāla* tree; but ROTH suggests it may be originally derived from *sākhā* (branch), later assimilated to *sāla*.
11. Perhaps 29 000–7000 BCE. For a good range of photographs and discussion, see donsmaps.com/venus.html#ukrainevenus.
12. PEREGRINE *et al.*, pp. 329–330; VARADPANDE, p. 5. An upper paleolithic floor in the Son valley decorated with an stone triangle surrounded by ochre concentric triangles has been interpreted via ethnographic parallels as a shrine for goddess worship, but this seems much less certain.
13. AGRAWALA, p. 16, 23*ff.*; KINSLEY, pp. 213–4; KENOYER. There are earlier images from Mehrgarh, Nausharo, and Pirak in Pakistan, which were continually occupied from 7000–500 BCE and are regarded as the forerunner of the Indus Valley Civilization. The prevalence of

highly stylized female figures suggests a goddess cult, but there is insufficient evidence to be conclusive.

14. See discussion on the exaggerated 'eye-index' of early human figures in JAYNES, pp. 169–171.
15. See discussion in KINSLEY, pp. 212*ff*. The emphasis on the head can be read as a hint at the special interest in consciousness found in all Indian spirituality.
16. This is Indus seal M-1186. Indus seal M-488C contains a comparable scene, with a similar head on an altar, only it is next to a typical Indus-style shamanic figure. See discussion in CAMPBELL, *Oriental Mythology*, p. 169.
17. WIJESEKERA, pp. 213*ff*.
18. PARPOLA, www.harappa.com/script/parpola12.html
19. Such signs are normally interpreted as a linguistic script, an interpretation that has recently been challenged by FARMER, *et al.*
20. www.harappa.com/script/parpola8.html
21. www.harappa.com/indus/34.html
22. In Harappa, excavations revealed a group of about 20 tightly packed skulls, together with animal bones and implements interpreted by the archeologist Vats as suggestive of ritual sacrifice. At Mehi, three Kulli goddesses were discovered placed inside a human skull (AGRAWALA, p. 26).
23. See CAMPBELL, *Oriental Mythology*, p. 155*ff*.
24. Picture taken from 200 year old wall-painting at the well known monastery of Kelaniya Vihara (about 5 miles east of Colombo), by a local artist, Solius Mendis.
25. Kāliṅga Jātaka (№ 479, 4.228–236).

Chapter 2 A Myth of Origins

1. Scholars who have commented on the Mahāpajāpatī story and have either asserted that there are significant historical implausibilities, or at least have referred sympathetically to such a notion, include the following. GNANARAMA, p. 66–79; KOSAMBI DHAMMANANDA (*Bhagavan Buddha*, Colombo 1968, cited by GNANARAMA); ANĀLAYO, 'The Four Assemblies'; KREY; KUSUMĀ; CHUNG, p. 87–8, who cites HIRAKAWA, Hae-ju CHUN, and Nancy Auer FALK; KABILSINGH, 'History'; METTANANDO; HEIRMANN, *Discipline in Four Parts, Part 1*, p. 65; HEIRMANN cites Ute HÜSKEN, *Die Vorschriften für die buddhistische Nonnengemeinde im Vinaya-Piṭaka der Theravādin*, Dietrich Reimer Verlag (Monographien zur Indischen Archäologie, Kunst und Philologie 11), 1997, pp. 345–360; TSOMO, *Buddhist Women*, pp. 54–5; GREEN quotes Kajiyama YUICHI 'Women in Buddhism' (The Eastern Buddhist, 1982); WILLIAMS; SPONBERG, who cites VAN GOOR, *De Buddhistische Non* and I.B. HORNER, *Women under Primitive Buddhism*, p. 105; NATTIER; E.J. THOMAS, p. 110; FAURE, p. 23; ARMSTRONG, *Buddha*, p. 138–42; SINGH, p. 211; GROSS, *Patriarchy*, pp. 32–38; PAUL, p. 81; WILSON, p. 236, note 15.
2. E.g. http://www.accesstoinsight.org/lib/authors/Ṭhānissaro/bmc2/bmc2.ch23.html. Notice that Ṭhānissaro, attempting to present a rational explanation for the Buddha's behavior, omits the similes of the diseases destroying the crops.
3. ROTH, p. 12, text and note 9.
4. Most editions here have 稽首 'bow', but the 聖 edition has 致二 'second devotion', which is required by the context. It seems this line is referring to the well known episode (found e.g. in the Vessantara Jātaka, № 547, pp. 246–247) when Suddhodana bowed to his son

while he meditated under the rose-apple tree. This episode is not mentioned in the early canonical account; our current context must be one of the earliest references. As often, the Pali tradition reserves for the commentarial literature episodes that the other schools found room for in their canon.

5. The Mūlasarvāstivāda (ROCKHILL, p. 60) has the Buddha encouraging Mahāpajāpatī to live a virtuous lay life, as our Mahīśāsaka version encourages Suddhodana above. The admonition here for Mahāpajāpatī to live effectively the life gone forth while at home is peculiar, however it is also found in the Sarvāstivāda Gautamī Sūtra (T1, № 26, p. 605, a17–18; T1, № 60, p. 856, a14–15). She is normally depicted as shaving and donning the robes with her 500 followers of her own volition (Lokuttaravāda at ROTH, p. 6; Mūlasarvāstivāda at ROCKHILL, p. 61; Dharmaguptaka at T22, № 1428, p. 922, c18; Pali Vinaya 2.253).
6. According to the Sarvāstivāda Gautamī Sūtra, the Buddha wandered off after the vassa, when the time for sewing robes was over (T1, № 26, p. 605, a19–24; T1, № 60, p. 856, a16–19).
7. The Pali is set at Vesālī; the Mūlasarvāstivāda (ROCKHILL, p. 61) is at an obscure town apparently near Vesālī, the Sarvāstivāda is at 'Na-po-ti' (?那摩提。住那摩提揵尼精舍 T1, № 26, p. 605, b9; 那那婆提。住那婆提耆尼舍 T1, № 60, p. 856, b6–7), while the Dharmaguptaka (T22, № 1428, p. 922, c16) and the Lokuttaravāda (ROTH, p. 6) agree with the Mahīśāsaka in placing the events at Sāvatthī. Modern folk tradition, however, agrees on Vesālī. There is a strong tendency for events to be situated at Sāvatthī, which became the 'default' setting for redactors who were unsure of the actual setting. In cases where the settings conflict, then, it is safe to assume that the place that is not Sāvatthī is more likely to be correct.
8. Mahīśāsaka Vinaya, Bhikkhunī Khandhaka (T22, № 1421, p. 185, b7). The translation was assisted by Bhikkhuni Samacittā. This last passage includes yet another peculiarity of this version: nowhere else, so far as I am aware, does a bhikkhuni act as preceptor in an assembly of bhikkhus.
9. Bhikṣunī Mahāprajāpatī Sūtra (T24 № 1478, p. 946, a26); Mūlasarvāstivāda Vinaya (T24 № 1451, p. 350, c13); Dharmaguptaka Vinaya (T22 № 1428, p. 923, a02); Gautamī Sūtra (T1 № 60, p. 856, b29); Sarvāstivāda Gautamī Sūtra (T1 № 26, p. 605c05); Pali Vinaya 2.256. This simile is absent from the Lokuttaravāda and Mahāsaṅghika.
10. Similar claims are found in the Haimavata Vinaya Mātikā (T24, № 1463, p. 818, b18–c4); Sarvāstivāda Gautamī Sūtra (T1 № 26, p. 607a16–b07); and the Gautamī Sūtra (T1 № 60, p. 857, c18–c27).
11. Bhikṣunī Mahāprajāpatī Sūtra (T24 № 1478, p. 946, a29–b4); Mūlasarvāstivāda Vinaya (T24 № 1451, p. 350, c13); Dharmaguptaka Vinaya (T22 № 1428, p. 923, a04); Lokuttaravāda Vinaya (ROTH § 8); Gautamī Sūtra (T1 № 60, p. 856, c04); Sarvāstivāda Gautamī Sūtra (T1 № 26, p. 605, c09).
12. Pali Vinaya 2.256, Aṅguttara Nikāya 8.51.
13. *Bhikkhuni Vinaya Studies*, ch. 6.
14. CAMPBELL, *Oriental Mythology*, pp. 110–111.

Chapter 3 The Death of the Goddess

1. GIRARD, p. 68.
2. JAYNES, p. 225.
3. CAMPBELL, *Oriental Mythology*, p. 140. CAMPBELL quotes the entire lament, and subsequent reconciliation with the god, at length.
4. Deuteronomy 31.17.
5. Jeremiah 18:17.
6. Jeremiah 33.5. See also Isaiah 8.17, Psalms 44.24.
7. Matthew 27.46. See Psalms 22.1.
8. Ṛg Veda 10.129. (DONIGER's trans.)
9. *Aeneid*, 4.208–10, 4.218.
10. Canda-kinnara Jātaka (№ 485, 4.282–288).
11. Phandana Jātaka (№ 475, 4.207–211).
12. Vinaya Mahāvagga 1.23.
13. MITCHELL, pp. 133–4.
14. *Aeneid* 3.111.
15. E.g. Kings 22.3–22.25. See discussion in CAMPBELL, *Oriental Mythology*, ch. 3.1 *passim.*
16. See SANDAY, pp. 216*ff.*
17. If Eve suffered a patriarchal reversal, a forcible divorce from her own divine aspect, this came to be reconciled in some later myths. For the Koranic tradition tells us that Mary, when her time grew near, approached a dry, barren palm tree and grasped it. When she did so, not only did she give birth to the Savior of the World, but the tree sprang miraculously into fruit. This is identical with the Indic *sālabhañjikā* tradition. The association of the woman and the tree continues in fairy tales. Cinderella, for example, is depicted by Joseph Southall clasping a tree in much the same way as Māyā. www.tate.org.uk/servlet/ViewWork?cgroupid=999999961&workid=13655&searchid=11058
18. NEUMANN, *The Great Mother*, p. 151.
19. http://www.ekantipur.com/news/news-detail.php?news_id=302477
20. http://www.guardian.co.uk/world/2009/nov/24/hindu-sacrifice-gadhimai-festival-nepal
21. 'Killing for "Mother" Kālī', *Time Magazine*, July 22 2002, Alex Perry ATAPUR. www.time.com/time/magazine/article/0,9171,501020729-322673,00.html
22. See http://en.wikipedia.org/wiki/Devi_Mahatmyam

Chapter 4 The Little Stick Collector

1. Kaṭṭhahāri Jātaka (№ 7, 1.133–136).
2. Bhaddasāla Jātaka (№ 465, 4.144–157).
3. It would seem highly implausible that a Khattiya clan such as the Śākyans would refuse to give their daughter in marriage to another Khattiya, both clans claiming to belong to the Solar Dynasty fathered by Ikśavāku ('Sugar'), which incidentally was the clan of Rāma also. Perhaps this anomaly is to be explained as indicative of a primitive social survival. The idea of the four classes, as promulgated by the Brahmans in the Buddha's time, emphasizes a pan-Indian social structure. But India, then as now, was riven by thousands of tribal divisions of all kinds. And the basic, ancient position of most tribes was endogamy, only

allowing marriage within the tribe. So this attitude of the Śākyans would be well explained as showing that their perception of themselves was still primarily tribal, and the class system was secondary.

4. Notice here how milk is the liquid of purity, which is replaced by blood in the revenge fantasy. The dual imagery of milk/blood will be a recurring theme of our inquiry.
5. It seems this happened shortly after the Buddha's death, although several sources depict it as occurring in the Buddha's life. A Chinese Dhammapada says that after killing the Śākyans, the Buddha said Viḍūḍabha would be taken to hell. To escape his destiny he fled to sea, only for the sea itself to ignite with the fires of hell. (T4, № 211, p. 583 a-b; WILLEMEN, pp. 55–7. See T4, № 211, pp. 590c-591b; WILLEMEN, pp. 105–7.)
6. Here, as with all Jātakas, I retell the story based on the traditional translations from COWELL, *et al.* I have checked these against the original Pali, and change or update when it seems useful. I am trying to convey a story, and so I do not offer a literal translation except where it is necessary.
7. Bhaddasāla Jātaka (№ 465, 4.148): *mātugottaṁ nāma kiṁ karissati, pitugottameva pamāṇanti porāṇakapaṇḍitā.*
8. Saṁyutta Nikāya 3.17.
9. Mahā Ummagga Jātaka (№ 546, 6.336–7).
10. There is a similar background to the romance between king Pasenadi and his favorite queen, Mallikā. She was a simple flower girl who was collecting flowers in a park when the king heard her singing (Kummāsapiṇḍa Jātaka introduction, № 415, 3.405–406).
11. Homeric Hymn 2 (abridged), trans. EVELYN-WHITE. http://www.theoi.com/Khthonios/HaidesPersephone1.html
12. JAYNES, pp. 361*ff.*
13. NICHOLSON in his 'The Soma Code' draws parallels between the descriptions of Soma in the Ṛg Veda with contemporary meditation visions.
14. GRAVES, *The White Goddess*, p. xii.
15. LONG.
16. *Aeneid*, 10.4.
17. Rāmāyaṇa, p. 12.
18. MILLER, p. 74, referring to Ṛg Veda 2.9.4, 4.11.3, 5.8.6.
19. NEUMANN, *The Great Mother*, p. 296.
20. PLATO, *Io* 534, quoted in JAYNES, p. 370.
21. Such themes recur throughout the Jātakas, e.g. Maṇicora Jātaka (№ 194, 2.124), Rājovāda Jātaka (№ 334, 3.110–112), Vessantara Jātaka (№ 547, 6.487), Kurudhamma Jātaka (№ 276, 2.335–382).
22. Some examples of magical conception are found in Jātakas 281, 497, 509, 526 (5.281), 523 (5.526), 540.
23. Ion 430–450, trans. George THEODORIDIS. http://bacchicstage.com/Ion.htm
24. CALASSO, *Marriage*.
25. For example, Zeus and Semele at OVID, *Metamorphoses* III.308–312; HYGINUS, *Fabulae* 179; NONNUS, *Dionysiaca* 8.178–406; or Moses and Jahweh at Exodus 33.20 ('You cannot see my face; for there no man shall see me and live'; but contradicted at Exodus 33.11).

26. JUNG, *The Integration of the Personality* (1939), p. 59. Quoted in CAMPBELL, *Hero*, p. 202–3 and *Oriental Mythology*, p. 46.
27. Speaking of a similar shift in Egyptian mythology, CAMPBELL (*Oriental Mythology*, p. 98) says: 'Its sunny atmosphere of play is characteristic of the mythic mood of solar as opposed to lunar thought. In it the old, deep, vegetal melancholy of a dark destiny of death and of birth out of decay has disappeared and a fresh, blithe breath of clean air has come blowing into the field, scattering shadows all away. A masculine spirit has taken over: boyish, somewhat; comparatively superficial, one might say; but with a certain distance from itself that makes a play of intellect possible where before all had been depth and woe.' Later (*Oriental Mythology*, p. 164) he refers to the dark Indian goddess 'of the long red tongue who turns everything into her own everlasting, awesome, yet finally somewhat tedious, self.'
28. BAMSHAD, *et al.*
29. This story bears comparison with the curious legend of ancestry related by the Buddha at Ambaṭṭha Sutta (Dīgha Nikāya 3.1.15–6). A Śākyan slave girl Disā ('Direction') gives birth to a black baby, who as soon as he was born cried out 'Wash me, mother, free me from this dirt!' 'Black' is said to have been a term of abuse in those days—though not, it seems, in the Buddha's time—and the story is told to humble the brahman student Ambaṭṭha's pride. But the Buddha redeems the story by saying that the black baby went on to become a mighty sage, who married the king's daughter. This might be the earliest reference to the story of Kṛṣṇa ('Black', spelt *kaṇha* in Pali). The story is also folkloristically interesting in that it recounts what appears to be a garbled form of fertility/regicide rite where the king points his arrow at the earth, then the sky, then the crown prince.
30. *Sā kira mahānāmassa sakkassa dhītā nāgamuṇḍāya nāma dāsiyā.*
31. As suggested by KARVE and GADKARI (p. 101). The *nāgas* are not the tribe called by that name in modern times; these are later arrivals in India, and their name (of uncertain origin) was given by outsiders only recently.
32. This uncertainty regarding the form of the name is reflected in the manuscript traditions, where 'Viḍūḍabha' occurs in various forms such as 'Viṭaṭubha' and the Sanskritic 'Virūḍhaka'.
33. Uddālaka Jātaka (№ 487, 4.293–304).
34. Chāndogya Upaniṣad, 4.4.1–5. The Upaniṣads were a class of spiritual literature produced by the brahmans. The earliest of them, including the Bṛhadāraṇyaka and the Chāndogya, probably predate the Buddha by a few centuries.
35. www.guardian.co.uk/politics/2008/aug/01/freedomofinformation.childprotection
36. This is not always true. We have already seen a famous test of true motherhood. The Nigrodha Jātaka (№ 445, 4.37–43) and Ghata Jātaka (№ 454, 4.79–89) deal with cases where the mother deliberately hides the child's parentage. However, this usually requires a substantial effort to conceal the truth or else a set of unusual circumstances, whereas parental uncertainty is the norm.
37. One of the earliest lineage lists is found in the Mahāsaṅghika Vinaya. FRAUWALLNER (*Earliest Vinaya*, pp. 61–3) has shown that this list mirrors exactly the form of a list found in the earlier Bṛhadāraṇyaka Upaṇiṣad.

38. Cetiya Jātaka (№ 422, 3.454–461).
39. The 'Great Elect'; he first occurs in the canonical Buddhist myth the Aggañña Sutta, Dīgha Nikāya 27.
40. As in the famous lines from the Mettā Sutta: 'Just as a mother would give her life for her only child/So too one would develop a boundless heart for all beings.' Sutta Nipāta 143–152.
41. In the *Iliad*, by contrast, the goddesses are the main provocateurs.
42. Takkāriya Jātaka (№ 481, 4.242–255).
43. Khaṇḍahāla Jātaka (№ 542, 6.129*ff*).
44. See ZIMMER, *The King and the Corpse*, pp. 202–235, for a discussion of this theme.
45. A standard device in fables, e.g. *Rāmāyaṇa* p. 458: Sītā recognizes Rāma's ring and is as happy as if reunited with him.
46. *Cf.* Jupiter's justification for marrying Cupid and Psyche (APULEIUS, p. 113, see below ch. 29.51).
47. A version of Kṛṣṇa's story is found in Ghata Jātaka (№ 454, 3.79–89), and here as in the Brahmanical accounts he dies of a wounded foot. See ch. 29.40.
48. FRAZER, ch. 60.
49. Vessantara Jātaka (№ 547, 6.251).
50. Majjhima Nikāya 56.29, verse 1 (1.386). In Tesakuṇa Jātaka (№ 521 Tesakuṇa, 5.110.24), Vessantara is also a proper name, in this case a bird who is adopted as son by a king, and identified with Sāriputta.
51. The Pali Text Society Dictionary (p. 738, note 1.) notes that the Pali commentators appear to have been unfamiliar with the very common Sanskrit word *viśva*. This is one of two Sanskrit words meaning 'all', the other being *sarva*. But while *sarva* has its regular Pali counterpart *sabba*, *viśva* hardly appears in the expected Pali form *vissa*, which is confined to just one verse.
52. VON SCHIEFNER, *Tibetan Tales*, p. 257. MONIER-WILLIAMS, p. 994.1 (there spelt Viśvāntara) and 993.1 (analyzed as *viśva-ṁ-tara*, noted as used for the Buddha, kings, and in Jātakas, and described as 'all-subduing', although I think the normal meaning of *tara* as 'crossing over' is preferable).

Chapter 5 A Magic Birth

1. In the Suttas *dhammatā* is found infrequently. At Majjhima Nikāya 48.11–2, it refers to the 'nature' of a person's character—certain things that, as an enlightened disciple, they may or may not do. At Aṅguttara Nikāya 10.2 it refers to the 'natural' way that wholesome qualities will proceed from one another. At Saṁyutta Nikāya 6.2 (verse 563) it refers to the 'natural' fact that all Buddha's, past, present, and future, will dwell revering the Dhamma. *Dhammatā* is similar in meaning to *dhammaṭṭhitatā*, which describes the 'regularity' of such principles as dependent origination (Saṁyutta Nikāya 12.20) or impermanence, suffering, and not-self (Aṅguttara Nikāya 3.136).
2. Summarized from the Mahāpadāna Sutta (Dīgha Nikāya 13). Repeated with slight development, in the Acchariya-abbhuta Sutta (Majjhima Nikāya 123). Also see Aṅguttara Nikāya 4.27.
3. Ṛg Veda 1.154.
4. Majjhima Nikāya 123.22.

5. Aṅguttara Nikāya 4.41.
6. Pali version at Dīgha Nikāya 14. The Sutta exists in Pali, Chinese, Sanskrit, and Uighur versions. See http://www.suttacentral.net for full list of versions.
7. Majjhima Nikāya 123/Madhyama Āgama 32 at TI, № 26, p. 469, c20. Detailed comparative studies in Minh CHÂU, *The Chinese Madhyama Āgama*, p. 159*ff.*, and ANĀLAYO, *A Comparative Study* V^OL 2.702.
8. Also, the list of miracles in the Acchariya-abbhuta Sutta is expanded with the addition of extra details about the Bodhisatta's stay in Tusita heaven. This confirms that the borrowing is from the Mahāpadāna to the Acchariya-abbhuta, not the other way around.
9. NEUMANN, *The Great Mother*, plate 97: a painting of the Virgin Mary, Upper Rhenish Master, Germany, *circa* 1400 CE.
10. www.patriarchywebsite.com/bib-patriarchy/Jerome-Against-Jovinianus.txt
11. www.newadvent.org/cathen/02767a.htm
12. www.msnbc.msn.com/id/23254178/
13. BLOK, p. 313. NEUMANN (*History*, p. 133.) says: 'Virginity simply means not belonging to any man personally; virginity is in essence sacred, not because it is a state of physical inviolateness, but because it is a state of psychic openness to God.'
14. The texts emphasize that his conception was a result of the Bodhisatta's decision: Mūlasarvāstivāda Vinaya (ROCKHILL, p. 15); Lalitavistara (MITRA, p. 88); Mahāvastu (JONES, V^OL II, p. 1*ff.*); Nidānakathā (RHYS DAVIDS, p. 148). None of the sources, to my knowledge, attribute the conception to intercourse, and indeed in the Nidānakathā (p. 149), Mahāvastu (p. 5), and Lalitavistara (p. 89) Māyā is sleeping separately from Suddhodana when she conceives.
15. Mahāvastu 1.98, Lalitavistara (MITRA trans.) 88–90. The Chaddanta Jātaka (№ 514, 5.36) revolves around the motif of the six-tusked elephant, a beast of majesty and magical potency, who is murdered by a queen due to her grudge from a past life. See discussion at ch. 36.44*ff.*
16. The Oedipal story appears explicitly in Buddhist texts, for example the Sarvāstivādin Mahāvibhāṣa's story of the evil monk Mahādeva (T27 № 1545, p. 510, c23–p. 512, a19. Translated in *Sects & Sectarianism*, ch. 5.2–25); and the account of conception found in the Mūlasarvastivāda Saddhammasmṛtyupasthāna Sūtra, VASUBANDHU's *Abhidharmkośa*, and the Tibetan *Book of the Dead*. Also compare the third story in the Kunāla Jātaka (№ 536, 5.428–30). Here the baby is abandoned twice, once in the field to be rescued and raised by goatherds, a second time cast into the river. Like Oedipus, he is raised in a royal family. But the family is his; or at least the mother is. She has abandoned him, since the child's father was a conquered king murdered by her new husband, and she was afraid he would be rejected. After returning by accident to his home and growing up, believed by all to be a low caste fondling, he falls in love with the daughter of the house—his own half-sister. A scandal ensues, until the mother is possessed by the spirit of the true father, and reveals the truth. An investigation reveals the facts of the matter much as in *Oedipus Rex*. The foster-father is, oddly enough, delighted, and so the two children are married. Rather than marrying his mother, it is his half-sister; and rather than killing his father himself, it is his foster-father who does so. In the end, he is given his father's kingdom.

17. An analysis and philosophical discussion by David LORTON at www.geocities.com/Athens/Academy/1326/ontology.html.
18. HESIOD, *Theogony*, 2.147–206. www.gutenberg.org/files/348/348-h/348-h.htm
19. See ZIMMER, *Myths and Symbols*, pp. 102*ff*.
20. As in the discussion between Socrates and Euthyphro regarding Cronos, discussed by Andrew LANG, *Custom and Myth*. http://en.wikisource.org/wiki/Custom_and_Myth/The_Myth_of_Cronus#cite_ref-2
21. To see how the earliest Greek novels dealt with mythic themes, see REARDON.
22. The riddle is from Apollodorus, *House of Oedipus* III.5.7.
23. See GOLDHILL, p. 216.
24. See GILLIGAN, *Birth*, p. 51.

Chapter 6 How Māyā Became a Goddess

1. Udāna 5.2.
2. The rate of maternal mortality has plummeted in the 20th century from perhaps 1 death in 100 births to around 0.25 in 100 births. The vast majority of these are in developing countries. The *lifetime* risk of maternal death in sub-Saharan Africa is 1 in 22, while in developed nations it is only 1 in 8000. http://www.unicef.org/progressforchildren/2007n6/index_41814.htm
3. Such references to Siddhattha as the Bodhisatta are a late development. In the early strata of the Suttas, he is only referred to as Bodhisatta after his going forth to actively seek Awakening. In these texts there is no hint that Awakening was his destiny from the time of birth (and earlier).
4. PIAGET, p. 11.
5. PIAGET, p. 351.
6. PIAGET, p. 13.
7. CAMPBELL, *Primitive Mythology*, p. 67–8.
8. CAMPBELL, *Primitive Mythology*, p. 70–1.
9. http://www.healthsystem.virginia.edu/internet/personalitystudies/home.cfm
10. Dīgha Nikāya 14.1.12: *Mayhaṁ bhikkhave etarahi arahato sammāsambuddhassa suddhodano rājā pitā ahosi, māyādevī mātā janetti. Kapilavatthu nāma nagaraṁ rājadhānī.* She is also named (possibly somewhat later) in the Theragāthā verses 534–535: *Suddhodano nāma pitā mahesino, buddhassa mātā pana māyanāmā/Yā bodhisattaṁ parihariya kucchinā, kāyassa bhedā tidivamhi modati./Sā gotamī kālakatā ito cutā, dibbehi kāmehi samaṅgibhūtā./Sā modati kāmaguṇehi pañcahi, parivāritā devagaṇehi tehi.*
11. The commentaries claim, implausibly, that Māyā was in her forties or even fifties when the Buddha was born; but this would entail that her sister Mahāpajāpatī was unreasonably old when she took ordination. Royal marriages typically took place at sixteen. Mingun Sayadaw (p. 248) derives the imputed age of 56 years, 4 months, and 27 days from a calculation based entirely on mythic logic; an excellent example of how such 'historical' details can be manufactured in the absence of troublesome facts.
12. There are too many examples to list, but the Mahāgovinda Sutta (Dīgha Nikāya 19) is typical. There are seven kingdoms for seven kings (to signify the mythic space), with seven brahmans and seven hundred students; and a wait of seven years, reduced to seven

days (stock: as in Satipaṭṭhāna Sutta (Majjhima Nikāya 10.46), Udumbarikasīhanāda Sutta (Dīgha Nikāya 25.22), etc.), to signify cosmic time. Compare Ṛg Veda 1.164.3: 'The seven who on the seven-wheeled car are mounted have horses, seven in tale, who draw them onward./Seven Sisters utter songs of praise together, in whom the names of the seven Cows are treasured.'

13. NEUMANN (*The Great Mother*, p. 160) suggests that the number seven is associated with the lunar hero, twelve with the solar.

Chapter 7 She Who Ate the Children

1. The canon says this was Tusita heaven, which is the same domain from which her son has so recently departed. For some reason, later tradition finds her downgraded to Tāvatiṁsa, where she perhaps enjoys the company of Sālabhañjikā.
2. Theragāthā-Aṭṭhakathā Dasakanipāta Kāḷudāyittheragāthāvaṇṇanā: *devūpapatti pana purisabhāveneva jātā.*
3. The close association in the Theravāda between Māyā and the Abhidhamma raises some interesting psychological and philosophical issues. See my *The Mystique of the Abhidhamma* for some further ruminations. An astonishing account of the ritual implications of the Abhidhamma as 'mother' in Thailand is found in MCDANIEL, *Gathering Leaves*, ch. 8.
4. T № 386 p. 1976 b15–c5. See T2 № 125 p. 706a.
5. T № 12, p. 383. Translation by Jennifer Rowan, based on Noel Peri's version in *Hariti la mere-de-demons*, 30–31. http://www.uoregon.edu/~jrowan/hariti/mahamaya.html. Also see T № 383, p. 1006, c18–1007, a3.
6. *Yakkhinī* stories at www.uwest.edu/sanskritcanon/Sastra/Roman/sastra76/Sa-76R-1-1.html
7. In the introduction to the Kacchapa Jātaka (№ 178, 1.79), there occurs the notion that one can escape malaria by making a hole in the wall and leaving the house. Disease was imagined to be a malicious entity who guarded the doors.
8. The Sudassanavinayavibhāsā only knows of Hārītī and her children: 呵梨帝耶夜叉尼有五百子 (T24, № 1462, p. 685, b4–5).
9. See http://en.wikipedia.org/wiki/Hariti.
10. Similar themes are found in Indic myth generally, such as the conversion of the *nāga* Kāliya by Krishna (ZIMMER, *Myths and Symbols*, p. 83*ff.*), not to mention the entire war of the *Rāmāyaṇa.*
11. Saṁyutta Nikāya 10.4. The Buddha, incidentally, disagrees with this sentiment, telling the *yakkha* that enmity can only be overcome with loving-kindness, not by mindfulness alone.
12. Saṁyutta Nikāya 10.12.
13. Saṁyutta Nikāya 10. 9–11.
14. Saṁyutta Nikāya 10.8.
15. Saṁyutta Nikāya 10.7.
16. Saṁyutta Nikāya 10.5. Verses below from BODHI, *Connected Discourses*, p. 309. The background story is found in the commentary, and retold by BODHI.
17. Vinaya Mahāvagga 1.23.
18. The war between the Gods and Titans, for example, which is depicted with such virulent depravity in the Greek myths, here is won by kindness. Sakka (who is Indra, the ferocious Vedic war god) is in full retreat from the victorious armies of the Asuras (Titans), when

his chariot comes to a forest with little birds nesting. He tells his charioteer to turn back, as he doesn't want to harm the baby birds. But the Asuras, seeing him reverse, think that he wants to re-engage them in battle, and flee in fear (Saṁyutta Nikāya 11.6).

19. T24, № 1448, p. 41, a28–b24; Gilgit Mss. 3, pt. 1:xviii-1. See STRONG, *Upagupta*, pp. 34–37.
20. E.g. Dīgha Nikāya 23.21. The motif is not confined to India. We have read of Ion, Apollo's son who was raised in his temple. This was already an accepted custom at the dawn of literature. In *Gilgamesh*, the goddess Ninsun says: 'As a priestess takes in an abandoned child, I have taken in Enkidu as my own son.' (MITCHELL, p. 102.)
21. Nigrodha Jātaka (№ 445, 4.38).
22. Kuntani Jātaka (№343, 3.311*f*).
23. MALALASEKERA, www.palikanon.com/english/pali_names/ku/kuntani_jat_343.htm.
24. WITZEL, 1.2.
25. MONIER-WILLIAMS, p. 1046.
26. Vaṭṭaka Jātaka (№ 35, 1.212).
27. Dhammapāda 92.
28. See discussion in WARNER, ch. 4.
29. WARNER, p. 401.
30. Bṛhadāraṇyaka Upaniṣad 4.3.19.
31. Similarly, the obscure monk Kuṇḍadhāna shares his name with the *yakkha* Kuṇḍadhāna. http://www.palikanon.com/english/pali_names/ku/kundadhaana_th.htm http://www.palikanon.com/english/pali_names/ku/kundadhaanavana.htm
32. WILLIS, p. 224, 226. Also spelled Hāritiputa.
33. Translation by Jennifer ROWAN. Available online with many more resources regarding Hārītī at: http://darkwing.uoregon.edu/~{}jrowan/hariti/samyuk.html. I have not been able to trace the exact location of this passage.
34. The notion that sacrificial victims might be redeemed, and become the source for special devotees, mirrors the Biblical story of Jephthah's daughter. (Judges ch. 11) Filled with the spirit of God, Jephthah destroys the Ammonites, devastating 20 towns, and in gratitude for his victory he vows to sacrifice to God whatsoever comes to greet him at the door when he returns home. Jephthah grants her two months to wander the hills and mourn with the other girls, then he fulfilled his vow. However, the medieval rabbinic commentators soften the harsh story: the daughter was not sacrificed, but was forbidden to marry and remained a spinster her entire life, fulfilling the vow that she would be devoted to the Lord.
35. Perhaps it is no coincidence that the regions of 'Theravāda' Buddhism where temporary ordination are prevalent are also those that worship Upagupta. Upagupta is unknown in the Pali tradition and in Sri Lanka, and seems to have drifted into northern Theravāda lands directly from India, rather than following the 'official' route via Sri Lanka. Upagupta is associated with the (Mūla) Sarvāstivāda tradition. He is, however, found also in texts belonging to the northern branches of Buddhism generally, so should be regarded as a regional rather than sectarian personality. See STRONG, *The Legend and Cult of Upagupta.*

Chapter 8 The King Sacrificed

1. CAMPBELL, *Oriental Mythology*, p. 167–8; *The Hero with a Thousand Faces*, pp. 93–94; FRAZER pp. 274–275. Original report in Duarte BARBOSA, *A Description of the Coasts of East Africa and Malabar in the Beginning of the Sixteenth Century*, Hakluyt Society, London, 1866, p. 172.
2. www.newadvent.org/cathen/05573a.htm
3. FRAZER, ch. 24.3, pp. 274–5.
4. AGRAWALA, p. 26, regarding the Kulli goddesses.
5. When I visited the Laotian capital, Vientiane, with my mother, we were shown one of the main temples in the city. In the center of the temple grounds was a large pillar, similar to an Aśoka pillar. Our guide told us that the pillar was established in this temple to mark the foundation of the city as a royal capital. At the opening ceremony, as the pillar was about to be installed, a young man and woman threw themselves into the pit, and the pillar was lowered on top of them, crushing them. Their bones are there to this day.
6. Maṇicora Jātaka (№ 194, 2.121–125).
7. Sutana Jātaka (№ 398, 3.325–330).
8. T4, № 211, p. 607b-608a; WILLEMEN, pp. 215–8. Here I give a summary based on WILLEMEN's translation. The story of Āḷavaka the child-eating *yakkha* is a famous one in Pali, though as far as I know the events leading to his rebirth as an ogre are not found in the Pali tradition.
9. The fall.
10. The exile; hunter-gatherer society.
11. Sympathetic magic; presence of sacred/tabooed person guaranteeing fertility of the land; grain as basis for civilization and prosperity.
12. Population increase; intensified cultivation; the role of the 'big man' or chief to redistribute wealth; potential for conflict and exhaustion of resources.
13. Sacred relationship of king to land; government by consent of the people.
14. Law is higher than personal authority of king; growing inequality and specialization; men in power gain access to women, for pleasure and progeny; increased production results in growth of trade and need for regulation.
15. Urbanization; ego inflation of ruler; increasing workload as population grows and civilization develops.
16. Tyranny; conflict; class struggle.
17. Regicide; betrayal by associates (Devadatta/Set/Judas motif); wilderness as 'free zone' outside the conventions of society.
18. The power of the will.
19. Fear of the dead; scapegoat; retributive justice.
20. Death without proper rites leads to disaster.
21. An unusual motif. Normally in Buddhist belief the old body decays and the reborn being takes a new one. This may be a remnant of a folk belief, or perhaps merely a mistranslation. We have already met Āḷavaka above. The Pali sources, so far as I know, know nothing of his colorful past life.
22. *Suttee*, i.e. ritual murder of the king's retinue; regicide.
23. I am not sure of the significance of this, but it must be a folk ritual of some kind, perhaps related to the *yajñopavītam* thread, which is worn by Brahmans from the time of their coming of age *upanayana* ceremony.

24. King who temporarily relinquishes the throne to a substitute.
25. Cannibalism; belief in the dead as source of death; fear of ancestors, who must be placated with offerings.
26. Periodic human sacrifice; literal belief in gods who eat food; destiny (all must die) versus chance (in the lottery).
27. This is an unusually explicit evocation of the symbolism of the bowl as womb. Compare the story in the Vinaya where a woman gives an aborted foetus to a bhikkhuni, who carried it away in her bowl (Pali Vinaya 2.268–9).
28. See ch. 4.34.
29. Saṁkicca Jātaka (№ 539, 5.261–277). Similar motifs recur, for example in Jātakas 193, 223, 234, 338, 373, 497, 530, and 543.
30. Compare the proper name Yaññadatta, 'Sacrifice-gift'.
31. Pali Vinaya 2.185.
32. Saṁyutta Nikāya 3.1.1.
33. Western examples include Lilith in the Hebrew tradition, the Greek Furies and Gorgon, and in modern times, Wagner's Kundry. An array of images from a Jain context is found in VYAS, *et al.*, pp. 65*ff.*
34. Pali Vinaya 2.190.
35. This follows the precedent of various versions of the battle between Indra and the primeval serpent Vṛtra, where the gods flee the onrush of the monster, and only a few have the courage of their faith.

Chapter 9 The Real Māyā

1. See Thomas NAGEL, 'What is it Like to Be a Bat?', in HOFSTADER, pp. 391–414.
2. See André BAREAU, 'Un personnage bien mystérieux: l'épouse du Buddha.' In HERCUS, *et al.* Summarized in André COUTURE, 'Survey', p. 14.
3. www.palikanon.com/english/pali_names/r/rahulamata.htm
4. E.g. Saṁyutta Nikāya 1.5.9, verse 548; Saṁyutta Nikāya 48.41; Dhammapada 147.
5. Here Calasso is alluding to Lalitavistara 12.34*ff.* (MITRA, p. 198). Gopā answers for her own behaviour with a series of verses, such as: 'A thousand folds of cloth cannot hide the nature and mind of him who has not modesty and a sense of propriety manifest in him. But he who has those qualities and is ever truthful—he may roam about everywhere in nudity, like a jewel unadorned.'
6. CALASSO, *Ka*, pp. 351–352.
7. APULEIUS (trans. GRAVES), *The Golden Ass* (*Metamorphoses*). www.jnanam.net/golden-ass/ga-11.html
8. All 1000 names are listed at www.sacred-texts.com/hin/kmu/kmu12.htm.
9. EURIPEDES (trans. E.P. COLERIDGE), *Helen*. http://classics.mit.edu/Euripides/helen.html
10. HERODOTUS, *Histories*, 2.113*ff.* Herodotus quotes passages from the *Iliad* and *Odyssey* to show that Homer was familiar with this version of events, but did not emphasize it for narrative purposes. http://www.perseus.tufts.edu/hopper/text?doc=Hdt.+2.113
11. Detailed discussion of the parallels between Helen and Sītā in DONIGER, ch. 1.
12. This part of the *Rāmāyaṇa* is absent from the short version of that tale found in the Dasaratha Jātaka (№ 461, 4.129.). However a very similar tale is found in the Sambula

Jātaka (№ 519, 5.88–98). The viceroy is exiled due to leprosy, and his virtuous wife insists on following him to the forest, where she attends on all his needs. One day she is accosted by a *yakkha*, but refuses him. Sotthisena suspects her, so she performs an Act of Truth and by the power of her virtue his leprosy is cured. Even after they return to the palace and are anointed King and Queen, he does not respect her, until he is exhorted by his retired father (the Bodhisatta). Compare the introduction to Nigrodhamiga Jātaka (№ 12, 1.145). A faithful woman was with child, but not realizing this, gained the permission of her husband to go forth. In all innocence she went forth among the followers of Devadatta. When the signs of her pregnancy became clear, Devadatta, being without compassion, made no inquiry into the matter, but thinking of his reputation expelled her immediately. But she had the wisdom to go and see the Buddha, who ordered a medical examination overseen by respectable lay followers. Finding that she had gone forth after being pregnant, he allowed her to stay and made provision for her child's upbringing in the nunnery. In this case Rāma's caddish behaviour bears more in common with Devadatta than the Buddha.

13. Sītā means 'furrow', and the *Rāmāyaṇa* tells us that she had been discovered when a plough had dug her up as a baby. The Mahā Ummagga Jātaka (№ 546, 6.364) riddles on the idea that a plough makes two out of one.
14. *Adhyātma Rāmāyaṇa* 3.7.3–4. This version of events has precedents in the Kūrma Purāṇa and Brahma-vaivarta Purāṇa. It is expanded on in Tulasidāsa, *Rāmacaritamānasā*, a 15th century Hindi version of the *Rāmāyaṇa*. Discussed in *Rāmāyaṇa*, introduction, p. liii, and DONIGER, ch. 1.
15. Devī Bhāgavata, *skandha* 5.
16. In the Buddhist version of this tale, included in the Kunāla Jātaka (№ 536, 5.425–427), she is said to have taken five husbands because of her sexual voraciousness.
17. GILLIGAN, *Birth*, p. 153.
18. SOPHOCLES, *Oedipus at Colonus*, 1727–8.
19. SOPHOCLES, *Oedipus at Colonus*, 1762–5.
20. Kusa Jātaka (№ 531, 5.278–312). Found in several variants, including a Mahāsaṅghika version in the Mahāvastu (2.419*ff.*), and a Mūlasarvāstivāda version (translated in VON SCHIEFNER, *Tibetan Tales*, pp. 21–28).
21. ZIMMER, *Myths and Symbols*, p. 34.

Chapter 10 Let's Play

1. HUIZINGA, p. 5. Quoted in CAMPBELL, *Primitive Mythology*, p. 23.
2. *Ibid.*, p. 22.
3. Udāna 4.4.
4. Saṁyutta Nikāya 11.6.
5. CAMPBELL, *Oriental Mythology*, p. 96.
6. See ARMSTRONG, *The Battle for God.*
7. HEESTERMAN, *The Broken World of Sacrifice*, p. 2.
8. VALERI, *Kingship and Sacrifice*, p. 233.
9. Ch 8.16*ff.*

10. Details from JOLLY, pp 133*ff*. For a popular account, see: www.vanuatutourism.com/vanuatu/cms/en/islands/pentecost_maewo.html. Footage of the rite may be viewed at http://www.youtube.com/watch?v=KQ-_Ksf6IFY.
11. See Majjhima Nikāya 64.3. The unconscious may also be concerned with a certain aspect of 'consciousness' (*viññāṇa*). This is described in the early discourses as a 'seed', and this metaphor was developed in the Yogacāra notion of the 'storehouse consciousness' (*ālayaviññāṇā*), which possesses all seeds (*sarvabījaka*). In a striking parallel, JUNG said: 'Moreover we know, from abundant experience as well as for experiential reasons, that the unconscious also contains all the material that has not yet reached the threshold of consciousness. These are the seeds of future conscious contents.' (*Aspects of the Masculine*, p. 74 §204).

Chapter 11 Perception, Symbol, Myth

1. Saṁyutta Nikāya 22.56, 57 (= Saṁyukta Āgama 41, 42, 46) define *saññā* as six classes of *saññā*, from the six senses. Saṁyutta Nikāya 22.79 defines *saññā* as *sañjānāti*, i.e. the noun is a verb: perception is not an entity but a process. (*Sañjānātīti kho, bhikkhave, tasmā 'saññā'ti vuccati. Kiñca sañjānāti? Nīlampi sañjānāti, pītakampi sañjānāti, lohitakampi sañjānāti, odātampi sañjānāti.* http://tipitakastudies.net/tipitaka/13S3/1/1.2/1.2.3/1.2.3.7) This is essential, of course, but does not distinguish *saññā* from other factors, as other dhammas are treated in the same way. The same passage goes on to say: 'It perceives blue, it perceives yellow, it perceives red, it perceives white.' This might be meaningful, but is not easy to decode. It associates *saññā* with visual experience, which suggests that we seek to understand it in terms inferred from visual perception in particular. Distinguishing between blocks of color is of course one of the chief jobs of visual perception. The corresponding Sarvāstivādin Sutta, preserved in Chinese translation, says: 'All perceptions are the aggregate of perception with attachment. What perceptions? Few perceptions, many perceptions, countless perceptions, perception of nothingness as "there is nothing". That is why it is called the aggregate of perception with attachment.' 諸想是想受陰。何所想。少想・多想・無量想。都無所有。作無所有想。是故名想受陰 (Saṁyukta Āgama 46 at T2, № 99, p. 11c 4–6; trans. CHOONG, p. 27). This is even less helpful than the Pali; but it influenced later authors such as Asaṅga.
2. Saṁyutta Nikāya 22.53–4.
3. E.g. Bṛhadāraṇyaka Upaniṣad 2.4.12–14.
4. Compare, for example, Sutta passages such as Dīgha Nikāya 16.1.23–4 which say that one's confidence both in an assembly and internally stems from one's ethical conduct, which is *saṅkhārā*.
5. http://wps.prenhall.com/wps/media/objects/213/218150/glossary.html
6. http://tinyurl.com/7shvhqg
7. In Buddhist usage 'perception' is a stage in the assimilation of sense experience, and is not used for the process of 'sense perception' as a whole.
8. Aṅguttara Nikāya iii 413: *Vohāravepakkaṁ, bhikkhave, saññaṁ vadāmi. Yathā yathā naṁ sañjānāti tathā tathā voharati, evaṁ saññī ahosinti.* http://tipitakastudies.net/tipitaka/16A6/2/2.1/2.1.9
9. Pali Vinaya *nissaggiya pācittiya* 10: *So ce dūto taṁ veyyāvaccakaraṁ* ***saññāpetvā*** *taṁ bhikkhuṁ upasaṅkamitvā evaṁ vadeyya'yaṁ kho, bhante, āyasmā veyyāvaccakaraṁ niddisi* ***saññatto*** *so*

mayā, upasaṅkamatu āyasmā kālena, cīvarena taṁ acchādessatī'ti. http://tipitakastudies.net/tipitaka/1V/1/1.4/1.4.1/1.4.1.10

10. Analyzed in Ñāṇananda. Majjhima Nikāya 18: *Cakkhuñcāvuso, paṭicca rūpe ca uppajjati cakkhuviññāṇaṁ, tiṇṇaṁ saṅgati phasso, phassapaccayā vedanā, yaṁ vedeti taṁ sañjānāti, yaṁ sañjānāti taṁ vitakketi, yaṁ vitakketi taṁ papañceti, yaṁ papañceti tatonidānaṁ purisaṁ papañcasaññāsaṅkhā samudācaranti atītānāgatapaccuppannesu cakkhuviññeyyesu rūpesu.* http://tipitakastudies.net/tipitaka/9M/2/2.8
11. These terms found in the analysis of sense experience in Dīgha Nikāya 15 Mahānidāna Sutta: *adhivacanasamphassa* and *paṭighasamphassa.*
12. Vibhaṅga 6: *Paṭighasamphassajā saññā oḷārikā, adhivacanasamphassajā saññā sukhumā.* http://tipitakastudies.net/tipitaka/30Vbh/1/1.1/1.1.3
13. Pali Vinaya *pācittiya* 61: *Pāṇe pāṇasaññī jīvitā voropeti, āpatti pācittiyassa. Pāṇe vematiko jīvitā voropeti, āpatti dukkaṭassa. Pāṇe appāṇasaññī jīvitā voropeti, anāpatti. Appāṇe pāṇasaññī, āpatti dukkaṭassa. Appāṇe vematiko, āpatti dukkaṭassa. Appāṇe appāṇasaññī, anāpatti.* tipitakastudies.net/tipitaka/2V/1/1.5/1.5.7/1.5.7.1
14. E.g. *A Leg to Stand On.*
15. E.g. the 'ten perceptions' of the Girimānanda Sutta (Aṅguttara Nikāya 10.60): *Aniccasaññā, anattasaññā, asubhasaññā, ādīnavasaññā, pahānasaññā, virāgasaññā, nirodhasaññā, sabbaloke anabhiratasaññā, sabbasaṅkhāresu anicchāsaññā, ānāpānassati.* http://tipitakastudies.net/tipitaka/17A10/2/2.1/2.1.10
16. Majjhima Nikāya 128: *obhāsañceva sañjānāma dassanañca rūpānaṁ.*
17. As well as modern studies. See, for example, Potter, p. 64; McGovern, p. 86.
18. A reference to Udāna 68–9.
19. *Path of Purification*, XIV, 130 (p. 520).
20. Abhidharmasamuccaya, p. 3.
21. Vasubandhu, *Pañcaskandhaka-prakaraṇa*, included in Anacker, *Seven Works of Vasubandhu*, p. 66.
22. Quoted in Boisvert, p. 78, note 9. This distinction is not found in the Pali canonical passages.
23. Vasubandhu, *Abhidharmakośa* 1–11b. Quoted in McGovern, p. 86.
24. Saṁyutta Nikāya 22.95: *marīcikā.* The same Sutta likens each of the aggregates to something equally insubstantial or delusory. Consciousness is compared with a magic trick, *māyā.* The point of these similes is not that these things do not exist; something is there, but it is not what it seems.
25. Knight, *et al. Cf.* M. Carrithers, 'Why Humans have Cultures.' Man 25, pp. 189–206, 1990; J. Bennett, *Linguistic Behaviour.* Cambridge University Press, 1976; H. Grice, 'Utterer's Meanings and Intentions.' Philosophical Review 78, pp. 147–77, 1969.
26. *Ibid.*
27. Miller, p. 47–8.
28. Śatapatha Brāhmaṇa 2.2.2.1; 3.8.2.4; 4.3.4.1; 11.1.2.1.

Chapter 12 On Using Jung

1. JUNG, *Aspects of the Feminine*, pp. 103–4, §149.
2. E.g. JUNG, *Psychologische Typen*, p. 598, quoted in CAMPBELL, *Primitive Mythology*, p. 32. Also see *Man and his Symbols*, pp. 57–8.
3. NEUMANN, *Origins*, p. 24.
4. NEUMANN, *Origins*, p. xxi. Neumann was trying to buttress the 'scientific' nature of his theory by denying that the archetypes acted in ways parallel to the then-discredited concept of inherited characteristics. However, while this is still the mainstream position, more recent biology is coming to accept the existence of inherited characteristics in at least a few contexts. This fits better with the Buddhist idea of interdependence rather than linear cause→effect chains. See http://tinyurl.com/88ajt22.
5. JUNG, *Aspects of the Feminine*, p. 80 §303. Jung, however, attributes to the Buddhists the Hindu notion of *ātman*—a bad mistake.
6. CAMPBELL, *Hero*, pp. 257–258.
7. Sāketa Jātaka (№ 68, 1.309; also № 237, 2.235.)
8. WARNER, p. 279.
9. JUNG, *Aspects of the Feminine*, pp. 100, 103–4.
10. WARNER, p. 417.
11. The following discussion is based on www.praetrans.com/en/ptf.html. From Ken WILBER, *Sex, Ecology, Spirituality*.
12. Wilber doesn't offer any example here, but how about this: 'The unconscious is not just evil by nature, it is also the source of the highest good: not only dark but also light, not only bestial, semihuman, and demonic but superhuman, spiritual, and, in the classical sense of the word, "divine".' JUNG, *The Practice of Psychotherapy*, p. 364 (1953). http://en.wikiquote.org/wiki/Carl_Jung. Also see ṬHĀNISSARO, 'The Roots of Buddhist Romanticism.' http://www.purifymind.com/BuddhistRomanticism.htm
13. In classical myth, the foremost archetype of this aspect of kingship is Theseus.
14. With the exception of certain aspects of Tibetan Buddhism. All traditional forms of Buddhism, of course, use ritual and myth extensively, but these are habitually deprecated by modernists, including those taking part in them.
15. E.g. TIYAVANICH.
16. Colin TATZ in his 'Genocide in Australia' (AIATSIS Research Discussion Papers, No 8. http://www.kooriweb.org/gst/genocide/tatz.html) quotes the following passage from an 1883 letter from the British High Commissioner, Arthur Hamilton Gordon, to his friend William Gladstone, Prime Minister of England: 'The habit of regarding the natives as vermin, to be cleared off the face of the earth, has given the average Queenslander a tone of brutality and cruelty in dealing with "blacks" which it is very difficult to anyone who does not know it, as I do, to realise. I have heard men of culture and refinement, of the greatest humanity and kindness to their fellow whites, and who when you meet them here at home you would pronounce to be incapable of such deeds, talk, not only of the wholesale butchery (for the iniquity of that may sometimes be disguised from themselves) but of the individual murder of natives, exactly as they would talk of a day's sport, or having to kill some troublesome animal.'

17. Jung believed that Westerners should not follow Eastern religions, as they had a deeper connection with their own mythos. I believe he was wrong on two counts: firstly, he overestimated the importance of the mythos; and secondly, he underestimated the compatibility of the symbolic language of Europe and India.
18. See SHARF.
19. To denigrate so-called 'Hīnayāna' as narrowly monastic in comparison with the universal salvation of 'Mahāyāna' is a silly error, the perpetuation of which in countless popular accounts is yet another sign of the divorce of modern Western Buddhism from realistic engagement with the reality of lived Buddhist life. In fact, 'Mahāyānist' Tibet was the most monastic culture ever developed.

Chapter 13 The Dhamma of Gender

1. June CAMPBELL has argued that a similar evolutionary pattern may be discerned within Tibetan religion.
2. An argument made by ELLER. Criticized by MARLER and DASHU, among others. These critiques and Eller's response to them are at http://cynthiaeller.com/mmpreviews_new.htm
3. See SANDAY, ch. 1.
4. GOLDBERG.
5. This case is argued in SANDAY's detailed and nuanced study.
6. MAGEE, pp. 6–7, quoting from the Kūlacūḍamaṇi Tantra and the Bṛhad-nīla Tantra.
7. June CAMPBELL's *Traveller in Space* discusses this dynamic within Tibetan Buddhism. Reviewed at www.buddhistethics.org/4/lang2.html
8. See SANDAY, Appendix E, for an example of how to assess women's status in society.
9. E.g. PAYUTTO, in the context of a discussion of women's ordination, says: 'Women's biological nature has placed them socially at a disadvantage. And because of this biological predestination, it is more difficult for women than men to live a life that is free and independent from society.' When presented with the feminist idea that such disadvantage is primarily a social construct, he responds, 'Women are child-bearers.' *Bangkok Post*, Sept. 22, 2001. It seems to have escaped his notice that celibate nuns would not be bearing children.
10. This idea has its Buddhist forebears; canonically in the rebuke of Bhikkhuni Somā to Māra (Saṁyutta Nikāya 5.2) and later in such passages as the Vimalakīrtinirdeśa.
11. E.g. Carol Gilligan. Criticized in KERBER, *et al.*, and by Margaret TALBOT at www.powells.com/review/2002_07_18.html
12. FINE uses the term 'neurosexism' for those who try to locate 'essential' gender differences in 'male' and 'female' brains.
13. Pali Vinaya 3.35. The issue is dealt with in several Vinayas.
14. See YOUNG, 'Female Mutability' and discussions in SCHERER & JACKSON. Classical examples include the story of Soreyya or Sāriputta's gender change in the Vimalakīrtinirdeśa.
15. Gender essentialism becomes an issue for the Abhidhamma theorists, and became one of the grounds for criticism by the Mahāyāna. I have not attempted to trace its early development, but for a late example, the 11th century Pali Abhidhamma text, the Abhidhammatthasaṅgaha, includes gender among a standard list of phenomena that 'exist' in the ultimate sense: *Itthattaṁ, purisattaṁ bhāvarūpaṁ nāma*. ('Feminimity, masculinity, are

called gender-form.') See NĀRADA, *Abhidhammattha Saṅgaha.* http://www.palikanon.com/english/sangaha/chapter_6.htm

16. This is not to imply that biology and social factors have no role in sexuality. Of course they do. Early Buddhism explicitly states that kamma is only one of many different kinds of causes.
17. However, Dīgha Nikāya 21.1.11 tells of a Śākyan girl called Gopikā, who, being virtuous and full of faith, became dispassionate towards her femininity and developed masculinity (*Sā itthittaṁ virājetvā purisattaṁ bhāvetvā*). She died and was reborn as the male deva Gopaka in Tāvatiṁsa. So far, so sexist. But the sting is that she was born in a higher heaven than three monks, who had become mere *gandhabbas*, indulging themselves with the heavenly nymphs. Gopaka gives them a good old telling off, saying they were a 'sorry sight' (*duddiṭṭharūpaṁ*). Two of them gain mindfulness and are reborn in a higher realm; the other lagged behind.
18. See G. WATSON.
19. NEUMANN, *Origins*, p. xxii, note 7.

Chapter 14 Mythic Fact, Historic Fiction

1. http://uktv.co.uk/gold/stepbystep/aid/598605
2. SALLUST, *Of Gods and Of the World.*
3. A.K. RAMANUJAN, 'Three Hundred Rāmāyaṇas', included in *Many Rāmāyaṇas*, Paula RICHMAN, ed., Oxford University Press, 1994. Quoted in Rāmāyaṇa, introduction p. lv.
4. Edmund LEACH, 'Lévi-Strauss in the Garden of Eden.' In E.N. HAYES and T. HAYES (eds.), *The Anthropologist as Hero* (Cambridge, Mass. 1970), pp. 50–51. Quoted in LARSON, p. 14.
5. Kuṇāla Jātaka (№ 536, 5.412–3).
6. Ambaṭṭha Sutta (Dīgha Nikāya 3.1.15).
7. Ona-Land. Review of E. Lucas BRIDGES, *Uttermost Part of the Earth*, DUTTON, *Time*, Jan. 2 1950. www.time.com/time/magazine/article/0,9171,780243-2,00.html
8. CAMPBELL, *Primitive Mythology*, p. 315–6. CAMPBELL is quoting Lucas Bridges.
9. www.time.com/time/magazine/article/0,9171,780243-2,00.html
10. CAMPBELL, *Primitive Mythology*, p. 322–3.
11. Some examples at Jātakas 481, 505, 538 (6.9–10), 542, 527.
12. Sanitsuda EKACHAI, 'Phra Dhammakaya Temple Controversy.' *Bangkok Post*, December 21, 1998. www.rickross.com/reference/general/general644.html
13. Oldenberg, Vinaya VOL 1, xxiii. Quoted in CLARKE, 'Monks who have Sex', p. 35.
14. *Bhikkhuni Vinaya Studies*, ch. 3.87–96.
15. See discussion in SCHOPEN, *Business Matters*, ch. 14.

Chapter 15 The Other First Bhikkhuni

1. Lewis CARROL, *The Hunting of the Snark*, Fit 1, Stanza 2; Fit 5, Stanza 9.
2. Quoted in WARNER, p. 409.
3. This belief is stated within the Jātakas themselves (Hārita Jātaka, № 431, 3.499).
4. Vānara Jātaka (№ 342, 3.133); Mahā-Ummagga Jātaka (№ 546, 6.428, 6.431, 6.439, 6.443, 6.454); Vessantara Jātaka (№ 547, 6.541).

5. I personally believe in rebirth, and that the Buddha may well have told some stories of his past lives. But this has nothing to do with the question of whether the Jātakas as we have them record genuine past life events. Even leaving aside the absurd and impossible details, and the known fact that many of them derive from Indian folklore, almost all the Jātakas assume a cultural, social, and linguistic background that is assumed to be 'timeless' and is the setting for hundreds of 'past lives', but which historically only existed in India for a few hundred years at most.
6. An accusation levelled against the Buddha and refuted in the Mūlasarvāstivāda Vinaya; see ROCKHILL, p. 58.
7. Therīgāthā 107.
8. Therīgāthā 108.
9. Therī-Apadāna 680.
10. Therī-Apadāna 681.
11. Therīgāthā 109.
12. Adapted from Therī-Apadāna 682–684.
13. Patricia DAVIS (p. 18) in a study of modern American teenage girls, concludes that 'girls have trouble being understood & being taken seriously by the adult world that has so much power over them ... girls must be [nice], even when they are feeling nasty or are angry, and even when they are threatened: 'girls who speak frankly are labeled as "bitches".'
14. After her conversion by Sāriputta, Bhaddā goes that same evening to see the Buddha, who teaches her and she gains arahantship (PRUITT, p. 136). It is clearly impossible to get from Sāvatthī to Rājagaha in a single day.
15. This directly contradicts her Apadāna verses, quoted within the commentary itself; for they say that Bhaddā's ordination followed her seeing a decaying dead hand. Seeking an answer, she sought out the Śākyan sons and was taken to the Buddha (PRUITT, p. 189–140). Both versions contradict Bhaddā's own verses. Furthermore, there is no mention in the Apadāna of Sāriputta or the debating contest. Nor do the Apadāna verses suggest that she had rejected the Jains, as stated in the commentary. Again, the Apadāna version of her attaining arahantship (seeing the water disappear) completely contradicts the commentarial notion that she became enlightened listening to the Buddha.
16. PRUITT, p. 106. Quoted in WILLIAMS, 'Whisper', p. 172.
17. This is the Vinaya of the school known today as 'Theravāda'. I generally try to avoid 'Theravāda' in historical context, as it creates the impression that the ancient school, or even the pre-sectarian community, is identical with the Theravāda of today. The most precise term for this school is the Mahāvihāravāsin, the 'Dwellers of the Great Monastery' [in Anuradhapura, Sri Lanka], which is the term they used of themselves and is conveniently unambiguous. But in this work I bow to popular usage and generally refer to the 'Pali', dubious though it is to name a school by its language (for other schools, for all we know, may have used the same language).
18. Pali Vinaya 4.214.
19. PRUITT, pp. 380–1.
20. T24, № 1461, p. 668, c21: 一由善來比丘尼方得，律二十二明了論.
21. T4, № 200, p. 238, b25*ff*. Also see T53, № 2122, p. 557, c21, etc.

22. T22, № 1428, p. 714, a17.
23. T40, № 1808, p. 499, b12.
24. T24, № 1463, p. 803, c1–2: 聽汝於我法中善修梵行盡諸苦際，毘尼母經.
25. T40, № 1810, p. 540, c24.
26. WILLEMEN, pp. 13, 68.

Chapter 16 A Buddhist Femme Fatale

1. I will be referring to this text from time to time. It is one version of the events from the Buddha's Awakening to the conversion of Sāriputta and Moggallāna. I use the title of the Sarvāstivādin Sūtra simply because the narrative as found more normally in the Vinayas does not have a distinct title, and is found in a chapter that is titled differently in the various Vinayas. Most of my remarks will apply to this generic body of texts, and I will make it clear when I am referring to the specific Sanskrit text. The Titus edition, which is based on Waldschmidt, is at http://titus.uni-frankfurt.de/texte/etcs/ind/aind/bskt/cps/cps.htm. However, this only covers the text up to the point where the Buddha encourages the monks to go forth and teach. Kloppenborg's translation continues until the Buddha quietens the unrest of the people of Magadha following the conversion of Sāriputta and Moggallāna. The Sanskrit text at the unfortunately-named 'Digital Sanskrit Buddhist Canon' is deficient, as it only includes the first of 22 pages of the Titus edition; it is also mistakenly classified as a 'Mahāyāna' sutra. http://dsbc.uwest.edu/node/3763
2. I follow the Dhammapāda Commentary, which is most detailed here; other versions have her speaking to her father.
3. Bhaddā's story is told, with many differences in detail, in the Therīgāthā Commentary, 99–108 (trans. PRUITT, pp. 132–143), the Manorathapūraṇī (Aṅguttara Nikāya Commentary), 1.368, and the Dhammapāda Commentary, 2.217–227. Pruitt's notes mention the main variations. Sattuka the murderer is given a detailed backstory in the Manorathapūraṇī account; the seven-storied palace comes from the Dhammapāda Commentary, a fitting fairy-tale motif for such a popular text. My version is based on MALALASEKERA: http://www.palikanon.com/english/pali_names/b/bhadda_kundalakesa.htm.
   I have expanded the text with details from the various tellings, and added the final verses from PRUITT, p. 139.
4. The text says 'Just like in the Kaṇavera Jātaka', which we look at below.
5. Sulasā Jātaka (№ 419, 3.435–9). Retold by MALALASEKERA: www.palikanon.com/english/pali_names/s/sulasa_jat_419.htm
6. An interesting sidelight on relations between servants and masters: the lady of the house was quite happy to lend priceless jewelery to her servant for a day's outing with a group of slave-girls (*dāsigaṇena*). Little wonder that Megasthenes declared that in India there was no slavery.
7. In the Pali this is 'Bhadda'!
8. *Visaññaṁ katvā.*
9. Kaṇavera Jātaka (№ 318, 3.58–63). Retold by MALALASEKERA: www.palikanon.com/english/pali_names/ka/kanavera_jat_318.htm
10. Andrew LANG, *A Collection of Ballads*, 3. www.fullbooks.com/A-Collection-of-Ballads3.html. This is a variant of the very common folk/fairy ballad, classified under Roud #21, 'Lady

Isabel and the Elf Knight.' While the very wide distribution and possible eastern provenance of this tale are well known, I am not aware that the connections with the story of Bhaddā have been noticed in modern scholarship.

11. See also WARNER's discussion (pp. 249–251) of 'The Subtle Princess', where Finessa likewise tricks the bad man into the death he had prepared for her.
12. The preference for mutually chosen marriage appears in modern works such as the Mahānirvāṇa Tantra, which are apparently under Christian/Muslim influence. See URBAN, pp. 63*ff.*
13. GILLIGAN, *Birth*, p. 194.
14. WARNER, ch. 2.
15. The method of scattering poetry across the land in hope of reaching one's lover was also used by Majnun. His songs for Layla, written in his desert cave, would be picked up by travellers, and on rare occasions a traveller might sing of Layla as he passed by the palace walls, within which she lay listening.
16. This account is summarized from the commentary to Bhaddā's verses.
17. The right answer, by the way, is: all beings survive on food. See e.g. Saṅgīti Sutta (Dīgha Nikāya 33.1.8.1). A Vedic precursor at Ṛg Veda 1.164.6.
18. Cūḷakāliṅga Jātaka (№ 301, 3.1–8).
19. Therīgāthā Commentary, p. 87; trans. PRUITT, p. 115.
20. KRISHNA MURTHY, p. 102. Nīlakesī means 'blue-hair'. In the Indic tradition it is common for black skin to be painted as blue, or for perfect hair to be described as blue-black. Given the evident links between Bhaddā's story, as well as other Indian tales such as 'The Brahman Girl who Married a Tiger', and the western tale of 'Bluebeard', I wonder whether the 'blueness' of the beard, which folklorists are at a loss to explain, might not be an Indian feature.
21. Therīgāthā 110–111. Trans. PRUITT, p. 141.

Chapter 17 The Weaving of the Web

1. The other three being food, shelter, and medicine.
2. Some examples from the Suttas are found in the Bāhitika Sutta (Majjhima Nikāya 88) or the Mahāparinibbāna Sutta (Dīgha Nikāya 16.4.35). The latter concerns the offering of two golden robes to the Buddha when he was near his death. After putting them on he became especially radiant. Here we see the strong symbolic role of the cloth. The clothes we wear create an aura around us, which here becomes literalized as an actual halo of light.
3. Dakkhiṇavibhaṅga Sutta (Majjhima Nikāya 142).
4. The Mahīśāsaka, Pali, and Mūlasarvāstivāda (ROCKHILL, p. 60) versions depict Mahāpajāpatī asking three times and being refused three times. This is unconventional: normally a request made three times is granted on the third request. WILLIAMS ('Whisper', p. 169, also note 3) is misleading here. She says that: '[Mahāpajāpatī] repeats her request for a second, and a third time, after which, following the established pattern, the Buddha refuses three times.' In the examples she gives in the note—a *sāmaṇera* requesting higher ordination, lay people requesting precepts—the third request is granted, not refused. To refuse the third request is highly unusual, if not entirely unknown. It is perhaps significant that Ānanda's three requests for the Buddha to live on for the æon were not granted

(Dīgha Nikāya 16.3.39–40), although even then on the third time the Buddha does not deny Ānanda outright but engages him with a question, and says that if Ānanda had asked when the Buddha raised the matter, he would have consented on the third request. But in the Sanskrit version Ānanda asks just once, so it perhaps best not to insist on such details. (http://fiindolo.sub.uni-goettingen.de/gretil/1_sanskr/4_rellit/buddh/mpsu_w_u.htm 18.6–9) Likewise, in the story of Mahāpajāpatī's ordination, the Dharmaguptaka (T22, № 1428, p. 922, c12–13), Lokuttaravāda (ROTH, p. 5), and the Sarvāstivāda (T1, № 26, p. 605, a11–19; T01, № 60, p. 856, a10–16) mention just one request.

5. Although it also appears as a Sutta in Aṅguttara Nikāya 8.51.
6. For example the Pali Dakkhiṇavibhaṅga Sutta (Majjhima Nikāya 142). As well as the Mahīśāsaka version translated here, this sutta has a wealth of parallels (of varying degrees of congruence) in all Buddhist languages, indicative of its importance for the Buddhist community. Chinese translations include a Sarvāstivāda version at MA 180 (T1, № 26, p. 721, c21) and an individual translation from an unknown school (T1, № 84, p. 903, b23). Tibetan version at D 4094 (mngon: ju 253b)=Q 5595 (tu 289a). ROCKHILL (p. 58*ff.*) translated from the Tibetan Mūlarvāstivāda Vinaya the story of the first bhikkhuni, but the robes are not mentioned (although much later legend is). Several manuscript fragments, according to ANĀLAYO, represent the early part of the text: SHT III 979 (SHT 1965 (VOL I), 1968 (VOL II), 1971 (VOL III), 1980 (VOL IV), 1985 (VOL V), 1989 (VOL VI), 1995 (VOL VII), 2000 (VOL VIII), 2004 (VOL IX). Sanskrithandschriften aus den Turfanfunden (Verzeichnis orientalischer Handschriften in Deutschland), L. SANDER, E. WALDSCHMIDT, K. WILLE (eds.). Wiesbaden: Franz Steiner.) Uighur fragment TEKIN, Sinasi 1980: 69. Maitrisimit nom bitig. Die Uigurische ...bersetzung eines Werkes der Buddhistischen Vaibhāṣika Schule. Berlin: Akademie Verlag. Two individual sutra translations of unknown schools (T4, № 202, p. 434, a01; T4, № 203, p. 470a) develop the legend so that the robes offered by Mahāpajāpatī eventually end up with the future Buddha Maitreya, a unique honor that further reinforces the ambiguity of the story.
7. As noted above, the Sanskrit fragments represent only the first part of the sutta, so they offer no evidence either way.
8. Āśvalāyanagṛhyasūtra 3.8.1. Also see Śāṅkhāyanagṛhyasūtra 3.1.18, Gobhilagṛhyasūtra 3.4.2. At Manu 2.246 other gifts are mentioned: land, gold, a cow, a horse, parasol and shoes, a seat, grain, vegetables. Almost all of these are specifically proscribed for Buddhist monks, except of course the cloth.
9. Pali Vinaya 4.332 (bhikkhuni *pācittiya* 77).
10. This agrees with the opening of the Pali version of the robe offering, where the Buddha does not refer, as in the Mahīśāsaka, to receiving 'great fruit', but to respecting the Sangha.
11. Pali Vinaya 2.183.
12. Pali Vinaya 2.292.
13. Majjhima Nikāya 62.3, Ekottara Āgama 17.1.
14. See BODHI's note to Majjhima Nikāya 62.3 in *Middle Length Discourses*, p. 1266, note 641.
15. E.g. Pali Vinaya 2.210*ff.*
16. Pali Vinaya 2.255: *Sace Ānanda Mahāpajāpatī Gotamī aṭṭha garudhamme paṭigaṇhāti sā v'assā hotu upasampadā.* Note the use of *upasampadā* here to refer to the full ordination, rather than

the term regularly used in the bhikkhuni *pātimokkha*, *vuṭṭhāpana*. This is a clear linguistic sign of the lateness of this passage. Other versions that depict the laying down of the *garudhammas* as specifically constituting Mahāpajāpatī's ordination include the Bhikṣunī Mahāprajāpatī Sūtra (T24, № 1478, p. 946, b22); Mahīṣāsaka Vinaya (T22, № 1421, p. 185), Lokuttaravāda Vinaya (ROTH § 14), Gautamī Sūtra (T1, № 60, p. 857, a22), and Sarvāstivāda Gautamī Sūtra (T1, № 26, p. 606, b4). However, the Dharmaguptaka Vinaya (T22, № 1428, p. 923, a27), and Mūlasarvāstivāda Vinaya (T24, № 1451, p. 350, c26) say the rules are laid down for 'women' and do not mention that this is Mahāpajāpatī's ordination.

17. Udāna 5.2. See discussion, ch. 6.
18. NEUMANN, *The Great Mother*, p. 230.
19. NEUMANN, *The Great Mother*, p. 227.
20. The title of an early Buddhist scripture. See SKILLING, V^OL II, p. 227*ff*.
21. Aṅguttara Nikāya 6.61/Saṁyukta Āgama 1164.
22. Bṛhadāraññaka Upaniṣad 3.6.1, 3.8.1*ff*.
23. Quoted in GILMOR, p. 84.
24. Ṛg Veda 10.18.11. Quoted by NEUMANN, *The Great Mother*, p. 223. Neumann gives the reference Ṛg Veda 10.18.45, which is incorrect.

Chapter 18 Fears of the Future

1. This is the most basic meaning of the Indo-European √**ar* from which 'rational' is ultimately derived. www.bartleby.com/61/roots/IE22.html
2. See ANĀLAYO, 'The Buddha and Omniscience.'
3. E.g. Dīgha Nikāya 29.27, Majjhima Nikāya 71.
4. Aṅguttara Nikāya 5.77–80.
5. At Dīgha Nikāya 2.20 fatalism (*niyativāda*) is ascribed to Makkhali Gosala, who the Buddha described as the most harmful man alive (Aṅguttara Nikāya 1.319, Aṅguttara Nikāya 3.137), as he denied the efficacy of action.
6. See discussion in TAN, 'The Dharma-ending Age.'
7. The 'elements', or more accurately 'physical properties' are regarded as basic aspects of the material world. The world can be brought to an end by a major imbalance in any of them, as by a flood, a universal conflagration, and so on.
8. Saṁyutta Nikāya 16.13.
9. Dīgha Nikāya 16.3.35; *cf.* Dīgha Nikāya 16.3.8.
10. It is in fact found in this place in the Sarvāstivāda Catuṣpariṣat Sūtra.
11. Dīgha Nikāya 16.5.3.
12. Vacchagotta Sutta (Majjhima Nikāya 73.13). A similar statement can be found in the two Chinese parallels Saṁyukta Āgama 964 (T2, p. 247, a11) and Saṁyukta Āgama 198 (T2, p. 446, c10). Translation and references from ANĀLAYO, *A Comparative Study*.
13. Dīgha Nikāya 29.12–14.
14. In the late, elaborated Pali version of the Lakkhaṇa Sutta, the sheathed penis (*kosohitavatthaguyho*) is said to be the result of reuniting long-lost family and friends. If one with such a mark becomes a king, he has over a thousand powerful sons, and as a Buddha likewise; these are his followers. This suggests the mark is a sign of virility, but the main import of this mark itself is to *hide* the Buddha's gender. John Powers in his *A Bull of a Man* emphasizes

how the Buddha was depicted in highly masculinized ways in Indian texts. He was, after all, a man, and it is only appropriate that he should be depicted as the embodiment of masculine ideals. The point is, how does that masculinity relate to the feminine? And more important, is the Buddha defined by the masculine and feminine, or are they simply partial aspects of his fully integrated person? The early texts depict the Buddha's masculinity in generally subdued ways. Most of the 32 marks are not gendered at all, while several strike me as being quite feminine—cow-like eyelashes, legs like a gazelle, tender hands and feet. Also note the spiritual progression in one of the key early devotional texts, the Sela Sutta (Majjhima Nikāya 92). The brahman Sela, when he first met the Buddha, praised him under the influence of the brahmanical values, focussing on his glorious body, with its gold skin and auspicious marks (92.16). Later, when he had attained arahantship, his praise was solely of the Buddha's spiritual liberation (92.28).

15. He is proportioned 'like a banyan tree', his height being the same as his arm span. But this is normal human proportion, and it contradicts one of the other marks, which is that he can touch his knees while standing and not bending.
16. There is no proper parallel for this discourse. The partial parallel at Madhyama Āgama 59 (T1, № 26, p. 493, a24) has an extra introduction, and lacks all the detailed explanations. The commentary claims that Ānanda composed the verse portions, but the whole text clearly stems from a later stage of doctrinal and literary development and was quite possibly composed in Sri Lanka, perhaps 200–300 years after the Parinibbana. As such, it cannot be seriously taken to represent the Buddha's own views. Nevertheless it represents a mainstream attitude within at least part of the early community; and it is no coincidence that the composition of the Sutta is closely associated with Ānanda, the champion of the bhikkhunis.
17. Dīgha Nikāya 30.1.8.
18. Dīgha Nikāya 30.1.17, 30.2.11, 30.2.14, 30.2.18, 30.2.20, 30.2.23, 30.2.30.
19. Also found in the Sarvāstivāda (T1, № 26, p. 605, c5–6; T01, № 60, p. 856, b29–c10), Dharmaguptaka (T22, № 1428, p. 923, a1–2), Mūlasarvāstivāda (ROCKHILL, p. 61), and Pali (2.256).
20. Saṁyutta Nikāya 20.3.
21. ROCKHILL, p. 157.
22. STRONG, *King Aśoka*, p. 195.
23. www.invasive.org/browse/subject.cfm?sub=11182
24. NEEDHAM, V^OL 6, p. 258.
25. *Bhikkhuni Vinaya Studies*, ch. 2.
26. HENSHILWOODA *et al.*
27. FRAZER, p. 557.
28. FRAZER, pp. 429–30.
29. FRAZER, p. 438.

Chapter 19 The Flood

1. A Buddhist version of the classical flood myth is told in the Samudda-vāṇija Jātaka (№ 466, 4.158–166).
2. Saṁyutta Nikāya 15.3/Saṁyukta Āgama 938/(Smaller) Saṁyukta Āgama 331/Ekottara Āgama 51.1.

3. www.luangta.com/English/site/talks.php
4. Saṁyutta Nikāya 15.4/Saṁyukta Āgama 939/(Smaller) Saṁyukta Āgama 332.
5. Saṁyutta Nikāya 15.13/Saṁyukta Āgama 937/(Smaller) Saṁyukta Āgama 330/Ekottara Āgama 51.2. In Therīgāthā 496 the bhikkhuni Sumedhā echoes the same theme when she recalls how she persuaded her family to let her go forth on the eve of her royal wedding: 'Remember the tears, the milk, the blood, the journeying-on/as being without beginning and end.'
6. Majjhima Nikāya 38.27.
7. See NEUMANN, *The Great Mother*, p. 31.
8. PURKISS, p. 125.
9. ISIDORE, *Generation of Animals*, 4.8.
10. Jacques GUILLIMEAU, *Child-birth*, 1612.
11. ZIMMER, *Myths and Symbols*, p. 60.
12. The rule says discreetly 'water-cleansing', but the *vibhaṅga's* gloss on this says 'washing the place for urination.' (*Udakasuddhikaṁ nāma muttakaraṇassa dhovanā vuccati.*)
13. Pali Vinaya 4.261.
14. PURKISS, p. 97, quoting CIXOUS & CLEMENT, *Newly Born Woman*, p. 35.
15. MUCHEMBLED, p. 89.
16. NEUMANN, *The Great Mother*, p. 24.
17. Such a strategy is found in the halls of Academe just as in the monasteries. PURKISS remarks: 'Jeanne Favret-Saada [*Deadly Words: Witchcraft in the Bocage*, Cambridge, Cambridge University Press, 1980.] claims that accounts of the cultural difference between the academic anthropologist and those who 'believe in' witchcraft function to construct the believer as the dark other of the academic. The witchcraft believer is credulous, where the academic is sceptical.... These oppositions construct an identity for the believer in witchcraft which affirms the identity of the academic who recounts those beliefs.' PURKISS, p. 60.
18. [PURKISS' note] Elizabeth GROSZ, *Volatile Bodies*, Bloomington: Indiana Press, p. 203.
19. PURKISS, p. 120–1.
20. *Avisadatā*, a term used in the Pali sub-commentaries: see *Path of Purification*, p. 20 (1.53) note 14.
21. PURKISS, p. 124.
22. PREUSS, *Nayarit-Expedition*, Vol. 1, pp. 50*f.*, from PREUSS, *Die Eingeborenen Amerikas*, p. 41. Quoted in NEUMANN, *The Great Mother*, p. 128.
23. NEUMANN, *The Great Mother*, p. 120.
24. CAMPBELL, *Primitive Mythology*, p. 62.
25. Ṛg Veda 6.61 (selected verses). In this and other passages from the Ṛg Veda I have used GRIFFITH's classic translation. This is, however, so archaic as to be barely comprehensible to many modern English speakers. In deference to linguistic evolution I have taken the liberty of modernizing the prose, and have occasionally changed the renderings. Sarasvatī and other goddesses of the waters are discussed in PINTCHMAN.

    The Vedic worship of Sarasvatī may be compared with the distinctly more martial worship of the water-goddess Anahita in that other ancient Indo-Iranian document, the Avesta. The fifth section (Aban Yasht) is a series of prayers to Anahita, 'the wide-expanding and health-giving, who hates the Daevas and obeys the laws of Ahura, who is worthy of sacrifice in the material world ... Who makes the seed of all males pure, who makes the womb of all females pure for bringing forth, who makes all females bring forth in safety, who puts milk into the breasts of all females in the right measure and the right quality; The large river, known afar, that is as large as the whole of the waters that run along the earth; that runs powerfully from the height Hukairya down to the sea Vouru-Kasha.'

She is invoked for spiritual as well as worldly victory: '..."May I smite of the Turanian people their fifties and their hundreds, their hundreds and their thousands, their thousands and their tens of thousands, their tens of thousands and their myriads of myriads." Ardvi Sura Anahita granted him that boon, as he was offering libations...' http://www.avesta.org/ka/yt5sbe.htm

26. *Vṛtraghnī*. This is the only time that Sarasvatī is called by this name. Normally, as we shall see below, it is an attribute of the emphatically male Indra. GRIFFITH had 'foe-slayer' here, and it may be that this is more accurate, since the epithet may have become so worn down as to lose its connection with the myth of Vṛtra.
27. CALASSO, *Ka*, p. 336. Also see discussion in NEUMANN, *Origins*, p. 70*ff*.
28. 'The Lament of Quetzalcoatl.' Quoted in NEUMANN, *The Great Mother*, p. 208.
29. NEUMANN, *The Great Mother*, p. 217.
30. Another tale has the serpent act in service to the great goddess Isis. She sets him down in the path of her father Ra, so that the snake bites him with its poison. Pretending innocence, she says she can dispell the poison with her healing powers, but only if Ra will reveal to her his true name. In the utter reaches of agony, he consented; and his name left him and passed over to Isis. These two stories in FONTEROSE, pp. 186–8. This chapter is an excellent, detailed comparative study of the dragon-fight episode in Indic, Egyptian, and Greek myth. Especially useful for those not yet convinced of the closeness of mythic parallels across cultures.
31. NEUMANN, *The Great Mother*, p. 187.
32. Ṛg Veda 4.26–7.
33. Ṛg Veda 1.132.
34. Ṛg Veda 1.32.1–14. The final verse refers to the guilt that is associated with the killing of the sacrifice. In later literature it was said that Indra was guilty of a terrible crime needing expiation, since Vṛtra was a brahman. This motif has various parallels. For example, Apollo fled in guilt after slaying the serpent Typhon. See FONTEROSE, p. 198*ff*.
35. Śatapatha Brāhmaṇa 1.6.3.16–17. For the implications of Vedic 'food' imagery, see LOPEZ.
36. Taittirīya Saṅhita 2.4.12, 2.5.2; Śatapatha Brāhmaṇa 1.6.3.1–11.
37. Ṛg Veda 1.32.2, 4.19.3–4. Like the Nāga-king Nandopananda, *Path of Purification*, 12.106–116.
38. Greenebourne argues that Vṛtra is a Indo-European myth, connects Vṛtra with *ahi* (snake, dragon) and *dāsa* (servant, primitive), and suggests the myth has a historical root in the subjugation of the pre-Indo-European peoples.
39. Ṛg Veda 2.24.3. See discussion in MILLER, pp. 29*ff*.
40. Ṛg Veda 2.23.3: *jyotiṣmantaṁ ratham ṛtasya*.
41. Ṛg Veda 8.15.7.
42. Ṛg Veda 1.32.13.

43. Ṛg Veda 10.124.6.
44. Rāmāyaṇa, pp. 67–8.
45. Ṛg Veda, 1.164.42.

Chapter 20 The Serpent

1. E.g. *Rāmāyaṇa*, pp. 119, 285. Similarly, Greek drama frequently stigmatizes women as reptilian. GILMOR, p. 74. In one of his less pleasant essays, JUNG (*Aspects of the Feminine*, p. 63, § 251) speaks of how single women bear the burden of society's trauma (he is writing in post WW 1 Germany), and as a result when they see those who have achived wedded bliss, 'The possessors of that bliss must be ousted, not as a rule by naked force, but by that silent, obstinate desire which, as we know, has magical effects, like the fixed stare of a snake. This was ever the way of women.'
2. E.g. *Rāmāyaṇa*, p. 141. The snake as shape-shifter appears in Saṁyutta Nikāya 3.1.1. Compare *Aeneid* 5.84–96; when Aeneas made funeral offerings for his father, a giant snake with seven coils, shimmering like a rainbow appeared from beneath the shrine, tasted the offerings, and disappeared. The 'rainbow serpent' is an important figure in many Australian aboriginal creation myths.
3. There may be a genuine historical basis for this. Women, it is thought, are weaker and hence less likely to attempt murder by stabbing or strangling; at the same time they have easy access to food and drinks in preparation. Poison therefore becomes the woman's murder weapon of choice. K. WATSON (pp. 45*ff.*) has a nuanced discussion of the situation in Edwardian Britain. She finds that the total number of poisonings by men and women are roughly the same. However women commit far less murders in total, so proportionately they choose poisoning more often than men. This is, of course, affected by social factors such as the availability of suitable poisons.
4. GILMOR, pp. 74–76.
5. Aṅguttara Nikāya 3.68–69.
6. Aṅguttara Nikāya 5.229.
7. Aṅguttara Nikāya 5.230.
8. E.g. Aṅguttara Nikāya 1.1. 1–10; 7.48; 8.17, 18; Dīgha Nikāya 31.30.
9. E.g. Saṁyutta Nikāya 5.3. The exception, of course, is the assertion that women cannot be Buddhas discussed above.
10. Saṁyutta Nikāya 35.127.
11. ALLEN, *et al.*
12. The details are fuzzy, since not everyone clearly identified themselves as holding grudges or not, but offered reflections around how they dealt with it. But roughly 9 out of 12 women and 12 out of 19 men admitted having problems with grudges.
    http://www.socialanxietysupport.com/forum/f35/do-you-hold-grudges-71809/
13. BAUMEISTER, *et al.*
14. SUCIU; FOX; research by Dr. Charlotte DE BACKER reported at
    www.science20.com/news/let_s_talk_about_sex_turns_out_men_love_gossip_too.
15. LEVIN, *et al.*
16. BJÖRKQVIST.
17. WIEDERMAN.

18. ATWOOD & SCHWARTZ, Journal of Couple & Relationship Therapy, 2002. www.menstuff.org/issues/byissue/infidelitystats.html
19. ANĀLAYO, 'The Bahudhātuka-sutta and its Parallels.'
20. Madhyama Āgama 181.
21. Aṅguttara Nikāya 2.6.10.
22. Aṅguttara Nikāya 4.80.
23. Majjhima Nikāya 44, Aṅguttara Nikāya 1.14.
24. Aṅguttara Nikāya 1.14, Udāna 7.9.
25. Majjhima Nikāya 73.
26. ANĀLAYO, *A Comparative Study of the Majjhima Nikāya* (unpublished draft).
27. E.g. *Rāmāyaṇa*, p. 187, 239, 274.
28. NEUMANN, *The Great Mother*, p. 144.
29. Paṇḍara Jātaka (№ 518, 5.75–88).
30. Koṭisimbali Jātaka (№ 412, 3.397–400); Bhūridatta Jātaka (№ 543, 6.177–8).

Chapter 21 The Deepest Taboo

1. See GUTERMAN *et al.* for a general survey.
2. For example, see HARRIS, *Cows*.
3. FRAZER, pp. 595–598.
4. PLINY the Elder, *Natural History*, Book 28, ch. 23, 78–80; Book 7, ch. 65. www.womenpriests.org/traditio/unclean.asp#law
5. Or at least, this is the injunction to Ānanda placed in the Mahāparinibbāna Sutta by the Theravāda tradition, though absent from the Sanskrit.
6. PAUCAPALEA, *Summa*, Dist. 5, pr. § 1 v. www.womenpriests.org/traditio/unclean.asp#law
7. www.womenpriests.org/body/ranke.asp
8. Pali Vinaya 2.270–1; Pali Vinaya 5.302 (bhikkhuni *pācittiya* 47).
9. In popular Buddhist usage, the term 'Brahmanical' or 'Hindu' doesn't necessarily mean literally Brahmanical, but can refer to any non-Buddhist superstition. This usage, while neither accurate nor politically correct, is common. Menstrual taboos are found commonly in Brahmanical texts, e.g. Manu 5.85. (See discussion in WILSON, pp. 50*ff.*) However, such taboos are a near-universal feature of pre-modern societies, and menstrual taboos in modern Thailand probably derive as much from archaic Thai customs as from any 'Hindu' influence.
10. Ven. Chatsumarn KABILSINGH (Bhikkhuni Dhammanandā), 'Women in Buddhism, Questions and Answers.' www.buddhanet.net/e-learning/history/wbq21.htm
11. www.ohbliss.org/freethought/menstruation.html (As of 1–2–2009 this site no longer exists.)
12. A Chinese Dhammapada has Mallikā, the forthright and intelligent queen of Pasenadi, attribute her own female form to her little merit, saying 'the impurity of this [female body's] sensual nature day and night accumulates like a mountain.' (T4, № 211, p. 585b; WILLEMEN, p. 72.)
13. Dharmacari JNANAVIRA, 'A Mirror for Women? Reflections of the Feminine in Japanese Buddhism.' www.westernbuddhistreview.com/vol4/mirror_for_women.html
14. 'Tenzin Palmo ... a search for spiritual enlightenment.' www.purifymind.com/IV8.htm

15. Ei Moe KHINE, 'Shoulder To Shoulder.' Originally published in TODAY Magazine (VOL 7, Nov 1999). www.burmalibrary.org/reg.burma/archives/199912/msg00416.html
16. G.K. UPAWANSA and Rukman WAGACHCHI. 'Activating All Powers in Sri Lanka Agriculture.' http://goviya.com/activating-powers.htm
17. Carla RISSEEUW, 'A Women's Mind is Longer Than a Kitchen Spoon.' In *Report on Women in Sri Lanka*, Leiden, 1980. Quoted in SENEVIRATNE, p. 58. The statement that men are not ever unclean is unusual, as the Dharmaśāstras give many occasions for a man's uncleanliness. This is especially associated with emission of semen. If Risseeuw's claim is correct, it throws doubt on the often-heard claim that chauvinistic prejudices in Buddhism are derived from the Dharmaśāstras. In fact both Buddhism and the Dharmaśāstras draw on much more ancient roots.
18. Yasodhara Newsletter on International Buddhist Women's Activities, 4/1/2004. http://goliath.ecnext.com/coms2/summary_0199-418197_ITM
19. Richard DAVIS, p. 66.
20. Details taken from Chang NOI, 'PAD saves the nation from supernatural attack'. *The Nation*, Nov 10, 2008. http://ads.nationmultimedia.com/option/print.php?newsid=30087963.
21. Such 'tacks' or 'pegs' are part of ancient Indian geomancy (*vatthuvijjā*, *feng shui*), referred to, for example, in the commentary on the establishing of Pāṭaliputta (An, *Last Days*, p. 58).
22. The pun in this sentence, sadly enough, is an unintended artifact of the translation.
23. Chang Noi, 'PAD saves the nation from supernatural attack'. *The Nation*, Nov 10, 2008. http://ads.nationmultimedia.com/option/print.php?newsid=30087963. See also: http://blog.newsweek.com/blogs/ov/archive/2008/11/26/bangkok-s-bizarre-power-struggle.aspx. The original speech (in Thai) is here: Youtube user thaienews, 'Sondhi Places 6 Used Tampons on Stature of King Rama 5', http://www.youtube.com/watch?v=e0f0RdfIUAw. This protest was followed, in March 2010, by the more widely publicized protest from the Thaksin-supporting 'Red Shirts', who collected blood from their supporters, and with monks and Brahman priests doing blessings, poured it in front of various Government buildings. http://www.guardian.co.uk/world/2010/mar/16/thailand-human-blood-protest
24. TERWIEL, p. 99.
25. Bhikkhu saṅghādisesa 2: *otiṇṇo vipariṇatena cittena*.
26. J.V. HEFELE, *Conciliengeschichte*. 2nd ed. (Freiburg, 1873–1890), VOL 3, pp. 45*f*. www.womenpriests.org/traditio/can_aux.asp
27. *Encyclopedia of Religion*, Macmillan Reference USA. www.bookrags.com/research/menstruation-eorl-09/
28. 'Responsa ad interrogationes Marci' [Intern 35]; *cf.* Ida RAMING, 'Der Ausschluss der Frau vom priesterlichen Amt', p. 39. Quoted in RANKE-HEINEMANN. www.womenpriests.org/body/ranke.asp
29. John MIJNGAARDS. www.womenpriests.org/traditio/unclean.asp
30. For menstrual taboos on amulets and tattoos (!) in Thailand, see TERWEIL, p. 78, 182, 243.
31. Mahāsupina Jātaka (№ 77, 1.337).
32. NEUMANN, *The Great Mother*, p. 31.
33. MAGEE.

34. The Pali word for the formation of an embryo (*sammucchati*) means to 'coagulate'. See discussion in SCHMITHAUSEN, 3.3.1.1– 2. Also see NEUMANN, *Origins*, p. 55.
35. NEUMANN, *The Great Mother*, p. 290. He is influenced by Robert BRIFFAULT's *The Mothers.*
36. KNIGHT *et al.*

Chapter 22 How to Kill a Dead Nun

1. *Bhikkhunīnam'ovādo pana idāni tāsaṁ n'atthitāya n'atthi.*
2. I am thinking of the climax of the Iliad, when Achilles initially refuses to allow his arch-enemy Hector a proper burial until beseeched by his father Priam; or Antigone's courageous burial of her brother Polyneices outside the walls of Thebes in defiance of Creon's edict.
3. This origin story has much of interest, and has been exploited by Gregory Schopen in his essay 'The Suppression of Nuns and the Ritual Murder of Their Special Dead in Two Buddhist Monastic Codes' (SCHOPEN, *Business Matters*, p. 341), an essay which delivers almost as much as the title promises.
4. Translated by SCHOPEN, *ibid.*
5. Kakacūpama Sutta (Majjhima Nikāya 21).
6. This and following versions were not noticed by Schopen. The first half becomes the background for a rule forbidding bhikkhunis from entering a bhikkhus' monastery without permission (Dharmaguptaka bhikkhuni *pācittiya* 145); the second half is the origin for the following rule, prohibiting abusing bhikkhus (Dharmaguptaka bhikkhuni *pācittiya* 146). In the Pali, these two rules also follow on from one another, but the origin stories are not related. By removing the rule material from Dharmaguptaka *pācittiyas* 145 and 146 we are left with a story that broadly parallels the story behind Pali *pācittiya* 52.
7. HEIRMANN's translation has 'kind of smiths'.
8. HEIRMANN, p. 879, 882–3.
9. T22, № 1421, p. 90, b2–12.
10. T23, № 1435, p. 340, a15–b4.
11. Abusing a bhikkhu, T22, № 1425, p. 532, c26–p. 533, a8; entering a bhikkhu monastery, T22, № 1425, p. 538, c17–p. 539, a10.
12. ROTH, *Bhikṣuṇī-Vinaya*, pp. 230–231, 262.
13. Majjhima Nikāya 104.2, Dīgha Nikāya 29.1.
14. SCHOPEN, *Business Matters*, pp. 337–339.
15. FRAZER, ch. 66, 67.
16. BEAL, *Buddhist Records*, pp. 180–181.
17. SCHOPEN, *Business Matters*, pp. 348–349.
18. Mahāvaṁsa, ch. 20, GEIGER's translation, slightly adapted.
19. BEAL, *Buddhist Records*, xli. Xuan-zang mentions this episode, but does not mention a stupa (BEAL, *Buddhist Records*, I 204).
20. BEAL, *Buddhist Records*, xliv.
21. BEAL, *Buddhist Records*, II 2.
22. BEAL, *Buddhist Records*, II 68.

Chapter 23 A Very Grievous Text

1. As Rāma was described by Shulman, quoted in *Rāmāyaṇa*, xliii.
2. See RHYS DAVIDS, *Buddhist India*, ch. 11. Available at http://fsnow.com/text/buddhist-india/chapter11.htm.
3. We have already seen the Bodhisatta as a murderer, thief, and traitor. A less lurid example is the Vissāsabhojana Jātaka (№ 93, 1.387), which depicts the Bodhisatta encouraging a hunter to smear a doe with poison to kill a lion. Such incidents did not go unnoticed by the traditions; a list of such ethical lapses is compiled at Apadāna 299*ff.*
4. Aṇḍabhūta Jātaka (№ 62, 1.289).
5. Aṇḍabhūta Jātaka (№ 62, 1.295).
6. Anabhirati Jātaka (№ 65, 1.298).
7. In the chapter entitled *Raihai tokuzui* ('Prostration to Attain the Marrow') of his major work *Shōbōgenzō* ('Storage of the Eye of the Right Dharma'). [ROMBERG's note:] Gudo Nishijima GUDO and Chodo CROSS (trans.), *Master Dōgen's Shōbōgenzō*, 4 vols, Woking, Surrey: Windbell Publications Ltd. 1994, I, pp. 69–83. This chapter was probably written around the year 1240. However, Dōgen seems to have changed his attitude later in life when, in his late writings, he states that a nun who has served the sangha all her life has to bow before a newly ordained monk. This represents the Theravāda view. [Sujato: In fact the view of all the early schools.] It is not clear whether Dōgen actually changed his mind or whether these later texts are apocryphal writings, added during the establishment of a male-dominated Zen Buddhist institution. [Sujato: The two views are not inconsistent. Dōgen may have believed that women were equal to men, but that social harmony demanded that they act in a subservient manner. This is the view of many Buddhists today.] On the authenticity of Dōgen's writing see Steven HEINE. 'The Dōgen Canon, Dōgen's Pre-Shōbōgenzō Writings and the Question of Change in His Later Works', Japanese Journal of Religious Studies, 24 (1–2), 1997, p. 39–85.
8. GUDO & CROSS, p. 78 (quoted in ROMBERG, p. 166).
9. Kunāla Jātaka (№ 536, 5.412–456).
10. GILMOR, pp. 79–81. Compare the discussion on this point between Zeus and Hera (HYGINUS, *Fabula* 75; OVID, *Metamorposes* III; APOLLODORUS 3.6.7).
11. DhA.i.324*ff.* http://www.palikanon.com/english/pali_names/s/soreyya.htm
12. Asātamanta Jātaka (№ 61, 1.285).
13. As was Athena in the *Orestia.*
14. Śatapatha Brāhmaṇa 1:1:1:20.
15. Taittirīya Brāhmaṇa 2.4.2.6. Quoted in MILLER, p. 137, from MUIR, *Original Sanskrit texts on the origin and history of the people of India.* O.S.T. London, 1868–70.
16. Without, it seems, considering the kammic consequences for his poor old mum of dying immediately after attempting to kill her son.
17. This Jātaka is retold by Hellmuth HECKER in his hagiography *Mahā Kassapa*. Brought in to illustrate the sterling qualities of Bhaddākāpilānī and Mahākassapa, it misrepresents the misogyny of the text. Saying, wrongly, that the son 'wanted to become an ascetic', Hecker says that the mother wanted him to 'know the worldly life before she would permit him to become an ascetic.' But that knowledge came in a 'drastic way', as the teacher's mother 'fell passionately in love with him and was even ready to kill her son.' Hecker's

re-imagining of the text shows the lengths that the modernist, rationalizing mind will take to edit out what it finds disturbing. Thus Mahākassapa, the ascetic rigorist, in both lives warns Ānanda of the dangers of women. We shall hear more of their stories later on.

Chapter 24 The Hero Departs

1. NEUMANN, *Origins*, p. 339.
2. CAMPBELL, *Hero*, p. 30.
3. In addition to his treatment in *Hero*, CAMPBELL returned to the Buddha's life story in *Oriental Mythology*, pp. 15–22, 252*ff.*
4. Even before the birth, the Jātakas appropriated endless tales and made the Bodhisatta hero of them all. But for now we shall restrain ourselves to Siddhattha's final life.
5. The Buddhist version of Rāma's story is the Dasaratha Jātaka (№ 461, 4.129.), which tells the story of the exile, but not the abduction and subsequent war. It is depicted in stone at Nāgārjunakoṇḍa, and hence probably older than Vālmīki's version. See KRISHNA MURTHY, ch. 2.
6. GILLIGAN, *Birth*, p. 163.
7. press.princeton.edu/books/lyons/chapter_1.html#ref25
8. See W. PÖTSCHER, 'Hera und Heros,' RM 104 (1961) 302–55 for the etymology of Hrôs and its connection with Hera, as well as his 'Der Name der Göttin Hera,' RM 108 (1965) 317–20. D. Adams, 'Hrôs and Hra,' Glotta 65 (1987) 171–78, taking a different line, sees both words as linked to Hebe.
9. O'BRIEN, p. 113–19.
10. HOUSEHOLDER and NAGY, pp. 51–52.
11. NEUMANN, *The Great Mother*, p. 28. See *Origins*, p. 42; John Bebe's introduction to JUNG's *Aspects*.
12. CAMPBELL, *Hero*, p. 308. See Majjhima Nikāya 123; Dīgha Nikāya 14. (*The Life of the Buddha*, pp. 2–5.)
13. CAMPBELL, *Hero*, p. 311.
14. On duplication in myth, see RANK, p. 89.
15. While from a Western perspective Jesus in the manger is the most obvious point of comparison, this is a common motif; for example Apollo and Artemis were born to their wandering mother Leto on the isle of Delphos. Birth while the mother travels back to her parental home is a standard trope of Indian story, as for example Mahā Panthaka and Cūḷa Panthaka in Cullakaseṭṭhi Jātaka (№ 4, 1.114). In these cases the ancient motif of birth on a journey is combined with the Indian cultural norm that the mother should give birth in her parents' home.
16. CALASSO, *Ka*, p. 365.
17. Sutta Nipāta 3.11, 685–704. (*The Life of the Buddha*, pp. 6–7.) See JAYNES, pp. 362*ff.*
18. Sutta Nipāta 691.
19. One still finds the belief that the Sutta Nipāta is a specially early and authentic collection of Buddhist texts. This is false. While certain sections, such as the Aṭṭhakavagga, Soḷasapañha, Khaggavisāṇa Sutta, etc., have a strong claim to be among the earliest texts, the collection as a whole includes verses from all canonical periods. Each section must be considered

independently. Nor are there good reasons to believe that the early sections are earlier than the early prose suttas from the four Nikāyas.

20. E.g. Dīgha Nikāya 16.4.2; Saṁyutta Nikāya 48.21; Majjhima Nikāya 128.32; Majjhima Nikāya 4.22.
21. Aṅguttara Nikāya 3.38; Majjhima Nikāya 36, 85, 100. (*The Life of the Buddha*, pp. 8–9; 21.)
22. Majjhima Nikāya 36.31. Full references and comparative discussion in ANĀLAYO, *A Comparative Study.*
23. Majjhima Nikāya 26, 36, 85, 100; Sutta Nipāta 3.1, 408–427. (*The Life of the Buddha*, pp. 10–11.)
24. Sutta Nipāta 939–943.
25. Aṭṭhasālinī Nidānakathā: *uyyānakīḷāya gamanasamaye anukkamena jiṇṇabyādhimatasaṅkhāte tayo devadūte disvā sañjātasaṁvego nivattitvā.*
26. Disguised divinities are a major feature of Greek myth. But Indian deities, apart from Māra the master of disguises, might hide their real nature, too, as when Sakka disguised himself as a poor man so as to offer alms to Mahākassapa (Udāna 3.7). In an isolated and curious passage, the Buddha claims that he frequently disguised himself so as to enter assemblies of various kinds for debate (Dīgha Nikāya 16.3.22–23).
27. AŚVAGHOṢA (trans. JOHNSTON) *Buddhacarita* 5.47–67 (selected verses). This text is translated from the Sanskrit and Tibetan. A translation of the parallel passage from the Chinese by Samuel BEAL is verses 384–394 at http://www.sacred-texts.com/bud/sbe19/sbe1907.htm.
28. http://www.sacred-texts.com/bud/sbe19/sbe1907.htm. This, of course, is the *sālabhañjikā.*
29. *Rāmāyaṇa* 5.2, p. 419–420.
30. Majjhima Nikāya 26, 36, 85, 100. (*The Life of the Buddha*, p. 10.)
31. Majjhima Nikāya 26.14. Incidentally, this passage should not be used to cast doubt on the idea that the Buddha's birth mother died, and he was raised by his aunt. Both could be called 'mother' (*mātā*), and the more specific term for the natural mother was *janettī*. In addition, the phrase 'mother and father' (*mātāpitu*) is a conventional one, which just means 'parents'.
32. Pali Vinaya 1.82–3.
33. Kumbhakāra Jātaka (№ 408, 4.375–383).
34. Bhayabherava Sutta (Majjhima Nikāya 4).
35. *The Life of the Buddha*, pp. 16–19.
36. Majjhima Nikāya 51.10 (1.344). Freud and following psychologists believed that a shaven head was a symbolic form of castration. This was argued in the case of Buddhist monks by Gananath OBEYESEKERA in his *Medusa's Hair*, p. 38, saying 'the Buddhist monk is sexless, a neuter. And this idea is represented in the castration symbolism of shaven head.' In the Vedas, hair was equated with vegetation, and the ritual of shaving was performed as an act of sympathetic magic to promote the regrowth of the 'bald' fields (VAJRACHARYA). See discussion and references at WILSON, p. 153.
37. Cakkavattisīhanāda Sutta (Dīgha Nikāya 3.67).
38. Chaddanta Jātaka (№ 514, 5.27).
39. Khantivādi Jātaka (№ 313, 3.41), Cūḷadhammapāla Jātaka (№ 358, 3.179).
40. Mahākapi Jātaka (№ 407, 3.227).
41. Khaṇḍahāla Jātaka (№ 542, 6.79).

42. GILLIGAN, *Birth*, p. 79.
43. Mahāsaccaka Sutta (Majjhima Nikāya 36.26).
44. The Lomahaṁsa Jātaka (№ 94, 1.389–391) relocates the story of the Bodhisatta's austerities to a remote past life. When he is passing away, he sees a vision of the hell that awaits him as a result of his delusory acts; but the wisdom of the moment freed hm and he was reborn in heaven.
45. Bodhi Sutta (Majjhima Nikāya 85.10). This view is attributed to an ascetic of the past in a Jātaka-type story at *Tibetan Tales*, p. 251, with apparently no comprehension that the view was denounced by the Buddha.

Chapter 25 The Hero Wakes

1. Majjhima Nikāya 26, 36, 85, 100. (*The Life of the Buddha*, pp. 13–14.)
2. Sutta Nipāta 425–449.
3. Majjhima Nikāya 36, 85, 100. (*The Life of the Buddha*, p. 21.)
4. TERWIEL, p. 155–6.
5. Or Nandā and Nandabalā, according to the Mūlasarvāstivāda Vinaya, Divyāvadāna, and AŚVAGHOṢA's Buddhacarita. These sources seem to share a common tradition, and all treat the episode quite briefly. The Abhiniṣkramaṇa Sūtra calls her Sujātā, daughter of Nandika (BEAL, *Romantic Legends*, 186). But Nandā and Nandabalā, daughters of Seniyana, occur as well, repeating the story (BEAL, *Romantic Legends*, 191). And a third time, with Sujātā again, this time one of two daughters of Sujāta; and she offers the milk that had been fed to cows repeatedly, as in the Sinhalese version (BEAL, *Romantic Legends*, 193). As usual, Sujātā's identity recedes the closer we look. The Pali Suttas say a certain Sujātā Seniyadhītā was the first female disciple to go for refuge (Aṅguttara Nikāya i.26). This may well be the only canonical reference to the same Sujātā. In the Abhiniṣkramaṇa Sūtra Sujātā's story is told adjacent to that of 'Seniyana', but no relationship is suggested (BEAL, *Romantic Legends*, 186). She is further identified with Yasa's mother, which is less plausible, as Yasa lived near Benares, not Bodhgaya. Yasa's mother—we have no personal name in the Pali Vinaya account—was the first to go for the three refuges, there not yet being a Sangha present while the Buddha was in Bodhgaya.
6. Jātaka Nidāna 1.68–9.
7. BEAL, *Romantic Legends*, p. 186.
8. Mahāvastu II, trans. JONES, pp. 191–193.
9. CALASSO, *Ka*, p. 335.
10. NEUMANN, *The Great Mother*, p. 48.
11. Kaṭha Upaniṣad 2.3.1.
12. Asko PARPOLA suggests that the inverted tree springs from the Indus Valley Civilization's derivation of the fig sign from that of the North Star: the Bodhi tree is literally 'planted' in the heavens. www.harappa.com/script/parpola11.html
13. Ṛg Veda 1.164.20–22. GRIFFITH's trans:
    http://www.sacred-texts.com/hin/rigveda/rv01164.htm
14. Saṁyutta Nikāya 4.24–25. (*The Life of the Buddha*, pp. 61–64.)

15. E.g. Saṁyutta Nikāya 5; Therīgāthā 312–399. The story of bhikkhuni Subhā who ripped out her eyes as a gift for her admirer is also found in the Christian story of Saint Lucy. The two names have the same meaning, 'light'.
16. Sutta Nipāta 3.2 Padhāna Sutta.
17. Majjhima Nikāya 36; Saṁyutta Nikāya 12.65; Saṁyutta Nikāya 22.26. (*The Life of the Buddha*, pp. 22–28.)
18. Aṅguttara Nikāya 5.129; Majjhima Nikāya 36, 26; Saṁyutta Nikāya 12.65, 22.26. (*The Life of the Buddha*, pp. 22–29.)
19. As recounted in the Introduction by John FREEMAN, pp. v-vii.
20. Dhammapada 153–4; Udāna 1.1–3, 1.4, 2.1 (*cf.* Pali Vinaya 1.1–4); Udāna 3.10. (*The Life of the Buddha*, pp. 29–34.)
21. Udāna 1.1–3.

Chapter 26 The Hero Returns

1. Translated by KLOPPENBORG.
2. Full text translated by L.W. KING at http://eawc.evansville.edu/anthology/hammurabi.htm
3. Aśoka, of course, normally referred to himself as 'beloved of the gods'.
4. See JAYNES, pp. 198–200.
5. Pali Vinaya 1.5 (*cf.* Majjhima Nikāya 26, 85); Saṁyutta Nikāya 6.1. (*The Life of the Buddha*, pp. 37–39.)
6. Pali Vinaya 1.21–22; Saṁyutta Nikāya 4.24–5 (*cf.* Sutta Nipāta 3.2); Dīgha Nikāya 16.3 (*cf.* Aṅuttara Nikāya 8.70, Udāna 6.1). (*The Life of the Buddha*, pp. 52–4; 60–64; 303.)
7. Saṁyutta Nikāya 4.24–5.
8. Dīgha Nikāya 16.3.8. According to ANĀLAYO, *A Comparative Study*, parallels to this passage may be found in the Dharmaguptaka Dīrgha Āgama T1, № 1, p. 15; the individual sutras T1, № 5, p. 165, a19 (which mentions the nuns only implicitly by speaking of the four types of disciples (四輩引子)); T1, № 6, p. 180, b27; T1, № 7, p. 191, b28; and in their Sanskrit and Tibetan counterparts as listed in Ernst WALDSCHMIDT, *Das Mahāparinirvāṇasūtra: Text in Sanskrit und Tibetisch.*Berlin, Akademie-Verlag, 1950–1951, pp. 208 and 209.
9. Catuṣpariṣat Sūtra, ch. 4.6, p. 11 of KLOPPENBORG's translation.
10. Saṁyutta Nikāya 45.174: *idaṁ saccābhiniveso kāyagantho*. Also see Majjhima Nikāya 72.3: *idam'eva saccaṁ, mogham' aññaṁ*. ('Only this is true, everything else is silly.')
11. Pali Vinaya 1.7*ff.* (*The Life of the Buddha*, pp. 40–42.)
12. FRAZER, pp. 586–7.
13. Pali Vinaya 1.9*ff.*, Saṁyutta Nikāya 56.11. (*The Life of the Buddha*, pp. 44–45, 52.)
14. Saṁyutta Nikāya 22.87.
15. See NEUMANN, *Origins*, p. 337.
16. VASUBANDHU, *Viṁśatikākārikā.* Trans. ANACKER, p. 163.
17. See Lalitavistara, ch. 12 (MITRA's trans.).
18. Ṛg Veda 4.18.1–2. See BANERJEE.

Chapter 27 Building the Legend

1. HARTMANN.
2. E.g. T45, № 1852, p. 10, a7.
3. Commentary to Lakkhaṇa Sutta: *Etā pana gāthā porāṇakattherā 'ānandattherena ṭhapitā vaṇṇa-nāgāthā'ti vatvā gatā.* 'The teachers of old have said, "The explanatory verses were included by Ānanda Thera." These verses are absent from the Sarvāstivādin version of this sutta (T1, № 26, pp. 493, a24*ff.*) This fact, together with the late style of the poetry, make it virtually certain that the verses were considerably later than Ānanda, and should be attributed to his 'school', or more generally the devotional tradition of which he was the major early exponent.
4. *Khandhaka* just refers to a 'group' of texts, and means little more than 'chapter'. Different schools use different terms, such as *vatthu, paṭisaṁyutta,* etc. As usual, I use the Pali form. Frauwallner used the Sanskrit *Skandhaka.*
5. FRAUWALLNER, *Earliest Vinaya*, pp. 52–53.
6. This notion was foreshadowed, in the context of the Jātakas rather than the canon as a whole, by C.F. RHYS DAVIDS, *Wayfarer's Words*, Vol 3, p. 812: 'Taking then the motley Jātaka-mass, with its introduction, it is scarcely an overstatement to say that, for all the much foolishness found in them, the oddities, the inconsistencies, the many distortions in ideals and in the quest for them, they are collectively the greatest epic in literature of the Ascent of Man.' (Quoted in WICKRAMASINGHE, pp. 73–4.)
7. Other obvious examples include the reference to the Buddha's first teachers, the association of 'Kassapa' with fire, the homage of Brahmā, the debate with Māra, sevenday time spans, earthquakes, and an encounter with a lone wanderer on the road.
8. HUME, §10.1. This basic principle of empiricism is better known as Carl Sagan's 'extraordinary claims require extraordinary evidence'. It is fundamental to Buddhist epistemology in such texts as the Cūḷahatthipadopama Sutta (Majjhima Nikāya 27) or the Caṅkī Sutta (Majjhima Nikāya 95).
9. See Kate BLACKSTONE, 'Damming the Dhamma.'

Chapter 28 The Wicked Stepmother

1. GILMOR, p. 72–73.
2. GILMOR, p. 73.
3. NEUMANN, *Origins*, p. 94.
4. A deeply controversial figure. www.leaderu.com/ftissues/ft9706/articles/finn.html
5. BETTELHEIM, p. 68–69. Quoted in WARNER, p. 212.
6. Warner, p. 212–3; in more detail in ZIPES, ch. 6.
7. Bṛhadāraṇyaka Upaniṣad 3.9.17.
8. 'From the Sutras: Life Stories of the Historical Bhikshunis'. www.geocities.com/zennun12_8/nunhistories.html
9. See PRUITT, pp. 180–201.
10. That is, in her own right; occasionally she appears in a list of other prominent women from the Buddha's time.
11. Culladhammapāla Jātaka (№ 358, 3.178–182).

12. *Kāsāyavatthanivattho.* The same robe monastics wear.
13. *Papañcaṁ akatvā hatthe chedāti.*
14. For more on the dark side of fairy tales, see TATAR's discussion of the 'hard facts' of the Grimm brothers' tales.
15. FRAZER, p. 428.
16. FRAZER, p. 432.
17. Vepacitti, the king of the *asuras*, is called *pubbadeva* ('older god') by Sakka at Saṁyutta Nikāya 11.5. The story of how the *asuras* were ejected from heaven is found in the commentary to Saṁyutta Nikāya 11.1.
18. Culanandiya Jataka (№ 222, 2.199–202).
19. Aṅguttara Nikāya 4.88.
20. See Dīgha Nikāya 1.21.1*ff.*; Pali Vinaya 2.139.
21. JAYNES, pp. 236–239.
22. *Pali Text Society Dictionary*, p. 737, note 3; referring to Sutta Nipāta 1022.
23. Bhikṣunī Mahāprajāpatī Sūtra (T24 № 1478, p. 946, a6–a10).
24. See Kate BLACKSTONE's perceptive essay on these issues.
25. Ṛg Veda 1.164.32. GRIFFITH has 'bosom' for *yoni*, which I correct to 'womb'.
26. NEUMANN, *Origins*, p. 91–92.
27. GILLIGAN, *Birth*, p. 169.
28. NEUMANN, *Origins*, p. 140–141.
29. Using the parallels with the five aggegates that we developed in chapter 11, this is the shift of focus from *saññā* to *saṅkhāra* as the prime locus of identity.

Chapter 29 The Princess & the Dragon

1. NEUMANN, *The Great Mother*, p. 104.
2. NEUMANN, *The Great Mother*, p. 54, note 27. Here and generally I prefer the terms 'masculine' and 'feminine' where Neumann frequently uses 'matriarchal' and 'patriarchal', as these terms are derived from structures of power within societies. The idea of a universal social stage of matriarchy has been widely dismissed, with much evidence suggesting that there are in fact no matriarchal cultures at all. Neumann has derived this usage from earlier authors, notably Bachofen, although he explictly repudiates the idea that his stages of consciousness correspond with actual historical situations, for example: 'It should not be forgotten that "early mankind" and "matriarchal stage" are no archaeological or historical entities, but psychological realities whose fateful power is still alive in the psychic depths of present-day man.' (NEUMANN, *The Great Mother*, p. 43.)
3. NEUMANN, *Origins*, p. 198.
4. As we have already seen in the battle between Indra and Vṛtra.
5. NEUMANN, *The Great Mother*, p. 12.
6. This retelling is based on http://en.wikipedia.org/wiki/Perseus, rewritten using the sources at http://www.theoi.com/Heros/Perseus.html, especially Pseudo-Apollodorus, whose account is the most coherent. I've spiced up his dry version with details from other sources. The choice of this myth to illustrate the higher/lower dynamic in myth was inspired by the treatment in NEUMANN, *History*, pp. 213–9.
7. This mytheme is also connected to Ares, Oenopion, Eurystheus, etc.

8. PSEUDO-APOLLODORUS, *Bibliotheca* 2.26, suggests a less exalted parentage: Acrisius' hostile twin, Proitos, was the real father. It is typical of the Greeks to maintain a rationalizing explanation side by side with the miraculous.
9. 'Graeae'. Like the Gorgons, they were daughters of Phorkys.
10. NONNUS, *Dionysiaca* 26.52.
11. See KERENYI, 1959, p. 49–50.
12. Compare the Indic motif of the rishis who fly through the air until they see a beautiful woman; their concentration falls away, and so do they.
13. This account of the battle is after OVID; others say he merely exposed the monster to the Gorgon's gaze and turned it to stone.
14. According to PSEUDO-HYGINUS this took place on Seriphos and the dead father was in fact Polydectes.
15. See the story of Persephone above, ch. 4.24–25. Polydegmon and Polydectes are variant forms with the same meaning.
    http://www.mythindex.com/greek-mythology/P/Polydegmon.html
16. That this is not an arbitrary association is shown by WIJESEKERA (p. 295–7), who refers to several passages in the Ṛg Veda where the discus is specifically compared with the sun: Ṛg Veda 2.11.20, 1.130.9, 4.16.12, 1.174.5, etc.
17. This is the version of PSEUDO-APOLLODORUS. PSEUDO-HYGINUS says it was a blow to the head, which is medically more plausible but less mythically apt.
18. Ghata Jātaka (№ 454, 4.79–89).
19. 'Kaṁsa' is Pali for 'bronze', and it seems to be a western, perhaps, Babylonian, term. Mahākaṁsa ('King of Great Bronze') plays the role of Acrisius in the story of Perseus, whose crucial deed was to lock Danaë in a 'bronze tower'. The name of Mahākaṁsa's daughter is similarly suggestive: it means 'Divine Womb', which is mythically exact, given that Danaë was fertilized by Zeus in the bronze tower, which thereby became precisely a 'divine womb'. Obviously, the prominence of bronze in the story suggests a 'Bronze Age' setting; Mahākaṁsa/Acrisius may have originally been culture heroes associated with the introduction of bronze, who were demonized when the story was recast in its current Iron Age forms. This is supported by the fact that Acrisius is said to have quarrelled with his brother Proetus even in the womb, so Proetus developed the buckler, a small bronze shield that was an important part of Bronze Age combat.
20. Vāsudeva is a popular name for Kṛṣṇa. In the verses he is called Kaṇha (the Pali spelling of Kṛṣṇa). Kṛṣṇa's brother is Balarāma (= Baladeva) and his mother is Devaki (= Devagabbha), whose brother is Kaṁsa.
21. The elaborate quest of Perseus to overcome the Lower Feminine is absent, unless there be a faint echo in the story of Ghatapaṇḍita's pretended quest for the rabbit in the moon.
22. The actual deadly weapon is the leaf of an apparently harmless shrub, which had been the subject of the prophecy. This motif is identical to the famous death of the Norse god Balder at the hands of Loki using a sprig of mistletoe.
23. See WIJESEKERA, pp. 293–305. He points out that the discus is closely associated with Kṛṣṇa in later mythology, and that Ṛg Vedic, Avestan, and Greek references, together with archeological finds of discuses, make the Indo-European use of the discus as a weapon likely.

Wijesekera notices the use of discus as weapon in the Catudvāra Jātaka (№ 439, pp. 3–4), but not in the Ghata.

24. Note that the Greek Perseus is dark-skinned, which is the meaning of 'Kṛṣṇa', while the Ethiopean Andromeda is pale.
25. Such depictions are common. See, for example, the images at http://commons.wikimedia.org/wiki/Andromeda_(mythology).
26. NEUMANN, *Origins*, pp. 354–5.
27. NEUMANN, *Origins*, p. 348. We have seen examples of this assimilation in the absortion of the *yakkhinī* cults within Buddhism. A similar process was going on among the Hindus, for example in the overcoming of the serpent Kāliya by Kṛṣṇa. (See ZIMMER, *Myths and Symbols*, p. 83*ff.*)
28. APULEIUS, p. 113.
29. NEUMANN, *Origins*, p. 201.
30. Dasaratha Jātaka (№ 461, iv.124).
31. Akitta Jātaka (№ 480, 4.237–242). The sister is not identified in the story, but her name is Yasavatī, which is one of the names of Bimbā.
32. NEUMANN, *Origins*, p. 199.
33. NEUMANN, *Origins*, p. 199.
34. NEUMANN, *Origins*, p. 206.
35. NEUMANN, *Origins*, pp. 339–340.

Chapter 30 The Sacred Stepmother

1. Pali Vinaya 2.256–259.
2. For example, the question about the difference in treatment regarding the rules shared in common between the monks and nuns presupposes a developed form of the bhikkhuni Vinaya, which must have taken a considerable time to develop.
3. Pali Vinaya 2.257–9, slightly abbreviated.
4. E.g. Majjhima Nikāya 37.
5. In the Dharmaguptaka version, Mahāpajāpatī herself doubts her ordination (T22, № 1428, p. 926, a29–b3).
6. E.g. Saṁyutta Nikāya 35.95. Sometimes the attainment of arahantship is omitted, e.g. Saṁyutta Nikāya 35.76.
7. *Esā buddhāna vandanā*. This echoes the famous line from the Ovāda Pāṭimokkha: *etaṁ buddhānasāsanaṁ* (Dhammapada 183–185). I have noted before (*Sects & Sectarianism*, ch. 5.37–8) that the verse closely associated with the heretical doctrines of the root-schismatics, the Mahāsaṅghikas, ends with this same line, and the verse as a whole is clearly constructed as a reformation of the original verse. The story has it that the verse was uttered in the fortnightly *pāṭimokkha*, just as the original verse is. It seems likely to me that Mahāpajāpatī's verse here is also a revisioning or implied comment on the original verse. She is subtly suggesting that true homage comes from diligent practice of the Dhamma rather than from insistence on *pāṭimokkha* rules. One reason for thinking these verses must be connected is that they have a distinctive grammatical peculiarity. *Buddhāna* is not the normal dative/genitive form, which would be *buddhānaṁ*. It is usually taken to be simply a poetic abbreviation, which is possible. But there is no reason to introduce the plural 'Buddhas'

here. The original verse has a variant reading *buddhānusāsanaṁ*, where *anusāsana* is in fact the more normal term for the 'dispensation' of the Buddhas. Adopting this reading the Buddha becomes singular and there is no grammatical problem. However, this does not work in the Mahāpajāpatī verse, for *anuvandanā* is not a normal term. It would seem, then, that she adapted this line with its incongruity. The ambiguity may be very old.

8. Therīgāthā 157–162.
9. See, for example, Devadhamma Jātaka 9 (№ 6, Vol i.127); *Rāmāyaṇa*, p. 118, etc. In the idealized world of the *Rāmāyaṇa*, even the stepmother Kaikeyī could not directly betray Rāma. Instead, she is goaded on by her hunchback maid Mantharā, of unknown origin, who is the 'crone of crones', so to speak.
10. PURKISS, p. 132, quotes GUILLIMEAU, *Child-birth*, p. 7: 'The milk (wherewith the child is nourished two years together) hath as much power to make the children like the nurse, both in body and mind, as the seed of the parents hath to make the children like them...'. This belief is also found in the Mūgapakkha Jātaka (№ 538, 6.3), which enumerates various faults of wet-nurses that must be avoided if the child is not to inherit their problems.
11. Does this exchange hint at a connection with Devadatta's attempt on the Buddha's life?
12. T2, № 125, p. 592, c10–28. This translation originally published as Ekottaragama XXI, Buddhist Studies Review 13.2, 1996, p. 149–150. Translated from the Chinese version by Thích HUYÊN-VI and Bhikkhu PĀSĀDIKA in collaboration with Sara BOIN-WEBB. I have made a couple of minor amendments.
13. Pāsādika translated this as 'broad-mindedness and extensive awareness'. But this is too literal a rendering of the Chinese (T2, № 125, p. 592c27).
14. Mūlapariyāya Jātaka (№ 245, 2.260).
15. See Haimavata Vinaya Mātikā (T24, № 1463, p. 818, b17–c4); Gautamī Sūtra (T1 № 26, p. 607, a16–b8); Sarvāstivāda Gautamī Sūtra (T1 № 60, p. 857, c13–c27). The last two are similar in this respect to the Mahīśāsaka Vinaya passage translated above ch. 2.43–44.
16. BUCKNELL.

Chapter 31 Rescuing the Hero

1. GILLIGAN, *Birth*, p. 16.
2. NEUMANN, *Origins*, p. 310.
3. NEUMANN, *Origins*, p. 348–9.
4. NEUMANN, *Origins*, p. 186–7.
5. NEUMANN, *Origins*, p. 64–5.
6. NEUMANN, *Origins*, p. 178–181.
7. JUNG, *Aspects of the Feminine*, p. 21 (§ 401).
8. Jung used *libido* to mean, not just sexual energy, but psychic energy in general.
9. JUNG, *Aspects of the Feminine*, p. 22 (§ 402). Jung further remarks that: 'If the libido connects with the unconscious it is as though it were connecting with the mother and this raises the incest taboo.' JUNG, *Aspects of the Masculine*, p. 14 (§ 450).
10. JUNG, *Aspects of the Feminine*, p. 20 (§ 399).
11. JUNG, *Aspects of the Masculine*, p. 121 (§ 147).
12. JUNG, *Aspects of the Masculine*, p. 30 (§ 776).
13. JUNG, *Aspects of the Masculine*, p. 33 (§ 784).

14. JUNG, *Aspects of the Masculine*, p. 221 (§ 459).

Chapter 32 The Hard Twin

1. This is not the case in Sri Lanka, where Moggallāna is sometimes depicted with dark, blue-black skin; according to Buddhavaṁsa 1.58 his skin was the colour of the blue lotus or the rain cloud. (*Gajjitā kālameghova/Nīluppalasamasādiso.*) See an example at: http://www.gavihara.org/wp-content/uploads/2010/01/Gbvimage.jpg
2. NEUMANN, *Origins*, p. 95*f.*
3. Vimalakīrtinirdeśa, trans. Robert THURMAN: http://www2.kenyon.edu/Depts/Religion/Fac/Adler/Reln260/Vimalakirti.htm.
4. Dṛdhādhyāśayaparipṛccha Sūtra, quoted by SPONBERG, trans. José I. CABEZÓN in 'Women and Illusion: Toward an Aesthetics in Buddhism,' a paper presented at the 1987 meeting of the American Academy of Religion, Boston, p. 10.
5. MIGOT, p. 409. Quoted in COUTURE, p. 20.
6. They are remembered in other branches of Aryan mythology, such as Iranian and Greek. Astronomically, PARPOLA identifies the seven sages with the seven stars of the Great Bear; their wives are the Pleiades. www.harappa.com/script/parpola12.html
7. Rāmāyaṇa, p. 131.
8. Ṛg Veda 1.164.16.
9. MILLER, p. 66.
10. *Kaśyapo'gnisamaprabhaḥ, adityā sahito* (*Rāmāyaṇa* 1.31.9, SCHLEGEL's ed.)
11. He is typically said to have ordained shortly after the events of the Catuṣpariṣat Sūtra, but this is not, so far as I am aware, attested in any early texts.
12. John 20:22–23.
13. Compare John 8.1–11 or Luke 7.36–50, where the sinners' own faith and acts saved them, and Jesus simply declared the fact. The *Catholic Encyclopedia* on 'absolution' cites the vague declaration in Matthew 19.19 and 18.18. www.newadvent.org/cathen/01061a.htm
14. www.newadvent.org/bible/joh020.htm#22
15. According to the *Catholic Encyclopedia*: 'From Scripture we learn that the Apostles appointed others by an external rite (imposition of hands), conferring inward grace.' www.newadvent.org/cathen/11279a.htm
16. Leviticus 16:21.
17. www.newadvent.org/cathen/07698a.htm
18. AQUINAS, *Summa Theologica*, Question 83: Of the Subject of Original Sin. http://www.sacred-texts.com/chr/aquinas/summa/sum220.htm
19. Matthew 26:26–28, etc.
20. www.newadvent.org/cathen/05573a.htm
21. Frazer used the terms 'contagious' and 'homeopathic'.
22. www.newadvent.org/cathen/07402a.htm
23. Saṁyutta Nikāya 16.11.
24. T № 202 and T № 203.
25. *Rāmāyaṇa*, p. 45.
26. Dasabrāhamaṇa Jātaka (№ 495, 4.365). See the English translation, 4.230, note 1.
27. Vatthūpama Sutta (Majjhima Nikāya 7.20).

28. As, for example, METTANANDO.
29. *Mandāravapuppha*. The *mandārava* is both the ordinary coral tree and one of the five celestial trees.
30. This story is often cited as a historical event, but it cannot be traced earlier than the koan compilation 無門關 (*Wúménguān*, often rendered in English as *The Gateless Gate*), compiled by the Chinese Zen master 無門慧開 (Wumen Hui-k'ai) and first published in 1228.
31. Theragāthā 1062–1071. Trans. HECKER & NYANAPONIKA.

Chapter 33 The Sage & the Golden Maiden

1. Bhaddā Kāpilānī is not related to the Bhaddā Kuṇḍalakesā we have discussed earlier. Bhaddā is a common woman's name.
2. Apadāna 265, 266.
3. Apadāna 273.
4. Apadāna 274.
5. Apadāna 291.
6. Apadāna 265, 272, 278, 290, 292, 294, 297.
7. Apadāna 295–298.
8. This famous story is retold here from the Pali commentarial version, which is found very similar form at Aṅguttara Aṭṭhakathā 1.92*ff.*; Saṁyutta Aṭṭhakathā 2.135*ff.*; Theragāthā Aṭṭhakathā 2.134*ff.* The story was a popular one, not confined to the Pali sources. A Tibetan version is recorded in VON SCHIEFNER's *Tibetan Tales*, pp. 186–205. This tells very much the same story, with the usual playful freedom in developing narrative details.
9. Cullabodhi Jātaka (№ 443, 4.22–27).
10. Cullabodhi Jātaka (№ 443, 4.23).
11. The Kusa is attested very early at Sañchī, so may be earlier than the Kassapa/Bhaddā story. The details of the nurse by the bathing place, etc., are not found in the Tibetan version of the Bhaddā/Kassapa story; and the golden image motif is missing from the Tibetan version of the Kusa Jātaka. The Pali version of the Kassapa/Bhaddā story includes one isolated reference to the nurse as a 'hunchback', which appears for no reason in this narrative, but is a central part of the Pali Kusa Jātaka.
12. Dhammapāda Aṭṭhakathā 3.281–4.
13. Sutta Nipāta Aṭṭhakathā 67*ff.*; Apadāna Aṭṭhakathā 1.126–7.
14. Udaya Jātaka (№ 458, 4.104–113).
15. Ananusociya Jātaka (№ 328, 3.92–97).
16. Sāma Jātaka (№ 540, 6.71–95).
17. VON SCHIEFNER, *Tibetan Tales* p. 202. The translation speaks of the 'Nirgrantha Pūraṇa', and it is not clear to me whether this simply means the followers of Pūraṇa, or the Jaina community. If the text was not late and unhistorical, one might suspect it was from an early period in the development of Jainism, when Mahāvīra and Pūraṇa had not yet parted ways. It is also unclear to me what these monks were supposed to be doing as they 'enjoyed her company every day.' Chatting? Basking in her beauty? Or something more intimate?
18. The Mahāsaṅghika Vinaya relates another episode when Bhaddā Kāpilānī had to endure the leering of five Licchavī youths while bathing in a river. It became the occasion for telling yet more of her past lives, revealing the source of her extraordinary beauty, at the

end of which the Buddha laid down a rule requiring nuns to have a bathing cloth of a suitable size. (Mahāsaṅghika bhikkhuni *pācittiya* 75; T № 1425, pp. 528c-529b; HIRAKAWA, pp. 253–258.)

19. Therīgāthā 63–66.
20. Pali Vinaya 5.289 (bhikkhuni *pācittiya* 33).
21. Pali Vinaya 5.291 (bhikkhuni *pācittiya* 35).
22. Saṁyutta Nikāya 16.10; Saṁyukta Āgama 1143; (Smaller) Saṁyukta Āgama 118. The date is not made explicit in the text, but it starts by saying that Mahākassapa was dwelling at Sāvatthi; the omission of the Buddha in the origin of a Sutta is often an indicator that it occurred after the *parinibbāna*. This is confirmed by the commentary. The following, closely related, Sutta is set in Rājagaha, and both of these seem to be setting the scene for the First Council. The Chinese versions (Saṁyukta Āgama 1143 at T2, № 99, p. 302, b3; (Smaller) Saṁyukta Āgama 118 at T2, № 100, p. 417, a24) are both set in Rājagaha. It's likely, then, that these events took place in Rājagaha and the setting in the Pali version was 'normalized' to Sāvatthi.
23. Thullatissā apears nowhere else. 'Tissa/Tissā' is perhaps the most common Pali name, and 'Thulla' is a derogatory epithet meaning 'fat'. The next Sutta we discuss has a similar confusion. The bad nun is called Thullanandā in the Pali, Tissā in SA 1144, and Tissanandā in (Smaller) Saṁyukta Āgama 119.
24. Needles were an extraordinary achievement in technology at the time, so to surpass an expert needle-maker was a feat of legendary difficulty. Which, of course, means that the Bodhisatta had to do it. In the Sūci Jātaka (№ 387, 6.281–6) he made an amazing needle whereby he won the needle-maker's daughter in marriage.
25. The Pali has *bālo mātugāmo*, which Bhikkhu BODHI translates as 'Womenfolk are foolish'. But this fits neither the context, in which many bhikkhunis have just delighted in the teaching and only one criticized, nor Ānanda's character. In fact, *mātugāma* is used both of womankind in general and of individual women. The Chinese versions here say nothing of 'womankind', simply remarking that she has been foolish: Saṁyukta Āgama 1143 (T2, № 99, p. 302, b24); (Smaller) Saṁyukta Āgama[2] 118: (T2, № 100, p. 417, b18). The Pali words *mātugāma* and *itthī* are both used to mean 'woman', but *mātugāma* has a slight derogatory connotation about it. Hence in the Vinaya, *itthī* is used in a neutral sense as contrasted with *purisa*, while *mātugāma* is used with *bhikkhu*, typically in rules where she plays the temptress.
26. Saṁyutta Nikāya 16.11; Saṁyukta Āgama 1144; (Smaller) Saṁyukta Āgama[2] 119. The date after the parinibbana is mentioned in Saṁyukta Āgama 1144; the Pali commentary adds that Ānanda was on his way to the First Council.
27. This detail, found in all three versions, is one of the places that make it clear that Ānanda was much younger than the Buddha, who had just passed away at eighty, despite the Theravadin assertion they were the same age.

Chapter 34 The Soft Twin

1. Also Aṅguttara Nikāya 4.129 .
2. In the Pali version, this is mentioned in brief in the context of the Mahāparinibbāna Sutta, then expanded in luxuriant detail in a separate long Sutta, the Mahāsudassana Sutta. The Sanskrit version keeps the Mahāsudassana story to a more modest length, and retains in within the Mahāparinibbāna Sutta itself.
3. Dīgha Nikāya 17.2.10.
4. Dīgha Nikāya 16.4.37.
5. Kāliṅgabodhi Jātaka (№ 479, 4.228–236). See Paduma Jātaka (№ 261, 2.321–323). See ch 1.
6. Aṅguttara Nikāya Commentary 2.533.
7. Aṅguttara Nikāya 4.159.
8. Pali Vinaya 4.91.
9. See e.g. Saṁyutta Nikāya 47.10, Aṅguttara Nikāya 6.44 (= 10.75). (Note that in this Sutta the Buddha criticizes a foolish woman. The word he uses here, *ammakā*, is not a standard word for woman, but is a diminutive of a term of affection. Perhaps it could be rendered 'aunty'.) This tradition continued in later times, as for example Dhammapada Commentary 1.415*f.*
10. Theragāthā 1042: *Paṇṇavīsativassāni, Sekhabhūtassa me sato; Na kāmasaññā uppajji...*
11. Mahānāradakassapa Jātaka (№ 544, 6.219–255). See also Dhammapada Commentary 1.327.
12. Pali Vinaya 2.195. The Cūḷahaṁsa Jataka (№ 533, 5.335–6) and a Chinese Dhammapada text (T4, № 211, p. 596b*ff.*, WILLEMEN, pp. 144–5) give same past life for this event.
13. Aṅguttara Nikāya Commentary 1.239.
14. Pali Vinaya 2.290.
15. Mahāsāra Jātaka, № 92, 1.382.
16. Pali Vinaya 4.158.
17. Guṇa Jātaka (№ 157, Vol 2.24–5).
18. On other occasions Ānanda was offered a robe (Pali Vinaya 3.195) and a bowl (Pali Vinaya 3.243), and immediately wished to give it to Sāriputta.
19. Theragāthā 1039.
20. Dīgha Nikāya 29.15–18.
21. It is well known, and confirmed in the Mahāparinibbāna Sutta, that Ānanda was still not fully Awakened, and yet he was the bearer of the scriptural transmission. That he should become an arahant is therefore demanded by the tradition, which needs to authorize the texts as being infallible.
22. METTANANDO alleges that this item relates to a brahmanical taboo on the use of the bathing cloth. However, while the foot is certainly regarded as unclean in some cases, such as contact with food, I have been unable to find evidence of a taboo specifically on touching the bathing cloth with the foot. Moreover, there were many different sets of brahmanical codes, and these evolved over time. Hence the mere fact that a brahmanical taboo is mentioned in a particular text, while interesting, does not prove that this was relevant in the time and place of the First Council.
23. In widely separated areas, women are told to leave the death-bed of a loved one because of their excessive emotions; e.g. Rāvaṇa's death in the *Rāmāyaṇa*, p. 626, or Socrates' death in *Phaedo*, 59E, 117A.

24. The extension of the life span is closely associated with the Sarvāstivāda, with their characteristic doctrine that 'all dhammas of the past, present, and future, exist'. The Pali version of this story has Ānanda taking his sitting cloth when going with the Buddha on the occasions when he announces his ability to live until the end of the æon. This detail may be as innocuous as it seems; but the sitting cloth is almost never mentioned in the Pali suttas, while it is normal in the Sarvāstivādin suttas. Perhaps, then, this episode is a Sarvāstivādin interpolation. This would explain the Theravādin commentaries' evident discomfort with the idea, preferring to explain 'æon' here as meaning 'the full normal span of 100 years'.
25. Saṁyutta Nikāya 16.5.

Chapter 35 What a Woman Wants

1. Sigmund FREUD, letter to Marie Bonaparte, as quoted in Ernest JONES, *Sigmund Freud: Life and Work* (1955), V^OL 2, Pt. 3, ch. 16.
2. Aṅguttara Nikāya 6.52. Compare Madhyama Āgama 149 (TI, № 26, p. 660, c01), Ekottara Āgama 37.8 (T2, № 125 , p. 714, b13).
3. Mahājanaka Jātaka (№ 539, 6.38.)
4. This section is greatly abbreviated.
5. Based on ZIMMER, *The King and the Corpse*, pp. 88–95, with reference to the original text edited by Thomas HAHN at http://www.lib.rochester.edu/camelot/Teams/ragnfrm.htm.
6. The original is Gromer Somer Joure. The etymology of *gromer* is uncertain. It is sometimes taken as 'man' (= 'groom'), but I follow PARTRIDGE (p. 1334) in relating it to 'grim'. Partridge, however, also suggests it may be connected with 'grin'.
7. Hahn glosses 'nag'.
8. This line is in ZIMMER, but not the original, which is missing a leaf at this point.
9. http://www.maryjones.us/ctexts/eochaid.html
10. *Jones' Celtic Encyclopedia*. http://www.maryjones.us/jce/loathlylady.html

Chapter 36 The Heroine

1. Ghata Jātaka (№ 454, 4.79–89), discussed above, although here it is Sāriputta who is identified with Vāsudeva (= Kṛṣṇa), while the Bodhisatta is identified with the wise brother Ghatapaṇḍita.
2. Dasaratha Jātaka (№ 461, 4.124–130); *cf.* Sambula Jātaka (№ 519, 5.88–98).
3. Kunāla Jātaka (№ 536; at 5.27 Ajjuna is identified with Kunāla, and at 5.456 Kunāla is identified with the Bodhisatta.)
4. Jātakas 495, 413, 515.
5. Samudda-vaṇija Jātaka (№ 466, 4. 158–166).
6. Sigāla Jātaka (№ 148, 1.501–504), retold in the Pañcūposatha Jātaka (№ 490, 4.326–7).
7. Naṅguṭṭha Jātaka (№ 144, 1.494–495).
8. There are too many parallels to mention all. As model of self-sacrfice and love in the face of violent death there are the Chaddanta Jātaka (№ 514, 5.36–57), the Khantivādi Jātaka (№ 313, 3.39–43), and the Sasa Jātaka (№ 316, 3.51–56). Various of Jesus' most famous miracles are found, e.g. the loaves and fishes (introduction to the Illīsa Jātaka, № 78, 1.347–350), walking on water (Pali Vinaya 1.32).

9. The closest parallel is probably the Mahājanaka Jātaka (№ 539, 6.30–68). The hero is cast adrift, alone on the ocean for seven days. Like Odysseus, he is only saved by the intervention of the goddess. The goddess leaves him in the care of the nymphs of the sacred grove, as Odysseus is cast ashore into the care of the wise maiden Nausicaä, all the while under Athena's guidance. On his return home, his resolve to take back the kingdom is thwarted by the many suitors for the Queen's hand. But the Bodhisatta, like Odysseus, is the only one who can pass the tests of stringing the impossible bow, and identifying the marriage bed. Some other Odyssean motifs are: as castaway clinging to plank, Sīlānisaṁsa Jātaka (№ 90, 2.111–113); use of a false betrayer as strategem to win seige, Mahā Ummagga Jātaka (№ 546, 6.406); in archery contest, Asadisa Jātaka (№ 181, 2.87–91) and several of the biographies. The Raṭṭhapāla Sutta also contains several Odyssean motifs, especially the idea that Raṭṭhapāla is not recognized when he returns home, but is identified by an old serving woman because of the distinct marks on his hands.
10. Javanahaṁsa Jātaka (№ 476, 4.212–219).
11. Jātakas 208, 342; *cf.* Jātaka 57 (= 224).
12. Some sources here: http://tibeto-logic.blogspot.com/2009/08/monkey-croc-turtle.html
13. See discussion at ch. 22.24.
14. Jātakas 57 (= 224), 159 (= 491), 208 (= 342), 224 (= 57), 281, 292, 309, 338 (introduction), 342 (= 208), 389, 400, 465 (introduction), 482, 491 (= 159), 501, 502 (=534), 514, 534 (= 502), 545.
15. Vidhurapaṇḍita Jātaka (№ 545, 6.255–328).
16. Dabbapuppha Jātaka (№ 400, 3.332–336). The tale is also found in the Mūlasarvāstivāda Vinaya (VON SCHIEFNER, *Tibetan Tales* № 34, pp. 332–4). This version, however, lacks the distinctive characteristics of the *dohaḷa* cycle, as the jackal just appears on the scene without being instigated by his wife. Variants of the story are widely distributed.
17. Chaddanta Jātaka (№ 514, 5.36–57). This is represented in a terracotta from Shunga as early as the 1st century BCE (Calcutta University Museum).
18. This note of editorial skepticism is found in the text itself. This passage, which here is much condensed, is an extraordinary description of abseiling techniques. After seven years, seven months, and seven days, the hunter found his target. He dressed himself in the ochre robe of an ascetic, concealed himself in a pit, and when the Bodhisatta came by with his herd, he took his mighty bow and loosed a poisoned shaft. The Bodhisatta trumpeted with pain, and the herd fled in fear.

Chapter 37 That Indefinable Yearning

1. Chavaka Jātaka (№ 309, 3.27–30).
2. SINGH, *Encyclopaedia of Jainism*, p. 3796.
   http://www.jaine.org/Stories/Preceptor/article_505.php
3. In Dhammapāda Commentary 5.15b and 6.5b32 a boy is conceived in the womb of the wife of a supporter of the Elder Sariputta; the expectant mother longs to entertain the monks, and so satisfies her longing.
4. For example, a woman wishes to drink the moon, and the husband arranges for her to be tricked by seeing a reflection of the moon (BLOOMFIELD, pp. 23–4, quoted from the Jaina text Parisistaparvan 8.225*ff.*) This episode reinforces the archaic nature of *dohaḷa*. The Ṛg

Veda identifies the moon with King Soma, so in drinking the moon she is really drinking the elixir of life.

5. GILBERT, p. 132; DURT, p. 49; PENZER, p. 231.

Chapter 38 The Flowering of the World

1. Mahā Mora Jātaka (№ 491, 4.332–343).
2. *Ibid.* 4.340: *samanabrāhmaṇānaṁ atthibhāvaṁ.*
3. Ṛg Veda 10.121.
4. Ṛg Veda 10.121.3.
5. Ch. 4.34.
6. The Mūgapakkha Jātaka (№ 538, 5.3–120) tells of the extraordinary stillness of the Bodhsatta, who as a baby prince stayed motionless so they would not make him king, where he would have to make decisions that would take him to hell.
7. A Chinese Dhammapada tells how the Buddha converted a primitive hunting tribe and introduced them to vegetarianism and the arts of cultivation. (T4, № 211, p. 581b-c; WILLEMEN, pp. 45–7.)
8. Chaddanta Jātaka (№ 514, 5.42).
9. The knowledge of the quest is passed down through writing inscribed on gold. No such items are known from such an ancient time, although in later years they are found. It is possible that kings before the Buddha did indeed use such plates, but none have been found so far.
10. This famous symbol, curiously enough, is attested in Roman iconography 700 years before appearing in China. http://www.estovest.net/tradizione/yinyang_en.html#t24
11. This is the first of the arguments for rebirth, not only in our Jātaka, but in the canonical Pāyāsi Sutta (Dīgha Nikāya 23.5).
12. ARISTOTLE, *Metaphysics* 4.8: 'And so the sun and the stars and the whole heaven are ever active, and there is no fear that they may sometime stand still, as the natural philosophers fear they may. Nor do they tire in this activity; for movement is not for them, as it is for perishable things, connected with the potentiality for opposites, so that the continuity of the movement should be laborious; for it is that kind of substance which is matter and potency, not actuality, that causes this.' *Metaphysics* 7.8: 'For the nature of the stars is eternal just because it is a certain kind of substance, and the mover is eternal and prior to the moved, and that which is prior to a substance must be a substance. Evidently, then, there must be substances which are of the same number as the movements of the stars, and in their nature eternal, and in themselves unmovable, and without magnitude, for the reason before mentioned.'
13. Kauśītāki Upaniṣad 1.2.
14. Majjhima Nikāya 95.14.

Chapter 39 Her Dreaming

1. Ruru Jātaka (№ 482, 4.255–263). ĀRYASŪRA's Jātakamālā № 26 (pp. 234–244 of SPEYER's trans.) is similar. Cariyapiṭaka 2.6 has the basic story without the *dohaḷa* motif.
2. Rohantamiga Jātaka (№ 501, 4.413–423).

3. Our text actually refers to the Mora Jātaka at 4.414.
4. Haṁsa Jātaka (№ 502, 4.423–430).
5. Mahāhaṁsa Jātaka (№ 534, 5.354–382).
6. E.g. Jātakas 167, 263, 348, 423, 433, 435, 477, 491, 507, 523, 526, 543, 546.
7. Kunāla Jātaka (№ 536, 5.427–428). Saccatapāvī was a female ascetic, so rigorous she dwelt in a cemetery and abstained from four out of five meals. But this did not stop her from having sex with a goldsmith.
8. See NUGTEREN, pp. 98–102.
9. Parsvanatha Caritra 6. 796–7. Quoted in BLOOMFIELD.
10. Vasavadatta 133 and 138. Quoted in BLOOMFIELD, pp. 1–3.
11. The following discussion is based on DURT, who gives full references. The relevant passages are from the Saṅghabhedavastu of the Mūlasarvāstivāda Vinaya. Māyā's *dohada* is also referred to in HARIBHAṬṬA, Jātakamālā 35.3.

Chapter 40 Things Hidden Since the Beginning

1. In his careful and detailed study of early Buddhist artistic history, KARLSSON has shown that they belonged to the common fund of Indic images, were adopted by the Buddhists, and only gradually came to acquire specifically Buddhist associations.
2. NEUMANN, *The Great Mother*, p. 262.
3. See CAMPBELL, *Oriental Mythology*, pp. 40, 291.
4. NEUMANN, *The Great Mother*, p. 289.
5. NEUMANN, *The Great Mother*, p. 123.
6. NEUMANN, *The Great Mother*, p. 130.
7. NEUMANN, *The Great Mother*, p. 158; GIMBUTAS, *Living Goddesses*, xvii.
8. By contrast, the *yab/yum* images of late tantric Buddhism make the gender integration entirely explicit, and hence lose their hidden power.

www.ingramcontent.com/pod-product-compliance
Lightning Source LLC
Chambersburg PA
CBHW021941240426
43669CB00046B/52
9781921842030